'twas Calhoun who divined
How the great western star's last race would run

—Allen Tate
"Fragment of a meditation," 1935

CALHOUN'S PHILOSOPHY OF POLITICS

A Study of

A Disquisition on Government

GUY STORY BROWN

MERCER UNIVERSITY PRESS

2000

ISBN 0-86554-680-0
MUP/H503

© 2000Mercer University Press
6316 Peake Road
Macon, Georgia 31210-3960

First Edition.

Library of Congress Cataloging-in-Publication Data

Brown, Guy Story.
Calhoun's philosophy of politics: a study of A disquisition on government / Guy Story Brown.—1st ed.
Includes bibliographic references and index.
ISBN 0-86554-680-0 (alk. paper)
1. Calhoun, John C. (John Caldwell), 1782-1850.
Disquistion on government. 2. Political science. 3. United States—Politics and government. I. Title.

JC212.B76 2000
320.473—dc21   00-39417

TABLE OF CONTENTS

For

M. E. Bradford

Foreword

IT IS A COMMONPLACE THAT JOHN C. CALHOUN IS AMONG AMERICA'S greatest and most controversial statesmen.[1] As one historian notes, "He was first nominated for president in 1821—at the age of thirty-nine—and was considered a serious candidate for that office in every election from 1824 to 1848." In the meantime, he was the only vice-president in the nineteenth century to be elected to two terms, one of which he resigned ("Calhoun was Vice-President because he was important, not important because he was Vice-President"), and he also served two terms as secretary of war ("If ever there was perfection carried into any branch of the public service it was that to which Mr. Calhoun carried into the War Department") and a term as secretary of state ("Calhoun was obviously the man for the crisis").[2] At the beginning of his political career in Washington he was hailed already upon almost his first speech in the House of Representatives as "one of those Master Spirits who put their stamp on the age," and, at its end, Daniel Webster, in his eulogy of "much the ablest man in the Senate," spoke of the "age" of Calhoun: "He is now an historical character. Those of us who have known him here...will indulge in a grateful recollection that we have lived in his age, that we have been his contemporaries, that we have seen him, and heard him, and known him..." These and related biographical facts are sufficient to distinguish Calhoun from most of his peers, as well as other politicians and men of state. One does not need his *Disquisition on Government* to know this, or to follow the drama of his long and often almost melodramatic public career. To do so, one only needs a certain awareness of elementary American history.

But apart from such facts as these is the still further fact that he was also a "political theorist" of the first rank and was remarked as such when the term itself was still hardly known. (Among others, John Stuart Mill spoke in the midst of the nineteenth century of Calhoun's *Disquisition on Government* as the greatest work of political theory since the *Federalist* in the previous century, and Lord Acton held a similar view.) This fact alone, as much as his whole public life, also sets him apart from all his peers. It also has certain brute implications beyond those imposed by even the most careful study of American history.

The first and clearest of these implications is that the student of *A Disquisition on Government* should be something of a political theorist, or at least to some extent genuinely open to becoming one under the guidance of that work. The second is that, since in its presentation the kind of political theory sketched by

Calhoun seems identifiable at first glance with the kind of political theory familiar among European thinkers since the original attempt by Thomas Hobbes to establish "civil philosophy" on what was thought a solid and true foundation, that is, a foundation compatible with Newtonian physical science, one should have some familiarity with that school of thought. That school of thought, which one may summarize as the "social contract philosophy," remains by far the dominant political thought of our own day and age. It is very much "our" political thought. Indeed, what in the wake of the Soviet collapse is sometimes referred to as the "end of history" (or "destiny") is merely the powerful, once-and-for-all globalization of the European social contract philosophy, including its tensions. An initial question or apparent complication arises immediately, however, when it is recalled that Calhoun was not an adherent of the social contract philosophy, which according to him is not merely unscientific but a "delusion."

This evident complication is pointedly depicted in another context in a commentary in *The Biglow Papers* by an earnest champion of Manifest Destiny, James Russell Lowell: "Mr. Calhoun has somehow acquired the name of a great statesman, and, if it be great statesmanship to put lance in rest and run a tilt at the Spirit of the Age, with the certainty of being next moment hurled neck and heels in the dust amid universal laughter, he deserves the title."[3]

Calhoun did not flinch in the face of the challenge presented him by the Spirit of the Age. One may characterize *A Disquisition on Government* in the first place as an individual or single-handed attempt to replace the whole "social contract" school of thought with genuine political science, that is, as the attempt to found, once and for all, and hence particularly for the future, the true science of government. It represents the greatest and most ambitious undertaking of Calhoun's life. It is an undertaking that is in a sense the most Herculean and in also a sense the most typical of Calhoun.

The study of political forms and institutions originally arose out of the failure of those forms and institutions. In Calhoun's case, as we will observe in the following pages, *A Disquisition on Government* is "preliminary" to his much longer and more historical *A Discourse on the Constitution and Government of the United States*. The *Discourse*, which at length presents the historical example of the culminating and most complex of constitutional forms of government introduced by the *Disquisition*, is especially concerned with (and celebrates) the American present, specifically and even narrowly construed, in all its parts, while the *Disquisition* surveys all human history, including (besides much else) particularly, European history from the time of the Copernican Revolution to the global empire of Great Britain, whence the United States seceded.[4] It is fitting, therefore, that the *Discourse* should contain the bold constitutional suggestions concerning the government of the United States for which it is famous. They exemplify the prescription of a Founder or constitutional statesman. Yet, we know that Calhoun himself little anticipated their implementation (least of all in his own absence), or anything remotely similar.

On the contrary, as one recent historian describes, after Calhoun's last speech in the Senate (March 4, 1850), even while he was continuing his work on the text of *A Discourse on the Constitution and Government of the United States* as we have it in the days just before his death (March 31, 1850), "at this time, Calhoun with uncanny clarity prophesied almost the exact order of events over the next decade or so that he thought would bring about the destruction of the Union."[5] Whatever else may be said of it, surely the least that might be said is that his uncanny clarity "at this time," the most famous prediction in American political history, is a more than sufficient suggestion that Calhoun intended his posthumously-published writings, the example of the *Discourse* and especially the foundational *A Disquisition on Government*, primarily for a posthumous and even post-bellum posterity, a posterity that is, moreover, in no way restricted to North Americans. (Mill and Acton, for example, are not North Americans.) Actually, as we will indicate in this connection in our discussion of the relevant parts of the *Disquisition*, Calhoun's envisioned readership is one that will increasingly find itself in the midst of what he identified (with Hegel before and Whitehead after him, among others) as a global "period of transition," already well begun in the advanced countries of the world, and which, however, he characterized (in terms resonant with Nietzsche's predicted twenty-first century "total eclipse") as increasing "uncertainty, confusion, error, and wild and fierce fanaticism" (and domination by banks). It is this period that provides the immediate context of *A Disquisition on Government*.

For finding one's way in this period, according to Calhoun, the most needful thing, the thing with which all true piety is intimately compatible, indeed, almost the only real hope for the human race and the real object of the best in humanity, is a science of government. This is perhaps as ambitious a claim on behalf of science as has ever been made. Calhoun's foundation in *A Disquisition of Government* of the true science of government is meant to make accessible to all the necessary foundation for the future, if there is to be a truly human future.

CHAPTER ONE

Calhoun's *Disquisition on Government*

"I am pretty well satisfied. It will be nearly through-out new territory, and, I hope, lay a solid foundation for political science."

June 15, 1849[1]

CALHOUN'S *DISQUISITION ON GOVERNMENT* HAS BEEN GENERALLY REGARDED FROM THE time of its publication as the greatest American work in political theory.[2] The present study is intended as an aid for those with the interest and opportunity to explore this challenging composition at leisure. I assume the work is always before them.

A Disquisition on Government is preliminary to *A Discourse on the Constitution and Government of the United States*. The two works were first published in one volume and were meant to go together as well as stand apart. *A Discourse on the Constitution and Government of the United States* presents at length the character of the United States constitution and government and completes the examples of aristocratic, monarchic, and democratic constitutional forms introduced in the *Disquisition*.[3] The popular constitution, according to Calhoun, is most complex constitutional government yet known, and in this sense the most extreme constitutional form. We learn from the *Disquisition* that all governments of whatever character have a constant tendency to simplify, that is, if not checked, to degrade or decline into simpler and simpler forms. This tendency is stronger the more complex and elevated the regime. Hence we may suppose it is strongest of all in the most complex regime yet known. Both these works arise out of the author's own sustained engagement—existential or historical—with the career of the complex constitutional form and from his conviction that its course was part of a larger movement of world history.

A Disquisition on Government is a "preliminary" or necessarily first inquiry into political science, as though its working title might have been "Prolegomena to All Future Work in the Science of Government." In it, as everyone knows,

Calhoun presents his theory of "concurrent majority," or constitutionalism. We may tentatively conceive this presentation as a sort of constitutional correction of Rousseau's famous social-contract doctrine of the "general will." In any case, the presentation of the *Disquisition* is preliminary to any discussion of what is to be done, of what courses of action are better and worse, of who should rule, of what the universally right order of society, so far as ascertainable by human reason or science, ultimately is. The disquisition is undertaken for the sake of presenting in the plainest and most direct manner the true elementary or radical understanding of government as such, and, therewith, the foundation of the science of government or political science.

Of the old questions, what is the origin of human society? what kinds of human society are there? and what is the best kind? Calhoun teaches that society originates in the nature of man, that it is original with man, and that the best kind of society is that which is most in accordance with the whole of human nature and which completes or perfects original human nature. To the question, what is human nature? Calhoun replies in terms of natural "inclinations and wants" (or "love") — the native human "faculties," or natural means by which these are achieved, and of the twofold "form" or "constitution" in which these are given. The *Disquisition* is in the first place a disquisition on the passions. The natural human inclinations and wants, "both physical and moral," produce society, which is necessary for the development and perfection of the natural human "intellectual and moral faculties." Man is distinguished from all other forms of life by precisely these inclinations and faculties, or by "the love of truth and justice" and the "love of country." He agrees with Aristotle that man is the political animal.[4] With all other animals, naturally, he shares the inclination to self-preservation and feels more strongly what affects himself directly than what affects others. He agrees with Plato that the human body is the most "private" of all things.[5] In no other form of life is this latter feeling stronger than in man. He agrees with Nietzsche that "Man is more an ape than the apes," and that the more man is an ape the less he is man.[6] This "twofold constitution" of human nature, in which the higher part is in tension with the lower, is the origin of government, which is aimed at harmonizing these parts and ruling this tension, and the point of departure for the science of government as laid down by Calhoun.[7]

The characteristic problem undertaken by the science of government is thus the problem of the proper organization or constitution of government. All human societies are characterized by the institution of government. To the question, what is the best form of government? Calhoun answers that it is that form which is most conducive to the perfection of the highest aims of society, the perfection of man as a rational social animal. This is "constitutional government," the government most in accordance with the constitution of man. However improbable it may be, constitutional government is everywhere and at all times possible in principle and is always the standard by which all existing governments should be judged. Languages, customs, pursuits, positive laws, and so on may diverge greatly from society to society or even within a single society. It is rather the principles of government which remain the same and are transferable from one case to another. By reason of all the variations and differences just mentioned, as well as others, Calhoun admits that "In applying them to practical uses, all elementary principles are liable to difficulties." Hence the foundation of the science of government does not obviate the need for statesmanship in the fullest sense. The application of elementary political principles requires judgment and experience. This means that good and wise government finally depends upon good and wise individuals. The science of government does not overcome chance.

Recognizing that the "high and glittering prize" of government acts as a powerful stimulus to them, the primary aim of the science of government is to mold the most ambitious individuals to the common good of the whole community.[8] Hence, the aim of the government most in accordance with the constitution of man is the formation of the character of the best man. Of course, government is a question of more than a moment or even of a single lifetime, however wise and just that lifetime might be. Who knows what will happen in even ten year's time? As Calhoun observed in another context, "A man of remarkable character, it is said, is at the head of [a certain] government. Things may go very well in his time, but how they will be managed afterwards, who can tell? Look at the subject."[9] The formation of statesmen or rulers is the purpose of the regime or form of government itself. Much is naturally beyond the control of rulers, however wise and powerful. In all cases, however, the more truly remarkable the statesman or ruler may actually be, the more his statesmanship or rule will accord with the elementary principles of government.[10]

A Disquisition on Government is preliminary also in the sense of being new: it is, according to Calhoun's letter to Anna-Maria, "nearly throughout new territory." The precise character of Calhoun's own new coverage, however, is less immediately clear than his intention. It is not to be found in any particular items of Calhoun's supposed originality, many and perhaps all of which can be found in predecessors, but inheres in the whole. We do not yet see this whole clearly. Popular commentaries on Calhoun or the Disquisition which stress contemporary or later political thinkers or schools and find in his thought however remarkable a precis of Hegel's famous constitutionalism; or a "Marxism" of a master class; or one of the "fathers of behaviorism" or of contemporary "interest group theory," provide little glimpse of it.[11] Useful as such studies doubtless are in many respects, it is obvious that Calhoun's thought is hardly comprehended by reference to the new universal and homogeneous state in which all are free and equal, much less to the view that essentially history is "rational" or is the "history of freedom"; to the new classless society, brought about by a cadre or party, in which each perfection is accessible to all; or to an idealization of science broadly characterized by reduction of the terms of the soul to the terms of the body. Calhoun clearly means to present another, almost opposite, state, society, and science. Perhaps his newness is hard to clarify because it is still "new."[12]

The Context of Calhoun's Philosophy of Politics

To begin to appreciate the newness of the territory covered by Calhoun it is useful for a time to concentrate less on contemporary and later political thinkers and schools and more on the territory as he first saw it himself, the "old" or commonplace territory familiar to the early European nineteenth century. The old or commonplace territory as found by Calhoun is the familiar territory laid out by Hobbes: Hobbism and all its variants: the state, society, and science as presented by Hobbes and his successors, including his contemporary successors today. The intent, then, of the *Disquisition* may be provisionally conceived first as the transcendence of Hobbes, not for the sake of mastering or overcoming Hobbes or his successors but merely for the sake, in the first place, of founding the new science, that is, the true political science which Hobbes claimed to have founded but, on the showing of *A Disquisition on Government*, did not found. To this end, which is Hobbes' own, Calhoun begins with the same ground, science, even "modern" science, and presents "new" ground, politics, or the political in place of the civil.

We can most succinctly state our opening thesis in this respect by saying that whereas Locke, Rousseau, and others had attempted to go beyond Hobbism primarily by correcting its beginnings, that is, its doctrine of the "state of nature," and transcend Hobbes' fundamental thought by more or less radically qualifying or inversing it in various respects, Calhoun attempts to do so primarily by correcting its end, and by dismissing its beginning in the hypothesis of the "state of nature" root and branch. In so doing, he arrives at a new place, the "new territory" that is the true and fundamental ground of political science. He undertakes to do this for the sake of statesmanship, surely, that is, for the sake of politics and political ends, for the sake of the whole human being, but primarily for the sake of science itself, for the perfection of the "highest attribute of the human mind," and the human attribute most admirable for its own sake. Political science as understood by Calhoun is incomparably the greatest achievement of that human attribute.

At least provisionally, then, it might thus be reasonably supposed that the extent to which he transcends Hobbism, or succeeds where Hobbes failed, is the standard by which, on his own terms, Calhoun must be judged. Yet, in a sense, these are already more (or, perhaps, less) than Calhoun's own terms. Certainly, it is true that Calhoun's attention to Hobbes might seem obvious enough at the beginning of the *Disquisition* in the inaugural reference to the science of astronomy and the science of government (par. 1); or in the middle of the *Disquisition* in the critique of the "state of nature" doctrine and the "Galilean hypothesis" of the "social contract" (par. 89); or, perhaps, even at the end of the *Disquisition* in the interpretation of Britain (paragraphs 140ff). It is "obvious" throughout the *Disquisition,* among other things, in the affirmation of unitary and undivided sovereignty and in the consistent emphasis upon the strength of the "individual" or "selfish" feelings as against the "social" feelings, or upon "self-preservation," the "all pervading and essential law of animated existence." But Calhoun never mentions Hobbes. While instructive sketches of Calhoun's relation to Hobbes or to other thinkers have readily been made, Calhoun himself does not point to any such studies but immediately to the matter. The truth of the matter, "the facts in their bearings on the subject under discussion," is his standard, and the standard by which he must be judged. He never mentions other thinkers by name. Almost the first thing that strikes the reader of the *Disquisition* is its lack of reference to *any* previous or contemporary authors or works. No authoritative figure or school is explicitly named anywhere in it. No names are named at all. Calhoun could seem to be open to the criticism that Mill made of Bentham for attempting to reconstruct "all philosophy *ab initio* without reference to the opinions of his predecessors."[13] This is surely curious in a thinker who speaks so often of "progress," the most common depiction of which is standing on the shoulders of others. Calhoun stands on no one's shoulders. At any rate, he is not a historian of ideas. The *Disquisition* presents itself not so much as a work of great learning, even useful learning, although it is that, but as a work primarily of original or pure thought. Gathering too quickly around questions of Calhoun's relation to others (a gathering already dependent in any case upon a presupposed assessment of the others), much less on his supposed place in an imaginary "history of ideas," not only risks blurring his plain intention actually and once and for all to "lay a solid foundation for political science" but, what is the same thing, his challenging invitation to the reader of the *Disquisition* to stand up, in like manner, on his own feet. In carefully thinking through the presentation of the *Disquisition,* the inquirer at length becomes an adept in political science himself, a participant in its achievement, and formed by it. *A Disquisition on Government* has no close parallels. It is a new experience, and the commentary is not intended in any way to distract the reader from that experience or otherwise rob him of it.

Given the silence regarding the names and works of others, especially in the face of his (admittedly private) statement according to which his own work covers "new territory," the reader might reasonably expect the name or "presence" of Calhoun to be correspondingly loud in the *Disquisition*. This expectation is not rewarded. The author is plain, direct, and brief—almost the opposite of a Saint-Simon or Comte. He compares himself to no one. The author of *A Disquisition on Government* intrudes as little as the author of the Platonic dialogs (if not less, as there is no setting or plot). All emphasis is upon the new science rather than upon the founder, who is himself tacitly presented as all but simply accidental to it. The new science, political science, is not "John C. Calhoun's new science." *A Disquisition on Government* can be read and its principles grasped without ever having heard of John C. Calhoun. As in the case of astronomy, where the apparent centrality of earth itself must be seen and overcome as merely accidental to that science, it is accidental that the science of government is founded by an American or that that American is John Calhoun.

In this regard it may be observed that it is not actually true that, as we have said, no names are named in *A Disquisition*. Many names are named, but they are the names of countries or nations, peoples, and not of persons. Calhoun names such names as the Jews, Iroquois, Chinese, and so on (*Disquisition*, 18). Peoples or communities (regimes) and not individuals (or "civilizations") are the proper subject of the science of government. "The absolute ethical totality is nothing other than a people."[14] However crucial a particular individual may be in the life of a people or regime, that individual will not alter or overturn any of the general principles pertaining to peoples or regimes. Nor, certainly, is it entirely true that Calhoun himself does not stand on the shoulders of others. As he repeatedly insists in other contexts, Calhoun, like all other men, stands, where Providence cast his lot, on the shoulders of his "community"—what we may for the moment call "society"—or, more precisely, on the shoulders of all the particular "laws and institutions of the country where born" and where he drew his first breath.[15]

For Calhoun, the knowledge that is necessary for and that is sought by the science of government is possible and immediately accessible to men as men on the basis merely of the prior knowledge possessed by each man that he is. The method entailed in ascertaining this knowledge, whether through radical doubt, cogitation, comparison, and discussion with others, "searching within oneself," experience, or all of these, is adequate to ground the science of government. This fact accounts for the absence anywhere in *A Disquisition on Government* of any acknowledgement of the centrality of the problem of knowledge, or epistemology, which has dominated modern thought, for the philosophy or science of government. This absence, which is a key to some of the assumptions of the work, is almost as striking as the absence in the *Disquisition* of names of any prior thinkers, if not moreso, and, in view of the fact that Calhoun studied the writings of Hume all his adult life and as a youth had even taught himself to read using Locke's *Essay Concerning Human Understanding*, hardly short of amazing. For Calhoun, Creation is naturally intelligible to the rational creature. Hence for him the question of "method" is never primary.[16] However, the capacity men as men possess is not sufficient to complete political science. If it were, perhaps that science could be found everywhere there are human beings, including among, say, the Iroquois, whose constitution and practice is otherwise so highly praised in the *Disquisition*. But it is not. What is found everywhere there are human beings is only government. Nor, apparently, does Calhoun find the foundation for political science laid in his favorite authors — Aristotle, whose *Politics*, he said, was "among the best" introductions to political or human life, or Burke, whom he regarded as "the wisest of modern statesmen, and who had the keenest and deepest glance into futurity."[17] In order to prepare to see political science as Calhoun sees it, the following observations may be useful.

A *Disquisition on Government* is meant to provide "a solid foundation for the science of government" (par. 1). Calhoun takes the term "solid foundation" from the preface to David Hume's *Treatise on Human Nature*, where Hume sets forth what is necessary for a "comprehensive science of man" and how it can be attained, what is necessary for its "solid foundation." He takes the term "science of government" from Burke's *Reflections on the Revolution in France*. (These writers, and especially Burke, are acknowledged by all to have been among his favorite authors.) Calhoun understands the science of government to consist of two parts, a more theoretical, rational, or strictly logical part, which is the science or philosophy of government or political philosophy or science in the strict sense, and a practical or applicative part, which is the art of government or the art or science of legislation. His position can be described as follows: he takes the theoretical or logical part of the science of government from Aristotle and the practical or legislative part of the science of government from Burke. (These two writers are particularly noted by historians to have been Calhoun's favorite writers.) Yet, if Calhounism — constitutionalism — is Aristotelean and Burkean, it is not simply Aristotle or Burke. The aim of the science of government is the perfection of the human moral and intellectual faculties, that is, the common good of the community as a whole and knowledge of the science of government itself. The science of government is the kernel of the science of man described but not arrived at by Hume.

According to Hume, "the science of man is the only solid foundation for the other sciences." It is the "solid foundation" because "there is no question of importance whose decision is not comprised in the science of man; and there is none which can be decided with any certainty before we become acquainted with that science." And, "the only solid foundation we can give this science itself must be laid on experience and observation."[18] It is the aim of the *Treatise on Human Nature* to introduce this foundational science and show all that is necessary to provide it with the "solid foundations," without which the most fundamental deliberations and decisions are vain, by introducing the "experimental method of reasoning" from physical into moral subjects. To the skeptic, since the latter are more comprehensive in their human import than the former, and since they cannot be purposely premeditated and manipulated like the former, it would appear that in the arena of the new science of man the proverbially "slow but sure Baconian method" may prove even slower than otherwise, as well as always of questionable surety. Hume, in any event, is already sure that the science of man itself is composed of the "four sciences of Logic, Morals, Criticism, and Politics." These comprehend "almost everything which it can in any way import us to be acquainted with, or which can tend either to the improvement or ornament of the human mind." As outlined by him, "the role of logic," the first or introductory part of the science of man, "is to explain the principles and operations of our reasoning faculty, the nature of our ideas: morals and criticism regard our tastes and our sentiments: and politics consider men as united in society, and dependent upon each other." It is hard to see how all or any of this could be known "by experience and observation," to say nothing of "logic" alone. But be this as it may, Calhoun's position is much the other way around. As viewed by him, political science is itself and alone precisely the crowning or ruling human science, the science to which, willy-nilly, all others finally point or lead, and, so far as what Hume calls the "improvement or ornament of the human mind" is concerned, on which they all ultimately depend.[19]

The import of this observation may be illustrated in the following way. Given his celebrated rejection of the Hobbsian doctrines of the "state of nature" and the "social contract," on the one hand, and his celebrated reference to Newtonian gravitation and the "solid foundation" of political science at the beginning of the *Disquisition*, Calhoun's closest point of contact with Hume in this respect is, not surprisingly, found less in the *Treatise's* outline of the new "science of man" than in its development of Newton's principle of gravitation in Hume's treatment of the natural origins of human society. Like Calhoun, Hume rejects all "state of nature" and "social contract doctrines." He writes: "The cohesion of the parts of matter arises from natural and necessary principles.... We must allow that human society is founded on like principles...for is it more certain that two flat pieces of marble will unite together than that two young savages of different sexes will copulate?"[20] That is, according to Hume, it is the ever-repeated experience of human sexual attraction, or that part of what Calhoun at the beginning of the *Disquisition* calls "physical wants and inclinations," that acts in the human as the principle of gravitation acts in the material sphere and gives rise to human society. In so doing, through the generation of offspring and the "family," this "principle" gives rise to what Calhoun in the same place calls the "moral wants and inclinations." Calhoun tacitly rejects this account as insufficient. That is, Calhoun approved of Hume's rejection of the Hobbsian doctrines, but believed that Hume did not go far enough in rejecting them. Hume did not arrive at the origins of society because his account of those origins remains on the same plane as Hobbes' account. He is, therefore, open to the same kind of fundamental criticism, which for Calhoun is final, that Montesquieu levied against Hobbes: he attributes to the physical or most animal inclinations, albeit for the sake of once and for all rejecting the doctrine of the state of nature, the experience and practice of established society, the "family," its "sympathetic feelings," and "moral wants and inclinations," and traces the origins of society to that generalized experience and practice.[21] It is not enough.

However much an improvement Hume's account may be over Hobbes' in this regard, the Humean "science of man" does not arrive at political science. Near the beginning of the *Disquisition* Calhoun, all but ignoring sexual attraction and all other mediated familial feelings, explains in almost so many words that the most immediately familial of all human feelings, maternal love (which is natural), and with it the family itself, is not the primary or the ultimate foundation of human society and that it does not represent the rational or "solid foundation" of political science, however inseparable family and society may be. He mentions this familial feeling explicitly only to contrast it with that solid foundation. When he later and for the second and last time in the *Disquisition* alludes to the family as such, in connection with the authority of the laws of the land, he does not allude at all to the affection of parents for their offspring. He alludes to the family only to remind the reader of parental authority or, in other words, to emphasize these duties and responsibilities, among others, of children. To use Aristotle's language, the family is first for us but not first by nature. Moreover, finally, when Calhoun in other places goes so far as to refer to the "human family" itself, that is to the human race as such understood as ultimately biologically kin, it is by way of explaining that this most exhaustive of all human kinship groups, the human race, is not comprehended in and will never provide the basis for a single society or community. However small and restricted or large and inclusive it may be seen to be, the familial relationship is neither the primary political relationship nor does it give rise to it.[22] It therefore cannot provide the basis for political science or a "science of man."

More importantly, however (at the very beginning of the *Disquisition*, paragraph 2), Calhoun asserts that, while "his inclinations and wants, physical and moral, irresistibly impel" man to associate with his kind, he immediately observes (in the same paragraph) that this association is necessary for "a full development of his moral and intellectual faculties." He specifies that, even if it were possible, as it is not, for mankind to exist otherwise, that is, even if human sexual attraction could somehow sustain the race apart from the family and human society, human society would nevertheless still be necessary for the development of the distinctively human faculties, the faculties by which man raises himself "above the level of the brute creation."[23] In other words, there is no question of human physical wants and inclinations giving rise to moral wants and inclinations or providing the "solid foundations" for them. "Sublimation" is a myth. Rather, it is these and only these distinctive moral and intellectual faculties, which, as such, are prior to any human inclinations and to everything to which human inclinations give rise or to which they irresistibly impel men, including human society, that themselves give rise to these human inclinations. For Calhoun, therefore, the "physical wants," however elaborated and generalized, do not adequately provide the "like principles," that is, the fundamental law of gravity in the realm of matter and motion and its likeness in that of human society and government, asserted by Hume, on questions of cohesion or order in the material and that in the human world. We here leave open the question as to the extent to which Hume's understanding of these principles may be determined by his "Baconian" or "experimental method" of reasoning.

The opposite position had, seemingly, been set forth by Hobbes, who, however, based his own "civil philosophy," which he understood to be and always presented as the first true political science, on similar ground, but in accordance with the Galilean and Euclidean methods of reasoning. Where Hume speaks of the attraction of physical pleasure as the passionate basis of society, Hobbes had spoken of fear of pain, or imaginary pain, as its rational basis. Hobbes taught that "every man is desirous of what is good for him, and shuns what is evil, but chiefly the chiefest of natural evils, which is death; and this he doth by a certain impulsion of nature, no less than that whereby a stone moves downward."[24] This likeness of Newton's principle of gravity in the material world is generalized by Hobbes into the animal law of self-preservation, upon which human natural right and human society and government are rationally based. It is on this basis that all the claims that Hobbes makes for his new science of government are themselves based. "Galileus in our time...was the first that opened to us the gate of natural philosophy universal, which is the knowledge of nature and motion.... Natural philosophy is therefore but young; but civil philosophy is yet much younger, as being no older...than my own book *de Cive*."[25] Hobbes' various statements of this claim, as well as the stress that he characteristically lays on Galilean and Euclidean methods in the various presentations of his new science, give rise to the controversy as to whether "civil philosophy" is to be taken, and accordingly understood, as a contribution to natural philosophy or science on a par with Galileo's, or as a separate but equal branch of knowledge.[26]

The substance of this whole Hobbsian controversy as it bears on and prepares us, via Hume's attempt to lay the solid foundation for the science of man, for the understanding of the solid foundation of Calhoun's science of government may be illustrated by reference to the private and public methodologies of British Utilitarianism, which arose on the shoulders of Hume.

John Stuart Mill's principal criticism of British Utilitarianism as that doctrine was formulated and handed down to him by Bentham and his father James Mill was not that these advocates ignored the opinions of their predecessors but, rather, that they had adopted the wrong methodology in their thinking. For his part, John Mill straight-forwardly asserted that "the backward state of the moral sciences can only be remedied by applying to them the methods of Physical Sciences, duly extended and generalized."[27] Bentham himself had also asserted the applicability of those methods to the moral sciences. When speaking of his own predecessors, he typically speaks in precisely these terms: "What Bacon was to the physical world, Helvetius was to the moral. The moral world has therefore had its Bacon, but its Newton is yet to come." Bentham himself hoped to establish the final or Newtonian perfection of social science through the principle of the "greatest-happiness" applied to utilitarian calculations of political economy. Nevertheless, however valuable Bentham doubtless perceived the doctrines of Helvetius to be, it is equally doubtless, as well as more important, that he thought he found that "the foundations of all virtue are laid in utility" not in the doctrines of Helvetius but, explicitly, in Hume's rejection of the "fiction" of the social contract." "I well remember," he wrote (in terms reminiscent of Kant's reaction to Hume), that "no sooner had I read that part of [the *Treatise*] which touches on this subject, than I felt as if scales had fallen from my eyes. I then, for the first time, learnt to call the cause of the people the cause of virtue."[28] Thus awakened by Hume from his intellectual slumber, Bentham claimed that "Any work of mine…on the subject of legislation or any other branch of moral science is an attempt to extend the experimental method of reasoning from the physical branch to the moral."[29] The ultimate results of this extension has long been summarized under such Benthamite watchwords as "the greatest good for the greatest number" and "representative government," or the resolution of the problems of government by the extension of the franchise and institution of regular elections. It all but goes without saying that, as seen by Calhoun, all these results are but an elaborate variant, even if at the same time, perhaps, the peak achievement, of the attempt to justify the political supremacy of the numerical majority.

According to Calhoun, of course, this justification is inadequate. It goes too far in its policy and not far enough in its principle. We may here for the moment limit ourselves simply to the initial observation that, according to Calhoun, "it is a great and dangerous mistake to suppose, as many do," that the right of suffrage, "the right on the part of the ruled to choose their rulers at proper intervals and to hold them thereby responsible for their conduct," however widely it is extended and however well-guarded and "enlightened" its practice may be, can alone form a good and happy government, or, ultimately, anything other than an absolute government.[30] Numerical majoritarianism will fail in the aims of government. Connected with this, however, is, one further issue connected with Utilitarianism, as it is set forth by John Stuart Mill, which has not been widely noticed but which represents, or may at least be taken to represent, one of Calhoun's prime concerns. This issue is identified by Calhoun as a "new and important political element."[31] In order to see this new element as it appears in Utilitarianism, we must turn briefly to James and John Stuart Mill.

John Stuart Mill criticized James Mill and Bentham principally on the ground that their work was not properly methodical. Bentham, however, had laid particular claim to scientific method. James Mill had also taught, both generally and to John Stuart Mill in particular, "the methods of physical science as the proper model for political."[32] In so doing, he had been explicit about the principal precursor of the "new science of politics" represented by Utilitarianism. The principal precursor was the political science of Hobbes, as made possible by the astronomical and physical discoveries of Galileo and by the geometry of Euclid, which the political science of Hobbes exemplified. According to James Mill, Hobbes' greatness lay in his applying these disciplines to human nature:

> Hobbes began his *Treatise on Human Nature [De Homine]* in these words: "The true and perspicuous explication of the elements *[sic]* of laws natural and politic which is my present scope, dependeth upon the knowledge of what is human nature".... Going, as he was, to expound the elements *[sic]* of political government, he saw, and he was the first to see clearly, that the elements *[sic]* of political government were the principles of human nature.

James Mill held that Bentham's Utilitarianism represented the completion of this application. It did so not only because it completed the application of the new scientific method to the understanding of human nature, begun by Hobbes, but primarily because it immediately and "without varnish" applied the results obtained by means of this application to practice, as recommended by Hobbes.[33] This latter application, which becomes primary in Benthamism and which is the genuine and characteristic impulse of Bentham's Utilitarianism (and which, it goes without saying, could hardly be more opposed to the intention of Hume), is far from limited to expounding Hobbes' writings in the schools, but itself becomes a conscious program of public exhortation to and "education" for "scientific" politics, not to say "scientific individualism" or Utilitarian democracy.

For this purpose, on the basis of what Calhoun in the *Disquisition* calls the new "diffusion of knowledge" and Bentham called the "spread of learning," Bentham and James Mill founded the *Westminster Review* in 1824. According to

Bentham, the spread of scientific learning was both increasingly revealing the essential equality of all men in truth and contracting "mankind to a level with each other" in fact. The *Westminster Review* was founded specifically to accelerate the spread of this scientific learning, which was understood to be equivalent to Utilitarianism, and the diffusion of all its beneficent effects, which were understood to be self-evident. John Stuart Mill became the "most frequent contributor." "When I first read Bentham," he records, "and especially from the commencement of the *Westminster Review*, I had what might truly be called a purpose in life." Having learned from his reading of Bentham that "all previous moralists were superseded" by the union of science and morality, or theory and practice, in Utilitarianism, this purpose, founded on the basis of this union and armed with the weapons it provided, not the least of which was the new hope of imminently diffusing certain happiness for all, was "to be a reformer of the world" on the model of Bentham. As recorded in his famous *Autobiography*, this purpose in his life collapsed.[34]

From the beginning James Mill had clearly seen that achieving this purpose, which was the *raison d'etre* of the *Westminster Review* itself, would (to say the least) require a certain sustained effort without which it would not come about. It was because this purpose was not flourishing on its own, in spite of the continuing "spread of learning" and all of the "discoveries and improvements" that were everywhere in evidence, that provided the object in founding this "radical journal," implicitly bent on promoting the Hobbesian mission of enlightenment, in the first place. The utilitarianist union of science and morality must thus be further and finally unified with activist periodical journalism in order to hasten and insure the achievement of its purpose. It is a sort of Hobbism for the people. According to him, and he was originally followed in his views by his young son, this state of affairs was primarily due to, or forced by, the opinions of long entrenched "sinister interests." These were the interests of the present rulers, the "people in power," which is to say, the rulers by inherited right or tradition or anything but scientifically demonstrated and utilitarian right. Mill explains the connection as follows. "A periodical production must sell immediately," if it is to be profitable and successful. "Every motive, therefore, which prompts to the production of anything periodical, prompts to the study of immediate effect, of unpostponed popularity." Since it is dependent for its success upon this "immediate applause," periodical literature must conform to prevailing "fashion." The deepest stratum of the prevailing fashion is political fashion, for political fashion, what Whitehead will later call the "climate of opinion," exercises the greatest power. Mill then asks, "But what is the class most instrumental in setting the fashion which exercises the greatest control over the opinions of men?...The people in power compose it." Since "[t]he favorite opinions of people in power are the opinions which favor their own power.... To these opinions periodical literature is under a sort of necessity...of serving as a pander."[35] It merely serves as the voice of sinister, or what Marx will call "ideological"—because "non-scientific"—ruling interests. In contrast to such literature, the *Westminster Review* was intended to counter this fashion, correct these opinions, and change these people as part of the comprehensive and systematic Utilitarian program of social policy. As this program increases in its success, Utilitarianism will to that extent educate and control the opinions of men in the name of science.

James Mill's own conception and description of the Benthamic union of philosophy or science, morality, and journalism—in short, the movement of Utilitarianism, with emphasis upon publicity—exemplifies what Calhoun has identified in the *Disquisition* as a "new and political element": public opinion formed by a mass press that is driven by party feeling, or secular propaganda. It is an opinion that takes the place formerly occupied by "superstition," and is similar in its character. According to Calhoun, "Its influence is in the present day on the increase, and it is highly probable that it may...in time effect great changes—social and political."[36] Calhoun's term for this powerful new element is neither novel nor especially revealing. It is merely "the press" or the new "power and influence" of the press in an age of increasing diffusion of information (112). As an "organ of public opinion," that is, the "opinion of the whole community," considered and weighed from all its parts, the press is as false as opposed to true public opinion. It is now "usually" the voice merely of "a small but energetic and active portion," and used actually "as a means of controlling public opinion and of so molding it as to promote...peculiar interests and to aid in carrying on the warfare of party." Calhoun emphasizes the possible beneficence of a free press, yet it is precisely the influence just described, which is not beneficent, that is now increasing and that is most likely to increase in the future. The term that is introduced by John Stuart Mill himself to denominate this phenomenon in his mature account of his own career at the *Westminster Review* has become familiar. It is the term "propagandism." "It was my father's opinions," he wrote, "which gave the distinguishing character to the Benthamic or utilitarian propagandism."[37] This secularized religious term denominates what Calhoun calls the "new political element," the characteristic element of society and politics, of the "present condition of the world." Both Mill's later writings and *A Disquisition on Government* are offered within this present condition as providing the only genuine means for its enlightenment.

What increasingly appeared to J. S. Mill as shortcomings in the union of science and morality or theory and practice represented by Utilitarianism led him to complain most particularly of the unsuitability of the method used to achieve it. Bentham and James Mill, he wrote, "though right in adopting a deductive method, had made a wrong selection of one, having taken as a type of the deduction, not the appropriate process, that of the deductive methods of natural philosophy, but the inappropriate one of pure geometry." This was what was "fundamentally erroneous in my father's conception of philosophical method, as applicable to politics."[38] This error, once discovered, for him explodes Bentham's Utilitarianism. For it means that the "new science of politics" or Benthamism is, in truth, not political philosophy or science at all but only and merely a kind of politics which does not and perhaps cannot see itself as merely a partisan politics. Arising within the ever-increasing diffusion of intelligence and learning and claiming to transcend all partisanship in the name of reason and virtue, it in fact only enshrines partisanship in the polemical doctrines of a pseudo-scientific ideology or orthodoxy. The Baconian interest in control of physical nature easily becomes also interest in the control of opinions about nature. There is, therefore, no new union between the "new science," as such, on the one hand, and true "morality" and hence actual practice, on the other, such as Benthamism publicizes. There is only the new partisanship and its increasing publicity.

Having turned away from Betham's Utilitarianism, Mill writes: "If I am [now] asked what system of political philosophy I substituted for that which as a philosophy, I had abandoned, I answer, no system: only a conviction that the true system was something more complex and many-sided than I had previously had any idea of." Establishing the true system depends on discovering the true methodology. His mature "system" or "philosophy" becomes, then, the system of properly determining philosophic methodologies, including the "Logic of the Moral Sciences," by the "mode of tracing causes and effects in physical science." This turn in the younger Mill's utilitarianism constitutes, in effect if not in name, a return toward Hume and even toward the skepticism of Hume: a return toward all that in Hume which Bentham had "gone beyond" once Hume had removed the scales from his eyes.[39] However, its upshot is, no less than in original Benthamism itself, the turning of Hume's profound Toryism into Liberalism. Mill stresses that he has no systematic political philosophy in the sense represented by Bentham's Utilitarianism, which he rejects because of its unsuitable methodism. If such a genuinely true political philosophy is possible at all, according to him, it is not yet possible. He merely continues and liberalizes Hume's position in the Preface to the *Treatise on Human Nature*. The mature Mill hopes that the philosophic methodology he has at length established on the basis of his tracing causes and effects in physical science will perhaps be useful for determining the basis, at which he does not himself arrive, or pretend to arrive, of a genuine, political philosophy in "the next two or three generations of European thinkers." The Liberalism of today, although perhaps modified on the point of what he called "advanced nations," remains largely on the ground established by Mill.

The collapse for Mill of the utilitarianism he inherited was not limited to his discovery that the scientific morality represented by utilitarianism was not properly scientific but was at the same time his discovery that its morality was not properly moral. On the contrary, according to him, its influence was "more pernicious" than the conventional or inherited morality it was intended to replace and in fact perverted the "whole moral nature" of those it attracted.[40] Its great "mistake," distinct but not separate from its mistaken methodology, was "presenting in systematic shape, and as the treatment of a great philosophic question, what should have passed for what it was, the mere polemics of the day."[41] Thanks to the efforts of the Benthamite followers of Hume in England, one side of these polemics to some extent acquired the apparent support and influence of "science," much as they acquired the apparent support and influence of reason among Hume's later continental students and rivals in Germany. The consequences of this popular success have now to be dealt with. Mill's most famous work, the *Essay on Liberty*, is devoted to this task.[42] In effect, the necessity to counter or disarm what Mill calls "propagandism," specifically, the propagandism of Benthamism or numerical majoritarianism in an advanced social state, becomes the central theme of the *Essay*. This is because, as seen by Mill, the very success of propagandism, the character of propagandism as such, is, now and for the first time, in Willmoore Kendall's words a century later, "the central problem of all civilized societies—the one to which all other problems are subordinate because of the consequences, good or ill, that a society must bring upon itself as it adopts this or that solution to it."[43]

What Calhoun called a "new political element" and Mill saw as characterizing his own time and country, has thus already apparently become for everyone the central and highest and almost only political problem. Willmoore Kendall, however, does not present the "central problem" of the *Essay on Liberty* as the specific problem of propagandism, as Mill sees it, or of Calhoun's new political element. He identifies it only as Mill's concern with "the entire 'communications' process in any civilized society ('advanced' society, as Mill puts it)—and the question he raises about it is whether there should be limitations on that process."

However, Mill distinguishes between civilized or advanced societies and "those backward states of society," that is, primitive or what Kendall calls "traditional" societies, nowadays typically labeled "underdeveloped" societies, which, according to him, readers of the *Essay on Liberty* "may leave out of consideration" as irrelevant to the central problem of civilized societies. Mill leaves them "out of consideration" because none of the "rights," including the supreme right of freedom of speech, which *On Liberty* is concerned to defend, concerns them (or "children or persons underage"). "All the nations with whom we need concern ourselves," he writes, are only the "advanced," or what Calhoun calls the civilized, societies, the societies characterized by the pervasive influence of modern natural science.[44] These societies are those in which the "spread of learning" made possible by modern natural science and flowing from modern natural science seems to be "raising mankind to a level with each other," in the Philosophical Radicals' terms, and in which, as a result, propagandism in more or less extreme forms is increasingly the characteristic mode of learning, and, therefore, of establishing "public truth," that is, forming public orthodoxy. These societies, the "advanced" societies, are to be understood in the first place in contradistinction to any "traditional" or "closed" society. Hence, when Willmoore Kendall observes that Mill's "doctrine of freedom of speech is...the perfect weapon— perfect because of its alleged connection with the quest for truth—to turn upon the traditional society that he must overthrow," we must replace Kendall's term "traditional" with Mill's term "propagandistic" in order to avoid the pitfalls and grasp the full thrust of Kendall's insight. "For," Kendall continues, "he who would destroy society [i.e., Mill's propagandistic society] must first destroy the public truth it conceives itself as embodying; and Mill's doctrine of freedom of speech, to the extent that it gets accepted publicly, does just that." It is only in this way, Mill believes, that there is any hope that the tyranny of propaganda, or of propagandistic society, of what he calls the "yoke of public opinion" or the "tyranny of the majority," may be thrown off or at least withstood.

In this connection we may summarize Mill's own description of the collapse of his original purpose in life as a reformer of the world by saying that, when considering whether, were all mankind actually to be reformed in perfect accordance with the greatest-happiness principle and the whole world managed in accordance with the principle of the greatest happiness for the greatest number, he would then actually be happy himself, he discovered and admitted that he would not be.[45] Since Benthamism held happiness to be the aim of human life, this discovery was unsupportable, and Mill immediately became unhappy with Benthamism. He began, then, to reformulate this aim in terms of the personal quest for truth and the conformation of feelings to authentic moral excellence. He became a partisan for excellence. This is because, according to him, the knowledge of the truth provides the greatest possible pleasure. Since the achievement of this pleasure, which is the highest human good and therefore the highest human aim, and which is inseparable from the quest for truth, requires freedom of thought, and freedom of thought depends on freedom of speech, or liberty, for its practice and dissemination in a propagandistic society, in which the "tyranny of the prevailing opinion and feeling...enslaves the soul itself," Mill, on these grounds alone, advocated public adoption of radical freedom of speech. His effort has the effect of making certain elements of the party of Philosophical Radicalism more radical than they originally had been, in particular, the advocacy of freedom of speech and the press.

Willmoore Kendall seems correct, therefore, in holding that Mill's advocacy "conduces to a negation of the very idea of a public truth" in these circumstances, except for that "truth" according to which there is no public truth or only private (or, in Mill's terms, "internal") truths. And he seems further correct in holding that "when Mill's followers demand the elevation of scepticism to the status of a national religion, and the remaking of society in the image of that religion, they are not reading into his position something that is not there.... They are, rather, merely making specific applications of notions that, for Mill, are the point of departure for the entire discussion." Such a climate of opinion may undermine a community or political regime while leaving what is called "civil society" intact. This effect, coupled with praise of individual excellence, is the hallmark of Liberalism from its inception. For his own part, Hume, also in the face of triumphant rationalism, had held that human society could exist and even thrive without modern natural science, which, on its own terms, he showed, was — as, on its terms, human society is not — irrational. Hence it has been well said that "since the time of Hume, the fashionable scientific philosophy has been such as to deny the rationality of science.... In other words [science] has remained blandly indifferent to its refutation by Hume,"[46] as numerical majoritarianism has remained indifferent to the collapse of Benthamism. For considerations like these, Kendall writes that, "assuming both a society willing to adopt Mill's proposals and a population willing to act in the manner they require...I contend that the society will overnight become the most intolerant of possible societies and, above all, one in which the pursuit of truth...can only come to a halt."[47] That is, such a society will be in the strongest sense of the term a "closed" society. Mill, too, of course, is concerned about just such intolerance. Still, Kendall's contentions help us to see that what is truly in need of defense.[48] For Calhoun's part, moral excellence, the achievement praised by J. S. Mill, is not genuinely possible in the open and almost subpolitical society Mill promotes (in effect Locke's "civil society"), anymore than unqualified intellectual excellence is possible in non-civilized regimes. Besides, according to Calhoun, "freedom of speech" is not "liberty," and in any case freedom of thought, or, in the highest case, philosophy or science (Mill's ultimate concern), is not dependent upon freedom of speech, still less on radical freedom of speech, and, furthermore, freedom of speech, radical or otherwise, is no effective check on what Mill identifies as the tyranny of the majority.

The most extreme statement in a work characterized by extremism and radical intent is the famous sentence in the *Essay on Liberty* according to which "If all mankind minus one were of one opinion, and only one person were of the contrary opinion, mankind would be no more justified in silencing that one person, than he, if he had the power, would be in silencing mankind." Truth is no respecter of persons, still less mere numbers. This is the most extreme claim Mill can make in balancing the many, the largest possible majority, against one, the smallest possible minority, such as a philosopher, on the scales of liberty and truth. These are meant by Mill to be political scales, of course, yet his presentation points one not to the discussion of the "general principles" of political science in Mill's own *Considerations on Representative Government* but rather to the presentation in *A Disquisition on Government* of what Calhoun himself calls an "utmost extreme," an example of government not limited to speech but extending to actual political life, "that would be thought impracticable had it never existed." This is the example of the "unanimity principle" in the constitution of Poland.[49] What may seem impossible in speech is not always simply impossible: action may sometimes be stranger (if often less humorous) than the extremes of the most rigorous thought. "Every member of her Diet...possessed a veto on all its proceedings—thus making a unanimous vote necessary to enact a law or to adopt any measure whatever." The freedom to disagree publicly, which for Mill is inseparable from the quest for truth and justice, and which, because of the elusive and progressively receding character of the truth and justice, must be absolute, is here balanced with the necessity for public agreement, which is itself inseparable from human society, the character of which is permanent and equally absolute.[50] The constitution of Poland shows that this balance is actually possible, even when the "principle" is carried to the "utmost extent." The genuine union of theory and practice is, perhaps, both beneficial and effectively possible, although it must be admitted that the Polish example is not yet one of a civilized propagadistic regime. Calhoun observes that "This government lasted in this form more than two centuries, embracing the period of Poland's greatest power and reknown (sic)," including the career of Copernicus, whose revolution ultimately launched the contemporary world.

The example of the constitution of Poland is the most extreme example of constitutional government offered in *A Disquisition on Government*. In its presentation may be clearly discerned the points along which Mill and Calhoun diverge. Mill's presentation of society as language and human life as a "free discussion" of truth, beauty, and justice (what Kendall calls a "debating society"), rests on the ideal of "Athens" as drawn by Mill from his reading of Plato's dialogues and his adaptation of the political to the speculative life: John Stuart Mill "writ large," as it were. This vision underlies and guides the aspiration of Mill's *Essay on Liberty* and to a large extent (i.e., to the extent that it is not tempered by his reading of *A Disquisition on Government*) also his *Representative Government*. Calhoun himself never refers to Athens in the *Disquisition*,[51] but the example of the actual extreme form of the Polish constitution replaces the example of the ideal of Athens in Plato's dialogues as Mill read them, as, for political science, the example of principle taken to the "utmost extreme." It will be helpful to grasp the character of this replacement for the understanding of the science of government as it is presented in *A Disquisition on Government*.

The Polish constitution lasted in this extreme form as long or longer than that of Athens over the period of Athens' greatest power and renown. Calhoun observes, in a fashion that is quite unusual for him, that "twice during its existence she protected Christendom, when in great danger, by defeating the Turks under the walls of Vienna and permanently arresting thereby the tide of their conquests westward." These feats, and not only the principle of liberty depicted by Mill, which are Poland's most splendid feats, are themselves on a par with the most splendid feats of Athens, which are the two great defeats of the ancient Turks, i.e., the Persians, at Marathon and Salamis, which permanently arrested their conquests westward in that age. It is of course more important for Mill that Athens also came to be a center of science or philosophy, which is his true point of reference. Calhoun, in observing that "This government lasted in this form more than two centuries, embracing the period of Poland's greatest power," adds "and reknown (sic)." As we have indicated, part of its great renown includes the great renown of Copernicus himself, whose "new astronomy," according to which the correct point of reference in astronomy is not the earth but the heavens, inspired the scientific revolution leading to the "astronomical philosophy" of Gallileo and Newton.

The divergence of the worlds of the *Essay on Liberty* and *A Disquisition on Government* may be more expressively shown in this regard by reference to the immediately following example which Calhoun presents after discussing the constitution of Poland. This example, he says, is "not so striking" as that of the constitution of Poland. Although it exemplifies the same principle of constitution, it does not carry the principle to a similarly striking extent. It is a more moderate example. Calhoun's moderate example is particularly striking, however, in its contrast to the purview specified by the *Essay on Liberty* with respect to "advanced" and "backward" states of society, for it is the example of the "Confederacy of the Six Nations who inhabited what is now the western portion of the state of New York," that is, the Iroquois Confederacy (par. 110). The Iroquois were a people of the most admirable moral excellence. The united consent of all the nations in the Iroquois confederacy was required for action on questions relating to the common welfare. "In a word, as a result of its political organization, the League of the Iroquois exhibited the highest development of the Indian ever reached by him in the hunter state."[52] According to Calhoun, then, we are thus to understand that the principle in question is not limited to "advanced" or civilized societies, but fully extends to what are called "backward" or savage societies, however understood: to all the "traditional" or Kendall's "closed" societies in which, according to Mill (following Comte), "the race itself may be considered as in its nonage." Rather, the utmost in human nobility and political achievement is fully obtainable and has been developed by the race "in its nonage," and this aim remains the standard for all ages, a fact that is important to recall in the wake of contemporary civilized political visions such as those presented in works like Golding's *Lord of the Flies* and others.

As we will see, this achievement is because the principle of constitution in truth is not based on any abstraction of political rights that are supposedly antecedent to human society, on the one hand, and because it is not in any way determined by the progress of human society understood as the progress of modern natural science and its material or human applications, on the other. So far from the principles of constitution being, as might seem to be implied in the course of the *Essay on Liberty's* pronounced concern for liberty within a civilized proagandistic society, inconsiderable in "backward" as distinguished from "advanced" societies, that is, in societies which are not characterized by high development of arts and sciences, or what Calhoun calls "civilization," as distinguished from societies which are, it is, rather, according to Calhoun, easier to sustain in the former kind of societies than in the latter kind. What the civilized Rousseau thought of as the "noble savage" is thus according to Calhoun in no way traceable to the savage as savage but, rather, to the "many high qualities," including the highest qualities of patriotism and virtue, that are exhibited in members of such non-civilized societies as are characterized, like the Iroquois, by "free institutions." As we will note in the proper place, Rousseau's own influential thoughts on the noble savages and what they represent for the "natural" man and human society were apparently based primarily on reports about none other than the Iroquois in North America, that is, about the people of a constitutional political regime. It is true, Calhoun says, that "Such institutions are more easily sustained among a savage than a civilized people. Are we to overlook this great fact?"[53] In other words, according to Calhoun, the spread of civilization—the high arts and sciences—which explodes traditional or non-civilized societies, is more likely than the spread of liberty, and yet liberty must accompany the spread of civilization if the spread of civilization is to be more than the spread of destruction and absolutism, beginning with the methodical propagandistic destruction of liberty as seen by Mill or of nobility as seen by Rousseau.

It is obvious that the progress of civilization, the advance of science and technology and wide diffusion of knowledge, powerfully influences politics in civilized societies as much as superstition ever has among savage societies. Calhoun identifies this advance as ultimately providing the "new and important political element" of contemporary society, the communications environment of "On Liberty" and the modern world (*Disquisition* 18). To the extent that it has attained it, contemporary communications theory has not advanced beyond the ground laid out in the *Essay*. That the progress Calhoun identifies profoundly affects more than the politics or institutions of what Mill terms the less "advanced" societies, and what its actual bearing is, is discernible in Calhoun's example of the Iroquois Confederacy. They are extinguished. The people and the regime are extinct. The immediate context in which this example occurs provides one of the most dramatic moments, if one may so speak, in the reading of *A*

Disquisition on Government. It is the comparison of practicable constitutional governments (*Disquisition* 108-111), and, more particularly, of the most extreme example of the principle of liberty that is given in the *Disquisition*, the constitution of Poland, and a more moderate example of the same principle drawn from a savage or non-civilized people, the Six Nations. This comparison is also a contrast. It is a contrast not of the nobility of the people or the principles in virtue of which these governments are compared, which are comparable, but rather of victory and defeat, a contrast of the splendid and the tragic.

The more libertarian example was finally subverted, Calhoun points out, as a consequence of its very extremity. This extremity, not of any tendency of the constitutional principle itself but of the extent to which its form and circumstances afforded opportunities for treason and intrigue—in short, all the vices observers typically associate with the ancient Greek cities—led to its own dissolution.[54] Thus, even though it resulted from a flaw traceable to the extremity of the application of the principle of constitution in developing circumstances, this subversion does nothing to blemish the greatness of the constitution and the honor due to it in virtue of its splendid feats and the salvation of Western Christendom. The more moderate example, on the other hand, was strong, intrinsically or constitutionally stronger, even, than the more extreme example. This fact led the most knowledgeable student of the Iroquois in Calhoun's time, Morgan, who never thought of the constitution of Poland at all in this connection, explicitly to compare their political organization and history favorably with that of ancient Athens, and to conclude that the constitution of the Six Nations was superior on this ground. Indeed, according to this authority, at their highest, the government and politics of the Iroquois compares with those of the Romans themselves "in the majestic days of the Republic" (cf. *Disquisition*, paragraphs 110-111).[55] Calhoun merely points out that the government of the Iroquois was characterized by "harmony in council and action" and, also, by "great increase of power." It was healthy in every respect. He thus does not remark on its dissolution, for, unlike those of Poland or the Roman republic, its dissolution had nothing to do with its constitution. Because it was healthy and vigorous, "the Six Nations, in consequence, became the most powerful of all the Indian tribes within the limits of our country." They carried their conquest and authority far beyond the country they originally occupied." The paragraph Calhoun devotes to the example of the moderate Iroquois constitution concludes with the sentence just quoted. The following paragraph (111) turns to the "most distinguished" of all constitutinal examples, the example of the Roman republic itself, which Calhoun then immediately sets aside. Where, only a few sentences earlier, in regard to the more extreme constitutional example of Poland, he had referred to the splendor of repulsing the westward tide of oriental despotism and saving Western Christendom from eastern invaders, Calhoun is here silent.

The Confederacy of the Six Nations did not repulse the tide of westward European conquest or the expansion of European Christendom, which are here, rather, primarily the spread or conquest of British civilization. They were unable to withstand that expansion. As Calhoun's reference to the "limits of our country" implies, it was, on the contrary, they who, by an alien race with alien languages, religion, customs, and arts, were conquered and finally extinguished altogether as a people.[56] Theirs was a constitutional government overthrown by external force, the only such example in *A Disquisition on Government*. To repeat, Calhoun admits that the example of the government of the Iroquois Confederacy is not so striking in the extremity of its constitutional principle as that of the government of Poland, "but," he at once adds, it is "deserving of notice." We stress this because we know from experience and from Calhoun's explicit testimony elsewhere that "it is not my habit to stop and illustrate by example," unless he regards the example to be of special significance. In this case, the significance is found in the fact that, thanks to their "federal system," "in the drama of European colonization, the Iroquois stood, for nearly two centuries, with an unshaken front, against the devastations of war, the blighting influence of foreign intercourse and the still more fatal encroachments of a restless and advancing border population."[57] In the end, they lost. But, for Calhoun, this accident in no way consigns them to what certain of Morgan's putative successors (e.g., Engels) have called the "ash-heap" of history or to any sphere "in which the race itself may be considered in its nonage." On the contrary, they and their political arrangements have earned our most careful respect and attention. They are "deserving of notice," according to Calhoun—and he means the notice of the highest minds, or what Rousseau means by the "thinking mind" in speaking of the constitution of Poland—even in the same breath with the most splendid and distinguished human examples, not because they happen to be savage but because they are noble. They are noble because they earned for themselves to the fullest extent possible for them what cannot be given, what Calhoun himself calls "the greatest praise and the proudest distinction" of "an all-wise Providence," which is liberty, and which self-sufficiency, according to him, is always reserved as "the noblest and highest reward for the development of our faculties, moral and intellectual."[58]

For Calhoun, therefore, the constitution of the Iroquois Confederacy is deserving of notice because it is itself a sort of essay on liberty as well as liberty in deed or in fact. For this reason, even in defeat however tragic and total, the Confederacy is, as much as others might be in victory however splendid and long-lived, forever an example to all other governments and men. Where is their equal in nobility? Although it cannot and does not avoid these things, the science of government as such is not primarily concerned with who wins and who loses or with the progress of civilization but primarily with the kind of governments that actually promote development of the human moral and intellectual faculties and, hence, liberty (Plato, *Laws*, 638a-b).

The issue that provides the "central theme" of Mill's *Essay on Liberty* does so precisely because it is the central problem of "my own time and country." "Modern reformers" now propagate "a despotism of society over the individual" surpassing anything contemplated in the political ideals of ancient philosophies and religions.[59] What lies behind Mill's statement of this problem in the *Essay on Liberty* is the recognition that the obverse of his celebrated youthful statement in the *Westminster Review* on the freedom of the press—"Conceive the horrors of an oriental despotism, from this and worse we are protected only by the press"—may be also and equally true. The free press may also be an agent of despotism. This is Mill's closest point of contact with Calhoun in the *Essay on Liberty*. As Kendall observes, "Mill preserves a discrete silence as to the detailed institutional consequences of his position."[60] The *Essay* makes its case on the basis of the distinction between thought or speech and deed, on temporarily abolishing deeds from consideration or understanding human society primarily as an expression of language. "No one pretends that actions should be as free as opinions."[61] Yet the *Essay* is meant to point to action, to society in the larger and true sense, in other words, to what Mill calls "representative government," and the detailed institutional consequences of Mill's position, on which he is largely silent in the *Essay on Liberty*, are, presented in his *Considerations on Representative Government*. The *Considerations* applies the principle set forth in the *Essay* to the question of the constitution and administration of government in Mill's time and country. It "borrows from political philosophy only its general principles."[62] This generality concerns primarily and above all the principle of liberty, the principle of constitutional government or, in Calhoun's famous phrase, of "concurrent majority." Mill explicitly states this principle in its most Calhounian form only toward the end of the *Considerations* (near his reference to the *Disquisition* as the greatest work of political theory since the *Federalist*). "That there should be, in every polity, a center of resistance to the predominant power in the Constitution—and in a democratic constitution, therefore, a nucleus of resistance to the democracy—I have already maintained; and I regard it as a fundamental maxim of government."[63] This is the general principle of concurrency or constitution, which Mill takes from Calhoun. The central theme of the *Considerations on Representative Government* concerns what Mill calls the "practicability of any real check to the ascendency of the numerical majority," and, therewith, to the "tyranny of the majority." The author's well-known provisions of proportional representation of minorities and plural or weighted voting on the part of certain minorities all point to this end. The immediate parliamentary reforms which the *Considerations on Representative Government* was in part intended to promote were unsuccessful. Nevertheless, Mill's borrowing and application of the general principles of political philosophy in the *Considerations* represents the best introduction we have yet had to Calhoun's *A Disquisition on Government* or to the science of government as established by Calhoun.[64]

The issues and controversies adumbrated in the preceding pages are merely representative items of what we have called the "old territory" or ground of "political science" as confronted by Calhoun. They may all be found in Hobbes and Hume. Each expression of the "new science" from Hobbes onward is characterized by its emphasis upon a new and improved or more systematic "scientific" methodology and some scheme of education or publicity. Calhoun's presentation of political science is characterized by the absence of any such emphasis. As has been previously indicated, *Disquisition* all but opens with the author's implicit dismissal of epistemology from the central place in philosophy since the time of Descartes and Hobbes. As the whole of Creation is held to be not unintelligible to the mind of the most thoughtful creature, the so-called "problem of knowledge" is not a problem in the *Disquisition*. The political animal is at the center of the constitution of nature or laws of the physical universe, and not marginalized as a bundle of "secondary qualities." As for a scheme of education, whether as familiar from Plato's *Republic* or Bacon or Locke's ideas of civic education or Rousseau's *Emile*, Calhoun takes an entirely different tack, for according to him, the essential constitution of our nature whence government naturally arises is impervious to all such schemes. "No increase of knowledge and intelligence [hence, e.g., no amount of popular "enlightenment"] no enlargement of our sympathetic feelings, no influence of education, or modification of the condition of society [i.e. no quantity of social reform or redistribution of wealth or stations] can change it" (*Disquisition* 114). The place of preoccupation with methodology is taken by the development of elementary principles and precepts of statesmanship. In the place of this whole question in these new social sciences are found methodological disquisitions and school or party tactics: the epistemologist and the revolutionary replace the founder and the statesman.[65]

We may conclude this initial survey of the "old territory" as confronted by Calhoun by noting the place of its opposing Hobbsian and Humean poles in regard to the origins of human society and the aims of government. These poles are, on the one extreme, reason in the service of passion (or grounding human society and government directly in reasoning from man's fundamental aversion to death and the "state of nature" — and extending also to the romanticization of the human will and reason and history via the doctrines of "Idealism" and others ultimately arising from Hobbes' hypothesis of the "state of nature") — and, on the other extreme, passion or physical wants themselves, or, Hume's empirical denial of Hobbes' hypothesis, providing this ground directly on the sentiments generated by the repeated phenomenon of the physical inclination to reproduce. This is the ground, the calculation from fear and the sentimentalization and the calculation of sexual love or physical desire, that Calhoun wishes to transcend in the *Disquisition* by providing the "solid foundation" described but not arrived at in Hume's *Treatise*. Hume and—after Hume had removed the scales from their eyes in rejecting the fiction of the "social contract"—the Utilitarians do not arrive at this foundation. In his own attempt to show the necessary foundation, Calhoun takes a similar point of departure to that taken by both Hobbes and Hume, namely, the relationship of the law of gravity in the realm of matter and motion (as established by Newton) to that of "like principles" in the realm of human society and the aim of government. Calhoun draws this relationship not from any tenet or discovery or "law" of natural philosophy or science but directly from the human faculty that gives rise to natural philosophy or science itself and that, as such, is prior both to what is called the "structure of science" and also to the "structure of scientific revolutions."

The "Philosophical Inquirer"

In the short opening paragraph of the *Disquisition*, Calhoun presents the study of government as a certain study of nature. The "nature and object" of government is derived from "our nature"—from human nature and that of which human nature is a part—and is ancillary to it. The first question, therefore, necessarily concerns "our nature" as it gives rise to government. In the central sentence of the first paragraph, Calhoun compares this study to the study of astronomy, particularly in regard to the relationship of the law of gravity to the science of astronomy. All studies must have a solid starting point if they are to arrive at a "just conception" of the subject and attain to science or knowledge. All science is admirable *qua* science. However, the science of astronomy itself, the ancient queen of the sciences, is not, for Calhoun, merely one science among others. He understands by astronomy the highest branch of physics or the science of bodies, that is, of "natural philosophy" or "natural science." Calhoun always discusses this physical philosophy or science in terms of metaphysics and always and above all in comparison with the science of politics.

Calhoun, it may appear, is a dualist. For him, all bodies or brute matter are eternally lifeless. They are not "dead." To be dead means that there has been life. For them there is only motion, or, more specifically, being moved. The only thing living is mind, which is self-moved. From this follows two things: the desirability or need for study of a science of bodies, or more strictly, of matter and motion, and the desirability or need for study of a science of mind. The highest form of the science of bodies or motion is that of the whole, of which our world itself is only a part and is not at the center: the science of astronomy. This science is one in which the whole is not only seen from within, that is, with our naked eye from the vantage of the earth, but also and more accurately from without by means of mathematics and mechanics and optics and the instruments arising in the course of developing these disciplines. The highest form of the science of the mind, on the other hand, is that of which we are ourselves a part and of which our own politics and nature are the center: the science of government. These two sciences represent the highest forms of knowledge to which man as man can aspire.

Yet, what Calhoun calls the "world of mind" is not exhausted by the extensions and limitations of the human mind. Beyond the highest science of motion and the highest science of mind, the highest things possible to human beings, there is a further or higher science, which, however, can perhaps only loosely be called in any sense a "science" because its object lies beyond the knowledge to which man can aspire. Men can be aware of this object but they cannot attain demonstrable knowledge of it. For Calhoun, it is the highest thing of which men are aware, because it is necessary comprehensively to conclude both these other sciences, but either its achievement is not possible to men, either because what he describes as the "limited reason and faculties of man" are inadequate for this task, or, what comes to the same thing, it is somehow confused with something else. For Calhoun, then, it is not human science, or if we may use non-Calhounian terms, it is a "supernatural" and "superhuman" "science." In any case, Calhoun nowhere calls the human awareness or consideration of this a science, nor does he even outline it specifically in *A Disquisition on Government*. Yet, after the opening paragraph, his attention to it there, in connection with the science of government, is actually more in evidence than is his interest in the science of matter and motion. Toward the conclusion of the *Disquisition*, he clearly poses the question of its import, from the perspective of the science of government, as is appropriate, for both these sciences. Certainly, Calhoun leaves no doubt as to the object of this science. Its object is the "Infinite Being" (or "Being" or "the Infinite"), the "Creator of all," the origin of all motion and mind and the world of which man is a part, hence of all human faculties and inclinations, and, therefore, of all human origins and ends. This attention is traditionally known in the West as "metaphysics." Calhoun hardly speaks about it in the *Disquisition*, but, even in saying so little he leaves no possible doubt as to its rank. The being itself of this infinitude, the "constitution" or "law" of the whole as whole, has the character of "divine ordination," and its working or becoming the general character of "Providence." This ordination is always characterized by Calhoun as "wise" and "beneficent,"[66] although it may be questioned (paragraph 137). There is therefore apparently an intimate connection between this ordination and its apprehension. Calhoun discoursed on this subject, or some of its branches, among his friends and associates, but he left

little trace of his formal reflections in any of his public writings. We are thus
dependent on the incomplete reminiscences of others for reports of them. As
might be expected, these typically affirm little more than that "Mr. Calhoun's
deity was of the most philosophical type, from all accounts."[67] In any event, it is
clear in *A Disquisition on Government* that Calhoun intends to produce or
reproduce neither physical science, which had already been founded, nor divine
science, or metaphysics, which is perhaps beyond our capacity as men or at any
rate the subject of a separate effort, but human science, which is, *par excellence*,
man's proper and noblest task. For purposes of illustration, we may say that *A
Disquisition on Government* sets forth this human science as the "physics" or
nature of politics. These sciences (physics and politics) necessarily point to what
is beyond them.

As it is conceived by Calhoun, the relation itself between these lower but
highest possible human sciences, the science of bodies or motion and the science
of mind, involves a particular feature that helps define Calhoun's view of the
science of government altogether. It consists, first, in the fact that both the science
of astronomy and the science of government are themselves "of the mind." They
thus differ not at all in their nature but merely in their different objects and
instruments. This fact may be overlooked. Calhoun in another place describes the
feature in question, a certain power of the human mind, in terms of metaphysics.
He says: "the power of analysis and combination—that power which reduces the
most complex idea into its elements, which traces causes to their first principle,
and by the power of generalization and combination, unites the whole in one
harmonious system...is the highest attribute of the human mind."[68] This
description, although it was given apparently *ex tempore* and in the context of a
public debate, appears to be a close restatement, in a single sentence, of the
"Method of Analysis" and the "Method of Composition" as set forth in
Newton's *Principia* and *Opticks* as "Rules for Reasoning in Philosophy" or the
procedures of natural science.[69] It appears, similarly, to be a restatement of the
"resolutive" and "compositive" method originally used by Galileo to establish
physics, including astronomy, as a systematic science, and from whom,
according to *de Cive* and *de Corpore*, it was adopted by Hobbes for the express
purpose of establishing his own "civil philosophy," that is, political science.[70]
Both these men, Galileo and Newton, understood this method in
contradistinction to "metaphysics" and as being for the sake of physics.
Calhoun, for his part, identifies this power as metaphysical but explicitly
distinguishes its operation from scholastic disputations involving "distinctions
without difference."[71] He understands it and identifies it not as itself a
"method," although it may analyze and combine itself into many methods,
including the method of disputation, but as the most characteristic attribute of
the human mind, the "method of man," which allows man to perceive and grasp
wholes as wholes and parts as parts, and by virtue of which, aided by logic,

experience, observation, and comparison, he can harmonize them, that is reconcile or order them, in accordance with general principles or "laws." Hence, as this power in the hands of Galileo and Newton has given rise to natural science, so the same power may in other hands give rise to political science.

Calhoun characterizes this metaphysical faculty or power in two ways. First, "it is this power which raises man above the brute—which distinguishes his faculties from mere sagacity, which he holds in common with inferior animals." This distinction is one between different kinds, higher and lower kinds, and not merely a distinction of degree within one and the same kind.[72] Sagacity is here an inferior power, including self-interest, foresight, prudence understood as "enlightened" self-interest, "conditioned" behavior, and so forth, which rises from and is broadly oriented toward the law of self-preservation that governs all animal life.[73] Hence it is specifically the metaphysical power Calhoun identifies and not sagacity which provides the possibility of the science of man or government. The one power is more vertical and theoretical, looking to what always is and to the whole, the other is more practical and horizontal, looking to immediate circumstances and to the past and future. It is this power that tells Hume the categories before the study is begun that may take the rest of time to complete. Here Calhoun makes no reference to any human wants or inclinations, morals or passions, will or feelings, or to any other human powers or attributes or habits as serving to distinguish man from brutes or inferior animals. It is, rather, this and only this particular human "intellectual faculty," the particular metaphysical power of the human mind, which fundamentally distinguishes man. This thought is underlined and further developed in his second, immediately following, description of this faculty.

Calhoun first emphasizes the distinction between men and beasts not because this distinction is itself the highest but because, in this context, it involves the first distinction for us as men. However like them we are, or however attracted to them we may be, men cannot help distinguishing between ourselves and beasts. We are distinguished by our bodies and by many kinds of considerations related to our bodies. But there are higher and more fundamental distinctions. Of these, the highest and most distinctive is the power of the human mind that Calhoun describes. This way of distinguishing between men and beasts is not original with Calhoun. According to the same principle, Calhoun immediately distinguishes between some men and others. Human beings possessing most completely the highest attributes of the human mind are distinguished from other men just as men as men are generally distinguished from beasts: they are most truly human. They are exemplary in this respect, which is the decisive respect. The particular men whom Calhoun here mentions by name in this connection are Newton and Laplace. Calhoun gives credit where credit is due. He says that "it is this power which has raised the astronomer from being a mere gazer at the stars to the high intellectual eminence of a Newton or a

Laplace, and astronomy itself from a mere observation of isolated facts into that noble science which displays to our admiration the system of the universe." The natural philosopher as astronomer, what Galileo and Kepler called the "astronomer philosophical," is as much above the mere astronomer as the astronomer is above the "mere gazer at the stars." This seems true individualism: the pinnacle of nature. The figures of Newton and Laplace, as distinct from all mere stargazers who are themselves distinct from all mere animals, represent the most fully human development of astronomy or natural science. We note in passing that Calhoun says "it is this power which has raised" Newton and Laplace, and, therewith, the pursuit of astronomy to the rank of science, not the other way around. Their "intellectual eminence" is the result both of the honor that is naturally paid by men to the highest and most admirable that is in man, and which, as such, is prior to any particular man, and of the admiration men naturally have for the order of nature. Laplace, as distinguished from Newton, did not hold this view. Be this as it may, Calhoun's immediate and explicit concern is not to establish here the priority of reason to the reasoner but to establish, within the limits of the immediate context, the relation of the science of government to the science of astronomy as an object of reason, or the most fundamentally human thing.

Newton and Laplace represent for Calhoun the author and finisher in principle of natural science as based on human reason. The heights they have attained Calhoun here claims as proper objects for political science. Metaphysics may, as it were, be brought "down to earth," to the arena of politics and legislation, with no loss of the dignity it enjoys by virtue of its attainments in the heavens. And it should be brought down. Calhoun goes much further: this is necessary, as well as desirable for science — for man — for, according to Calhoun, the political whole which man completes is itself necessary for the completion of the whole of which man and politics are themselves but a part. It is in this absolutely small but relatively decisive way that man himself approaches most closely the Creator of all. For this completion to be "worthy of the name" and thus to command the highest admiration, the principles and objects of government must first be understood: political science is necessary. Calhoun admits that human wisdom, including the most godlike "metaphysical" intellectual powers, may not be adequate for this divine task. It and not natural science is the true pinnacle of nature. It is thus a higher task than the task that is represented by any natural science. Nevertheless, it is the highest ordained task, the profoundest duty, of man as man.[74] Hence it is inseparable from the highest potential in man.

It is in this connection, and not in connection with science or metaphysics as such, that Calhoun here refers to "Galileo and Bacon." Galileo and Bacon are here to be distinguished from Newton and Laplace. Newton and Laplace represent "intellectual eminence," the heights to which it is given man to reach.

They show what science is, what the metaphysical power of man is. They show that the world of material nature speaks in the language of mathematics and can be understood in that language. It is true that Newton holds and Calhoun holds (as Laplace does not hold, or rather, holds that it is not necessary to hold) that a kind of *primum mobile* is entailed or participates in this fact. For the purpose at hand, including the distinction being drawn between Newton and Laplace and Galileo and Bacon, this disagreement is, as it were, immaterial. On the other hand, rather, Galileo and Bacon represent the great "martyr" and the great "prophet" of natural science. They represent the political impact and the public face or authority of natural science and the political "science" that is based upon it. Calhoun mentions their names primarily in connection with "prejudice and denunciation" and with immortal fame, that is, in short, in connection with the religion or faith of science or philosophy, the systematic advancement of learning, as against, and in more or less explicit conflict with, all other religions or faiths. The very fact that he mentions their now "immortalized names" testifies to the success of the advancement of their learning, the learning of natural science and of the application of the discoveries of natural science.

Between the representatives, not to say the author and finisher, of pure natural science, on the one hand, and the representatives of the faith of natural science, on the other, Calhoun places the "philosophical inquirer" into the "first principles" of political science, the "high purpose of political science and legislation" and the laws to which they are subject. This unnamed philosophical inquirer is Calhoun. It could seem that the political philosopher is in the same position as Galileo when he committed his crime and Bacon when he first unfolded his educational project, but he is the herald of a different science.[75] It could seem, then, also that Calhoun sees himself simultaneously as author, finisher, martyr, and prophet of this political or human science. Philosophy in its own name enters the assembly, if only as exhortation or, rather, a kind of defense. (Calhoun had been charged with being "metaphysical.")[76] In any event, in this speech in the Senate Calhoun predicts not merely that political philosophy is possible, as well as desirable, but that the time will someday come when political science will prevail, that is, when philosophy will guide the assembly in its own name.

Calhoun calls the science of astronomy both "noble" and "admirable." It is noble because the exercise of the highest human intellectual power is noble in itself, and "admirable" because its object, the "system of the universe," is admirable in itself. For both these reasons, the science of astronomy, as represented by the thought of Newton and Laplace, is of very high dignity. Its system and laws are prior to man and independent of everything he does or may do. Calhoun does not in this place, as he does in the *Disquisition* and elsewhere, refer to the application man can make, for good or ill, of his knowledge of these laws, that is, to technology. But this thought leads here appropriately to

Calhoun's immediate point. This point concerns, at least in part, "legislation," which is that part of the science of government which involves the application of the knowledge accessible via "a philosophical turn of mind" or that is provided by political science. The science of government is noble and admirable for all the reasons that the science of astronomy is noble and admirable, then, as well as others that are outside the scope and capacities of the science of astronomy. Its object is what is good for man as man. "This high power of the mind," says Calhoun, should be applied to the "high purposes of political science and legislation. I hold them to be subject to laws as fixed as matter itself, and to be as fit a subject for the highest intellectual power," therefore, as the science of government. Although it uses the same metaphysical power of the mind in its operation, the object of political science and legislation is of higher dignity than that of the science of matter and motion, whose object, however admirable, is itself less than human. "Progress in matter" implies no moral progress, whereas, as Calhoun makes plain in the *Disquisition*, the object or "high purpose" of political science and legislation is "to perfect what the wisdom of the Infinite ordained as necessary to preserve the race" and the human moral and intellectual faculties.[77] For Calhoun, the conception of political philosophy presupposes the possibility, in some sense, of moral and intellectual progress.[78]

The superiority of the science of government to the science of astronomy, as well as its application to the astronomer himself in so far as he is a man, is also evident from a further consideration. The discipline of the science of government is similar to the discipline of the science of astronomy in that just as the astronomer must step outside the vantage that is first for him or that comes most naturally to him, namely, the vantage that is provided by his own eyes and by his place upon the earth itself, in order to establish the science of astronomy, the would-be political scientist (who is no less implicitly governor than governed) must step outside the vantage that is first for him or that comes most naturally to him. This step is not a step that is outside human society as such: for Calhoun, this is not a step that is genuinely possible. This is because "society" is naturally central to men and to the knowledge of man in a way that the earth is not central to the nature and object of astronomy. Nor is it first of all even a step outside of the government under which he actually lives. Wherever and whenever he lives, there will be government. Man always carries government with him. For man to step outside the vantage that is first and most natural to him means to step outside himself, as a personal or private individual. This first and most necessary thing he can only do to the extent that he is able to overcome his own self-interestedness or self-centeredness, in short, that selfishness which, according to Calhoun, animates all the realm of the living "down to the lowest reptile or insect," and which is strongest in man. He must master or rule himself completely by mastering, through the highest attributes of man as man (attributes that Calhoun insists are limited or weak), the attributes that are strongest of all in man as man. He must begin personally to ascend what Calhoun calls the "scale of liberty."[79] He must, however falteringly, begin to know and transcend himself, that is, to undertake his own moral self-government. The would-be political scientist must take a step that seems impossible in all but the most "peculiar constitutions" (*Disquisition*, paragraph 6) but that is the only possible path if the science of government is to be established. In so doing, he must achieve not merely as much as the astronomer in his thought but more than the astronomer in his means, for he must achieve in truth and for himself what the astronomer only pretends or seems to achieve through his sense-altering instruments. The natural philosopher as astronomer does not discover the law of gravity in order to check or transcend it, but to understand the admirable material system whereby the bodies of the universe mutually act on each other and are held in their respective spheres. The result is that the science of government raises a question, about which the science of astronomy as such remains oblivious, or may even seem to close, as to whether the scientist himself or the object of his science is truly superior.

The greatest possible achievement of the science of government, the aim of the science of government, involves rendering the individual more like the political philosopher, more capable of self-government, more possessed, ultimately, of "knowledge, wisdom, patriotism, and virtue," which complete the natural and most distinctive human faculties and which, in their various forms, are as ubiquitous and natural throughout the various forms of human society as the phenomemon of government itself.[80] To repeat, the science of government differs from the science of astronomy or natural philosophy or science in this respect. The establishment of the science of government, which is the overarching science of man, the highest and only possible such science in the absence of the superhuman, supernatural science already mentioned, will improve men in the direction of the fulfillment or perfection of ordained human nature. The discoveries of natural philosophy or science do not alter in any way the principles or operations of material nature. The most these discoveries, or rather the human application of those discoveries in what Calhoun calls the "control of material agents," can do is to affect these principles or operations as these principles or operations, in turn, can affect human society. But precisely in this case such applications should and must fall only under the jurisdiction of political and not natural science.[81]

The Text and Context of
A Disquisition on Government

A Disquisition on Government is preliminary, as we have noted, in that it explicitly prefaces or prepares for the constitutional presentation made in the Discourse on the Constitution and Government of the United States. Calhoun explained to an English interviewer in 1845 that "I have made an allotment of these years: a portion for America, a portion for my own private affairs (for I am a planter, and cannot afford to be idle), and a portion I have reserved for peculiar purposes connected only with myself." Calhoun puts his personal or most individual purposes last. In the same year, he informed a friend more explicitly of the purposes that were peculiarly his own. He had begun, he wrote, while serving as the Secretary of State, "an enquiry into the elements of political science, preliminary to a treatise on the Constitution of the United States, but I know not whether I shall ever have time to finish it."[82] This work, A Disquisition on Government, is the peculiar purpose connected only with Calhoun himself, with the part of himself that he reserved to himself, distinct if inseparable from his public life and from all of his private affairs. In it, Calhoun turns to what is by nature first and, in this sense, prior to what is first for Calhoun.

The Discourse or rather the important subject that is set forth in the Discourse, and not the transcendence of Hobbes or Hobbism or all political pseudo-science, is thus the immediate, practical occasion for the inquiry that is presented in the Disquisition. Following Aristotle in the sixth and tenth books of the Nicomachean Ethics, Calhoun divides political science into two branches, political science proper, the higher and theoretical branch which deals with elementary principles, and "legislation," the practical branch which is concerned with statesmanship or the actual application of the elementary principles in given circumstances. As we have already noted, Calhoun observes that the latter effort is always liable to difficulties. While this fact does not impeach political science proper, it does mean that political science proper alone is not enough, and, furthermore, that even the coincidence of political science and statesmanship may not be enough to secure the aims by and toward which political science is oriented. This is particularly true in the United States itself, owing to the great complexity of its constitution and government. "To legislate for our country," Calhoun wrote in 1817, "requires not only the most enlarged views but a species of self-devotion not exacted by any other."[83]

The two works, A Disquisition on Government and A Discourse on the Constitution and Government of the United States (and the latter followed by all of Calhoun's public papers and speeches, beginning with the lost commencement address on the subject of the perfect statesman), seem to correspond to the division of political science just described.[84] The former, which is meant to stand alone, is always referred to by Calhoun as preliminary to the latter, which reflects it, but, because it stands alone, the *Disquisition* is also meant to be introductory to more than the *Discourse* or to Calhoun's own statesmanship. It is meant as preliminary to understanding politics or political practice as such "in the present condition of the world," but in principle on any occasion. Political science *qua* science, or reason, is anonymous and common to all men and in no way peculiar to the United States, whether to the United States of Calhoun's time or of any other time. The *Discourse* does not provide and is not meant to provide a "solid foundation" for political science. (*The Discourse on the Constitution and Government of the United States* is easily distinguished from *A Disquisition on Government*. It opens with the word "Ours.") Nevertheless, it is Calhoun's intention that it should be judged on the basis of political science.

In spite of the fact that Calhoun composed this work in the midst of one of the most intense periods of his public life, (a fact that many find reflected in some of his contemporary speeches), *A Disquisition on Government* presents itself as of whole cloth, without any obvious seam or division into parts. It appears to be written all in one breath as a homogeneous unit of thought, as a "sentence" or single "complete thought," in a remarkably plain or Lockean style.[85] Calhoun uses no jargon but he uses plain words strictly — within the structure of his argument, even "technically" — and he reasons closely. One of its most perceptive readers, Lord Acton, observed in this connection that the *Disquisition* is very difficult to summarize or to abbreviate. The longer one studies the work, the more one inclines to the view that that Acton was right. This difficulty arises from the fact that another contemporary (a famous devotee of Compte's "sociology") was probably also right when in the 1830s she said that "Mr. Calhoun's theologies of government, which are almost the only subjects that occupy his soul.... are the compactest that ever were made." *A Disquisition on Government* is difficult to summarize because it is already a summary.

This difficulty is in a sense compounded by the further fact that, as noted earlier, Calhoun refers by name to no authorities or previous thinkers anywhere in the *Disquisition*. This means two things (in regard to the second of which, at least, this commentary may be of use to some readers). *First*, and above all, it means that, according to him, one does not need to know anything about any other authorities or previous thinkers in order to understand the science of government for oneself from the beginning. (Calhoun's political science is meant as a true science, not a fraternity or guild.) One has merely to follow the argument attentively and think carefully for oneself from the beginning. Only the natural human moral and intellectual faculties are required.

Second, it means that those who do *not* know something about, say, the history and historiography of ancient Rome independently of *A Disquisition on*

Government, will be unable to recognize that Calhoun's inimitable presentation of the constitution of the Republic of Rome in the portion of the *Disquisition* devoted to examples of constitutional government is based on his own study of Livy, from whose text he draws (paragraphs 144-145), and, among others, Polybius' *Histories* and Machiavelli's *Discourses on Livy*. (In this connection, a glimpse of the character of Calhoun's intended addressee is possible at paragraph 142, first sentence; cf. paragraph 152.) Or, if one does not know much about the history or historiography of Great Britain, then one must fail to recognize that Calhoun's presentation of the British constitution thematically follows the thesis of Hume's *History of England*. Or, if one does not know much about the history of modern philosophy, one will not think of modern philosophers like Hobbes and Locke and Rousseau and others (the "social contract philosophers") when reading Calhoun's paragraphs explicitly criticizing those who have set forth the "hypothesis" of the "state of nature" and made it seem universally persuasive (paragraph 89), much less when considering crucial arguments elsewhere, particularly near the beginning of the *Disquisition*, that bear direct on that hypothesis even when Calhoun does not explicitly say so.

Although the appearance of seamlessness in the *Disquisition* will gradually decrease in the course of closer study, the impression of singular unity or wholeness will increase as this thought is penetrated and understood. It is possible to analyze each of the work's sections into ever further subdivisions until one arrives at Calhoun's own subdivisions, namely, each one of the paragraphs in order, and, finally, at each sentence in each paragraph from the beginning to the end, or until the *Disquisition* is reconstructed. There is, so far as I am aware, no superfluous word, nor any out of place. In an explicit manner befitting the new age of information and open inquiry for which it was composed, it reflects as perfectly or transparently as possible the order or constitution of Calhoun's own thought. It does not and cannot (and need not) take the place of government itself or of the various secondary kinds of public education schemes referred to above, but presents the science of government *qua* science plainly for those who are interested. The difficulties are those which naturally inhere in the subject and its thinking through; there is nothing "hidden" though much that is "deep," nothing cryptic, though much that is gnomic. The method necessary for a constructive reading, then, is the same as that used in its composition and that is described by Calhoun as "analysis and combination," which "reduces the most complex idea into its elements, which traces causes to their first principle," and which "unites the whole into one harmonious system." The text as we have it was "given to the public with no other comment than that made by himself in a letter dated the 4th of November, 1849" —

I wish my errors to be pointed out. I have set down only what I know to be true; without yielding an inch to the popular opinions and prejudices of the day. I have not dilated,—but left truth, plainly announced, to battle its own way.[86]

A Disquisition on Government comes to just over one hundred pages in Cralle's edition of Calhoun's works. It is roughly comparable in length to such contemporary political writings as Mill's On Liberty or Marx's Communist Manifesto, or, among earlier works in politics, to Rousseau's Social Contract, Bacon's Great Instauration and New Atlantis, or Machiavelli's The Prince, among others.

The preliminary study consists of 165 paragraphs of varying lengths which exhibit no obvious external divisions. If we take A Disquisition on Government and the Discourse on the Constitution and Government of the United States as detachable parts of one whole, it becomes somewhat easier to begin to grasp the order of the Disquisition itself and make our way in it. In the absence of any other external divisions or guides, we may begin by orienting ourselves from the part in which the Disquisition begins most clearly to look toward and prepare the way for the Discourse. This point is reached in the part (beginning with paragraph 140), which Calhoun opens by saying, "I shall, in conclusion, proceed to exemplify the elementary principles which have been established," in "simple regimes." These examples of the simple constitutional regimes are the most distinguished examples offered in the Disquisition. Calhoun specifies that this exemplification of elementary principle is presented as "...preparatory to an exposition of the mode in which they have been applied in our own system." The United States, to which reference is made here and there in the work, is a "complex" regime. As such, according to him, it represents the most distinguished of all possible popular constitutions or regimes. The theme of the Discourse is thus the exposition of the elementary principles which have been established in a "more complex system," including certain of his own posthumous recommendations. This part concludes at the end of the Disquisition in paragraph 165, where Calhoun says: "I have finished the brief sketch I proposed...and shall next proceed to consider the character, origin, and structure of the government of the United States."

This part, (i.e., the paragraphs devoted to exemplary constitutional regimes concluding A Disquisition on Government), is thus apparently the central part of the whole composed by the Disquisition and the Discourse taken together. As such, it appears as the bridge between elementary principles exemplified in distinguished examples, on the one hand, and the extended treatment of "our own government," on the other. There are, accordingly, three plainly distinct parts of these works taken as a single whole. These concern, respectively: 1) political science proper (paragraphs 1-139 of A Disquisition); 2) the greatest simple constitutional regimes of the past (paragraphs 140-165); and 3) a fragile complex constitutional regime in the present day (*Discourse*).

This cursory survey of Calhoun's arrangement proves inadequate, but it may serve as a guide to a more adequate introduction. For, of course, one of the "simple" constitutional regimes discussed at the conclusion of the *Disquisition*, Great Britain, is not, and was not considered by Calhoun to be, a regime of the past, although its constitution emerged before the present day. And, while his presentation of the examples of the greatest simple constitutions at the conclusion of the *Disquisition* may provide the appropriate guide for some future reader in reading or studying his presentation in the *Discourse*, what of the more extreme and more moderate examples of constitutional regimes, Poland, in which the new science of astronomy originated, and the Iroquois Confederacy, that are presented some thirty paragraphs earlier, toward the middle of the *Disquisition*? Would not a combination of their simple institutions be a complex constitutional regime? This consideration alone is enough to entirely separate the *Disquisition* from the *Discourse*. The *Discourse*, which speaks much of history — including illustrious personalities and careers like those of Washington, Madison ("the ablest and most sagacious man of the convention"), Hamilton, Jefferson, Adams, and Monroe — and very little of nature, needs the *Disquisition*, which speaks much of nature and of history; the *Disquisition* does not need the *Discourse*.

The constitutional examples Calhoun offers in *A Disquisition on Government* as extreme and moderate occur in the context of his discussion of the practicability of constitutional government, which is the same as the question of the effective attainability of the "high ends" for which government as such is ordained or of the actuality of what is given by natural ordination. The discussion of practicability begins in paragraph 99. Immediately following the example of the Iroquois Confederacy, Calhoun pauses explicitly to "pass by" the moderate example of the Roman Republic in order first to take up the subject of public opinion and its effectual role in promoting the attainment of these ordained ends. He explains that he will show the virtue of the Roman Republic "hereafter." He takes up this example, along with that of Great Britain, in paragraph 140. If we provisionally take all the intervening paragraphs as bearing on the effectual attainability of the highest and distinctive ends of human government, that is, the possibility of constitutional rather than absolute government (which is the same as the herding rule among all merely "social" as distinct from "political" animals), the arrangement of the *Disquisition* may be presented as follows: 1) political science proper, paragraphs 1-98, and 2) public opinion and simple and complex constitutional governments, paragraphs 99-165, followed by the *Discourse*.

Once this is seen, it is a relatively easy matter to discern the principal division of the primary part of this whole. It occurs at the point at which Calhoun seems to interrupt the course of the argument near the middle (paragraph 89) to repeat at greater length, in the famous passage on the "purely hypothetical" character of all "state of nature" doctrines, what had already been laid down at the very beginning of the *Disquisition* as the first axiom of the science of government (paragraph 2): the "state of nature" doctrines represent so many confusions of physical and political science. They amount to a rejection of human nature in the name of natural science. It is thus almost literally as well as thematically accurate to say that the rejection of the hypothesis of the "state of nature" stands at the center of the science of government as established by Calhoun. But it is not enough to suppose that in a sense Calhoun tacitly plays Laplace to Hobbes' Newton in finishing what Hobbes had begun while having no need of his hypothesis. For Hobbsianism is nothing if not its crowing conception of the "state of nature." Indeed, it is hardly an exaggeration to say that Calhoun's whole effort in the establishment of political science is itself little more than the exposition of what the rejection of the Hobbist "state of nature" entails. And, indeed, the statement of this rejection is almost itself a thematic summary of Calhoun's philosophy of government. Calhounism is an attempt, on a similar basis and by a similar method, to replace Hobbes and what Hobbes had begun.

Hobbes had introduced the state of nature hypothesis on the basis of Newtonian natural science as the foundation for absolute monarchy, calling this foundation the "first philosophy of civil government," and pitting this new science against Scholastic political thought, which it rejected. Calhoun begins by establishing an analogy between Newtonian natural science (the "principle of gravitation") and the science of government. His intention in replacing Hobbes' Newtonian foundation for political science—which is essentially a science of matter in motion or bodies moved by other bodies in accordance with "natural law"—is to restore political science to what he elsewhere calls "the world of mind," the specifically human world which is "self-moved"—the most self-moved portion of "all animated existence." The basis of this movement is not matter (or mind understood as essentially material) but reason (or mind understood as essentially rational or logical), which has its ultimate origin outside man in the cosmos itself of which man is a part. This position carries Calhoun beyond Hume in two ways. First, where Hume had also rejected the state of nature on the experiential grounds of natural human sexual attraction and the need of all living things for preservation, Calhoun rejects this basis (although it is true) as insufficient to account for human social and political life. These exist, rather, out of and for the sake of the natural human moral and intellectual faculties themselves and their perfection. Hume's rejection of Hobbes and the Hobbist state of nature does not go far enough to arrive at genuine "political" science. Second, Hume is the great empiricist and, therefore, the great skeptic. Calhoun considers empiricism primarily as pertinent to the art of legislation in the light of reason itself: he is only a "practical" skeptic or "pessimist." Having its origin in the cosmos or order of which man is a part, "reason" has the character of natural law. Because the existence of such a law implies a lawgiver, or creator, it is more precise to say that it has the character of "divine law." For Calhoun, therefore, it has the character of divine law, and the political condition of man is a divinely ordained condition. It is in the perfection of this condition, through the perfection of constitutional government, that man is most godlike and most free. Calhoun's natural theology is superior to Hume's natural theology.

The second great "social contract" thinker, Locke, is also the most influential. He is also a great empiricist. Locke modified Hobbes' state of nature hypothesis in such a way that the basis of government, the social contract, concerned not so much the fear of violent death and hence reasonable self-preservation, but the accumulation and protection of property. His civil philosophy has the effect of turning Hobbes' doctrine of sovereignty upside down and making all (property-owning) individuals little sovereigns in the place of Hobbes' one absolute sovereign. A Lockean majority has natural rights over against the political "rights" of the "one" or monarch. The result is the presentation of civil society — essentially economic man in the market society — in the place of the political community. This is what Locke means by conflating the civil and the political in his famous chapter in the *Second Treatise* "Of Civil and Political Society." He completes the thought of Hobbes' terms "civil philosophy" and "civil government." According to Locke, the purpose of society is the secure accumulation of property, and thus the purpose of government is ultimately the protection of property. Calhoun's rejection of the state of nature is aimed at Hobbes, but as it were *through* Locke. His opening sentence alludes to this: Calhoun's "a clear and just conception" replaces Locke's famous emphasis on "a clear and distinct idea" (i.e., organized sense impression). The terms "property" and "fear," the very watchwords of Lockeanism and Hobbism, do not even occur in *A Disquisition on Government*, for society and government are not based on them and the aims of society and government cannot be derived from them. Calhoun replaces "civil society" as the highest natural human association with the political association, and the numerical majority of quasi-absolute sovereigns with the sovereignty of the political whole and the principle of concurrency.

If he has been often contrasted to Locke, Calhoun may naturally be compared with Rousseau, for the concurrent majority and the general will seem quite similar, not to say practically identical. Hence it is necessary to consider whether Rousseau, who embraced the state of nature hypothesis in a form more radical than Hobbes in order to transcend Hobbes and Locke in the direction of the truly human or political, or Calhoun, who rejected the state of nature altogether, is more persuasive, because in embracing the extreme form of the state of nature hypothesis Rousseau had to argue that reason was not natural, whereas, for Calhoun, it is first "in the order of things," and the basis of the good of the whole. As we will have occasion to note, the denial of the naturalness of reason to man is ultimately the same as the Hobbian mind of matter in motion. Hence, Rousseauism, in attempting to go beyond Hobbes on Hobbes' own basis, only carries us into a more exaggerated or extreme kind of absolutism than Hobbes had conceived. It is not sufficient merely to desire the truly political and disdain the merely civil: one must also follow Calhoun's fundamental distinction between absolute and constitutional government. This cannot be done on the basis primarily of original human will but requires primarily reason. Human liberty is not in the origin of man but only in the end of constitutional or self-government.

For all these reasons, one's study of Calhoun's thought cannot be limited to the discovery and superficial elaboration of these similarities, if only because the similarities noted, as we have adequately indicated, are already sufficiently obvious. Since, as Calhoun observes, "Nothing is more common than that things closely resembling in appearance should widely and essentially differ in their character," since "arsenic resembles flour, yet one is a deadly poison, and the other that which constitutes the staff of life," the reader who would learn from Hobbes or Calhoun is bound to consider wherein these obvious similarities contain essential differences or only "distinctions without difference."[87] This is the fundamental *desideratum* in beginning the study of Calhoun.

Dividing the *Disquisition on Government* – provisionally or merely by way of orientation – in accordance with what comes before and what comes after this famous passage on the "state of nature" hypothesis, one may say that the former concerns primarily establishing "solid foundations" for the science of government, or political science proper, while the latter concerns primarily, in Calhoun's words, the "greater solidity of foundation on which constitutional governments" (as against all others) "repose" (paragraph 106). The first object entails the understanding of the form of constitutional government in accordance with the natural ends and objectives of human society, and the latter object entails the establishment and effective maintenance of such a government. We have already noticed that it is not Calhoun's habit, in his words, "to stop and illustrate by example." Hence, we take particular note of the fact that four examples are found in each of the parts of the *Disquisition* thus divided. In the first part, all four examples occur in the space of a single paragraph (18). The other four take up almost one third of the second part.[88]

Calhoun unfolds the argument in his familiar manner of a "professor of mathematics" as a series of deductions from axioms that are assumed or laid down in the opening paragraphs as irrefragable. These axioms are that mankind, the human race, is social in nature (paragraph 2); that human society is political in nature (paragraph 3); and that men individually are by nature (for the sake of their survival and maintenance) narrowly self-centered (paragraph

5). This last axiom is admittedly susceptible of exception, as, we may say, Newton and Laplace are exceptions to the general run of mere stargazers, but the exceptions are very few and only serve to prove rather than to overpower or supplant the general rule (paragraph 6). Nevertheless, it is true that, as axioms do not admit of exceptions, this fact has the character of a general rule rather than an axiom. It must be supplemented to become truly whole or "axiomatic." Yet the only supplement possible for the general rule are the exceptions themselves. For the same reason that "people are not in the habit of looking back beyond immediate causes," any of these exceptions are "regarded as exceptions to some general and well-understood law of our nature, just as some of the minor powers of the material world are apparently to gravitation."[89] For example, the constant tendency is for governments of whatever form or character to decline or simplify themselves; the opposite tendency is also present and perhaps equally constant, but it is weak and, in respect to the stronger tendency, comparatively minor. Calhoun presents the former as characteristic of all governments, while he presents the latter as, in the highest and unprovisional case, ultimately, a trait of the rarest individuals. As we have noted, Calhoun refers not to individuals but to peoples. The problem of government, then, becomes primarily the problem of checking the tendency of government to decline. Calhoun's whole intention appears to be to discover and base the philosophy or science of government on a law of political gravitation (paragraph 1). This means, in the first place, that he intends to base political science on the general rule and not on the exception, on the "well-understood law of our nature," with all emphasis on "well-understood," and not on less understood or misunderstood or controversial or, for some, non-existent "minor powers" of our nature which "apparently" contradict it. Anything less is too insubstantial to provide a solid foundation for the philosophy of government. In an age of more or less open inquiry when intelligence is so widely diffused, political science cannot be based on anything that is not open to man's understanding, if not generally "well-understood" (cf. paragraph 18). The science of politics must be plain and present a "clear and just conception" of its object (paragraph 1).

As we have suggested, the *Disquisition on Government* falls into two parts of unequal length dealing, respectively, with political theory or nature (paragraphs 1-98) and with political history or practice (paragraphs 99-165). In the beginning, these parts may be respectively understood as being on "constitution" and on "construction." The first part is subdivided as follows:

i. Constitution (1-98)

Necessity and the Possibility of Human Perfection (1-18)

Human perfection consists primarily in constitutional government (1-3, 12-14, 18)

a) The Nature and Perfection of Constitutional Government (19-52)

The principles of constitutional government (19-37)

The appearance and the reality of the constitution (38-52)

b) Constitutional Government and the Perfection of Society (52-98)

The lower and primary end of all government (53-70)

The higher and core end of all government (71-78)

The highest end and final perfection of all government (79-98)

ii. Construction (99-165)

The general practicability of constitutional government (99-111)

Extreme example (108-109) and savage example (110)

c) Constitutional government and the element of modern society (112-139)

Good government and "progress in knowledge" (112-117)

Prolegomena to construction of good government in the future (118-131)

"Progress and civilization" and good government (132-139)

The practicability of constitutional government in civilized society (140-165)

Republican (142-150) and monarchic (150-162)

This is the order of *A Disquisition on Government*. As we have indicated and will go on to present in following chapters, it may also be further subdivided.

In the first part, on theory, Calhoun explains and corrects certain common errors in regard to the subject and explicitly digresses to rebut the common or typical alternative to his own argument, or what we have called the "old ground." The old or alternative argument is that mankind or the human race is not social by nature, that human society is not political by nature, and that man is naturally or incurably "selfish" or vicious. In this light, the task of political science appears to be that of manipulating this vice in such a way that, not being virtue, it turns out to be as good as virtue or that its consequences are the same as or similar to the consequences of virtue, or at least not harmful to anyone else (or at least not to non-consenting children and adults). For Calhoun, the question of morality or virtue is an organic or intrinsic and not a technical or mechanical question (cf. paragraphs 19, 6). Hence celestial mechanics cannot supply political mechanics. Celestial mechanics already applies to men in so far as men are material. If man jumps up, he will fall down. This fact—all the material explanations there are—does not tell us anything about man or human society or the ordination of government. There is, therefore, no material "law of social or political gravitation" (cf. paragraph 81).[90] In the place of such, Calhoun establishes something else. It is important always to bear in mind what is at stake in Calhoun's correction of the "common errors" in apprehending this subject. These errors are very common. The prevalent errors (and not Calhoun's corrections) in other words, represent the general rule, the strong tendency to which experience and almost every page of history testify. His argument is to the general rule as the minor to the major powers of matter (paragraph 6). Hence, although he teaches that political science must begin with the general rule and not with the exception, he gradually brings it around to the exception. However much the exception proves the general rule, so much does the mere recognition of the general rule prove the exception. The exception is not so much "minor" (except numerically) as it is elusive. The exception itself, the philosopher of politics, is what completes the "solid foundation" of the science of government. But government itself, the natural object of this science, is not an exception. It is axiomatic.

In the second part of the *Disquisition*, Calhoun answers the most plausible objections to the argument he has laid down in the first part. These are, first, that constitutional government is difficult if not impossible to construct, and, second, that, even if it could be constructed, it would not be what it was supposed to be, that is, it would not fulfill the aims for which it was intended and ordained. In other words, it might be "constitutional" in accordance with theory but in practice it would not be "government," for it would fail in its primary duty, which is to provide security. With regard to the objection that constitutional government is difficult of construction (which has been his theme from the beginning of the work), Calhoun observes that it has already been "sufficiently noticed," but here goes on at some length to describe how its construction might be even more difficult today than it has ever been before. With regard to the second objection, which appears plausible, that constitutional government is theoretically sound but impracticable, Calhoun observes that constitutional government has existed in the past. The greatest regimes known to all of mankind (not merely to modern Western men or to civilized or European or white men), the exceptions to the general rule that are admitted by all, have all been constitutional regimes. Constitutional government today, when intelligence is so widely diffused, supplemented, guided or aided by the elementary principles set forth in *A Disquisition on Government*, will both promote all the ends of government and contribute to their actualization to the fullest extent possible to men.

Calhoun insists that constitutional regimes are rare, that is, exceptional or atypical regimes. They cannot be taken for granted. On the contrary, it is the general run of governments that can be taken for granted. They can hardly ever be avoided and will always tend to predominate. It is for this reason that constitutional governments have made a "deep impression" on men (*Disquisition*, 6, cf. 18, 148). Yet, admittedly, this is less or even not at all because they are constitutional than because of their great and impressive achievements: their longevity and power, including above all their "moral power." It is

Calhoun who traces these achievements, and above all their moral power, to their constitution. At the same time, we must likewise bear in mind that Calhoun's most "distinguished" examples of constitutional regimes also were, or became, examples of empires, and even "world empires." Three out of the four constitutional examples he gives in the second or constructive part of the *Disquisition* are examples, also, of empires. The exception, the Polish constitution, which is the first in order, is distinguished by its own extremism and also by the fact that, not being an empire itself, it repelled an empire, even a would-be "world empire." Its not being an empire itself is part of its extremity. The pressing if tacit question of the second part of the *Disquisition,* in a sense almost the whole problem of the second part in so far as it does other than discuss the application of principles already determined and prepare for the presentation of Calhoun's proposals in the *Discourse* itself, is whether there is a way to combine the virtues of the first two examples: the power of the Polish constitution with the politics of the Iroquois constitution. More specifically, the question concerns a way to combine the power of the Polish constitution with respect to self-defense from external attacks with the virtue of the Iroquois constitution within, and the moderation of the Polish constitution with regard to empire with the liberty of the Iroquois, to constitute a people powerful, virtuous, moderate, and free. This combination, the object of the philosophy of government and with the foundation of the philosophy of government, would satisfy from every point of view the highest aims for which human society is ordained. While all these issues are today profoundly complicated by the unprecedentedly widespread civilization and diffusion of intelligence, Calhoun's whole thesis is that they might be resolved, indeed, can only be purposefully resolved, by human knowledge of the kind presented in the *Disquisition.*

If the subject presented in the *Discourse* is the immediate or efficient cause of *A Disquisition on Government,* as it surely is, what may be called its formal cause is hardly less immediate, for, in Calhoun's own terms, it is what provides the immediate context of the former. This "cause" or purpose is connected with the distinction just drawn between science *qua* science, on the one hand, and the technology or technologies that are derived from it, on the other: the theoretical and practical parts of that science. For it is less the establishment of the Newtonian science itself than the diffusion of intelligence and related technologies that have grown and are growing out of it that, for Calhoun, make the establishment of the science of politics now not merely desirable or even necessary in principle for the most mindful human beings, as many philosophers have taught, but actually and practically necessary for politics itself, if not for every human being, for every community.

Few if any of his contemporaries in any country were, on the one hand, as impressed by the new technologies as Calhoun, or, on the other, as critical of their possibilities. In the 1817 speech already quoted, Calhoun had said that,

"The mail and the press are the nerves of the body politic. By them, the slightest impression made on the most remote parts is communicated to the whole system; and the more perfect the means of transportation, the more rapid and true the vibration."[91] Almost a generation later, he had extended this same thought thus:

Never in history has a period occurred so remarkable as that which has elapsed since the termination of the great war in Europe, with the battle of Waterloo, for the great advances made in all these particulars. Chemical and mechanical discoveries and inventions have multiplied beyond all former example—adding, with their advance, to the comforts of life in a degree far greater and more universal than was ever known before. Civilization has, during the same period, spread its influence far and wide, and the general progress of knowledge, and its diffusion through all ranks of society has outstripped all has ever gone before it.

This period—the period between the defeat of Napoleon in Europe and the settlement of the Oregon Territory on the Pacific frontier of North America—represents for Calhoun an historical turning point in human society, which, he said, inaugurated and made clear to all who have eyes "the dawn of a new civilization," namely, a global technological civilization. This new era or new global horizon is due, according to him, to the advent of the technologies derived from the physical sciences which preceded them.. Together, they have given rise to what he called "a new political element," a new element for human society connected with the diffusion of intelligence and opinion at this time or epoch (*Disquisition*, paragraph 132). This new element, part of which Mill called "propagandism" and the underlying condition of which Calhoun in one instance simply calls "electricity," thus, still has something of the character of opinion. This turning point or epoch has superannuated much prior thought on politics and policy not because it has led to any change in human nature or in the essential nature of politics—"it cannot change...our nature" (paragraph 113)—but because the effect of technologies in question, has decisively altered the condition and circumstances of social life, and not in one place only but, in principle, everywhere:

The two great agents of the physical world have become subject to the will of man, and have been made subservient to his wants and enjoyments: I allude to steam and electricity, under whatever name the latter may be called. The former has overcome distance both on land and water to an extent which former generations had not the least conception was possible. It has, in effect, reduced the Atlantic to half its former width, while, at the same time, it has added three-fold to the rapidity of intercourse by land. Within the same period, electricity, the greatest and most diffuse of all known physical agents, has been made the instrument of the transmission of thought, I will not say with the rapidity of lightening, but by lightening itself. Magic wires are stretching themselves in all directions over the earth, and when their mystic meshes shall have been united and perfected, our globe itself will become endowed with sensitiveness — so that whatever touches on any one point will be instantly felt on every other.[92]

What helps to insure that an extended, even continental, republic might be truly republican — or alternatively, might in Calhoun's terms become "national" — might also help to insure the same for what, a century before McLuhan, he explicitly terms the global or electronic village.[93] This may be the first reference to what is taken for granted today as "our world," that is, the "real world" — Mill's globe come willy-nilly of age, even if only apparently so. Calhoun's critical summary of such developments and what they and probable continuing developments in the same line mean for the world is contained in the section of the *Disquisition* that immediately precedes the conclusion (paragraphs 132-139). As is clear from this summary, what we have called the turning point in human society is, according to Calhoun, still turning, and is not something beyond which we, any more than he, can effectually harken back or otherwise escape.

The meaning of this summary is nothing other than his warning call for the gravest attention to the science of government, indeed, for those who are capable of it, the same heroic "species of self devotion" referred to in his 1817 speech. The progress of civilization to which he refers and its diffusion has neither made political science possible nor desirable in regard to the highest ends of society. These ends have always existed. But Calhoun believes that it has made political science necessary in a way that it has never been necessary before. For he observes that these causes — the numerous discoveries, inventions and applications that have altered "the art of war" and have "increased many-fold the productive powers of labor and capital" — and "many others, probably of equal or even greater force [that are still] to be brought to light" — and which have already produced the greatest changes or effects in the history of the world, "have as yet attained nothing like their maximum force." He sees that they have hardly even begun to produce "their full effect." Their power was at that time still fresh and markedly increasing, with their full effect yet to come. Certainly, their effect would, as he saw, long outlive him and the generations immediately succeeding him. "What will be their final bearing, time can only decide with any certainty." But the possibility is already certain, he wrote, that they may ultimately or finally prove "the cause of permanent evil, and not of permanent good" (*Disquisition*, paragraph 137). The outcome is now in the balance. Political philosophy may in some sense have always been necessary and desirable for the attainment of human perfection; it now in its first or primary sense of science of government seems necessary to insure human preservation.

One might suppose that if there is such ultimate risk involved in technological progress, it would perhaps be better foregone altogether. Surely the potential good envisioned from such a project—he conquest of space, the diffusion of intelligence, the increased comfort and convenience of daily life, the sensitive electronic global society—is less than the equally potential evil that Calhoun envisions from it. Yet, such an understandable and appropriate hesitation does not reach the problem. On the one hand, the problem rises naturally from the highest and most fundamentally human inclinations as they have always been, from man at his best. On the other hand, at the same time, according to Calhoun, foregoing this progress, however ambivalent it may now be supposed (or may by some have always been supposed), is not now a practical alternative, any more than, say, overcoming the problem of scarcity without division of labor ever was. Hence, it can be said in passing that Calhoun provides a kind of beforehand answer to the Fugitive-Agrarians, who are often thought to be in some ways his closest political kinsmen in this century: Agrarianism as a program is now no better or, at any rate, any more effectual than a desire, say, to restore the vanished Iroquois Confederacy.[94] Such proposals are, at best, "purely hypothetical" proposals, since the progress and diffusion here in question is actually propelled by the prospect of war and subversion, and hence unstemmable. In a brief sketch of what has since grown to be called the history of science or modern technology, Calhoun tacitly shows that, practically, such proposals have not been an available option since before the colonial settlement of the North American Atlantic coastline (paragraphs 133-134). It has been from long before the time of Calhoun what he calls in a related context "one of those forward movements that leave anticipation behind," with all the attendant risks and uncertainties of such a promising condition. Anticipation is without reasonable guideposts in such periods.

Technical innovations in the art of warfare foreseeably insure victory (at any rate survival) for those who possess technical mastery, and therewith foreseeably insures the survival of that mastery at progressive levels.[95] If the question of ultimate survival itself cannot be said to have been "forever settled" by the progress of technological mastery, or even if it is precisely the diffusion of technological mastery that may jeopardize ultimate survival most radically, it has nevertheless been, long since, immediately settled that this mastery will both survive and continue to progress so long as the question of ultimate survival remains an open question (paragraph 134, cf. paragraph 95). According to Calhoun, this clearly and explicitly means that in the future such mastery will of necessity increasingly become one of the acknowledged aims of every government, and require "large establishments...both civil and military," or what a century after the publication of the *Disquisition* became familiar in

Eisenhower's celebrated phrase as the "military-industrial complex" (paragraph 28, cf. paragraph 95). It must be noted that, while technological capabilities are both necessary and can be a blessing, and may bring other blessings in their train for the relief of man's estate, they will not do so necessarily. Possession of these same capabilities may also coincide with the "most absolute and despotic governments," especially, of course, as Calhoun indicates elsewhere, with "a military despotism." High civilization is compatible with the armies of great and small Napoleons and with diverse cults or schools of ideologues.[96] Because of this fact, it is necessary for the purpose of gaining or sustaining independence in what Calhoun refers to as "the present condition of the world," and it is practically synonymous in the present condition with what is now called "superpower," yet it may also be the cause of losing independence and all that makes independence meaningful and worthwhile.

In this condition, Calhoun says, in which Creation itself may prove ultimately evil and human existence essentially meaningless, the only way in which these capabilities may ultimately prove of permanent good is if the ultimate political effect of their action "shall be to give ascendancy to that form of government best calculated to fulfill the ends for which government is ordained": that is, if they shall, whether by chance or Providence, or by human knowledge, choice, and dedicated art, in fact give rise to the substance that is conveyed in *A Disquisition on Government* itself as the reasoned insight into all human ages or epochs (139). The author takes in hand the education of the whole period or age. To complete his undertaking, he would have to go further and show how the capabilities and forces in question might be optimized. This may not be possible. Their contemporary workings certainly seem to be against such desirable ascendancy as Calhoun posits, and it seems to him "not improbable that many and great but temporary evils will follow the changes they have effected and are destined to effect" in the immediate future. Many regimes will be utterly destroyed, including, it goes without saying, noble constitutional regimes of admirable worthiness. Here Calhoun observes a law that appears to obtain equally for both the sciences of physics and of government: "It seems to be a law in the political as well as in the material world that great changes cannot be made, except very gradually, without convulsions and revolutions—to be followed by calamities in the beginning, however beneficial they may prove to be in the end."[97] However, Calhoun offers no example of good government that arises simply as a consequence of calamity.

This "present condition of the world" is called by Calhoun himself a "period of transition," which time, he says, "must always be one of uncertainty, confusion, error, and wild and fierce fanaticism."[98] The global society itself has emerged in this period. "The governments of the more advanced and civilized portions of the world," according to him, those possessed of more highly developed arts and sciences, "are now in the midst of this period." The phrase "in the midst of this period" means increasingly lost and disoriented amid the flux of political opinions and principles, except of course for such orientation (or what is now called "persistent bias") as may be provided by continued diffusion of technological progress and related intelligence, within in it. As for the peoples (whether constitutional, like the Iroquois Confederacy, or absolute) of all the less technologically advanced or civilized portions of the world who are not yet politically lost and disoriented, they will either be conquered outright or be impelled into this transitional period as their own progress follows course and civilization becomes increasingly diffused among them, and their existing regimes or communities thus more or less quickly extinguished. It is, thus, a global or universal period of transition with ambivalent issue. It may very well also retard the progress of political science, as Calhoun observes, even while control of the material elements of nature apparently accelerates. His conclusion is that this period of "temporary evils," a sort of extended dark age which coincides with unexampled technical and material progress, will actually endure in effect either until such time as both "the governing and the governed" shall grasp the natural ends of government and the principles of the science of government and apply the latter to their communities for the sake of the former, or until it in fact congeals in "permanent evil."[99] The outcome is open and to some extent in our own hands. (All reference to chance is dropped in this concluding statement.) The claims of political science could not be put more eloquently or more urgently.

The assertion that has just been set forth, with its attendant premises and implications for better and for worse, including the strong implication that their should be many different forms of constitutional regimes and not one regime (cf. "all the circumstances in which communities may be respectively placed") brings Calhoun to the end or concluding section of the *Disquisition on Government*, beginning, as we have already indicated, with his statement, "I shall, in conclusion, proceed to exemplify the elementary principles which have been established" in the prior sections of the enquiry. These elementary principles constitute political science proper, as established once and for all by him. The *Disquisition* contains the whole of political science as it bears on the organization of government and its proper aims and as oriented by these aims. Calhoun elsewhere calls this whole the "philosophy of government."[100] "Science of government" and "philosophy of government" are equivalent and inter-changeable terms. To this philosophy we now directly turn.

CHAPTER TWO

Nature and Political Science

Being assured that nothing will interfere between these causes and their effects, we venture to extend our views into futurity, and contemplate the series of events which time alone can develop.

Laplace[1]

THE SCIENCE OF ASTRONOMY EXPLAINS THE WONDROUS ORDER IN WHICH THE CONSTI-tution of the visible material world is ordained or given. It is the purpose of the *Disquisition* to provide the same kind of explanation for the constitution of human government. This is what is meant by "science." This formulation need not itself provide the answers to every political or human question, but it must clearly present those pertinent to government which essentially are no longer the occasion for scientific or rational debate and clarify the ground for ultimately answering the other important questions.[2] Apart from what we have already noted in respect to the composition of the opening paragraph, we may now note above all that Calhoun is intrested here in astronomy in the first place because of its place in the new civil philosophy of Hobbes, in which individuals are presented as properly resembling at best small bodies in the presence of an overpowering sun.[3] The commentary and annotations that follow are meant primarily as an analytic and constructive guide to the exploration of *A Disquisition on Government*. As such, it is far from exhaustive.

Paragraphs 1-18

The science of government necessarily begins with "a clear and just conception of the nature and object of government." To arrive at such a conception, the *Disquisition* opens with a question that is framed in a certain comparison of the "constitution or law of our nature," on the one hand, and the "constitution or law of the material world," on the other. This comparison depends on the prior distinction between "our nature" and the "material world," and corresponds to the familiar distinction that is traditionally drawn between the "soul" and the "body," although it may be important to note that Calhoun here does not explicitly draw the distinction in these terms. Indeed, he does not use the term "soul" or, except in regard to the "bodies composing the solar system," the term "body" anywhere in the *Disquisition*, yet the distinction in question is consistently maintained throughout.[4]

In order to arrive at "a clear and just conception" of the "nature and object of government," it is necessary first to arrive at a clear and just understanding of what it is in our own nature that constitutes the origin of government or that makes government necessary, and without which government would not be necessary. Arriving at this understanding is itself also the first and most important step in the self-understanding that is meant to accompany the study of the *Disquisition* throughout. The first group of paragraphs in the *Disquisition* is devoted to this end: i.e., understanding the origin of government in our nature (paragraphs 1-8). The second group, then (paragraphs 9-12), is devoted to a clear and just conception of the nature of government itself, and the third group, finally (13-17), is devoted to a clear and just conception of the object of government. In the midst of the latter group (paragraph 15), Calhoun introduces the "important and difficult question" which will come to occupy the following or second part of the *Disquisition* on "constitutional government" (19ff). The examples of ancient constitutional regimes offered in the eighteenth paragraph complete the opening or first part of the work as a whole, and complete the necessary conception required in the opening paragraph of the origin, nature, and object of government. In the concluding paragraph of the first part (18), the comparison with the "science of astronomy" or natural philosophy with which the *Disquisition* opened is replaced by political history or reference to the greatest regimes of the remotest past (cf. 13). The constitution of the great regimes of human history takes the place of the bodies composing the solar system, or of the constitution of the material world.

Paragraph 1:
Natural Science and the Science of Government

In view of the opening section of the *Disquisition* as just sketched, one may note a certain divergence in the constitutions that are compared in the opening paragraph. In the first place, one cannot help noticing that while the solar system does not vary at all within itself and has one Creator, the ancient regimes of the past, indeed, all regimes everywhere and always—as numerous as the stars—each have a founder or founders and differ more or less radically among themselves, often to the point of actual war. The comparison might seem one of order and chaos. Little wonder that such a standard as the law of gravity has been desired. Unless we have some independent standard by which to compare and judge the regimes, we have no way of distinguishing and weighing their qualities except for our own wishes and tastes, and these will have already been more or less decisively formed for better or for worse by life under some one or another government, and so we will probably merely dig up what we have buried and in one way or another select our own or an approximation of it. This means that we truly have in that case, so far at least as we are concerned, no more discretion in the matter than if there were merely one regime in the first place. In the same connection, we may also note that whereas all human regimes, including constitutional regimes, according to Calhoun, have a tendency to decline (paragraph 69), and hence require constant human maintenance, the solar system or material world itself exhibits no such tendency and requires no such human maintenance (paragraph 12). The law of gravity, on the other hand, is no respecter of founders however wise or of any human governments and operates universally whatever the government may be and whatever the founder or anyone else may wish or say to sustain. Hence it is necessary to find a similar human law that operates similarly in all human governments if it is to be possible to speak of "political science."

In the *Federalist* Publius says that government would not be necessary "if men were angels." As they are not angels, government is a necessary evil. Kant said that good government is possible "even for a race of devils, if only they have intelligence."[5] These are long questions. Perhaps angels have government; surely they have duties: even if they are not ruled by what rules us, they are not unruled. We simply do not know what government of angels might amount to, but we do know that human government is something above and beyond self-defense against unusually wicked men. The very name of the Roman patriot Publius already points to this universally recognized fact.[6] On the other hand, however, it is surely hard to see how, apart from despotism, good government is ever possible among devils, however intelligent, and surely the more intelligent they are the more despotic it ought to be. Despotism or absolutism is the best government for devils. Calhoun does not speak of angels or of devils, but he derives government from the nature of man, which is no less than angels or devils distinct from the "material world."

The comparison of "our nature" and "the material world" is drawn at the point at which they are most comparable, namely, in their obedience to law. The comparends obey these respective laws whether there is any understanding of them or not. Hence, in order to understand "our nature" fully or accurately it is necessary to understand the constitution or law which it obeys. The laws obeyed in the material world are the laws of motion. The laws obeyed in the non-material or self-moved world, the world of spirit, or what Calhoun in a later paragraph calls "all animated existence," are the laws of motivation. The animate world is self-moved, it moves itself; the inanimate world is merely moved by or in accordance with something else. To lay any solid foundation for the science of government it is therefore necessary to understand the laws of motivation as the science of astronomy must understand the laws of motion.

The laws of motion "according to which the several bodies composing the solar system mutually act on each other and by which they are kept in their respective spheres" are known generally as the law or force of gravitation (paragraph 6). Knowledge of this law or force is what has firmly established the science of astronomy, because the universal formula of gravitation explains the observed order and regularity of the universe. It does not explain the origin of the universe or its end but only its maintenance by means of this presumably permanent law or force. The firm establishment of the science of government, however, on the contrary, absolutely requires an explanation of the origin of government, as well as its end or object, beginning not with the observed order of human governments in their variety but with that constitution or law of human nature "in which government originates."[7] Accordingly, Calhoun says in the conclusion to the opening paragraph that ascertaining this constitution or law is "the first question to be considered" in investigating the nature and object of government. However, after stipulating it, Calhoun does not immediately address this first of all questions to be considered. He does not even attempt to do so until after he has again restated the question in the fourth paragraph and turned to the fifth paragraph, which begins with the phrase, "The answer will be found...." In the intervening paragraphs, rather, Calhoun continues his consideration of the "first question to be considered." In considering this necessarily first of political questions he lays down the axioms which, so to speak, govern this question and all of the elementary questions of the science of government (paragraphs 2-3). These are the axioms stipulating the sociability and essential perfectibility of man as man, or the axioms assuming his "political" nature.

In looking from the first paragraph to the presentation of these axioms in the third and fourth paragraphs, several observations are in order. Ultimately, as Calhoun will later make clear (paragraph 12), these great axioms cannot help pointing above all to the divine science mentioned in the previous chapter, the science of things above the contrivance of human language. For this very reason, however, the divine science is not political science, and Calhoun does not take it up anywhere in the *Disquisition*. Metaphysics itself, the definitive capacity of human reason, is not divine science, but no more than the way to it. It is not more divine than physics is physical.[8] Between these spheres, and blending them, politics and government are the proper sphere of man as man, the sphere of the human moral and intellectual faculties as such, and the only condition in which they can be perfected by him. Man is the political animal (paragraph 14).

We know from his speeches and other writings (as well as from the relevant paragraphs of the *Disquisition's* opening part) that, according to Calhoun, the object of government is ultimately to maintain society or the political sphere as the solar system itself is maintained, admirably and harmoniously holding its constituent moving parts in their appropriate spheres, and thus to fulfill the law of the whole or to perfect the whole as such. We know that, further, this maintenance of government is itself the greatest task of the greatest human beings, given the natural and constant tendency for human government to decline. It is in this activity that man is most godlike, or perhaps, most "angelic." For while the thought of the Infinite Being sustains itself, that is, is self-sufficient, this is not the case with man, whose sustenance requires his own action, through politics, the most characteristically human activity, as well as through thought, the most characteristically human attribute, for his constitution is "twofold" (paragraph 9).[9] Thus, if the astronomical order may be said to complete itself or to be its own end, human understanding is not at all completed by the existence of the solar system or by the science of astronomy. The most important and difficult questions for man, the distinctively human questions, yet remain (paragraph 15). Hence, in the first paragraph Calhoun's emphasis is no less on the "clear and just conception" than it is on the "nature and object of government."[10] One may then ask whether it is only the perfected order of government that completes the whole, or whether perhaps something more is yet necessary also, such as the science of government. We may simply annotate Calhoun's intention on this point by referring to Mill's admission that "the most effective mode of showing that the science of politics may be constructed would be to construct it," and not merely praise it.[11] The purpose of the *Disquisition* is to provide this construction.

Paragraph 2:
The Social Nature of Mankind

"In considering this" — "the first question to be considered" — Calhoun introduces in the immediately following paragraphs two assumptions which he describes as "incontestable" and "unquestionable." These assumptions should be examined closely. He appeals not only to reason or nature but also to experience and observation in presenting these as necessary assumptions in this context, that is, as elementary facts, and even as "self-evident" elementary facts. The first of these is the fact that man is "so constituted as to be a social being" (paragraph 2). All men are equal in being so constituted. The reference to constitution brings it to our attention that man is a being composed of elements or parts, he is an order or system of parts. Calhoun's first expression of these elements or parts is in reference to man's "inclinations and wants," that is, to his native orientation or predispositions and his desires, or, in contradistinction to the motion of the inanimate material world, his original self-motivation. Inclinations and wants are not the same things. These inclinations or his wants, or both, may be either physical or moral, or both. As a being composed of such dissimilar and unequal parts, man differs in an essential or radical way from the bodies of the material world. His inclinations and wants constitute man as a social being and "irresistibly impel him to associate with his kind." He is social by nature.

It is important to see that this explanation of the first sentence in the second paragraph is also a restatement of the question that is raised in the first paragraph along the following line: being constituted as he is, that is, socially or for society, what necessarily follows from this constitution, that is, from the necessity human society? What is the nature and decisive object of human society, of man's social nature? It follows from what has been said that the object would be morality or virtue and perhaps what is now called "physical culture." This being the case, we can say that the term "man" and the term "society" (or sociality or sociability) are equivalent and—except for the difference implied in number, which is the only particular in which they differ and which arises only from the usage of general or abstract nouns—also interchangeable terms for Calhoun. They merely refer to original human inclinations and wants as such. As such, they are names for the law of self-motivation that distinguishes the whole material or inanimate world as this "law" is found in humanity as distinguished from all other "social" animals. This question, the question of specifically human animation, is the underlying theme of the opening paragraphs of the *Disquisition*. This is what he wishes to isolate in plain terms. It is important to see that this specifically human animateness has nothing to do with any exercise of the human will. The human composition or construction is a given predisposition. It is not willed by man any more than animateness is willed by the non-human portion of the animated world. This is not to deny that this limitation or binding can be ignored. One can choose to act otherwise, or select between alternatives, etc., the human will has this essential capacity.[12] But this is already social in the sense described. It is not the ground of right, much less human society. It is the ground ultimately, rather, of the assertion that might or capacity makes right. It is only in this sense that the human will can be "apolitical," that is, by implicitly projecting into humanity itself the "law" of the rest of the animated world, which is precisely the lower part of the animated world and without the human will because there right and animation simply coincide.

Calhoun's first axiom stipulates that human society originates in the nature of man and is itself an association of like beings. Accordingly, he immediately observes (in the same sentence) that in every "age and country" man has been found in this particular state, the state of society, and not in any other, hypothetical state. It was on the basis of observations like these that Hume rejected the hypothesis of the "state of nature" as the origin of human society via the "social contract" and sought to put in its place a solid foundation for the strictly human sciences in the *Treatise of Human Nature*. In the first paragraph of the section of the *Treatise* treating "Of the Origin of Government," the term "state of nature" merely means anarchy, as a tendency toward dissolution in the given or pre-existing civil society, or precisely how Calhoun uses the term "anarchy" throughout the *Disquisition*. The state of society is the state of human nature, which, while it may be more or less artful, is always social. The social state in which man is found is necessary for human preservation, that is, for physical existence, as it is among all social animals, but, Calhoun here adds in the same breath that, even if it were not necessary merely for human existence, it is further necessary for human perfection. That is, setting aside his physical inclinations and wants altogether, Calhoun lays it down that the social state is necessary for man to "attain to a full development of his moral and intellectual faculties." These are what constitute the essential and social nature of man. Hence Hume does not go far enough. The empirical or experimental outline of the human sciences and their study in the *Treatise* only point toward this. Human perfection consists in the perfection of these faculties as the purpose of human existence. The aim of the science of government is to perfect the orientation of these faculties or to provide the necessary conditions for their perfection (paragraph 14). However, it cannot do this with exact precision because it cannot possibly know all the human and non-human circumstances of changing times and "in every age and country" (cf. paragraph 41).

The moral and intellectual faculties are the characteristic and hence definitive human faculties, and their development is therefore the characteristic and definitive object of the social state. Calhoun's replacement of the reference in the second sentence of the second paragraph to "man's physical and moral inclinations and wants" by that in the third sentence to the "full development of his moral and intellectual faculties" is, therefore, not insignificant. The phrase in the second sentence is as much of a bow to man's physical inclinations and wants — the appetites and drives to achieve sexual connection and avoid hunger, thirst, and pain dwelt on by other writers — as Calhoun ever makes in presenting the axioms of political science on the point of his social nature. They are superseded by man's intellectual inclinations and wants. The reference to man's "moral and intellectual faculties" completes the original reference to his "physical and moral inclinations and wants." More fully and accurately stated, the fully developed state of these faculties, particularly the intellectual faculties which replace the physical inclinations and wants, is man's "natural state," the state toward which human nature points. The science of government is thus in the first place the science of specifically or distinctively human government, of what is necessary for the government of man as man, of man as distinguished from herds of beasts.

Calhoun indicates in the same (third) sentence that the development of these faculties is itself not simply natural or given. Their development is neither axiomatic nor instinctual and requires more than the social state or a social nature. The social state is natural in that it is given by the constitution of man; the full development of the parts that compose man, all his inclinations, wants, and faculties, is not given but must be acquired by organization and practice and art or science, that is, "intellectual and moral culture" (paragraph 7). Culture is the aim of human society as such. The arts and sciences, broadly, or as distinguished from all that is not man-made or given by nature, and for which society is necessary, are the means by which man raises himself from what is merely given, namely, the original and brute irresistibility of the social state. This irresistibility or nature alone is never simply sufficient to complete the highest or distinctively human faculties. Culture is necessary. Were it otherwise, it would be impossible to distinguish between different human societies, for all human society would be equal and indistinguishable from itself. Instead of being many, human society would be one, like the associations of other animals, which, wherever and in whatever age they might be found, differ only by number, and we could speak of "society" interchangeably with any particular community or culture or regime. Art, the work of man's intellectual and moral faculties, is necessary to complete what nature has begun and to raise man in what Calhoun here calls the "scale of being" from one social being among others to a fully developed or perfect moral intellectual, as distinct from an angel or a "superman," a finished human being, or what Calhoun would doubtless call a constitutional statesman. To use for purposes of illustration the familiar scholastic or Aristotelian terms which Calhoun does not use, man is by nature actually social and potentially a perfect moral intellectual (cf. Aquinas, *Commentary on Aristotle's Politics, Proemium*, paragraph 1).

The second paragraph moves from the irresistible social being of man, through his physical and moral inclinations and wants in time, that is, "in any age and country," to the easily resistible development of his moral and intellectual faculties according to nature, that is, to the "scale of being," the ascent of which requires effort. The "material bodies composing the solar system" that are moved in accordance with the laws of motion in the analogy set forth in the first paragraph are replaced in the second by the "social being" or self-motivation specific to man "in any age and country," and the "respective spheres" or order of the solar system are replaced by the "scale of being." What it is that must yoke and finally unite these unequal and dissimilar beings in order to complete the analogy, or what must make that which is easily resistible as much as possible irresistible—government—is not yet mentioned in the second paragraph. Our attention is thus drawn again to the disparity between the constitution or law of the solar or physical system, by means of which the system is a system, and that within man and society which makes government necessary, but which alone is insufficient to perfect man and society, or to produce the moral intellectual, which is the aim of human sociability or nature. This disparity provides the distinction between Creation, on the one hand, as admirable and harmonious in its order, and, on the other, as merely brute, as Calhoun refers to it in connection with the scale of being in the second paragraph, or ignorant of any order or causes, including its own. Ultimately, this disparity, the original brutality, must be overcome through reason or development of the highest intellectual faculty, the knowledge of causes, and by the will to act in accordance with that knowledge. This is in accordance with nature, but it does not itself occur simply by nature. If it did, there would be no need for government.

Paragraphs 3-4:
The Political Nature of Mankind

Calhoun therefore immediately turns to the axiom about government in the following (third) paragraph. This assumption flows necessarily from man's social nature, but is based on experience and observation. The institution of government characterizes human society in all ages and places and among all human beings, and itself expresses the fundamentally or essentially single and unchanging nature that has been and will be shared by all humanity always. The phenomenon of government is in no respect limited to any particular historic moment or epoch. Rather, it defines the human epoch. The Republic of Rome itself has incomparably more in common with another human community of any description than with all other forms of Creation taken together.

In laying down the axiom about human government, Calhoun distinguishes between the enlightened and the savage human being and between the idea of human society (the natural or merely social state of humankind), and that of community. All these are elements of the universal experience of mankind. It is easy enough to see that the distinction between the enlightened and the savage is related to the level of development of the arts and sciences in the community, considered as we have done in connection with the preceding paragraph, and, as we have already suggested, it is enough for the moment to say that the enlightened is identical with the civilized, or possessing high arts and sciences, and the savage with the uncivilized, or possessing no high arts and sciences. As for the distinction made here between human society and community, we may say that, while every community is a society and society is what all communities indigenously, commonly, indiscriminately, and equally share, human communities as such are separate, distinct, unique and unequal. "Society" as such is merely the social nature of man wherever he is found, as distinguished not from an hypothetical asocial nature but primarily and precisely from "community," and refers, as has been indicated, to essential or "original man" and his necessary association with his own species.

These plain words must be seen as almost like technical terms in *A Disquisition on Government*. In so far as the nowadays familiar term "societies" (which is not found in the *Disquisition*) might be used loosely or vaguely to refer to any or all of the various independent political or cultural wholes actual or potential wholes into which mankind is divided or through which humanity is expressed, and differing among themselves by "language, customs, pursuits, situation, and complexion," and so on (paragraph 16), it actually means or refers to so many particular "communities" or would-be communities. Human society as such is essentially completed by government as such, or to express it more fully, by the particular ends or aims of the government. It is for this reason that the incidence of the term "society" itself becomes relatively uncommon, to say the least, in the *Disquisition* after Calhoun has completed the account of the origin of government (paragraph 9), while the term community then becomes quite common (see paragraphs 16-17). Reference to "community" replaces (completes) reference to "society." Communities are particular social orders or regimes with particular governments. The term "community," thus, may refer to the order of all these human or social phenomena or attributes either plus or minus government (e.g., paragraphs 13-14). In short, it means throughout the *Disquisition* what the term *"polis"* means in Aristotle's *Politics*, i.e., the fullest and most complete human association, and it is subject to the same kinds of objections and hypothetical criticisms. Government (which Aristotle discusses primarily as the form of government) is an isolatable element but it is the critical or decisive element (paragraph 19). Without due attention to it, contemplation of politics tends to lose or rather assert itself in considerations of topics like "civilization" as usually understood, "education," "aesthetics," "communications theory," and so on.[13] Accordingly, Calhoun says that "universal experience" shows government necessary for the existence of the social state, which itself is necessary for man's existence and "the full development of his faculties," already mentioned. Human sociability naturally inclines toward community, and hence government is necessary and natural for man, whatever may be the level of development of his distinctive faculties (paragraph 9).

As will become clearer as the study of *A Disquisition on Government* proceeds, the "community"—polity, regime, political order, culture, constitution—which term Calhoun uses interchangeably with the term "people," or what he also sometimes calls the "state" (e.g., paragraph 17, in the same sense in which the Greek term *polis* is often translated as "city-state"), is the particular "form" of society, which is its "matter" (paragraph 14). The distinction that is drawn here by Calhoun between society on the one hand and government or the constitution of the community as a whole, "constitution in the comprehensive sense," on the other, is present in earlier political philosophy as the familiar distinction between the private and the public. There is perhaps an unavoidable ambivalence or apparent paradox entailed in using the terms "society" and "private" in this way, for each can refer equally to what is by nature, which is common, and by virtue of which Calhoun says that society is of higher rank or dignity than government, but also to what is merely individual and not truly or fully common, and, as such, of less rank or dignity than government. We have seen the ambivalence before, for example, in Calhoun's reference to the duties of his public life as a statesman, on the one hand, and the duties of his private life as a planter, on the other, in the same sentence in which he refers also to his equally private work on the *Disquisition* itself as, in his terms, "peculiar to myself," whereas of course the science of government is by its nature also something common and an object of admiration and interest to all men as men, even though it is also in a sense unique to Calhoun. The distinction made is not new but is essentially the same as that found in the *Nichomachean Ethics* and the *Politics,* along with the notion that the constitution (or "polity") is the form and society, understood both as the original sociability of man as constituted by his distinctive faculties and feelings and what, following Hobbes (and usually under the banner of Locke) is now known as "civil society," that is, an ordered and orderly marketplace, is the matter. But this simple ambiguity itself is often complicated and blurred in our time (and with it the foundation of political science as set forth by Calhoun), by the common understanding of the distinction of "state" and "society" — or the individual versus society or man versus the state, or individualism versus socialism, and so on — particularly with respect to his point about the form of the community and the aims of society, which is its substance or matter. Because the distinction is crucial for understanding Calhoun and the science of government, it will be useful here to pause and review it at some length in connection with the political thought of Hegel on the modern or "rational" constitution, with whom Calhoun's idea of constitution and political science has been compared.

Excursus on the Relation of Calhoun to Hegel and Marx,
   or the German "Philosophy of Freedom" (pp. 62-78)

FOR HEGEL, "WHAT IS RATIONAL IS ACTUAL, AND WHAT IS ACTUAL IS RATIONAL."[14] FOR
Calhoun, the case is not as Hegel puts it. According to Hegel, the distinction in
question above arose as part of the unfolding in modern times of the principle of
the infinite individual, the complete determination of the concept, and the rest of
the Hegelian system and its apparatus. In the middle of his *Outline of Natural
Law and the Science of the State: Principles of the Philosophy of Right* (paragraphs
182-185A, and *Remarks* on paragraph 185) Hegel says that the idea of the
"social," which includes privacy, the idea of the individual and individuality,
and so on, and therewith the idea of "civil society" itself, could not and did not
exist in antiquity because antiquity lacked the necessary foundation in principle
for its full emergence, although they as it were tried to emerge. In the Hegelian
system, it was Christianity and the Roman Empire which gave rise to the
principle of individualism generally, and, to paraphrase, Protestantism, if not
Lutheranism, that then in turn gave rise to capitalism particularly. Hence the
rational could not become actual at the time of the Greek polis. In a famous
sentence, Hegel writes that "the creation of civil society is the achievement of the
modern world which has for the first time given all determinations of the idea
their due" (paragraph 249). The ancient philosophers (Hegel here has in mind
particularly Plato) were necessarily limited to what they called the "political"
because they were essentially limited to the world and experience—the
"spirit"—of the Greek polis. Lacking the principle upon which to do so, instead
of properly distinguishing the political from the civil state, they left these things
conflated, undetermined, and unarticulated in the idea of the political itself, and
the civil state could not become actual. Except as having been necessary in their
own time and philosophizing in the shadows, these ancient philosophers are
irrelevant to the concrete science of government or the philosophy of right, for
which the actualization of "civil society" is necessary. It is the intention of the
Philosophy of Right to present the political here and now, for the first time, as
made sufficiently possible and necessary by the actual emergence and
flourishing of civil society and by Hegel's own *Science of Logic*, for what it
actually is (*Philosophy of Right*, Preface).

Hegel sees that all states were founded not on a "social contract," for such a
concept already implies an existing consensus. (This view is of course not
original with Hegel, nor is it due to anything especially "modern," as is clear
from the fact that he takes the term "consensus" ultimately from Cicero.) He
holds, rather, that all states were founded originally as tyrannies in which a
"people" is created out of existing mass society by the work of an extraordinary
man. This view is, and Hegel explains that it is, "Machiavellianism." As the
people progress, tyranny in time (perhaps a long time), becomes superfluous,

having served its purpose, and is violently thrown off by the people as superfluous. (Only the tyrant refuses to recognize this superfluity out of his own subjective desire and lack of universality.) In this way there emerged out of tyranny, and on the basis of popular assertion, the Greek polis.[15] The polis, which beautifully expresses the happy liberty of the people, however, also remains ignorant of universality. It is essentially "Greek" and essentially "ancient," and must be transcended. The primary reason for this is that it knows not yet the proper distinction between the polity or state and civil society, or between the public and the private, and it is therefore undifferentiated, the individual being subsumed in the political. On the one hand, this results in a kind of totalitarianism, for the self-consciousness of the individual is essentially identical to the unself-consciousness of the polity. On the other hand, the result is that the opinions which characterize the life of the polis are merely accidental and not necessary, that is, are of essentially the same character as those which properly always characterize "civil society" and the marketplace, where circumstances are always variable. The emergence of Christianity, on the one hand, within the expanse of the Roman Empire, on the other, provide for the emergence of the principle of the self-conscious individual and of "civil society" in their own right, as such, only in modern times. It is on the basis of civil society, then, including the emergence of the practical science that is its characteristic expression, that it becomes possible and necessary to transcend civil society in the direction of the state.[16] For now — for us — the problem is not that the political ignorantly if necessarily subsumes the civil in an undifferentiated way but, rather, that the properly political itself is sunk in the civil, which has now emerged in its fullness, and remains undetermined. It is the work of the *Philosophy of Right* to effectualize this determination and therewith complete or end human history and hence bring to light the true or final human individual (viz., the political philosopher Hegel). We should hasten to note that civil society, that is, the marketplace and the wealth of nations as understood by Adam Smith and others, is not and does not become superfluous for the state in the way original tyranny becomes superfluous for a people. It can not be thrown off. It is always necessary, and, now that it has emerged, it will exist so long as man exists. History as the culmination of the system of wisdom, human history properly so called, will end, and in principle has already ended, with the thought of the *Philosophy of Right* and the battle of Jena, but civil society and its affairs will not end. There will be accidents. To be fully human, man must recognize this necessity and identify himself with it, just as it is understood by Smith. The civil or economic society must be transcended in the modern state but it cannot be overthrown. (This is Hegel's beforehand answer to Marx.)[17]

This is more or less how Hegel accounts for the emergence and necessity of "civil society." But if civil society thus understood, that is, understood as the marketplace or the home of Smithian man, is necessary, according to Hegel, it is not yet sufficient for man as unqualifiedly man.[18] Only the state itself transcending civil society is sufficient as the actualization of man's essential self-determination. "The rational end of man is life in the state," that is, the "ethical community" as such (paragraph 75A). Given the freedom of the individual, on the one hand, and the rule of law, on the other, as these are drawn from civil society and transformed in the state to a common end, the state is a complete moral (private) and ethical (public or common) whole, represented ultimately and finally by the will of the monarch. Hegel pauses to note that the monarch himself may be and doubtless will be in every respect an undistinguished (that is, undetermined or unindividuated) individual (280-281A). Nevertheless, the principle of the constitution—transcending civil society, which makes it possible, and completing in the monarch the principle of the self-conscious individual, which makes it necessary—is the "higher principle of the new age, which remained unknown to the ancients." It recognizes itself in its own realization, which is the actualization of man as unqualifiedly man.[19] Therefore, the constitutional monarchy of the modern European Christian state is both the most necessary and the most free or rational regime, the best regime according to the nature or history of man.

It is true, however, that man's self-determination and self-realization and self-recognition are not entirely exhausted by the existence of this state, even the most necessary and rational state, or by the will of this constitutional monarch. Man needs also, according to Hegel, art and philosophy, and, for Hegel, most especially philosophy. These, like religion, transcend the state in directions beyond merely human life, even though they are not possible for man outside the state. In the past, philosophy was not possible in the state, *sensu strictu*, although it was necessary. Now it is possible in the state. The place of philosophy in the rational state is primarily in the state civil service (including academia, where Professor Hegel himself was). The civil service, which occupies the place of reason in relation to the monarch's will, the will of the state, is the modern field or dimension of the extraordinary men who, in earlier or "original" times, were the founders of states in accordance with Machiavelli's understanding of the founder or legislator. This class is called by Hegel the "universal" or "absolute" class, and either in the form of bureaucracy or some other, is necessary to the modern state, as Weber, following Hegel (and Comte), has said. Its essential responsibility is the management of all the affairs of the state for the good of the whole (289ff, Preface). Philosophy, as it resides in this class, will search all things that lie beyond the state, but Hegel seems reminiscent of Calhoun in holding that it will always focus on the state and the philosophy of the state, for it is in this philosophy that man is most unqualifiedly man.[20]

Hegel is always original and sometimes also engaging in the way he speaks about anything, but it remains that his dialectical method, which is the most characteristic feature of his thought as a whole, in the end loses altogether the elementary concrete distinction between absolute and constitutional government. It is merely absorbed into the history of the concept of the consensual state, which is supposed to account for it. Yet this distinction is fundamental for the science of government *qua* science, as, Calhoun says, all governments, whether ancient or modern, are either one or the other (*Disquisition*, paragraph 19).[21] For Calhoun, therefore, with all his discussion, Hegel has not shown—and is even unable to show—that the Modern European Christian Constitutional Prussian Monarchy is constitutional. He would agree with Marx in saying, "Why is he entitled to conclude that 'this organism is the state'? Why not 'this organism is the solar system?'"[22] The distinction in question is, ultimately, as Hegel's remarks on Fries in the Preface make clear, what provided the occasion for the publication of the *Philosophy of Right* itself, and, ultimately, also what is behind the controversy among Hegel specialists as to whether the *Philosophy of Right* is not merely an apology for the post-battle of Jena Prussian monarchy (i.e., as to whether, as a defender of genuine constitutionalism, Hegel was born not, indeed, "before his time" but in the wrong country). Is power amenable to rational direction, or is such apparent direction the self-deceiving rationalization of holding rule? Hegel's project does not arrive at more than the admittedly important insight that government is a positive good. In principle he advances no further than J. S. Mill in his *Considerations on Representative Government*. Whether or not one must understand the *Science of Logic* and the *Phenomenology of Spirit* and the *Encyclopedia* and the *History of Philosophy* or, in other words, the whole system of wisdom according to Hegel, that is, Hegel's own individualism, in order to understand the place of the *Philosophy of Right* in that system is, so to speak, neither here nor there for the fundamental question at hand. The fact remains that one cannot distinguish concretely between absolute and constitutional regimes on the basis of the Hegelian system of wisdom or his science of the state. For this reason alone, his *Philosophy of Right* cannot be said to arrive at the science of the state.

This fundamental defect in Hegel's political thought is shown in another way, also, in what is thought to be the most searching "dialectical" critique of the *Philosophy of Right*, the *Critique* by Marx, with whose doctrines Calhoun's philosophy of government has also been compared. For Marx, all human history is the history of class struggle.[23] For Calhoun, the case is not as Marx puts it. Marx is closest to Calhoun in his statements like "The [Hegelian] state is an abstraction; the people alone is the concrete" (comment on paragraph 279), and his typical criticism of the Hegelian constitutional state throughout the *Critique*, that it is merely formal or abstractionist, and so on, is the same criticism that Calhoun would make of it.[24] It is not worthy of the name "constitution." Yet in Marx's *Critique* this criticism serves little purpose. In his *Critique of Hegel's 'Philosophy of Right,'* Marx, who follows Feurbach's dialectical transposition of the Hegelian subject and predicate and wishes, using this "method," to turn over the Hegelian system or stand it up on its feet and arrive at the true science of "socialism," also does not arrive at the crucial political distinction mentioned above but merely transposes Hegel's terms of absolute and concrete. Hegel's method, which for Marx is the "true method," is, according to Marx, in Hegel's hands merely "allegory." "At the most profound and speculative level... it is evident that the true method is turned upside down" (comment on the remark to paragraph 279, see the comment on 304).[25] Such a "critique" remains on the same plane as its object—to the extent that it attains it—the Hegelian system, and depends on that object for whatever rational value it may be thought to possess. He surely goes no further than Hegel, although he loses Hegel's insight that government is a positive good in the procedure of turning the system over. It is the same procedure initially taken by John Stuart Mill in seeing that the Benthamite Utilitarians had been wrong in their interpretation of politics and, therefore, in their "selection" of a method for philosophizing about politics, and replacing this incorrect method with the correct one of material physics. Marx retains the Hegelian system after altering it to his own satisfaction.[26] Throughout, Marx entirely agrees with Hegel on what Hegel himself takes to be the fundamental point about the necessary modernity (if not futurity) of the state itself, and hence of the science of government.[27]

It is not surprising, therefore, that the most important sections of the *Critique*, and perhaps also the most famous, are those which have nothing to do with the Hegelian system and do not in any way depend on it or Feurbach or anyone else, namely, the sections on the civil service as presented in the *Philosophy of Right*. Perhaps Marx's own language unwittingly signals this in opening the critique there by saying "what Hegel says about 'the executive' does not merit the name of a philosophical development" (comment on paragraph 297). As is well known, in those sections Marx observes that the civil service does not and will not play the role in the modern state that Hegel says it does or that the Hegelian system assigns to it, namely the role of the "universal class" whose aim is the superintendence or management of the state as a whole for the good of the whole, but only the role of petty agents of the government interest or party. (Marx associates the civil service with a priestly or mandarin class.) Marx thus arrives at the insight set forth in the twenty-eighth paragraph of *A Disquisition on Government* as to the partisan character of the government interest or party. On the basis of this insight, Marx makes on this point the same kind of critique of the Hegelian state that Calhoun would make. This insight is, in fact, the only positive thing the *Critique of Hegel's 'Philosophy of Right'* achieves. Yet this important achievement remains inert, for Marx does not pursue this insight or develop it in the manner of Calhoun. He cannot do so, given his prior dependence on the Hegelian system. He merely criticizes Hegel for mistaking the civil service, which is in fact the master class, for the "universal class," and goes on to assert that it is not the civil service as seen by Hegel but the "proletariat," or slave class, as seen by him, that is the true and final universal class which, come the revolution, will administer things for the good of "society" as a whole ("Introduction" to the *Critique*). Marx thus overlooks the brute fact that this party, too, is only a partial or partisan party—or, if you like, he does not overlook this fact but rather embraces it: the point is immaterial, it nonetheless remains a brute fact (*Disquisition*, paragraphs 29-33).

We may note in passing that it is in terms of some of Calhoun's arguments presenting the necessity to check or counterbalance such aggressive partisanship or interests with other parties or interests for the sake of the common good that some academic historians have found in Calhoun what they understand as a proto-Marxian system or thought. Thus one writer observes that "Calhoun laid down an analysis of American politics and the sectional struggle which foreshadowed some of the seminal ideas of Marx's system.[28] However, Calhoun's position is more subtle and is concerned primarily with the political, the whole or the common good itself, whereas Marx simply wishes to abolish or annihilate a part of the community in order to leave a merely partisan good in the place, *io nomine* or "allegorically," of the whole or common good. His attitude and his method is already that addressed more than a half-century earlier in the tenth *Federalist*, where Madison says, also in the context of securing the "public good," that there are "two methods of curing the mischiefs of faction: the one, by removing its causes," which are "sown in the nature of man" and the protection of which "is the first object government," the other, by controlling its effects," which are liberty, which is "essential to political life," and inequality. The whole argument of *Federalist* 10—the developed argument of factions and interests checking and controlling factions and interests, particularly "majority factions," concerns the latter method. Marx's wish to remove the causes of faction and thus secure the social good by abolishing property and hence inequality and interests is, according to Madison, a cure that is "worse than the disease" or, in short, a quack remedy.[29] It is not political but merely absolutist. It is easy to see from a study of the tenth *Federalist* that the argument could be made—and, in fact, it actually has been made—that Madison also "foreshadowed some of the seminal ideas of Marx's system." "Madison's whole scheme comes down to this," says one historian, "the struggle of classes is to be replaced by the struggle of interests.... Madison gave a beforehand answer to Marx."[30] All that these kinds of arguments or notions—which are admittedly more or less innocent of Marx, to say nothing of Calhoun—can be said to intimate is that American political thought in this period is more interesting and provocative than it has been before or since, as well as equal or superior to that of contemporary Europe. Were it not for the gravity of the issues involved this whole argument could seem absurd. Nevertheless, it points in the right direction. Marx's opinion was that, once he had appropriately corrected the theoretical "beforehand answer" of Hegelianism, the remaining or practical "beforehand answer" to Marxism was, precisely, England: "political economy can remain a science only so long as the class struggle is latent," and this is the case in England, according to him, "because its political economy belongs to the period when the class struggle was as yet undeveloped" (*Capital*, vol. 1, beginning.) The "period" in question is, according to Calhoun, in fact ("historically") the period of constitutional monarchy (*Disquisition*, paragraph 160). So long as constitutionalism holds firm in Britain, the Marxian "class struggle" will always be undeveloped, that is, will never happen. When and if the constitution breaks down, assuredly something like it will happen. This is, certainly, Calhoun's whole point, and it is also Madison's point. The true aim of the struggle or competition of classes or parts of the whole, or Aristotle's struggle between the few and the many, is constitutional government (*A Disquisition on Government*, paragraphs 151-159). Constitutionalism is not merely a beforehand answer to Marx and the embrace of partisan interests for their own sakes—under whatever pretext or mask—it is also the afterthought that remains after the partisanship has run its merely typical and predictable course. Constitutionalism outranks all "isms"; it is the first and last political "ism": all others lead more or less quickly to Caesarism.

For Calhoun, just as for Marx, the end of Marxism is from the beginning a foregone conclusion, although Marx is mistaken about the conclusion because he is mistaken about the beginning, namely, that ultimately mind is matter and that freedom and hence "humanity" is ultimately only and necessarily material. That this position—that there is, therefore, no common good but only the good of the proletariat class—cannot and will not for a moment be sustained is, therefore, also foregone. It will necessarily disintegrate into the position that there is no genuinely common or "species good" for the proletariat class as a whole outside the good of the relatively minute "vanguard" of the proletariat class as a "whole," that is, the ambitious or warlike intellectuals espousing Marxism. These are the true species-proletariat, although it goes without saying that they are not "proletarians" and have, so to speak, nothing in common with the proletariat. Marxism thus amounts to replacing the "universal class" of Hegel's government bureaucracy with the "universal vanguard" of the party bureaucracy: *la lutte glorieuse* of the organization men. And the "common good" of this initially small group will quickly boil down to the good of merely of the vanguard of the vanguard, the leader—chairman, secretary, *dux* – and the "class struggle" will play itself out in the struggle for leadership of the party: Marx but not Lassalle or Bernstein or Saint Simon or whoever else; Lenin and no one else; Stalin and no one else; and the rest (*Disquisition*, paragraph 65). This dynamic, so far from being essentially "modern," or awaiting modern technological civil society to emerge, is the characteristic dynamic of "Caesarism," as opposed to "Republicanism," and of the "purge" of the Second Triumvirate. Republicanism, commitment to the common good (*res publica*), is the beforehand answer to Caesarism (Cicero, *Republic*, III, 45 and context), and it is also the ineluctable nostalgia that remains after Caesarism has run its foregone course.[31] Caesarism is "alienation." What is new, in this case, is that it clothes or masks itself as philosophy or, rather, "science." (Because it has been successful in doing so among *arriviste* academics, some have come out like Cato swinging blindly at philosophy itself as the enemy of the "open society"—except, of course, for positivism. Positivism cleansed of the *Furherprinzip* may make society safe from philosophy. This amounts to a blind or senseless but not at all irrational recovery of Hume, even though it still leaves us with organization men.) For the purposes at hand, it is enough to observe that, as everyone knows, according to Marx, the proletariat ultimately will play no role in the life of the state, for with their rule—or administration—the state itself will necessarily wither away. In that day, everyone will participate in all the most human things that Hegel had said were impossible independently of the state—particularly art and philosophy—without the oppression of the state. Man will then, without the state, be truly and unqualifiedly man.[32] Yet, according to Calhoun, the day has never been and will not come when man is without a "state," and, apart from reason, the partisanship Marx himself embraces is alone enough to ensure the perpetuity of an increasingly aggressive state. Hence what Marx's argument shows, insofar as it may be said to show anything, is that the "proletariat," *qua* proletariat or as distinguished from this or that party, will never play any role in the life of a state.

We cannot leave it at this, however, for Marx's critique of the Hegelian state, understood as the modern and hence true state, is at the same time and above all meant as a critique of philosophy, understood as the modern and hence true philosophy. Marx sees that Hegel makes all the attributes of the contemporary European Christian monarch into absolute self-determinations of the will, and that the final decision of the will as the will of the monarch is a "metaphysical axiom." He sees that Hegel constructs out of sovereignty and will the idea as "one individual," the "personality of the state" within and without, and that the medium for all this construction is the "word of the philosopher." He observes that "Hegel takes pleasure in having demonstrated the irrational to be absolutely rational," and quotes him (paragraph 33, cf. 31-32): "This transition from the concept of pure self-determination into the immediacy of being and so into the realm of nature is of a purely speculative character, and the apprehension of it therefore belongs to logic." He sees that the concrete justification for the Modern European Christian Constitutional Prussian Monarchy is the justification in the *Philosophy of Right* of the abstract or formal rule of the philosopher-king Professor Hegel behind the scenes in the civil service or *"le republique prete."* [33] The justification could serve, or be easily adjusted to serve, just as well for the rule of the Egyptian Pharaoh mediating the divine *maat* or the Chinese Emperor mediating the yin and the yang—or the Rector-Professor Heidegger mediating the inward "relation to Being" of the German *Volk*—as for the final decision of the Prussian monarch. The term "constitution" for Hegel ultimately means nothing more than the form of government in which philosophy and power (kingship, executive branch) abstractly coincide in the state with the public support of the state (Plato, *Apology*, 36d-37a; *Critique*, 98: "Thus, philosophy is also essentially dependent upon the government treasury."). In modernity this is possible; Plato was unaware of it. For Calhoun, of course, in such a case, the king must be checked or balanced in some way. For Hegel, the king must be weak, that is, in a sense not a true king. He leaves it at this. (This is why he pauses to point out the mediocrity of the king himself in the Hegelian state.)[34] For Hegel, the public responsibility of philosophy is quite serious. This is also why Hegel is serious about the defense of monarchy, if primarily of "constitutional" monarchy, and would not dream, as Marx does, of seeing in history primarily the dialectical rise of democracy or democratic socialism through the class struggle. For democracy is of all regimes the most hostile to philosophy, and hence history as the rise of democracy would be irrational.

Marx is not satisfied with the rule behind the scenes of the philosopher civil servant as set forth by the would-be philosopher king of Hegel. This is an imaginary or allegorical rule. It is yet to be made actual or concrete. The philosophy of Hegel is genuine (for Marx), but the rule of philosophy is not genuinely actualized in the modern state as set forth (correctly) by Hegel. The liberation of the nation is not brought about by the liberation of one individual, which is necessarily private. "That a Scythian was numbered among the Greek philosophers [Anacharsis] did not enable the Scythians to advance a step toward Greek culture," according to Marx, and this advance is the important thing, the decisive thing ("Introduction" to the *Critique*, 135). Hence not the historical rationalization of the Hegelian constitutional state but the revolutionary rise of Marxian democracy is the only true end of the state because it is the only true coincidence of political power and philosophy. The modern state as set forth by Hegel is only satisfactory in an imaginary or illusory way, like religion or like Plato's *Republic*, or philosophy altogether. Feurbach was right: the essence of philosophy and Christianity and the state are the same (132). Once this is understood fully through the critical interpretation of Hegel's speculative philosophy of right, it becomes categorically imperative—Marx never says that it is desirable, much less that it is necessary—in practice to change or to modernize what is not yet modern in the modern state, that is, to make it essentially philosophical and philosophy essentially partisan. This transvaluation of philosophy is achieved by the method or "weapon" of Hegelian criticism stood upright and turned into a properly material force, a mass force, by assuming the form of *ad hominem* propaganda aimed at the realization of the absolute, that is, the abolition of existing conditions and institutions in the name of the "universal rights of society" ("Introduction," 137). It is in this way that the rule of philosophy will be actualized in the transformation or degradation of philosophy. It is a commonplace that this propaganda never did become a mass force. Its appeal is not to the "masses" or the "proletariat" but primarily to ambitious intellectuals (e.g., Lenin, Mao). *Ad hominem* critique is the opium of intellectuals. (Cf. Plato, *Euthydemus*) "Now it is the philosopher in whose brain the revolution begins" ("Introduction," 138; cf. Heidegger, "The Fundamental Question of Metaphysics," last paragraph).

Criticism thus understood—that is, as according to Mill, Bentham saw the polemical propagation of Utilitarianism ("the principle of happiness")— according to Marx, "is no passion but is rather the brain of passion. It is not a scalpel but a weapon. Its object is its enemy, which it wishes not to refute but to annihilate." It is the weapon of the Grand Inquisitor (Marx makes this comment in the context of a critical "executioner" and a philosopher or non-critical criminal). "Criticism [i.e., thought] is no longer an end in itself but now simply a means. Indignation is its essential pathos, denunciation its principal task" ("Introduction," 133). It is at such passion and indignation that the argument of *On Liberty* is directed.[35] Marxism—no less than Compteanism ("materialism consists in explaining what is above by what is below")—is a religion of man and no less than any other religion does it escape the condemnation by Feuerbach of the essential abstraction and idealist projection of religion. Prometheanism is as much an ism as Totemism. It is more, for totemism does not see itself or understand itself as an ism. It thus remains true to the essential mystery of man, of which it is a genuine human expression. Paraphrasing Feuerbach, one would have to say that it is the mysterious oxymoron of "dialectical materialism" and the indignant critique that closes man in the name of an abstraction of universality and infinity, enslaves the human condition in the name of a projected human freedom, sets up a vanguard to act as *"le republique prete,"* prohibit speculation in the name of orthodoxy, and the rest. It is Calhoun, not Marx, who reminds us that there are thousands on thousands, millions on millions, not shadows, but real persons under these abstractions and who will have to carry their weight. Before we act, let us examine things as they really are and not as we might imagine them in the fervor of debate.

The "emancipation of man" aimed at by Marxism is one and the same as the emancipation of the new and future class—the "not yet" class—of the "proletariat." "The head of this emancipation is philosophy," transvalued as dialectical materialist critique or polemic, "its heart is the proletariat," transvalued as the absolute ideal of creative modernity. "Philosophy cannot be actualized without the abolition of the proletariat, the proletariat cannot be abolished without the actualization of philosophy." By these means, philosophy will be fulfilled in the political sphere and society will abolish the political sphere. Philosophy will reign, announced "by the crowing of the Gallic cock" ("Introduction," 136, 142, cf. 132: "French chronology"). This passion, including its "brain," is what Calhoun calls "false philanthropy," "false philosophy," or "French philosophy." It is not—any more than Benthamism or Comteanism—philosophy, and its various prophets and parishioners are not philosophers. It is merely academic or intellectual partisanship wearing the mask of philosophy because it wishes to clothe itself in the noblest public robes, the robes of man as man, and to speak with the authority accorded science as the highest and distinctive human faculty, and which raises man above the brutes in the scale of being. It therefore must logically distort philosophy in the name of what is unqualifiedly lower than philosophy, while history testifies to its distortion of human society. The transvaluation or mistranslation of the idea of the philosopher king into the idea of the intellectual tyrant results in the actualization of tyranny wearing the mask of "philosophy" or "science." The "idea" of the philosopher-partisan is as oxymoronic as the "idea" of dialectical materialism," which is its "direct efflux." In order for this idea to have sense, it would be necessary to reconceive tyranny as rule for the good of all, including those whom Marx calls "noble, or of equal rank, or interesting," for it is only in this way that tyranny could be good also for the tyrant. Yet the happiness of most of the others, even all the others but one, is not the same as the happiness of the one, as Mill realized in his reflection on the aims of Utilitarianism. It is for this reason that the philosopher does not wish for absolute rule (Plato, *Republic,* 519c4-520b4, and related passages), which is in Plato's sense impossible. Perhaps, had these or similar questions ever occurred to Marx, the result would have been the same as they were for Mill. They did not occur to him, with the result that philosophy was abandoned and tyranny embraced in the name of "emancipation" and "liberation."[36] The rule of the philosopher-partisans is an illusory liberation. It does not enable society to advance a step toward Greek culture as imagined by German thought; it outlaws such steps. The political Marxification of the modern state is, rather, the Scythification of the modern state. Withal, it is a sweeping achievement that would have embarrassed the Scythians. The critical means annihilate the decisive end.

Calhoun's concern is not with a new political class (there is none) but with the new political element of public opinion as affected or controlled by the new means of mass information, and which may decisively strengthen the tendency of governments toward absolutism under the illusion of a "free press." The translator of Marx's *Critique* reports:

> In becoming theoretical praxis, philosophy [i.e., Marxism] in Germany of the 1840s uses the popular press as its medium of expression. It gives up its solitude and ascetic existence and enters public life through the more conventional means of the newspaper and journal of social criticism. The philosopher becomes a journalist without ceasing to be a philosopher. Political society is the prime object of his attention. He

brings his understanding of the foundations and purposes of society, law and the state to a public discussion [sic] of the deficiencies of the existing socio-political order.[37]

As has been observed, the result of this activist journalism will not be the emancipation of society by throwing off the yoke of the state but merely a more aggressively absolute government or state than has yet been seen. This is achieved not by actually or literally transcending philosophy by the actual or literal annihilation of part of the society itself, beginning – as Mill discerned and as Marx boasts in the *Critique* – with the annihilation of philosophy itself in the direction of sophistry. Thus would be achieved, on its own terms, an actual absolutism or totalitarianism undreamt of by citizens and men of the Greek *polis*.[38] It goes without saying that this was not exactly the original intention, but good intentions are not enough, and it must be the inevitable result whenever thought is no longer understood as an end in itself and is reduced to simply a means. In Calhoun's terms, in such a case, it is necessity, not parties, that will ever provide the actual end.

For Hegel, reason is not simply a means to some other end but an end in itself. It was partly for this that Marx abandoned Hegelianism for a life of journalism in the quest to modernize what was not yet modern in the modern state. Yet the understanding or recovery of philosophy, beginning with the philosophy of government, does not entail a return to Hegel. Hegel does not arrive at the science of government, ancient or modern. Political science is not dependent on Hegelianism or historicism of any kind, and still less, if possible, on the emergence of the modern idea of "civil society." This independence can be clearly seen in Aristotle's *Politics* if not "already" at the "beginning" (the armor of Diomedes cost only nine oxen, but the armor of Glaucus cost an hundred oxen: *Iliad* vi. 236). Aristotle was no less aware than Hegel of what is now (as we have noted, following Hobbes) called "civil society" – the human association primarily comprised of families or guilds or traders concerned with "mine and thine," profit and loss, buying and selling, and in which affairs are carefully managed by contracts and treaties, in other words, what is generally called the "marketplace" and all its rules and regulations of productions and commerce.[39] Yet, instead of conflating this "society" or partnership or association with the political association, on the contrary, he explicitly distinguishes it, along with the family itself, if you will, as sub-political or pre-political or "not yet" political. The political is still "future" for the merely civil society. This distinction is a characteristic of Aristotle's whole political thought. Both the existence of such society and the distinction in question are implicit both in his critique of the theoretical proposals of communism in the second book of the *Politics*, especially the proposal of Phaleas of Chalcedon, who was the first to assert that "all factional conflicts arise" from inequality of property, and in the proposals themselves (*Politics*, 1265a35ff). His review of the regime in Crete in a similar context is a consideration precisely of whether it is properly called a "regime" rather than merely a "dynasty" (1271b20ff). These questions occur in the context of the oligarchic argument about the regime and which typically associate the regime primarily with the property they have in the regime. For Aristotle (certainly no less than for Hegel), the market association—however elaborate—is not yet a polity in the comprehensive sense; it is less articulated formally and substantively than a polity; it does not have the distinctive aims of a polity; so far as it limits itself to the calculus of the marketplace thus understood, it will never be a "polity"—and, as soon as invasion or war of some sort is threatened, all its intrinsic shortcomings will show up immediately and clearly.

> It is obvious, therefore, that the city [*polis*, political association] is not a partnership in a location and for the sake of not committing injustice against each other and of transacting business. These things must necessarily be present if there is to be a city, but not even when all of them are present is it yet a city, but the city is an association in living well both of households and families for the sake of a complete and self-sufficient life.... Living well, then, is the end of the city, and these things are for the sake of this end. (*Politics*, 1280b29ff.)

Certainly, Aristotle would welcome the intent of the *Philosophy of Right* so far as it means to go beyond the phenomenon of "civil society" and arrive at the political, that is, at man as man, or a conception of "living well" (humanly) that is not exhausted by *habitus* of aggressive consumerism. Whether or not Hegel is unaware of this or merely misconstrues it, and whether or not this is alone enough to explode Hegel's historicist system, it is not the "ancient" philosopher Aristotle, to say nothing of his younger contemporary Calhoun, with whom Hegel has here first to contend, but, rather, with the modern philosopher Locke, whose most famous chapter in the *Second Treatise* is entitled "Of Civil or Political Society," and whose intention it is there, following Hobbes, precisely to remove the distinctively "political" as such from the sphere of human society, to "reduce" the political to the "civil," or to say, *pace* Aristotle, that the market society, more or less what Plato (following Homer) in the *Republic* called the City of Pigs, not the political regime or constitution, is the natural human association, the association that is best and most by nature.[40]

Locke's intention is merely to turn his predecessor Hobbes' doctrine of sovereignty upside down or stand it up on its feet, as Marx wished to do with Hegel's dialectic. Lockean man is Leviathan writ small.

Absolute Monarchs are but Men, and if Government is to be the Remedy of those Evils, which necessarily follow from Men's being judge in their own Cases, and the State of Nature is therefore not to be endured, I desire to know what kind of Government that is, and how much better it is than the State of Nature, where one Man commanding a multitude, has the Liberty to judge in his own Case.... Much better it is in the State of Nature wherein Men are not bound to submit to the unjust will of another.... (*Second Treatise,* 13.)

Hence it is clear not only that "civil society" as understood by Locke is not necessary for the establishment of political science, as we have already seen, but also that wanting to go beyond the "civil society" as understood by Locke in order to arrive at political science is not enough, for Locke would obviously have many of the same criticisms of Hegel's "constitutional" monarch as he has of Hobbes' "absolute monarch," although he would perhaps approve of the liberal and neutralistic tone of the state as presented by Hegel. Thus Locke would not be argued out of "civil society" *cum* "political society" and his own argument for monarchy into the Hegelian monarchical state in the Hegelian manner (i.e., "dialectically"), for Hegel's dialectical "science of the state" does not reach far enough: there must be more solid ground. Hegel's monarchy has nothing to show Locke that Locke has not already seen more and better of in Hobbes' monarchy, besides which, neither Hobbes nor Locke would be impressed with Hegel's praise of war—although it may be admitted that the Hegelian executive hardly seems energetic enough to carry out its own functions, much less undertake a war (he is more likely to become an instrument of the most powerful estate). Lacking Calhoun's fundamental distinction between absolute and constitutional government, Hegel's genuine insight that government is a positive good (what Popper calls Hegel's "Platonizing worship of the state") only leads him off into the argument that war is a positive good. (One cannot avoid noticing, also, therefore, that while he does not omit the praise of war, Hegel forgets to make any recommendations about military preparations and education and spirit and who would make them.) Neither Hobbes nor Locke—setting aside Aristotle or Calhoun—will have any of this.

For his part, Locke achieves his "revolution" of the Hobbian sovereignty by replacing the Hobbian ground of "fear" with the new basis "property." Human society and hence government is grounded in the rights of property, and hence in individual rights, which are the natural issue of sovereignty, and not on the rights or "final decision" of the monarch. For Calhoun, however, this Lockean revolution is itself only an apparent and not a genuine advance toward the philosophy of government, if it is not merely a convenient mask for the original Hobbian ground. According to him, "property is, in its nature, timid, and seeks protection, and nothing is more gratifying to government than to become a protector."[41] Locke attempts this revolution by beginning not where Aristotle had begun but where Hobbes himself had begun, from the hypothesis of the "state of nature." The result is that he arrives at a certain kind of association he holds to be the human association most according to nature, but not at politics or political science. He arrives at government as almost a kind of afterthought, as a protector of property, even though his true and fundamental interest is not human "society" as such (still less "property") but, just as for Hobbes or for Hegel, government or constitution or the "state" itself. Whatever one might have to say about his imaginary history of ancient political thought and philosophy, Hegel's historicist "science" on its own ground does not grasp this Lockean argument. Calhoun, America's profoundest student of Locke, sees the core of Locke's whole contract argument precisely as a conflated or "unarticulated" argument not primarily about society but primarily and above all about government, and hence the first sentence of *A Disquisition on Government* takes its aim ("a clear and just conception") directly at that argument. *Hic Rhodus, Hic salta*.[42]

The noted similarities between Hegel's attempt in the *Philosophy of Right* to present political science or the science of the state and Calhoun's presentation in the *Disquisition on Government* may be accounted for in two different but related ways. The first is found in the fact that for Calhoun the political is historical and the historical is political.[43] One would begin to consider this orientation not by looking to the historicism of Hegel but, with Calhoun himself, to the politics of Burke, or even Cicero. Secondly, and here more importantly, they may be traced to Hegel's well-known rejection of the "state of nature" hypothesis. Like Hume, Hegel did not accept the "state of nature" doctrine as a basis for human society and government, and what is most valuable in his doctrine of the concept of constitution derives directly from that rejection.[44] Yet, his insightful presentation in the *Philosophy of Right* of public opinion or the press and its role in legislation in the modern state goes no further, if so far, than Hume's view that the progress of popular opinion as to the progress of science and arising from the progress of science is no more than the history of an opinion. As in the case of Hume, he did not carry his rejection of it far enough. For the Hobbian "state of nature" is actually what lies behind the idea of "right" throughout the *Philosophy of Right*, which presupposes not only the *Science of Logic* but also the *Phenomenology of Spirit*, including the crucial chapter on "Lordship and Bondage" and the Hobbist "struggle for recognition" or honor.[45] But there is no natural right of "recognition," merely the history of a particular opinion about it that emerges in Hobbes, if not in what Hegel calls "Machiavellianism" and leads toward the doctrine of the "will to power."

The struggle in the human soul that is natural to man and that occupies Hegel so characteristically need not and should not be characterized as Hegel repeatedly characterizes it. It is familiar to all, and "recognized" by all. It arises from what Calhoun calls man's "twofold constitution" or what Hegel calls the "two worlds" in which man lives.[46] When Calhoun says "I hold the duties of life to be greater than life itself.... I regard this life as very much a struggle against evil, and that to him who acts on proper principle, the reward is in the struggle more than in the victory itself, although that greatly enhances it," he is pointing to the same universal phenomenon that Hegel limits to and in fact distorts as the "struggle for recognition."[47] The little victories that are actually achieved are but "moments," in Hegel's terms, in the life that is continually formed by such a quest, while the aim is the happiness of the whole life. The unceasing effort to perfect and enjoy one's intellectual and moral faculties is not the same as the unceasing quest for recognition. The latter both requires and remains ever on the plane of the political or of the state itself and hence cannot see ("recognize") the political or the state for what they are, as in fact the *Philosophy of Right* does not. This is what Calhoun means when he says in the *Disquisition* that the "love of truth and justice, when not counteracted by some improper motive or bias," that is, by any of the correlatives of the Hegelian "struggle for recognition," "more or less influences all, not excepting the most depraved" human beings" (paragraph 104, cf., 100: "pride of opinion").

The Hegelian struggle for recognition originates not in nature but in passion, like Hobbes' artificial society originates in fear. It is more aristocratical, where Hobbes' is more vulgar or democratical, but it is just as much passion. The struggle in question, the true "state of nature," as taught by Calhoun, is the struggle for the political whole, the community. Man is naturally oriented to the true, via the intellectual faculties, and the good, via the moral faculties, to happiness. These are the natural ends of his moral and intellectual faculties, the distinctively human ends, although, as Calhoun acknowledges, they may in individuals be counteracted by ignorance and stronger feelings or passions. The necessity of government itself arises as the natural necessity to control these counteractions for the sake of the natural human ends (*Disquisition*, paragraphs 8-9). It is Calhoun's contention that the struggle for the political whole is best understood as a struggle for the government. Only if the passions are understood as unequivocal and unproblematic inclinations toward the true and the good as such is it proper to say that reason ought only to be the slave of the passions, including the passion for recognition.[48] So long as the divine transcends man it is not possible that human wisdom become absolute.

So far as the discussion of constitutional government in Hegel's own *Philosophy of Right* is any guide, we cannot say that essence is adequately distinguished from existence or (certainly) that the Hegelian system of wisdom itself is absolute, for the *Philosophy of Right* does no more than point to constitutional government (that is, to contemporary American rather than Prussian government), or to an epoch in which liberty in some sense (sc. "recognition") would be no longer the privilege of only a single individual or of a narrow class, but granted to all the elements of political community. For this, each element must possess an effective check on every other. To be specific in regard to the case that is explicitly set forth in the *Philosophy of Right*, it is not sufficient for Hegel to have said that "the constitution is essentially a system of mediation" in the differentiation of the concept in the moments of which mediation is synthesized the individualism of civil society and the universality of the state through the disinterested administrative sense and temper of the civil service as organizing the legislative will of the great estates, and so on, and throwing in the "final decision of the monarch" that, the student is informed, Plato never thought of. While all this may be fine as far as it goes, it is not far enough to arrive at the object Hegel and Calhoun have in mind. One now has yet to go one step further, following Calhoun, and clothe each of the estates — in this given, Prussian case, the agricultural class and the business class — with a negative on the other (*Disquisition*, paragraph 52). The effect of this would be to render the government substantively or materially constitutional, rather than merely nominally or "allegorically" (or "rationally," in Hegel's sense) constitutional, and the object in view genuinely achieved or completed ("actualized"). In such a case and only in such a case, the constitution would be, in Calhoun's terms, "worthy of the name," that is, a constitution in word and deed. Otherwise, it will remain, in Hegel's Rousseauan language, "alienated," while, in the meantime, in the "modern," Smithian civil society, the business class also takes over the agricultural class. Hegel does not go so far, however, but limits himself to the Calhounian observation that the "separation of powers" is insufficient to make the constitution.[49] The Hegelian final state is, as Hegel exposes it, not final but merely another state on the path of absolutism, not to say to Spenglesian decline, albeit with an expert and patriotic civil service, including Splengerian the professoriate.

We have sketched Calhoun's relation to Hegel and to Marx here because this subject has often been raised by others and because the views of the latter on society and government, or those upon which they are based, particularly in regard to the distinction between the state and society, are today quite familiar. Calhoun does not hold these views, which *A Disquisition on Government* is meant generally to provide the way for correction, and he does not make this distinction. He speaks of the "state," the community as a whole as it looks outward to other "states," only in the context of other states (17). Within, the community is many and diverse, but in relation to others — to "the world" — it is one.[50] Within, the self-consciousness of the citizen is by no means necessarily limited or identical to the polity. Government is ultimately what preserves and perfects or determines the "society or community." It is clear in the third paragraph, then, that what remains to be isolated and examined or, to use a Hegelian term, differentiated, is precisely government. Government is suspended between the two terms of the phrase, being implied in the first and subsumed in the second. So now Calhoun is ready actually to take up the first question of political science as he framed it in the first paragraph and examine the origin and object of government.

In the fourth paragraph, then, "without further remark," Calhoun asks why it is that natural sociality or original human self-motivation is not sufficient and hence that government is necessary for man. As sociality is necessary for the perfection of the distinctive human faculties, the first question of political science necessarily involves the understanding of human imperfections, including imperfections of the distinctive human faculties, for it is in these that the necessity of government will be found. In the sentence Calhoun wishes to complete correctly in the science of government, Hobbes had said that human beings fundamentally or most humanly act "by a certain impulsion of nature, no less than that whereby a stone moves downward."[51] When Calhoun speaks in this connection of the guiding principle of the science of government that is most like the law of gravity for the science of astronomy in the material world, we may perhaps begin to grasp his view of Hobbes by asking what is it that is being held or that "moves downward," or why is it that the distinctive faculties of human nature that so transcend the brutes in the scale of being do not simply or naturally soar to their natural ends?

Paragraphs 5-9:
The Practical Necessity of Government
(Feelings)

THE DISQUISITION'S NEXT FIVE PARAGRAPHS ARE DEVOTED TO ANSWERING THE QUESTION why natural sociality is not sufficient for mankind. This is the section of the *Disquisition* which deals with man's elementary condition, and extends from the paragraph beginning with the phrase "The answer will be found..." to the paragraph beginning "It follows, then..." (5-9). This section or group of paragraphs, which explains the necessity of government, is followed by another of five paragraphs, which argues, somewhat strikingly, that government would be just as necessary as it is and always has been even if original human nature were just the opposite of what it is and always has been: it is a divine condition (paragraphs 10-12) that is left for its perfection by man (paragraphs 13-14). That section (paragraphs 10-14) begins and ends with reference to human reason. Together, these sections complete Calhoun's answer to the first question posed for the consideration of the beginning political philosopher or student of politics.

According to what is said in the first of these sections, the law of motivation that most corresponds in the animate world to the prime law of motion in the material or inanimate world, the law or force of gravitation, is selfishness, the force of the individual "selfish feelings" (paragraph 5). For this very reason, however, those who appreciate the affinities between Rousseau and Calhoun must remember that the law of selfishness alone cannot be the origin of government: sociality, including the distinctive human faculties composing it, is prior. Sociality is not absent, it is merely weaker. This law or force of selfish feelings is not specifically human but seems to Calhoun to be "essentially connected" to the "great law of self-preservation which pervades all that feels." It arises from the faculties of the animate body as such and distinguishes the animate from the inanimate world.[52] It is the lowest common denominator, the spiritual "atom," as it were, of the animate world. Many who seek to understand human society and government may thus be more or less easily led astray by analogies drawn from the animal world or by projections of what is human into the animal world. Certainly, man is the crowning creature or greatest animal of the animate world, in nothing that feels are these feelings "stronger" or more forceful than in man (paragraph 7). The section of the *Disquisition* that is inaugurated by the fifth paragraph is, therefore, about "feelings," particularly the strongest human feelings, as these are distinguished from the "sympathetic" or social feelings.[53]

Paragraph 5

There are more famous and more often-quoted passages in the *Disquisition* than the fifth paragraph, but none, I believe, are more important for understanding the work. In it, Calhoun explicitly begins to answer the first question of political science. In this paragraph, also, and not in any other, Calhoun explicitly refers to his own object in regard to this question and all that hangs on the answer to it, the foundation of the science of government. His "peculiar" object ("my object," he says) concerns precisely how this foundation is to be laid with respect to understanding the origin of government, namely, by following only nature or reason. The science of government can properly proceed only on the basis of this foundation. Otherwise, it is not possible to speak of it as science. To summarize, for Calhoun, government is not a necessary evil or any kind of punishment. It is not primarily an enlightened or artful contrivance for the manipulation of natural depravity or vice. Government is natural and does not arise from human depravity or vice, but merely from the imperfection or incompleteness of the original human faculties. In other words, it is for the sake of perfecting and completing these faculties, or for the sake of virtue. Hence, Calhoun explicitly intends here to avoid deriving government from vice. For Calhoun, government is a positive good. Its mere existence in every age and country is itself a reflection upon the natural human orientation in very age and country toward the good and capacity for good. Nor are its good effects limited to the community as such or to the best men in the community, that is, individuals who take "an active part in political affairs" (cf. paragraph 78). All benefit, including those who are not interested in political affairs.

This is indicated in the following group of paragraphs in the explicit association of government with divine ordination (paragraph 12). It is part of the purpose of the introductory paragraphs of the *Disquisition* to show that it is above all the problem or task of constitutional government that represents the actual completion of the universe or cosmos itself (paragraph 14).

In finding the answer to the question of the necessity of government in the "selfish feelings" of individual men in the fifth paragraph, Calhoun says that it arises from the fact that, although a social being by nature, man is "so constituted to feel more intensely what affects him directly than what affects him indirectly through others." This thought is not original with Calhoun. Men as social beings have individual or "anti-social" bodies: he is naturally self-centered.[54] Calhoun here interrupts himself to point out that he intentionally avoids the expression "selfish feelings" because he intends to avoid the implications attached to this expression in common usage, namely, the implications of depravity or vice, when this expression is applied to persons and then generalized. "My object is to avoid such inference." This is the same as saying that he intends to avoid grounding the necessity or origin of government in depravity or vice or asserting that man is naturally depraved or vicious. At the same time, Calhoun's intention here is not hypothetical or concerned with hypothetical states. His intention is "to restrict the inquiry exclusively to facts in their bearings on the subject under consideration." For the moment, the primary fact that it is necessary to bear in mind is the fact that Calhoun intends for the reader to exclude the implications attached to what he describes as "an unusual excess in the individual over the social feelings," that is, the implication of depravity or vice, when he is speaking only of individual affections being naturally stronger than sympathetic feelings.[55] The implication of depravity or vice is not applicable to this fact. It is a natural occurrence, and also a commonly accepted one.[56] We note in passing that, while Calhoun's procedure here is clearly reminiscent of Hume's Is-Ought distinction, it must not obscure his intention to present a non-Machiavellian origin of human society. Calhoun does not deny, that an "unusual excess" of "selfish" over social feelings in a person is depraved and vicious. He accepts it. Indeed, his care not in suppressing the term in question ("selfishness" or "selfish feelings") but, rather, in drawing the reader's attention to his avoidance here in this place of its common implications in excessive instances, shows clearly, and also draws attention to the fact, that the common or usual inferences are generally correct where this excess is concerned. The implications that are commonly or usually drawn from this view or excess are merely implications that men are by nature capable of vice, and therewith, with the necessary effort, which must be sufficiently great to overcome the stronger feeling, are also naturally capable of virtue.

Calhoun does not here suggest what such an effort just mentioned of the weaker against the stronger part of our constitution might involve. Obviously, the weaker, to be successful in overcoming the stronger, must combine with or be supported by something other than itself. One is reminded of the weak horse pulling upward and the strong horse pulling downward in the image of the charioteer in Plato's *Phaedrus*. Government takes the place of reason in this conception, but it is not an image and it is not human reason or any kind of individual calculation, and this is why Calhoun calls it "divine." Indeed, the Platonic charioteer is as fine and exact an image as one could wish for what Calhoun will call the constitutional or concurrent majority. The will must choose or act in accordance with disinterested reason. For the moment, it is enough to say that natural sociality or the faculties that compose it combine with government in producing human community. Elsewhere on a similar subject Calhoun refers in a political context to the human will and the "arts of persuasion" over against our selfish or individual feelings, which, although they are stronger than the sympathetic or social feelings, are "the weaker part of our nature."[57] The phenomenon of government itself represents the stronger part, but the science of government as such is not a branch of rhetoric, and the *Disquisition* itself is not a rhetorical work. It is not addressed to the weaker part of our nature. This is the distinction of the whole work. In any case, "stronger checks" are necessary because not all are equally open to persuasion (e.g., paragraph 100). Nevertheless, it is important to see that Calhoun moves immediately from considering what men feel "directly" and "more intensely," or the senses, in the fifth paragraph to what makes a "deep impression," or the imagination, which helps order perception and is the particular object of rhetoric, in the sixth paragraph. The deep impression made by the moral intellectual might even override or guide what is otherwise felt "more intensely." Calhoun stresses these rare and extraordinary occasions that make such powerful impressions precisely as representing exceptions to the well-understood "law of our nature," the law that is among mankind as unquestionable as the law of gravitation in the material world (paragraph 6). Government is not founded on the extraordinary or exceptional individual case, however striking, whether the case in question is one of unusual excess of the individual over the social feelings, depravity or vicious selfishness, or one of unusual excess of the social over the individual feelings, openness or virtuous benevolence. This is not to say that virtue and vice are reducible to these, although these are their roots, but only that the science of government itself begins the understanding human feelings as "phenomena appertaining to our nature," for government naturally originates in these phenomena.

Paragraph 6

In the sixth paragraph, Calhoun discusses "peculiar relations" and "peculiar constitutions" which overpower merely individual or self-centered feelings. The specifically female occasion overpowers these feelings in the direction of maternity and the family or posterity (paragraph 89, end).[58] The specifically human occasion overpowers them in the direction of what Calhoun later calls the "love of truth and justice" and, also, the "love of country," or what the community itself shares in common (paragraph 104). These loves, not excluding the love of one's children, are the natural and ultimate root of a human community, and the community that is most sufficient for these is the best, the most according to nature. Setting aside the question of community, men as men are the same, more or less, in virtue of their particular individual or self-centered feelings, but men as men are equal, more or less, in virtue of the "love of truth and justice," in which is united the specifically human "moral and intellectual faculties," for this love "more or less influences all, not excepting the most depraved," irrespective of country or community.[59] However, these loves, which are the decisive human feelings, are not yet knowledge. In this context Calhoun mentions "habits," acts repeated until they become "strong." These already require the existence of government and are not the origin of government. Calhoun is only secondarily concerned in the *Disquisition* with the particular individual disposition from which these examples spring, as science cannot ultimately account for it, and is primarily concerned, rather, with the human predisposition that, for its part, is promoted by these habits.[60] The essential human predisposition consists of the love of truth and of justice. The human individual is dependent upon human community and thus on government, which is Calhoun's immediate subject when he comes to mention these loves. The task or art of legislation is to assimilate the love of oneself, which is not essentially human although it is strongest in humans, by promoting or influencing certain habits (paragraphs 77-78), to these other, more essentially human loves, and particularly the highest or specifically human love, for the good of the whole, including the country or the whole man (paragraph 106). One might consider, therefore, since the "peculiar constitutions" mentioned by Calhoun are known prior to the philosophy of government, whether the philosophy of government may take the place of government in providing perfection for them. We have already seen that, according to Calhoun, education alone is never sufficient to bring about what is desirable, except apparently in these exceptional instances, but, even then, Calhoun's reference to education and habits is primarily a reference to the fact that the perfection in question does not occur thanks to nature alone but requires effort, "moral and intellectual acquirements."[61] The concept that unifies the exceptional examples acknowledged in the sixth paragraph is the concept of obligation or duty or, in the larger sense, culture, including the efforts and habits required for it. *A Disquisition on Government* does not become henceforth a disquisition on intellectual and moral culture, although Calhoun immediately refers to it (paragraph 7). Such a disquisition is not strictly necessary for the science or philosophy of government and would more or less rapidly or gradually lead away from such a science (cf. paragraph 19).[62]

The fact that everyone can refer to these striking exceptional cases proves the general and well-understood rule. Government grows out of the ordinarily human and not out of the extraordinarily vicious or virtuous case which all ordinary men can see, illustrative as these are. The exceptionally virtuous case is an aim of culture rather than the beginning of government. Government is thus constructed neither upon the fear of evil nor the hope of good in nature, although it acknowledges both. Hobbes had asserted that "Men have no other means to acknowledge their Darknesse [sic], but only by reasoning from unforeseen mischances that befall them in their ways."[63] But, carried very far, such excellent reasoning, which is the ground of the Hobbian enlightenment, only dims or dissipates the light that already governs their ways, and without which their ways would not be "ways." By obscuring the light there is in the ways of men, it cannot attain to a clear and just conception of government because it cannot attain to a clear and just conception of the nature of man.[64]

Paragraph 7

In the central paragraph of the section of the *Disquisition* devoted to human feelings (paragraph 7), Calhoun goes farther. He asserts that the phenomenon appertaining to our nature that makes government necessary in men is itself a "phenomenon not of our nature only, but of all animated existence throughout its entire range so far as our knowledge extends," beyond good and evil or where virtue and vice as such are unknown. He begins by saying, "I might go farther," less because he is extending an earlier assertion or observation than because the subject of the paragraph, the "all-pervading and essential law of animated existence," itself goes farther than what is strictly essential to the immediate question, what makes government necessary in man. In moving away from the strictly or essentially human, from government, it could almost seem a digression. For, although this phenomenon is not limited to "our nature only," it is only in "our nature" that it issues in or constitutes the necessity of government and, in light of human sociality, points the way to specifically human government.

The essential law of all animated existence, including human existence, "pervades all that feels, from man down to the lowest reptile or insect." He does not mention plants, which might be more extreme examples even than man. Perhaps one might say that reptiles and insects are insignificant not to themselves, thanks to this great law, but because the powers in the service of their own self-centeredness in relation to other beings, particularly man, are insignificant, and, besides, unlike higher beings, they apparently do not notice their offspring. However, he does not mention plants not because the self-centeredness of plants is ordinarily irrelevant to all other beings, for they have their allotted place in the scale of being, as well, but simply because they are generally not "social" beings. For, even though in plants a masculine and feminine power is found, in plants these are joined in the same individual.[65] For their part, the insects and reptiles are lower in the scale of being because they are more automatic and stupid than mammals. In no feeling being is this all-pervasive and essential feeling stronger than it is in human beings, the most social and political beings, who are also the most powerful feeling beings. In any case, throughout all animated existence this law itself provides only what is most felt and most wanted, not what is necessarily deserved or what is actually gotten.

In the less powerful social beings, in which this feeling is weaker than in man, this law ultimately results in the rule of the strongest among them or a kind of "absolute" rule. One may think of the kingdom of the ants or bees at the absolute bottom of this scale.[66] The non-human stations of animated existence beneath man do not possess reason. It is precisely the "all-pervading and essential law of animated existence," the "great law of self-preservation," that makes specifically or essentially human government not only unnecessary but also impossible throughout the remainder, that is, all the non-human stations, of animated existence. In these stations or conditions, perfection is "given," the is and the ought simply coincide by original nature. The stations above man, if any, no doubt transcend man in virtue of the same coincidence. The specifically human law is, rather, therefore, in some sense other than the simple law of self-preservation: a kind of "law" not only of self-preservation but also of self-perfection, the fully and distinctively human "law," which, however, does not take precedence over or nullify the law of all animated existence, as one might suppose on the argument that it would or should (cf. paragraph 85). It does not. I believe that it is for this reason that the following paragraph (8) is the only one in the course of the answer to the first question of political science which begins with the word "but."

Human self-perfection entails full development of the "moral and intellectual faculties" (paragraphs 2-3). In the seventh paragraph, Calhoun indicates what such full development means. It means "high intellectual and moral culture." Such culture consists essentially in the pursuit of knowledge of causes and the cultivation of virtue, of moral and intellectual excellence. Man is the culture-maker, that is, the cultivator of the moral and intellectual faculties with the aim, ultimately, of attaining true wisdom and genuine virtue or goodness, toward which his nature is originally inclined, and he is, also, the culture-made animal.

The distinction between man and the rest of animated existence is in this way, as well as the others we have indicated, fundamentally a distinction in kind, not merely in the degree of feelings.

This is the only explicit reference to culture in the *Disquisition*, that is, to the comprehensive end of human nature. As becomes clear in the subsequent group of paragraphs, the reason for this is that "culture" and "community," although inseparable, are not always simply identical or synonymous. Community does not always mean what is shared or having everything in common or being ready to be of service together in everything, for it also means diversity and peculiarity.[67] The aim of government is not the perfection of culture itself, which is the aim of community, but the perfection of specifically human or political community (paragraph 14). Culture both exists in the human community and is the distinctive aim of human community, but it also points beyond the human community in the direction both of what simply transcends it, or the "higher, the divine as such, and of what descends from it, the "lower," the mundane and ultimately merely material. In this way, culture, the distinctive aim of the human community, points beyond the human community to the whole of which the political whole is but a part. It is thus higher in dignity than the human community, including its manner and mores, from the form of which it is inseparable and which is perfected by government. Hence the question what is the best government may easily be mistaken for a question about the best culture, or simply the best completion of the natural and human whole.[68] This is not surprising, for this whole, intellectual and moral community, which is the distinctive and only truly human aim of society, of the social nature of man, finds its highest expression, to be sure, only in the full development of the arts and sciences, not simply or without qualification, but, specifically, in the science or philosophy of government and the art of legislation, and all such questions ultimately point to this science. The science of government is the ultimate expression of culture.

It is for this reason, also, that the problem of civilization, the power over agents of the material world, which, as we have noted, is the highest problem of culture, does not here arise. Its place is here taken by the science of government itself, and, within the science of government, by the prior question indicated above and set forth in Calhoun's observation that all the expansion and force of high intellectual and moral culture does not overcome the original and lower phenomenon of the force of the selfish feelings. As we noted in connection with earlier paragraphs (esp. 3), human nature and hence human society and government can be discussed without any reference to "civilization" as we understand it today or as Calhoun understood it. The *Politics* of Aristotle is sufficient proof of this, aside from the further fact that the science of government is perfectly applicable to savages or barbarians, even though it cannot arise among them. Nevertheless, in due course, the problem of civilization, in part, a crucial element in human self-perfection and itself the occasion for the founding of the science or philosophy of government, must be taken up (cf. paragraphs 95, 132ff).[69] Calhoun, never speaks of "civilizations" as the subject or true ground of human reflection, but only of "communities" or particular constitutions.[70] The basic and highest "unit of study" is constitutional government.

The tension in question arises naturally in consequence of the different pace and practice belonging to each of the parts of which the community is composed. Calhoun admits that under certain optimal conditions, which he describes in terms of physical, intellectual, and moral inclinations, wants, and faculties, or high intellectual and moral culture, that which in human nature makes government necessary among men can perhaps almost be finally countered and overpowered. But still it cannot be finally overpowered. It is constant. The establishment of the science of government itself, therefore, will not overcome or remove the necessity of government. To say nothing of other things, the science of government obviously does not remove the presence in society of infants, children, and others who, as such, are incompetent and in need of exceptional attention, and it does not nullify the great law of animated existence: *Si vis pacem, para bellum.*[71] Stated differently, the exceptions to the general rule presented in the previous paragraph will always be exceptions of the general rule and not themselves the general rule.

Paragraph 8

"But," says Calhoun, for the reason we indicated above, in the following paragraph (8), each individual in consequence of his constitution wishes or aims at his own safety and happiness, and hence tends to come into passionate conflict with other individuals and their wishes or desires or values, or with other aims of safety and happiness, because there is inequality of the human moral and intellectual faculties among men. When there is such conflict, each is ready to sacrifice the interests of others to his own.[72] In sum, each has a "greater regard for his own safety or happiness than for the safety and happiness of others."[73] This is the first occurrence of the term "interests" in the *Disquisition*, together with the first occurrence of the term "happiness." The strength of these individual affections, which is connected in the manner Calhoun has explained with the individual or selfish feelings, looks and attaches to the notion or end of happiness, over and above mere safety or self-preservation. Happiness is more than the sum of individual physical experiences, plus safety. Physical deprivation is often endured and safety itself risked for it. This concern, the sum of the human moral inclinations in happiness or the good, is what constitutes each individual's "center of gravity," and their tendency to conflict constitutes the true field or "space" of politics and government.[74]

Paragraph 9

The tendency to universal conflict between individuals is no less natural than sociality itself, although it is secondary. This does not mean that nature is simply a war of all against all, as the Hobbian saying is, for there is always the prospect of rest and peace, that is, happiness. On the contrary, the bodies composing the solar system itself, which is natural, are not at war. They mutually and naturally act on one another in such a way that "they are kept in their respective spheres." Nor is human nature such a war: happiness is possible. The tendency in question means, rather, that government, which checks it, is equally if not even more natural to man and for the sake of man, more so, even than most individual men.[75] It arises from the "twofold constitution" of human nature (paragraph 9). If it is not restrained or controlled by reason or by government in some form, the tendency to conflict itself, because it is attended by powerful passions growing out of human self-centeredness and nourished by the strength of human self-centeredness, then necessarily tends both toward "a state of universal discord and confusion" and also toward government of some form, Calhoun says, "wherever vested or by whomsoever exercised."[76] He will later show that this tendency is ordinarily to government of a certain form that is hard to distinguish from the mere rule of the strong, or typically animal rule (paragraph 5, cf. paragraphs 57, 63-66, 109). Here, he speaks only of the natural or irresistible human tendency to form government. This tendency is no less original and irresistible than human sociality, of which it represents the highest part, the rational part, for controlling unreasonableness and selfish passion. Government represents the human state, being necessary for safety and happiness, "the sympathetic or social feelings constituting the remote" cause, that is, happiness, and "the individual or direct the proximate, cause," that is, preservation and safety (9).

By preserving the weaker and more remote against the stronger and more immediate part of human nature, the naturalness of government itself plainly shows strength and purpose in the place of the weakness of individual human nature. Hence, the mere existence of government is itself the profoundest testimony we have or need as to human nature and its potential for goodness. Government is a positive good.

Summary

Calhoun traces the necessity of society to natural human physical and moral needs and inclinations. Human society is originally distinguished from all other kinds of "societies" because it is necessary to satisfy these and precisely these needs and inclinations (paragraph 2). Society is also necessary to develop the moral and intellectual faculties and raise man in the scale of being much above the level of brutes with whom he otherwise shares equally, albeit much more forcefully, what is merely common to the animate world, "so far as our knowledge extends." In the latter formulation, the physical needs and inclinations, which as such do not develop and do not need development, and which are, in any event, the least essential of the human characteristics, are replaced by the intellectual faculties, which are the highest and most essentially human, and relatively boundless, or which reach all the way to the heavens, in company with the moral inclinations and faculties. The moral inclinations and faculties are, thus, the central and irreducible fact or phenomenon of human nature (paragraph 3). In every age, including ages of unrelieved savagery, we always find government wherever we find men (paragraph 4). This is because both the physical or bodily needs and inclinations, on the one hand, and the intellectual capacities or faculties, on the other hand, are each "private" or "individual" in a way that the moral inclinations and faculties are not. Everyone knows that excessive selfishness is bad, whether or not they have ever heard of the law of gravity, much less understand it. The most common feature among men and the most decisive feature for the philosophy of government, therefore, because it is the immediate root of human community, is the moral nature of man (cf. paragraphs 83, 96-98). This is the stage on which the tension or struggle between the selfish and the social feelings plays itself out or in which the tendency toward individual conflict arises, making government necessary for the preservation of the natural ends of full moral and intellectual development (paragraphs 5-9). The "state of nature," properly understood, the original human condition, is already a moral state.

Paragraphs 10-14:
The Theoretical Necessity of Government:
Calhoun's Relation to the British and
French Philosophy of Nature

CALHOUN HAS NOW COMPLETED THE LOWER OR MORE STRICTLY EMPIRICAL OR sensualist part of the answer to the first question of political science. The necessity of government is rooted in the individual and social "feelings" of man which are natural to him as part of his original constitution, and their affects. It is at least as convincing as similar kinds of arguments aiming at other conclusions. He has shown that government is reasonable. In the following section (paragraphs 10-14), he presents his higher or more strictly rational or theoretical account of the necessity of government. In this group of paragraphs, Calhoun proceeds from an alternate constitution of human nature, from a hypothetical human "other." In the previous section, he began with the human body or with the senses. Here, in conceiving this alternative constitution, he in effect begins with "mind." He presents what he later calls a "purely hypothetical" state, namely the hypothetical "state of nature" (paragraph 89). He has in mind this hypothesis and its representatives throughout the section, although it is not limited to them. His intention is to show that government is not merely reasonable but also, and more importantly, rational. Hence these paragraphs contain the profoundest strains of Calhoun's whole critique of the "state of nature" hypothesis.

Paragraph 10

If man were constituted according to these alternate conceptions of his nature, Calhoun initially says, and were other than he actually is, there would then be no necessity for government. First, if we accept a calculating or "egoistical" kind of hypothesis, following Hobbes, according to which men were originally created without sympathy and without dependence on others for his safety and existence, there would then be no society and hence no government. For human government does not arise outside of human society. Calhoun's argument is near to that put forth by Montesquieu in his Preface to the *Spirit of the Laws* as the refutation of Hobbes' "state of nature." (Montesquieu is surely the closest of all European philosophers to Calhoun, but this subject must be taken up in another study.) Calhoun does not here indicate whether men would be free and equal in such a state as he describes. Near the center of the *Disquisition*, he admits that men would, "by supposition," be free and equal in this state, as Locke has it, but it is clear in both places that they would not be real men (paragraph 89). Man is freest in mind. Men would have enjoyed or rather feared equally the freedom in the state that is described by Hobbes in the Leviathan as "liberty." The problem with such a state is not, as might be supposed, that it is "purely hypothetical," and therefore contrary to the hypotheses *non fingo* of the Newtonian method, or to what appears at first glance to be the elementary procedure adopted in Hume's *Treatise*. Plato's *Republic* and other dialogs contain hypothetical regimes, for example, yet Calhoun never speaks of them as anything "unfounded and false." On the contrary, he praised them.[77] It is possible for hypotheses and other fictions to be well-founded and useful, although in a sense false. To speak in terms that are currently fashionable, they can be true in the "meta" sense and false in the "object" sense. Rather, the problem with this particular hypothetical state, the Hobbian state, called by "great misnomer" the "state of nature," is that, "of all *conceivable* states, it and no other is the most opposed to his nature" for it consists essentially in the denial of the distinctive human faculties, that is, of human nature (paragraph 89, emphasis added).[78] It is false in every sense. It amounts to no more than materialism or the simple union of the will and reason in matter. It might almost be said not merely to imply but actually to aim at government without community, as if the existence of government were its own end, like the existence of the solar system, and in so doing to destroy community and its most distinctive ends, beginning, obviously, with fraternity, but including that of intellectual development, which is its own professed aim ("enlightenment").[79] This is the fundamental error of absolutism (and also of would-be "anarchists"), that ultimately human society is for the sake of the government (i.e., for the sake of the governors), whereas government is for the sake of the community, including the governed and the governors. Hence, it is an ill-founded hypothesis. Here, Calhoun merely says, first, that, given a natural constitution omitting sympathy and positing physical independence, human society, and therewith of course government, would be no more necessary for men than for reptiles or plants. In making this admission, he naturally omits any reference to man's faculties and speaks only of his animal "safety and existence." Man's faculties would be no more an issue in such a state than they are in the case of reptiles or plants, and the hypothesis itself would no more occur in the case of human beings than it does in the case of the others. These creatures could presumably preserve themselves, if they came to be, but they could not come to be. Hence, according to Calhoun, they would have to be "created." But, if they were created in such a manner that they could preserve themselves by calculation, as implied in the hypothesis, they would be social by nature, and possessed of all the natural sociality which the hypothesis wishes to deny. We therefore cannot avoid the conclusion that man was created as a social being with sympathetic feelings, as Calhoun observed in the second and third paragraphs, and so we must abandon the hypothesis as unfounded and regard any conclusions drawn from it as simply fallacious. It is a false hypothesis.

Or, rather, there remains perhaps yet one possible way to avoid this otherwise unavoidable conclusion, that is, by taking the hypothesis to a still further extreme and denying logic or reason altogether in order to void the authority of these unavoidable conclusions. We could deconstruct them. Admittedly, it is hard to see how this way would not also void the authority of the hypothesis itself. In any case, Calhoun takes up this way in the following, second or "extreme" or moralizing version of the original (already "extreme") calculating hypothesis. If we accepted a more moralizing kind of hypothesis according to which man were originally created—or if they were educated in accord with Rousseau's idea of the individual will and the general will, and hence according to Kant's argument about moral imperatives—so as to feel more intensely, or even equally, what affects others than what affects himself, there would, apparently precisely on the showing of the previous section, be no necessity for government and none would ever be.

For Rousseau, man in the true "state of nature," that is, in the Lockean hypothesis taken to its extreme, is willing but lacks human reason and language, rather like, say, the great apes (cf. *Discourse on Inequality*, note J). In their place, for man, is openness or "perfectibility." The moralizing "state of nature" hypothesis also replaces Hobbist selfish pride with the natural "virtue" and sentiment of compassion or pity, which are anterior to reason. Thus provided, it repaints the hypothetical state of nature that is a projection of a factual state of war with a hypothetical *cum factual* "state of nature" that is a state of sweet peace, without conflict or competition. It is important to see that this argument about the "state of nature" is not more extreme than the former in virtue of its replacement of the strength of the selfish feelings by the strength of the sympathetic feelings. In this, it merely projects from the sympathetic feelings observed in already socialized man no less than, according to him, the former hypothesis projects from the selfish feelings observed in already socialized man. In this respect, the Rousseauan hypothesis remains on the same plane as the hypothesis of Hobbes. In fact, the former hypothesis is more accurate in regard to this point, for it is more according to nature and the whole range of animated existence. This version of the hypothesis is the more extreme version only because it abandons reason altogether in favor of sentimentality anterior to reason. Without reason, Rousseau must retain and strengthen the sympathetic feelings observed from already socialized man in order ever to arrive at society from the asocial "state of nature," however elaborate the chain of happenstance that might befall him. In the case of natural peace and sweetness, a state without conflict or competition, although Calhoun does not say so, human society would, at least on this supposition, perhaps come to exist and thrive, although this seems dubious on its face unless all spent their time preserving someone else. (It is not surprising that Rousseau wants citizens to be very busy with their duties.) Human society, if it could be, would be and could only be only a mutual preservation society, but it could therefore only be at the same time a mutual destruction society. It could go no further, if it could preserve itself.[80]

It is important to notice that Calhoun himself does not here say anything about society; he says only that there would be no government. He does not here speak about society at all, because, as opposed to the earlier or first case in which there could be no government because there would be no society, in this case there would be no society because there could be no government. For Calhoun, government is necessary, because human society is necessary, but the perfection of government depends on human reason and also, even primarily, on chance. For Rousseau, the existence of human society and hence government and also of human reason itself depends on chance. Only the freedom of the individual man is natural and, therefore, it is the only necessary end. Confronted with this more extreme—and also perhaps more self-satisfied—form of the argument, Calhoun interrupts himself in the midst of the first paragraph of this section just as he had done in that of the previous section. He does this in order to attack the argument at its highest and also most vulnerable point, that is as it concerns relationships and "feelings." The Rousseauan argument finds its meaning in formal or abstract relationships ("freedom"), on the one hand, and concrete individual feelings ("selfhood"), on the other. In the previous instance of interruption, the interruption was made in order to point out that he intended to follow nature or reason and not convention in his investigation of the necessity of government, although it turned out that reason and convention did not diverge on the immediate point. Here, the interruption is to indicate "the order of things," that is, nature or what is rational and in accord with reason. In the previous section, the order of nature or scale of being is present most obviously in the form of the "whole range of animated existence" which man distinguishes or crowns as the culture-making and culture-made animal, the potential moral intellectual or wise and virtuous animal. In this section, it concerns what it is that distinguishes or crowns the nature of man, reason. Although society and government are intimately connected and mutually dependent, and although they originate in nature and coexist in time and space, they differ in rank and object. Society, the natural sociality of man and the distinctive human faculties, is the greater. "It is first in the order of things and in the dignity of its object," which is both "to preserve and perfect our race" through the perfection of the intellectual and moral faculties of man, that is, through culture, and, specifically, the cultivation of the moral intellectual or the truly free man. Calhoun and Rousseau are at opposite poles, so to speak, on the question of the "order of things," or reason. For Calhoun, reason is what is definitive in man's nature, because it is prior; for Rousseau, individual sentiments "anterior to reason" are definitive, because these are prior. All the significant and well-known tensions and contradictions and apparent imprecisions and fluctuating attitudes in Rousseau's works, as well as the sermonizing quality of much of it, are traceable to this assertion that reason is not prior. In order to better follow Calhoun's argument about the "order of things," let us turn immediately to the next paragraph.

Paragraph 11

Having explained the respective ranks and objects of society and government, Calhoun returns in the next paragraph (beginning with the phrase, "I have said...") to the hypothesis he was discussing before he interrupted himself. This hypothesis, the more Rousseauan or Spinozistic one, is the most important for the whole question of the theory of government as such. It is the conception of our constitution according to which selfishness was abolished or canceled and we would feel more strongly or even equally that which affects others than what directly affects ourselves, and enjoy the consequential harmony of essentially ungoverned society, or a human "society" in which we all directly govern ourselves and also everyone else. According to this hypothesis, what was shown in the previous section of the *Disquisition* would itself be "hypothetical." Here, in the eleventh paragraph, Calhoun reminds readers that the contrary to what is being proposed is actually necessary for the preservation of "beings of limited reason and faculties," that is, for the whole range of animated existence, including man with such reason as he actually possesses, never mind being without reason altogether. He then attacks the extreme argument at its most vulnerable point. The hypothesis wants above all to retain the "fact" of the natural sovereignty of the individual as this is arrived at by Hobbes and Locke on grounds of egoistic calculation, while abandoning the primacy of selfishness and practical reason. Practical reason, absent in the "state of nature," where it exists only as the Rousseauan category of "perfectibility," can be accounted for by Rousseau, on the basis of Hobbes' saying that men have no other means to acknowledge their ignorance but by reasoning from unforeseen mischances that befall them in their ways.[81] Hobbes' thought is the origin of Rousseau's concern with history. Reasoning on happenstance events as they occur is, for him, the long and winding road from contented ape to rational if repressed man. Hence human society and thus government arise only from chance, because, ultimately, for Hobbes and Locke, human reason arises only from chance: human psychology is a branch of Newtonian physics, that is, of matter in motion (*Leviathan*, 6 passim; 1, paragraph 4; 9; *De Corpore*, I, 6, 6).

For Calhoun, on the contrary, practical reason alone will never arrive at theoretical or metaphysical or hypothetical reason. Man does not make what is called theoretical or metaphysical or hypothetical reason: it is a gift of nature or the Creator. What is called practical reason is a gift not of chance but of theoretical reason. It is only for this reason that man can ascend from practical reason to theoretical reason. For this reason, also, it is inescapable in some form. It is the ground of every hypothesis. It, too, is merely projected into the extreme "state of nature" hypothesis from already socialized man—which, according to Calhoun, is "man"—along with the strong sympathetic or social feelings. The necessary result of the denial of reason as prior would be the collapse of what Calhoun in the previous paragraph had called "the order of things" into disorder, indistinguishability, and destruction, in short, a nasty, brutish, short-term state indistinguishable from and bearing all the same effects as irremediable anarchy or irrationality or blind chaos. The attempt to remove the Hobbist self from the "great law of self-preservation" also removes preservation. Society would not thrive if it could not be preserved, which is the same as saying that human beings require government for their preservation.

For Calhoun the preservation in question is precisely the preservation of the rational or specifically human world, the world of distinctions, order, and reason, however limited, whence originates this particular hypothesis and whence originates also what is called common sense. The consequence of such a "rational" hypothesis about human feelings is merely the impossibility of any hypotheses, inferences, deductions, meaning, or truth. The subjective and finite would disappear into the objective and infinite, and the latter would themselves be imperceptible, for they would disappear with the disappearance of the former. Calhoun observes that "all individuality would be lost and boundless," and hence the wished-for freedom of the natural individual, for the sake of which Rousseau stakes everything and which depends on anterior reason for its conception, is, with the abandonment of reason, thus lost in a nihilistic condition of absolute servitude. "Remediless disorder and confusion would ensue," for the capacity to grasp relationships of any kind, or to be free, would be impossible. From the absence of any particularity, the rational vacancy that, except for sweet sensibility and pity, is arrived at in the hypothetical "state of nature" would be "generalized" into society itself as a categorical sort of vacancy, an emptiness, a mere *nihil obstat* that would present itself as "duty." But, "on the supposition," there would in fact be not even the possibility of such generalizability or categoribility. Universalization disappears with particularization, the absolute with the relative. Hence Calhoun characterizes this state of unreason as merely one of "conflicting emotions" writ large—not sweet peace but merely alienated desires. Passion or wishing or wanting would be all there is—not a will to power, not a categorical will, not an individual or general will of any kind, for one could not speak at all of will, which requires choice and hence awareness of possibilities and alternatives as possibilities and alternatives and hence reason—but only blind desire or wishes without object. This is not a natural condition anywhere along the scale of animate existence. The best of intentions, if one may speak of "intentions" at all in such a context, are perfectly compatible with the darkest ignorance.

In theoretically hypothesizing sweet and subrational individual freedom as the final nature of man, one merely reverses the order of things in order to deny the order of things, and this hypothetical reversal merely blurs and obscures the order of things, including the rationality of man and the will of man and, therewith, the actual freedom of man. The more moralizing hypothesis, impatient with the petty reason and freedom of the more calculating hypothesis, which denies the political, goes even further the way of the calculating hypothesis, and loses all reason and freedom in a political vacancy that preaches only absolute "duty." This is the result of Rousseau's desiring to make freedom "easy": virtue becomes impossible. According to Calhoun, all this amounts to a "state of anarchy." It is not a "state of nature" but merely a careless state of mind. The hypothesis of the original "asocial" man is merely an apology for an already very socialized (not to say bourgeois) "anarchic" man. In this anarchic state of being, government, naturally, would again emerge and loom as the most urgent and necessary thing. (One may imagine a Heidegger painstakingly brooding and "preparing the way" for it.) Yet it would be, if possible, not less but even more necessary than it actually is, but it would be absolutely impossible. It could never be arrived at by "chance." It would have to be invented or created by man, of course, and could not be. The transvaluation of all values would have to mean first the transvaluation of nothing into a "value," and hence means making way for teleology *ab origine*.

If government were not natural and necessary, it could not be created by art, for there would be no purchase for it. There would be no purchase for "art" — for this most crucial art or for the "fine arts" of music and literature that Rousseau himself was personally interested in. If, through some *deus ex machina*, government actually could exist, "its object would be reversed." Following the officious meddler in the affairs of all others, Calhoun sketches the Aristophanic manner which government would have to pursue its new object. In so doing, he both tacitly corrects the educational project of the *Emile* and indicates clearly the manner in which government must (and actually does) pursue its actual object, namely, by rewards and punishments calculated to affirm and encourage moral interests and actions, in other words, virtue (cf. also, paragraphs 76-78).

We can summarize Calhoun's argument in these paragraphs by saying that it is true that if there were no reason there would be no government. The existence of either affirms the other. Hence there is no possible venue beyond good and evil, although, perhaps, there is a possible venue beyond evil. Prior experience or awareness of good, however inarticulate and unfathomed, is necessarily presupposed in our becoming aware of evil, but the opposite does not hold. There is no need of awareness of evil to experience or be aware of good. This is shown by the playfulness of puppies and calves, by dolphins running the surf, and so on.

The portion of the whole scale of animate existence that is without knowledge of good and evil nevertheless experiences good. The existence of evil, made possible by the existence of free will, is necessary not for experience or awareness of good but for knowledge of good. The faculties obviously regarded by Calhoun as highest in character and dignity, the intellectual faculties, the perfection of which is the highest aim of society, belong, as such, to the province not of government but of society, or to the most developed intellectual faculties, the province of society as it considers its own government and the science of government. The science of government is itself the highest expression of human knowledge of the good.

In order to understand what it means that government "is," and to understand more clearly why Calhoun interrupted or explained himself at this place, and what he finds in the place of the extreme hypothesis—that is, what is truly natural—it is necessary to look more closely at the explanation and recall once more that in the prior instance he had indicated his intention to follow reason or nature and not convention or common opinion (paragraph 5). In that place the immediate issue involved facts or phenomena and the necessary selfishness or individuality—the subjectivity—of human nature. The immediate issue was a "perspectival" issue related essentially to the body and the senses, and it was necessary to be objective. Here, on the contrary, the issue is not "facts," for these have been set aside or suspended in order to entertain or consider explicit hypotheses. The issue involves hypotheses and sympathy or sociality—the objectivity—of human nature. It is thus necessary to be subjective, "for there must be something to which other things are related." Perhaps both practical reason and experience are sufficient to resolve the issue of the moralizing hypothesis. But, if so, this is only the lower of two issues that are involved. The remaining or higher issue is the character of human reason or nature itself, as such. Calhoun's purpose in interrupting himself is to introduce into the discussion of this confused hypothesis the logic of rank, or "the order of things," that is, to recall natural or rational equalities and inequalities, and in reference to which experience alone is, so to speak, out of its depth. For it is not a question of perspective, but purely rational and objective. We know that the perfection of human society, the end for which society is ordained, is culture or the development and perfection of the definitive native human faculties—the promotion of knowledge qua knowledge and of virtuous life. Hence society is "first" in the order of things and in the dignity of its object, that is, in nature, which is served by government. While these things—society and government—are coexistent and interdependent, government is "next," not "first," in rank. It is important to follow nature and not mistake it, as in the case of the unfounded hypothesis under consideration. The end—perfection of society by government (i.e., community)—is native and hence prior to human society, which serves it. This prior or natural end is the perfection of the human intellectual and moral faculties, that is, of man, the perfect moral intellectual, but this individual is, therefore, not found in the "state of nature" but only in community.

In another place Calhoun explains that, "although [in time] the human race cannot exist without society, nor society without government, yet in the *order of things* [i.e., in reason or nature] man must have existed *before* society, and society *before* government" (emphasis added).[82] Man so "existing" — that is, "formally" or "necessarily" (paragraphs 2-3) — is to human society as nature is to convention, which is the imperfect human attempt to preserve and perfect it. This distinction in rank between the natural "human being" and "society" is, according to Calhoun, the formal distinction between nature and convention. Hence it is perhaps not surprising, as conventions vary so widely among communities, that the Sophists and also the modern state of nature thinkers should have mistaken the necessary distinction in rank between nature and convention for a simple division or opposition, like the division between the few and the many or the king and the people. However, since the existence of man necessarily implies society and hence convention, in the same way, society is to government, which is the imperfect human attempt to preserve and perfect it, also exactly as nature to convention. This, "society" and "government," is, for Calhoun, the material distinction between nature and convention (paragraph 10). This is why so many see the distinction in rank between society and government itself as essentially oppositional, that is, as the usurpation or oppression of government, or as the necessity of evil, and wish to revolutionize the government in the name of society or to work toward abolishing it altogether by removing or abolishing what they suppose makes it necessary "sinister interests." Still others perceive this same distinction as a reason to ignore government and pursue the pleasures of culture as more dignified and worthy, often while complaining about government, even though they and indeed culture itself depend in every way on it for their own preservation. Furthermore, however, since the existence of society necessarily implies government in the same way, government is to community — the imperfect human attempt to perfect the moral intellectual, or culture — also exactly as nature to convention. For Calhoun, this distinction between "government" and "community" is the efficient distinction between nature and convention (paragraph 14). In this respect, government can be isolated from all other aspects of human "society or community" (paragraph 3), and itself considered as the universal object of human science or philosophy (paragraph 1). Indeed, given the distinctive human faculties and the natural inequality of men, there is no other purchase than the phenomenon of government for a genuine "science of man." Finally, moreover, since the existence of government necessarily implies the possibility of the perfection of man the formal perfection of government (constitutional government worthy of the name) is the actual perfection of man, or, in other words, the genuine unity of nature and convention or human liberty, with nature being first, and convention or human liberty next in rank (paragraph 14). This distinction between nature as divinely ordained and the perfect moral intellectual is the final distinction between nature and convention. Nature is superior to man, since man can rise to freedom only in artfully following nature, which is given. It is only from this vantage, reason, "the order of things," that we can speak of good or bad government or of good or bad men or of well-founded or unfounded hypotheses or of anything else. This reason is the most divine thing about man, and is his proper and most fitting state. Government is the great means to this end. Calhoun's disquisition on government, therefore, is necessarily oriented toward both the nature or origin and the object of society, for the object of government is to preserve and perfect society. Both are equally necessary to human beings living and living well, and divine.

The most distinctive human thing, government, points beyond itself not only to the perfection of man or the human faculties but to the larger order in which it is but a finite point, and hence to the limitation of man in his allotted condition, however perfected.

Paragraph 12

In the central paragraph of the section on feelings (7) Calhoun had gone "farther" and extended the argument to speak of the "great law" of all animate existence the force of which is stronger in none than man: none other than man himself is the great exemplar of the great law, although he is subject also to other laws. Man crowns all that is beneath him in the scale of being. Here, in the central paragraph of the following section (12), Calhoun brings the argument to its natural end and speaks in an identical manner of man's "great capacities and faculties, intellectual and moral" by the development of which he raises himself above the brutes, and which also necessarily points beyond itself as finite. Of "every class of animated beings," man is also the great exemplar of these great capacities and faculties and their development—that is, of intellectual or moral culture or self-perfection, the weaker but higher law by which we are aware of the divine or of what transcends the merely human and, therewith, of our place in the natural or cosmic whole, which is knowable by human reason. Together these determine man's "allotted condition." His allotted condition is, "social and political," and the political condition, which is open to the whole of which man is but a part, is rational and divine. Since living and living well for man entails human society and government, the Creator has ordained these and rendered them indispensable for the human attainment of wisdom and goodness, which is the end of Creation.[83] This creating being or divine legislator is superior to the ultimate perfection of created human being, that is, to the outstanding and distinguishing feature of humanity or human nature understood as the "highest attribute of the human mind."[84]

Paragraph 13

As does its parallel in the previous sections, the following paragraph (13) similarly begins with the word "but." The speculative argument of the previous paragraphs has merely successfully returned us to the prior conflict not of mindless and sightless desires or wishes but to the very mindful conflict of the calculating and moralizing desires presented in the eighth paragraph, on the one hand, and to the condition of government presented in the ninth paragraph, on the other. It has merely confirmed that government as such is a positive good. Its mere existence neither changes the condition of man nor perfects society, but only preserves it, including its natural ends or its "potential." This is all that the existence of government implies. Calhoun has thus far only established or accounted for what is already given in the existence of government, and, although this account is sufficient to answer the first question of political science (paragraphs 1, 4), as well as the "old ground" or modern political philosophy, there are other important questions to consider. This is why he begins the new paragraph with the word "but." The necessity of government is not itself sufficient for good government. In other words, the mere existence of government does not actualize or achieve the potential it sustains any more than mere existence or original human nature achieves the development of the characteristic or natural human faculties that is its end. And, even as regards mere existence, as in the rest of animate existence, the "feelings, instincts, capacities and faculties" that are necessary for preservation do not themselves guarantee preservation. The sustenance necessary for some may always be consumed by others, either of the same kind or by other kinds, and some may themselves be consumed by other kinds or by others of their own kind. The natural conflict of self-interest which arises from the all-pervading and essential law of animated existence is, for Calhoun, evidence not of Darwinian selectionism or Spencerian survivalism, but of the natural tendency of each individual to promote or perfect his given attributes according to his condition and functions and, hence, the tendency toward government.[85] These attributes are those "best adapted to its natural condition." Nature tends toward perfection most characteristically in individuals, not merely for the sake of preservation but also and primarily for the individual to be what it is: this kind of plant or insect, that kind of fish or reptile, a kind of mammal, and so on. In Aristotelian language, "all things desire and love existence, but we exist in activity, since we exist by living and doing. This is in fact a fundamental principle of nature: what a thing is potentially, its work reveals in actuality."[86] Things are happy with themselves in their allotted condition. This happiness is what Rousseau sees as the sweet sense of natural life, and which exists there easily because the is and the ought coincide, except for man, because he is by nature incomplete, or in Rousseau's terms, "alienated" by social life. It is this natural sense, then, that Rousseau wants to bring into social life. However, as we have already seen, the Rousseauan alienation in human or social life is but the unreason he has already projected into the so-called "state of nature," whence, in his scenario, man emerges into reasonable and artificial society through the natural "perfectibility" that he possesses in the place of reason, or in other words, through chance, with the result that he never arrives, but only remains ever alienated or originally "incomplete." This "perfectibility" is the root of the evolutionism we find in Kant and Hegel and others following Rousseau and which received its classic expression in Darwin's *Evolution of the Species*, the perfectibility stemming merely from aggressive self-preservation. Darwin is to evolutionism as Newton is to mechanism. The British thinkers are incomparably the classic expression of modernity, from Hobbes and Locke to Hume and his successors; from Newton to Gibbon to Darwin and his successors. For Calhoun, the happiness or sweet sense of nature for man is originally available to him in his admiration of and openness toward the whole of which he is a part. This is the natural human happiness, the happiness appropriate to his allotted condition. According to Calhoun, the coincidence of natural means and ends for man is metaphysics or reason, above all as it is applied to government or the political whole of which he is a part and which is the completion of Creation.[87]

However, the same twofold constitution of man which makes government indispensable for the preservation and perfection of society makes government itself tend in like manner also toward disorder and abuse of the power, until it becomes perhaps no more than an "instrument of oppression" of the rest of the community. Government is limited or ordered in accordance with the ends for which it is ordained by nature, but this ordination is "weak" and "remote," like the social or sympathetic feelings of individuals. Government is divinely ordained, but it "must be administered by men" who are not divine. Ordinarily, these men are no more wicked or vicious than those discussed in the fifth paragraph, but they are also not so virtuous as the exceptional cases discussed in the sixth paragraph. The condition necessarily arises in which the power necessary to control the tendency toward decay in the community must itself be controlled if the government is to succeed in the direction of its highest object instead of seeming a curse. Recognition of this fact, however dimly, is evident in the appeals to justice or the common good by all parts of the community, however mild those appeals may be. That by which the decay of government is prevented and the perfection of society attained, "by whatever name called, is what is meant by constitution," in its most comprehensive sense. In the following paragraph, Calhoun, who sometimes elsewhere speaks of caring primarily "not for the name but for the thing," moves from the introduction of the political constitution "by whatever name called" to characterize the constitution that is "worthy of the name" (paragraph 14).

In its most comprehensive sense, constitution refers to the care and superintendence of the Infinite Being, the Creator of all, or divine reason in the fullest and most unequivocal sense. In the same sense, when the term constitution is applied to government, both of which originate in the same principle of our nature, it refers to human reason in its highest sense. It stands as reason stands to the form and matter of government and society (paragraph 14; Cf. Rousseau: "One should remember here that the constitutions of the state [society] and that of the government are two very distinct things."[88]). However, in contrast both to the ordination of the solar system, which could not be other than it is, and to the ordination of government itself, which is divine and simply given or necessary, the perfection of government by constitution is "permitted to depend on our volition." It is the undetermined "space" of the cosmos, the openness to which nature only points and does not complete or finish its own intrinsic order, the order of the cosmos. The human community is, potentially, what spans this uncompleted dimension of creation, which is, therefore, potentially the dimension of freedom. The perfect completion of the political constitution would be the rational completion of the whole cosmic order, so far as our knowledge extends, or, in other words, would be the regime most in accordance with nature or the whole of which it is itself a part. Its completion and human freedom are the same thing. Yet, although it is left to and depends on human volition, it is nothing easy and cannot be simply willed, but depends further on development of the moral and intellectual faculties, for which man himself is responsible. While this development depends on society and provides the highest object of society, which is divinely ordained and necessary, constitutional government is, *par excellence*, the "contrivance of man." It depends decisively on human art or skill. This is the heart of Calhoun's vision of the human condition: man is left to imitate nature in order by his own effort to complete or fulfill nature. He "is left to perfect what the wisdom of the Infinite ordained as necessary to preserve the race." It is an exceptional condition distinct from the whole lower range of animated existence and which, for its perfection, requires exceptional effort. For reasons he has made abundantly clear, the perfection of government provides the natural occasion for this task that is at once the distinctively human and the most nearly divine task, because it is the task in which man most nearly imitates the divine or in which man may become a *Cooperator Dei*.[89]

According to Calhoun, however, man may not be adequate for this task. Rather, it is entirely possible that this great task, the only task that is commensurate with the perfection of the greatest and most noteworthy human endowments, is insuperable, however dedicated the effort. Hence the first question that was posed by Calhoun (paragraph 1) in a way leads to not only the "next" question that is posed by him (paragraph 15), for it leads also to the question of human wisdom.

For Calhoun, the question of human wisdom is the same as the first question of political science. Hence, for the purposes of the *Disquisition* the place of that question is occupied by the original reference to the science of astronomy, on the one hand, and by the whole of the *Disquisition* leading up to the question noted in the fourteenth paragraph, on the other. Still, if it is not merely volitional, the mere possibility of constitutional government or the perfection of government in accordance with nature is more than sufficient to provide all that is necessary for what is variously called the "art of the possible," the unique "space" of politics, the "middle ground" and "in-betweeness" characteristic of the political, genuine human liberty. Government must always exist with man. "Humanity" is not infinite; government provides a natural human limit or border: its existence is not a matter of choice. "There is no difficulty in forming a government." However, to form "a constitution worthy of the name" is "one of the most difficult tasks imposed on man." A perfect constitution, "one that would completely counteract the tendency of government to oppression and abuse and hold it strictly to the great ends for which it is ordained," has never existed. Its formation "has thus far exceeded human wisdom, and possibly ever will." It is the definitive human task.

Summary

If one characterizes the first of these two groups of paragraphs (sc. 5-9) according to its beginning and ending in reference to an answer that is certain (5 and 9: "the answer will be found..."; "it follows then..."), then one may characterize the second (10-14) similarly in accordance with the fact that it begins with the phrase, "If man had been differently constituted..." (10) and ends with reference to the wisdom which may ever exceed human reason and abilities (14). The description which perhaps most accurately captures the relation of their composition is that of form (10-14) to matter (5-9), or of theoretical to practical reason. The essential character of Calhoun's thought here consists in a tension between the founding of the philosophy or science of government on the ordinary and not the extraordinary case, on the "all too human case," on the one hand, while firmly orienting that philosophy toward the perfection of the whole, that is, upon the exceptional or extraordinary case *par excellence*, which in Calhoun's own words is possibly impossible, on the other. He thus aims at a truly "normal" political science in the sense that combines the usual with the normative while holding the usual "strictly to the great ends" for which politics is ordained. For this foundation to be successful, that is, true, it is necessary only that the potential for the extraordinary case, the exceptional exemplar of the intellectual and moral faculties, must exist in the ordinary case, or at any rate the ordinary government.

Paragraphs 15-17:
The Improbability of Constitutional Government

THE DISQUISITION ON THE NECESSITY OR ORIGINS OF GOVERNMENT IS COMPLETED (1-14). Government is a continuing or constitutive human condition. The following group of paragraphs (15-18) begins with the phrase, "with these remarks I proceed to the consideration of the important and difficult question." On the basis of the understanding of government reached, the remainder of the work is devoted to the problem or question of the perfection of government. The section introducing this question (15-18) resembles the opening section on the axioms of human nature (1-4), and completes Calhoun's introduction or foundation of the philosophy of government (1-18). The order of this foundation recapitulates the order of the whole, through the presentation of the great examples with which it closes.

The concluding section of the *Disquisition's* prologue is primarily concerned with the "powers of government," with the "amount of power" of government, or what he elsewhere calls "quanta of power." (If I am not mistaken, the term "power" or "powers" occurs fourteen times in the space of these three paragraphs; "community" occurs eleven times.)[90] Yet the section is, also, about the limits of government. Although it is not without significant ambiguities, it is clear that the concluding section of the prologue, as might have been expected following the presentation of the fourteenth paragraph, is as much about art as it is about nature.

Calhoun poses the "important and difficult question" and then immediately reformulates it, "to express it more fully," just as he had done in the beginning with the first question to be considered (compare . 1, 4, and 15). It is perhaps easier to see than it is to say how clearly and quickly in Calhoun's mind the primary and important question turns or grows into the second "important and difficult" question: *quis custodiet ipsos custodes* (cf. Plato, *Republic*, 403c)? Can the people, the human community or political whole, govern itself? He poses the latter question, first, as a problem of government, or of the form of society, potentially and ordinarily subversive of its perfection, and, "more fully" or proximately, as a problem of the men in government, or of the matter of society, potentially and ordinarily subversive of its preservation (paragraph 15).

Calhoun typically characterizes the political problem elsewhere in Clausewitzian terms as one of "warfare by legislation." Politics and governance is ordinarily merely war, carried on by other means, between the stronger and the weaker interests or parts of the community. Government, which is naturally meant in the first place to control the natural tendency toward individual conflict, ordinarily only seems to do what it is meant to do, or does only partially what it is comprehensively ordained to do. Actually, it ordinarily expands the individual tendency toward conflict to classes, parties, or whole portions of the community. A "system of hostile legislation" against the weaker arises from the stronger part:

> Warfare, by legislation, [is] commenced between parties, with the same object, and not less hostile than that which is carried on between distinct and rival nations—the only distinction [is] in the instruments and the mode. Enactments, in the one case, would supply what could only be effected by arms in the other; and the inevitable operation would be to engender the most hostile feelings between the parties, which would merge every feeling of patriotism—that feeling which embraces the whole—and substitute in its place the most violent party attachment; and instead of having one common centre of attachment, around which the affections of the community might rally, there would in fact be two—the interests of the [stronger portion], to which those who constitute [it] would be more attached than they would be to the whole—and that of the [weaker portion], to which they, in like manner, would also be more attached than to the interests of the whole. Faction would thus take the place of patriotism; and, with the loss of patriotism, corruption must necessarily follow, and, in its train, anarchy, and, finally, despotism, or the establishment of absolute power in a single individual, as a means of arresting the conflict of hostile interests; on the principle that it is better to submit to the will of a single individual, who by being made lord and master of the whole community, would have an equal interest in the protection of all the parts.[91]

According to Calhoun, constitution worthy of the name is one in which the tendency in question is genuinely controlled for the sake of the whole.[92] The problem as two aspects. The essential difficulty arising in the tendency toward vice and dissolution in government is evident in the fact that it cannot be counteracted or prevented by disinvesting the government of its powers and reinvesting them elsewhere (as happens in a coup or a revolution), as though perhaps then the problem posed by government would be corrected or managed or go away. Considerations along these lines led Hobbes to propose absolute monarchy as the best possible government. Nor can it be counteracted or prevented by simply reducing or limiting the powers of government, as though perhaps then the problem posed by human society itself, the problem of conflict or power itself, would be corrected or managed or go away. Considerations along these lines led Locke to propose a monarchy limited or "fenced" by the power of the numerical majority as the best possible government. The government "wherever vested" (8) is the highest power in the community The proposal to institute a higher power is therefore merely to "change the seat of authority and to make this higher power, in reality, the government." Because this higher power, for example, an eldership of some kind, ecumenical council, or other corporate body or committee or advisors behind the scenes, is in reality the government, Calhoun observes, it will then exhibit "the same tendency" already identified as the essential problem of government. Hence the answer necessarily lies in the direction of somehow limiting the government.

Calhoun's presentation makes it as clear that he is not without qualification a proponent of what are called (and were popular long before him) "limited government" doctrines. Good government obviously cannot be achieved simply by advocating "limited government," whether understood primarily as restriction of government by rules or as exclusion of government from various segments of community or communal action. The unequivocally true and right rule is not simply "limited" rule.[93] Calhoun notes of limiting the powers of government that "it is a sufficient objection that it would, if practicable, defeat the end for which government is ordained." This is because the powers of government themselves arise from the necessity to control the same tendency in the mass of society that constitution must control in government itself. To illustrate, there is ordinarily something like a necessary equilibrium between these tendencies in society and government in which the balance of power is always in favor of the government or controlling power (paragraphs 8-9, cf. paragraphs 81-85). Calhoun makes explicit here in the last sentence of the fifteenth paragraph what we now see was already fully present but only implicit in the last sentence of the eighth paragraph: the selfsame powers that are necessary for government to exist necessarily "will ever prove sufficient" for the self-aggrandizement of the governors at the expense of the governed, or for the governors to organize the government over against the governed in the conflict of interests. What makes government necessary for the sake of society makes it also almost impossible to limit or control in the name of society. Put another way, what makes the political whole possible is also itself the principal threat to the political whole. The existence of government is necessary but not sufficient to perfect the community or the political whole for whose sake it is. The question of how government may be controlled is thus the question of how government may be limited by the whole of which it is itself the necessary and definitive most necessary part. If it is not so limited, one can speak positively of the governors or rulers but only equivocally or nominalistically of the political "whole." The government for its own sake, the rule of a part, takes the place of the political whole. It rules the community for the sake of preserving and aggrandizing itself. Hence one cannot simply follow nature to arrive at man's natural ends or at liberty, for controlling or limiting the government amounts to controlling or limiting nature.

Paragraph 16

Up to now he had spoken of the internal and intrinsic objects of society and of government and of the dangerous tendencies which naturally beset these. But the amount of power required by government must be greater than that necessary to control the dangerous tendencies of conflict in society. It must also be powerful enough to defend the community against external dangers. External dangers limit the community, and may extinguish it altogether. Hence Calhoun turns for the first time to the threat of external dangers to complete the statement of the problem in question. It is in this context that he speaks of the community with the term "state." It is also in this context that he makes it explicit that society and government, human community, the political whole, is an "organism" of a certain (divine) kind (cf. paragraphs 18-19). The political whole is itself a species of animated existence, stronger than man and higher than man, because less incomplete than man. Communities are like a human individual writ large, or, rather, like a human individual writ large would be who contained both masculine and feminine parts. The "great law of self-preservation which pervades all that feels" (paragraph 7) is the "supreme law as well with communities as with individuals" (paragraph 17).[94] The former have all the same feelings and inclinations as the latter, with the qualification that the feelings are strongest of all in the former. The "controlling power" of government is, thus, also the commanding power of the full resources of the community for its defense in conflicts with other communities.

In the sixteenth paragraph Calhoun presents in terms of the tendency toward conflict between the communities of the world much of what he had presented in the eighth paragraph in terms of the tendency toward conflict between human individuals in society. The tendency toward conflict is global or universal because humanity is universal. The origin of these tendencies is identical, except that the tendency toward conflict between independent communities is "even stronger," for it is counteracted by even weaker sympathies. Locke and others had tried to overcome this weakness by making the political association ("civil society") as much as possible like a new joint-stock company and attaching individual sympathies as much as possible immediately to all "humanity" or the "natural community," as though political life itself, as distinct from "civil" or mere life, were the cause of the weakness.[95] For Calhoun, this hypothetical order is inverted and fallacious. "Mankind," "humanity," is a generalization: "it" exists only as a variety of so many nations and regimes. Government is that which is common or universal to man, or to these nations or regimes, the revealing or proof of a "human" being or nature ("existence"), and, at the same time, in every case that which also has the greatest determination (indivi-duation) and concreteness and uniqueness. It is the most human thing because it is in each case the most distinctively human creation. A Disquisition on Govern-ment is meant to provide an account of the universal dimension of government or of the universal principles of government, and to render an understanding of the most human achievement and duty. Calhoun does not deny that we may have sympathetic or social feelings for men of other communities or indeed for all men, but the less familiar they or their communities are the weaker these feelings will be. We have more feeling for our dead ancestors than for contemporaries living on the other side of the earth. Everyone cannot be at the same place at the same time. "Those who understand the human heart best know how powerfully distance tends to break the sympathies of our nature. Nothing—not even dissimilarity of language—tends more to estrange man from man."[96]

The tendency toward conflict between independent communities is, there-fore, constant: it is the strongest and hence the most characteristic of human tendencies outside of the tendency toward government itself. They are actually parts or dimensions of the same original tendency. The tendency toward govern-ment in human society becomes fully expressed as ultimately an imperial tendency of the community. The problem of limited government leads neces-sarily and inexorably toward the question of world government (paragraph 16). If government is natural for man as man, then it is reasonable that the best government for man is the best government for mankind. The fact that there is one human nature, one "human race," points to the natural inference that there should be one government, a world government, for the sake of the safety or preservation of the race.[97] Since this is the case, to anticipate, the science of government would naturally culminate in a global constitutional regime on the basis of "concurrent majority," with one semiglobal governmental interest or interests checking others, as the only true completion and crown of creation. One great human organism would envelop and express the whole sensitivity of the globe.

Calhoun does not explicitly say but otherwise makes it clear that his object, to adopt his language from the fifth paragraph, is to avoid this inference. Calhoun foresees precisely this. This is perhaps why he uses the term "state," meaning the independent and proud community in its posture toward others, for the only time in the Disquisition in this context. For Calhoun, such a completion as just described might come about by chance as the progress of current technologies increasingly overcome the natural "difficulty of intercourse" and various similar things that have previously acted as barriers to world community, particularly the barrier of distance. So far as these things are concerned, according to Calhoun, there is no ultimate barrier to world community, or at any rate to world government (paragraphs 132-139, 140-165). But this aim and the circumstances which excite it are fatal to genuine moral development, and hence to community. Hence, such an "achievement" would be far from the crowning or true finish of creation, for it would not be brought about by human reason and its responsiveness to human reason would be questionable. It would not be a true community, which is the aim of government. It would not fulfill the highest ends for which society and government are ordained. On the contrary, the result would be what has come to be called a "cold war" in the place of a just and lasting peace. It would be fragile, ever threatening deterioration, rather than harmonious and strong, and it would be characterized by enmity rather than friendship and concord — in short, by what is already attested as typical on almost every page of history. We must here leave it with the mere assertion (although a review of most of his speeches that touch on the subject of Britain intimate it clearly) that Calhoun himself believed it probable (primarily for intrinsic reasons, but also on the example of the Punic Wars) that, if every care were not taken (and perhaps even so), the United States and Great Britain would achieve just such a global division between them, in principle, by the turn of the next century, and that the division would be short-lived. All this must be a study for another occasion, but it is this pre-vision of global convulsion (though not this only) that lies at the heart of what he calls his "dread" that the modern progress in what pertains to matter will "retard or even arrest" progress in what pertains to politics and morals.

The task represented by forming a constitution is one of the most difficult tasks imposed on man in even the smallest and most homogeneous community (cf. paragraph 27). For this reason, a perfect constitution has never been formed, and may never be so. The larger and more various the community is or becomes, the less possible its achievement is or becomes, and the more utterly it depends on chance (paragraph 25). In this context, Calhoun says that, although the human race is comprehended in its social nature, "it must not be overlooked that the human race is not comprehended in a single society or community," but in a multitude of diverse independent and conflicting communities (paragraph 16). The human race is not a political whole but a natural whole of a certain kind. The human race has a nature in virtue of which every human being is equal, that is, a member of "our race." This nature is the decisive thing that defines humanity and that makes human individuals human, as against all other beings or natures. It is essentially composed of the "wants and inclinations, physical and moral," and the "moral and intellectual faculties" appropriate to them. Hence, our race has "one common interest running throughout," namely the perfection of these wants and inclinations by means of these faculties. This interest actualizes itself in "society," and, in so doing, defines the ends for which society is ordained. The natural and universal equality of men finds its full and complete expression in the natural and universal phenomenon of society, that is, in the sociability of man. This is all it can do. Society, however, is composed not of one common interest running throughout but of "various and conflicting interests." Not natural sociability but characters vary from community to community, and even within communities. It is this fact that naturally produces governments (paragraphs 62, 15, 3; cf. Plato, *Protagoras* 337c-d). Just as society is prior in human nature, a community of some description is prior to the actual human individual. This multiplicity of communities is a natural condition or limitation, a future as well as an historical fact that human reason cannot overcome not because it lacks the technique but because it lacks the reason, faculties (including moral qualities), and strength to do so (cf. paragraph 119). It is substantially impossible to know what to do and how to do it, even though, as Calhoun foresaw, global technology may be developed that nominally or apparently overcomes this essential defect. Technology alone will never overcome it. Consideration of the question of limited government, which leads to the question of world government, leads also to the acknowledgment of limited human reason itself as the true barrier to world community. The "limited reason and faculties of man," understood as the highest and most essential aspects of man as man, are themselves incompetent to attain true world community.

The tendency or inclination toward conflict in man's nature may be checked or overcome by government (paragraph 8), the same tendency or inclination in government, which is the tendency or inclination toward either internal or external aggrandizement, toward conquest or oppression, may be balanced or checked by forming a constitutional government. Ultimately, then, the preservation of the race according to reason will depend primarily on each of the many communities forming its own constitutional government, and not primarily on the formation of a constitutional "world" government.[98] If each of the many communities succeeded in forming its own constitutional government and then joined or combined in a constitutional world confederation or union, only then would there be a reasonable facsimile of "world community." Yet, it would remain even then but a reasonable facsimile. Hence, when Calhoun speaks of "barriers" or "ancient barriers" in this context, it is always in reference to barriers not to world community, which is not attainable for other reasons, but to world dominion, which is attainable, by a single power or interest, or "universal monopoly." "The ambition of a single country can destroy the peace of the world." The "common interest of mankind," by which Calhoun means "reason and the general convenience of nations," or "neutral [non-partisan] rights" of sovereign communities as against belligerent powers, are, thus, naturally opposed to world despotism, including the "peace of despotism," that is, an unjust peace, no less than to a world war.[99]

The prospect just mentioned is no more imminent now than it ever has been, although the overcoming of distance via the progress of technologies continues to accelerate. Even so, the greatest danger is not progress in what relates to matter or the overcoming of distances, but the humanitarian political thought which has come to accompany these developments, with which it is commonly associated (which Calhoun calls "misguided philosophy and false philanthropy"). It becomes the voice of a party speaking in the name of the whole. This ambition and self-seeking, and not technological progress itself, is more likely to retard the former "than all other causes combined." He explicitly calls this "philosophic" philanthropism, both when it is associated with external aggrandizement and when it is associated with internal aggrandizement, a "delusion" or a "delusive hope."[100] Nevertheless, it is hard to see how the desired progress of political science is to be achieved in this context in as much as one cannot help noticing that the greatest examples of ancient and modern constitutional regimes presented in the *Disquisition* are also the greatest examples of ancient and modern empires. Here in the sixteenth paragraph, with regard to external dangers, Calhoun leaves it at speaking of the "protection and preservation of the community" and the power necessary "to repel attacks from abroad."

Calhoun lists three sets of factors in order of importance and difficulty as barriers to world community. First and, one might also say, final among these are the "limited reason and faculties of man." He does not even pause to allude to what he elsewhere suggests are the decisive differences in the reason and faculties of individual men, such as between, a Newton or a Laplace, and uncounted multitudes of mere stargazers. He means human reason at its unequivocal height, that is, at the height of the unequivocally true science of government and the unequivocally wise and virtuous statesman, understood as the pinnacle of nature. It is too limited or weak. Hence there will never be a genuine world community. The second barrier Calhoun lists is the "great diversity" of communities now existing. They differ in language, customs, and pursuits, and in situation and complexion.[101] These differences, whether due to cumulative human effort or merely to accident or both, are all difficult to overcome: the natural love or sympathy for one's own as opposed to others' is very strong. Man's moral faculties are inadequate to overcome this diversity, for they depend upon community for their development and perfection. Hence there will never be genuine world community. Finally, "difficulty of intercourse and various other causes" are mentioned as having also been significant barriers. These difficulties are less hard than the others to overcome in themselves, but actually overcoming them alone does not necessarily lead to peace or even free trade, much less community, and, hence, in a manner of speaking, it is ultimately neither here nor there, except as the inconveniences such difficulties actually do represent, or except as overcoming them might itself actually prove to pose a threat of some kind. A more or less regulated global market is possible. In the last two sentences of the paragraph Calhoun returns directly to the moral and intellectual faculties, and treats the problem as though distances and related conditions were altogether overcome. These sentences culminate in the reference to "almost incessant wars" for plunder or revenge among "contiguous communities." That is, they refer above all to the communities that are the most familiar, and in some ways perhaps the most similar—in "language, customs, pursuits, situations, and complexion"—to one another. Familiarity breeds contempt.[102]

Paragraph 17

Nothing Calhoun depicts might seem so near to the Hobbian "state of nature" as the condition subsisting among the variety of independent communities. "Human history is war history."[103] This condition is not so much a state without society as it is a state with only the rudiments of government. Calhoun elsewhere typically discusses these elements under the rubrics of "international law" ("laws of nations") and "mutual interest" ("free trade").[104] These topics are not even mentioned in the *Disquisition*. As there is no appropriate constitution-making power, this state of things is apparently remediless. Of course, leagues and confederacies of independent communities or states are possible. At the parallel place in the previous group of paragraphs, Calhoun had begun what followed with the querying conditional phrase: "if man had been differently constituted..." (paragraph 10). Here, he begins with the declarative conditional observation: "so long as this state of things continues... ," which means, "foreseeably," if not "from now on" (paragraph 17).

Generally speaking, the ordinary state of things is the diversity and forces of political life as it has always been known. This is the state of things to which "all experience and almost every page of history testify," and which almost cries out for and in every way leads toward the desirability of constitution (paragraph 13). Hence constitution easily first comes into light as recognition of the need for a limiting of governmental power. In turning in the previous paragraph (16) from the subject of the power of government sufficient to aggrandize the men in government to that of the power of government necessary for government to repel external assault, Calhoun had restored the question of the perfection of constitution as it was first posed in the fifteenth paragraph, with the qualification that the government is like the community writ large, which is like the complete or hermaphroditic human being writ large. The virtue of the government reflects the virtue of those in the government. Virtue or the specific feature in anything that is organic is finally the definitive and hence decisive element. In the next paragraph (18) Calhoun's subject is in fact the subject of the virtue of the best and wisest men, whose virtue as men is unsurpassed, in other words, the genuinely extraordinary and striking cases. The ordinary necessarily points toward the extraordinary. It is perhaps the characteristic beauty of Calhoun's style that his thought never seems more than a sentence away from either the most elementary general rule or the most striking exception. The first part of the *Disquisition* explicitly culminates in the subject of the exceptional case, the founders of communities and governments, who, as such, are prior to them, and preservers of communities and governments, who keep them to their principles. This subject, for Calhoun, is, at the same time, the comparison of historical constitutions, or the most exceptional governments to which the pages of human history testify. In the *Disquisition* this subject naturally takes the place of that of the virtue of the exceptional individual as such.

Paragraph 18:
Examples of Partially Successful
Constitutional Governments

THE EIGHTEENTH PARAGRAPH IS WITHOUT PRECEDENT IN THE FIRST PART, INDEED, IT IS like none other in the *Disquisition*. In a sense it is the exception, as well as the conclusion, to what has gone before. It seems to abbreviate and to gloss rather than to compress its argument in Calhoun's usual style. It proceeds in a manner that is elliptical rather than "clear and just," or plain. It has primarily to do with what is historical while the preceding paragraphs all had to do with reason or what could be made reasonable. The conclusion that is at the same time the peak of the first part of the *Disquisition* is the subject of the wise men and good foundations of the past that is at the same time the greatest human subject—the human foundations that are most reminiscent of the order of the solar system itself because they are most revelatory of its true reason: the reason of the animate and inanimate whole.

The eighteenth paragraph represents the difficulties involved in perfecting constitution in a different way than had the immediately previous paragraphs, and that unites and completes the immediately previous paragraphs (15-17). Previously, Calhoun had discussed the place and power of government within its own community, whatever its condition, in reference only to *quanta* of power, without reference to its forms, and the difficulty faced by human art or skill in limiting or controlling political power (15). As we noted, the art of rhetoric does not complete this art or skill (7). One cannot control nature with words. Then he discussed the disparities among mankind and the conflict of independent communities (16, cf. 8), and restated more fully the essential problem of constitution, in connection with the fact that the higher ends of government and all other considerations must ever give way to the lower for the sake of preserving the organism itself (17). In the eighteenth paragraph this problem emerges into its own in connection with both the question of forms of government and given social conditions.

Calhoun names four organisms, four particular occasions of the consummate wisdom and skill with which the most remarkable constitutional devices were applied, as striking exceptions to the general run of human governments (cf. Plato, *Laws*, 715a3-4), and demonstrating the historical possibility of constitutional construction. In pointing to them, he names only the names of the people among whom this wisdom and skill of application occurred and not the names of the devices that were applied or the names of the men who devised and applied them. The "permanency of their effects" is, for him, one of the prime aspects of their remarkableness. His is a centuries-long perspective (cf. Hegel, *Philosophy of Right:* a true constitution is "not a contrivance but the work of centuries"). The list of exemplary constitutional regimes is remarkable for the diversity it contains. Calhoun's point is that difficult of achievement as it emphatically is, constitutional government is possible and has actually existed among diverse religions, races, regions, and so on. Withal, for example, are presented representatives of what are commonly thought of as divine compacts, including a compact between mortal and immortal gods; a compact between the classes of being; a compact between the people and Providence; and a compact between children and parents. Among them are what have been called pantheistic, atheistic, polytheistic, and monotheistic religions. They involve, withal, worship of a mortal god for an eternal reward; of an immortal god for a temporal reward; of mortals for a temporal reward; of the immortal world for an eternal reward. Most involve monarchy or a more or less prominent desire for monarchy, as well as other institutions, such as the institution of slavery and, by whatever name, privileged priestly classes.[105] What is further noteworthy about them, apart from their permanency, is the fact that all possess writing. The science of government, like the possibility of an effectual constitution, is independent of the question of race or religion.

What emerged in and with the "early dawn of civilization," therefore, was not the problem of constitution as such, which has engaged the highest capacities and best efforts of wise and good men "from the earliest ages," but rather only certain advancements in the arts and sciences, including writing, which allowed greater perfection of the intellectual faculties and which allow this wisdom and skill to be transmitted.[106] The question of constitution and its perfection is not new, but has existed and it is coexistent with "man." Already at the very dawn of civilization the competence of man in the most important matters was such that afforded "consummate wisdom and skill," even though the materials which that early age afforded were sparse. The author manages to refer no fewer than three times to the wisdom and goodness or skill of antiquity in the space of seven sentences, and to trace, "fairly," all "the subsequent advance of our race in civilization and intelligence" directly to it. He distinguishes between our age and the earliest age primarily on the ground of the advance of civilization and intelligence in matters pertaining to matter, that is, "enlightenment," and not at all on the ground of any wisdom and skill in matters pertaining to constitution, which are the most decisive and important matters for man as man, and hence for us. Other regimes and individuals are singled out for praise in *A Disquisition on Government*, but Calhoun never refers to our age as in any sense an age of wisdom, and he never praises any modern men as wise or good.

Here Calhoun draws our attention for the first time to the idea or the event of "progress," to the great gulf which separates the men of today not merely from the men of "the earliest dawn of civilization" but from the men even of yesterday.[107] This progress is not the progress of time but, as progress within time, it requires time. Progress takes time, which is to say, "stability [of] political institutions." This "stability," it all but goes without saying, is itself an active and not a passive condition. Indeed, the more active it is the more stable and sure it is.[108] For progress within time, just as for historical or political stability, the decisive factor, the absolute factor or *sine qua non*, is precisely the constitution or rule. All that Calhoun can here be said to indicate is that some constitutions promote stability or moral perfection (e.g., Egypt, and others at the early dawn of civilization), and others (e.g., Great Britain), in a period of high civilization, hasten primarily the perfection of man's intellectual faculties in regard to the agents of material nature. These are the two kinds of exceptional cases represented by constitutional governments in the *Disquisition*, and, taken as they are, that is, separately, they represent precisely what Calhoun means by referring to the only "partial success" achieved hitherto in the consideration of constitution. What it is necessary now to see, therefore, is that, in naming the particular names he names in the eighteenth paragraph, Calhoun has named the names only of such constitutions as are remarkable for promoting stability over (for human regimes) extraordinarily long periods of time, that is, for their particularly morality. He is entirely silent about the other kind, although he points to the other kind in several obvious ways. The other kind will be introduced in later sections of the *Disquisition*.

In the course of *A Disquisition on Government*, Calhoun provides constitutional examples from the primordial or savage states, or least civilized, to the most civilized regimes of the present moment. These may and do even exist for a time in the same moment or age. Yet, in speaking here of the progress of civilization in which "we now" enjoy the benefits, Calhoun means by this reference "we contemporary men and women," modern or enlightened humanity, heirs of (Western) Christendom, but including, more especially, the contemporary West (and even, most especially, the United States itself:

paragraph 131, last sentence, with 18, last sentence). In contemporary hindsight, the history of the West conventionally falls into two broad epochs, the ancient and the modern or enlightened. The ancient epoch culminates above all in the Roman Republic and the individual Cicero, and, finally, in the triumph of Christianity. With the conquest of Byzantium, the Roman Empire in the East, by the Turks in 1453 AD, antiquity, if not Roman Christendom (paragraph 108), is finally extinguished. Between the fall of Constantinople in 1453 and 1565, when the Manila galleon was able to establish a round-trip voyage between Acapulco and Manila and connect the cities of Catholic Spain in Western Europe with the cities of imperial China and what is now called the Pacific rim generally, the world of the present was born. These years cover most of the important discoveries and applications discussed at length by Calhoun in paragraphs 132-135, including the publication in 1543 the *De Revolutionibus Orbium Coelestium* of Nicholas Copernicus, as well as the Protestant Reformation and, of course, the discovery of North America. The present state of the world is characterized by an ever-increasing diffusion of communication and intelligence throughout the globe and all ranks of society. As observed in this paragraph, the relation that is characteristic of former times between philosophy or science and enlightenment, on the one hand (that is, in the terms of the eighteenth paragraph: "wisdom"), and politics or the community, on the other, is somewhat altered. Philosophy or science is today a commonplace, a utilitarianism, almost even a religion of reason, and, as it had increasingly become toward the fall of the Roman Republic, is on everyone's lips indiscriminately. In *A Disquisition on Government*, Calhoun addresses this new enlightened world plainly and directly, in its own terms and on its own grounds. However, he does not use the term "philosophy" in the work. Philosophy in its primary sense is beyond *A Disquisition on Government* both as something to which it necessarily points, that is, as we have noted, to "metaphysics," the Infinite Being, Pure Spirit, and something more rare to which it points more contingently, to the complete human life itself, or to a way of life that represents the perfection of all the natural human faculties, i.e., to statesmanship.

So far as the great constitutional regimes here set forth are concerned, the effects of the permanency mentioned above are now clear from their own consequences. For Calhoun, therefore, the crucial thing is not so much the advance of the stages of intelligence and civilization themselves but rather their diffusion and the effects of their diffusion. The fact that Plato derived his presentation the best regime from a "plan laid up in heaven," while he in fact knew nothing whatever of celestial mechanics or the plan of the heavens, is, so far as concerns Calhoun, neither here nor there. In that age of limited diffusion of intelligence, he might have known all that Laplace knew and still say what he said. The important thing is merely to note, as has always been noted, that there has always been supposed an order in the heavens, that is, an order of Being or of Creation, and it is Calhoun's intention, as the most divine task, to demonstrate and help complete this order in constitutional government. Just as constitutional government is not unique to this or that religion or grouping of humanity (18), neither is it tied to any particular dogmatic physical science, including the science arising out of the Copernican revolution, i.e., Newtonianism, compared with which all other relations to the world are thought simply inadequate or collections of superstitions, and, if possible, still less, to the characteristic paradigm of humanity and community erected thereon: Hobbsianism in whatever version or revision. Not at all. If this science, Newtonian physical science, were, in truth, the only true science, the only science worthy of the name, there could hardly be any profound divergence in its diffusion between progress in what pertains merely to matter and progress in all that pertains to human affairs, including not only material science and technology but, above all, knowledge and development of the non-material whole of which the human being is a part and the character and aims of the constitutional "organism" (paragraph 19). Yet nothing is more manifest. It is, therefore, radically inadequate. In truth, it cannot be more than the handmaid or even the footstool of the science of government, however impracticable such subordination may be in an age of its wide diffusion.

To repeat, it is Calhoun's purpose in the *Disquisition* to outline or establish the foundations of this true and final human science (paragraph 1), once and for all, here in the initial throes of an unprecedented era of material development and rapid transformation of long-established social organization. At the culmination of the opening or primary part of this work, we now see that this means that political science must look to and encompass something of the "consummate wisdom and skill" of earlier ages. To follow Calhoun's distinction between the thought of the earlier age of wisdom and skill and our own age, one may best compare this paragraph with the paragraph devoted to progress. Calhoun explicitly mentions diffusion of information no fewer than three times in that paragraph (134, cf. 132-139). Such diffusion finds its highest and noblest expression in imperialism, the spread throughout many lands and peoples, which, of course, is also its most dubious and problematic expression. None of the constitutional regimes named by Calhoun in the eighteenth paragraph are decisively characterized by imperial expansion, but it is undeniable that they include empires. The least one might say is that Calhoun's list of early constitutional regimes, although they are empires, is not primarily a list of empires.[109] Hence the contrast is less between empires and non-empires than between more explicit and uncontrolled imperialism and more implicit and controlled imperialism. It is interesting in this connection to see the progressive alteration in Western travelogues and reports of China in the eighteenth, nineteenth, and twentieth centuries, to-date, as the old regime declined and was revolutionized. In the mid-nineteenth century, Tocqueville could still write:

> I do not exaggerate in affirming that not one of them [sc. physiocrats] does not fail to praise China grandiloquently in some part of his writings.... They were enraptured at the sight of a country...where a literacy examination has to be passed to qualify for all positions, and which has a philosophy as a religion and men of letters as aristocrats.

Today, a little more than a century later (although it is apparently no longer a crime punishable actually by death or imprisonment), hardly a Chinese official is to be met with who has even heard of Confucius or Mencius, to say nothing of philosophers or men of letters. They speak of Marx, if not Stalin (although, admittedly, less and less of either). Now, for them, "most favored nation," so far from pointing to the central station between heaven and earth, is a term referring to nothing more than an advantageous commercial status.[110]

What the constitutional regimes here named have most in common, as Calhoun observes, is that they were all wisely devised precisely for a stage of civilization and culture in which intelligence was so partially diffused. They are well suited to that stage from the point of view of stability of political institutions, or, in other words, from the perspective of the aim of society toward perfection of men's moral faculties. No higher praise is to be found anywhere in the *Disquisition* than for the wisdom and goodness of these statesmen. We may exemplify this by a reference to one of these examples. Calhoun repeatedly indicates not that the discovery of the mode of making gunpowder but precisely "its application to the art of war" has been momentous for making a degree of civilization and therewith diffusion of intelligence a given in the contemporary world (paragraphs 95, 133-135). It apparently equalizes otherwise unequal communities as well as unequal men. One of the regimes Calhoun names is, among other things, well known for the discovery and long possession not only of printing but of what came to be called gunpowder, without, however, ever having applied it to the art of war. But it has since been so applied, and application now is become necessary for any community's survival. We refer to this example as a positive way of stating his conclusion on this point because Calhoun ordinarily if not always referred to the necessary evil of war as usually "a positive evil." "War may make us great; but let it never be forgotten that peace only can make us both great and free."[111]

Summary

Each sentence of the prologue to the *Disquisition*, from the question of the science of government (paragraph 1) to the necessity of government (paragraph 9) to the exemplifications of constitutional governments (18) could be fruitfully annotated beyond anything we have said. To summarize, Calhoun states the first question of political science (1), and then its elementary axioms (2-4). The discussion of human feelings (5-8) leads necessarily to government (9), and that of human reason (10-13) to the question of the constitution of the whole (14). He states the next question of political science, the problem of constitution or the need to control nature for the sake of freedom (15), and then its limits, including some distinguished early exemplifications of constitutional government (16-18). In what follows he presents his theory with respect to the question raised in paragraph 15 ("the most important question," 19-53), then shows its advantages with respect to preservation and the perfection of the human intellectual and moral faculties (paragraphs 54-98), and discusses and rebuts apparent objections to its practicability, including moderate and extreme examples of constitutional effectiveness (paragraphs 99-139). He concludes with a discussion of the most distinguished exemplifications of constitutionalism that are yet known (paragraphs 140-165), and, finally, offers his practical recommendations regarding the greatest and most complex and unique popular constitutional example (*A Discourse on the Constitution and Government of the United States*).

CHAPTER THREE

Empire and World Government

> I think there is not one of us but felt when he last addressed us from his seat in the Senate...who did not feel that he might not imagine that we saw before us a Senator of Rome, when Rome survived.
>
> Webster[1]

THE NINETEENTH PARAGRAPH OPENS WITH THE PHRASE, "IN ANSWERING THE IMPORTANT question under consideration...," that is, with a phrase reminding of the opening of the fifth paragraph. From this and other observations, one might suggest that the first part stands to the rest of *A Disquisition on Government* as the first four paragraphs stand to the rest of the first part of the work (paragraphs 5-18). The culminating paragraphs of the first part (15-18) are devoted to the "difficult question" of constitutional government, which defines the field that, according to Calhoun, wise and good men above all wish to address. He explicitly refers to "wise and good men," statesmen, but to no man in particular. It is likely that he thought of more than one man in each of the cases named. Perhaps most notably in this context, he also does not refer in these paragraphs to that "most sagacious of the men of antiquity," who carefully distinguished the "constitution-making from the law-making power," that is, to ancient political philosophy,[2] to men who philosophized about government and community. Nor does he refer to himself, but only to "our race" (twice). Indeed, after the opening sentence stating the question in the fifteenth paragraph, there is not even a first person reference anywhere in the "consideration of the important and difficult question" of constitutional government (15-18). It is in the paragraph following (i.e., 19) that Calhoun is prepared to say ("In answering the important question under consideration..."), "what I propose...." In so doing, he joins those whom he has identified as "wise and good men," while at the same time distinguishing his own position. And, he speaks no longer of the science of astronomy, or the constitution of the whole of physical creation in the highest sense, but of "organism."

With his gentle if firm proposition, Calhoun gracefully and all but explicitly enters the lists of the political philosophers. Of course, as we have observed, his concern to replace the "civil philosophy" of Hobbes or the "social contract" school is implicit from the opening paragraph, and through the whole opening part of *A Disquisition on Government*. This focus is maintained throughout the work. Calhoun returns to it explicitly in discussing the hypothesis of the "state of nature" at the close of the section of the *Disquisition* introduced by the nineteenth paragraph. Elsewhere, Calhoun associates this hypothesis, and particularly its influence in the United States, with Locke, or with Locke and Sydney.[3] In place of the "state of nature" hypothesis in the opening or introductory part of the *Disquisition*, Calhoun presents the assumptions and orientation of traditional or classical political philosophy, that is, of the thought of Plato, Cicero, and Augustine that peaks in Aquinas, and against which, particularly Aristotle, Hobbes originally delivered his "civil philosophy." Hence one may reasonably if provis-ionally suppose that Calhoun aims at a recovery or restoration of the traditional or classical political philosophy displaced by Hobbes and his successors. How-ever, in Calhoun's own proposal, which he describes as "limited," his aim ap-pears rather differently.

Paragraph 19:
Calhoun and the "History of Political Philosophy"

THE PORTION OF *A DISQUISITION ON GOVERNMENT* THAT BEGINS THE PRESENTATION OF Calhoun's political thought proper opens with a distinction between that thought and traditional or classical political thought. Calhoun here begins by saying that in answering the question under consideration it is not necessary "to treat of constitution in its most comprehensive sense," that is, in the manner of traditional or classical political philosophy, and especially in the manner of Plato in some of his dialogs. When Calhoun says that what he proposes is "far more limited," he apparently means, specifically, that it is far more limited than the undertakings of ancient political philosophy.

Constitution in its comprehensive sense, when applied to human government, involves the whole "intellectual and moral culture" that is the defining aim of the community (7, 14 first sentence) and includes all the means by which are prevented the governmental tendency to disorder and abuse (13, 15). Such means include all the devices named in the prior paragraph on the great constitutions (18)—superstition, ceremonies, education, religion—and the various matter named in the earlier paragraph on external relations (16)—the reason and faculties of the community, language, customs, pursuits, situation, complexion, and various other things. According to Calhoun, entering into such a comprehensive treatment of constitution "is not necessary" to answer the question under consideration, ultimately, how to secure the end for which human society is ordained: the highest possible intellectual and moral culture (7, 12, 14; cf. 78 end: "religion," "education"). Nor is it necessary to enter into an examination of the devices by which the particular constitutional governments just named in the eighteenth paragraph achieved control of the tendency to disorder and abuse. (Indeed, Calhoun does not even refer to those regimes again.) Government is coeval with human society, and, although every actual form of it owes its rise to the existing community or social system or order, (and is, therefore, contingent), the elementary principles of constitutional government are not limited to any particular culture or regime. Calhoun proposes that these elementary principles will emerge from a consideration of the nature of government itself, of what is necessary and universal, however the matter mentioned above (paragraph 16) might be found. In elucidating these elementary constitutional principles, Calhoun does not disagree with Plato that "A constitution, to succeed, must spring from the bosom of the community and be adapted to the intelligence and character of the people and all the mutilfarious relations, internal and external, which distinguish one people from another" (*Disquisition*, 119; cf. *Republic* 426eff).

Most particularly, in the present connection, a comprehensive consideration would necessarily include what Calhoun in the eighteenth paragraph calls "organic arrangements in the government and community." We can see that Calhoun sets aside as unnecessary for consideration all of the elements just mentioned above, as well as the latter element here—organic arrangements in the community. These include such things as, for example, an institution of monogamous marriage, an institution of slavery, an establishment of social orders or ranks in the community, and so forth. He limits himself, rather, only to a consideration of the organic arrangements in the government, and, specifically, to that arrangement which makes the government constitutional, to the constitutional organism. This may easily appear as a contraction of the concerns of traditional or classical political thought from the community as a whole to the arrangement of the government. For Calhoun, on the contrary, it is merely a concentration on the decisive part of the most important element of the community (any community) as a political whole, whatever its social institutions. For, just as society is for the preservation and perfection of the race, and government for the preservation of society, the constitutional organism is for the preservation and perfection of the government (14). The question is how a genuinely constitutional government may be achieved (15). It is certainly important not to suppose that this concentration represents in any sense a turning away from the high question of the moral formation of the people or of the outstanding individual (statesman). Rather, according to the closing sections of this part of *A Disquisition on Government*, it is precisely the operation of constitutional government, and in particular the operation of the constitutional organism itself, that, beyond all other considerations, most surely (typically, ordinarily) achieves the perfection of the moral faculties of the people and community leaders (6, 72-98; cf. 104-107).

Today, as we have noted, Calhoun is understood by some of their representatives as primarily a founder of some one or another twentieth-century or "post-modernist" political philosophy, if not of some kind of "Marxism" or other variant of Hegelianism or Smithism. The rise of these various schools may blur for us the position of Calhoun as it was seen in his own time or shortly after his death. At that time, he was judged by some writers, including Acton and Mill (whose thought is also for us often somewhat hidden by the rise of these schools), to be in some sense the culminating figure of the school of political philosophy stemming from Hobbes and, especially, Locke, if not from "medieval freedom."[4]

The most explicit statement of this view was made less than a decade after the *Disquisition on Government* was first published (1851), the point just made was drawn out at length by a contemporary of Calhoun, from the new perspective of positivism, or what he called "sociological ideas," in the conclusion of a ten-part article that was published in New York in a learned journal of the day under the title "Review, Historical and Critical, of the Different Systems of Social Philosophy" (1860).[5] As this article is unknown today, it will be useful to sketch its outline as a guide for our beginning to study Calhoun's proposal.

According to the author of the "Review, Historical and Critical, of the Different Systems of Social Philosophy," there are two great classes or schools of social philosophy. These are the ancient school, beginning with Plato, which emphasizes virtue, and the modern school, beginning with Machiavelli and Hobbes, which emphasizes preservation, individualism, and *laissez faire*.[6] Together, these schools constitute the whole of Western "social philosophy." In this version of Western intellectual history, what is termed the "first class" of political thought, the modern school, beginning with Machiavelli, is denominated essentially as that of the "philosophers of liberty," and what is termed the "second class," or ancient school, beginning with Plato, is denominated essentially as the "philosophers of virtue." The most comprehensive of the modern class, out of many examples cited from Machiavelli through Calhoun, is Locke's two-part *Essay on Civil Government*. Calhoun, who is understood as the polar opposite of Locke in this school, while on the same plane, is presented as the most distinguished philosopher of the modern class, the "philosophers of liberty." The ancient school, according to the author, is both superior and inferior, but inferior in the decisive respect, to the modern. The "philosophers of virtue" are fuller or more holistic in their concerns than the moderns, but they overestimate the role of government and hence do not arrive at or understand the effectual truth of government. The "great exemplars" of this ancient class of thinkers, according to the author, are Plato and Aristotle, who speak for all. The "philosophers of liberty" are narrower and less holistic in their concerns than the ancients, but they correctly estimate government and understand its truths. The broad distinction that is drawn between these two classes, the "Ancient" and the "Modern," is presented both at large and as primarily and most acutely a distinction between Calhoun himself, on the one hand, who speaks for all, and Plato and Aristotle, on the other. The author summarizes Calhoun's position in the following way.

When we compare the clear and direct disquisition of Calhoun with the vague and pointless ones of many antecedent political inquirers, we are almost tempted to exclaim that political philosophers before his time were striving to find out, and to declare, what it was they were aiming at, and at last found expression in Calhoun.

However, it is on these same grounds that Calhoun is most properly criticized. "Yet even in him they find only half a tongue. For Calhoun does not inquire, or scarcely at all, *what government should do for society, but* [only] *what is to be done to prevent government from transgressing its legitimate province, and inflicting injury on society.*" The writer concludes that "this latter question, however, is much more difficult than the former, though to common observation it may not appear so," that is, without the benefit of Calhoun's guidance.[7]

The ancient social philosophy, rather, aims at improving the social condition to a greater extent and somewhat more fundamentally than the legitimate function of government can ever improve it, and to an extent which is possible, though not very likely to be attained, and which, as a means of attaining this end aim at a political system, or organism, which transcends the legitimate function of government.

This criticism of the ancients, which is characteristic of the whole review, is essentially that levied by Hegel throughout the *Jenaer Realphilosophie* and the *Philosophy of Right*. However, in contradistinction to the moderns, according to this author, the ancients at least "recognize the importance of far more fundamental influences than those of the mere legitimate function of government." The ancients are unqualifiedly superior to the moderns in this important respect—"one of the only two important points in which the two classes differ from each other." The following passage deserves quotation in full:

The theory or general scope of the first class of ideas would appear to be this: that all which it is of any great importance for the social philosopher to aim at is a government capable of completely discharging the proper duties or legitimate function of government—a government which protects all the individual rights and interests of the community—a government, in short, which, according to the views of Calhoun, the most clear spokesman of all the philosophers of that class, at the same time that it is invested with the full command of the resources of the community, for the purposes of protecting it, is so arranged, by its own interior structure, or organism, as to resist its inherent tendencies to abuse power [i.e., *Disquisition*, paragraph 19].

The social philosophers of the second class, of whom Plato was one of the most strongly marked and illustrious exponents, very justly assert, on the contrary, that this is very far from being all that demands the serious and particular attention of the social philosopher—that the moral character and industrial pursuits of the community, their habits and occupations, their theological notions and religious beliefs, as well as their mental culture, demand attention.[8]

In all of this, "the philosophers of the second class have decidedly the advantage over the first, that they distinctly recognize the importance of attention to all of these influences." These philosophers seek to actualize, for mankind, the grand end of their being, that which the Grecian philosophers seem to have been aiming in all their speculations, the *To agathon*, or, as the Romans styled it, the *summum bonum* of human life—that exalted sentimentality or spirituality of character the aspiration after which, in modern times, is resigned almost to the religious meditations of individuals, or a purely contemplative philosophy.

Perhaps because they published on a wide variety of subjects, the author does not here reflect on any disjunctive relation between what he calls "all their speculations," on the one hand, and "a purely contemplative," private, or "non-social" philosophy, on the other. In any case, he concludes (with Hegel) that these philosophers "commit the grand error of aiming to make the government, or political authority of society, the instrumentality for seeking to actualize these influences."[9] They are, thus, inferior to the modern philosophers.

In short, the social philosophers of the first class have this great advantage over those of the second, that what they aim to do at all they aim at wisely and well, whereas those of the second class, while they aim at accomplishing a great deal more, mistake the true method of accomplishing anything.

The former, more comprehensive, aim too broadly or too high for the means of government, according to this writer, and the latter, more acute, aim too narrowly.

Calhoun's particular argument about the political "organism with extensively disseminated self-checking powers," and, generally, that "all constitutional governments, of whatever class they may be, take the sense of the community by its parts, through its appropriate organ, and regard the sense of all its parts as the sense of the whole," represents the *terminus ad quem* of the class which began with Machiavelli and Hobbes, or of modern "social philosophy" as such. Accordingly, in conclusion, the author supposes that Calhoun's completion or conclusion of political philosophy leaves us with "only one question," a last or final question which he reduces to one of social engineering: "into how many parts is it expedient to partition a community, with a power in each part, through its appropriate organ, to speak out and hold in check all the rest." By answering this final question, perhaps the two great schools of Western social philosophy could be united or synthesized, or even transcended. However, the writer himself is modest and enough not to attempt such a project. For, ultimately, this "only remaining question" and all its ramifications "open up such a vast and varied field for consideration that no one who is not deeply read in the principles of social philosophy should presume to pronounce judgment on them. They will not be considered in this Review" ("Review," no. 5, 671).

So far as *A Disquisition on Government* is concerned, the number of such parts is unimportant (cf. paragraph 41). What is important is that the constitutional organism must "spring from the bosom of the community," including all the circumstances in which it is found. "If it does not, it will prove in practice not to be a constitution," but will be speedily superseded and laid aside (paragraphs 119-120).[10] The author of the "Review, Historical and Critical, of Social Philosophy" lucidly if perhaps unwittingly exhibits all the tensions of the impact of the new school of positivism and sociological ideas on the progressive mind of the day, and presages the emergence of both American legal positivism and the idea of "social engineering." As a result, however useful the "Review" may be in discussing the subject of Calhoun's place in a schematic of the history of philosophy, it is not an accurate expression of the substance or argument of the *Disquisition*, which is quite otherwise than the author supposes it in his statement of its conclusion, and in the expression of the "only question remaining" after having formally reached this conclusion. With his admitted deference or hesitation before the "vast and varied" difficulties involved in answering this last question, the author of the "Review" arrives practically not at the last question after Western social philosophy as concluded by Calhoun, but, once again, at the beginning of *A Disquisition on Government*.

Moreover, in a sort of ersatz foreshadowing of the doctrine of eternal return, he arrives not merely at the beginning of *A Disquisition on Government*, understood as the culminating political work of the "modern school" of Western social philosophy, but also in the same manner and for the same reasons at the beginning of Aristotle's *Politics*, understood as the great political work of the "ancient school." More precisely, in this connection, it returns us to Aristotle's account in book two of the political speculation of one Hippodamus of Miletus (or Thurii), a celebrated astronomer and architect of the day, explicitly about the best or true partitioning of a human community or polis, and how many parts there should be in order for the community or polis to be most according to nature (*Politics*, 1267b21-1269a27).[11] Hippodamus was the first man who was not himself engaged in politics to speculate publicly on these questions in Greece.[12] Turning from the *Disquisition* to the *Politics*, we find that Hippodamus has completed his study of nature and political thought, and has the answer for the sociologist's last question. He has made a proposal about how many parts the best community, in principle, all communities, should be partitioned into. It is precisely this kind of speculation and related matters and its increasing currency in his time that is Aristotle's own explicit point of departure in the *Politics* (1260a30ff).

By far the most striking of all the striking items Aristotle adduces from Hippodamus' proposal is the partitioning of the whole community into three classes or interests: the soldiers or warriors, who must defend the community, the farmers, who must feed the community, and the artisans, who support or supply the community, as well as innovate or discover ever more useful things; all the community's land into three parts, and all the community's laws into three categories. The proposed population of 10,000, which has a Persian look about it, is '3 times 3,333', plus one. Because this trinitarian partition is the most striking thing about the proposed community, Aristotle has presented it first, and also because this particular partitioning and none other is understood by Hippodamus as itself the end or perfection of the community. It is that in which the perfection of the community consists. The number three stands for natural or divine reason, and is that by which reason is possible. Merely by adhering to this formal pattern or rule, therefore, categorically renders the community perfect, the only rational or "true" community. Because the number three is a key to the understanding of the whole of nature or in a sense is the "rule" or right of nature or contains the whole reason and perfection of nature and the cosmos — or because it is particularly related to other numbers that do so — the partitioning of the community in accordance with it is the perfect way of being or the way which most immediately imitates nature. Nature's end is in this city, and this city is the end of nature. The existence of the community upon this plan of partition is what constitutes its perfection and what makes the city and man one with divine nature.

Shall we suppose that this is the answer to the "last question," the post-Calhoun question? Would our speculative sociologist accept it as a reasonable answer? Or, would he perhaps want there to be some other number than three underlying the partitioning of the community, say four or two, or some other? Hippodamus partitions the community into three interests. These are necessary classes or interests or parts of any community, under whatever name. Aristotle never contests this. Priests, for example, need not constitute an interest unto themselves; they might come from any or all of the classes. Allowing that someone might want to add a partition here or remove one there on the basis of some other understanding of nature — even though this would perhaps destroy all its rationality and beauty for Hippodamus (although it is possible that Aristotle himself has already imbalanced its perfection by adding one more to the specified citizen population and thus destroyed the whole enterprise) — we are justified in taking Hippodamus' proposal here as in principle answering the last question as put by the positivist historian. Any answer to that question would amount to an answer of this kind.

The manner of Hippodamus' partitioning of the community ensures that it will immediately become a tyranny. This is the first thing Aristotle points out about the proposal, and it would be the first thing that Calhoun would point out about it. Beneath the most striking thing in the proposed regime is merely the familiar absolute regime. This is not new or novel, although Hippodamus presents it as new, but old. It is what Calhoun refers to as the testimony of almost every page of history (cf. Plato, *Laws*, 715a). Disseminating mutual checks on each of the interests would improve the condition. Without such checks, Aristotle begins his critique of the Hippodamian regime with the immediate observation that the military class will rule it. It is obviously not to say that morality grows out of the barrel of a gun to observe that the warrior class, who have all the weapons, will not pay any attention to Hippodamus' natural or divine numbers but will disregard them as mere abstractions, and, in violation of justice and morality, will overcome the other interests and rule over them just as they please (*Disquisition*, paragraph 51). The government will be for the rulers, and its end will be the pleasure of the rulers. It will not be the accord with nature that Hippodamus represents by the trinitarian partition that he devises, which will be instantly subverted by the conquest of the warrior class, for whatever purpose it wishes, as "natural." That end will be the first thing to go, and all the other provisions will follow suit. The whole is destroyed by the rule of a part. Withal, it is a poor hypothesis and worse art—what the New Critics called the "naturalistic fallacy." It is not three but one.

The whole question or theme of the *Politics*, the whole question or theme of the *Disquisition on Government*, concerns the political whole. Tyrannical rule, the rule of a part in its own interest, is not political rule (e.g., *Politics*, 1255bff; *Disquisition*, paragraph 57). Hence it is unwise, and, as Hippodamus' proposal demonstrates, also dangerous, merely to replace the question of the political whole with the question of the parts, or, in other words, to lose sight of the whole or otherwise take it for granted, for the parts depend on the whole, which means, in the first place, on government and on the ends for which government is necessary and ordained, beginning, as we have indicated, with morality or virtue. It is "pre-political." There is no public in Hippodamus' proposed regime, and hence no public or common good or justice but only so many private interests. (Hippodamus has ignored all kinds of laws concerning public crimes or crimes against the *polis* itself.[13] In the place of these he puts "new discoveries.") In replacing or forgetting that question, one will only arrive, willy-nilly, at some more or less elaborated number of parts, but never at the whole itself, which is the object of the science of government or the science of man.

These brief remarks on part of Aristotle's criticisms of the proposed partitioning of the community by Hippodamus of Miletus do not exhaust that criticism, but they are sufficient to show the agreement of Aristotle and Calhoun (if not of all the exemplars of the ancient, or more expansive, and modern, or more restrictive, schools of social philosophy) on at least the practical or legislative aspects of the question about partitioning as these relate to the science of government. Both Aristotle and Calhoun place incomparably greater weight on this aspect than does Hippodamus, and for the same reasons. Another aspect of the sociologist's last question may be illustrated by reference to a related assertion that Calhoun's treatment of constitution in the strict sense in *A Disquisition on Government* is not limited enough. Let us turn to this assertion with the sociologist's question in mind.

A leading historian of economic theory, according to whom Calhoun is the "one major political theorist" to have provided a "profound analysis of the constitutional problem" — referring to the "famous doctrine of the concurrent majority" advanced by him as the only solution for the problem of absolute government — has written that Calhoun "does not push his path-breaking theory on concurrence far enough."[14] This defect arises because, according to the author, Calhoun has apparently overlooked the crucial point that the principle of concurrency must, obviously, not only apply to the government but also to the "states." In considering this objection it should be borne in mind that Calhoun in the *Disquisition on Government* does not make any distinction between the government and the state beyond the distinction made in the nineteenth paragraph between the constitution in the comprehensive sense, the organization of the community considered in all its aspects and conditions, and the constitution in "the strict or more usual sense," the organization of the government itself in light of its natural ends. The core of Calhoun's political philosophy as presented in paragraphs 19-98 thus begins with this fundamental distinction between the "community" and "government" as the fundamental distinction between "convention" or culture and "nature." There is no other kind of distinction between the government and the state. But the writer is of course thinking primarily about the American federal government and the individual states that make up the American Union. There is no explicit discussion of this subject in the *Disquisition*. (Calhoun addresses the issue here raised in the *Discourse*, of which the writer is unaware). However, according to Calhoun, government of every kind or description in communities or political states of every kind or description is perfected — circumstances permitting, but in principle everywhere and always — by its constitution, or by what Calhoun calls the constitutional principle or "principle of concurrency." This includes the governments of the individual states composing the American Union, as well as the federal government, because they are all governments. So far as Calhoun is concerned, it would also include all the states that might make up a future

United States of Europe or of Africa or of Eurasia. If this elementary notion is not grasped, nothing about the *Disquisition* can be grasped. Any omission or apparent exemption or contradiction on Calhoun's part is merely apparent or, rather, lies only in the mind of the writer, who is unaware of other writings and speeches of Calhoun where the subject is treated at length, or who, in a familiar enough practice, wishes to use the *Disquisition* for other purposes.

The confusion would thus seem to be straightforward. The writer is primarily concerned with the political state itself as "almost universally considered an institution of social service," and with which estimation, as a libertarian theorist, he adamantly disagrees, but his work peaks in the section on Calhoun's *Disquisition* and the American government, as illustrating his broader theme. He is thus concerned with the federal government, on the one hand, and the individual American States, on the other, as representatives primarily of state power.[15] He comes to the *Disquisition*, then, in connection with the federal government being a judge in its own case in the United States Supreme Court, particularly in regard to the constitutional legitimacy of the New Deal, and as representing the greatest expression of the old American school of state rights. Having found the correct way to solve the problem of absolute government in the *Disquisition*, the "last question" of the libertarian theorist is, then: "What is to prevent the Calhoun system from working in reverse, with states tyrannizing over their citizens and only vetoing the federal government when it tries to intervene to stop that state tyranny? Or for the state to acquiesce in federal tyranny?"[16] For Calhoun, of course, the principle of concurrency would prevent it. This is the point. The principle of concurrency does not have a "reverse"; it is itself the reverse or "negative" power, and not a "positive" or legislative power (*Disquisition*, paragraph 54; cf. Rousseau, *Social Contract*, IV.5). However, it is certainly of equal importance to note that not the *Disquisition* but the *Discourse* is the great expression of the American school of state rights—in so far as Calhoun may be considered the definitive spokesman for that school. The *Disquisition* is silent about state rights. The *Disquisition* is preliminary to the *Discourse*, it is true, but Calhoun means for the *Disquisition* henceforward to be preliminary for any discourse on constitution and government anywhere, including the *Discourse*. The *Disquisition* is the *prolegomena* to any future work on constitution and government.

These observations may not satisfy the libertarian theorist, for he is here in fact only incidentally interested in the issue of state rights, and he is not interested in any of Calhoun's other writings. He is interested only in the *Disquisition*, which contains the profoundest analysis yet given of the constitutional problem. The omission of any reference to the American states in the *Disquisition*, while everyone knows Calhoun was an adherent of the state rights school in his politics, leads the writer to see that the *Disquisition's* constitutional doctrine or teaching actually confines its checks to the agencies of government itself or, in other words, that it treats of constitution in the strict sense. It is this restriction, according to him, that flaws critically the otherwise profound analysis. This criticism is the same as saying that Calhoun should have taken up first the question of the constitution in the comprehensive sense and not limited himself to the constitution in the strict sense—or, in short, that he should have begun by first abstractly determining into how many parts the community as a whole should be partitioned. Hence it is not surprising that—having to his own satisfaction neatly trapped Calhoun in the obvious contradiction entailed in having apparently exempted the individual American states that make up the federal union from the principle of concurrency, to all of which it must necessarily be applied for the sake of consistency—the writer goes on to assert that, since all this is so, it must also apply willy-nilly to all the individuals who make up the states who make up the union, and who are, in their capacity as human individuals, the true sovereigns, for whose service the state is a putative service institution. On the basis of this reasoning, the author is able to show the whole position in the *Disquisition* exploded, because Calhoun does not carry the point far enough, namely, "down to the individual."[17]

State rights thus go the way of any other government "rights," which is the familiar libertarian thesis: state rights of whatever kind (except property police) are a conventional usurpation (backed merely by force) of natural individual rights. Therefore, according to the writer, "why stop with the states?" The veto principle should be carried to every individual and the community—or, rather, "society"—should be thus partitioned into as many separate human beings as happen to be within its range—in principle, into an infinite number; in principle, into the whole of mankind—who will produce goods and trade, "mixing their labor" with resources, to innovate and advance their "standard of living." Universal human rights must replace all parochial state rights. Government, if it should exist at all, should be constructed with these ends in view, and hence should be held to a merely nominal or minimalist "police level," for the sake of securing individual rights to property and dignity, and, of course, to prevent homicides. Orphans or others who are hopelessly destitute or helpless might also be supported to some extent, perhaps, if there is anything deserving about them or if anyone wishes to take on this burden. This is the most natural state and the only one that is right by nature. By this argument we are led to see plainly that Hippodamus was merely mistaken about the number of partitions, which, given his time and place in pre-modern history, is surely understandable, if not "historically necessary." In most respects, however, he was "before his time" or "ahead of his time."

The argument of libertarian economism also lets us see clearly what the positivist sociologist had meant by suggesting a hundred years earlier that Calhoun's social philosophy arose out of a thoroughgoing Lockeanism as the powerful reaction to Locke.[18] For the libertarian merely interprets the

Disquisition "in reverse" or toward the other, original Lockean "pole," much as Marx interpreted Hegel or as Locke had interpreted Hobbes. This apparent "polarity," as we have sufficiently shown, is what must be investigated in Calhoun's case with a view to discovering whether it is a difference merely in plane or in fact a difference in kind. That is to say: Calhoun's answer to the first question of political science must be taken seriously, that is, as the true or absolute answer. If it is not true, according to him, one can forget about genuine political science, to say nothing of constitutional government and genuine liberty. Equally importantly, however, the "reverse" interpretation of the theorist (admittedly unwittingly) also lets us in a sense get a brief, inverted glimpse of the true Calhounian man—constitutional man: the perfect moral intellectual, the completed and sovereign political animal—or of what Calhoun means by "liberty" in the highest sense, which is an individual sense, and for the sake of which highest end government is. This man and only this man transcends the community because he fulfills the community.

But what should not be obscured by this brief glimpse is that this "libertarian" critique of the *Disquisition* in fact originates in a certain understanding of the Lockean hypothesis of the "state of nature," not in an understanding of the political nature of man of the *Disquisition* itself. According to this writer, men have no such nature. In his own somewhat loose version of this doctrine, men are "born naked," and come out of the "state of nature" into society for the sake of property and convenience; society and government are based on property; and the science of government is best understood as economics, while the government itself at best is essentially a police force to protect accumulated wealth from thieves.[19] Calhoun's *A Disquisition on Government* is in this connection useful mainly for showing how the self-aggrandizement of the government actually works, and how it might be minimized, which is necessary if it is to be held to its high purpose of protecting property (including, doubtless, in Calhoun's case, property in slaves) instead of stealing it, although Calhoun does not push this important theory far enough. Ultimately, Calhoun's most fundamental or substantial omission in the *Disquisition,* then, according to the reasoning of this writer, or in the science of government as set forth by Calhoun, is the "omission" of the "state of nature" hypothesis as its own foundation. Without this foundation, Calhoun is, therefore, blind to the need first to determine the partitioning of the community or the constitution in the comprehensive sense, or, which is in this case the same thing, to extend the principle of constitution, the veto or negative power, much further than he does, namely, to every human being, not to say to every child at birth.

Yet, it should be mentioned in Calhoun's behalf that he extends this principle very far. The example adduced by Calhoun of the constitution of Poland, which answers formally in almost every way the wishes of the libertarian theorist, will no sooner emerge or endure for an instant on the putative basis offered by the schematic libertarian critique of the *Disquisition*, certainly, than it would on the reasonable appeal of Mill's *On Liberty*. Indeed, we can go even further and say that Calhoun is perfectly willing to extend these principles as far as they can possibly go. This is his original point in providing the example of the Polish constitution (paragraphs 108-109). According to him, however, the principle of constitution or liberty applies theoretically only to man (paragraphs 2-3), and in practice it cannot be gratuitously extended to all actual men, because of the natural inequalities of actual men. Nevertheless, it is a standard for all men in all times. Liberty is the highest end of man. It can be extended very far in its application to all communities, but, in like manner, circumstances of one kind or another may prevent—and, historically speaking, almost always have and will prevent—its genuine political emergence in most communities.[20] It is, rather, a supremely difficult task and not anything that can simply be lavished hither and yon, for it cannot be alienated, but only "lost." It has the character of a telos or reward, not of a gift. In short, it is not a thing that can be "extended" or "given," although it can be learned. Recognition of this fact and the popular confusion and zealotry concerning it—the highest human end—is the occasion for the *Disquisition on Government* itself for what Calhoun calls the "period of transition," which period will last until this question and the world itself is settled (paragraph 139).

Calhoun's rejection of the "state of nature" hypothesis, and his sustained argumentation concerning the moral and intellectual dimension of human nature in the full light of that rejection, is not any kind of omission but the substance of *A Disquisition on Government* itself and the solid ground of political science or the science of government, including the principle of constitution and the principle of liberty. To recall one feature of this argumentation, the term "property," so far from providing the basis of government or providing the essential ends whence the necessity of government itself is derived, does not even occur in *A Disquisition on Government*. Calhoun's whole introduction to the science of government as such can be read and grasped without even so much as having ever heard of individual property rights or of any of the modern theories of property. By its failure to have grasped these fundamental facts, one is led back again by the critique of the *Disquisition* from the viewpoint of libertarian theory to the beginning of the *Disquisition* as a whole, just as inexorably as one is led there again in the case of the "only remaining question" of the sociological or positivist survey of the history of philosophy as a whole. Positivism and economism do not provide solid ground for the science of government because they do not provide the true ground of knowledge or of liberty.

Finally, the same point is arrived at, also, via the other, anti-Lockean side of the Hobbist hypothesis. For, if we say, with Locke, that, coming out of the "state of nature," government is based on private property, what do we say then of those who have no property? All those others from whom the property owners have erected their government in order to protect all their property are left still in the "state of nature" without even any government to call their own. Upon what can they base government, then? Locke says they must stay in the "state of nature" while the others get to go have a government, and that this will be fine, because "it injures not the freedom of the rest; they are left as they were in the Liberty of the state of nature" (*Second Treatise*, 95). But they have moral and intellectual faculties to perfect just like the others. They need government, too. Are they merely to sulk about, forlorn, without any hope of a government for them? This cannot be. After a time, they will say that private property is wicked, and that they want nothing whatsoever to do with property, or anyway as little as possible, and that they are going to figure out a way to base government on just what they have that is already their own, and they will think how to base it on their own natural freedom or will. They have to do this, of course, but they will try to put a good face on it and make every virtue out of necessity, disparaging the others who already have a government as petty, hypocritical, insincere, and whatever else. But somehow, in due course, only the familiar government and property emerges, and the explanation for it amounts merely to saying—with the Englishman who so explained the British acquisition almost of the government of the whole world—that it came about out of absence of mind. This is essentially Rousseau's position. It turns out that while government should protect everyone from the fatal influence of property, in the meantime it should also be limited government. So all are again joined together, though with lingering recriminations, and we come to the same thing as in Locke, except as Calhoun is considering, that there seems to be no way to limit the government. It will not will its own limitation, because the will itself is unlimited. We may here catch a glimpse of the fact that Calhoun's limitation of government is, thus, ultimately the limitation of avarice.

As has been indicated, in the nineteenth paragraph, Calhoun is explicit about what he omits from his explanation of the only means whereby government might be limited. He will omit an examination of the constitution "in the comprehensive sense," including the composition of the society, on the one hand, and its culture, on the other—or any investigation of the particular organic arrangements communities may make or may have made as to their preservation and the perfection of their moral and intellectual faculties. These arrangements are the same as the purpose of the community as a whole and complete the community. He will limit himself to the constitution "in the strict and more usual sense," the organization or organism of the government itself. The internal organism of the government, that by which it is a government, is what is definitive of the community as a whole (cf. *Politics*, 1278b10-12). For the science of government as set forth by Calhoun, two things only are prerequisite, for these require and presuppose society: the intellectual and moral faculties—reason, as the faculty for knowing causes—and the knowledge or capacity for seeing that an excess of the selfish over the social feelings is evil. All see this, even if they would wish to exempt themselves. Of these, the former is higher rank or dignity. It is first in the order of things. It is to government itself as government is to community (paragraph 13). Hence it is not necessary to speak of constitution in the comprehensive sense in order to explain the principles upon which government may be perfected (paragraph 19).

Those who have been most diligent in the pursuit of this perfection in the past, among them Socrates in Plato's *Republic* and Hegel in the *Philosophy of Right,* have spoken mainly of the constitution in the comprehensive sense, yet they have not arrived at political science. This is because they too often see the community as a whole or the constitution in the comprehensive sense as an animate being that is like a man writ large. But it is not the same thing as man. The constitution in the comprehensive sense is an animate being, but it is an organism that is more complete than man and stronger than a man (paragraphs 16, 7, 6), and it is what constitutes man's place in the scale of being (paragraphs 13, 3). It is implied by the idea of man, and it is for man, as man is for it (paragraphs 14, 4). The dialectic rooted in rational nature, Socratism, loses too much of the specifically political nature of the human community in best understanding the idea of the human community as "philosophic kingship," or the soul of Socrates writ large, and thus according to nature. This is the underlying thought of Aristotle's critique of the theoretical communities of the *Republic* and the *Laws*. The dialectic rooted in rational history, Hegelianism, loses too much of the specifically political history of the human community in understanding the concept of the human community as the rationalized history of the community—even as the end of all Hegelianized history—or the soul of Hegel writ large, and thus rational. Neither of these ways arrives at human or political community, but make it "too much one." They seem to mistake their own reason or their interpretation of the community for the reason of the community itself. Rather, the political rationality of the community is present not in the logical heuristic or aporiatic method of Socrates (that is, in speech), or in the immanent or external disclosing or revealing method of Hegelianism (that is, in historicism), but, constitutionally, in the political organism's own process or method—which is more complete than in a man—of "checks and balances" in the "composition of power," and, particularly, the harmony of the "positive" and "negative" powers (paragraphs 54, 15, 9), in which its internal contradictions are resolved in moderation. This process and only this process is the true "reason" of state. The governmental process is the reason of the specifically political organism: the community as a whole or the constitution in the comprehensive sense.

It is for this reason that Rousseau speaks of *"terms"* and *"middle terms"* and *"correspondance"* [sic] in the definition of constitutional government. Generally, Rousseau says: "What is government? An *intermediate* body established between the subjects [parts] and the sovereign [whole] for their mutual correspondance" (*Social Contract*, III.i, paragraph 5, emphasis added, *Disquisition*, paragraph 14). And, more particularly—that is, in absolute or "unfree" governments, where a part rules the whole and the general definition is no more than a solipsism—constitutional government occurs as follows: "When an exact relation cannot be established among the constituent parts of the state [i.e., the whole]...a special magistracy is instituted [i.e., through human art] which replaces each term in its true relation, forming a middle term between the [legislative and executive]," or between the indivisible sovereignty of the whole and the government (*Social Contract*, IV.v, paragraph 1, *Disquisition*, paragraph 54). Rousseau calls this "special magistracy" the "Tribuneship," which appellation he takes from the Roman *tribuni plebis* and which, according to Calhoun, was specifically what formed the "solid foundation" or constitution of the *res publica* of Rome, the greatest human government. In other words, there is no difference in the principle of concurrency as taught by Calhoun and the "general will" as taught by Rousseau from the point of view either of the constitution in the strict and more usual sense or of the spirit of the laws of the constitution in the comprehensive sense—that is, from the point of view either of Calhoun's strict constitutionalism or of Montesquieu's understanding of the "general will" in his presentation of the spirit or logic of the laws regarding constitution in the comprehensive sense, whence Rousseau originally took the term. Rousseau differs from Calhoun and from Montesquieu in his not seeing, or his pretending or wishing not to see, that reason is first in the order of things, believing this inversion to be the only ground for going beyond Hobbism and arriving at the political nature of man. It thus comes about that he inverts the end terms while leaving the middle term in its correct or natural place, although, as Calhoun has sufficiently shown, it is impossible ever to arrive at the middle term from Rousseau's beginning, even given Rousseau's insistence on every kind of chance and happenstance or accident of history, because Rousseau's rejection of Hobbes does not go far enough. He does not reject the "state of nature" hypothesis and begin at the beginning with the social and political nature of man, and hence, like Montesquieu, with the reason of the community and the nature of government and the spirit of the laws. Therefore, because the reason of the community is seen most immediately and clearly in the organism and action of the government itself, Calhoun lays it down that it is not necessary to examine the logic of the laws in all the circumstances that Montesquieu has set forth in order to explain its principles but only to investigate the organism of government itself.

Having arrived at this point in our consideration, let us now turn at once to a consideration of the great constitutional examples with which Calhoun concludes the *Disquisition* as a whole, those of the Roman Republic and Great Britain (paragraphs 140-165), in order to see firsthand what he sets aside as unnecessary to the investigation begun in the nineteenth paragraph, and to prepare ourselves more readily for his disquisition on the constitution in the strict sense. The examples as presented are summations of the argument, including that part of the argument according to which no perfect constitutional government has yet been known. The examples of the greatest constitutional successes thus are also guides to their own imperfections, that is, to the original problem of constitutional government. In the examination of these constitutions, which are the most sustained examples that he provides in the work, what he includes as decisive for its bearing on the subject of constitutional government and what he considers unnecessary to it will be clear.

The concluding section of *A Disquisition on Government* (paragraphs 140-165) is the most exemplary part on the principles that are expounded in the work and, from the point of view of the *Disquisition*, the part that most obviously prepares the way for the *Discourse on the Constitution and Government of the United States* (paragraphs 140, 165), which follows upon it without any connective or referential remarks in the *Discourse*, and which, like the *Disquisition*, has no formal internal divisions.[21] Taking the two works together as one whole, this concluding section of the *Disquisition* would be the central part of the whole. There are no imaginary examples, or Platonic, Baconian, or Augustinian cities or islands. It presents no "philosophy of history." Using the "most remarkable and perfect" examples known of the kind, the object is expressly to demonstrate applications of the constitutional principles that have been laid down in the preceding paragraphs in the greatest aristocratic and monarchic regimes. The choice of examples is not representative of a "Western" bias in Calhoun's thought. Rome and Great Britain are, according to him, simply greater regimes than ancient or medieval or modern Egypt, India, China, Israel, Poland, or the Iroquois. They are more fully human in their development and display of the moral and intellectual faculties, although Calhoun does not praise their founders as he does those of the regimes listed in the eighteenth paragraph, and they are also more powerful. As a result, their political influence, as it were, knows no bounds. However, as Calhoun has previously explained, because of their characteristic social arrangements, which are absent in popular regimes, these are simpler constitutional applications than is possible in popular governments, which are necessarily more complex (paragraphs 121-122).

Paragraphs 140-141:
History and Natural Circumstances

THE CONCLUDING SECTION OF THE *DISQUISITION* EMPHASIZES MORE THAN ANY OTHER the historical and natural circumstances pertinent to all communities—their intellectual, linguistic, moral, economic, social, ethnic, racial, and geographic features, in short, the matter of the constitution in the comprehensive sense (cf. paragraphs 16, 119). However, for the most part, it does so only tacitly: the examples themselves represent this more comprehensive emphasis. Calhoun will abstract the elementary principles from all this mass. The penultimate and antepenultimate sections of the *Disquisition* have explicitly emphasized such features (paragraphs 108-111, 119, 130-131), and the immediately preceding section on global progress, which, as Calhoun emphasizes, is itself historical, closed with reference to constitutional government "under all the circumstances in which communities may respectively be placed," in other words, to every kind of circumstance (paragraph 139). The emphasis is implicit in the question of construction in connection with practicability (paragraph 99).

It appears from Calhoun's demonstration in the following paragraphs that in the greatest of constitutional regimes, ancient or modern, aristocratic or monarchic, the principles of constitution are the same. "The difference in their application resulted from the different situation and social condition of the respective communities" (paragraph 140). The principles of constitution cannot always be applied in the same way. "Every form of government is not fit for every country," as Montesquieu has shown once and for all (*Social Contract*, III.vii). In the cases here in question, the principles were modified to conform to these respective conditions, and these modifications are what account for the remarkable success of their respective peoples (paragraph 41, cf. paragraph 18). Both these regimes also exemplify the emergence of the people into constitutional participation in communities that are characterized by hereditary orders (paragraphs 124-125, 128-129). The object and the means of application are also the same—to blend or mix them and thus politically harmonize the conflicting interests of the community, and to achieve this harmony by taking the sense of each class or order through its appropriate organ, considering the concurrent sense or will as the sense or will of the whole (paragraph 141). For these reasons, of course, they do not and cannot exemplify the emergence of popular constitutional government, where the general will or the will of the whole and the will of the people are the same, and where a more refined and artificial form is necessary for ensuring equal majority and minority participation in the powers of the government.

Calhoun begins his presentation of the first example by saying that his first observation about the social division of the Roman people is "well known to all, the least conversant with their history." Indeed, everything that he says about Rome, as about Poland or the Iroquois, so far as the historical details are concerned, is "well known to all," at least to all who have ventured upon some study of their own of these subjects. Yet, characteristically enough, Calhoun's beginning differs considerably from those of other famous considerations of the grandeur or republic of the Romans, and perhaps more than one study could be made of his unusual presentation of this subject. It will repay the minutest exploration. We can here not pretend to more than outline the argument. His polite disclaimer about his brevity should not be allowed to obscure the fact that what immediately follows in the *Disquisition* is a constitutional outline or digest, an "abstract," of the whole political history of the Roman Republic, the study of which, including its imperial decline and fall, occupied Calhoun all of his life from the time he first learned to read.[22] It is probably accurate to say that this study occupied for him the place often given by his contemporaries to the French Revolution and similar subjects, although, to be sure, it is true that he also studied closely Burke's work on the revolution in France. Nevertheless France has given but little, whereas Rome appears, for Calhoun, to be *the* great regime (cf. paragraph 163). And, if we may be permitted to venture, the decline and fall of Rome, that is, the shadow of the vanished Republic, is, for him, all but equally "striking" (cf. paragraph 130). It is, from beginning to end, the greatest political event ever known, the greatest political story ever told. No matter what the age, Montesquieu says, "it is impossible to leave the Romans behind."[23] Wherever a regime worthy of notice may go, it will find Rome on her way back. Calhoun takes up this subject—the first great exemplification of constitutional principles—as he had taken up the question of constitutional government itself, by excluding what is extraneous to it, that is "Rome" in the "comprehensive sense," or, here, the Polybian sense, including almost all of the historical and political detail. With the object immediately in view, "it is not necessary to enter into a minute account" (paragraph 143, cf. paragraph 19), Calhoun says, of any large part of it. The student must bear in mind all that Calhoun has said up to now on the subject of what is not necessary, as well as his proviso that his accounts will be brief (paragraph 140).

Paragraphs 142-150:
The Republican Constitution of Rome

OF THE NINE PARAGRAPHS THAT ARE DEVOTED HERE TO THE ROMAN EXAMPLE, THE first three concern the fall of the Tarquins and the oppressive interval that followed. The following three are on the emergence of the plebian tribunate and its character. The final three are devoted first to summary praise of Rome under the tribunate, then to its decline into party strife, and, finally, to various patrician institutions in light of the power of the tribunate. Calhoun sees the

Republic and hence Rome primarily in the light of the tribunate (cf. Cicero, *Laws*, III.19-26).[24] However, only the central paragraph (146) describes the concurrency of the Roman constitution, as flowing from the *lex sacrata* and the *concilium plebis tributum*, as "the solid foundation of Roman liberty and greatness."

Calhoun begins not with the founding of the city or the division of the tribes or with the claim of Livy that the Twelve Tables was the fountain of the whole law or the claim that it was the body of the whole law or the *mos maiorum*, but with the plain fact, known to all, that the Roman people consisted of two classes, the tax-consuming class, or patricians, the noble rich, and the plebeians, the vulgar poor or tax-paying class (paragraph 33), between which was drawn a line of distinction as strongly marked as that between the Tarquin dynasty itself and the populus. Calhoun stresses in his first sentence that intermarriage between these classes was prohibited.[25] A history of Rome could be written, and in a sense has been written, as annotation to this opening sentence.[26] It is at least as effectual a beginning place as others that have been suggested. Patrician indignation toward Tarquin oppression, which was of the same sort they visited upon the plebeians and others themselves, led to the overthrow and expulsion of the monarchy, which left the government exclusively in patrician hands and, as soon as fear of a Tarquin restoration passed, the patricians ushered in a reign of "oppression and cruelty" surpassing that of the Tarquins.[27] Loving their own honor more than the city, not the Tarquins but the patricians were the worse tyrants. The character of tyranny in this connection is set forth in Shakespeare's *Lucrece,* on the rise of the patrician power.[28] Throughout, Calhoun is silent about Servius Tullus or Publius Valerius.

It is at this point in the prehistory of the republican emergence in Rome — that is, the point where Calhoun says that "it is not necessary, with the object in view, to enter into a minute account of the various acts of oppression and cruelty" to which the *plebs* were then subjected (paragraph 143, first sentence) — that Machiavelli says in the *Discourses on Livy*, "I shall not pass over in silence the disturbances that occurred in Rome from the time of the death of the Tarquins to that of the creation of the Tribunes...for these Tribunes were established as the most assured guardians of Roman liberty." "If the troubles of Rome occasioned the creation of Tribunes, then they cannot be praised too highly" (*Discourses on Livy,* I.4, first and last sentences). Machiavelli continues at length in the *Discourses* on the point that not absolute tyranny but the tension and conflict between the patricians and the plebeians was good for the republic. Machiavelli is more silent about oppression and cruelty. Calhoun restricts himself to a description of the increasing impoverishment and indebtedness of the *plebs* under the rule of the tax-consuming class, which he here actually calls "savage provisions," by which he means not merely unjust (i.e., partial or incompletely just) but ignorant and inhumane, or brute, in short, tyrannical (paragraph 143). The impossibility of legal recourse from certain impoverishment and debt, a sort of patrician "Roman system," as it were, were essential provisions in the increasingly unendurable regime of this period, and its abominations were suffered to continue for less than a generation.

The next two paragraphs (144-145), on the increasing spiritedness of the Roman plebes, are drawn by Calhoun directly from the passages of Livy's *Annals of Rome* on the period of the plebian secession. Calhoun's narrative of the "old soldier" in these paragraphs — "squalid, pale, and famished" — is surely the most extraordinary description to occur anywhere in the *Disquisition*, and reflects the Livian or Machiavellian character of all his paragraphs on the Roman Republic. It was, in Livy's account, the appeal of this decorated veteran that ultimately led, under a certain Sicinius, to the secession of the plebes from the city and, aiming only at release from patrician oppression and not at political power, to the contemplation of founding a new city of their own.[29] After violent threats and desperate uncertainty, the alarmed patricians finally sent an envoy, the plain Menenius Agrippa, to treat with the withdrawn plebeians. He finally secured their compromise with his famous speech "The Belly and Its Members," referring to patrician grain prices, as well as to the fact that the body politic cannot subsist without all its parts.[30] After this appeal, the plebes consulted and consented to return only on condition of participation in control of the powers and honors of government. This compromise issued in the *lex sacrata* and the organization of the *Concilium plebis tributum*, and, with them, the foundation of the republic (paragraph 145).

These actions, then (and those above all of the moderate Sicinius) were the true origin of the Roman Republic (paragraph 146). Its solid foundation was at last laid in the concurrent and joint participation of the whole Roman people in the powers and honors of government, the patricians having the positive power in the Senate and the plebeians the negative power in the Tribunate. This simple change converted the regime from an absolute into a constitutional government, providing the solid foundation to be afterwards matured and perfected (cf. paragraph 120). The negative power is the crucial element (paragraph 54). "The tribunship, [that is, the negative or veto power], wisely moderated, is the strongest support of a good constitution" (*Social Contract*, III,v, third paragraph). There is no stronger support.

"A superficial observer," Calhoun observes, would suppose a concurrent government feeble, impracticable, dissolute, and inglorious, because he would forget that the positive power is everywhere and always ready; it is the negative power that is rare (paragraph 147). The result, then, is strikingly otherwise (paragraph 148).[31] For the only time before or since, the various and diverse countries lying about the Mediterranean Sea, and beyond, were unified, a thing as striking then as it would be today.[32] The Roman conquests "elevated the Roman name above all others," provided for the establishment of Christendom, which continues "to the present day," and lasted for almost two thousand years, until, its formative influence having already reached as far as Kiev in the north and nourished the beginnings of the modern humanistic Renaissance in Italy in the West, the Eastern portion of the empire finally fell to the Turks (cf. paragraph 108: "Christendom"). All this is due, ultimately, to the Roman constitution, and thus most particularly to the plebian tribunate, which formed the constitution in the republican government. But so little is this far-reaching legacy and fame its true glory that Calhoun does not even allude to it again after the middle of the paragraph. According to him, the conquest of however many "insignificant" states—"whose names and existence would have been long since consigned to oblivion had they not been preserved in the history of her conquests of them"—is merely incidental and does not add up to true glory or to the glory of Rome. Save for her constitution, Rome herself—Rome under the Tarquins or under the patricians—was but one of these same insignificant states, however many times she conquered them. (In the same way, by the standards set forth by Calhoun, not merely the Volscians or the Aequians but the likes of Babylon and Persia and the rest are insignificant. Calhoun's only mention of the Turks is in reference to their defeat, twice, by Poland. It is precisely and even above all in this context that Calhoun's reference to the Iroquois as "deserving notice" is to be understood.) The central features of the summary praise of the Republic here offered are those of the substitution of devotion to the whole in the place of devotion to a part, the united strength of the whole in emergencies, and the elevation to power of the wise and patriotic (cf. paragraph 97). In this way is nature united with liberty. This is the true glory of Rome, and not merely the everlasting legacy she left as testimonial of it. One should therefore not be distracted from the true glory of Rome and its effectual cause, which is justice and moderation in a time of chaos, by the glory of its great legacy in the manner of a superficial observer. That is, one should not mistake the mere love of glory or recognition, which is common, for the true cause of glory, which is the intelligent love of the common good, and which is rare (Cicero, *Pro Sextius*, 45).

These and the other internal features Calhoun mentions, the moderation of internal conflicts, the mixing and harmonizing of interests, and virtue, are what is owed by all the Romans to their constitution, that is, to the principle of concurrency or what Rousseau in this sense, following Montesquieu, calls the "general will." The "general will," that is, the will of the whole, is indestructible (*Social Contract*, IV, i), but it cannot become actual without the solid foundation of the constitution. This, then, is what the Romans owe to their constitution. What all posterity owes to the Romans, the humanizing influence of Roman laws and institutions (including Roman writings), is due, likewise, to the Roman constitution and the extension of Roman authority (cf. paragraph 18, end, also paragraph 110, end). Her "imperishable renown," in short, all that distinguishes Rome above other regimes is due to her constitution, and her constitution is due, in turn to a wise and concessionary course adopted at the time of the plebian secession. It resulted thanks not to "cunning," including the "cunning of reason," but to the moderation of the plebeians and the patricians (especially Sicinius and Agrippa) and to the fortunate turn which events then generally took. Had it been otherwise, and an appeal to arms been made, "whichever order might have prevailed," whether the plebeians or the patricians, it would have resulted in cruel and petty tyranny and ultimate extinction under others, whether neighbors, Carthagenians, or Gauls, as the expulsion of the Tarquins actually had done. (Cf. Montesquieu, *Romans,* chap. I, paragraphs 14, 33). The actions of men, moderate men, influence the turn of events, including those which turn out to be the greatest or most fundamental events in human history, even if they can never simply control them. Moderation of this kind, political moderation, brings uncountable and unreconstructable blessings.

However, the Republic fell. "What is called a body politic is a very equivocal thing," Montesquieu writes in the most obviously Calhounian passage of his *Considerations on the Romans*:

> the true kind is a union of harmony, whereby all the parts, however opposed they may appear, cooperate for the general good of society — as dissonances in music cooperate in producing overall concord. In a state where we seem to see nothing but commotion there can be union — that is a harmony resulting in happiness, which alone is true peace. It is as with the parts of the universe, eternally linked together by the action of some and the reaction of others.[33]

But the body politic is not eternal, and Calhoun notes that such extinction ultimately occurred in any event, centuries later, even after Rome was raised to "a height of power and prosperity never before equaled" is not due to the tribunate itself. Given the patrician Senate, the plebian tribunate formed the republican constitution, although, admittedly, in the process of time it, too, became "one of the instruments" by which Roman liberty was overthrown (paragraph 109, *Social Contract,* III, iv, paragraphs 5-8). However, this had nothing to do with the tribunate but was the result of what Calhoun significantly calls "new dangers." The "new dangers" are the theme of this paragraph. The new dangers are the new territories. The new dangers are not simply new but are "new" only and primarily in the particular sense that they are the dangers represented to constitutional government by its own success.[34] As explained by him, these new dangers were the many social changes which arose in the relations of the patricians and the plebeians as an indirect consequence of the constitution and against which the tribunate furnished no effective guard. They arose in the process of time within Rome itself. The tribunate fully accomplished its original end of protecting the plebeians against patrician oppression and abuse of power, and therewith the whole against a part, the sovereign from the executive, but it could not withstand the social changes that grew out of the increased wealth and dominions to which it led and that undermined the political relation of these orders. Hence the constitution decayed (paragraph cf. 119 end).

Calhoun identifies two related causes of the corruption and dissolution of the tribunate, neither of which has anything to do with Machiavellian *fortuna* or with Providence. These are crucial to understand because the art of government itself depends upon a clear knowledge of them.[35] These causes are, first and decisively, external and, then, secondarily but fatally, internal to Rome, yet both arise from the original internal success of the constitution, which led to the original extension of Roman authority and dominion. Externally, the tribunate could not protect the people in the new territories to which Roman authority was carried, because its reach did not extend to them, and who were then typically plundered by the consuls and proconsuls. The patricians merely extended what had been their former absolute or preconstitutional rule in Rome outside of Rome, where it was unchecked. As Montesquieu says, "So great was the share the senate took in the executive power, that, as Polybius informs us, foreign nations imagined that Rome was an aristocracy."[36] This policy, which in general is praised by Machiavelli, will ever prove fatal. The constitution must extend as far as the authority of the government extends. Otherwise, not only the constitution in the strict sense but also in the comprehensive sense—the political whole—will necessarily be subverted by the aggrandizement of the government interest. The indestructibility of the "general will" depends on the health and stability of the political whole of which it is the general will.[37] The new territories were often numerous and wealthy, and provided Rome with new citizens as well as many resources. Internally, the tribunate could not protect against the resultant debasement of "the people." (Calhoun characteristically does not distinguish between patricians and plebeians in this respect. He is not concerned about any class or interest except as it bears upon the whole of which it is a part, which must be the first object in view.) The formation of factional parties bent on possession of the government "irrespective of the old division of patricians and plebeians," which innovations increasingly superannuated the object of the tribunate, and hence the constitution, led in the end to the overthrow not of the plebes or patricians but the whole of Roman liberty.[38]

In a particular sentence not to be overlooked Calhoun refers to the "eminent individuals" who struggled to restore the primitive Republic (cf. paragraph 124). Like the description of the old Roman veteran four paragraphs earlier, this reference is unique in the *Disquisition*. It represents the highest praise in the *Disquisition* after that of the wise and good men earlier singled out in the eighteenth paragraph. It points not to certain peoples or countries or governments but explicitly to certain eminent individuals. There are more individuals in the Roman example than anywhere in the *Disquisition*. Rome is where human individualism finds its true peak. Calhoun characteristically does not name the names of these eminent individuals. He observes that the Republic then had decayed to the point that it existed in reality only in this small but patriotic body of individuals and the hope of their endeavors, and who sacrificed their lives on its altar and their names to its name (c.f. paragraph 105). This thought and its formulation is drawn from the opening of the central book of Cicero's *Republic* (V. I. 1-2, cf. *Pro Sestio*, 21). The names of these eminent individuals are well known to all, "the least conversant with their history," as synonymous with the name and greatness of the Roman Republic, and its virtue and nobility. To say nothing of other things, those who are conversant with their history will necessarily be led to think above all of the orator who had so unforgettably prosecuted senatorial abuses in the provinces as an indictment against the Senate and Rome itself in his accusation of Gaius Verres that Burke modeled his own impeachment of Warren Hastings and irresponsible British rule in India on that procedure. He is the noblest Roman, the most eminent individual simply. A minority of patriots may exist even in the most ferocious and corrupt periods. Their action, whether moderate or extreme, may not be sufficient to influence the immediate turn of events. Men, however good, however wise, however eminent, cannot control events (cf. Cicero, *Laws*, III, 30-32).[39] Yet, even in defeat they may prove themselves equal and more than equal to them, and the virtuous and noble efforts of these men will ever equal Roman renown.[40] *"Moribus antiquis stat res Romana virisque."*

It is on this occasion, too, in the *Disquisition*, the description of the collapse of the Republic from before Marius and Sulla to Pompey and Caesar into despotism, that Calhoun for the only time uses the word "sad." It recalls the example that immediately preceded Calhoun's first mention of the Republic of Rome (paragraphs 110-111). There is a profoundly tragic quality in the greatest expressions of human achievement, however sweet. Yet, on the former occasion, the end had come from defeat by foreigners; in this case the defeat suffered is from within. Despotism was by then sadly necessary because "the Republic had in reality ceased to exist long before," namely, as the tribunate became less and less able to fulfill its original function. Instead of extending the blessings of the constitution, the interval was as feral and corrupt as the absolutism of the Tarquins or even the patricians had been. The problem is similar to that generally presented by an extended republic. In order for this state of things to have been avoided in Rome, it would have been necessary originally to have carried not merely Roman citizenship into the new territories, as was done, but to have extended the original Roman constitution itself into the new territories. Not being extended into the continually added territories, the fate of the constitution of Rome itself is foregone: in such circumstances it is a matter of time. The extension of the citizenship, then, to say nothing of the influx of new populations, itself merely becomes another and more aggressive agent of the disease, rather than a stabilization. To save the constitution, it would have been necessary for perhaps some sort of joint or federative constitutional government to have been adopted, or for the tribunate to have been extended in some manner to the conquered peoples, or, in short, for an altogether more complex constitutional form to have been applied. Without this, all other wisdom and valor notwithstanding, the end of the Republic was more necessary than the beginning. As it was, the new territories and all the new wealth and citizens they represented could not be politically assimilated or embraced in the community, and hence the community itself in the course of time was gradually absorbed into an imperial monarchy (cf. paragraph 130), that is, into one man.

It will be noted that Calhoun's presentation does not exactly parallel the presentation of Montesquieu on the central issue. Montesquieu's considerations on the Republic pivot in the career of Pompey the Great and his criticism of Cicero (*Romans*, chaps. vii-xii), the latter being incomparably the most eminent of the individuals to whom Calhoun refers. According to Montesquieu, Cicero absorbs the Republic into himself as much as Caesar. The Montesquieuan critique of Cicero in the central chapter of the book in terms of *amour de soi* and *amour-propre* provides Rousseau with his fundamental understanding of human nature and his orientation to what is therefore first in the order of things. It is Montesquieu's understanding of Cicero that Rousseau has taken into the "state of nature" in order to return with perfected ancient or republican virtue. Rousseau's critique of Cicero in the *Social Contract* is almost literally the same as Montesquieu's critique of Pompey, which introduces and culminates in the critique of Cicero (IV.6). What is called Rousseauism is thus originally or at its deepest root an attempt at the final critique and correction of Cicero, or the resolution of the "problem" represented above all by Cicero. This interpretation is the "true" Rousseauan "state of nature," and the critique of the character of Cicero is what provides the clue, for him, of man's original nature. Montesquieu follows Machiavelli in his interpretation.[41] After Cicero, the thought and character of the West has perhaps always gone according to whether the interpretation of Cicero has been more of Boethius or of Jerome, more Erasmian or more Machiavellian.[42]

Thinking of the inevitable end of the Republic, Calhoun recalls us once more to the fact that it was the plebian tribunate that had been the formative element in the republican constitution (paragraph 150). It was not the only element. The Senate, which was the principal patrician organ, perhaps could not have itself been expected to be easily adaptable to the new dangers without corruption. After all, if unchecked power corrupts, to paraphrase Acton's paraphrase of Calhoun, then unchecked patrician power in the new provinces provided every opportunity for corruption. Originally, the Senate is of the most particular character—the most peculiarly Roman, character—and hence apparently the least generalizable or common.[43] It did prove flexible and assimilative, and was steadier and more consistent whereas the tribunate was apparently more irregular. Even so, its corruption would seem of less moment to the constitution than the corruption and superannuation of the tribunate, if these things could be separated. For its part, the Senate was easily able to protect the patricians from any oppression or abuse of power from the tribunate. Looking toward the community in the comprehensive sense, that is, particularly toward the plebes from the point of view of the Senate, Calhoun identifies six important elements of patrician authority and control of the plebes, half of which are primarily religious and official in character and half of which are political or official. The religious features of the patriciate are mentioned only in connection with their political features. Calhoun follows Polybius (VI. 56. 6-12). However (unlike Polybius, but like Montesquieu and Rousseau), he stresses that the leading Senatorial power was the emergency power of appointing a dictator during periods of imminent danger, as this is the best way of insuring steadiness and consistency in such periods.[44] Together, Calhoun concurs that the powers of the Senate and the tribunate constituted "an iron government," but he returns to underline the point that without the tribunate that government was "one of the most oppressive and cruel that ever existed" anywhere at any time, while with it, "one of the strongest and best." Apart from other examples named in the *Disquisition*, the only ancient constitution that compares with Rome in these terms is Sparta, which Calhoun does not mention here at all (see *Discourse*, 393; Polybius, VI. 50. Cf., Rousseau, *Social Contract*, III.15.9-10).[45]

The patrician features are mentioned last by Calhoun because the patriciate deserves to be mentioned last, and the patrician censorship last of the last. The patriciate is the constitutional channel for the "new dangers" which vanquished the whole people. The censorship, whose leading responsibilities included management of the census and hence, above all, stewardship of the rank of citizenship, became as superannuated as the tribunate, and, so far as that goes, citizenship itself.[46] In order to see the particular failure of the patrician element in the constitution, a failure against which the plebian tribunate could not guard, and hence to grasp more clearly the "new dangers" to which Calhoun has drawn particular attention as leading to the failure of the constitution, which are the highest theme of this section of paragraphs, it is helpful to investigate further when it was, "in reality," that the Republic had ceased to exist (paragraph 149). Calhoun himself does not say precisely when it ceased to exist, except to indicate that it was in fact long before the great deeds done by its gallant rear guard, and that it was in no part the fault of the plebian tribunate. As a constitutional government takes time to mature, it also takes time, more or less time, to pass away completely (paragraph 25). Constitutional government has a long tail. It is not surprising that we find the terms "multi-cultural" and "multi-civiliza-tional" first used in this context. Hence one must investigate not the interval between the end of the Republic in reality and the establishment of the Empire, which Calhoun describes, that is, the Social Wars, but the period between the actual beginning of the Republic and its effectual if not formal demise in reality, and in connection with which Calhoun speaks primarily of the "new dangers." To begin this investigation, we may turn first to Calhoun's immediate sources in order to become more conversant with his history.

Calhoun's reading of Livy's *Annals of Rome* and of Machiavelli's *Discourses on Livy* in the Republican paragraphs of this section is easy to see, yet it is for this reason that his reading of Polybius is far less easy to see. This is because he does not see Polybius through the eyes, so to speak, of Machiavelli, or in the light of the *Discourses*, which is so easy for us to see, but, rather, he sees the *Discourses* in the light of the *Histories*, which we can barely see. Those who see the Republic or Polybius (or Livy) primarily through the eyes of the *Discourses on Livy* and its borrowings from Polybius may have difficulties due to inattention or to Machiavelli's own persuasiveness. Yet, perhaps Machiavelli's agon is not immediately with Livy but with Polybius, whom he follows in the beginning but does not mention, and above all Cicero, whom he mentions in the beginning (*Discourses*, I.4). For those who have such difficulties, we may for the moment set aside Polybius and yet perhaps arrive again at the same thought merely by observing that Calhoun here goes far beyond Livy, whom he follows most easily and literally in the Republican paragraphs. It happens that Livy's original *Annals*, which tell the story of Rome up to the time of Octavian, break off, as they have come down to Machiavelli and Calhoun and to ourselves, abruptly at the battle of Pydna and the celebration of its triumph (*Annals*, xlv). The remaining books have disappeared. It happens that Polybius himself, who was taken to Rome in consequence of it, begins the crucial part of his *Histories* with this battle (*Histories*, iii. 4-7). According to Polybius, it was the victory at Pydna which finally established once and for all the "universal" and forever unsurpassable power of the Roman empire, the empire of the Republic.

It may be useful to consider the battle of Pydna in the perspective in which Hegel saw the battle of Jena. It is the "end of history" event before the fact, as it were, in connection with which Polybius presents his "natural history" and the necessary cycle of all regimes. At any rate, for Polybius, it is the end of the Republic event before the fact. It is fair to say that Calhoun had a much higher regard for Polybius than is generally found today, and that he admires Polybius even when he differs with him or fails to follow him. Whether this fact is ultimately due to how the *Histories* may have been understood and taught in Calhoun's own time is a matter of conjecture. Polybius follows Thucydides (cf. *Histories*, i. 1; Thucydides, I. i.), and Xenophon (cf. *Histories*, iii. 4. 12, *Hellenica*, VII. 5. 27), and Plato (cf. *Histories*, vi. 47, 7-10 and context; *Timaeus*, 19b-c and context). But he especially follows Thucydides, the most expert writer on war, who had the opportunity to see the war between the Athenians and the Spartans, the "greatest motion" in the world from both sides.[47] For his part, Polybius, an expert on rule, had the opportunity to see Roman imperial rule, the rule of the world, from both sides, that is, the side of the rulers and the side of the ruled (*Histories*, iii. 4. 1).

It is true that this is not the beginning theme of the *Histories*. The beginning theme of the *Histories* is "how and because of what kind of constitution" Rome achieved world dominion, a theme Polybius explores with care. "Who is so thoughtless and so irresponsible as not to wish to know by what means, and under what kind of constitution, the Romans succeeded in subjecting nearly the whole inhabited world to their sole rule in not quite fifty-three years, an event unique in history."[48] The *Histories* is written not primarily to those "who are so thoughtless and so irresponsible," but primarily to those who are both thoughtful and responsible. That beginning theme becomes also how Roman world dominion would be preserved, of whether Roman dominion of the world was just (*Histories*, iii. 4). The *Histories* is addressed to thoughtful and responsible world rulers, or at least potential world rulers, who may, however, like Polybius, actually be ruled. These themes are connected by such Polybian comments (as distinct from, say, Scipionic comments) on fate of empire as refer to the fateful (Carthagenian) belief "that there is one method by which power should be acquired and another by which it should be preserved; they had not learned that those who preserve their supremacy best are those who adhere to the same principles by which they originally established it" (X. 36. 2f., cf. Montesquieu, *Romans*, IX end).

The aim of the *Histories* is the understanding of empire and world government, including whether these things are necessarily cyclic and foreordained, or are to some extent open to human influence and choice, and including what is necessary if they are to be open to human influence and choice.[49] This theme, what we may here call the Polybian theme, is the highest theme of the last section of *A Disquisition on Government*, not only the paragraphs on the Republic of Rome. It is, however, not the highest theme of the *Disquisition*, if only because the last section is "pragmatic." It is the highest theme of Calhounian pragmatism. Calhoun has already indicated that these things are in principle not foreordained, only in practice the most difficult things (paragraph 14). Calhoun is a pessimist, so far as his pragmatism is concerned, and perhaps the most "pessimistic" as well as thoroughgoing and consistent exemplar of the much celebrated American pragmatism, but even the most complacent historians freely admit that he is by no means merely pessimistic.[50]

It is possible to be precise about the end of the Republic according to Calhoun, by working our way back to the beginning of the constitution in the light of what he has said. In so doing, we certainly will not be far wrong if we place the crucial period of infection around the time of the new constitution of Sulla, which attempted to restore the strict, pre-republican patriciate. Among other things, its reconstruction of the government explicitly and severely restricted and all but dissolved the plebian tribunate, as well as the censorship. The *lex Valeria* made Sulla dictator not, as Calhoun says in connection with the original institutions, "for a limited period," but "indefinitely," Caesar *avant la lettre*. But the Sullan constitution itself cannot be the beginning of the end of the Republic. Sulla in the end stepped down from the dictatorship, and, if the tribunate was superannuated given the new citizenry and organization of Rome, it might have been well to dissolve it. In any case, the Sullan constitution was short lived; it is already more an effect or symptom of what had gone before, the Social Wars and the rivalry with Marius, who had extended the citizenship, that foreshadowed the rivalry of Pompey and Caesar.[51] Nor is the introduction of new cults the source of the new dangers. The rival parties do not want justice and virtue themselves; they want to rule. They want the distinction of controlling the honors and powers of government. The new cults and their new understanding of virtue and justice do not significantly affect this. Besides, as is well known, the elder Cato saw at the time that the new understanding was, so to speak, "false philanthropy." The Greek schools—Epicureans and Stoics, and others—(sometimes *contra la lettre*) do not want justice and virtue themselves, they want pleasure, or rather, pleasure and peace, or rather, pleasure with maximum honor and peace.[52] The introduction of new foreign cults is itself merely another symptom or effect of new Roman conquests.

Calhoun's "new dangers," the dangers proceeding from the strength of the constitution as well as its weakness, are presented in Livy's *Annals* under the reference to "*nova sapientia,*" the "new wisdom" not of foreigners, much less new Greek schools, but of the familiar old patrician ambition and avarice, loosed and newly rationalized or masked *avant la lettre* as *raison d'etat* in the affairs of foreign conquest, and in Polybius' *Histories* under the rubric of "pretexts," the specifically Polybian addition to Thucydidean "causes."[53] The "new wisdom" emerges from the strength of the constitution (and hence ultimately, at least in a sense, from the plebian tribunate, which forms the constitution) because constitutional governments are much more vigorous and powerful than absolute governments (paragraph 96: "augmented power"; Montesquieu, *Romans*, IV, 15). It emerges from the weakness of the constitution (and hence ultimately from the patriciate) in the handling of this power in foreign affairs, where the patriciate is constitutionally unchecked (*Disquisition*, paragraph 149). The new wisdom is the unchecked voice of a new party (*Romans*, IX, 8). Thus, the origin of the "new dangers" against which the constitution was unguarded, and hence the beginning of the end of the Republic, occurs when the idea of world empire and the law of selfish interest is loosed in the Roman victory at Zama (*Histories*, I. 3. 6; cf. XXXVIII. 22;). This aim was achieved in the Roman victory at Pydna, after which there followed "a period of transition" (*Histories*, I. 4. 12ff; cf. *Disquisition*, paragraphs 138-139). Plutarch, in what may be called the domestic perspective, most closely approaches Calhoun in his presentation of the debate between Scipio Nasica, according to whom Rome needed a rival or balancing power in the world, and Cato, according to whom Carthage should be destroyed, on the declaration of the last Punic war. For Polybius, according to whom the Roman constitution is that of a complex mixed regime, the position is carefully stated in his own "ecumenical" perspective by the famous *novis homo* and tyrant, Hiero of Syracuse: "We should never contribute to the attainment by one city of a power so dominant that none may dare to dispute with it even for its own liberty" (I. 83. 4).[54] Ultimately, the "new dangers" point to the need for constitutional empire.[55]

Machiavelli recommends the foreign policy of the Roman Republic to princes.[56] This is a questionable recommendation. Calhoun has explained why this policy is inadequate. That which debases and corrupts the community in its foreign affairs must debase and corrupt the community in its domestic affairs. Hence it can only lead to "falsehood, injustice, fraud, artifice, slander, and breach of faith," followed by all their corrupting and debasing influences, subverting the constitution and culminating in Caesarism within as well as without (paragraph 76). At the same time, it restricts the human intellectual faculties essentially to instruments of cunning, manipulation, and treachery. It is not enough to remonstrate that Machiavelli was himself a patriot who gave all this advice for the sake of the common good, for the means determine the end, and by these means there will be no common good. Nor is it sufficient to say that Machiavelli recommended using virtue as well as vice for the sake of glory, etc., for the Roman foreign policy itself neither did this nor, according to Cicero's speeches, did it have this effect; Rome was hated by those it conquered. Who could mistake what was merely the vice of the conquered for the true virtue of Rome? Its glory is empty. It traded gold for bronze. In the end, it "commanded armies that had forgotten Rome, and were degenerating into the manners of the Persians" (cf. Livy, IX. 18. 4). Its glory and renown passed to those eminent individuals who struggled past all hope against its abuses. Calhoun makes it as plain as he can that the difference between Rome and its insignificant neighbors is not its power but only its constitution (paragraph 148). In his interest either to restore Roman glory to Italy or to establish his own personal glory Machiavelli was right in his judgment of contemporary appeals to virtue and religion (paragraph 78 end), but he was wrong in his appeal to a new vice and cunning. The Roman glory depended not upon any special or lucky vice or cunning but upon the constitution. Hence Calhoun looks directly to the origin of the Roman constitution. That origin is quite common and humble, indeed, in Calhoun's striking description it is almost dramatically humble (paragraph 145). It could hardly be more humble. But just for this reason it is not special or unique, much less spun from some sophistical *nova sapientia*. What people can not equal this? The love of truth and justice more or less influences all, not excepting the most depraved (paragraph 105). Humility is not incompetence (cf. paragraph 14). Its origin was in plain reaction to oppression or injustice, in moderation, and in compromise. According to Calhoun, even though all the parties did not intend selfless justice, constitutional governments necessarily have their beginnings in justice, toward which compromise is the first step: they are necessarily as dependent upon actual justice and the openness to moderation of their own constitutive elements as they are upon the force of chance. Even dependent as they may be upon the promptings of fortune, these beginnings in the natural social as well as individual feelings are thus more than enlightened self-interest, without yet being as much as consummate wisdom and pure justice. But they may become wisdom and justice.

We are now at a somewhat better vantage for seeing the problem of consti-tution as it was seen by Calhoun. It concerns the relation of the constitution in the comprehensive sense and in the strict or more usual sense. Specifically, it occurs in the relation of the organism of the constitutional government, which is the voice of the whole (*vox populi*, paragraph 61) or the constitution in the comprehensive sense, to the internal mechanism of the government itself, the constitution in the strict sense. In other words, it consists in the internal tension of the "organic mechanism" that arises from the fact that the organism grows, in accordance with its nature (the Greek word for nature is a word for growth, for nature means growth from beginning to end), while the mechanism, which is a work of art, if not extended simultaneously with this organic or natural growth, remains the same (i.e., merely "mechanical"), and hence increasingly threatens to fail in its original or constitutional task.[57] Hence the perfection of government or constitution in the strict sense through its own success naturally leads, without statesmanship or the intelligent extension or adaptation of the constitutional mechanism, to its own decline. Thus the constitution in the strict sense depends ultimately on the science or art of government, that is, on virtue or statesmanship.

We may note in passing that Calhoun has already shown that the constitutional problem is not on the level proposed by Kant in the "Idea for a Universal History from the Cosmopolitan Point of View," according to which "the problem of establishing a perfect civil constitution is dependent upon the problem of a lawful external relation among states and cannot be solved without a solution to the latter problem." This "idea" is merely an attempt to change the seat of authority and make that the government (*Disquisition*, paragraph 15). The perceived need for a categorical government is in the political expression of categorical ethics and amounts equally to an empty or infinite regress. Whether it is resolvable or not, the problem is otherwise. The twofold constitution of our nature which makes government necessary also makes political constitution necessary if the ends of our nature are to be perfected in society. As Calhoun elsewhere says, "divided within, we present the exterior of undivided sovereignty": "within we are many—to the world but one."[58] As Montesquieu says, following Polybius, "Greece maintained itself by a kind of balance, but the equilibrium was upset by the coming of the Romans" (*Romans*, V). At the same time, therefore, the perfection of the government or constitution in the strict sense, to the extent that it is successful, necessarily points outside of itself, as one among many, to empire of some kind.

On the showing of the Roman example, there are two difficult problems arising from this. The first of these is that the internal perfection of the government promotes the extension of the political whole. Controlling the parts internally, it does not control the ambition of the few. The problems arising from this can be avoided and even work to the common good so long as there is an effective external check or limit in the world (such as relative isolation or Carthage). When and if this check is overcome, however, then the failure to extend the constitution at the same time that the authority of the government is extended, leads, as Calhoun has indicated, to the dissolution of the political whole or constitution in the comprehensive sense and, therewith, the government or constitution in the strict sense. It is with this thought in mind that Montesquieu quotes Livy to the effect that the world cannot contain Rome, but, as a result, now Rome cannot even defend Rome (*Romans*, III, penultimate paragraph). The result was the fall of the Republic and, ultimately, that there is no tyrant but neither is there liberty: that is, there is what Locke will "discover" as "civil society," which Montesquieu presents in the Romans under the terms "commercial power," vanity, and "imperial rule," and Plutarch presents under the term "ecumene." Hence either the authority of a republican government should not be extended at all, or, if it is extended, then the constitution should be extended also. Otherwise, the extension will merely prove oppressive and cruel and gradually bring the constitution itself to an end. In the case of Rome, before the authority of the patricians was extended outside it the constitution provided an "iron government" for the whole and, so long as the tribunate remained effectual, it was one of the strongest and best governments ever known.

Paragraphs 151-161:
The Monarchic Constitution of Great Britain

After reference to the iron government of Rome with the tribunate, Calhoun turns to Great Britain without further remark. Roman power, as we know, had reached Britain before the time that the Empire was established. Calhoun, however, makes no reference to Roman Britain.[59] Nor does he refer to Catholicism or Christianity, Celtic or Roman (Bede). He begins his "very brief sketch" of the British constitution not with Roman Britain but with the Norman conquest. However great the political story of the Roman Republic and its influence, there is nothing particularly Roman about constitutional government as such.

Because of the Roman experience, it was necessary to speak of foreign affairs in discussing the corruption and decline of the constitution of the Roman Republic. As Calhoun has previously explained, aristocratic constitutions are less suited to empire than monarchic constitutions. The Roman Republic itself is an example of this fact (paragraph 130). The influence of the British empire, though as yet shorter in duration, is already greater than that of Rome, and, for Calhoun, it has not yet reached its maximum effect. Britain rules the world more completely than did Rome, and also more of the whole world than did Rome. She rules the world in principle by ruling the ocean itself, the Homeric or poetic limits concretely or literally referred to by Glabrio. Britain is mistress of the seas. The sun that illumines the whole world never sets on the British empire. The route of the sun itself is the limit of the British Empire. The world commerce of which Calhoun has spoken earlier and which diffuses all the blessings of modern civilization is primarily British commerce. The application he has described earlier of the recent discoveries and inventions to practical use is primarily British industry. Newton and Bacon themselves—and Hobbes, to say nothing of Locke, Hume, and Smith—are British. Modernity is British; Britain is modernity.[60] The name and influence of Britain rivals and surpasses those of Rome. There have been few who significantly resisted British power and still fewer who resisted successfully. The most powerful and "enlightened" absolute monarchy yet seen anywhere on land or sea fell before Britain. In considering the British constitution, Calhoun does not dwell on such facts. He does not so much as refer to them. The British influence in his own lifetime was certainly no less than it is in our own, but he does not here mention it. He does not refer at all to the sea, or to the importance of sea power in politics or history, shipping, travel, or, particularly, commerce, still less to empire, scientists, or philosophers. He does not refer at all to world government. True world government begins humbly, as we have seen, not with a bang but almost with a whimper (paragraph 145). First, one must learn to rule oneself. Hence Calhoun discusses the origin of the British constitution, which is exponentially closer than was Republican Rome to actual world government, much as though Britannia were merely another neighbor of Tarquinia.

All this is merely assumed by Calhoun because empire is less problematic for monarchic governments, including constitutional monarchies, than for other forms of government, whether constitutional or absolute, and because for Calhoun the immediate and crucial question always concerns not empire but constitutional government, or in other words because the question of world government is merely a blurred way of raising the original question of constitutional government. Government is necessary for society, including world or universal "society," should there be such a thing. It is in the concluding section of the *Disquisition on Government* that the full dimension and import of the first question of political science, the question set forth in the work's opening paragraph, becomes concretely clear.

It is not entirely true that foreign affairs is simply omitted from the sketch, for the sketch begins, after all, with explicit reference to the Norman conquest. Calhoun thus omits discussion of the whole period between the dominion of Rome and the Norman invasion. The fact that there are more Roman ruins in Britain than anywhere else except Italy is altogether ignored, as is the establishment there of the Christian religion. The Christian religion (i.e., the New Testament) does not choose constitutional government over other forms, and it does not protect constitutional government from declining into other forms: it does not care anything about the forms of government.[61] Britain is thus in no way an example of colonies from constitutional governments adopting a particular form of government (paragraph 66, last half). Yet, in ultimately arising from the Norman conquest, the British constitution ultimately arises from foreign affairs. It could seem perfectly distinct from the origin of the Roman constitution, then, were it not for the fact that the "old veteran" of the prior sketch is an old veteran of foreign wars. (Calhoun observes that he is a "decorated" veteran, and gives Livy's count of twenty-eight battles. The secession to the Sacred Mount included most of the army.) In the case of Britain, the Normans followed the Danes who had followed the Anglo-Saxons who followed the Roman Britons who followed the Celts. Britain is "multi-ethnic" from the beginning. Foreign affairs and all that follows in its train implicitly overarches the whole sketch.[62] With due allowance for these and similar kinds of elisions and omissions, then, it is fair to say that Calhoun's survey of British political history (paragraphs 152-155) implicitly if inimitably follows Hume's *History of England from the Invasion of Julius Caesar to the Abdication of James the Second, 1688* almost throughout.

William the Conqueror brought feudal law to Britain and established an hereditary monarchy and nobility (paragraphs 152, 129, first half).[63] The people or serfs "lived in a state of absolute slavery or villainage."[64] They were serfs. After 1066 AD, conflicts followed between the monarch and the nobles which led, "in the process of events," to the gradual elevation of the people to power. Perhaps Calhoun's surprising omission in the consideration above of the Roman constitution of any reference or allusion to the Twelve Tables will have prepared the reader somewhat for his omission in the consideration here of the British constitution of any reference or allusion to Magna Carta, the most celebrated British political document. According to Hume, Magna Carta (1215 AD) became in the course of time "a kind of epoch of the constitution." He admits, however, that the Great Charter "introduced no new distribution of the powers of the commonwealth, and no innovation in the political or public law of the kingdom." Indeed, Hume specifies that "though the royal authority was confined within bounds, and often very narrow ones, yet the check was irregular, and frequently the source of great disorders, nor was it derived from the liberty of the people." Like Shakespeare in *King John*, Calhoun ignores it altogether. At this time, the serfs or people did not yet possess, in Hume's terms, "a negative voice against the king and the barons."[65] Whatever its import must be, therefore, and whatever must be said about the circumstances of its achievement or about both its immediate and more remote consequences, Magna Carta is not the constitution. According to Hume, among other things, this famous deed "either granted or secured very important liberties and priviliges [sic] to every order of men in the kingdom; to the clergy, to the barons, and to the people." Although it was not established in fact for some time thereafter, this was achieved because "the barons, who alone drew and imposed on the prince this memorable charter, were necessitated to insert in it other clauses of a more extensive and more beneficent nature: they could not expect the concurrence of the people without comprehending, with their own, the interests of inferior ranks of men; and all provisions, which the barons, for their own sake, were obliged to make, in order to insure the free and equitable administration of justice, tended directly to the benefit of the whole community."[66] In short, then, Magna Carta, like, to take another example not mentioned by Calhoun, the Petition of Right, is a particular instance of communities in such circumstances beginning to settle on "some fixed law of action" by which "increased protection and security are acquired by all" (paragraph 129, last half: perhaps Calhoun has Magna Carta there in mind).

In the progress of events, the influence of the serfs became so palpable that they were summoned to provide delegates to a meeting of parliament, more as consulted observers than as an order, estate, or constituent interest of the body politic. Calhoun specifies two instances in this connection. The first fixed "on a more democractical basis than any which had ever been summoned since the foundation of the monarchy." This summons, for two delegates from each borough or town, which was "most remarkable," for this was "an order of men which, in former ages, had always been regarded as too low to enjoy a place in the national councils," came from the Earl of Leicester, who led a rebellion of nobles against the crown 1258-1264, in 1265.[67] The second summons, to the "Model Parliament," also for two delegates from every borough, came from Edward I, the "English Justinian," while he was engaged or wished to engage in wars with France, Scotland, and Wales, saying, "it is a most equitable rule, that what concerns all should be approved by all, and common dangers be repelled by united efforts." Hume stresses that those so summoned "composed not, properly speaking, an essential part of the parliament." However, the union of the representatives from the boroughs gave gradually more weight to the whole order, and by means of the necessary attentions of the king and the nobles, "the third estate, formerly so abject in England...rose by slow degrees to their present importance."[68]

From this "humble beginning" (paragraph 153), that is, originally an ethnically and religiously mixed population of conquered serfs and slaves ruled by stronger and more refined foreigners, the commons became an estate of the realm. The political foundation of the British constitution was thus laid in the Model Parliament of 1295. Participation did not guarantee more for the commons than it had for the nobles or for the crown, however, and in the long struggle among all of these to secure such guarantees—marked on the part of the commons in the course of time by such failures as those of Wat Tyler (1381),[69] Jack Cade (1450),[70] and of no "considerable person" (1525),[71] for example—the commons finally overpowered the other two estates in the period of colonial establishment in America, and concentrated all power in themselves in the Long Parliament (1640).[72] This concentration led to the organization of Cavalier and Roundhead factions, and to the involvement of France, Scotland, and Ireland in the ensuing English civil wars. After the establishment of the Committee of Public Safety in 1642, and the execution of Charles I, Stuart, the Parliamentary Army and Lord Protector Cromwell concentrated all power to themselves.[73]

Cromwell's son could not hold his father's power, and was deposed in 1659.[74] In the following year, the colony of Virginia proclaimed Charles II, Stuart, king, and the Long Parliament dissolved itself. The Cavalier Parliament met in 1661. The restored Stuarts expanded their dominion to Tangier and Bombay, and elsewhere in Africa and the Americas, while the relation between the estates remained unclear (paragraph 154).[75] In the Glorious Revolution, the crown passed from the Stuarts to the House of Orange and the House of Hanover. It happens that "the short interval" here mentioned roughly includes the period, on the one hand, of the siege of Vienna by the Turks and, on the other, the beginning of the European confrontation of the Iroquois, as well as the publication of Nathanial Bacon's "Declaration of the People of Virginia." The accession of the House of Orange was accompanied by the Declaration of Right.[76] In this manner, "through a slow but steady process of many centuries," one of the essential connecting threads of which throughout is the issue of taxation, or the conflict between the tax-payers and the tax-consumers, the British constitution was finally perfected on its original foundation, that is, the foundation of the feudal law (paragraph 155).

The survey given in the previous paragraphs (152-155) describes how parliament became the supreme political power in Britain and how all the factions or interests, including the last and least, came to partnership in the control of its action. The following paragraphs (156-159) take up the constitution in the perspective of Montesquieu, as a contemporary regime as well as the exemplification of a form of government. Calhoun's discussion differs somewhat from that of Montesquieu in most points.[77] He agrees with Montesquieu that it is a certain kind of monarchy, namely, a constitutional monarchy, and not a "parliamentary democracy," as some have supposed. This confusion is due in part to the reminiscence in the British constitution of Aristotle's description of "polity," in which the powers of government are mixed, or, as Calhoun says in the following group of paragraphs, "blended."[78] The monarch acts through intermediaries or agents. Calhoun is no more interested in regard to the British constitution in the judicial power than he had been in regard to the constitution of Rome, and he gives even shorter shrift here than he had earlier to any idea of the separation of powers (paragraph 52). The judicial power is *"en quelque facon nulle."* The judges must be independent of the judged (paragraph 156, cf. paragraph 102). The deliberative and magistrative functions are possessed to some extent by all the parts.[79] One should not become lost in legalism and lose all sight of the true powers that constitute the regime. The powers of the lords and commons extend virtually to partnership in the executive department of the government, as well. The powers need not be divided or separated at all so long as all participate in controlling them. The action of the government throughout its entire range may be fairly considered as the concurrency or action "in concert" of the whole (paragraph 156, *Spirit of the Laws*, XI. 6).

Hence, as we have indicated, a question arises naturally about the king, or about what in particular the kingship is in this case, that is, the exemplary case of constitutional monarchy. The following paragraph (157) takes up this question. The beginning of this paragraph is unique in the *Disquisition*. Calhoun has in mind among other things a certain error, but he does not notice this error in the way he has earlier noticed great or radical errors, or gravely mistaken opinions.[80] The imperfect and false view of the subject in question, the kingship, concerns the doctrine of divine right. The kingship does not represent divine right any more than does a numerical majority, but it does represent both natural and conventional might. In the British case it is reasonable. Calhoun explains that the king represents what Calhoun again specifies as "in reality" the strongest interest under every form of government in all civilized communities, the interest that grows out of the action of the government in the process of time, whatever the form of the government may be, and that is sustained by the ongoing action of the government. This is the government interest or class or party, as distinct from the people as a whole or the commons in particular (cf. paragraphs 29-36). In all civilized communities, the tax-payers and tax-consumers are the two fundamental classes of the community, who are in antagonistic relations with respect to the fiscal action of the government. The government interest is, naturally, strongest, and, naturally, it must be checked.

The strongest interest is naturally represented by a single head, for by this means the distribution of government honors and emoluments proceeds with the least discord and most unity (paragraph 158). The tax-consuming interest therefore tends to monarchy and unity, the tax-paying interest to democracy and variety. In Britain, the king represents the former, the House of Commons represents the latter (paragraph 159). To prevent the conflict toward which these classes or interests constantly and strongly tend, the House of Lords is interposed (paragraph 160).[81] It is the moderate and conservative power of the government. As part of the government party, its own condition can only decline if either of the conflicting estates comes to dominate the other. Thus, the nobility and its parliamentary organ, the House of Lords, make the British constitution.

Paragraphs 161-165:
Comparison of the Great Constitutional Governments

THESE PARAGRAPHS COMPARE THE EXEMPLARY ANCIENT AND MODERN, ARISTOCRATIC and monarchic constitutions, conclude the *Disquisition* as a whole, and introduce the extreme example of the *Discourse*. He refers twice more to the brevity of his sketches (paragraphs 161, 165). Brief as they are, they are sufficient to demonstrate the conformity of the regimes discussed to the constitutional principles that he has set forth in the earlier sections of the *Disquisition*. The first paragraph (161) of the comparison is devoted to the fortunate origin of these illustrious constitutional regimes; the second (162) to the principle of concurrent government and its effects in both; the third and fourth (163-164) to the relative effects in this respect of each; and the last (165) emphasizes the differences between popular constitutional government and both of these forms. Of these, the penultimate paragraph is one of the longest in the *Disquisition* as a whole and the most important of this group.

Both the Roman and the British constitutions originated in circumstances arising from the conflict of interests aiming at removing oppression or at control of the government (paragraph 161). Calhoun has indicated that as a rule ordinary human wisdom and virtue is unfortunately insufficient for the founding of constitutional government. That they had some idea of it is shown by the speech of Agrippa in the former case (even if Livy's is an imprecise account) and the remark of Edward I in this case (even if it is dissembling). Better government was certainly intended in so far as, for their part, the outs wished for more justice and, for theirs, the ins wished for stability and preservation. As Calhoun has shown earlier, the more these wishes can be extended the closer to constitutionalism affairs will become. Yet, constitutional government was not their aim, but their own immediate interests. Hence, while wisdom and moderation were necessary and present in both cases, so far as concerned the immediate objects, neither of these governments originated so much in them as in fortune or prompting necessity. Moderation provides unseen—extraordinary or even extreme—rewards.

Both the Roman and the British constitutions are constituted by an internal organism by which the voice of each interest is taken and unanimity is required for action (paragraph 162). The effects in both cases were similar. The conflicting interests were harmonized in the action of the government, attachments to the whole itself were strengthened, and all partial sentiments were commensurately moderated. Unity in adversity and elevation of the feelings of nationality were strengthened. Hence, most importantly, both developed physical and moral power to an extraordinary extent. In coming to this, Calhoun carefully distinguishes between the two constitutions on the basis of their respective organisms and historical circumstances.

In Great Britain, the orders are blended in the Parliament and its actions. In Rome, there is a positive and a negative power (paragraph 163). Each has advantages. Calhoun does not here mention any advantage in the case of Britain, but defers entirely to Rome. The advantage of the Roman constitution was to develop more fully public spiritedness, the love of country and the feelings of nationality. "Perhaps," observes Calhoun, Rome has never been equaled in this respect by any government, not excluding Sparta. The Roman Republic is of all known regimes the most public spirited. For this reason, in Rome, also, was more fully developed the power of community (paragraph 164). Everything considered, given the relative "state of the arts" in both countries, Rome developed more physical and moral power than Great Britain ever has or will. Calhoun admits that the power of Great Britain is "vast." Yet it does not equal the power that was developed by Rome. "Perhaps," he observes, Rome has not been equaled in this respect by any government, not excluding, in particular, Great Britain. Great Britain is inferior to Rome in respect to moral power. It is not in morality that Great Britain most excels. As Hume said, "It may be justly affirmed, without any danger of exaggeration, that we in this island have ever since [the accession of Orange] enjoyed, if not the best system of government, at least the most entire system of liberty, that ever was known amongst mankind."[82] But its morality and hence its liberty is inferior to the peak of Roman morality and liberty. The iron government of the Republic is the superior "system of government" from the point of view of love of country and moral power, and thus is decisively superior. "Hence the mighty control she acquired from a beginning so humble." Yet, that control in the end corrupted and controlled Rome, which was also one of the most oppressive and cruel governments.

One might suppose that it is in this respect and this respect only that the constitution of Great Britain is superior to the constitution of Rome. The British empire is equal to that of Rome primarily in extending almost to the whole world. The Roman regime began to show "marks of decay" as soon as she had extended her sway beyond Italy, while Great Britain holds an empire equal to that of the Roman Republic at its height without any sign of decay. This superiority is due to its constitutional structure, which is inferior to the Roman in point of spiritedness and morality. Its hereditary structure prevents factional conflict for the whole and protects against the corruption of patronage. As Calhoun observes in several speeches, patronage, especially as concerns the claims of patronage arising from foreign affairs, strengthens the British regime. The conservative element of the government, which is not limited to England, will use patronage to conserve the government instead of change it. Together, these causes render Great Britain the most capacious of all governments for subjecting extensive dominions, not excluding Rome, which is in other respects, as regarded from the perspective of the true ends of government, superior to Britain. With these advantages, Great Britain is the strongest government ever known, if not the greatest. She defeated the Spanish empire at her peak, the greatest modern religious power, and Napoleonic France, the greatest modern secular power. In short, with these advantages, Calhoun finds it "difficult, indeed, to assign any limit to its capacity in this respect." The rule of Great Britain could extend in fact to the whole world.

However, Calhoun immediately thinks of a certain limit that might be assigned. Such a limit is essentially internal. This is the lesson of the whole political history of the British constitution, born and bred, as it were, in the cradle of foreign affairs. In spite of the great internal strengths the British constitution has developed, the taxation that will be necessary to acquire and govern such vast dominions might prove too heavy a burden for the British laboring and producing population. Britain as well as Rome would then be "crushed" under the weight of so vast an empire. (Calhoun uses the same terms with regard to each example.) This leads to two considerations. The first is that Britain has not escaped and will not escape the necessary tendency that Calhoun has earlier explained of all regimes to divide into tax-paying and tax-consuming classes, and the tendency for the tax-consuming class to expand at a greater rate than the tax-paying class, thus more or less gradually or quickly subverting the original constitutional construction, if due care is not taken, by internal overextending the governmental power or authority (paragraphs 29-34). Once begun, this expansion has a natural tendency to promote itself. This tendency parallels the tendency exhibited so clearly in the example of Rome of the government to extend itself beyond the original construction externally by proceeding unchecked in foreign affairs. The Roman example represents this external tendency and its necessary effects if the authority of the constitution is not also somehow extended. In overcoming this external problem, Britain still has to overcome the internal problem. Secondly, if this is the case, Britain is ultimately not notably superior to Rome in regard even to the capacity to acquire and govern vast dominions (see Macaulay, "Warren Hastings"). In this case, Rome, with an equally vast empire and superior in public spiritedness and morality, is thus unchallenged as the supreme constitutional government. This thought necessarily leads us back to the question of the respective "state of the arts at the different periods," to which Calhoun drew attention at the beginning of the paragraph, in which Britain is unqualifiedly superior to Rome. British liberty nourishes this superiority above all, the superiority of the highest end of government, in the perfection of the human intellectual faculties, particularly instrumental or practical reason and the development of the laws that control the great agents of the material world, economics, and so forth.[83] Calhoun does not here address this question, except in explicitly setting it aside in order more accurately to compare Britain and Rome, although several earlier remarks in the *Disquisition* bear directly on it (e.g., paragraph 95).

With this thought in mind, let us briefly return to the fact that, in contrast to his presentation of the Roman example, Calhoun does not speak of any kind of cruelty or oppression in his presentation of the British constitution and the spread of its "vast" dominion, much less of the British government as one of the most cruel and oppressive governments ever known. Perhaps it is the case that, while Great Britain does not soar so high as the Roman Republic when possessed of the effectual plebian tribunate, neither does it sink so low as Rome without the effectual tribunate. Perhaps the British constitution is in this way a median kind of approximation of Rome, neither so high nor so low. This is an engaging possibility. A moment's reflection is sufficient to show, rather, that this contrast in Calhoun's presentations is due to the fact that the immediately previous section of the *Disquisition* – the section on modernity, which the example of the British constitution summarizes – has made it clear that in spite of the fact that Calhoun speaks openly of the "blessings of civilization," the "vast" spread of these dominions has also been and will be the most destructive, the most "annihilistic," that has ever been known on earth, and that this feature will continue to increase indefinitely into the remote future. Whole peoples everywhere will disappear, and, instead of either gradually becoming more British or "modern" or remaining what they are, will become nothing – or rather will become "proles" in the original Ciceronian sense of "breeders."[84] Where is the hope of any government of their own? To judge from the example of the British serfs, according to Calhoun, it may be six or seven hundred years into the future, if affairs go fortunately and moderation is abiding, which no one can foretell. The British ecumene is inferior also to the Roman *pax* in this crucial respect, which is the characteristically modern respect. We must here leave it at merely asserting that this is the reason for Montesquieu's apparently following Machiavelli's recommendation that the Roman foreign policy be imitated by modern monarchies. They need not destroy everything in order to preserve themselves.[85] (This was essentially the internal position taken by Solzhenitsyn in the *Letter to the Soviet Leaders*.) Yet Roman foreign policy will *not* be imitated in this respect. This is the characteristic feature of modernity. According to Calhoun, some kind of more humane and paternal system is therefore necessary if simple destruction is to be avoided during the whole period of transition, that is, of modernism.[86] Yet, this crucial consideration obviously can only be a secondary consideration. More importantly, constitutional government must be better understood in the first place, for one must first learn to rule oneself. As we have indicated, this recognition is the occasion of *A Disquisition on Government*. The natural tendency of constitutional government to expand is the particularly constitutional expression of the natural tendency of all regimes to decline, as Calhoun has previously explained, or the natural tendency of every community toward dissolution. It arises from the twofold constitution of our nature. It is for this reason that, according to Machiavelli, this expansion is simply necessary, that is, genuine vice is "natural" and, therefore, a "good," or at any rate necessary.[87] Machiavelli is wrong. Calhoun agrees, rather, with Polybius. It is a natural tendency, but it is not necessary. Constitutional government can, with the required effort, indefinitely if not eternally, calm or still or counterbalance the natural tendency to decline and death in the eternal cycle of regimes. It is open to human choice. The principles are eternal, if not the practice. The principles are divine, if not the practitioners. Nature can be countered, and hence completed in accordance with itself and perfected by man, but only if one holds fast to the principles of constitution. This is the only truly human choice there is: not to forsake liberty, to hold fast always to liberty, to aim always at liberty. Liberty is first in the order of things. Liberty is greater than death. The science of government is the true science of man because it is the logic of liberty.

Finally, we may note that Calhoun thinks of the limit on British dominion that is represented by the problem of taxation for the quite obvious reason that the issue of oppressive taxation had already provided one striking occasion in particular for the successful secession from Britain dominion and the repulse of British power, an occasion which presaged another, equally striking occasion. Great Britain, vast as she is, strong as she is, has been defeated—twice. Calhoun's study of the United States does not merely grow out of his study of Britain. At any rate, therefore, although the question for the moment remains open, it is clear that there is at least one power that can, if wisely guided, throw off British rule and withstand British incursions. The "Young Hercules" who carried the second war for independence on his shoulders will not have overlooked this.[88] That power is now growing more formidable. Wars are inevitable in "the present condition of the world" (paragraphs 17, 28, 138). Only constitutional government can ever hope to order or to some extent justify this fact. In the present condition of the world, the success of the popular constitution will determine whether the global alternative in future will be between monarchy and popular government, constitutional government "worthy of the name" or absolutism (paragraphs 131, 95). In the next and final paragraph of the *Disquisition*, Calhoun turns to the constitution and government of the United States.

The government of the United States differs more from each of the other constitutional governments than they differ from each other (paragraph 165). Although it is "an existing government of recent origin" and one need not be conversant with any ancient history at all to be aware of it, according to Calhoun, its character and structure deserves a fuller exposition than it has yet received. As Calhoun has previously explained, as the only purely popular constitutional government of any significance that ever existed, the government of the United States is more complex either than that of Rome or of Britain (paragraphs 121, 140), although, in its devotion to liberty and physical or material power, it is closer to Britain than to Rome, if it is not superior to Britain in this respect (paragraph 95).

This paragraph brings to an end, as abruptly and as modestly as it was begun, the text of the *Disquisition on Government* and Calhoun's foundation of political science, and turns toward the *Discourse*. This foundation raises many questions, but it is complete as we have it from his hand. We may leave it to others whether it is finally best described as more Aristotelian or Hobbian in spirit, or a kind of stoical synthesis of these, or as something more and something else altogether, ancient or modern, and for better or for worse. Certainly, it is Calhounian. It is presented from the beginning by Calhoun in the plainest and most manly terms. As understood by him, political science is a humane science; it is *the* humane science. It is true that it requires almost superhuman talents, capacities, and labors—qualities and attention that Calhoun exhibited in the highest degree—but we need to see that it is partly only because of this requirement that political science can be the most humane science, and hence also the most humanizing science. This is not insignificant in an age as remarkable for inhumanity as it promises to be for humanity. For this reason alone it is also a science that, if it will not save us, as the claim of so much scientism has become, in any age will unerringly find us, and introduce us to ourselves. The apparent abruptness of the conclusion of the *Disquisition* and his comparison of the great constitutions should not distract us from the fact that it was not in Great Britain or by Hume that the solid foundation of political science was achieved, but in the United States and by Calhoun.

CHAPTER FOUR

Political Science and Government

It is evident, then, that all those governments which have the common good in view are rightly established and strictly just, but those who have in view only the good of the rulers are all founded on wrong principles.

Aristotle[1]

Paragraphs 19-98

THE PROBLEM OF CONSTITUTIONAL FORMATION AND THE EXTERNAL CONSIDERATIONS which bear upon it are framed by Calhoun in paragraphs 15-18. The explanation of the principles of internal formation are presented in paragraphs 19-40 and summarized in paragraph 41. Taken together, the section begins in the paragraph where Calhoun says that he will limit himself to an explanation of the interior structure or organism of constitutional government as such (19), and ends with the paragraph beginning: "In coming to this conclusion, I have assumed the organism to be perfect..." (41). This explanation is followed by a digression on the fundamental difficulties which prevail with respect to popular constitutional governments and which have the character of common erroneous opinions (paragraphs 42-52, cf. paragraph 22). Calhoun then turns from his comments on these common opinions to resume the question set forth in the fifteenth paragraph (cf. 21). He resumes at the point that had been reached in paragraph 42, namely, with the axioms of constitutional government (54: "as has been explained..."). He does not there allude in any way to proceeding to the question "without further remark" as he had upon stating the unquestionable phenomena of our nature (paragraph 4), but, on the contrary, stipulates that he will now go on to speak "more fully." This explanation, which develops and completes points made in the previous sections, occupies the following forty-five paragraphs, beginning where he says, "I shall next begin to explain more fully" (paragraph 53) and ending—after several steps and a marked digression—where he says, "...as has been fully shown" (paragraph 98). Taken as a whole, the sequence completes Calhoun's answer to the question set forth in the fifteenth paragraph, the most difficult question of political science. It is this answer that we take up in this portion of our comments.

I. Necessity and Power—
The Art of Government:
Paragraphs 19-52

Paragraphs 19-20:
The Organization of Government
and the Common Good

CALHOUN EXPRESSES THE RADICAL DISTINCTION BETWEEN ALL STUDY OF INANIMATE things and political philosophy by the introduction in the nineteenth paragraph of the conception of "organism." The organism is the essential and characteristic unit or structure of the animate as distinct from the inanimate world. As he stipulates, organism here denotes the internal organization of the community or political whole and its parts, the government.[2] In this part of A Disquisition on Government, understanding the formation of the organism of constitutional government takes the place of or completes the understanding of the completed solar system in the opening part, the part devoted to nature and the whole as such. Each study represents determinate, predictable causal sequences that are analogous and united, although they are not the same.[3] Constitutional government is the artful completion of natural creation. In the organic as distinct from the inorganic world, order, however contingent it may be, proceeds from and in accordance with something that is primarily internal no less than external.[4]

The remainder of the Disquisition is devoted to explaining and exemplifying the principles by which the political organism may resist its own natural tendency toward factional aggrandizement and dissolution. This limiting or controlling organism is what distinguishes constitutional from absolute governments, a distinction corresponding to Aristotle's distinction between political and nonpolitical kinds of rule at the beginning of the Politics (1254a 1-16), and is what is strictly meant by the term "constitution" in ordinary usage.[5]

The subsequent examination must include consideration both of defense against outside enemies, on the one hand, and of sustaining the necessary vital processes, on the other (paragraphs 16-17).[6] The community is an animate being, albeit "artificial" or *leviathan*, and, in the whole animate world, a lifetime of successful defense against outside enemies or of optimum health, or both, nevertheless naturally and more or less quickly ends in the cessation of life processes and death. Death itself, then, cannot be a more essential evil for an organism than failure to fulfill ordained ends.[7] These entail each other. Death is the natural termination of the living organism, which loves its life. However, the artificial organism, the highest example of which is constitutional government, may truly last, as the exceptional governments Calhoun mentioned in the previous paragraph themselves all confirm. This is among their most remarkable achievements, and part of the reason that their names are known among us. Amid ubiquitous examples of absolutist governments on every page of history, it is the constitutional governments that have made a "deep impression" (paragraph 18, cf. paragraph 6). More than any other human thing, the thousand-year constitutions seem, by virtue of their steady endurance and influence, to imitate the divine thought or laws according to which the cosmos itself proceeds and endures. They are the greatest and most admirable of all animate beings, because they live longest, and the most perfect animate things within the cosmos, for they exhibit the most comprehensive ends. The core of Calhoun's political philosophy begins with the distinction between "community" and "government" as the fundamental distinction between convention, on the one hand, and nature, on the other. His definition of the constitution in its strict and ordinary sense as the internal process by which the resistance to its own organic dissolution is sustained resembles Aristotle's celebrated definition of the soul: the whole soul holds together the whole body (*De Anima*, 441b-413a). Calhoun's *Disquisition on Government* may thus be thought of as the strict examination of the soul of the greatest of animate beings, the constitutional community. If the admittedly imperfect constitutional governments already mentioned can have lasted so remarkably, there is no apparent reason why others, with luck, could not do so just as well or even more remarkably than they have done if they were equaled or wisely improved. Indeed, if constitutional government were perfected, there is hardly any internal reason to suppose that it would not last as long as the portion of the human race comprehended by it lasts, and even that in time it would not ultimately extend itself, by example and otherwise, to the human race as a whole.[8] After all, the phenomenon of government itself extends to the human race as a whole: all communities exhibit government.

Calhoun has distinguished between governments which counteract the tendency on the part of the rulers to oppress the rest of the community and those which do not counteract this tendency (paragraphs 13, 19-20). It is constitutional government that makes explicit and concrete what typically remains implicit and may only rarely become explicit in the idea of government as such—that all government is ordained and exists for the sake of the political whole and represents the decision and action of the political whole, and not merely what is called the "authoritative part."[9] The political whole and the parts that essentially compose it are the truly authoritative thing, that is, what Calhoun calls "sovereign" (paragraph 23). He thus presents the relationship of the rulers and the ruled, the political relationship, as the beginning place of the examination of constitutional government.

Paragraphs 21-28:
The Action of Government and
the Common Interest

There is only one way that the desired relationship may be brought about. The weaker must be strengthened in regard to the strong, and the strong weakened in regard to the whole.

Paragraph 21

According to Calhoun, the ordinary relationship of rulers and ruled as an antagonistic relationship of the strong and the weak in regard to the action of the government that springs from the same constitution of human nature that renders government necessary. The constitutional organism must consistently and peacefully modify the tendency of the rulers to oppression with the tendency of the ruled to resist. Hence, constitutional government may appear, in the first place, as a certain limitation or redistribution of power. In so far as the relation of rulers and ruled is a power relation, constitutional government thus means, in the first place, taking power from the powerful and giving it to the powerless so that power can successfully resist power. It makes the weak like the strong in this respect. The successful systematic and peaceable resistance to power essentially means *participation in power*. In so far as this relationship is a common tendency toward selfish aggrandizement, it means the negation of the power to aggrandize. It makes the strong or powerful like the weak in this respect. The first step necessary in bringing about this relationship is the establishment of the fundamental principle of the responsibility of rulers to ruled. In accordance with this principle, constitutional government thus tends to equalize or "mix" the rulers and the ruled, or to place them in equilibrium with respect to the decision and action of the government. It makes it hard to say unequivocally who are the rulers and the ruled, or who, politically speaking, are the weak and who are the strong. It politically equalizes the parts, that is, the rulers and the ruled, with respect to the operation or process of the whole. The principle of responsibility of rulers to ruled, or right of suffrage or of representation or of participation, by whatever name it is called, is the original claim or purchase of the whole upon the part.

The twenty-first paragraph is the first in the *Disquisition* in which Calhoun uses the term "the people." "The people" takes the place of the distinction between the rulers and the ruled. For Calhoun, it does not identify a part but the whole. This mixture, the people as the communal or political entity, can be achieved, according to him, only by first establishing the principle of responsibility of rulers to ruled. Otherwise, the "people" is not the communal entity or the whole people but only parts. As he is speaking of the constitution in the strict rather than the comprehensive sense, Calhoun is thus here only implicitly speaking of a popular government in a community without artificial orders or classes of any kind. This is the most extreme or radical form of government. The same point could be made, as Calhoun elsewhere indicates, with respect to other arrangements and forms (e.g., paragraphs 121ff.). Here, the claim of the ruled upon the rulers or of the many upon the few is the same as the claim of the majority upon the minority. It is the right of the numerical majority. "It is an established principle of politics and morality that the interest of the majority is paramount to the interest of the few. In fact, it is a principle so radical that without it no system of morality, no rational scheme of government, could exist."[10] Its establishment is therefore the first element in forming constitutional government. So far as it goes, this right is the same thing as the rule of the fundamental law: *quidquid populo placuit legis habet vigorem.*[11] Those who make the laws are themselves subject to a more fundamental law, the organism of the constitution or community itself, than those laws which they make and execute and which itself authorizes the execution of the laws they make. It is the organism itself, the political community, which is strong and which rules, as secured by the right of suffrage. Perfected, then, it is proper to say, as is everywhere said, that constitutional government, the *solus conditor legis*, means first of all the rule of law, or, what is the same thing, the equality of the parts before the whole.

At the very outset of his discussion of constitutional government, Calhoun stipulates that a certain "enlightenment" must characterize the people if the first step of the establishment of this principle of responsibility of rulers to ruled is to be effective in securing its end (21, end). Otherwise, on the same principle, some other mode (absolutism) must be sought. Calhoun introduces the term "the people" in connection with this requisite enlightenment, and almost simultaneously introduces the term "interests of the community." Although the right of suffrage or citizenship may be gradually expanded very widely over the course of time, and so forth (cf. paragraph 70), the enlightenment here in question is not a trait to be desired in the future, but is a given necessity prior to the exercise of suffrage itself. Neither is it a vague or random kind of awareness or learning, but it must extend to certain specific and interrelated ends about which Calhoun is quite clear. Without this characteristic, the right of suffrage is null and, even, dangerous (paragraph 22). This enlightenment on the part of the people (the political whole) is Calhoun's true emphasis.

First, the people must understand their own rights, the right to choose their rulers: the duty or responsibilities of the rulers and the right of the people to hold the rulers accountable to them, that is, they must understand the subjection of the parts to the whole. Second, they must understand the "interests of the community." He speaks in the same breath of "the people" and "the interests of the community" because they are different ways of regarding the same thing. The interests of the community are plural, not singular, whereas the people is one. Reason is primarily pertinent to wholes and operates primarily in terms of wholes; as a result, what it distinguishes as "sense perception" is itself also primarily perception oriented toward identifying wholes. Third, they must understand the motives of the representatives whom they have chosen and judge of their motives and conduct accordingly, that is, in light both of the first and second subjects enumerated. They must possess prudence and be able to exercise judgment. Together, these capacities provide effective control of those elected, but, without the latter, the result will only be what Calhoun elsewhere repeatedly refers to as "instructions" (as in an "instructed delegation," and so on), in one or another form, instead of intelligent, reasonable consideration of immediate policies and events by those elected.[12] It is in virtue of these capacities that the people as a whole, the "citizen body," also discharge responsibility, no less than the rulers, to the whole, that is, to themselves.

Paragraphs 22-23

The right of suffrage alone is, under the conditions just identified, sufficient to establish the effective responsibility of rulers to the ruled and to retain sovereignty unimpaired in the community. The "whole community" (paragraph 24), the constitution in its most comprehensive sense, is the rightful or natural and rational seat of sovereignty. It is from their participation in the sovereign community that the people or parts of the whole individually derive their rights. These are the only rights that are mentioned or recognized by Calhoun in *A Disquisition on Government*. They are "political rights," the rights of citizenship, the political right of ruling and being ruled in turn. The aim of the right of suffrage is only the effective retention of sovereignty in the whole community, instead of abrogating it to a part, the rendering of otherwise irresponsible rulers responsible agents. It poses the question "who should rule?" as the question "who are the citizens?" or "what are the parts?" (paragraph 23)[13] However widely it may be extended, whatever the conditions, the right of suffrage alone, properly guarded and executed, or the principle of responsibility of rulers to ruled, itself, and the retention of sovereignty in the community, may (like peace and security), also characterize absolute governments, for it merely checks the irresponsible agents, not the internal tendency of government to oppression and abuse of its powers and, therewith, of the social state to dissolution. Calhoun explicitly stresses that enlightenment and the right of suffrage alone are insufficient to establish or maintain constitutional government (paragraphs 22-23). The mistake here described is an instance of the problem already explained in the fifteenth paragraph, when the fundamental question of constitutional government was first set forth. The principle of responsibility of rulers to ruled can be but the necessary and not the sufficient principle in the formation of constitutional governments, no matter how enlightened the people or how effective, systematic, and peaceable the suffrage in securing its end (paragraph 22). It is only the "first step" (paragraph 21).

Calhoun speaks here of the community in three distinct but inseparable senses. Firstly and above all, the community as such is "sovereign." Its sovereignty or authority is one and indivisible, deriving from the composition of the community and the ends for which society is ordained. Secondly, then, he speaks of the community as "the people," that is, the "body of the community," or citizenry. The terms "the people," "the community," and the "whole" or "country" are equivalent. They each refer to the same thing considered in its different facets or aspects. Thirdly, he speaks of it as the diffuse and here undifferentiated interests which the people as such embody: "society" or the actual matter or "mass of the community" (paragraph 23). This locution is necessary because the essential distinction between rulers and ruled, which are the essential political interests, has been effaced by the principle of responsibility of rulers to ruled. It is especially in this latter aspect, the "interests of the community," that "power must be resisted by power—and tendency by tendency," as the primary venue of the antagonistic relation of the rulers and ruled (paragraphs 21, 23). All these usages follow the analogy of the form and matter of constitutional government laid down in paragraphs 12-14 above. The problem is the effective resolution of these interests in the action of the government.

Paragraph 24

The following paragraph is one of the few in the *Disquisition* beginning with the conditional "if." As was the case when he began an earlier paragraph with this word (paragraph 10), Calhoun here argues, or admits for the sake of argument, what is not. If human society were constituted differently than it actually is and has been constituted, that is, if its interests were actually all the same, the retention of sovereignty in the whole, expressed in the principle of responsibility of rulers to ruled through the right of suffrage, would be sufficient for government, and constitutional government would then consist, as is its aim, in enlightened deliberation about the "common interest of the whole." "But," he says, "such is not the case," and the division of labor alone, upon which society itself rests, to say nothing of other divisions, is sufficient to insure that no political community ever was or will be so (paragraph 25).[14] It is enough to see that, other things being equal, according to Calhoun, all see and admit that the best, that is the "wisest and most capable of understanding," should rule. This is the most natural and the most widely conceded claim to rule. The essential point is not original and is stated equally well by Madison, among others: "If interests are all the same, the only question is who is best."[15] In cases where "interests are all the same," the judgment of the majority rightfully rules. However, the interests of the community are diverse. The theme of "enlightenment" and who is "wisest and most capable of understanding," explicitly mentioned in these paragraphs (21 and 24), will ultimately issue in the subject of the common good, to which they point. The theme of the interests of the community (paragraph 21) already points explicitly to the subject of the common interest. Effectively resolving the "interests of the community" in the action of the government means properly relating if not uniting these subjects.

In the twenty-fourth paragraph, Calhoun counterposes the interests composing the community, in themselves, to the "common interest of the whole." Introducing the principle of responsibility of rulers to ruled, Calhoun mentioned that the electorate must be sufficiently enlightened to understand, apart from the rights of the people and the motives and conduct of persons, the interests of the community (21). In the following paragraphs, he had mentioned the "tendency toward oppression and abuse" on the part of the "mass of the community" (22-23). Here, he opens the twenty-fourth paragraph with the clause, "If the whole community had the same interests...." In the next paragraph, he speaks of the "various and diversified interests of the community." These interests are always plural, and have a tendency to come into tension with the "common interest of the whole." The common interest of the whole is the health and prosperity of all of the interests composing the community, not that of one interest only. Hence, whatever promotes this health and prosperity is in the common interest of the community. The community is, regarded in this light, a commonwealth. We may illustrate the distinction between the common interest and the common good by saying that the common interest is the field or dimension of the community in which, following Franklin's dictum, honesty is primarily a policy, that is, in which traits or virtues otherwise associated with the wisest and best human beings are essentially means to something else. The common good, understood as comprehending, the higher ends for which government is ordained, comprehends or contains the common interest, and may often be confused with it. It is the aspect of the community which is an end in itself. The contrast restores the distinction originally blurred or reduced by Hobbes in his equation of the desired or merely consensual and the good. As distinct from the common interest, the particular interests, which are interested always in protecting and promoting their own interests, have a tendency to come into conflict with others. Interests divide the people.[16] They compete with one another on political grounds. They say that whatever seems best for themselves is best for the whole or is the same as the common interest.

Paragraph 25

Calhoun is not concerned with any particular interests in themselves but only in their political import or in their connection with the tendency to oppressive action by the government, that is, as an essential aspect of the relationship of rulers and ruled. For what largely accounts for the prevalence of absolutism and for the failure to arrive at perfection in constitutional government is the fact that nothing is more difficult for men than to equalize the necessary action of the government in reference to the various and diversified interests of the community (paragraph 25, cf. paragraphs 119ff.). The observations made about particular communities in the twenty-fifth paragraph point to the character of particular interests, and, all of the reasons already cited in the sixteenth paragraph in connection with the division of the human race into many communities apply, as well, to the division of the community into many interests. They may be understood as social or economic classes and pursuits, guilds, or what Hegel calls "corporations," orders, estates, and so on (cf. paragraphs 122-123). Ultimately (paragraph 26), one may characterize their political relevance in terms of the relationship of the rulers and the ruled or of the few and the many. Their competition or rivalry characterizes every political whole. This rivalry cannot be resolved by the right of suffrage alone, to say nothing of appeal to the common good or the spirit of the law.

This condition obtains in all regimes in all ages, however they might be characterized, but it obtains particularly in extensive regimes, and, then, moreover, most intensely of all in precisely those extended regimes in which it is likely that the presumption may be widely held that the principle of suffrage itself is *the* constitutional principle, namely, in extended popular regimes (paragraphs 25, 22). Extension in time, more than in space, provides the essential problem. For in time, through the tendency of interests to come into conflict with respect to the action of the government, the community will become openly divided into merely major and minor parties. This is the tendency of all governments based on majority suffrage. It is inevitable in such cases that what is actually most natural to society, the diversity of interests, itself actually becomes at the same time the natural enemy of society, not to say of the law. Thus, it cannot be enough to say merely that constitutional government means the rule of law, as if this denoted the substantive rule of the whole itself, for such rule may merely denote the rule of the major over the minor part, or the usurpation of the whole. This is why Aristotle denominates the kinds of regimes in accordance with the major or authoritative part, except for the mixed regime, which he calls polity or "community."[17] In order to denote the rule of the whole in truth, constitutional government must mean, then, the rule not merely of anything that may be called "law" — outright conquest is often attempted "under the color of law" — but of a true or certain kind of law, and equality of parts before the whole.[18]

To begin to look toward the kind of law in question, constitutional law in the strict and ordinary sense, one must first note what it is not. It is not law understood either primarily as merely a public mask for private interests, etc., or as a well-intentioned or effectively only abstract or ceremonial statute, whatever the legislative or judicial or executive trappings by which these may have been arrived at. A valid (or constitutional) law must carry the authority of the whole community and be directed to the common interest of the whole community in accordance with the ends for which government is ordained. This is not a merely procedural question. It is true that the "human heart is reconciled to do many things under plausible covering that it would not openly avow," that the human heart is of a "deceptive character," and, also, that men are often given over to wishful thinking. Constitutional law must attempt to check such tendencies, but, as Calhoun here makes clear, they do not exhaust the problem. In a statement made elsewhere, he is equally explicit: "It belongs to the human heart that...power will be abused; and, what is most extraordinary, those abusing it will," in ignorance of the nature and character of constitutional law, "often not be conscious of the abuse."[19] The tendency toward "legalized" or "institution-alized" oppression occurs even—nay, especially and most dangerously, because initially unintentional and impalpable—"under the operation of laws concluded in general terms, and which, on their face, appear *fair and equal*" (paragraph 25, emphasis added).[20] By the time these cases become palpably inequitable, the political lines and all the rest are already drawn and rationalized in major and minor terms. Yet, however long it may take, this division will occur not only (Calhoun emphasizes "even") "without preconcert or design" to be, "fair and equal." In spite of appearances, in many cases, such a law will be unfair and unequal in its operation, for it is "an imperfection incident to all human laws that" the best worded act must comprehend many cases within the letter that are not within the spirit or intention."[21] The aim or intention of fairness and equality is, over and above the need for security arising from the individual or selfish feelings, the natural root of government arising from the "social or sympathetic feelings" (paragraph 9). To see further what this means, which is the same as looking more deeply into the true nature of constitutional law, we must look more deeply into the "principle or constitution of our nature in which government itself originates."

Paragraph 27

To do this, Calhoun turns from the non-designing lawmakers interested in fairness and equality of the previous paragraphs (25-26) to those who are more immediately interested in appearances and less immediately interested in laws that are truly fair and equal (paragraphs 27-28). The former may be thought of as in some sense the best men, relative to the latter, but they, the majority, do not fulfill Calhoun's reference to wisdom (paragraph 21, end; paragraph 24). They are not the "wisest and most capable of understanding." On the contrary, rather, they do not understand. He lays it down that hostile division would arise, even if there were *no* various and diversified interests in society, and thus either no necessary reason for government itself and, hence, for constitutional government, on the basis of any inequality of condition, pursuits, or interests in society, merely from the desire for individual prominence alone. This desire, the love of honor and distinction, is the ultimate and most distinctive expression of the self-centered feelings that, of all the animate creatures, are strongest in men (paragraphs 7-8): "in single honor, whether vile or worthy."[22] It is the bloom of brute or given human nature. Given the social nature of man, then, irrespective of all other considerations, or, if all other considerations were annulled in every conceivable way by the most perfect possible equality of condition, circumstances, and interests throughout the community, by unequivocally perfect social and political equality, or by constitutional government, the incessant desire of individuals for honor and prominence alone, that is, for inequality in some sense, would itself generate the necessity of government, and the attraction of honor and position represented by the government, the interest that is constituted by the government itself, would naturally generate the whole difficulty of constitutional government (paragraph 27).[23] This is the decisive "condition" in light of which all the other considerations here mentioned are secondary or derivative. It is not primarily a question either of the interests composing the whole, or of the metaphysics of the whole, on the one hand, or of "self-interest" understood as wisdom and virtue, on the other. There is no necessary conflict between, say, the agricultural and the mechanical interests as such, or producers and shippers, but only between excesses or the desire for aggrandizement on the part of men pursuing them.

Paragraph 28

It would be hard to exaggerate the importance of this desire for Calhoun. It is the furthest thing from a "mere" desire among others. In the following paragraph, he opens his discussion of it in the same way he had opened *A Disquisition on Government* itself, as though he were beginning again, or beginning a new aspect of his subject (paragraphs 1, 28; cf. paragraphs 74, 105, and context). In a sense it is fair to say that he is. The action of government centers around the interests of the whole community; the philosophy of government naturally centers on this, as well, but also and no less on this prominent desire. Where he had spoken of forming a "just conception" of what is always the nature and proper object of government, he speaks here of forming "a just estimate of the full force" of the private advantages in government today, "in the present condition of the world." This force is an all but irresistible force of attraction among those who are susceptible to it: it is "the high and glittering prize" (paragraph 76). Calhoun obviously considers some among these, ultimately the ambitious intellectuals of the future, as constituting at least a part of the readership of the *Disquisition*, not to say simply that the work is composed with them in mind from the beginning as representing the primary audience for the philosophy of government.

Beginning here (paragraph 28) at the beginning that is the most obvious and agreeable to most of those who have taken up the subject of government—with the elemental object of providing protection from internal and external dangers—he succinctly and for the first time in a characteristically modern way describes the role of government in what for a time became known in the West as the "military-industrial complex" and in the "East" (or "Second World") as the "armed organization of the proletariat," including the state police. This phenomenon alone is more than sufficient to insure that the state will not wither away into "society." All such questions as might pertain "in the present condition of the world" to the value and import of a standing army, for example, including police, are, to say the least, settled. Necessarily entailed in the role of the government, therefore, are all the familiar revenues and disbursements, including, it need hardly be said, government contracts and licenses, involved in its support and all the stations of influence and patronage attendant to its administration and management.[24] Calhoun merely describes what is now already the necessary or minimal extent of government, without reference to any other consideration than defense. It is a minimalist outline, which in practice must necessarily swell and grow. In the present condition of the world—a condition of unexampled progress in the arts and sciences, including unexampled progress in the application of their new discoveries and inventions to warfare—it is only reasonable to expect that these "vast establishments" can and will only continue to increase and consolidate or centralize (cf. paragraphs 132-137). This inexorable tendency toward centralization or consolidation and its accompanying absolutism is the prime characteristic of the present condition of the world.

The two great hostile parties that are ultimately formed in the struggle to obtain control of the powers of government, which struggle either explicitly or implicitly characterizes political life, are themselves primarily formed around men's desire for honor or personal aggrandizement, even where one might suppose matters such as the defense of the whole would override such concerns. They but excite them. (The Romans, in their wisdom, instituted the office of dictator.) In a paragraph that emphasizes necessary arrangements for defense against external threats in the present condition of the world, it is, and in a manner that is entirely consistent with what he has earlier laid down, the violent internal conflicts of the hostile parties that spring from these passions and not any external threats or special conditions that Calhoun explicitly calls "evil." He here refers unambiguously to "something depraved and vicious" (cf. paragraph 5), the "ambition of the aspiring and the cupidity of the avaricious." The excessive force of these passions is rooted in the selfish and not the sympathetic feelings, but, as the author has emphasized, this evil would not be corrected by an excess of sympathetic feelings (paragraphs 10-11). It would require knowledge and habit. Avarice taken alone might be at least checked if not cured by appropriate measures, including the criminal law, but what of unbounded ambition?

Part of Calhoun's aim in *A Disquisition on Government* is effectively to attract the ambitious and aspiring and, by appealing both to their ambition and to their capacity to understand, to show how to contract the gap between political virtue as it is ordinarily understood and hypocrisy as it is ordinarily practiced. The reason for this extraordinary object is that any corruption in the public morals, where vice may be more or less effectively checked, extends quickly and inevitably to private morals.[25] As we will be discover, he discusses the distinction between apparent and true virtue generally not in the conventional terms of "public" (as false or superficial) morals and "private" (as true) morals but in terms of apparently equitable but actually inequitable laws, on the one hand, and that between personal duty or honor in terms of the relation of necessity and liberty or self-mastery, on the other. The aspiration to true virtue must be prefaced by *A Disquisition on Government*.

With respect to the effectual formation of constitutional government, since the honors and emoluments of government are available only to a few of the relatively many who desire them or who envy those who have them, to say nothing of the whole population of the community, the evil in question is not remedied by the right of suffrage alone.[26] Furthermore, as has already been indicated (paragraph 25) even if it were possible to equalize these prizes in every way throughout the community, without debasing citizenship, or even if debasing citizenship were necessary to achieve it, the impossibility of equalizing the elementary fiscal operation of the government would itself irresistibly lead, if by a secondary or more indirect road, more or less quickly to the same evil. This is to say, as Calhoun explains, that the good intentions of the lawgivers implied in the earlier paragraphs, or the essential neutrality of the composing material interests in themselves, is insufficient, even were there no excess of private ambition.

Paragraphs 29-37:
Justice and the Operation of Government

The following nine paragraphs are devoted to explaining the inevitability of the division of the political whole into hostile parts as a necessary consequence of governmental taxation and disbursement. This section follows naturally the preceding paragraphs, 27-28, because the "vast establishments" and bureaucracies of the government and all that is related to their support, administration, and management will form the basis of the gradual coalitions of interests mentioned in the earlier paragraphs (25-26). As these establishments grow and proliferate, the government interest will grow and consolidate power. This is the modern tendency of government toward absolutism. "Taxation is at the base of the nexus between governors and governed."[27] Calhoun's doctrine is that the fiscal action of the government, even when coupled with the principle of responsibility of rulers to ruled or with the right of suffrage properly exercised and protected, will itself create this division, and thereby actively promote factionalism and vice, by augmenting the governmental interest at the expense of the other interests of the community.[28]

Like the honors and emoluments of governmental office, the operation of governmental taxation and disbursement cannot be equalized in the community (paragraph 29). Taken together, this redistribution of wealth represents bounties to some, the recipients of the taxes that are paid, and penalties to others, the payers of the taxes (paragraph 30). This is a necessary result if the fiscal action of the government is taken as a whole, or if one part of it, disbursement, is not expended outside the community or otherwise lost (paragraphs 29, 31). We note in passing that governmental projects of "foreign aid" outside the community that are carried on by contracts to domestic manufacturers, suppliers, and experts are, to that extent, an instance of the same operation. For the community as a whole to be in the same position as the government in respect to the fiscal action of the government, it would be necessary for taxation to be levied outside the community, for example, in conquered lands or territories, and the bounties equalized among all the parts of the community. In any case, as income is redistributed from some to others, the wealth and population of the tax-recipients (as a sector or interest or portion) of the community will increase, as against those of the tax-paying sector or portion (paragraph 32). Government fiscal action itself thus divides all interests, willy-nilly, and, therewith, the whole community, into "tax payers and tax consumers," which interests Calhoun calls the "two great classes" (paragraph 33), and whether quickly or gradually, alters the whole in every way (paragraph 25). The power of taxation is the power of the rulers to revolutionize the community, that is, the ruled, in their own interest. "This is the great and disturbing principle in all governments, especially those that are free, around which all other causes of political divisions and distractions finally rally."[29] These tax-paying and tax-consuming classes, the fundamental classes with respect to the fiscal operation of the government "and the entire course of policy connected therewith," are always in an antagonistic relation (paragraph 34). This is the true stage upon which is played out the history and the future of all "class struggle," which is to say, the struggle of the predominant interests of the community, and, ultimately, the struggle of the governmental interest against the community and the rulers against the ruled.[30] In this struggle is displayed the course of every regime, and this is the reason why human history is essentially political history, for government exists in all communities. In other words, it is the necessary fiscal action of the government, which is rooted immediately in the natural constitution of man, and not in particular institutions of property or privilege or anything else, that is the ineradicable origin of "class struggle." On the contrary, many of the most celebrated historical champions of the various "classes" have typically been drawn from some other class than the one they champion.

For all these reasons (paragraphs 22-35) it is clear that the first principle of constitutional government, the principle of responsibility of rulers to ruled or of parts to the whole, is itself not even achieved and sustained merely by the establishment and protection of majority right by suffrage. The tendency to abuse and oppression on the part of the rulers which is unaffected by the form of government, "whether it be that of the one, the few, or the many," of the numerically dominant portion is not restrained but loosed by the right of suffrage (paragraphs 36-37). Both the struggle for honor, which is first in rank (paragraphs 27-28), and the struggle of the two great classes (paragraphs 29-36) — Calhoun treats all these conflicts under the general term of "party struggles" (paragraphs 27-28, 35-37) — inevitably vitiate the self-sufficiency of this first step in forming constitutional government (paragraph 21).

In all forms of government, however perfectly these ends are conceived, or however perfectly formed they may be in accordance with their principles, there is necessarily a governing and governed portion or class, and in all, the tendency to abuse and oppression on the part of the governing is the same, unless checked by the principle of responsibility of governing to governed, whatever the numbers, estates, corporations, divisions, interests, orders, portions, parties, or classes in question. In particular, the right of suffrage alone does not suffice to establish the principle of governing to governed or to check this tendency. In government by the many a majority rules, "for the time," over the minority, just as the aristocracy rules over the people in a government by the few or as the monarch rules over the subjects in a government by the one. The only difference between the forms of government in regard to this particular is that, so long as all their respective principles are effectively sustained, the rulers in a government by majority-rule, unlike the other governors and governed, may for a time become the ruled, and the ruled may for a time become the rulers, without the intervention of force or revolution. The rulers do not actually change, but only relatively in reference to each other, as when one pretender to a throne or dynasty overthrows another in a government of the one. So long as the principles that are characteristic of each of these forms are effectively sustained, then, the respective forms of rule do not change. The community itself is ruled absolutely by the government interest or the coalition of interests that has captured it. Any minority is a would-be majority, a baby lion tending to grow into a mature one.[31] The Lockean regime of absolute majority rule, or the rule of the many over against the one, with the addition of government for the sake of protecting the property of the few against the many, is, in particular, insufficient to establish the fundamental principle of responsibility of rulers to ruled. Hence the establishment of the principle requires some further step.

Paragraphs 38-43:
The Principle of Constitution
and the Common Interest

There is no form of government by "all" or by the community itself, as a whole, and no responsibility of parts to the whole, except in constitutional government. Other forms are forms of absolute rule. "The true idea of a constitutional government is...a government of the whole—a government which should fairly express the sense of every portion, and thereby the sense of the whole, and not one that expresses simply the voice of the numerical majority, or the numerical minority. Either one of them would be the government of the part over a part, and not the government of the whole."[32] In the following group of paragraphs, Calhoun turns to this idea, the idea of constitutional government or the government of the whole, with which he will always be associated as the touchstone of his political philosophy.

Paragraph 38

He begins with consideration of "that principle which *makes* the constitution, in its strict and limited sense," the responsibility of diverse interests to the whole that restricts the action of the government as an agent only for some interests, including itself (paragraph 38, original emphasis). This is the "most important and least understood" principle involved in all of the questions embraced in the science of government. The problem is that interests must be organically or internally prevented from usurping the powers of government according to the principles forming the organism itself. It is a version of the problem of culturing an individual to choose the right when there is no external pressure on him to do so. The evil is this: take any population you like, with whatever culture and blend or variety of interests you like, provide for the right of suffrage or representation or participation however you like, and you will get (always assuming safety from foreign conquest), either immediately or in the course of time, like it or not, an absolute government ruled by particular interests at the expense of the community and subject to the familiar disorder and abuse to which all experience and almost every page of history testify.

Paragraphs 39-40

It is now evident what it is that the strictly constitutional provision must accomplish, and why it is necessary (paragraph 39). It must carry further the principle of responsibility of rulers to ruled than does the right of suffrage alone, which is necessary but not sufficient to establish and maintain the sovereignty of the whole. Beyond compelling the responsibility of the rulers to ruled, or in order to do so, it must also compel the parts of the community to be responsible to each other by compelling them to consult each other and receive separate and concurrent consent. It must prevent the usurpation of the necessary and ordinary powers of government by any interest or combination of interests for its own aggrandizement and, therewith, the dissolution of the political whole. Its first object is the preservation of the whole.

Without such a provision, all the educational refinements upon theories of mixed republics or commercial republics or small or extended republics or democratic or "people's" republics, however excellent these may otherwise be supposed, will not provide an effective remedy for this evil in the future any more than they have in the past, and will follow the same course without contributing anything to our understanding. The provision can, certainly, have the character only of an active limitation or restriction upon the abilities of any interest or coalition of interests in respect to gaining control of the government. Majority rule cannot effect this any more than can monarchic rule.[33] If it is genuinely to be effective, such a restriction can, just as certainly, originate only in the sense of each and every affected interest, and in its particular consent upon the action of the government. Taking this sense and establishing this consent requires an appropriate organism within government, and, he further emphasizes, if it is necessary for the purpose, an organism also within the community or social institutions as such, that is, outside the agencies of government and hence outside the constitution in the strict or ordinary sense, such as a division of the community into orders or estates or social classes. In such an instance, it would be necessary to enter into a consideration of the constitution in the comprehensive sense, including the history of the case. Calhoun admits that a popular constitutional government lacking such orders or estates is the most difficult and complex of all, but his whole thesis is that, however unlikely it may always be, in principle a constitutional government is possible in some sense always and amid any institutions, customs, and mores, whatever the difficulties and whatever form it might take, in accordance with the principles here laid down (paragraph 41, first half; cf. paragraphs 18, 108-111, 121-122, 139, last sentence). Otherwise, one could not properly speak of human nature or of the object of government. To whatever extent it fulfills its end, whatever form it may take, constitutional government always has the same effects. Social institutions, customs, and mores, are as variable among different communities as government is invariable in all communities.

Calhoun is here no more or less illustrative with respect to the right of concurrency than he was about the right of suffrage (paragraph 21). One cannot be without pointing to an individual instance, like the Roman tribunate. The provision in question succeeds or fails in any community just in so far as it prevents or fails to prevent the control of the government by a particular interest or combination of interests, or in so far as it promotes or fails to promote the interest of "all" and the perfection of the whole. The provisions of suffrage and concurrency together, representing the principle of responsibility of rulers to ruled and of each particular interest to the political whole, which are the principles of constitution, are, therefore, what constitute the elements of constitutional government. Together, they prevent the self-aggrandizement of the rulers and of any part of the community at the expense of the community, and hence they are sufficient both to counteract the government's intrinsic tendencies to oppression and abuse and to "restrict it to the fulfillment of the great ends for which it was ordained" (paragraph 40).

Paragraph 41

This analysis concludes Calhoun's consideration of the "difficult question" to which he had turned in the fifteenth paragraph (paragraph 41, first sentence). To arrive at this conclusion, he has assumed throughout that both the organisms of participation were reasonably perfect and optimally exercised (paragraphs 21, 39, cf. 43). In particular, he here explicitly assumes the community in all of its parts to be duly enlightened and deliberate, as he had stipulated twenty paragraphs earlier with respect to the whole people. He is speaking of the perfect political form and substance. Here, Calhoun turns to the question of the specific extent of representation. He had not specified the extent of suffrage in laying down that provision and its rationale. Here, he says that if the division of the powers of government is carried out in perfect accordance with the distribution of divisions or interests in the community, the whole community will be fully and truly participant in the government. What is called the compatible sum of all the various and diverse interests of the community would be the government. To this extent, at least, the government would be inseparable from the "common interest of the whole." Whatever the extent of suffrage for the sake of rendering government fully responsible to the governed may be, then, the "concurrent voice" should extend inclusively to "each and all" of the community's divisions and interests.

Such extension is, admittedly, difficult to achieve in practice. The obvious difficulty to which Calhoun draws attention does not impeach the truth of the elementary constitutional principles themselves, any more than in other cases. The sphere of elementary principles and that of practice are united in human life. The most one can do is to live in accordance with elementary principles, which means, in their application in immediate existence. The individual is not a principle but a character; human life is personal practice. The sphere of practice or life is thus the same as that of opinion, which is the natural human orientation toward elementary principles. Every opinion is an application, in act or imagination, of elementary principles. The active discrimination of application is the highest form of human life, ultimately, the life of the statesman.[34] In carrying out the responsibility of reducing the principles of the relation of the whole and the parts to prudential political affairs, one must not expect mathematic or geometric perfection. Time and circumstances vitiate such precision. Still, they do not render the general form so vague and imprecise that it cannot be grasped. It is sufficiently clear. (Nevertheless, one might wish that the subject discussed third sentence of the paragraph receive fuller notice.) The element of suffrage rests upon the principle of responsibility of the rulers to the ruled or the obligation of the part to the whole. That of concurrency rests upon the principle of responsibility of the many to the one. It represents, in other words, what is usually called the rationale of monarchy, minus the figure of the king. According to Calhoun, it is sufficient that the organism take the sense of "a few great and prominent interests only," ultimately the many and the few, to fulfill, in large part, the end intended by the constitution. However imperfect the organism may be, it will, to the extent of its perfection, diminish the tendency of government to abuse and oppression and increase the likelihood of its further perfection in the process of time.

Paragraph 42

The inference is immediately drawn that it is concurrency thus understood which itself truly and fully completes the intention of the provision or right of suffrage. Calhoun's discussion of this completion occupies the whole paragraph (42). The subject concerns also the issue of enlightenment. His reference to what may be "readily inferred from what has been stated" in the preceding paragraphs is not here merely an affirmation of the need for reflective attention to inference and implication which must attend the proper study of political things or the text of the *Disquisition* itself, but an indication also that the inference immediately in question is perhaps not yet a common one outside this text.

The organism of concurrency completes the provision of suffrage. Suffrage aims at collecting the sense of the whole community to form and preserve government, or put it in motion, yet it regards the whole in the aggregate as though it were one common interest, and takes only the sense of the majority in reference to the entire mass, which is to say, necessarily only the larger number and the strongest interest or combination of interests. This it confounds with the sense of the whole for which it purports to seek, while disregarding the consent of the smaller number and the weaker political interests or combinations of interests. Concurrency regards precisely this number and these interests. Neither provision is meant to prevent diversity or dissent within the government or the community, but, together, to take the consent of the whole community in reference to the action of the government. Diversity and dissent within each interest, on such issues as whether or not to combine with others for a certain purpose, say, although possible and even probable, is politically insignificant with respect to the action of the government in relation to every other interest, and hence to the constitution as such. Otherwise, it would be impossible to speak of any class, say, the mechanic or agricultural class, or of the rich or poor, or any other, or of a class interest in political terms. The aim of concurrency is not to represent each individual as such but each political interest, each interest in regard to the action of the government. Citizens of each interest would in that capacity be fully and truly represented in the politically significant respect through its appropriate majority or organ.

Paragraph 43

The two modes of representing the political will of the whole community, by the organism or right of suffrage alone or as aided by the organism or right of concurrency, each take, in a different way or sense, the "sense of the majority" (paragraph 43). The former mode considers the whole as having one common interest throughout, as though the whole were but a single interest writ large, so to speak, but in fact takes the stronger interests or combination of interests to represent the common interest. This is all it can do. Alone, it represents the rule of a part in the name of the whole. Hence, this is called the numerical or absolute majority. The latter mode considers the whole as constituted by different interests, which are in conflict in relation to the necessary fiscal action of the government, collects the sense of each one separately through its own majority or appropriate organ, and takes the united sense of all as the sense or will of the whole. This is called the concurrent or "constitutional" majority, because it more truly construes the sense of the whole. Although those exercising rights via either mode are the same, the political difference between the resulting kinds of "majority" is profound, and they cannot be confounded without producing "great and fatal errors." For these two modes, the absolute and the constitutional, provide two different majorities and, thus, two different modes or senses of "majority rule."[35] The subject deserves further discussion.

In coming to this proposal (paragraph 43), Calhoun's evident sense of the importance of the subject and of the gravity of the consequences that must follow in the wake of continued ignorance or misunderstanding of it is noteworthy. Even apart from his reference to "political discussion," his stipulation here at the end of this paragraph recalls Socrates' famous assertion in Plato's *Republic* that error and disharmony will characterize kingdoms until absolute monarchs are philosophers, and resembles the requirement that all citizens of a popular constitutional government, beyond understanding their own political rights and the community's interests and appreciating the motives and conduct of their agents or representatives, must become philosophers of government.[36] One is tempted to say that Calhoun plays Locke to Plato's Hobbes.

Paragraphs 44-52:
Important Common Errors on the Subject

The subject of the following nine paragraphs is common errors, most importantly, the error involved in confounding the "two majorities." This is the error involved in the notion of the numerical or absolute majority itself, the presumption that might is right. In developing this consideration, Calhoun interrupts the positive exposition of the concurrent or constitutional majority, to which he will return in the fifty-third paragraph, and, so to speak, enters the political arena. This section of paragraphs, which properly concludes or is appended to the investigation of the question raised in the fifteenth paragraph, is the first of the *Disquisition*'s three main excursions: the excursus on popular or common or vulgar errors: ordinary errors that are long-standing and fundamental. Each one of the excursions or digressions might have served as starting places if the *Disquisition* were a Platonic dialog.

Paragraphs 44-45

At this place, particularly, we are afforded our clearest glimpse into the character of Calhoun's manner of thought. For, according to him, the first and leading error, which he insists is a "radical" error—one which goes to the very root, is very common (paragraphs 44-45). It is, so to speak, the opposite of any error that might be involved in here and there overlooking some of the angels on a pinhead. It is a gross error. Thus, on the one hand, while he explicitly bases the science of government on the common or ordinary case (paragraphs 5-6, 13), on the other hand, he at the same time provides an extraordinary and radical solution for the most serious ordinary problem, which is *the* political problem. In arriving at this solution, he mixes the two senses of the term "ordinary" in the same way he does with the term "majority." What he identifies as our almost "universal experience," and hence unquestionably true and the necessary context of the science of government, he also identifies as, in truth and in fact, a radical error (paragraph 44) that leads illusion (paragraph 45) into delusion (paragraph 46). He makes these identifications on the basis of the radical and extraordinary science of government itself, which is "ordinary" in the sense of providing the true or proper order, or universal or common reason (paragraph 47), that is, on the basis of what is truly common and not merely individual and particular. If this is not an instance of the "appeal to heaven," or even an instance simply of judging one's own case, it is, nevertheless, an entirely monarchic way of proceeding. It is the implicit question, "Who is deluded?," that the *Disquisition* answers and explains in terms of the political whole, including the dominant part or interest, and before the bar of the whole, that is, the bar of reason. The intent of the *Disquisition* is to replace through plain teaching, that is, to lead toward enlightenment through reasonable conviction, the ordinary or most common opinion with reason by observing the rule of reason, only, as ordinary. It could be asked, on the same grounds, whether the effect is not, actually, to treat unequals equally and equals unequally. The ultimate cause of this undertaking is Calhoun's desire to promote (posthumously) the actual establishment here and now, "in the present condition of the world," when intelligence and the applications of physical science are so widely and increasingly diffused, that to which all human society and government in principle or naturally points, and his conviction that the *Disquisition* presents the only way in which it can be understood.

In setting forth the common errors in the context of which the science of government naturally begins and from which it must rise, Calhoun continues to restrict his discussion to the most extreme form of government, constitutional government of the popular form, "in contradistinction to governments of the aristocratical or monarchical form." The first and leading error concerns the proper construal or identity of "the people," and hence of sovereignty. The people and the political whole are, rightly, regarded as interchangeable. This is the basis, the only true foundation, of the doctrine of "popular sovereignty." The first error, therefore, to regard the absolute or numerical majority, which is a part, as identical to the people, or as simply representative of them and thus the final agency of sovereignty, or to mistake a part for the whole. In this way, absolute rule is justified. It is, one might say, a "category mistake." Yet, if only absolute or numerical majority is recognized, this error is unavoidable, as, for example, following Hume, in Bentham's utilitarianism or positivist "social science." It leads to the radical assertion that the political whole is "merely the group tendency or demand represented [by] the man who talks of it, erected into the pretense of a universal demand of society," that is, to the claim that the political whole does not exist but only "parts arrayed against over parts."[37] To correct this, it is enough to note that where there are no wholes there are also no "parts." Hence, through no less than ordinary language, Benthamism surreptitiously points to the whole. Such familiar assertions are helpful indications of Calhoun's concern. The "people" as such, or the political whole, is hard to "sense" or "experience" except mediately. It is, for this reason, ever an object of potential controversy and susceptible of many claims and assertions.

According to Calhoun, this fact, the defective or uninstructed human perception on the part of many, is the root of the error under discussion: "those who regard the numerical as the only majority...can perceive no other way...." However, he does not here investigate this root either in terms of the traditional mind-body problem, of which this problem is an exemplary instance, or those of reductionist epistemologies, to say nothing of looking toward a new and now unknown kind of perception or knowledge either in the future generally or "after the revolution." No such investigation is necessary, because he does not consider ordinary or commonplace human perception in any case to deny but always only in some sense to affirm, as in the Benthamist case mentioned above, willy-nilly, the political whole. Hence, it is not *that* but only *what* the political whole is which is truly in question.[38] This question comes to light in the familiar everyday conflict of arguments and claims about justice, which are also arguments and claims about the political whole and the ends for which it is ordained, or the common good, to which the former necessarily point, including dynastic struggles, internal revolutions, and wars of independence. With this fact in view, Calhoun merely analyzes the common error in accordance with which the whole as such and its general sense and will must always be mistaken.

In the forty-fourth paragraph, Calhoun restates the Aristotelian distinction between the healthy or wholesome governmental form "polity" and the unhealthy or diseased form "democracy" as the distinction between "popular government" and the rule of the numerical majority. A perfect popular government would embrace the consent or sovereignty of the whole, that is, literally, of the "people," of all the citizens, where "all" is understood to comprehend "each," and in every respect. It would represent, with respect to the whole, the general will of the community, and not merely that of a part. This is its implicit aim, as it is, also, in the case of the other governmental forms. However, because unanimity is always or almost always impossible among all citizens on most issues (cf. paragraphs 27, 100) in a popular government, many regard the sense of the greater number, only, as if it were that of the whole, in contradistinction to monarchic and aristocratic forms. The sovereignty of the whole resides in the will of the majority, just as it is the judgment of the king that *makes* the state in the inherited practical or actual monarchy of Louis XIV or in the rationalized modern "objective" monarchy of Hegel. On this conception, that the will of the majority is assumed the will of the whole, is based all the familiar modern statements according to which democracy is not the best form of government, or even an intrinsically or truly good form of government, but only the least bad form, or a "necessary evil" to avoid still worse evils (i.e., anarchy). Yet, the essential problem is not in this case any more than the other's one of quantities or numbers—one, few, or many—or of political form—monarchy, oligarchy, or democracy—but of right or the status of the political whole (paragraph 13). The identification of the rule of the people as it actually is as merely the rule of the greater over the lesser part, that is, as merely the rule of the many in contradistinction to the rule of the few or that of one, provides the basis for the familiar doctrines of the "mixed" form of rule as the best practical form of rule. In the *Disquisition*, it provides the basis of the famous doctrine of the "concurrent" or "constitutional" majority, or the elementary theory of constitutional government.

The term "majority" commonly means the most or the largest part of a still larger whole, in contrast to the term "minority" as the least or lesser such part or quantity. This distinction is commonplace, and the term "major," which may also mean strongest or most important, derives from it. Calhoun sometimes uses the terms in this sense, as when he speaks of the majority as the absolute or numerical majority. The rules of the many, of the few, or of the one, whatever their number, are all so many majorities, the *force majeur*, in their respective governments, which are, as a result, absolute governments. The will of the major or stronger part is conceived or asserted as the will of the whole. The term majority may also mean legal or natural wholeness or completion, as when we refer to a man coming into his "majority" out of his "minority," and into the fullness of his mature faculties and accountability according to rights and duties prescribed in law. This distinction is also commonplace, and is observed in some fashion, whatever the terms, in the written and unwritten laws of all communities. It is this kind of fullness and accountability to which Calhoun refers in speaking of the constitutional or true "majority."

Paragraphs 46-47

The "radical error" to which Calhoun traces the fundamental and brute problem of forming and sustaining popular constitutional government is an original "misconception of the true elements of constitutional government" (paragraphs 45-46). If the numerical majority were the whole community or people, the right of suffrage, and, hence, the proportional representation of the tax-consuming and the tax-paying classes, or the major and the minor parts, including the government, would be adequate to safeguard the sovereignty of the whole. However, as the numerical majority is not the whole, the result of this misconception will not be a self-governed and governing people or political whole but merely the absolute rule of a stronger over a weaker part. A further consequence is the fact that, when a popular constitution may somehow have been formed, the conception of the numerical majority as the whole community or people leads easily to the conviction that any organic constraint on the will of the numerical majority in the organism of government, and potentially including even the existence of any minority or "difference" in the community itself, is only an offense against conformity or a constraint on the will of the whole community or people and, therefore, unjust and treasonous on its face. In such a case, the abolition or eradication of a deviant minority, any minority however defined, might well be undertaken in the name of the common interest—even in the name of "pluralism"—in spite of the fact that, as Tocqueville indicated, one thereby merely reduces the natural diversity and wholeness of the community in the direction of the sameness of simple or absolute homogeneity.[39] This reduction or sacrifice of the whole to the strongest part is already implicit in confounding the numerical majority with the people and hence confounding homogeneity of condition with justice. The political course of the French Revolution and of the Bolshevik, Chinese People's, and German National Socialist movements, for example, all of which understood the numerical majority, properly led, in contradistinction to the established aristocracy or monarchy or other minorities and as the whole community or people, each provides an illustrative case in point, whatever might have to be said about the fact that each was, also, the movement of a relative few, or about the further fact that such illustrations are not limited to these movements. The government, understood as the instrument of the majority, will not be controlled, as any such control must by definition be treasonous and unjust. Thus it is believed dogmatically that any problems arising in democracy can only be solved by ever more thoroughgoing democracy: democracy must be made more and more democratic (paragraph 46).[40] The common misconception of the numerical majority as the whole community or people is the root reason why there have been so few popular governments answering to the aim laid down in the fifteenth paragraph, and why, so long as it remains dominant, this condition will continue (paragraph 47).

Paragraphs 48-51

In the following paragraphs (48-51), Calhoun is led by the foregoing considerations to the subject of a written constitution. The illegitimacy or injustice and imprudence of the rule of the numerical majority or any other absolute majority has long been recognized and does not begin with Calhoun's *Disquisition* (e.g., Plato, *Republic*, bk. VIII). This recognition may be expressed in reference to a written constitution by which the government is supposed bound. The conception of constitutional government has always involved restrictions or limitations on the powers of government in respect to the community. A written constitution plainly spelling out governmental prerogatives and limitations is thus, an incarnation of the conception of limited government. It is not, in virtue of this, however, a constitutional government. Calhoun discusses this conception as related to the error of perception that has just been explained. It is, he says, an error "of a kindred character." By this he means less that it is equally prevalent than that it is equally radical. We may say that they are the errors, respectively, of the "feelers" and the "thinkers." Each of the two errors "contributes to much the same results," although of the two the former is the "first and leading" error. The former error, just treated, is that of mistaking a part for the whole. Its discovery is implicit in the idea of constitutional government. The error treated here is the inverse of the former: mistaking the name for the thing, or the sign for the thing signified. Its discovery, too, is implicit in the idea of constitutional government (paragraph 13). The two errors correspond in political terms to those of realism and nominalism.

Calhoun looks both to the actual seat of authority in his discussion of the question (paragraph 48, cf. 15). If there is no effectual veto or check on the ruling part, then the rule is unlimited, whatever may be written or otherwise provided or said by anyone to the contrary. He here explicitly identifies the rule of the many as the rule that must be limited or checked in a popular government. It would be the rule of the one or the few that must be checked in a monarchy or aristocracy. He does not mention the "tendency of the numerical majority" again in his discussion of the problem. It is replaced by the tendency of the government interest, the "major and dominant party," the "party in possession of the government," and "of the ballot box and physical force of the country" in respect to the minor party. These tendencies, here expressed in respect to popular governments, are one and the same in the emergence of absolute government in any form.

The tendencies of government must be controlled for the sake of society or protecting the parts of the community. Whatever may be acknowledged and arranged in the written constitution, if these parts are without effectual positive means of enforcing the limiting provisions, then there will be a tendency on the part of the major party not to observe them, and, in time, they will be altogether effaced (paragraph 49; Hobbes: "And covenants, without the Sword, are but words, and of no strength to secure a man at all."). In its own defense, the minor party will, in the same time, endeavor to strengthen and enlarge these restrictions on the major party, but, without effective means to force their observance, they can and will resort only to constitutional argument, to forensic interpretation and legal construction (paragraph 50). Calhoun is concerned with the internal structure of the organism. (Hence, he does not presently consider that the minor party might resort to conspiracy with foreign interests or governments in order to force the observances in question, etc.).

Construction will then be pitted against construction in the service of these parties. The minor party will adopt the strict construction, the narrowest and most literal, granting only the original letter. The major party will adopt the broad construction, the least literal, asserting only the current majoritarian spirit of the letter. At first, the minor party might enjoy some success. This would be primarily due to the respect and admiration its representatives command from the major party. It would be admitted that the strict construction was not illiberal but a truthful representation of the whole: the letter and spirit would not diverge, at least in the character of the leading representatives of the minor party. The constitution itself would reside primarily in them. In the progress of the contest, however, as the numerical majority becomes more absolute, the spirit will change. As it does so, the constitution itself will come to seem but a debate about the written constitution, in which the minor party will increasingly possess little more than the strict construction, and the leading representatives of the minor party will come to seem to be "mere abstractionists," seeking to defend an increasingly dead letter. To the extent that the *Disquisition* is meant as a preparation for the *Discourse, this* portion of the *Disquisition* presents the end of the written constitution, the beginning of which is presented in the *Discourse*. It is in this light that the position of the leading representatives of the minor party, the "mere abstractionists," not to say Calhoun personally, may be seen as corresponding to the position of the "small but patriotic body of eminent individuals" singled out for mention in the penultimate paragraph treating of the Roman Republic (paragraph 149). As we have noted, that paragraph includes the only occurrence of the word "sad" in the *Disquisition*. It is perhaps typical that the nearest Calhoun comes to referring to himself by name anywhere in the *Disquisition* is in his use of this familiar and deprecating personal epithet, the "mere abstractionist." This distancing is primarily for the sake of showing that such a judgment would be deserved and must always be the consequence of confounding the written with the actual constitution. From the basis of the written constitution alone, appeals to reason, truth, justice, and the obligations imposed by strict construction are ineffective in staving the conversion from constitutional to absolute government, not to say, to use the term Calhoun introduced in the same context in a previous paragraph, "delusive" (paragraphs 46, 51: "folly").[41] After all, if these were self-sufficient, government itself and thus constitutional government would be unnecessary, while society would be preserved and, even, perfected.[42] As they are not sufficient, the restrictions that are merely written will be more or less quickly eluded and, then, effaced (paragraph 51).

Paragraph 52

The fifty-second paragraph is the concluding paragraph of the excursus on popular errors and, therewith, of the section of the *Disquisition* beginning in the fifteenth paragraph, to which the excursus forms a kind of appendix. This appendix is, also, a kind of climax or peak in the *Disquisition*. To begin to see this peak for what it is, we may recall that the excursus is not merely on errors that are common but on certain fundamental or radical errors that are common. It is on the decisive errors that characterize human or political life as such, political realism and nominalism, and which arise directly from the natural faculties that characterize man or human beings as such. These are, also, the faculties by which they come to be discovered and known as errors—and only indirectly if at all from particular interests, material conditions, or accidents of birth, that is, from chance as such. It is on this basis that science is possible. As that which is necessary to man's existence seems fundamentally inimical to man's perfection, it thus comes about that the conflicting interests which necessarily compose society seem inimical to the aims of society, that they seem to be necessary enemies (paragraphs 25-27). This enmity reflects the original struggle in man. There is a war in man for himself, a struggle of good and evil. The science of government is founded to show the way that this antagonism or sickness is healed and man finally made whole.[43] This way is essentially understanding. The common errors and the actions and choices typically arising from them are fundamentally ignorant and irrational not in view of a given particular or immediate interest but in view of the political whole and only in view of the political whole, as opposed, say, to the universal nature of man, the "state of nature," Kant's *rechtslehre,* or other standards or hypotheses. Constitutional government and true *"raison d'etat"* are one and the same.

The fundamental political errors are common errors about the political whole, as a result of which the political whole is ever the center of controversy and struggle. The first error, the error of circumscribing the whole at which it aims, is the mistaking of the stronger part, which is easy to sense, for the whole itself, which is more remotely sensed and must be reasoned (paragraphs 44-46). It requires, as Calhoun says in another context, "a greater effort of reason," which few may undertake. It is the misconception of the true nature of the whole that leads to the struggle for the whole, the division of the community into major and minor parties, which characterizes political life. In the highest case, this struggle takes the form of a debate between the letter and the spirit of the law, or about the whole itself or justice, which openly pits the whole against itself in the claims of the minority and the will of the majority (paragraphs 48-51). The substantive positions are relative and could be reversed (paragraph 37). However, the principle or tendency in question, government, is not relative but limitless. It is itself lawless. The application of science or reason in all these controversies is weak. After all, if, as we have seen, a written constitution itself cannot prevent dissolution, what possible hope is there that a written doctrine about constitutionalism, such as Calhoun's own, may do so, however popular or widely known.

Calhoun addresses this question, which is related to nominalism, implicitly in the final paragraph of the excursus on fundamental errors, where it is presented as obvious—an error "too clear to require explanation." For the reason given in the forty-first paragraph in connection with the application of fundamental principles, it is not enough merely to recite or adopt a certain doctrine or law to establish constitutional government. The principle of concurrency or constitutionalism cannot be woodenly applied in any case but must be discovered, established, and sustained by men in each case.[44] The example given in the fifty-second paragraph, the philosopher Montesquieu's doctrine of the separation of powers, is especially pertinent. This celebrated doctrine is found in his *Spirit of the Laws*. It is a commonplace that Montesquieu himself always stressed that the composition of *The Spirit of the Laws*, like his other works, followed a careful and precise order from which the meaning of its parts is inseparable. However, it is equally commonplace among scholars and students of *The Spirit of the Laws* that this asserted Montesquieuan order is actually unknown and apparently nonexistent. This divergence is not merely a matter of careful study but of perception and wisdom.[45] In such a case, if it is too much to say that one may as well insert random passages from Pound's *Cantos*, it is obviously dubious to apply what may be supposed to be Montesquieuan doctrine as providing the rock of the constitution. Calhoun explains that a famous and influential doctrine, such as Montesquieu's "doctrine" of the separation of powers, when combined with a written constitution, may do very much to further efficiency and deliberate caution in the action of the government, which is desirable in itself, but it will not ultimately check the will or balance the power of the absolute majority. For this, that is, for the spirit and the letter of the law to be the same, which is the ultimate concern of *The Spirit of the Laws*, it would be necessary to go a step further and complete that doctrine as it is commonly and usually understood by making the separation of governmental powers into the separation of constitutional powers. This would amount to the establishment of constitutional government, but it cannot be achieved by reciting Calhoun any more than by reciting Montesquieu or any other doctrine. It requires the prevalence of genuine wisdom and understanding and good fortune (paragraphs 43, 47, 119, cf. 139).

The excursus on common radical errors, which is thus at the same time an excursus on the relative potency of reason, is an excursus precisely on the errors which naturally tend to check the spread of wisdom and understanding or which make absolute government typical or common. Even at the height of the age of common enlightenment, popular reason is relatively weak. *A Disquisition on Government* is an attempt to strengthen this reason. However, the philosophy or science of government here made public itself has no more power to change the nature of social or political causes and circumstances than the science of astronomy has to change the causes and circumstances by which the bodies of the solar system are as they are.

II. Power and Liberty:
Paragraphs 53-98

CALHOUN HAS ANSWERED THE QUESTION SET FORTH IN THE FIFTEENTH PARAGRAPH. IT is the action of the constitutional or concurrent majority that the abuse of the absolute majority may be prevented in government and the community or political whole preserved. Further, he has explained that it is particularly difficult to form and preserve constitutional governments of the popular form because of the common confusion of the numerical and the constitutional majorities. In the following paragraphs, he explains "more fully" what the constitutional or concurrent majority is and why it is indispensable to constitutional government of every form. This explanation, which begins by returning to the place in the argument arrived at in the forty-second paragraph (paragraph 54: "as has been explained") occupies the following forty-five paragraphs, beginning where he says, "I shall next proceed to explain, more fully" (paragraph 53), and ending, after several steps and a marked digression, where he says, "...as has been fully shown" (paragraph 98). It is Calhoun's intention now to distinguish more thoroughly than has ever before been the case between the constitutional majority and the absolute majority, and their respective tendencies, for the sake of preparing the most ambitious and aspiring men of the future for a life of reflection and active participation in politics.

The constitutional or concurrent majority, while effectually preserving the whole community, also effectively promotes the perfection of the human moral and intellectual faculties. Calhoun repeatedly said: "Of all earthly blessings, I place liberty in the first rank.... It is not in the power of any single or few individuals to preserve liberty. It can only be effected by the people themselves; by their intelligence, virtue, courage, and patriotism." The remainder of this section of *A Disquisition on Government* (paragraphs 53-98) may be seen as a completion of a certain strain of classical political thought. Plato writes, for example, that "even if someone should advance in the true political art," according to which what is common must be guarded or protected from the merely private or partial, and should then rule the city without being checked, and as an autocrat, he would never be able to adhere to this truth and spend his life giving priority to nourishing what is common in the city, while nourishing the private as following after the common; human nature will always urge him toward getting more than his share and toward private business (*Laws*, 875a ff.). Similarly, according to Aristotle, in the best possible case, the rulers "will rule in a just fashion because they will be subject to check by others. For to be checked, and not to be able to do everything according to one's own opinion, is advantageous. For the capacity to do whatever one wishes is incapable of guarding against what is base in each human being" (*Politics,* 1318b 33ff.). These thinkers thus concur with the principle that Calhoun has laid down in the *Disquisition* (paragraphs 6 and 27, and related passages), although their discussion is less thorough and developed.

Paragraphs 54-57:
Forms of Power

Power is the capacity to obtain ends. It may be positive or negative, the power to act or to arrest action, more like gravity or more like inertia. Calhoun has explained that men are affected more immediately by the individual feelings and more remotely by the social feelings. The individual feelings which are necessary to sustain individual life tend toward a condition of social conflict and anarchy. This positive tendency is effectively counteracted by the social feelings which abhor or are repulsed by anarchy. Society means the interests composing a community, and hence not interests alone but also the common interest of a people or community. This sympathetic tendency, which is positive toward society and negative toward anarchy, is the necessary condition for government. The government is the positive, controlling power among the interests of the community. It means the power to control the interests of the community, and hence not power alone but in the service of the whole people's interest (paragraph 54). The issue is thus not primarily one of power or might but primarily of limiting or restricting might, that is, of right: of empowering right in accordance not only with natural antipathy toward anarchy but in accordance with the natural ends of society, which are thwarted by the governmental "tendency to oppression and abuse of power."

Absolute government is constituted by the "single or one power" itself, monarchy or tyranny, unlimited power in its own behalf "which excludes the negative," and not by the particular number, one, few, or many, by whom or for whose interest that power might be wielded. This positive governmental power must be checked by or "mixed" with the negative power. It is this mixture or negative power which controls the positive power and makes constitutional government (paragraphs 55-56). The negative power, however it is called, equalizes the otherwise unequal parts of the whole in reference to each other within the fundamental law, which is not a written constitution but the sovereignty of the whole itself, and peacefully and effectively resists the natural tendency of the parts to aggrandize themselves through the sword of the government. It is the negative or "veto power," Calhoun elsewhere says, "which must, almost invariably, interpose a shield between the weaker and the stronger interests," and which shield makes the constitutional organism, the political *daimon* which tells the government what it should not do.[46]

In all absolute governments unlimited power is possessed by an irresponsible part whose will is taken as the will of the whole people or community. Such a community is a house divided against itself. All constitutional governments, government by consensus of the great and prominent interests, exhibit concurrent majority, and thus, directly or indirectly, they all rest on the principle of responsibility of rulers to the ruled. This relation is definitive of constitutional governments. However different in character they may otherwise be (e.g., Poland, Iroquois, Roman, British), constitutional governments of any form are organically more similar to each other in their effective possession of shared power, a constitutional or concurrent majority, than they are to absolute governments of any form (paragraph 57). Such an organism is the foundation of constitutional governments. The constitutional forms differ principally in regard to the material composition or organization of the community, that is, in regard to the constitution in the comprehensive sense; they are all essentially the same in regard to the operation of their respective constitutional organisms.

Paragraphs 58-62:
Power and Reason

As constitutional or concurrent government is a balance of power, or nullifies power alone (paragraph 54), it necessarily follows that the primary mode of its preservation is a kind of reasonableness or compromise, which it promotes, whereas absolute or unlimited government is itself a single or unmixed power (paragraph 55), and its characteristic mode of preservation is brute force. Constitutional government systematically promotes compromise. Absolute government systematically leaves no alternatives but acquiescence in oppression or open rebellion or secession (such as the secession of the Roman plebs, paragraphs 143-145). It is not the case, as has been said, that in constitutional governments the multiplication of interests leads to the "cancelling out" of particular interests, while the general or public interest remains intact and on top, and so on, or that the concurrent majority "creates" the general or public interest. In absolute governments, it is the dominant interest or coalition of interests that forcibly "cancels" other interests composing the whole. In constitutional governments, particular interests do not cancel interests; these remain intact, but independent power checks independent power and composes them together, and the general or public interest is sought and brought forward in debate and compromise, that is, reasonably. To use terms familiar from elsewhere, constitutional government by the operation of its internal organism synthesizes the antithetical claims of community and government. Its operation is most reasonable and most in accord with reason.

Concurrent government, like absolute government, presumes conflict, but it also presumes and nourishes a natural commonalty within or underlying the conflict that is ignored or destroyed in absolute government. This distinction in their respective conservative principles, reasonableness and force, is what impressively marks the difference between constitutional and absolute regimes, but it is a distinction of a secondary character that derives from the presence or absence of the constitutional or concurrent majority. It is secondary because the proximate cause is in neither case devotion to the common interest simply or the love of compromise (or of force) as such, but, rather, in the one case, the constant general suppression of anarchy and the promotion of respective prosperity and, in the other, the more equivocal fear ("dread," or fear mixed with guilt) of losing private or partial advantage (paragraphs 58-61). It follows that, historically, the point of constitutional origin is the same as the principle conservation in concurrent governments (cf. paragraphs 119-120). This is constant. It follows, also, that statesmanship, above all, is *always* necessary in constitutional regimes; and that it is promoted beyond all else in constitutional regimes—the more perfect the constitutional organism the more statesmanship is promoted (paragraphs 75-77); and that it is the highest achievement in constitutional regimes (cf. paragraph 18). It is the highest and ultimate human achievement (paragraph 14). It is the achievement characteristically promoted by constitutional government because this is the kind of government whose operation is most oriented toward reason itself.

This original orientation is rooted in or simultaneous with the avoidance of anarchy. As we have noted, the avoidance of anarchy is not presented by Calhoun as arising from an original fear of violent death, still less from a fear of competition or conflict. It arises from a natural aversion to "universal discord and confusion destructive of the social state" (paragraphs 8, 60). This condition—"anarchy"—is repeatedly identified by the author as the "greatest of all evils," the "greatest of all curses," the *summum malum* for mankind (paragraphs 60, 84, cf. paragraphs 138-139). This natural inclination away from anarchy that is decisive and fundamental, that defines and determines "human" nature (paragraphs 2, 9, 11). It is, with self-preservation, the strongest, the most "urgent and imperious" element of the human constitution (paragraphs 7, 61). The inverse of this immediate natural aversion or loathing of the anarchic state is a mediate but concomitant love that is equally naturally and definitively human, the "love of country" and the "love of truth and justice" (paragraphs 16, 104). This identification is a corollary of the understanding of man as a political animal, and follows necessarily from it. The love of truth and justice, which replaces the Hobbist fear of violent death or the Lockean desire for secure luxury and convenience, is the highest and most distinctively human affection. Yet constitutional government originally rises from and is ultimately preserved not by this love, which is more remote, but from and by its shadow, as it were, the more proximate loathing of anarchy (61).

In transcending "all partial and selfish interests" constitutional government is faithfully consistent with the pure sense of the whole as such, the supreme authority: the "voice of God." It is in the highest sense righteous and just. To say so, Calhoun goes out of his way to say, is not impious. To locate this voice anywhere else than in the political whole itself would be impious, for it would limit the whole to a part. It is all-encompassing and determinative for men in the scale of being. As Calhoun says in a related context: the voice of the whole is "the Deity of our political system," the "creating voice that called the system into existence" out of what was before merely potential parts: the "full, perfect, just, and supreme voice of the people," the voice of the whole political community become self-conscious in its government.[47] At the same time, it is important to note that this "voice," the immediate voice of God or the voice of the political whole, the "Deity of our political system," is not the same as the "Infinite Being" referred to at the beginning of the *Disquisition*. The Infinite Being is infinite and one, the "Creator of all" that is within the scale of being (paragraphs 12, 4, 2, 137). Political communities and hence political deities are many and finite (paragraphs 16, 82-83). The Creator is the Infinite Being behind all the political deities. The former is cosmic or "astronomical" in the strict sense; it has no temple, or rather, it is its own: the temples of the latter are in the cities, are the cities: the regime or community. The spheres of the latter are within the plenitude of the former.

Calhoun emphasizes that the discussion of the broad, secondary distinction between constitutional and absolute regimes assumes perfection in each kind. In fact, "few or none" of either kind have ever been perfect. There is no "simple" regime in the strict sense. Each kind of regime actually contains the preservative principle of the other as well as its own and, "in practice," exhibits and depends to some extent on both, that is, upon force and upon reason, in accordance with the predominative form in its own organization (paragraph 62). All regimes are "mixed" in this sense. Force cannot ever be dispensed with, however perfect the constitutional or concurrent government may become (paragraph 7). On the other hand, reason will be found in even the most benighted absolute regime, however depraved its population (cf. paragraph 104). Indeed, absolute government itself may sometimes be reasonable and necessary (paragraph 83). As a result, therefore, it happens that the possibility of establishing a constitutional government is never simply out of the question, whatever the actual circumstances at a given time. It may actually happen only on the rarest and most fortunate occasions, but the potential for it is in almost all political occasions.

Paragraphs 63-69:
Necessity and Power

Absolute governments by numerical majority present an apparent exception to the rule of force characteristic of absolute regimes, as has been explained (paragraphs 25ff., 35ff.), because in them the minor party may become the major party, and the major party the minor party, through the right of suffrage, and thereby change their relative positions without the intervention of force or violent revolution. They may appear to conform to the secondary distinction that is characteristic of constitutional governments and follow the principle of compromise as against that of force. In so far as it does so, government by the numerical majority is the least bad of the absolute forms of government, and the closest to the constitutional forms (cf. paragraphs 69, 43). The question arises whether the parties themselves may constitute a mechanism of concurrency and contribute to the stability of governments of the numerical majority.

Calhoun holds that this state must be more or less temporary, and that the duration and uncertainty of the tenure by which power is held cannot of itself counteract the tendency of unchecked power to oppression and abuse, and hence to decline into increasingly absolute forms. He discusses the question throughout in terms of the "process of time." The process of time is the operation of causes and the accumulation of consequences, including their operation and proliferation. He also uses the terms "progress" and "degenerate" to denote this accumulation. He takes the long, millennial view implicit in the examples of the great ancient constitutions. Unless organically checked somehow, a decline of government by the right of suffrage alone toward that of irresponsible force is inevitable, not in spite of parties but, in large part, because of them. However little pernicious the process may seem in the "earlier stages," the conflict between the major and minor parties "tends necessarily" to "settle down into" a struggle for the honors and emoluments of government (paragraphs 64, 27-28). "In process of time," the struggle necessarily concentrates party control in ever fewer hands and then converts the honors and emoluments of government into rewards for partisan service. We may note in passing that this problem is not overcome but only compounded by the establishment of what is called a "civil service," or what Calhoun called organized "public service," for such a bureaucratic establishment (whether technically "expert" or not) only extends the government interest along the lines he has already laid down and accelerates the centralization of the government (paragraphs 29ff.). At best, then, government is held in thrall by a mere majority of the major party, perhaps, assuming universal suffrage, amounting to no more than 27 percent, or even less (depending on voter-turnout), of the whole community (paragraph 64).

As the government becomes more explicitly one of party leadership and party usage, there is raised the issue of popularity ("leadership") in the place of "principle and policy," and conflict for control of the government will descend, in the process of time, into a vicious struggle of party leaders in the course of increasingly gross appeals to the "lowest and most worthless portions of the community" as to the most authoritative, because most numerous, part. The lowest portion of the community includes the poor and the ignorant. These will constitute the actual majority in all advanced regimes. The most worthless portion includes those receiving tax bounties and supported only by government revenues. To these portions or interests will the parties increasingly appeal, as the most numerous, the one more on behalf of the tax-paying class, the other more on behalf of the tax-consuming class. Therewith, parties themselves will have become but petty factions with but little distinction between them vibrating in excited public tension, and the community itself thoroughly debased and corrupted.[48] The honors and emoluments of government being at length too few to satisfy the ambition and avarice of proliferating party leaders, leaders will become as political liege lords, until, in the regular course of events, public "confusion, corruption, disorder, and anarchy," which no part of mankind will long stand, eventuates in an appeal to force, ending in a change in the form of government toward the more explicitly absolute. This is a sketch, "in brief," of the process of decline and degradation through which the government and community will pass (paragraph 65).

The process of time or "transition" that is involved in this decline will vary in accordance with elementary circumstances. Its progress will be shorter in those circumstances generally conforming to Hume's idea of a perfect commonwealth, and with developed arts and sciences and an advanced fiscal operation in the government, and longer in those appertaining in a small, simple community without such development and where the fiscal operation of the government is more modest, provided the (voting) majority is sufficiently intelligent and attentive to conventions of intelligent debate.[49] The author observes that government by the numerical majority might be the only form of popular government suited to the latter condition. The presentation is compatible with the familiar "small republic" doctrine of Montesquieu and others (*Spirit of the Laws*, II.2). Hence, colonies of constitutional regimes, if not conquered by others, often adopt governments of the numerical majority upon obtaining their independence. If there is no growth and development, and no change in conditions, and if the community is left to itself, then it may persist in this form indefinitely. On the other hand, as the small community develops and grows and becomes more diverse, it must either then follow the path of force, and hence absolutism, or that of government by concurrent majority (paragraph 66).

It plainly appears from this paragraph that, for Calhoun, government by numerical majority is the most natural form in the sense of being the earliest and least "artificial" or simplest form of popular government (cf. paragraphs 24-25). The radically opposite form of government, monarchic force or military power, is equally natural. The government of the many thus has a tendency to transform itself into its opposite, the government of the one, as the interests within it develop, in spite of the mutual repugnance and antagonism of these forms. In the process of time, the transformation becomes merely formal, following the substantial or material change occurring in the character of the community. Calhoun takes it for granted that, in the process of time, all interests, all foci of significant ambition and avarice in all societies, center increasingly and primarily upon the honors and emoluments of government (paragraphs 27, 67-68).

The result is that one may observe a natural or universal and constant tendency in governments to decay which is not checked by the love of country or by aversion to anarchy, and may even be stimulated by these in various ways, and which, in any case, always arises most strongly from the ambition of the aspiring, and most especially in popular governments. Constitutional governments of the one, few, or many tend to degenerate into absolute forms of the one, few, or many, and absolute forms of the few or many tend to degenerate further into absolute monarchy, which itself may then become characterized by dynastic struggles. Constitutional monarchies or aristocracies are strongest in resisting this degeneration, because their form is more obvious, and the great and prominent interests which characterize them are thus more immediately "jealous and watchful" of their rights in regard to one another. The absence of strongly marked orders or classes in popular constitutional governments, and hence of a strongly marked popular constitutional form, on the other hand, may make it hard for some to see that the increase in the power of the numerical majority, on the basis of the right of suffrage, is not an increase but a decrease in popular government. Men are more apt to err in such a case than otherwise, and "honest and sincere" patriotism itself may unwittingly nourish its degeneration (paragraphs 69, 25, 46). For this reason, constitutional democracy is the weakest, internally, of all the constitutional forms of government. Having noted this weakness, Calhoun goes so far as to observe that the numerical majority directly "perhaps should be one of the elements of a constitutional democracy," but not necessarily. The individual citizens could as well or perhaps better be represented through other organs than direct suffrage (paragraph 42). The decisive aspect on this point is to ensure the responsibility of the parts to the whole (paragraph 21). A direct numerical majority is not necessary to ensure this, and may even obstruct it. To make the numerical majority the sole or ultimate element in popular government, even for the sake of popular government, will therefore quickly defeat the aims of popular government (paragraph 22).

Paragraphs 70-98:
The Principles of Constitution and the
Preservation of the Common Good

The immediately prior paragraphs have presented the (indispensably) formative and (secondarily) conservative principles of all regimes, particularly, the responsibility of rulers to ruled and the relative empowerment of reason in the case of constitutional regimes, and observed their constant tendency to degenerate and ultimately to decline in the direction of some form of absolute monarchy. They provide the foundation and context of what follows. The following portion of the *Disquisition*, then, is clearly divided into three distinct sections that explicitly present, in the order of their rank, the particular virtues or advantages of constitutional government deriving from their form, and particularly of constitutional democracy, with regard to the specific natural ends for which human government is ordained. For, while constitutional democracy is in principle the highest, it is for this reason also the most difficult and complicated and hence the most fragile of all the constitutional forms (paragraph 69).

These three sections treat, first, of the advantages of constitutional government with regard to the first or primary and lower end of government, or the common interest (paragraphs 70-71). The second or central and much longer section treats of the means by which the ends of government are attained, and which means are, also, ends in themselves (paragraphs 72-78). The short final section treats of the other, higher and ultimate end of government (paragraphs 79-80). This treatment itself leads to or culminates in a discussion of the ultimate ends and origins of human community itself, including the explicit rejection of the political theories of Hobbes and his successors and, implicitly, the fundamental correction, and hence proper completion, of the project initiated by Hume, that is, so far as it is humanly possible, the perfection of genuine political science (paragraphs 80ff.). (This is why Calhoun has written about the *Disquisition* that it covered "new ground" and, also, that "I wish my errors to be pointed out."[50]) Taken together, these subjects (paragraphs 70-98) in principle comprehend the whole of political or human life and science: they represent the peak of *A Disquisition on Government* as a whole and of Calhoun's philosophy of government, to which every sentence and phrase of *A Disquisition on Government* heretofore has led.

Let us take a brief overview. Following upon the presentation just completed of the formation and conservation of governments, the implicit or "first question," formed and conserved for what? (paragraphs 1-14), is here taken up. The first end of government is again acknowledged as the fundamental and primary political end: the security or conservation of the political whole for its own sake, that is, for what it is (paragraphs 70-71). The principal or key word in the section is "safe." Security is the first and lowest end of government because preservation is necessary but not sufficient for the perfection of the whole. While preservation is of greater moment than the higher ends of government which are dependent upon it, the fact remains that preservation is always for the sake of the higher ends (cf. paragraph 85). How these ends are achieved and sustained involves the questions of means and morality. The perfection of political or human life is essentially a moral problem. Morality, the perfection of the human moral faculties, is thus the subject of the following section (paragraphs 72-79). The principal or key word in this section is "morals." Morality bridges or unites the lower and higher ends of human community in the "common good" (paragraph 75). Private morals are merely public morals writ small: it is the venue and not the substance that changes. Public morals typically establish or, what is the same thing, overwhelm private morals. Private morals reflect and are formed by actual public morals. This is why various schemes of formal or public education, however elaborate (indeed, the more elaborate they are, the less successful they will be) will not protect morality, any more than they will lead to insight or wisdom, on the part of the country or an individual. (The most educated man, however imperfectly, in the nineteenth century was, doubtless, the younger Mill, whose most mature thought is an effort to liberate himself from it.[51]) Calhoun explains this in what follows in comparing constitutionalism and absolutism and contrasting morality to each. The unity fostered by concurrency attaches the "strongest passions of the human heart," or individual desires and affections, to the "common good of the whole," or the public good, by promoting that upon which kind feelings and good will ("good faith" in more recent language) depends. Morality is both instrumental, in that it promotes or serves the first end of political life and hence of government, on which it depends, and constitutive of the good life as such, which is higher than the first end of government. This means that morality both is and is not relative to any particular form of government, whether constitutional or absolute, or the composition of any particular community, the ordained ends of all of which are everywhere the same: the people's physical or material security in accordance with justice and the formation of character in accordance with truth. Achieving these ends is what government is for. Government is the means to these ends.

Political or human life can be the good life, secure in the scale of patriotism and virtue, through compliance with the principles laid down in these sections and earlier—so much has been achieved in the historical past, particularly with respect to the great constitutional governments that have been praised—but it cannot be complete, or good, without further qualification or understanding. Without this specificity, it cannot be, strictly, the best life or the life that is truly the life that is most in accordance with human nature. For the completion of the good, fully human life it is necessary also to develop the intellectual faculties as such (paragraphs 2-3). This development is not primarily the cultivation of traditional liberal arts or religious education, for example, as in the case of all the great constitutional peoples that have been praised, but of knowledge of nature as such. This subject occupies the following section (paragraphs 80-98).

Paragraphs 70-71:
The Principles of Constitutional Government and the Preservation of the Common Interest

In these paragraphs, Calhoun explains the "other advantages" characteristic of constitutional government. These advantages lie beyond the fundamental advantages already established. The essential advantage of constitutional government is that of preserving or sustaining the fundamental principle of responsibility of rulers to ruled and of the parts to the whole over the process of time, which means that genuine progress is possible. The first of the advantages flowing from this superiority is that all constitutional governments, especially including constitutional democracy, exhibit a more wholesome and popular character than any absolute government, including absolute democracy. This is shown in the fact that the concurrent democratic government safely allows a greater extension of the right of suffrage than does that of the numerical majority. Indeed, with "ordinary exceptions"—Calhoun has in mind youths, convicted criminals, aliens, defectives, indentured or bonded labor, if any, rather than any specific statutory qualifications—it safely allows "universal" suffrage: every mature male citizen may vote his mind. This extension is considered by Calhoun as an "advantage" because it broadens participation in political life to the utmost extent, and, to that extent, perfects the people. In the case of absolute democracies, such extension will, in the process of time, only degrade the regime and people. As has been previously noted, it may be reiterated that Calhoun does not entertain the direct suffrage of women, who will be fully if indirectly represented through their men and families. In this connection, Calhoun himself did not, so far as contemporary reports have come down to us, especially vary his conversational subjects or themes or purpose of discourse from men to women or, indeed, even to children, including slave children, but, on the contrary, addressed all similarly, or in accordance with their individual interest.[52] He did not talk down to anyone, as we say nowadays. It was essentially this widely-remarked quality in him that has led on the part of some to the opinion that he did not understand human nature (particularly in the general run of men and women), and hence that he necessarily underestimated his own natural superiority to others.[53] Rather, he is distinguished by the fact that when he listened his attention was undivided and when he spoke he addressed only the best in everyone, man or woman or child. (The European figure most reminiscent of Calhoun in these personal respects is Kant, whose political thought evinces such remarkable similarities and contrasts.) These characteristics are themselves a part of his natural superiority, and which he, apparently, never either doubted *or* took for granted.[54]

The safety which Calhoun here stresses is related to the relative health of the people or the community as a whole (70). What makes such an extension "safe" is not that these citizens are intrinsically or by nature wiser or more just than those under a government of the numerical majority—they are the same—but that the extension itself is carried out under the counterbalance of the concurrent majority, and hence, also, of a relative propensity toward compromise or reasonableness. They differ by habit. Otherwise, in the process of time, as the community develops and grows, the government of the numerical majority will become increasingly merely the government of the poor and ignorant and dependent, led toward that end by wealthy and ambitious claimants, over against the wealthy and intelligent, and thus more or less quickly or gradually destroy the community and degenerate into a form of absolute monarchy. The distinction between the portions of the population will increase as progress continues, with the poor and ignorant and relatively dependent becoming ever greater in proportion to the rich and intelligent and relatively independent. It is constitutional rather than absolute democracy which is most popular in character, because, while it promotes the growth and development of the whole, it limits and hence tempers the effective designs not merely of the poor but, more importantly, of the rich, including the most ambitious and rivalrous among them (paragraph 71). It appears that in the process of time, as distinctions between the poor and the rich, the intelligent and the ignorant, the dependent and the independent proliferate and deepen, the organism to which Calhoun refers must most especially check those among the rich and intelligent who are also the most ambitious (paragraphs 27-28, 64-65). These, not the poor and ignorant, are the most dangerous. The decline is not due primarily to the ruled, that is, the poor and the ignorant, for they are both predictable in their behavior and either modest or do not know what they are doing, but rather to their opposites, who desire distinction and who corrupt the poor and ignorant in the attempt to attain it. The problem with absolute government is less the many than the few (paragraphs 71, 64, last sentence), and less the few than the most ambitious and aspiring.[55] Were it otherwise, the problematic relationship of rulers to ruled would be much otherwise than it actually is. As we have indicated, it is for these that *A Disquisition on Government* is primarily intended, for it is they who will rule in any regime.

The danger represented by the wealthy and ambitious is presented by Calhoun in terms of danger to the whole community, and particularly to the "more ignorant and dependent portions of the community," to whom the ambitious directly make their appeals. The interest of the poor and ignorant is no more served by the actual rule of the poor and ignorant than anyone else's interest. In any case, the ambition of the ambitious is ultimately not for the sake of the poor and ignorant but for the sake of advancing their own distinction. The interest of the ambitious, on the one hand, and of the poor and ignorant, on the other, is thus divergent, as ruler and ruled. The more successful the ambitious become in exciting and directing the poor and ignorant, the more divided their interests actually become, and the community is corrupted. It is only when numbers alone do not have absolute sway, allowing the interests of the wealthy and intelligent to ally and identify with the interests of the poor and ignorant of their respective portions of the community, that the wealthy and intelligent become the "leaders and protectors" of the poor and ignorant as of themselves, since what is in the best interest of their respective portion is in their own interest. Under concurrency, the ambitious can promote their own interest only by promoting the common interest. Otherwise, the ambitious will merely exploit and corrupt the poor and ignorant for the rulers' own ends. In this way, while retarding and modifying the division of the growing community merely into the few rich and the many poor, constitutional government nourishes genuine paternalism with regard to all of the most dependent portions of the community, and hence, also, the preservation of common unity among the different portions.[56] Since Calhoun's time, paternalism has become increasingly unpopular in explicit forms, but this obviously does not alter the fact that the reality which necessarily gives rise to it in any form or by whatever name is unchanged.

Paragraphs 72-78:
The Constitutional Principle and the
Perfection of the Moral Faculties

What Calhoun refers to as "another [advantage]" of constitutional government in the following paragraphs is, for the regime, actually a higher, derivative aspect of the advantage just explained, a particular that is usually associated with the peculiar quality of the "small republic" in regard to its superior tendency in promoting virtue. He here explains the tendency of concurrent government to unite rather than divide the portions of the community, however many and diversified they are and however great the differences between them may be, and therewith to strengthen and protect the whole (cf. paragraph 27). He discusses this tendency in terms of the "scale of patriotism and virtue" which occupies the place of the "scale of being" in the opening paragraphs (paragraph 78).

As we have noted, Calhoun understands the political whole, the "people," the "community," and the "country" as one and the same (paragraphs 72-75, 44ff.). The numerical majority divides the country according to the stronger force within it, which division is then justified by some rationale. This division arises only secondarily from the relative ignorance of the many. It is primarily the result of the ignorance of the few: the "ambition of the aspiring and the cupidity of the avaricious." These—avarice, ambition, rivalry—are the "strongest passions" arising from the selfish feelings (paragraphs 5, 11, 27-28), and from the partial and imperfect identification of the whole with a part of the whole (paragraphs 44-45). They attach naturally to parties, and, in the "progress of party strife," they take the place of the country (paragraph 65). These passions spring from our nature and cannot be abolished, whether by religion or by education, however important these might be in controlling them (paragraph 78), any more than can be mankind—including, above all, the honor-loving man, the would-be great man—but they can be tamed or ruled, or "educated" in the sense of being formed by the laws, their consequences purified, and the community itself thus made good and great. All government and all law naturally if implicitly points to this, even if it does not often actually tend to it in the most decisive cases. The explanation of this phenomenon leads to the fundamental moral stratum of Calhoun's political philosophy.

The ultimate goal which excites the strongest or ruling passions among the most talented and aspiring men is the "high and glittering prize of governmental honors and emoluments." This is the fundamental fact of political life. Such a goal represents, at least, perfect personal wholeness: the highest and fullest communion of the individual and social feelings: the best life here and now in truth. In every regime, the most certain means of acquiring this "high and glittering prize," therefore, or various aspects or fragments of it, are what most immediately form the character of those who are most desirous of it, and these ones are also those who, by their "energy, intellect, and position in society," are most efficacious in forming the character of the whole people. In every regime, beginning with such factors as climate, pursuits, language, and so on, there arises in this way a characteristic type. It is one of the most consistent features of human sociability that, by one means or another, one emulates most what one honors most, and seeks, by this means, a sense of personal achievement and recognition as good, and hence perfection or genuine identity and individuality. Thus is stamped the character of a community and its intellectual and moral culture. When all selfish or partial promotion at the expense of others or of the country is prevented through the internal action of the constitutional organism, then the selfsame passions which otherwise tend to divide the whole into parts tend rather to unite each with the other in devotion to the country. In this unity, the otherwise weaker or "social" feelings are rendered more than commensurate with the otherwise stronger or "selfish" feelings. So far as the union were perfect, so far would these feelings be difficult to distinguish. In the conciliatory operation of the concurrent majority, the rivalry and competition which naturally characterizes all regimes is in constitutional regimes essentially a rivalry and competition in genuine political virtue: "a struggle only for supremacy in promoting the common good of the whole," in which the name corresponds as much as possible to the thing. It is a mature rivalry in which "truth, justice, sincerity and moral obligations of every description" are the tissue of all social attachments, and for success in which "knowledge, wisdom, patriotism and virtue" are themselves most "highly prized" and most "assiduously cultivated" as the means for public esteem. Those who struggle publicly mutually surpass themselves in their rivalry, and the struggle for this supremacy purifies and regenerates from within. This struggle and the elevation it bestows is a way that is open to all, and not limited to the most rare or exceptional constitutions who may achieve it alone (paragraph 6). In this way—the assimilation of public honor to personal virtue—constitutional government serves the moral perfection of the people or the political whole, for the sake of which perfection, in large part, society or the social nature of man is originally ordained, and turns the "high and glittering prize" from the brass clutched at by the few to gold that is shared by all. Thus, the organism of concurrency renders as much as possible what was many, one, without annihilating the many; what was plural, absolute, without abbreviating its manyness; what was passionate self-interest, rational common interest; and what was merely interest, the love of country and of truth and justice (cf. paragraph 104).

In this context, Calhoun for the first time describes the country or whole as the "common center of attachments of all its parts" (paragraphs 74, 75), in contradistinction to the "center" each party or portion finds only "in itself" (paragraph 74) or to the "center" of the selfish or individual feelings (paragraphs 1, 5), while allowing the latter parts everything that is their natural due. By the "common center," Calhoun means the res publica, the genuinely "public," by virtue of which the community is a common unity or whole. It is "this community of feeling, which ultimately identifies the whole as a peculiar and distinct interest in the community."[57] This center, the "people," the "community," inheres above all in public morality. Politically, it is "constitutional" (Hegel: objectively ethical), socially or individually, it is moral. The whole is sustained through the constitutional majority, the equalized action of the government with respect to the constituent portions of the community, which is the essence of constitutional government.

This "unit," "common center of attachment," "people," or "community," then, is not a place, although a place is required for it and may be hallowed by it, nor in any particular interests or any competition or cooperation among them, although it arises amid and along with these, but in virtue itself, the love of the impartial and common good. It is this, virtue or moral perfection, that is the ultimate and true aim of all government and law—however little it may be attained and whatever the reasonableness, language, customs, pursuits, situation, complexion, commerce, superstitions, ceremonies, education, or religion of the whole people may be. This aim does not vary from age to age or from country to country. However much they may differ, the languages of all communities in all times and places contain words for "knowledge, wisdom, patriotism, and virtue." In absolute governments of whatever form and in whatever age, however, it is "little more than a name" (cf. paragraph 92), both in spite and because of the fact that its inculcation and primary support is left to religion or education, while the effectual formative process of the people's character goes on unheeded in the actual operation of the government itself and in the actual means by which its honors and emoluments are obtained. This is why, as Rousseau noted, education in the decisive sense is often no more than education in hypocrisy—inauthentic, alienated, and so on—and, also, why he thought Locke's educational reform program should be replaced. Among other things, this has also led to the familiar distinction drawn between true or private virtue, including actual vice or Machiavellian virtue, and public or merely political virtue. "It is not...wonderful," Calhoun here observes, that this is the case among absolute governments in which incessant internal hostilities are carried out under forms of law (paragraph 74). So far from conferring public benefits, private vices do not even confer private benefits. This whole notion is a fiction within the fiction of the "state of nature" doctrine. In fact, whatever politically corrupts and degrades the whole morally corrupts and degrades the parts, including each individual composing the parts. Debasing citizenship, for example, debases the citizens as citizens and hence as human beings. It *is* "wonderful" that this fact can be recognized and explained, and that constitutional governments surpass all others in this crucial particular. The wonder here expressed is the root impulse of Calhoun's political philosophy. His intent in setting forth the consideration here is to show that, finally, however extraordinary they may be, all constitutional governments, whatever their form and the character of their parts, more truly—and perhaps those based on the wide diffusion of knowledge most truly of all—unite the name and the thing, "virtue," to the greatest possible extent: the greatest theoretical and practical extent. It lets what exists in all speech be in its deeds. This condition, the health of private morals, is not only a means but a natural end in itself without the achievement of which it is not possible to speak of human completion or fulfillment.

Naturally, even if it were perfect the organism of concurrency itself cannot insure that all or even many of all those who assiduously cultivate virtue will actually fully and unequivocally attain it, however much progress they may make toward it, and it remains that the extent to which they do not actually attain it provides the denticulation for vice, to say nothing of the likelihood, over time, of unintentional mistakes on the part of those who do attain it (cf. paragraph 25). According to Calhoun, no contrivance can absolutely correct this circumstance; hence statesmanship is both the most necessary and the most desirable of all human things. Yet, constitutional government as much as possible provides in every way for the failures, including the variance that may often obtain between the name and the thing. The few who seek virtue as a means of supremacy under the wing of such a constitutional organism are those whose energy, intellect, and circumstances render them most likely to attain it, and having attained it, the least likely to develop merely personal or partial rivalries in the rivalry to contribute to the good of the whole, for this is their interest. It is less important that every person in the community come unequivocally to possess genuine political virtue if at least the great and prominent persons possess it (cf. paragraph 41). Their influence insures the influence of virtue among the people regarded individually, many (and perhaps most) of whom care little or nothing for politics, in so far as it lies within them to attain it. This influence gives the community its maximum strength.

However effective it may be in its operation, the organism of concurrency does not overcome the brute fact that the most honorable offices are fewer than those who compete for them. "Supremacy" in promoting the common good of the whole is still supremacy. According to Calhoun, the character of this fact is here decisively transformed, because it is freely recognized as supremacy in goodness. It promotes the willing sacrifice or overcoming of merely individual or private interests. It establishes the individual self as constituted by the discharge of moral obligations. The struggle for virtue is how one comes to be who one is or is not. The result of vice is ultimately indistinguishable from that of the "other" constitution of human nature discussed in the eleventh paragraph: apparently beneficent, it is hollow, there is no benefit or remedy in it. The nullification of the tendency of government to excess and abuse genuinely renders the attachments of all the political parts one unified whole or common interest, and this unity, given due enlightenment on the part of the people, renders the question of these relatively few positions or "who will rule?" as the common question: "who of us is best?" — the most fit, wisest, and capable of understanding (cf. paragraph 24). It thus both raises the participants above themselves, that is, above their merely selfish feelings, and subordinates as much as possible the natural rivalry for supremacy to the common interest, while simultaneously bringing forward the best into the ruling positions. This is by nature best and right. In so doing, it elevates the term "citizen" itself to honor (cf. paragraphs 97, 163), which is to say, the community as a whole.

Because it characterizes the community as such, its effects are not limited to political action in any narrow sense but extend outward to every sphere and rank of the whole community, including each individual, irrespective of whether or not they have a direct part in political action (paragraphs 74-78). It yokes the public and the private, unifying private politics and public morality. Public and private morals have a reciprocal influence upon one another, like the relational character of powers. They cannot be separated, and in life as it is actually lived, they are not. Everything that makes a regime selfish or partial makes the smallest and least significant parts of it selfish or partial, and vice versa: they are symptoms of the same cause (paragraphs 75-76). It follows necessarily that, for the reasons explained in these paragraphs (76-77), the operation of concurrent majority provides the most effectual means, including religion and education, for politically and morally improving the people or society "as a whole." This means is so sure that, if it were possible for a community to establish and maintain an effective constitutional government among them, that is, one that answered to the fundamental requirements laid down in earlier paragraphs (21, 39, 57), it would, for the reasons indicated, of itself purify and regenerate a corrupt and degenerate people, raising them in the "scale of patriotism and virtue" by restoring "regard for truth, justice, sincerity, and moral obligations of every description," however sunk in vice and ignorance they might be, while absolute government will gradually corrupt the most virtuous and intelligent of peoples absolutely (paragraphs 76, 78).

Paragraphs 79-85:
The Constitutional Principle and the
Perfection of the Intellectual and Moral Faculties

The unity and protection of society which is promoted by the development of the moral faculties that has just been explained is not yet its perfection but only its securest ground. In the following paragraphs, which are the central paragraphs of *A Disquisition on Government* as a whole, Calhoun takes up the subject of the perfection of society, that is, the intellectual and moral faculties of individual human beings, the highest end for which government is ordained (paragraphs 2-3, 9-10). To perfect society means to develop in individual human beings the intellectual and moral faculties characteristic of man as man (paragraph 80).[58] These faculties develop only from the base or in the context of sustained unity — community — achieved in accordance with the exposition of the previous paragraphs, in which politics and morality appeared primarily as a means. They are the means to this end.

Using a mechanical analogy, Calhoun says that the "mainspring" of the development of these faculties is the desire of individuals to better their condition, however their condition is conceived. This desire cannot be imposed from without, but must be internal or original. For Calhoun, the differences between men in this respect are beyond human control. It is not necessarily stimulated by what might otherwise be called necessity. It cannot be forced, but only encouraged. Without this original desire, development of the individual's intellectual and moral faculties is impossible. Centuries earlier, Hobbes and Locke and their successors had argued that this desire is universal. And, after the sweeping influence, especially in England and the United States, of the thought of Spencer a generation after the *Disquisition* was published, and the popular success of academic works like *The Mainspring of Human Progress* and innumerable imitators, we may be naturally tempted to take Calhoun's statement as merely the most natural and obvious thing and find it difficult even to conceive of individuals who do not desire to better their condition. However, for Calhoun, it is quite easy to conceive of such individuals. Indeed, according to him, they constitute the ordinary or typical case. What Locke calls the "restlessness of mind" is primarily typical of advanced or civilized society characterized by wide diffusion of intelligence, that is, the present epoch.[59] It will be useful to begin to anticipate Calhoun's digression on the "state of nature" (paragraph 89), and compare his view with the more familiar thought of Rousseau, according to whom the desire to better one's condition is altogether unnatural to man, for whom, indeed, nothing could be more unnatural, on the one hand, and Locke, on the other, for whom the desire to protect one's own property is natural.

For man, according to Rousseau, true or original man, man in the "state of nature," the elements cannot even be formulated that would begin to compose such a desire. Such a desire cannot even occur to him. In any case, the sweet sense of his original condition, mere existence or life itself, is too great. He only learns in civil society, in which competition, rivalry, *amour-propre*, the struggle of mine and thine, and everything that is associated with these things, including writing, combine almost to crush the sweet sense of existence. For Rousseau, the desire of individuals to better their condition occurs in society and is, alongside the inequality that is necessarily signaled by it and attendant to it, a primary characteristic of society. Like the fear of death, these characteristics are absent in the state of nature, where men are free and equal. The hypothetical absence of these characteristics and all that is attendant upon them is all that the Rousseauan "state of nature" amounts to, while "society" more or less means mere inequality, particularly inequality of condition. The gap between the state of nature and legitimate civil society as described by Rousseau is vast, if not simply an impossible bridge. His most famous sentences state that, although men are born free in the state of nature, they are everywhere now in the chains of civil society, and, while he does not know how this came about, he believes he knows how it can be made "legitimate."

In providing a sort of account of how this vast chasm between nature and human society is bridged or how human society (or, what is the same thing, human inequality) came about, Rousseau merely appeals from the sweet sense of existence, which all more or less actually share now, to an hypothetical "history," to emerge in due course with human society, complete with rivalry, property, inequality, and all the rest. The *Discourse on the Origins of Inequality* amounts to a discourse on the origins of man. Yet, as the absence of the term "equal" in the famous sentences indicates, Rousseau *does* know how human inequality came about. Assuming, for the sake of the argument, an original "state of nature," and setting aside the question whether men were in some sense free in this state, it is evident that they were not all equal in that state, whatever the hypothesis may posit. The conclusion is inescapable that some individuals in the "state of nature," at least, were not the same as the others in that they had a desire to better their condition in some respect. This inequality is, thus, natural (and hence "legitimate") even were it to have been limited to one original human being—a sort of necessary forerunner of the superior man, the "legislator," later so famously and eloquently celebrated by Rousseau himself. It is particularly important to see that the inequality in question is not limited to the presence or absence of the desire to better one's condition, nor does it even primarily consist in the presence or absence of this desire. The desire is altogether derivative and secondary, or symptomatic. As this hypothetical *reducto ad absurdum* condition, the "state of nature," is supposedly original or primal, there are thus no earlier examples to follow, no existing figures to emulate, as in the sense described in the immediately previous paragraphs of the *A Disquisition on Government*. Hence the original desire naturally arises and can only arise, whenever it did so and in whomsoever it did so, in the light of original reason or the natural human intellectual faculty, even if this original awareness is nothing more than the beginnings of a question. On Rousseau's own account, this knowledge, which is a kind of self-knowledge, is not natural to human beings, or at any rate it is not natural to almost all or (at least) to most human beings, or, if it is, which is more accurate (cf. *Disquisition*, paragraph 104), it is alone insufficient in most human beings to stimulate a desire to better their condition. This inequality, the diversity of the intellectual faculty in individuals, is the natural and inevitable ground of human inequality. Most human beings are imitators or emulators. As for the question whether individuals might be in some sense "free" in a hypothetical state of nature, according to Calhoun, it is nonsense to speak of unreason and amorality in the same breath with human freedom, or, if there is reason in this state, as there necessarily is, then it is in fact the political state, the original and primal human state, in which state only is there any hope of human liberty (paragraph 89).

Paragraphs 80-81

Calhoun holds that the desire of individuals to better their condition is characteristic of human society, the political community, where it is stimulated principally by emulation among the numerical majority, and not of an imaginary asocial "state of nature." Calhoun's presentation in the eightieth paragraph might appear to be blended easily into the Lockean position on the rights of property, upon which, according to Locke, civil society and hence government is contracted outside the "state of nature," but Calhoun's silence on property rights altogether makes it obvious that his concern is here only secondarily, if at all, with material conditions of any kind, much less with this or that opinion about property rights, and primarily with the development of the human intellectual and moral faculties as such, for the sake of which, according to him, society and government are ordained. Progress in "civilization," control of the material elements of nature, represents increasing perfection of the human intellectual faculty. Calhoun goes so far as to say that "progress, improvement, and civilization, with all their blessings" are simply derivative of this development, or secondary, for which the preservation or protection of society is primary, and not the other way around (paragraphs 79, 85). This is of a piece with his earlier observation in the eighteenth paragraph that the advance and benefits which we now enjoy are due ultimately to the success of ancient and long-lived constitutional governments. The aim of these paragraphs (especially 81-83, 91ff) is to show that these high ends, civilization and constitutional government, are in principle compatible: intellectual development (to the extent possible for each) and liberty may coincide in a constitutional people. We note also that Calhoun does not here or elsewhere observe any necessary association between wealth and intelligence or virtue. Were there such a necessary association, it would be a simple matter to print and give everyone money or long credit. Of course, one would no more achieve economic or other progress or virtue or intelligence in this way than one would perfect society by simply giving everyone liberty or the right of suffrage.

The desire of individuals to improve their condition is the mainspring for the development of the intellectual and moral faculties. In the first and highest and rarest instance, this desire stems from independent awareness of ignorance and shortcoming: original reason. There are various ways of attempting to improve one's condition, and the primary way of distinguishing among human individuals is by what they most desire and pursue to this end. As we have noted, throughout the *Disquisition* Calhoun speaks only of the perfection of constitutional government, government that is characterized by reasonableness itself or compromise and moderation, as the highest and most distinctive of all human ends and the object of the wisest and best men in all ages. It is the end in the pursuit of which the intellectual and moral faculties are most fully developed, on the one hand, and incomparably the most fully engaged with fortune and with one's fellows, on the other. It is the most fully human life, the most completely human being. Hence it is in no sense emulation. It demands what Calhoun calls the "active mind" and independence from the common opinions of one's fellows, not for its own sake but for the sake of attaining as far as humanly possible to first causes and truth, as well from the ordinary inclinations to personal aggrandizement. It is, in this sense, solitary and unique, genuinely "private" or "one's own," and hence the fullest attainment of individual liberty. At the same time, it is also fully "public," open and based or dependent on what is common or shared, and hence fully in the service of what is common and shared.

For most individuals, the desire to better their condition stems not from independent reason but from noticing the condition of others and emulating them in the things that seem to them most apt to serve their own interest and happiness. It is primarily imitative and habitual, as set forth in the previous section of paragraphs. This is no less the case among hunting and gathering peoples than among civilized peoples. If the community is internally divided into artificial orders or estates, the lower orders will imitate the higher orders. If it is without any internal divisions, the average man will hasten to keep up with the "ideal" or "above average" family. It is for this reason that improvement or progress in morality and politics requires much time, and cannot in any case be rushed (e.g., paragraph 86, last sentence). It is for this reason, also, as Calhoun observes in various other places, that the examples of successful constitutional governments are of great influence, even if they cannot simply be copied.

It is primarily the operation of emulation and rivalry, a desire to have what others have or to be like them and surpass them, and not primarily a desire for wealth or "materialism" that stimulates the desire of individuals to better their condition. Hence the desire for wealth characterizes some communities and not others. Wealth is also seen as the best way to improve and control one's fortune or chance, and it is often even called "fortune." The last three sentences of this paragraph seem to state the thesis of liberal economics and civil society perhaps as succinctly as it has ever been stated, but that thesis does not adequately capture Calhoun's meaning.[60] Calhoun's object is only secondarily "progress, improvement, and civilization, with all their blessings," for these only arise through the development of the human intellectual and moral faculties, which are primary. In the present condition of the world, the pursuit of wealth in advanced society may lead to the further diffusion of intelligence or, as was the case in former ages, it may not. This question is related in Calhoun's thought outside *A Disquisition on Government* to the emergence of banking or what is now called "finance capitalism" and its relation to economic development and "service industries." "The rise and progress of the banking system is one of the most remarkable and curious of the phenomena of modern times," for it is "the operation of the banking system, that peculiar description of property existing in the shape of credit or stock, public or private, which so strikingly distinguishes modern society from all that has preceded it." It is no longer merely a concern of moneyed corporations but has itself become a political institution (interest) that is all but as great *as the government itself*. The bearing of this system is objectionable because it tends to discourage individual industry or virtue "and to convert the whole community into stockjobbers and speculators." It rewards not individual virtue and industry but "those in on the secret" — what are now called "insiders." Hence,

> it allots the honors and rewards of the community, in a very undue proportion, to a pursuit the least favorable to the development of the higher mental qualities, intellectual and moral — to the decay of the learned professions, and the more noble pursuits of [natural] science, literature, philosophy, and statesmanship, and the great and more useful pursuits of business and industry.

> With the vast increase of its profits and influence it is gradually concentrating in itself most of the prizes of life — wealth, honor, and influence — to the great disparagement of all the liberal and [truly]

useful and generous pursuits of society. The rising generation cannot but feel its deadening influence. The youths who crowd our colleges, and behold the road to honor and distinction terminating in a banking house, will feel the spirit of emulation decay within them, and will no longer be pressed forward by generous ardor, to mount up the rugged steep of science as the road to honor and distinction, when, perhaps, the highest point they could attain—in what was once the most honorable and influential of all the learned professions—would be—the place of attorney to a bank.[61]

The "noble pursuits" mentioned by Calhoun in this connection are ranked by him from the lowest to the highest of the high possibilities of human life. The peak of the rugged steep is constitutional statesmanship. However, while the *Disquisition* is concerned with statesmanship, it is silent throughout on the subject of the financial system, even though the statesman must be concerned with it as an engine of avarice. It is not relevant to the subject, the "higher mental qualities." "For this purpose," Calhoun stipulates, that is, for the full development of the mental faculties, certain political conditions are requisite.[62]

The necessary political conditions include "liberty and security." The composition of these conditions is essentially the same: they are one condition, or two sides of the same thing that delimit each other. Liberty is political freedom as distinct from natural freedom (or from liberty or freedom as it is defined, say, by Hobbes or Russell). Liberty or political freedom is individual freedom within the power that is ordained to protect society. This power, the power of the whole or the "powers of the government," is here presented as "security," the provision of which is the first object of government (paragraph 17, cf. 77: "power—or, more correctly, influence"). "Security" here means the powers of the government plus what is now called, following Mill, "positive liberty." Its essential composition is as Calhoun has explained it in the previous section in connection with the community viewed in a public or political aspect: the security of the whole is in the parts, or the community viewed in a private or moral aspect, that is, it is "common," everywhere and nowhere, in the "character of the people" (paragraphs 76-78). Liberty in popular constitutional government is anchored in the political equality of each citizen in holding share in the government, or, more fully and accurately stated, in the attachment of each citizen to the "common center" (paragraph 75). The gravitational center of constitutional government is the just union of liberty, equality, and fraternity. What are called "negative" and "positive" liberties are merely the inside and outside of liberty. Behind this security are the powers of the government, which is specific. To allow individual or negative liberty a sphere of action beyond the limits of security will weaken the government and lead to insecurity. As has been explained, insecurity, the weakening of the common attachments described above, will, irrespective of education or religion, lead to an appeal to force, to be followed by a revolution or turning back in the form of the government toward absolutism (paragraphs 65, 76). For example, if liberty should be accompanied by disrespect for the law and an increase in criminality, and if criminals are not effectively punished by the government, it will become increasingly evident that liberty has been allowed a sphere of action more extensive than security will tolerate, and that sphere will eventually be contracted by expanding the powers of government into it, to that extent retarding or extinguishing the blessings that follow in liberty's train (paragraph 80, end).[63]

Paragraphs 82-85

From the foregoing, it might easily seem that the best arrangement would be that which maximizes power and minimizes liberty, or the most absolute form of government, as the surest means of protecting the community. This inference overlooks both the facts that the dangers to the community are external as well as internal, on the one hand, and that the highest ends of government are the development of the moral and intellectual faculties of the governed (paragraph 79). This latter cannot be imposed from without but can only come from within. The maximum expansion of the sphere of liberty consistent with security, that is, with the "common devotion to the country," is the best means to achieve these ends and, therewith, also to ward off foreign dangers. The withdrawal or receding of governmental power that is made possible by the virtue of the people exponentially augments the development of the power of the whole. The power of the whole — wealth, population, and other advantages — becomes greater, not less, with respect to external dangers. The cause of this is the development of the moral and intellectual faculties of the community, which ultimately depends on the security and character that is provided by the action of the government (paragraphs 75ff., 81). This is the primary end that provides the principle by which liberty and power, the higher and the lower, are assigned their proper spheres.

These spheres may vary greatly from community to community, in accordance with the preponderance of concurrency or absolutism in the construction of the government and the character of the people (paragraphs 78 end, 82). Protection takes the first place, or provides the limit, the residuum belongs to liberty (paragraphs 15, 17). This "residuum" is indistinguishable from the authority of the law or individual virtue. In the central paragraph of *A Disquisition on Government*, Calhoun observes that security may require that the sphere of liberty be all but entirely contracted in some communities. In such cases, however, even when government is most absolute and despotic, the higher ends of government may be served by promoting "a conception of liberty or of living" among the mass of the community that is beyond mere survival and self-indulgence. Not merely government but even despotic government is a positive good in such a circumstance. The relevant causes and circumstances that must be taken into account in this connection are diverse. They fall into two general classes, physical or external limits and moral or internal limits. Of these, the internal or moral limits are paramount, so much so that they may override all other circumstances, including wealth and population, however favorable or unfavorable they might otherwise seem. In all circumstances, self-government, or liberty, is a discipline or art. As such, it is not natural but, rather, the completion of nature in accordance with human political nature. It is the mastery of nature in the sense of being self-mastery.

The extension of the sphere of liberty of action, or what is the same thing, high moral and intellectual culture (paragraph 7) is, thus, the highest end of government and definitive of the best government. However, the extension of the sphere of liberty among a people not possessing the requisite morality and intelligence to sustain it and the concomitant underextension of government power among them—barring foreign conquest—merely prepares the collapse of both and the devolution of the form of government to one that is simpler and more appropriately absolute (paragraph 84). In all such cases, the extension of liberty is no more than the emancipation of selfishness and hence merely a curse that portends the still greater curse of anarchy, for it destroys those who possess it (cf. paragraphs 8, 69).[64] In turning to the dual nature of liberty, Calhoun speaks of it first as a "blessing." It is like the blessings of progress, improvement, and civilization, in that it depends, like them, on the advancement of intelligence and morals, from which they also flow; otherwise it is a curse.[65] He then speaks of enjoying liberty (paragraph 84, twice; 86). Liberty in itself is the highest human enjoyment. However, it cannot be enjoyed beyond the advancement of intelligence and morals: if more than this is allowed a people, they will soon fall into disorder and confusion, for they will mistake it and forsake it for other enjoyments with the ensuing consequences. The dual quality of liberty as both its own reward, on the one hand, and as a positive blessing and share in the government, on the other, however, means that it may in some circumstances be deserved or earned and possessed while circumstances prevent it being fully enjoyed. While this phenomenon may not be as unusual as it might seem at first glance (it is the characteristic theme of Epictetus), its reverse is impossible: more liberty than has been earned cannot be retained (paragraph 84, end).

The aim of liberty is the full development of the human moral and intellectual faculties—self-government and knowledge of the world and man—the enjoyment of which is the greatest human enjoyment and among the greatest of all blessings. This is the highest end of human society or of the human race, of all human individuals, as the distinctive human faculties find their ultimate perfection in individuals. However, liberty is not the greatest of blessings, as it is but the artful completion of the enjoyment of the sweet sense of natural existence, which, for all individuals, is necessarily prior (paragraphs 85, 82). When the two come into conflict, as they must often do, given the "different degrees of intelligence, patriotism, and virtue among the mass of the community," to say nothing of external menaces, the dependent or derivative must and rightly should yield to what is original and prior (cf. paragraph 16, sentences 3-5).

Paragraphs 86-89:
Digression on the Hypothesis of
the "State of Nature"

Having established the principle which assigns to power and liberty their proper spheres, Calhoun turns, in what amounts to the second excursus in *A Disquisition on Government*, to notice a series of "great and dangerous errors," intellectual and moral, in regard to determining the proper allotment of liberty (paragraphs 86-89). They include the opinion that all peoples are equally entitled to liberty (paragraph 86), that liberty and equality are indistinguishable (paragraphs 87-88), and, what is the contemporary origin of these, that political or moral equality and liberty are derived from physical equality and liberty, that is, from a hypothetical idea of the nature of man as drawn from the abstraction of man in an apolitical "state of nature," or, ultimately, from matter and motion (paragraph 89).

These errors differ from those discussed earlier in the argument (paragraphs 44-52) in that they might not or do not arise just anywhere or anytime but are relatively recent, and derive specifically from the doctrine just mentioned, and most influentially from the teachings of Locke.[66] In this excursus Calhoun peels back the features or layers of this doctrine to its cause. The former errors are "natural" errors, so to speak, whose understandable shortcomings, however profound, are hardly more than those of "common sense," and reasonable enough, while these are artificial: they derive not from careless or unaided reason but from the wide diffusion of elaborate philosophic doctrine, what Calhoun elsewhere calls "false philosophy" or pseudo-science. These artificial errors that arise from intellectual hypotheses, for their part, are just as dangerous as the less sophisticated or vulgar ones that arise from the many, and, hence, they compound political difficulties, as they present themselves today, beyond what these have always been "from the earliest ages." So far from presenting the progress of reason, they are "destitute of all sound reason," and leave one all but lost in disorder and confusion (paragraphs 89, 11).

Paragraph 86

It follows from all that has been stated that, while liberty is among the greatest of blessings, it is a great and dangerous error to suppose that all peoples are equally entitled to liberty. Liberty is a reward that is earned; it may or may not be "ours," but it is not, in any case, ours to "give." Like the "arbitrary" sovereign power discussed by Burke, it cannot be given. The fact that its appreciation and enjoyment is the highest political end, and hence the ultimate true end of "the progress of a people," of any and all peoples, of the human race as such, and, therefore, of human government as such, is its "proudest distinction" and its "greatest praise." It is, thus, the opposite of an original right or privilege or condition. If it were not, the development of the moral and intellectual faculties, maturity, and self-government or restraint would be of no moment. Nor, therefore, can it be released or forced by any external power. As no such power exists, one will merely be left with the powers which do exist, absolutism or force under some other guise (cf. paragraph 93). To attempt to precipitate the necessarily slow progress of any people in the scale of liberty, or, what is the same thing, attempt to abolish the scale of patriotism and virtue in respect to it, on the ground that liberty is the entitlement of all, will merely retard or permanently defeat that progress, or, even, annihilate the people as effectively as would a foreign conquest.[67] This is not to deny that "the true end of government is liberty" (Spinoza, *Theologico-Political Treatise and A Political Treatise*).

Two points in particular should be noted in connection with this paragraph (86). The first is that the paragraph makes it as plain as anyone could wish that all peoples aim at and may, potentially, in the process of time, attain to more or less liberty. All peoples are equal in this respect, if not actually or at the same time. In other words, the author's reference here to peoples "too ignorant, degraded, and vicious" to be either worthy or capable of liberty (and hence should be ruled absolutely) must be understood in light of the fact that the "love of truth and justice more or less influences all, not excepting the most depraved" (paragraph 104).[68] The eventuality in question depends principally upon whether constitutional government is established and effectively maintained among them. Calhoun is in the strict sense a cultural relativist, because he holds culture to its natural standard, which means that he is in no sense a cultural egalitarian. The former is strictly a political perspective, while the latter is only an imperial, and imperialist, one. Secondly, the upward progress of all peoples in what Calhoun calls the "scale of liberty" or the "scale of intelligence, virtue, and patriotism" does not necessarily proceed at the same pace as, or even in connection with, the progress of civilization or the diffusion of knowledge and intelligence as such. Hence the possibility emerges that the spread of civilization is more likely than the spread of liberty, and yet liberty must accompany the spread of civilization if the spread of civilization is to be more than the spread of destruction, beginning with the destruction of liberty wherever it may be found. The least one can say is that the Senecan or Burkean "law" to which Calhoun refers precludes only the elevation of any people in the scale of liberty by the force or fiat of others. It does not preclude in the slightest not merely the enslavement but the complete destruction of peoples who are fully deserving of such liberty as they have and can fully enjoy. (The example of the Iroquois noted in paragraph 110, who possessed liberty and hence the highest happiness afforded a people, is a case in point.) The signal terms in the eighty-sixth paragraph, following upon those in the eighty-forth, are terms derived from entitlement or reward (seven occurrences), which are contrasted with a variety of opposites: "a blessing to be gratuitously lavished" (i.e., a curse), "a boon," "a punishment," "abortion," "defeat." These terms represent the delineation of the scale of liberty, including the progress of a people along that scale, in contrast to the Hobbist conception of liberty as negative or scaleless or as merely the absence of effective opposition. As has been pointed out, the absence of opposition, that is, the *single* or absolute power, whatever the number in whom it is vested, is a definition not of liberty but of absolutism (paragraph 56).

Calhoun here speaks of general principles that are applicable without discrimination to all human beings and all regimes of whatever language, moral qualities, pursuits, complexion, and so on, or to what he repeatedly refers to in this context as the human "race" itself. This paragraph, in the context in which it occurs (paragraphs 80-85) presents the discussion of liberty and security "in the abstract." To the extent that it is conceivable as a discussion of "mastery and slavery" in the abstract, it is a presentation of reason and the passions in political terms. However difficult the application of general principles to immediate uses may be, they apply inexorably to all, that is, to the race (paragraph 18). There will not be one science of politics for one ethnic or linguistic group or race or and still others for other ethnic or linguistic groups or races. As it is, Calhoun offers the governments of different groups or races, the Poles, Iroquois, Romans, Chinese, Egyptians, and so on, as worthy of the attention and study of all humanity, regardless of "origin."

The first paragraph of this excursus on errors is meant to address or apply the substance of the foregoing paragraphs not primarily to contemporary Abolitionism, as some have asserted, but, above all to the contemporary "French philosophy" and the kind of hypothetical political thinking, or what is now called "ideology," represented, to take one example, by the "Christian" socialism of the Abbe Lamennais, in which lie the seeds not of reason and liberty but popular fanaticism, and which Calhoun believed was growing and would continue to grow.[69] The error addressed is the opinion that government is slavery, or that all existing governments are necessarily unjust and hence evil in their abridgment of the natural liberty of all human individuals "in the abstract." In the following paragraphs, Calhoun turns in like manner to what both underlies this error and is most noteworthy in the contemporary doctrines of Fourierism, utopian communitarians, and similar movements, namely, the ultimate extinction of liberty in the opinion that, as all men are equal, equality and liberty are the same (paragraph 87). One may provisionally characterize the difference between the first excursus and the second excursus of the *Disquisition* (i.e., paragraphs 44-52 and paragraphs 86-89) by saying that the first concerns obtuse or thoughtless errors that are common ("vulgar"), and that are correctable only by reason or science, and the second concerns sophisticated or clever errors that are increasingly common, and that are correctable by holding strictly to common sense and ordinary experience.

Paragraphs 87-88

The opinion now taken up in the eighty-seventh and eighty-eighth paragraphs amounts merely to the replacement of virtue by equality in the understanding of liberty, and in the consequential reduction of the understanding of vice to the denial of equality. The intention is to overcome vice by enforcing an equality of condition among all.[70] "Liberty" is assimilated to equality of condition. These oft-cited paragraphs inimitably (and apparently independently) set forth, and even extend a little further, the core relation of these principles that is more discursively adduced in Tocqueville's celebrated *Democracy in America.*

Calhoun stipulates that liberty and equality are necessarily united to a certain extent. They are united as the private to the public or the individual to society, as he has shown. Liberty in a popular regime is grounded in the political equality of citizens and their security under the law. This is implicit in the idea of free government (paragraph 44) and is extended to the fullest possible extent in popular constitutional governments (paragraph 70). However, the operation of personal liberty among citizens of various natural and conventional qualities and advantages insures a corresponding inequality of result between those citizens who possess these qualities and advantages and those who do not. The equality of citizens before the law,[71] which establishes liberty and unites the citizenry, also sustains (and may even increase) the inequality of conditions among the citizenry. Hence, the various natural and conventional inequalities and advantages among the population in a civilized community will always be reflected in unequal ranks (or "classes," "interests"). For the result of preventing the operation of liberty would only pervert the highest end of government, which is the promotion of liberty, and elevate the government itself, which must achieve and enforce the desired equality of condition, beyond its lower end, which is the preservation of the community. In that case, a new community will emerge in which the government itself will compose the superior rank. The governors will not share the same condition as the governed, and the intention in question, while perverting the highest aim of government, will not reach its own aim. While believing itself to be progressive, or as securing the final aim of equality, because its aim is the abolition of oppression and exploitation understood either as inequality of condition or as necessarily arising from inequality of condition, actually, it only progressively strengthens the inequality or distinction of the government interest and artificially arrests progress among the rest of the citizens. Otherwise, the "march of progress," true progressivism, subject to the explicit restrictions laid down in the previous section (and which invite further exploration, paragraphs 80-85), is open-ended among them.

What Calhoun calls progressivism makes allowance for the different capacities and advantages of different individuals and depends both upon the liberty of individuals to better their condition and upon the inequality of conditions to stimulate their desire to do so. It refers to the dynamic that is composed by the desire of the front rank of the community to lead the others and maintain its position in respect to them, and the eagerness of the rear rank of the community to catch up and take their place with the first. The "unremitting exertion of vigilance and attention" of individuals engaged in this emulating effort reflects the vigilance and active mind of the statesman, and the best from all ranks or parts will seek to obtain power, influence, and standing in the government (78). These ranks refer to the extremities of wealth and station or material condition in the mass of the community, or all those who are regarded as equal in the eyes of the law, the rich and the poor, understood as having the same desire throughout.[72] The result of their efforts over time will vary in relation to specific individuals in accordance with all of the ways in which they differ from one another, but it will not alter the relation of the ranks or classes, which will remain the same. However, for the same reason, over time, the ranks will not always be of the same composition.[73] Similarly, although the relative condition of the ranks does not change, the absolute well-being of each individual is greatly augmented by these exertions, that is, by the condition of society produced by the march of progress,[74] just as the whole population of the community (and not merely what Mosca calls the "political class," or those who participate equally in public life) is progressively elevated by the steady operation of constitutional government (78, first sentence, and context). In this way the benefits of equality and liberty may be increasingly harmonized throughout the community.

The march of progress consists not in any alteration of the relation of the ranks of society but in the increasing diffusion of intelligence and material well-being throughout all ranks or parts. It is the responsibility of the progressive statesman to sustain this condition for the whole community to the extent possible for it.[75] The principle by which the sphere of liberty must be assigned or restricted for the sake of safety or preservation has been discussed in the previous section. Preventing the results of liberty for the aim here intended by the means Calhoun describes will abolish progress along with liberty, while, also, failing to achieve equality. In other words, the destruction of liberty, which cannot be given, in a forced equality of condition, shows that equality, also, the social nature with which all men are born, cannot be given. It is as ineluctably relative and as elusive as liberty. If men are restricted to equality of condition, as the most easily quantifiable condition and hence satisfactory for the meaner capacities, then the government itself will exhibit this radically unequal nature. The project of the "welfare state" only means less welfare and more state. For the abolition of "ranks" in the community by the interposition of government will only establish the government itself as in every respect the first rank of the community, while all but insuring that those who are invested with the powers of government will not be the best but only party-men (paragraphs 27, 64-65).[76]

This will necessarily be the more or less rapid fate of all political claims on behalf of what are now valorized as "alternative" or "marginal" populations. These ultimately amount to the claim that the equality asserted on behalf of the less endowed and advantaged surpasses both the equality ("privilege") and the endowments and advantages of the more endowed and advantaged, that is, that the less endowed and advantaged are (*pace* the denial of what is called "essentialism") in essence, *more* equal, and, therefore, implicitly, should rule. The falsity of such a claim is beyond credible dispute, yet it may nevertheless come to possess political power. "While it is powerful to pull down governments, it is still more powerful to prevent their construction on proper principles." Its error discloses itself in the unlimited growth of government or absolutism.

Paragraph 89

With the presentation of the "march of progress," Calhoun arrives at the original error underlying the view of government or the restriction of human liberty as a necessary or unnecessary evil, on the one hand (paragraph 86), and the restriction of liberty in the name of human equality, on the other (paragraphs 87-88). These views are inspired by the "state of nature" doctrines of Rousseau and Locke — on analogy with which human liberty can be given or bestowed as a wild animal is given its "freedom" by releasing it from captivity or any artificial condition — and, ultimately, Hobbes, who used the argument of human equality to justify absolute monarchy, at which issue the eighty-eighth paragraph had arrived. Specifically, they originate in Hobbes' original attempt to understand human being or liberty strictly on the basis of Newtonian motion, or to define the animate or self-moved world in terms of the inanimate or merely moved world, as merely unimpeded action, that is, license. Such understanding reduces human liberty to obedience to the laws of matter and motion in the operation of which matter is, as material (or the will, as immaterial), ultimately or decisively the same or equal. They originate, therefore, in opinion, or in what Calhoun gradually identifies as "opinion" (twice), "assumption," "assertion," "supposition" (twice), and "hypothesis," that is, in theoretic or hypothetical reason, not in direct observation, and, in fact, contrary both to universal observation and to reason. They are, thus, not scientific by any modern or any genuine standard of science. They are no more related to human nature than the Ptolemaic universe is related to the physical universe or the doctrine of the flat earth to the earth. Their prevalence today is testimony to the fact that the invisible rules the visible and the brute power of abstractions. They, not modern natural science or material progress of any kind, clothe the emperor in the finest robes.[77]

Calhoun's theme in this paragraph is human origins: physical or universal and actual human "birth" (six times), and Creation or the human natural state, the social and political state (three times). His intention in the paragraph is to resolve the relation between the theme of conditions and the theme of equality as these have developed in the previous almost twenty paragraphs and in contradistinction to the hypothesis of the "state of nature." Specifically, he wants to isolate that in which the supposition that is contrary to universal observation nevertheless possesses what he calls "some semblance of truth." To reveal this semblance, he treats of the hypothesis in its most extreme (Rousseauan) form, according to which human equality itself ultimately consists in its condition—hypothetically asocial separation in the state of nature anterior to the social and political state—not in the essence or substance or content (there is none, by the supposition) of original man. It is not intrinsic. As soon as this condition of separation (nothing more) is altered and two or more men are gathered together, according to Rousseau, inequality emerges. Inequality is intrinsic to men. This opinion bears a semblance to the truth in that, thus understood, the mere condition of equality is indistinguishable from human social and hence political nature, which is also a formal condition, with the distinction that the social and hence political nature of man is not merely formal but substantial or intrinsic. It is in this way that all men are equal, and this equality is expressed in the universally observed phenomenon of human society and government, as Calhoun has explained (paragraphs 2-3ff). It is the human condition. The idea of human inequality has no meaning outside this condition; one could not even distinguish members of a human species. This natural condition, which Calhoun calls "humanity," is not sufficient to attain the virtue desired by Rousseau or the union of nature and freedom ("sociability") desired by Kant in his most Rousseauan moments.[78] For this, constitutional government, or government by the concurrent majority, is necessary, beyond mere humanity, as Calhoun has indicated. Up to now in the eighty-ninth paragraph, he has spoken only of universal observation and of the physical feelings and wants ("preservation and perpetuation of the race"). This is the ground of Hume (paragraph 2). To point to human perfection ("preserve and perfect his race"), or beyond the physical to the metaphysical, he refers, as he has in earlier paragraphs, to the Creator (paragraph 12), and hence original human reason. As he has indicated from the beginning of *A Disquisition on Government*, reason is the original essence or substance of man. Not inequality as such but reason is intrinsic and primary in original man, that is, human nature.

To grasp his meaning in the remainder of the paragraph it is necessary to recall that the "semblance of truth" to which he has pointed in connection with the hypothesis of the "state of nature" finds its ultimate expression in the post-Rousseauan idea of "history," which derives from it. As nature is replaced by a hypothetical "state of nature," giving impulse to the idea of nature as landscape and unimproved wilderness, this hypothetical state is itself elaborated and supplanted by an equally hypothetical "history," now solemnly bedecked in the fabulous robes of "philosophy of history," according to which the earliest ages were, necessarily, the infancy of the race.[79] History is thus the "anthropological" progress of the race from its infancy to its maturity, etc. Nevertheless, to repeat, the earliest ages were not ages of an imaginary "childhood" or "nonage" (Mill, Locke) of humanity but, rather, were characterized by all the essential antagonisms and problems of politics and government that characterize the present (paragraph 18). These are original and intrinsic. Childhood, as described by Calhoun, is that period of life characterized by yielding to "the impulse of present pleasure, however fatal," out of lack of self-knowledge and awareness. It obviously does not characterize the earliest stages of society — within which the savage who is without civilization also renounces, "sublimates," distinguishes, deliberates, educates children and worships — to say nothing of characterizing peoples such as the Iroquois or any form of constitutional government. It is true that intelligence was not then widely diffused (paragraph 18), but this fact is fully consistent with Calhoun's understanding of wisdom as always genuinely exceptional. Humanity was "already," in the earliest ages and in all stages (or material conditions) of society, possessed of religion and education and full grown or mature in the decisive respects, namely, all the respects confronting "philosophers of history" today in the immediate present in the "present condition of the world" (paragraphs 28, 95). To say the least, the present, in comparison, is no more "mature," nor will be the future. Otherwise, there would be no reason for government—which is *almost* Locke's own libertarian position—to say nothing of constitutional government and still less of the composition of *A Disquisition on Government* itself (paragraph 139).

Although it does not appear in the *Disquisition*, if we recall Calhoun's oft-quoted phrase, "the past is the parent of the present," we can easily grasp his intent at the close of the eighty-ninth paragraph. The present is in no sense mature but a child. The past overhangs the present. The present is ever under the authority of the past and carries its inheritance with it. Its task, the task of individuals living, is ever to discover for itself the principles and application most apt for given circumstances. These principles are not "historic" principles in any sense and cannot become "historic," but rational principles. It is the applications that are historic, and hence wise or not wise. The present has this crucial task because as the child of the past it is also the actual and unhypothetical parent of future. One might go so far as to say that in speaking of the "never was" and "never can be," Calhoun is in a sense the most historicist of all aspiring historicists, for, according to him, the present is itself "already" no less history than the past, and so, too, the future. Yet he is only interested in the past, the present, and the future (or, as he typically says, "posterity"), and not at all in the hypothesis "history."[80] Nothing is more characteristic of "philosophy of history"—or the hypothetical "state of nature" whence it arises—than that it abandons posterity, no less than the well-intentioned "religion of progress," or "futurism," with the same derivation, abandons the past. (This is why Calhoun here uses the phrase "most repugnant to his feelings.") For these reasons, the penultimate sentence of the paragraph redacts the familiar conversation of Plato's *Crito*, and also provides the only occurrence in the *Disquisition*, if I am not mistaken, of the term "authority." It is an authority embraced by universal observation as naturally right. This authority is not any kind of what is sometimes nowadays called "fictions of authority," of course, but immediate parental authority, the universal authority of parents (fathers *and* mothers) over infants and children, the old over the young, and, Calhoun immediately adds, the "laws and institutions of the country where born."[81]

The movement of the eighty-ninth paragraph and the digression as a whole is toward its final sentence. Be the hypotheses what they may, this is the universal and acknowledged truth. Calhoun means it as literally as it can be meant, as literally as Filmer meant it, and as literally as Locke meant it in his argument against Filmer.[82] To the extent that it is an acknowledgment that is shared by Calhoun and Locke, each further step illuminates not only the similarities and dissimilarities of their thought but those of Calhoun and the whole "state of nature" school. From the position set forth at the beginning of the *Leviathan* and the defense of the most absolute monarchy possible, Hobbes ultimately arrives at his proposal of "enlightenment," to be achieved by the study of his writings in the place of others, the ancient classics and Schoolmen, at the university level. From that set forth at the beginning of the *Essay Concerning Human Understanding* and his defense in the *Two Treatises on Government* of the most limited monarchy possible, Locke, arrives at his proposals concerning the education of the young.[83] The two differ only in these means, the purpose or end of both proposals is the same, the transformation, or, better, "conversion" of the English warrior class, the nobility, into a kind gentrified bourgeois, or what will become known as "economic man," the basis of the later abstraction of the "common man," and related notions. The aim of this project, whether the proposals of Hobbes and Locke are taken independently or together, is pacification of the warrior class. However, whatever the extent to which nobility is suppressed or curbed or rubbed away, no one can read Locke's *Thoughts Concerning Education* without being left fully aware that the intended education remains thoroughly English, *is* English. As many have overlooked, but as Rousseau above all did not overlook, what is called economic man is not "natural man" but a certain kind of Englishman. Economic man is an Englishman as conceived and educated by Hobbes and, especially, Locke. It is this insight that inspires Rousseau's attack on the Englishman as conceived and justified by Locke on behalf of the "noble savage" and the "true" natural man.

We have discussed these conceptions as they relate to Calhoun's doctrine of man as a political animal. Yet some light may be further shed on his position by referring to the most influential authority on the subject of the decisive absence of feudalism in early American history for the understanding of Locke's influence and sketching out Calhoun's view: "When Locke came to America because the basic feudal oppression [*sic*] of Europe had not taken root, the fundamental social norm of Locke ceased in large part to look like a norm and began, of all things, to look like a sober description of fact."[84]

This "sobriety" is not Locke's, and the fact itself is only a fact in the way a strictly controlled experiment produces a "fact." It requires a certain, almost willful blindness with respect both to the seers and to what is seen. This blindness replaces Locke's *tabula rasa* for the purposes of establishing this fact in the place of Locke's sober "norm." It means not seeing the seer as precisely a Lockean Englishman, on the one hand, and not seeing the other seers, the hosts of aboriginal Americans as equally men because they are not socially or culturally equal, that is, not English. To some extent, this is the way all peoples look at other peoples, but in this case the "norm" in question is universal reason, *the* norm, the definitive quality of all men. The norm must, then, be extended as right to the aboriginal peoples, to all aboriginal or less advanced peoples considered individually. Although it is difficult, one must, of course, take care not to confuse the extension of this norm with the "sober fact" of English imperialism. Otherwise, the "equality" thus extended will merely become the mask by which the less are exploited and defrauded by the more advanced in the name of reason. Calhoun is perfectly sensible of the material and psychic shock or awe represented by the appearance of civilized to uncivilized peoples. If possible, he is even more sensible that the experience of the civilized people is not that of Locke's "state of nature," and still less of the confrontation with equals (can it not be proven in a trice that the family who has lived on this or that plot of land and drank from this or that well for a thousand years do not hold title to the land according to English law?), but the experience of sheer, unchecked superiority. What is all but invisible in the passage just quoted is that the position it sets forth necessarily provides the ground either for the establishment of a kind of "feudalism," if it is to be made responsible, or for the extermination of the aboriginal hosts.

It is this fact, for example, to which Calhoun was referring in once speaking to the younger Adams, at Adams' instigation, of the American Declaration of Independence, according to which the rights of American colonists as Englishmen had been abused by the government of George III. When Adams asserted that the Declaration should be applied to Africans in the South, Calhoun said that, in the South, "we" do not think of them as applying to the Africans. They are not truly "Englishmen," that is, they are not Americans in the same way "we" are Americans; they have not the same background; they are not similarly advanced; they are not equal. The artificial condition in which they are maintained in the midst of a more advanced people is, in their circumstances, beneficent. Its contrary would not be beneficent but would compound their deracination.[85] The demand that the Lockean norm nevertheless be extended to them represents a severe contraction of the understanding of man, true or original man, to that, ultimately, of the Lockean Englishman, beginning with the *Essay Concerning Human Understanding*. According to Calhoun, this is a "sad delusion." As such, it arises, in Lockean England and the United States, not out of concern for the less advanced peoples but out of envy of the slaveowners as a rising aristocracy or new feudal class. It leaves the less advanced to one side, or worse. What inside England, or, if you like, inside "European feudalism," is a project meant for pacification of the warrior class, becomes, outside, a project of conquest of all peoples, as Conrad unmistakably saw, under the rubric of absolute "pacification." It becomes in the end, in Conrad as well as Twain: "exterminate the brutes," whether literally or merely as peoples.

Admittedly, this is perhaps not Locke's intention in his most judicious moments; it is even its opposite. Yet, be this as it may, it is also its necessary consequence, because it follows from the merely apparent if emphatic replacement of politics and the political by "civility" and economism. The "city" — the *polis*, the *political* community — is replaced by this emphasis — by empire. This is all the replacement of state rights by what are called "human rights" ultimately means. Locke's attempt to mitigate Hobbes' absolute monarchism in England effectually, if unintentionally, globalizes it — unless it is externally checked or collapses internally. The response cannot merely be political, however, for the universalizing hypothesis under which it marches, its abstractly or hypothetically "anti-absolutism," which is in truth only a counter-absolutism, must also be checked, that is, refuted on its own ground. This is the purpose of *A Disquisition on Government*, beginning with the rejection of the doctrine of the "state of nature."

There remains an urgent difficulty, which has nothing particularly to do with Locke or Lockeanism, which is, however, severely compounded by Lockeanism, and which Rousseau had attempted to resolve in tandem with his radicalization of Locke's doctrine of the "state of nature" and education, and his counter to the bourgeois gentleman, the "noble savage." Where the ultimate aim of Hobbesianism and Lockeanism is pacification—peace with comfort—Rousseau's aim is typically split between those of citizenship and community—political virtue—and the natural man. Among other things, he attempts to unify these aims in his myth of the legislator. According to Calhoun, as we have noted, they are actually or concretely unified only in the constitutional statesman. The urgent difficulty in question is the difficulty to which Rousseau attempted to point as represented by progress in the arts and sciences: "civilization." Calhoun begins his turn to this subject in the section's concluding paragraphs, which complete Calhoun's outline of the science of government.

Paragraph 90:
The Conclusion

The author now returns to pick up the thread of the discourse on perfection of the human moral and intellectual faculties at the point he had reached in the eighty-fifth paragraph in the discussion of the greatest of all blessings, protection or power and liberty or virtue. The more perfectly a government combines these, that is, the more perfectly a government arms virtue or virtue commands power, the better it is. It remains only to show that constitutional government promotes "a higher degree of power" and "a wider scope of liberty" than does absolute or non-constitutional government. Calhoun presents this explanation in terms of the development of the intellectual faculties, or "progress," and morals (paragraphs 91-98). The section is primarily a summation and culmination of what has been set forth (paragraph 91: "...as has been explained," "...as has been fully explained"; paragraph 94: "...has already been shown"; paragraph 98: "...as has been fully shown"). However, it contains a crucial element that is new, or that receives a new emphasis (paragraph 95), which we will discuss at the proper place in connection with Calhoun's understanding of "the present condition of the world" (paragraphs 16, 28). This element is not a summation of anything that has gone before. Although the rationale of these paragraphs (16, 28, 95, to name only these) is evident in their places, upon reflection it is clear that they could also be placed otherwise, and, taken together, they begin to exhibit a theme and dimension of the *Disquisition* that only becomes explicit toward the end of the work. For the full perspective of the *Disquisition* to emerge, they must be seen not only in light of their place in the order of the argument, but in light also of the second excursus taken as a whole (this group of paragraphs and the second excursus begin from the same place—paragraph 86: "it follows...," paragraph 90: "it follows...") and the "new political element" that is introduced below (paragraphs 112ff.). The whole of *A Disquisition on Government*, of course, is written as it were in the face of this new element or with this element in mind.

Let us attempt an overview. At first glance, it seems that this discussion (paragraphs 91-98) is divided by Calhoun into two parts. The first concerns the enlargement and security of liberty as the highest end of government (paragraphs 91-93); the second concerns, derivatively, the expansion and security of power, which is a lower end (paragraphs 94-95), or, in other words, what Calhoun has earlier called liberty's repayment of power with interest (paragraph 81). The latter is further divided into a discussion of the progress of civilization and hence physical power (paragraphs 94-95), and one of moral "power," which is independent of the progress of civilization and of greater moment (paragraphs 96-98). A free civilized people, a modern constitutional people, is the most powerful, as well as the noblest, of all peoples, and incomparably surpasses all others in respect to the moral and intellectual ends for which government is ordained. In the midst of this discussion, Calhoun is brought to mention two "striking examples" by name: "England and the United States" (paragraph 95). The modern world will be contested by these. These are the first examples offered by Calhoun since the ancient examples mentioned in the first or introductory section of the *Disquisition* as a whole (paragraph 18), which examples exemplified constitutional government in an age of partially diffused intelligence. With his reference to the new examples. as exemplary of the modern or enlightened age, and the close of the discussion in which they occur, Calhoun's outline of the metaphysics of politics or the foundation of the science of government is complete.

In studying the parts of this discussion, the reader may notice the remarkable artistry (if that is the best word), or beauty, with which this group of paragraphs, taken as a unit, closes the subject that was marked out in the nineteenth and twentieth paragraphs, where Calhoun had introduced the term "organism" as the living mechanism of the community. The initial paragraphs here (paragraphs 91-93), in the first of which occurs a reference to the "open and free" society, culminate in reference to this organism. They are about liberty, or virtue, and government. The closing paragraphs (96-98) are about community and moral power. Moral power *is* the community. It thus comes about that the close of Calhoun's discussion of the second question (paragraph 15) of political science culminates in the topic of moral power. Constitutional government is, ultimately, the intelligent empowerment of the human moral faculties. Both these sets of paragraphs concern the "inside" of the communal organism, the interior of the open and moral community. Together, they represent the two aspects or the "manyness" of the inside, or the interior order: its true "nature."[86] These two sets of three paragraphs, or this presentation, is interrupted, in a sense, in the middle, by two paragraphs on physical power. The longer of these two paragraphs (95) explicitly looks "outside." We draw attention to this aspect of the *Disquisition* in view of the work's initially strikingly apoetic quality. It is in this paragraph and its context that also emerges what might be called the sublime aspect of the argument, in the sense either of Burke or of Kant, as distinct from its beauty.

Paragraphs 91-93:
The Principles of Constitution and
the Promotion of Liberty

The ninety-first paragraph of the *Disquisition on Government* presents the earliest explicit reference to what has become celebrated as the "open society." Its public and its private are transparent and open to each other in freedom and without contradiction. However, it is necessary to see that here only what is "beyond" the proper limit of government, what Calhoun has earlier called the "residuum" (paragraph 82), remains within what Calhoun expressly calls the "bounds" of liberty. The open society is possible only as a closed community. It is a society with fixed and exclusive limits, upon the basis of which, and only upon the basis of which, the preservation liberty is possible. It is the tendency of liberty to pass beyond its proper limits that makes government necessary if the community is to be preserved, and the tendency of government to pass beyond its proper limits that makes constitutional government necessary if the community is to be perfected in accordance with the natural ends of society. The organism of the closed society is identical to the organism of the concurrent majority, for it is the organism of concurrency which binds liberty to security or the part to the whole, and, therefore, as he has shown, which makes the constitution and empowers the whole. Because the organism of concurrency prevents erosion of the common center of attachment of all it parts (paragraphs 75-78) and, in accordance with the principle assigning liberty and power their proper spheres (paragraphs 80-85), restricts the government to its primary end of protecting the community, government of the concurrent majority is better suited than absolute government to enlarge and to *secure* the bounds of liberty. Government leaves all that is beyond its primary end "open and free" to liberty. This is the "sphere of liberty," the highest reward for virtue or the development of the human moral and intellectual faculties. The action of concurrency tends to weaken the tendency of virtue to be sapped or drawn off by the stimulation of some partial or merely selfish motive, while absolute governments only affirm this tendency or "add to it increased strength." It is for this reason that such governments amount to an education in vice.

Paragraphs 92-93

All governments and regimes claim the promotion of virtue and the right in the character of the people, but as the reward of virtue is liberty and in absolute governments liberty is little more than a name, it follows that the virtue and right promoted among the people is, also, little more than a name (paragraph 92, cf. 48).[87] The name does not meet the thing: "knowledge, wisdom, patriotism, virtue" (paragraph 78). Constitutional government is the government of the whole for the good of the whole, and not merely in the name of the whole (cf. paragraph 14). The central paragraph of this initial part of the concluding section (paragraph 92) resembles the summary paragraph of the opening survey of concurrency (paragraph 42): the organism of the concurrent majority, whatever its form, avoids partiality and localism by taking the "full sense of the community." It restrains the government as the laws restrain individuals. In so doing, it protects the rights and interests of each individual and strengthens his sympathetic feelings.[88] It perfects the right of suffrage, while extending its spirit to the utmost possible extent. All have a common interest in the strength of the government and in holding the government to its primary end (paragraph 93). Individuals taken alone cannot achieve this. Without an organism of concurrency this aim cannot be met (paragraph 52). Revolution is no answer (paragraphs 15, 17). Force is rarely sufficient to establish liberty or to regain it when it has been lost.[89] Liberty itself, virtue or what Calhoun will call "moral power," grounded in concurrency is the only sure guard of liberty against power.

Paragraphs 94-95:
The Principles of Constitution and the
Present Condition of the World

These considerations concerning the defense of the community from the most threatening danger from within, vice, lead also to acknowledgment of the threat of overthrow from without, alien power, and the need to be prepared accordingly (paragraph 94). These dangers differ as nature and history (paragraph 95: "the pages of history"), or political as natural history in the Polybian sense. Calhoun has shown that the liberty favored by constitutional government tends toward the community's increasing attainment of better material conditions, growth in wealth and population, increase in efficiency, and diffusion of the arts and sciences. All this is what everyone understands by the idea of progress, but this understanding only partially captures Calhoun's understanding, which we will here try to sketch following the indications provided in the *Disquisition* and elsewhere.

As we noted in the beginning, the place of the human being in the scale of being, as it is understood by Calhoun, is the scale of independence from brute creation or material nature (paragraph 2). Civilization, "the advancement in the mechanical and chemical improvements in the arts," is the primary means of increasingly bringing matter under the "dominion of mind" and enlarging this independence to provide a solid foundation for learning and for the improvement of conditions in society. Although it "will be found in progress to react on the moral and political world" in a way that is great and salutary, it is secondary, and must be "subordinate to higher views of policy."[90] As he has shown, progress in the scale of being is primarily progress in the "scale of patriotism and virtue" or the "scale of liberty" (paragraphs 78, 86), or what he calls "high intellectual and moral culture" (paragraph 7). Thus understood, culture, as distinct from civilization, is the means by which the passions are brought under the dominion of reason, or self-government, and hence elevated. This is the aim of human society, given its place in creation. All creation proceeds from the Creator in order to make him known and that the creatures be perfected (paragraph 12). This knowledge, which, as has been noted, Calhoun elsewhere calls metaphysical knowledge, is the perfection of the human intellectual faculties. Creation is understood by Calhoun as manifestation, revealing to the mind the Infinite Being who cannot be known without understanding the laws of mental and material nature. This, creative mastery of the agents of material nature for the sake of raising the condition of man above brute creation, which, as such, is not in any sense free or self-sufficient but is absolutely subject to absolute laws or causal relations of which it is merely so many occasions, and which are themselves revealed for what they are in the progress of the arts and sciences, is the aim of the arts and sciences. This progress provides the foundation or context or, as it has been more recently suggested, "enframement," for the perfection of human society in accordance with the highest ordained end of human society or nature.[91] It is only by means of such progress that humanity both finds *and* makes its home in nature, its own nature or the true "state of nature," which is permanent and does not change, although human understanding may change. At the same time, humanity discovers that its own nature is not merely human thinking or making or doing but primarily "other" thinking or making or doing, that is, it discovers the Divine that is also ever beyond its manifestation in material nature and to which the human is subordinate: the Infinite, the Creator, and Providence, the highest purpose of which in relation to man is the perfection in freedom of man.

As we noted in the beginning, Calhoun only takes up this subject in the *Disquisition* except as it is immediately related to the perfection of government. All government ultimately points beyond itself to its highest aim. Humanity differs in this way from animals and plants. The aims of government are not so high as the aims of society, in the final or best instance, the metaphysics of mind. It is sufficient that the science or metaphysics of government be implicitly consistent with such a disquisition. It is as part of the primary end of government that Calhoun here discusses the progress of civilization, that is, from the point of view of the defense of the community in the present condition of the world. While one might suppose as a matter of course that all the things mentioned in this paragraph contribute to the increase of power, Calhoun nevertheless says that "it now remains to show" that they contribute to the increase of power (94). The following paragraph (95) provides the keystone of the *Disquisition*'s sketch of the universal history of the human race in terms of mastery of the material agents of nature and the increase of power.

Calhoun observes various "stages" in the development of human society.[92] The stages describe a continuum or scale of human progress "through which our race has passed" from the "earlier stages of society" to the "present condition of the world" (paragraphs 28, 18: "the subsequent advance of our race in civilization and intelligence"). Yet the stages are distinct from historical epochs. The stages refer not to time but to material conditions and, above all, to the extent of diffusion of intelligence among the people (paragraph 18). He presents three different general stages which are all equally social and political and which all have the same ends (cf. paragraph 3). Nature, including human nature and its ends, does not change. These stages include, first, the "earlier stages of society," which extend to all savagery and barbarism. This period is characterized, from the vantage of the high arts and sciences, less by the possession of liberty than by the absence of the high arts and sciences (cf. paragraph 18: "the earliest ages").[93] As we noted in the beginning of our study, according to Calhoun, it is in this period, that liberty, the highest human reward, when attained, is most easily maintained. Second, there is "a more advanced stage," a stage of civilization and commerce emerging and contending within that of barbarism, "when intelligence was so partially diffused" (cf. paragraph 18: "the early dawn of civilization"), in which stage, as Calhoun noted at the beginning, there were several remarkable constitutional regimes. Finally, there is a further or "more advanced progress" — perhaps a high noon of civilization — which is characterized by flourishing arts and sciences and wide diffusion of intelligence. In this stage there may eventuate the replacement of everything reminiscent of the conditions of savagery and barbarism by the blessings of science, including, above all, Calhoun's science of government. This stage may be the final and highest stage of human society, as distinct from merely the last historical period or epoch. The noblest or most noteworthy moments in all of the stages of human society are found in the constitutional governments which crown them. It is the emergence of the science of government itself, the disquisition on its elementary principles, which represents for humanity the greatest and essentially if not practically final moment of all time, even though or because the age of science has not yet actually (and may never) become the universal attainment of all the peoples on the earth, precisely because it is beyond time and circumstance. It is, thus, equal or superior even to the origins of the constitutional governments themselves, both because its origin is rational and self-conscious or in accord with nature and because its achievement is dependent not upon many but one.[94]

Liberty, which is the highest end of government, gives the greatest impulse to progress, which contributes greatly to the community's power. The present stage of society is beyond any other in development of power. It is the stage of power. This does not mean, as some may suppose, that the earlier stages, in contrast, were stages of liberty: all stages are equally social and political stages, that is, stages of liberty and power. The stages of human society do not represent changes in the nature of man. It does mean that the tasks of statesmanship are great in this stage of society, the stage of power, if liberty is to be guarded against power and unified with power (cf. especially paragraph 93, last sentence). In this paragraph, Calhoun touches on two aspects of power in the present condition of the world. We will take up the second of these aspects first, his reference to Great Britain and the United States. We may justify our doing so by observing that the immediate subject is the protection of the community from external power, and these examples are the most apt instances of foreign affairs and external confrontation.

Great Britain is, as we have noted, for Calhoun, the greatest of world powers. Her capitol is the center (Calhoun sometimes says, "the vortex") of world commerce, the net that increasingly enmeshes the globe. Her natural rival, from the time of William the Conqueror forward, France, is no longer a serious concern. In Calhoun's speeches, we find that the revolution in France led to the democratic Terror, an extreme form of "political correctness," confusion, and, finally, military despotism. So far from representing the spirit of freedom, the French spirit was dissipated in mere militarism. They were left neither great nor free. With France no longer a distraction, Great Britain, whose name is synonymous with material progress and its conditions, is come to the verge of a global dominion far surpassing the Romans. In so doing, she has become the natural rival of the United States. The "striking examples" of material progress, are, also, competitors.[95] Their power is ultimately drawn from the liberty afforded by their respective constitutions, which are superior to absolute regimes in this crucial respect. Calhoun turns to this subject in the following paragraphs. Such liberty is, thus, crucial for protection in the present stage of society, which is also the present condition of the world. It is, therefore, of the utmost importance. However, the other aspect of power which Calhoun mentions is, for him, even more important.

Calhoun indicates the signal difference of the present age in a striking way. In the past, the "more advanced stage" of society which emerged from time to time within barbarism had always to contend with predominant barbarism. The more advanced stage was, typically, overcome. The usual examples (Calhoun gives no examples) are the fall of the Greeks to the Macedonians, and, above all, the fall of Rome to the tribes of the north. The "pages of history" to which Calhoun refers relate mainly to such struggles. According to Calhoun, these declines and falls were due primarily to the internal moral collapses of the more advanced peoples and only secondarily to anything having to do with the less advanced peoples, who themselves quickly receded into the obscurity whence they had momentarily arisen. A still more advanced progress, however, has now settled this issue in favor of the more advanced stage of society. This is the most decisive fact in the natural history of human society, for it means that to a greater extent than ever before "numbers and individual prowess," and, therefore, the moral qualities which render a people capable of self-government, no longer are at all sufficient for protection from external enemies (paragraphs 83, 95, first sentence). Fifty barbarians with machine-guns might easily destroy thirty-thousand lesser-armed defenders of superior moral capabilities.[96]

To begin to understand what Calhoun means, it is necessary to notice that all of the stages of human society described by Calhoun may and actually do exist, or have existed, in the "present condition of the world." Three of the eight constitutional examples set forth by Calhoun, Poland, the Iroquois, and Great Britain, fall within the historical period that is marked by the emergence of this final or civilized stage. Its emergence is marked by the discovery of gunpowder and its application to war. These examples also represent the stages of society. The result of the progress under discussion is that in the present condition of the world, "communities the most advanced" occupy a superiority over the least advanced stages or communities that is "almost as great as that of the latter is over the brute creation" (cf. paragraph 2).

Calhoun's formulation of this relationship is as good as any we have yet seen to show why his literal language must first be followed with close attention if he is to be understood. Otherwise, his meaning is easily lost or assimilated to views he does not hold. For example, he does not here employ what was long since the commonplace comparison, in this connection, of human beings to animals or of adult human beings to children (much less of civilized men to natural men).[97] Rather, the least advanced communities are, in every sense, fully human or political communities, also with superiority over brute creation, but without advanced civilization. It is progress in civilization that has "forever settled the question of ascendancy between civilized and barbarous communities in favor of the former," whether the former are of a constitutional character or not. This means that the pages of history will not now simply go on as before. It means that the non-civilized communities, who, at the time of the writing of the *Disquisition*, not only remain the vast majority, but, more notably, some of whom are possessed of constitutional governments, all now must either imitate the civilized communities in some way or become assimilated or extinct.[98] The progress of the arts and sciences achieves not only striking power over the material agents of nature but, for those who possess it, an even more striking power over other peoples. Possessed of such unchecked and irresponsible power, it would be difficult for the civilized communities to hold government to its ordained ends and avoid engaging in as unthinking a tyranny as that famed as the sack of Rome. In such a context, it even begins to be possible to ask whether perfection of constitutional government may not be necessary not only for the perfection of the community but for its preservation.[99]

Whatever may have been the import of the discoveries of fire and of the wheel in the earliest stages of society, it surely pales before the import of the discoveries of gunpowder and steam and their application to war. These two discoveries are the discoveries specifically mentioned here by Calhoun in tracing the ascendancy of the civilized communities, but they must not be simply taken for granted. They occurred at widely different times and places, and should be considered separately. The elementary impact of application of gunpowder to war and the impulse it gave to invention and innovation is now well known.[100] It ushered in what Calhoun looked upon as the period of world conquest, the consequences of which are now the inheritance of all. In spite of the suggestions of Kant, among others, to the contrary, the development of "new and far more powerful and destructive" weapons of war has not antiquated war, and, according to Calhoun, will not do so in future (cf. paragraph 28).[101] After the application of gunpowder, the invention of steam power, centuries later, similarly marked an epoch.[102] With the application of discoveries to war for defensive purposes only and of steam power to intercontinental commerce, it is the epoch Calhoun wishes to promote, in the place of conquest or as an alternative to it, as that of world commerce and of culture. Calhoun hardly develops this possibility in the *Disquisition* (see paragraphs 134-135), but it is a common theme in his speeches under such themes as "free trade." In this paragraph such concerns are barely visible in his references to the "wealth" and "increased expenses" characteristic of the most advanced stage of society. Progress in technology, and not only in the development of new and more destructive weaponry, risks becoming irresponsible power. Irresponsible power and the corruption that follows in its wake is primordial and coeval with government, not new. All prior technology was effective and diffused to the extent that it operated on the same principles, and hence that they are the same in this respect, as nature is the same and does not vary with the historical epoch, and also the fact that modern technology, whether it is Newtonian or post-Newtonian, ultimately, like the earliest technology, remains dependent on the human observer.

The problem raised by technology is that, while the application of scientific discoveries to military purposes has assured the ascendancy of civilized over barbarous communities, it has done little to insure the ascendancy of constitutionalism over absolutism, or liberty over tyranny. It primarily aids in the defense of already free peoples against invasion or subversion and conquest. It may also aid in the preservation and expansion of absolute regimes. The settled ascendancy of civilized communities over uncivilized communities does not settle the question of the ascendancy of constitutional over absolute governments, although progress promotes the former. This question, which is inherent in the first communities, or in human society itself, is retained in all communities. With the continuing advance of civilization the not unambiguous struggle for ascendancy between barbarous and civilized peoples, which struggle "for a long period" had replaced the timeless struggle between barbarous peoples, is now characteristically replaced by that of increasingly civilized peoples. The condition brought about by the application of scientific discoveries to war will not now be lost, but the community Calhoun has described in the preceding paragraphs and the morality he describes in the following paragraphs, that is, the character of a constitutional people, may easily be lost. It is challenged by its very progress in wealth and power, a challenge which, Calhoun has indicated, only concurrency and the moral power of the people may meet.

The attainment and preservation of the civilized constitutional regime and its blessings, which, as such, while enlarging the peak achievements of other stages in the scale of liberty, is itself open-ended in respect to the development of the human intellectual faculties, is only in principle an attainment of "the race." It is particularly and actually an attainment of constitutional peoples. As such, it emerges not merely within and against the field of barbarism, like all civilization, but within and against the field of absolutism. This attainment cannot be given or transferred by the constitutional peoples to humanity or "the race," but must be developed from within each community. The end of this internal development, the simply best regime, the regime which most fully expresses the highest ends of nature and the elementary principles of the science of government, is the perfect civilized popular constitutional government, or constitutional democracy.

Paragraphs 96-98:
The Promotion of Liberty
and Moral Power

After emphasizing physical power to such an extent, Calhoun returns to the moral question with the word "but" (paragraph 96). Morality is the ultimate human question, whatever the powers that be or whatever the stage of society. The liberty secured and bound under concurrency, that is, by "knowledge, wisdom, patriotism, and virtue," itself bestows on the people considered individually an elevation, self-reliance, energy, and enthusiasm that exponentially augments the physical power at their disposal. It is these qualities which most tend to render a people and individuals truly and irresistibly free, that is, capable of self-government under even the most adverse circumstances. This capability or power is the greatest human power, the highest and most distinctive human power. It arises or is released by constitutional liberty itself as its concommitant or reward.

It should not be overlooked that the last quality named among those listed, "enthusiasm," is a term familiar during the "Enlightenment" as primarily denoting the passion of religion and the origin of fanaticism, which the leading Enlightenment figures wish either to abolish altogether or to enlist on the side of "acquisition."[103] Rather, Calhoun distinguishes between religion and fanaticism, and holds that fanaticism cannot be enlisted on the side of reason but is the absence of reason, and antithetical to virtue.[104] His concern has been to show how enthusiasm, which is natural and essential to humans, is brought into its proper sphere in the political community while aligning it with reason and virtue.

In the central paragraph of this concluding group, which almost begins with another "but" ("however"), Calhoun emphasizes that beyond these important qualities are still others, harmony, union, and devotion to country, that are even more decisive (97).[105] However, with one exception, he has already mentioned these kinds of qualities, and explained at some length how they are established, preserved, and perfected (paragraphs 72-78). The exception concerns their particular disposition, which, like the others, follows from the argument in the paragraphs just cited, although it is there passed over in silence. This disposition is the disposition "to elevate to places of trust and power those who are distinguished for wisdom and experience." It arises from the political virtues of constitutional peoples, which are the common ground that the people considered individually share with the exceptional individual described in the sixth paragraph, the simply rational man. Reference here to this disposition as the crown of moral power or the perfection of culture is the true intent of the paragraph and the positive aim of the organism of concurrency itself.[106] This is its true perfection. By this means and by this means only can the parts of the whole be selfless and yet remain wise, or retain the advantages of individuality (cf. paragraph 11). It is thus, also, that reason itself becomes whole. Through the promotion of all these causes, constitutional government promotes the optimum individuation in the "mass of the community," wherein lies the "maximum of power." It frees the whole to rise above itself, while absolute governments so sap the communities under their rule that these ever languish beneath themselves.

There has never existed, and may never exist, such a perfect regime as is here outlined. If it were to emerge, one may doubt whether, under the best of circumstances, it could ever actually become the simultaneous possession of the whole race. However, as it is presented in its elementary principles in *A Disquisition on Government*, it nevertheless remains in all circumstances the standard for the whole race. It is a standard that may be realistically approached or approximated to good effect, and has been by the most noteworthy communities in every age and stage of society. Because of its superiority, even when defective, to all other modes in developing the human political and moral faculties, including education and religion, the concurrent majority in some form is necessarily an indispensable element in the theory of constitutional government and the completion of the highest natural human potential, "as has been fully shown."

CHAPTER FIVE

Political Science and Progress

> In his *Disquisition on Government* Calhoun has expounded his theory of
> a constitution...with arguments which are the very perfection of politi-
> cal truth, and which combine the realities of modern democracy and
> the securities of medieval freedom.
>
> Acton[1]

CALHOUN IN THE REMAINDER OF THE *DISQUISITION* TAKES UP THE PRACTICAL PART OF
political science to consider the principle of concurrency from the point of view
of application, beginning from the essential fact of controversy and conflict of
opinion (paragraphs 99ff.). He treats this part, also, in an elementary way.
Together with the introductory part (paragraphs 1-18), the remainder represents
about one-half of *A Disquisition on Government*. Taking the closing section on
constitutional examples, which also opens onto the *Discourse*, as a part unto
itself, we may say that the *Disquisition* as a whole consists of four major parts:
the introduction, or foundation of the science of government; explanation of the
principles of constitutional government; application or problems; and working
examples. We here take up the section on problems.

The foregoing parts of the *Disquisition* have explained the principles upon
which government must be formed in order to resist by its own internal
structure the tendency to abuse of power (paragraphs 18ff.), and shown that the
concurrent or constitutional majority is an indispensable element both in
forming constitutional governments (paragraphs 53ff.) and in best developing
the "great elements of moral power" that are naturally present in all regimes or
"society" (paragraph 98). At first glance, the immediately following section of
the *Disquisition* (paragraphs 99-111) seems to be as sharply set off from what
follows it as it does from what it has followed (cf. paragraphs 98-99, 111-112).
Yet this section (paragraphs 99-111) also represents the peak of the whole work
from the point of view of purpose (cf. 41) or from the perspective of political
science itself (paragraph 1). It introduces (following the emphasis on wisdom
and experience in the prior paragraphs) the tasks of statesmanship in the present
condition of the world. What has gone before in this respect is summarized here

in the author's discussion of the relative weakness and strength of the foundation of governments (paragraphs 100, 107). This summary statement culminates in his assertion of the "greatest possible achievement of the science of government" (106), which concludes or closes his opening reference to the laying of a "solid foundation for the science of government" (101). At the same time, beginning with reference to "striking advantages," "objections," "diversity of opinion" (paragraphs 99, 100, "opinion" is mentioned nine times in paragraphs 100-102), and "impracticability" (paragraphs 99, 108, 110) and closing with the exposition of striking and worthy pragmatic examples (108-111), the section adumbrates all that will follow after it, including "public opinion" as a "new political element" (112, 132). The section may be treated independently, as a summation of the foundation of political science, or as a concluding statement of *A Disquisition on Government* up to this point, or as the introductory statement for the remainder of the whole. Were Calhoun's disquisition a Platonic dialog, it might have begun with the questions at issue here and worked its way at once forward and backward to the beginning and end of the presentation as we have it.

That the last possibility among those just mentioned — treating the section as a synthesis and introductory to what follows — is the best one is suggested by the author's initial reference to the objection to constitutionalism that has "already been sufficiently noticed" (paragraph 99) for purposes then more immediately at hand. This first or continuing and continual objection that constitutional government is always difficult of construction, which has already been sufficiently noticed, in fact appears to be the theme of most of the remainder of the *Disquisition*.

The science of government itself is explicitly mentioned only three times in the whole work. The first of these references occurs in the opening of the first part of the *Disquisition* (paragraph 1) in the discussion of what is necessary for the "solid foundation" of the science of government, and the third and last reference occurs here in the opening section of the last part as a whole (paragraph 106) in the course of the discussion of the "greatest possible achievement" that might be expected of the science of government once it has attained its true foundation. The central reference occurs in the center of the first section of what we have called the second part (paragraph 38). That section introduces the distinction between constitutional and absolute or numerical majorities, and concerns the problem of the "application in practice" of the essential principle of constitutional government, that is, the constitutional or concurrent majority. The great difficulty in forming constitutional government and all that goes with such difficulty arises first from ignorance of the distinction between merely numerical and truly constitutional majorities (paragraphs 19, 38, 47, 51). The argument there and in the subsequent paragraphs is intended to dispel this ignorance in every particular up to and including those most pertinent to the perfection of the human moral and intellectual faculties, and liberty. This accomplished, the foundation of the science of government is unfolded in accordance with the axioms that have been laid down in the opening paragraphs (1-4). This primary and, *sensu strictu*, ordinary achievement, however, Calhoun's own, is not yet the "greatest possible achievement of the science of government," and it is to that "extraordinary achievement" that the *Disquisition* now turns (paragraphs 99-165).

The author now observes or concludes in the first sentence of this part (paragraph 99) that the constitutional regimes have "many and striking advantages" over absolute regimes. He separates these quantitative and qualitative adjectives in order to give due emphasis to each one, and, as constitutional advantages have been enumerated throughout (e.g., paragraphs 70, 72), particularly to the latter. These, the "striking" advantages, are those which "from their very nature" make a "deep impression" not merely because they are apparent exceptions to the common run of human governments throughout time but also and precisely because they are the most naturally desirable in themselves (paragraph 97, cf. 6). The striking physical, moral, and intellectual advantages of constitutional regimes that are described in the immediately previous paragraphs are perfectly commensurate with the striking physical, moral, and intellectual particulars by reference to which constitutional government was originally distinguished in the fourteenth and eighteenth paragraphs. For Calhoun, the most striking or remarkable thing about constitutional government here is not merely that it is theoretically discernible as the government most natural to man as man, that is, to man in the fullness of his most distinctive faculties, but that, to some extent, with effort and luck, its attainment is actually possible to man as he is here and now (i.e., as he always has been), and, to some extent, with effort and luck, it always has been (paragraphs 14, 18, 78, 95). Scientific knowledge, genuine knowledge, of the phenomenon of politics or the human or political condition is attainable for man, and perfect constitutional government is for man at least no more impossible than it is possible, even if it is, certainly, improbable. That is, it is possible in the exceptional case. To the extent this is so, where the *Disquisition* and the philosophy or science it discovers may be said to have been more Apollinian, it now becomes, aptly, more Herculean, and no less subject to fortune than all such tasks. The part of the *Disquisition* introduced by the ninety-ninth paragraph is devoted to the conviction left by this impression by way of answering those who would attempt to gainsay these striking advantages on behalf of more ordinary or usual circumstances. As a result, it is, in certain ways, the most striking part of the whole work, if only because it is so strikingly characteristic of Calhoun himself.[2]

Paragraph 99:
Common Objections as to Practicability

This part of *A Disquisition on Government* opens with reference to two plausible objections to all that has been previously said. Of these two objections, one, that constitutional government is difficult of construction, is truly plausible, as the author has repeatedly insisted and fully explained (paragraphs 14, 38, 98). He says that the other objection, the objection that constitutionalism or concurrency is impracticable even if it were evidently plausible and could be easily constructed, is only apparently plausible, and arises from a "great error" (paragraphs 99, 108). Hence this section is on great but ordinary or common errors, like the first digression (paragraphs 44-52) and to which this section is related. He then selects some pertinent examples for the exposition of his point (paragraphs 108-111: Poland and the Iroquois Confederacy; paragraphs 111, 140-150: the Roman Republic). Both of the objections mentioned here arise directly from the problem addressed in the reference made to the science of government in the thirty-eighth paragraph. The author there observed that, "of all the questions embraced in the science of government," the sufficient principle of constitutionalism is "the most important and the least understood." This essential constitutional principle is the principle of concurrency, which he is there introducing for the first time and has now fully shown. He immediately goes on to say there, however, that, even when ignorance and common errors have been overcome and this elementary principle is well understood, it remains always the "most difficult of application in practice" (paragraph 38). There, he leaves it at that; here, it is the difficulty of application of the now fully-explained principle of constitution that he takes up.

Difficulty of application can be no objection to the principle. As Calhoun has already pointed out, understanding the principle is primary (paragraph 41). In his famous *Letter to General Hamilton*, which we have already mentioned, however, the author is somewhat more expressive in respect to this particular difficulty than he is either here or in the thirty-eighth paragraph. The analysis of the constitutional or concurrent majority, he says in the *Letter*, "is liable to one *almost* fatal objection, the tardiness and feebleness of its movements—a defect difficult to be remedied, and when not, so great as to render a form of government—in other respects so admirable—*almost* worthless. To overcome this difficulty was the great desideratum in political science, and the most difficult problem within its circle" (emphasis added). The great desideratum in political science, according to the *Letter*, is thus to correct the great error that is first described as plausible in the ninety-ninth paragraph of the *Disquisition* and following, and, in the *Letter*, as an almost fatal objection. Were the objection well-grounded, political philosophy, admirable in so many other respects—reminding as it more or less does of the rule of nature, including the law or constitution of human nature and its moral and intellectual faculties—would almost be but a myth or dream, and would, with however elaborate a presentation of constitution in its most comprehensive sense, whether as the perfect "person" or as the perfect "world," have to make do with absolute government as "best," which is to say, practically abandon the subject of the intrinsically best regime, along with the other questions, altogether. The correction of the error in question, then, would render political science evident in a way and to an extent beyond anything in the past, for all, not just for men like himself, a matter that the author thinks is of considerable import not only to patriots and contemporary or potential statesmen (cf. paragraph 51) but to potential political philosophers as philosophers in the future, if political philosophy is noticed in the future. Calhoun is confident that, if there is a future worth preparing for, which surely must be supposed, it will be (paragraph 139). Even so, it goes without saying that the clarification of this important problem, which takes up the whole last part of the *Disquisition*, is carried on in the shadow or, rather, in the light of his initial insistence that the foundation of the science of government will not and can not do much to make this application of the principle of constitutional easier in any future age than it has been in the past.[3]

Government cannot naturally or easily obtain unanimity on any line of policy among numerous and diverse interests, for, if it could, there would be no need of government, or, then, even if it could, the procedure for doing so would be too slow to provide the security in emergencies which is the primary original reason for government, and thus it would not amount to government (cf. paragraphs 15, 51, 70, 85). Hence there must be a controlling power or majority that can quickly act irrespective of any disagreement. Calhoun observes that this objection is plausible and deserves fuller notice than he has yet given it (cf. paragraph 38).

Paragraphs 100-107:
Plausible Objections

The author immediately restates the objection so as to add reference to the "diversity of opinion" that characterizes all politics, particularly in civilized regimes as he has described them (paragraph 100). Opinion is the root of governmental sluggishness. Opinion characterizes all government; diversity of opinion, conflict of opinion, characterizes all popular government. "Opinion is power."[4] Government will no more do away with power than it will do away with opinion. Checking opinion is no less necessary for the discovery of truth than checking power is necessary for the establishment of constitutional government. The last part of the *Disquisition* thus opens with reference to essential diversity of opinion, the theme which characterizes both popular government and the remainder of the work. Calhoun does not here trace the diversity of opinion on questions of policy only or even primarily to the diversity or number of the interests engaged, as for example, in the celebrated passage of the Tenth *Federalist*, and elsewhere, but primarily (and even merely) to spiritedness or "pride of opinion" (this is his basic position from the beginning, cf. paragraph 8).[5] He says that this is "natural." It follows from man's essential composition. He does not even refer to "interests" in this connection. Interest are entirely secondary. Calhoun explicitly says "he," not "interest" or "interests," etc.; so far from arising from "self-interest" pride of opinion may fly in the face of self-interest, however broadly enlightened or minutely elaborated and rationalized it may be (cf. paragraph 7; Hobbes, *Leviathan*, chapter 8). Hence, just as an individual may sometimes need guidance in the pursuit of his own good, so each interest and even the community as a whole surely needs guidance in pursuit of the common good. They all have the same character in this respect. The problem is primarily in the understanding, not in the material or non-material "interests."

Each interest no less than the government itself is led by individuals, and everything that Calhoun says of government in this regard he also says of other interests. When there is no urgent necessity, every individual may wish to do as he likes, selfishly resist agreement and concert, and pursue whatever course that seems to him pleasing. Calhoun admits that this tendency makes unanimity "difficult," because one must then depend only upon reason, which is no more equally distributed throughout the community than material goods, interests, and so forth (cf. especially, paragraph 51). When there is no urgent necessity to unite, from the point of view of the issue here in question, perhaps every kind of abstractionism or notion of what is best may be tolerated, however much this or that interest may actually suffer. But when there is urgent necessity, and some line of policy *must* be agreed to, then "reason and experience" both prove that — what is determinative from the point of view of the issue here in question — necessity will assume the place of reason that is lacking in the community and "force a compromise," whether the compromise be one of pride itself or any factious or merely partial interest. Under these circumstances, the circumstances requiring the provision of common security assumed by the objection, where compromise is indispensable to action, compromise will occur.

It is in this way that pride of opinion becomes more reasonable, and the subjective more objective.

Let us pause briefly to observe that, although upon reflection it is perhaps not surprising since he explicitly refers to the example of the Roman Republic at the conclusion of the section (paragraph III), it is worth pointing out that Calhoun's unstated immediate reference here is the passage in Polybius' natural history of the Republic where the author speaks most explicitly of urgent necessities impending from the outside (*Histories*, VI.18). Polybius there explains that, whenever this is the case, the Roman community's three great and prominent interests (the consuls, Senate, and people) mutually compromise in suspending or transcending their mutual checking and balancing and begin in earnest to compete with each other to see who can do the most to meet or check the threat to the commonweal (cf. *Disquisition*, paragraphs 75, 105). It is by this means, according to Polybius and Calhoun (paragraphs 142ff.), that Rome is able successfully to persevere and even triumph in the most unfortunate and urgently threatening circumstances.[6] The Polybian passage is acutely responsive to the objection under discussion.

Now, depending upon the attention the student is able to bring to bear on the text of the *Disquisition*, it is often more or less possible, as we have indicated in our notes, to determine the received text or texts (always unstated) underlying each Calhounian paragraph or series of paragraphs, such as, in this case, a particular passage in Polybius' *Histories*. In these cases, a reflective investigation as to why Calhoun might refrain from mentioning them (or, at least, from introducing immediately the relevant illustration) often leads—although, of course, such an investigation surely cannot always be concluded with certainty—to an improved understanding of Calhoun's own argument and purpose, and, even, of the underlying passage, for Calhoun does not simply "omit" reference to relevant texts.[7] In this case, for example, with respect to the former, it is not enough to say that Calhoun omits the reference because government must secure against *both* internal and external dangers, and hence Calhoun here has in mind both internal and external threats (cf. paragraphs 7-8, 15-16), whereas Polybius speaks only of external threats. After all, one might say that, in the terms of the immediate objection to constitutional government, an urgent threat, whether it is an internal or an external threat, is an urgent threat, besides which, in any case, internal threats may be more difficult to secure against than external threats. Calhoun's argument here (paragraph 100) and Polybius' observation both answer this objection in their own terms. Rather, Calhoun wishes to take what he in other places typically calls "higher ground," that is, ground pertinent here not merely to security from threats, which he has already argued and will almost immediately exemplify with examples of his own choosing (paragraphs 108-110) and which, while it is the ground of the objection in question, is merely the first and hence lowest if most obviously crucial ground in laying the foundations of government (paragraphs 79, 85), but ground that also is equally or even more pertinent, as well, to the higher ends of government (cf. paragraph 80, first sentence). In this case, the concern is particularly the perfection of the human moral and intellectual faculties as these ordinarily are politically summarized in the virtue of "justice," and the rule of reason. After all, if security against urgent threats were really all that were needful for the perfection of government, perhaps an absolute military dictatorship would suffice, which admits of relatively easy construction. We may note that the celebrated Sparta, whose regime was military in its orientation, was equally famous for its slowness to act. At any rate, Calhoun wishes to present the objection referring to urgent or extraordinary necessities or threats in what is apparently the most ordinary way, as, for example, in ordinary criminality and lawbreaking. For the moment, Republican Rome is remote from this intention. Hence, of "many" possible illustrations from experience, he selects that of trial by an impartial jury as "most familiar." It is not merely the urgent internal threat to the first end of government that is foremost in his mind but the internal perfection of the higher faculties of man for which the government is ordained that is foremost in his mind, and of which Polybius for his part is in the most relevant instance, and mostly elsewhere in the *Histories*, entirely silent. Polybius' own reasoning on this point does not confirm the important truth here in question. Obviously, the validity of this gloss cannot be demonstrated with finality. To say nothing of other things, it is but one gloss out of the many possible glosses from all paragraphs of the work. We may here leave it merely with the assertion that it illustrates a not unimportant part of what Calhoun means in once privately speaking of having covered "new ground" in the *Disquisition*.

Paragraphs 101-102

Montesquieu, Blackstone, and other writers with whose works Calhoun was well acquainted had described the peculiar educational value of jury service for civic affairs, either more or less generally or particularly in the United States, as does an immediate and once-celebrated contemporary.[8] Although Calhoun's illustration, as drawn from the most familiar experience, could almost be counted an explicitly American one, he is silent here about any special educational value it may have for participants, whatever their citizenship. (Calhoun is silent throughout his writings on any special distinction between "civil education" as such, which he has described in the section of the *Disquisition* on community, and some or any aspect of "education" otherwise conceived.)

Rather, he speaks only of its pronounced favorability to the "success of truth and justice," which are the highest political ends (paragraph 102). Even though it may seem an impracticable mode of trial to a "superficial observer,"[9] it is found in practice not only to succeed but to be the safest and the wisest and, hence, according to Calhoun, "the best that human ingenuity ever devised" (paragraph 101), because it unifies safety with truth and justice. "When closely investigated," Calhoun says, the cause will be found in the necessity to agree unanimously to find a verdict."[10] The true verdict that is found in this manner is not, per a Millian "open society" or a public Socratic seminar on justice, the truth or justice without specification or in imagination, but "according to law and evidence," which are both more circumstantial and more concrete—more political—than the truth or justice without specificity, and hence, at least in this sense, more true and more just. In promoting common opinion out of diversity of opinion in accordance with attention to truth and justice, this mode thus transcends social feelings and any kind of mere conformism, to say nothing of mere or partial and private "interests," in the direction of truth and justice. Where Plato and Xenophon would display the trial presentations, Calhoun would examine the jury instruction and its deliberations.

Calhoun stresses the "predisposing cause of concurrence," the "disposition to harmonize," that results from the necessity of being unanimous and promotes truth and justice. This disposition is to be distinguished from the peaceable attitude emphasized by Hobbes (*Leviathan*, xv), although it is surely peaceable. Necessity thus compensates, within the given parameters of the law and rules of evidence, for the defect of legal knowledge and a high degree of intelligence "on the part of those who usually compose juries" (paragraphs 101-102). The illustration is as much or more one of the thought underlying the concept of the concurrent or constitutional regime, the artful compensation of necessity for the unavoidable defect of reason in the diversity of human opinion, as it is of the safety and wisdom of trial by jury as practical, moderate, and relatively sure. So far from representing any kind of weakness, however, this is its truest and greatest strength. Calhoun's emphasis on selection without discrimination, an impartial hearing of both sides, and meeting not as disputants but "calmly to hear the opinions of each other and to compare and weigh the arguments on which they are founded, and finally to adopt that which, on the whole, is thought to be true," makes it clear—aside from the whole question of "education"—that he is not thinking of trial by impartial jury as merely an important check on absolute power that would necessarily abuse the law, and hence as a particular and important aspect of concurrency (cf. *Federalist*, 78), but also as promoting, so far as it goes, the actual consummation of the ends of political life itself, not only for the immediate participants but, indirectly, for the community as a whole. This is its genuinely "educational" advantage. It is not merely the participants who would suffer from crass majoritarianism in the findings of juries, then, but the whole community, for through majoritarianism no less than through an initially stacked or show-trial jury would enter all the partial interests of the day and "contaminate justice at its source," namely the social feelings and intellect, destroying the community itself as surely as a conquering invasion from outside might do, or even more surely than a conquering invasion from outside might do.

Paragraphs 103-105

The same disposition to harmonize found at the bar in trials by impartial juries under the necessity to find unanimous verdicts is found even more forcefully in the ordinary operation of governments of the concurrent majority under the necessity of keeping the government in motion, for the urgency is far more compelling. Politics abhor a vacuum, as we know, and, as has been established, the operation of government cannot be suspended even for "an inconsiderable period." Calhoun refers to earlier passages and offers no further examples beyond those already given. The Polybian passage mentioned above would not be apt: according to Polybius, action in extreme crises from external threat, not ordinary government, is the peak achievement of the Roman Republic. For Calhoun, the peak achievement of government is reasoning. No government, including constitutional government, obviates the need for reasoning: constitutional government most promotes reasoning in what some might look upon as ordinary circumstances as well as in what all will admit are extraordinary circumstances. It is, for this reason, the best government.

The theme of these paragraphs (99-111), the ultimate theme of Calhoun's political philosophy taken as a whole, is the mode of reason: unadorned or unimpaired human reason, the specifically human tool for achieving the specific ends of unadorned human nature. One might have thought this subject had been conclusively presented in the previous section in connection with the progressive development of civilization and of maximal moral power crowned by the rule of the wise and experienced. As power cannot be abolished or otherwise avoided or escaped, it is crucial that only the wisest and most experienced have anything to do with it. We see now that it was not concluded. The perfection of the ordinary human faculties—unadorned human reason—is not finally achieved by the progressive development of civilization, any more, necessarily, than is that of the human moral faculties. This intellectual perfection is shown not only or even primarily in the progressive development of civilization but primarily and above all in the kind of wisdom described in the first part of the *Disquisition* (paragraphs 18, 41, 47), the wisdom itself of the "wise and good men" whose extraordinary thought is as much above the popular superstition of that age and time as political philosophy is above the public or popular opinion of the age of progress and civilization. The consequences of this thought are the great constitutional regimes themselves, which include the organic arrangements of the constitution "in its most comprehensive sense." Calhoun discusses only the reason or principle of constitution. The perfection of this wisdom and goodness in itself, or what Mill in this connection in his *Considerations on Representative Government*, which, as we have indicated, is an attempt to apply the principles of the *Disquisition*, called in so many words the "true secret of human progressiveness," is here described by Calhoun, in the course of the explanation of the controlling principles of constitution "in its strict or more usual sense," in terms of its characteristic openness or receptivity to truth.

Unadorned—or unalloyed or unaided—human reason does not here refer primarily to ordinary this-worldly human reason unaided by otherworldly guidance or divine revelation, but, rather, to ordinary this-worldly human reason unimpaired by selfish interest, pride or person or opinion, or, in short, spiritedness: pure or dispassionate human reason, which shows passion for what it is and channels or directs it. If I am not mistaken, the first public statement on record by Calhoun on the point that is here at issue occurs in a speech he delivered in 1814. On that occasion, as we have already had occasion to note, he interrupted himself at a certain point to say:

> I must beg the attentive and deliberate hearing [of the audience], for a correct mode of thinking on [the] subject [is crucial].... I say an attentive and deliberate hearing, for it is not sufficient that the mind be fixed on the discussion; but it should also be free from those passions and prejudices unfavorable to the reception of truth. The fact that a discussion here assumes the form of debate produces a state of things unfavorable to dispassionate attention. In debate here, as between individuals, the opposite sides are much more disposed to find objections to an argument, be it ever so clear, than to receive it with a proper degree of assent. In their zeal...mere recriminations [are] made to take the place of earnest endeavors to discover and enforce the claims of truth.[11]

The specific "crisis of parliamentary democracy," and hence of political liberalism, in Schmitt's terms, is, according to Calhoun, on the one hand, already the tension of original human nature (*Disquisition*, paragraphs 8-9) and hence of all government, and, on the other, as it is later described and set forth by Schmitt, but the necessary "contamination of justice at its source" by numerical majoritarianism (*Disquisition*, paragraphs 48-52, 63-69).[12]

The above quotation from Calhoun's congressional speech, as he indicates, is an appeal. Apart from the question whether such appeals are usually successful, the appeal itself is not for assent or unanimity about the subject but for the appropriate "mode of thinking," which the speaker describes. The success of the appeal depends in the first place on some reasonableness or predisposition to harmonize, without which it is useless. The speech cited occurred in the midst of a great war. In the case at hand, the trial by jury, this disposition is necessitated by the artifice of required unanimity. On almost all questions of policy, human reason unimpaired by self-interest or passion is not ordinary but extraordinary. We must often rise above ourselves, as it were, or be taken outside ourselves, or dutifully resist and overcome ourselves, simply to think clearly. As in this case, necessity, which is in a way lower, is, thus, often the support of the higher.[13] We see common awareness of this reflected in common sayings like "necessity is the mother of invention" or unpredicted and often all but miraculous ingenuity and resourcefulness. In a manner of speaking, human nature itself necessarily is almost pointed at the miraculous as to its own rational and social end. Were it otherwise, and dispassionate reason ordinary and commonplace, there would be no need for government for the sake of attaining the natural human ends (*Disquisition*, paragraphs 13-14). Mere life would alone immediately attain liberty (paragraphs 10-11).

What is most miraculous in the illustration offered is not the fact that it fosters the disposition to harmonize, although it does so, for such a predisposition is implicit, if only implicit, in original human nature (paragraphs 2-3, 9). Nor is it the fact that fostering this disposition is practicable, which is Calhoun's immediate point, or, even, as he goes on to show, that it is compatible and intimately associated with patriotism of the highest and greatest spiritedness (paragraph 104, cf. paragraphs 96-98). What is most wonderful is the fact that by this means is so effectively compensated the defect of legal knowledge and a high degree of intelligence in the multitude that a group of individuals selected without discrimination often find a true verdict according to law and rules of evidence in cases where the ablest and most experienced judges continue to differ after careful examination. By these means, men may and will think and judge, as it were, above themselves, or discover themselves at their true best. In so doing, they stand for or are here Calhoun's example of the innermost core of the internal organism of constitutional government considered in its strict sense: reasoning, reasoning that is dispassionate, in the sense of impartial, but passionate in devotion to the truth and justice. This *is* the good of the whole, the *common* good, for, in the strict sense, it is only reason that is finally and truly common. Calhoun has elsewhere explained that, where government itself is concerned, what results from this same disposition to harmonize is "enlightened policy." Even when those deliberating may not be enlightened in the beginning, they will be, at least more so, in the end. In such a context, they will enlighten themselves by genuinely thinking. This is the true liberation or discovery of liberty, as well as one of its most useful guardians. It arises from the opposition of contrary opinions in free and open discussion in the context of common devotion to the whole, or patriotism, as he has already shown, and the disposition to harmonize, or moderation. It reaches in a sense beyond good and evil, but it is only the basis of virtue that gives it this reach, or truth this sense:

> Opposition simply [ultimately] implies contrariety of opinion; and, when used in the abstract, admits of neither praise nor censure. It cannot be said to be either good or bad, useful or pernicious. It is not from itself, but from the connected circumstances, that it derives its character. When it is simply the result of that *diversity in the structure of our intellect*, which conducts to different conclusions on the same subject, and is confined within those bounds which love of country and political honesty [virtue] prescribe, it is one of the most useful guardians of liberty. It excites gentle collision; prompts to due vigilance—a quality so indispensable, and, at the same time, so opposite to our nature—and results in the establishment of an enlightened policy and useful laws. [Emphasis added.][14]

Otherwise, it results merely in partial and hence unenlightened policy and laws that are partial, or "laws" in name only, whatever force may back them. We may note that in this passage it is easy to see what Calhoun himself ultimately most relishes in human relationships: what he identifies as the "diversity in the structure" of human intellects, genuine "*differance*," within the frame—let us say, the "enframing"—of virtue, including, as we know from his contemporaries and biographers, not only male but also female, and not only adult but also adolescent. This real difference is what Calhoun most seeks, and seeks to guard, in the present condition of the world, in setting forth the science of government, which is the science of liberty. Ultimately, neither is possible without the other. It therefore necessarily points beyond his political science, his metaphysics of politics, to his metaphysics simply. For the real diversity in the structure of human intellect, which is not final but political—the origin of the necessity of government that is beyond human ignorance and vice (per paragraph 5)—points necessarily and simultaneously to that difference in the different structure of intellect that *is* final, the difference between the Supreme Intellect and the human intellect, or between the divine or Supreme Being and the political or human being, of which human being has an ordained part only in its unalloyed reasonableness. That constitutional government, to the extent it is established and sustained, itself attains to this unalloyed reasonableness and lives by it is, to the extent that it attains it, its most striking and its decisive characteristic. Yet, however extraordinary and striking it may seem, in truth, this circumstance is not at all miraculous but the actual end that is aimed at by original human nature in the order of nature ordained for it and that is actually attained to the extent that constitutional government is perfected (paragraph 103).

The section of the *Disquisition* of which we are now almost in the midst is the most condensed section of this most condensed work of a man who is famous for the condensed presentation of his thought. This is because it is the peak of the work, its highest thought. It could almost be said to be about thought. It is certainly the part of the *Disquisition* in which one can almost see the author's own thinking in his very words. It is, to repeat, for the same reasons, the most striking section. These facts are often overlooked and hence left out of account because there are no external or formal indications of them and no obvious or explicit statements that identify them. But there are, nevertheless, many revealing statements. The author speaks of "wonder" or of what is most wondrous (paragraph 104), of forming just "conceptions" or "estimates" (paragraphs 104, 105), of what distinguishes constitutional government "so strikingly" from absolute government (paragraph 106), and, after all, of the "greatest possible achievement of the science of government" (paragraph 106) and "cheerfulness" (paragraph 107). Each of these statements is meant to contrast with those to which we have drawn attention in the second digression (especially paragraph 89: "opinion," "semblance," "repugnant," etc.). Hence, within the context of this section (paragraphs 104-107), each of these statements provides a good guide to the peak of Calhoun's science in the *Disquisition*.

The unitary quality of this group of paragraphs (101-107) is indicated by the fact that the first four paragraphs close with reference to common opinion, justice, or compromise, and the last three close with reference to the "good of the whole," the "common good." The beginnings and endings of these paragraphs are as follows:

Beginning	Ending
paragraph 101 "necessity for unanimity"	"common opinion"
paragraph 102 "potent influence of this necessity"	"justice at its source"
paragraph 103 "the same cause"	"compromise"
paragraph 104 "a just conception of its influence"	"compromise"

paragraph 105
"a juster estimate of its force"   "the good of the whole"

paragraph 106
"its source"   "the good of the whole"

paragraph 107
"greater solidity of foundation"   "the common good"

The central and longest paragraph of this group (paragraph 104) presents the most definitive and comprehensive human passions: the "love of truth and justice" and the "love of country." It describes what is, according to the author, in truth the most wondrous of all the advantages of constitutional government. This is perhaps the place to observe, in view of the assertions in passing of many writers to the contrary, that Calhoun is obviously not a Calvinist. Calvin and Locke may perhaps be useful places to begin the study of the thought of, say, Jonathan Edwards, but they are not especially helpful places to begin in arriving at any serious grasp of Calhoun, except to show what is not. Calhoun is no more Calvinist than he is Lockean.[15] After what has been established in earlier chapters, and, in light of this paragraph, it cannot be necessary to emphasize further the point that the intellectual faculty, specifically reason, as the highest and most definitive human attribute, which proceeds originally from the Creator and can only proceed from the Creator, is, as such, incorruptible. As man does not make himself, neither can he destroy or corrupt his essential nature or constitution, even should he corrupt or degrade his most characteristic love, or even annihilate himself by his own act. *Naturalia manent integra.* So far from representing Calvinism, Calhoun's teaching on this important point is all but indistinguishable from that of, say, Duns Scotus.[16]

Earlier, in the same context—forming a just conception of the powerful force of political antipathies—Calhoun had spoken specifically of what is given or evident and "not wondrous" and what is "not surprising" (paragraph 74). It is not wonderful, he observes, that in absolute government party struggles actually exhaust all sympathy and devotion to the common good by law, or, as he more accurately says, "under the forms of law," in vice and self-absorbed antipathies. From the point of view of political science this activity is not wonderful or surprising but humdrum and vulgar: "ordinary." Its motives and biases are petty and selfish and its true objects, masked this way and that, are the "glittering prizes" (paragraphs 74, 76, cf. paragraphs 5-6). What is wonderful here (paragraph 104, see paragraphs 58-61), is that, acting under circumstances much more favorable than those under which juries act, the impulse throughout the country to impartial compromise easily overpowers ordinarily all-absorbing antipathies. Prompting necessity supplements or empowers the common if weaker sympathies or social feelings on the side of good for the whole country (paragraphs 8, 14, 75). Without this necessity—setting aside more or less insignificant exceptions (paragraph 6)—pretensions of truth and justice only disguise ulterior personal motives, ignorance, or merely partisan biases, and the constitutive elements of human nature are corrupted and perverted away from their natural ends. With it, as in the case of the jury just mentioned, the love of truth and justice is emancipated, with the striking results just described. Without it, the powerful love of country, which comprehends "all the charities of all,"[17] is but the love of a part. With it, each part is not only more devoted to the whole than it is to itself but the love of country itself is augmented by truth and justice and each part loses itself in the whole or transcends itself in the direction of the whole, and what are otherwise thought of as sacrifices or compromises (stressing the conflict between merely selfish and common interests) are become willing gifts to the one that is in all and the all that is in each (paragraph 105). By these means (paragraphs 76-78), the whole is transformed or emerges as a true community of communities. This, the piety of citizens before the "altar of the country," the symbol—one of the rare symbols to be found in the *Disquisition* – of the oldest sacrifices to heaven, is the ultimate end the source and aim of which is the "voice of god," of the whole community, in truth, in reference to itself (paragraph 61).

This is the aim, however confused it may sometimes be, of all government as such. What is most striking about constitutional government as distinct from absolute government is not only that to the extent that it succeeds in its constitution it actually achieves this aim but that, in doing so, it naturally pushes or pulls forward and promotes the unqualifiedly best or most fit men, those men who above all are distinguished for "wisdom and experience," to the position of rule (paragraph 105). These, the wisest and best men, have unqualifiedly the best natural claim to prominence, whatever the composition of the community as a whole may be. By these means the government is perfected and transformed or emerges as a natural aristocracy (paragraphs 97, 24, 18).[18] In the end, constitutional government, the government most strikingly in accord with the whole as such, is necessarily the rule of the wise, the rule of the most extraordinary and deeply impressive human exceptions. According to Calhoun, it is for reason of all these exceptional features that constitutional government, government by reasoning, is in every way the most exceptional and most striking, and is the only true standard by which to judge all government and even government itself, for all communities, in fact, all politics, is ineluctably oriented toward it.[19]

Paragraph 106-107

Ignorance, pervasive ignorance, is almost the last word of the following paragraph (paragraph 106). Constitutional government enthrones the stronger argument, whereas the stronger feelings or passions always greatly tend to empower the weaker argument (paragraphs 8, 51). The latter empowerment is not wondrous but commonplace, "as all experience and almost every page of history testify" (paragraph 13). "It is not necessary to teach men to thirst after power," and hence "it is not even a matter of choice" whether government will exist among them or not.[20] But constitutional government is, to some extent, open to choice, as persistent questions and even differing errors about government itself indicate, as well as the fact that even ordinary governments are all to some extent mixed, and it is the aim of political philosophy or science to help enlighten or inform that choice and to sharpen reflection about it (paragraphs 15, 20). The greatest possible achievement of wisdom is the actual enlistment of the social feelings in favor of the true good of the whole, whether it is the whole individual or the whole community (paragraph 106).

This reasonable accord accounts also for the "greater solidity of foundation" on which constitutional governments are built. Not only is constitutional government superior in reason or speech but also in deed. Its patriotism is "exalted," that is, as much above the commonplace as the regime itself, and citizenship is the moral equivalent of friendship (cf. Aristotle, *Eudemian Ethics*, 1234b 31). This is because its sentiment and feeling are willing, earnest, and cheerful, for its character, the "constitution" itself, is written in the hearts of its citizens (paragraph 107) and expressed in government by reasoning. Its motives and aim are unqualifiedly the common good and happiness of the whole: the completion of the laws (cf. paragraph 8).

Having provided a just conception of constitutional government, Calhoun is now ready to answer the practical objection that such a government is too extreme or wishful in its conception and would be too tardy to meet with sufficient promptness the many and dangerous emergencies to which all communities are exposed. Such an objection amounts to saying, as many lawyers and others with similarly vested interests do say, that trial by jury as Calhoun has described it is inconvenient or would not work. In any case, the objection is unfounded because such governments have actually existed in the past, not in hypothetical suppositions but in time. He offers two concrete examples—"concrete universals"—of communities responding to external threats on the basis of the foundation just described.

Paragraphs 108-111:
The Most Illustrative Examples of the Principles of
Constitutional Government

Without repeating here what has been already said about the examples Calhoun now adduces, it should be noted that, according to him, "history furnishes many examples of such governments."[21] We know that of all examples he most admired those of Rome and Sparta, but he does not present these here. The two he actually presents are, thus, selected particularly. They are Calhoun's examples not of the greatest or of the most renowned but, we may say, of the "most natural" constitutions or regimes. For its part, the first example is most natural because it is, rationally, the most extreme. This is why thinkers like Rousseau supposed that it must engage the attention of "any thinking man," and thinkers like Burke referred to it as approaching "rude Nature." Although, to say the least, it has nothing to do with the Hobbesian "state of nature" doctrine, it is the most "individualistic" government in the historical record. It achieved this status thanks not to nature but to its constitution. The second example, which is not so extreme, for its part, is most natural because it lacks as much as possible any tincture of civilization, and particularly any tincture of modern mass or material civilization. It is the most thoroughly "communitarian" of regimes, so much so that it became the putatively "historic" inspiration for modern theories of "scientific socialism" in the very midst of advanced "liberal" technocratic civilization. Its character was due, like that of Poland, not to nature but to its political constitution.

The first is selected because it carries the principle of unanimity to the "utmost extent": "further the principle could not be carried." It thus shows the practicability of constitutionalism better than any other example. As Burke observed, "Until the other day, in the constitution of Poland unanimity was required to give validity to any act of their great national council or diet. This approaches more nearly to rude Nature than the institutions of any other country. Such, indeed, every commonwealth must be, without a positive law to recognize in a certain number the will of the entire body."[22] The impressive glory attaching to Poland during this time is commensurate with this fact, that is, with this extremism. Not once but twice, responding more quickly than the rest of Europe (divided by every kind of reluctance, hesitation, scruple, ambition, indifference, and uncertainty, not to say fear), she alone permanently broke the tide of the conquering Turks and preserved Western Christendom (paragraph 108). Hence, we may note in passing that, contrary to what has sometimes been asserted, Christianity is obviously not incompatible with noble boldness or with the best political government.[23]

As in all great victories, chance played a role in both the Polish defeats of the Turks and the Greek defeats of the Persians. We have mentioned that Calhoun does not notice the Greek cities in the *Disquisition*. In spite of her greatness, Sparta is not remarkable for development of the intellectual faculties. Nor does he mention Athens. This is not because he agrees with Morgan and others about the relative political substance of the Iroquois confederacy and the Athenian empire, but, in part, because he agrees with Polybius and others that the acme of Athens was merely circumstantial, arising suddenly at the time of the defeats of the Persian invasions, and rapidly eclipsed because of internal political decay (*Histories*, VI.43. 1-2ff.). He explains that the subversion of Poland was not due to weakness of the principle of unanimity, even though carried to the utmost extreme, but to other causes. This is strictly true. But the causes described must remind of the traitorous behavior of many of the ancient Greek cities and citizens upon the occasion of the Persian invasions, indeed, upon almost any occasion (cf. paragraph 130). It is also true that this form of government existed for two centuries in Poland, but, similarly, it did not last longer than two centuries because of internal intrigue or decay. In short, the example proves that the principle of unanimity carried to extreme does not alone provide, by the author's own admission (paragraph 109), all of the unity of community and oneness of will on behalf of the Estates of the kingdom that he has asserted on behalf of a perfect constitutional government in the earlier paragraphs. Perhaps the principle of responsibility was weakened by the extremity to which the principle of unanimity was carried. Perhaps everyone's will is no one's will. On the other hand, Montesquieu had criticized the Polish regime for placing the serfs in the status of slaves. It would then be in the position of Rome at the beginning of Calhoun's description of the development of the Roman Republic. At any rate, to attain the impressive longevity achieved not by the extreme but the great constitutional governments (paragraph 18), something else would seem to be required beyond the principles of suffrage and concurrency as established by Poland. Calhoun repeatedly stresses the extremity of the Polish example. To say the least, then, the example proves, apart from the other things he sets forth, also the need for artfulness or moderation even — or particularly — as regards the fundamental principles of even — or perhaps especially — the most natural regime. With this, the principle of unanimity perhaps could be compatible both with power and permanency of government. Even so, Calhoun's point is surely carried as regards the most immediate practical objection to constitutional government (paragraphs 99-100).

The more moderate and less striking example of the Iroquois confederacy, in which there are no problems from internal intrigue or decay, is not perfect for the reason mentioned above in connection with Sparta, but it is deserving of notice. Apart from its internal harmony in council and action, however, which represents the blessings he expects of constitutionalism in this connection and which the example fully exhibits, the principal result, on Calhoun's showing, is not merely the great increase of power he has previously explained but the great increase of Iroquois authority. At its height, Iroquois influence—Calhoun does not say "power" (cf. paragraph 77)—stretched from the Atlantic to the Mississippi River, a territory about the size of the African country of Zaire today. It is true (from what we know) that this expansion appears in every way beneficent, but the author does not elaborate on this provocative feature (paragraph 110).

The example is also deserving of notice because, if authorities like Sorel may be followed, it was the example principally of the Iroquois confederacy as it was described by European contemporaries that inspired Rousseau to his celebrated and still influential images of the "noble savage" and the "natural man," not to say the linchpin of his whole hypothetical doctrine.[24] Writing a century before Morgan, Charlevoix said of the Iroquois councils that, "We must admit that in these assemblies they proceed with a wisdom, a maturity, a skillfulness, and I would even say an integrity, generally speaking, that would have done honor to the Council of Athens or the Roman Senate in the finest days of these republics. There, no conclusions are arrived at in haste.... [In matters of diplomacy] everything is conducted with a dignity, an attention, I would even venture to say a capability, worthy of the most important matters."

Little wonder Rousseau seems to offer little respect to the advancement of the modern arts and sciences in this decisive regard. Yet the confederacy of the Iroquois is a complex or constitutional regime and not a simple or absolute regime, like that of, say, the Tupinamba. What Rousseau hypothetically traces to the "prehistorical" state of nature and an absence of knowledge and even reason, however, to say nothing of advanced civilization, Calhoun traces, rather, to the actual political constitution itself or the principle of concurrency, as demonstrated precisely here among the Iroquois. It is above all in the constitution, which, whether among savage or civilized communities, ancient or modern, of whatever race or circumstance, consists of human will and contrivance (paragraph 14), that one finds true man because it is in the constitution that one finds the true cunning of reason, moderation, and end of human nature. For Calhoun, constitutional man and only constitutional man *is* natural man or the true and whole human being.

Paragraph 111

With such thoughts in mind it is understandable that Calhoun turns in the following paragraph to the example of Rome or, at least, to the mention of Rome, for Rome is the greatest and most studied example of political glory, unity, and achievement, and it would both reasonably and artfully consummate the argument of the *Disquisition* at this conclusive point (paragraph 111). After all, apart from its own intrinsic qualities, the example of Rome is typically seen by most authorities as providing the most striking of political examples, whatever particular is being exemplified. As we have noted, Calhoun's own appreciation of the Roman example is hardly surpassed, and, as has been indicated, he refers to it in related contexts. It must here extraordinarily unite both the striking pinnacles of glory that are discerned in the success of the extreme Polish constitution and the not altogether less striking tragedy that is betokened in the decline and fall of the moderate Iroquois confederacy. Did not the fall of Rome leave a gloom as great as its glory? One might almost say that Calhoun necessarily turns now to the example of Rome.

Yet Calhoun does not here actually present the example of Rome, but defers it. He briefly draws our attention now to the example of Rome only to acknowledge its rightful place, and to say that he will, however, discuss it later in another place. There is for Calhoun a not unimportant sense, then, in which this place both is and is not the rightful place for the Roman example, or, in other words, a sense in which this place is not the conclusive place in the *Disquisition* that it might have seemed from the presentation thus far. Understanding why this is so, or what is still lacking here, is the best guide to the rest of the *Disquisition* up to the presentation of the comparison of Rome and Great Britain (paragraphs 140-164) and the subsequent *Discourse*. For the moment, we may say that the example of Rome both would and should conclude this section of the *Disquisition*, as Calhoun as much as acknowledges, and even the *Disquisition* itself, except for the "new political element" and all connected with it that he immediately introduces and discusses in the next section and following, that is, except for what we call—what, following Hegel, if not Voltaire, everyone calls—"modernity" (although, if we took Petrarch as seriously as Machiavelli took him, would we not have to say "post modernity?") and what Calhoun calls simply the "more advanced stage of society," in which and for which he is writing. It is with the following section, then, that the second part of the *Disquisition* begins in earnest.

However, with these and the considerations presented in an earlier chapter in mind, there remains a further reason for close attention to these examples, particularly as they bear upon the composition of the *Disquisition* itself, and that of the *Discourse*, and which we need but touch upon in passing. It is true that the most extreme example of constitutional government presented in the *Disquisition* is the example of the Polish constitution. This extremity is stressed by the author. But it is not in every sense the most extreme example of constitutional government that is mentioned in the *Disquisition*. The most extreme example that is mentioned, because of its complexity, is the constitution of the United States (paragraphs 121, 165). The Polish example points in this manner, extremity, as well as other ways, to the example of the United States, for Calhoun sees the

American states much as members of the Polish Diet, as the Iroquois example, historically, also does. Like Poland, the United States also twice threw off or repelled a great power from the east. The author himself, as we have noted, is particularly associated with the second of these victories, which secured the independence and established the honor of the country. One may wonder whether, if it were possible to combine them, the various extreme and deserving constitutional elements and principles that are presented in the examples of Poland and the Iroquois Confederacy would not find their most striking expression in the constitution and government of the complex regime that is the subject of the unfinished *Discourse on the Constitution and Government of the United States*. This must be another study.

Paragraphs 112-117:
The New Political Element and Progress

Having concluded his response to the direct objections to concurrency set forth in paragraphs 99-100, and described the animus and character of the reasoning government, or government by reasoning, Calhoun now takes up the counter-supposition as to whether there might not now be another easier, simpler means than government by concurrent majority to achieve all that is desired, namely, merely by means of the establishment of a free press as the organ for public opinion. In one sense, this may prove the greatest objection or barrier to the establishment and maintenance of constitutional governments. Given popular suffrage (paragraph 21) and a written constitution stipulating a careful division of powers (paragraphs 48-52), the objection runs, does not the establishment of a free press as the organ of public opinion make government by concurrent majority superfluous?[25] After all, as we know, a free press could act as the people's guardian, watchfully checking abuses of power and protecting their liberties, as well as educate them about their rights and duties and inform them of all the most pressing issues of the day.[26] Through the press, the community considered individually is informed and reasons about policy. Calhoun replies in the negative to this supposition on two grounds. Firstly, the press in fact does not do this (paragraphs 112-113). In the following paragraph (114), he explains why it does not and will not ever do so. Secondly, in fact it does the opposite (paragraphs 115-116). He explains why in the last paragraph of the section (117).

To grasp the purport of these paragraphs, it is necessary to ask why the author introduces this subject here, following acknowledgement of the diversity of opinion (100), the description of the reasoning government (101-107,) and the remarkable constitutional examples, the extreme, the moderate, and the most distinguished, just mentioned (108-111). These historic examples respond to a plausible but erroneous objection about the practicability of constitutional government. The supposition here introduced objects to the necessity of government in accordance with the principle of concurrency, that is, it takes us back to the beginning (paragraphs 19ff.). According to the supposition, it is a free press that completes or ensures and characterizes constitutionalism. The free press is the great check on the tendency of government to abuse its powers. This opinion has the same status as the opinion that the right of suffrage itself is the essential constitutional element or the opinion that a written constitution is the essential constitutional element (paragraphs 21ff., 36ff., 44ff.). Like the others, this supposition is erroneous. None of the remarkable constitutional examples just described or mentioned were characterized by a free press. A free, that is, unchecked, press may well strengthen opinion as against reason, that is, liberty.

What is called "public opinion," with the press regarded as its proper organ, is "new." It does not mean the settled opinions and habits on which the community is based, but presents itself as progressive and reformist in regard to those opinions and habits, that is, as authoritative. Among other things, such as urbanization and the increase of literacy, it has arisen in connection with the growth in influence of the doctrine of the "state of nature," including the derivative opinion that an informed and consensual society is the only legitimate or right human society. With the rise of democracy on these grounds is announced the diffusion of reason as protected and nourished by a free press. As has been observed, according to Calhoun, this Lockean rational right of the numerical majority has the same status as the Filmerian divine right of kings. However, it is not Calhoun's intention either to detract from the importance of the press (viz., newspapers and journals, but his observations may be fairly extended to the mass news and entertainment media generally, including those in which literacy is not presupposed) or to underestimate the great power and influence which the press has given to what is now called public opinion. On the contrary, this power and influence is so great as to entitle the press to be considered (Calhoun says, "I admit") as "a new and important political element," or estate. "Opinion is power." He does not yet discuss the origin or cause of this power but presents it only as another issue in the construction and practicability of constitutional government. (cf. paragraphs 132ff.). By the supposition, a free press antiquates the superstition and ignorance of less advanced stages of human society, including the authorities characteristic of these stages. In fact, it merely attempts to take their place or substitute itself for them.[27] An unchecked press is, to say the least, necessarily in tension with the community as a whole, if not with all its parts. Certainly, this new element may, "in combination with the causes which have contributed to raise it to its present importance," in time effect great political and social changes—Calhoun does not say "progress"—everywhere. It is powerful. It is even more an organ of power than it is of opinion, for it presents itself, like the government, as speaking in the name of reason and right, or of the public, the community, itself. It is for this reason a new political element.

As we have noted, this section of the *Disquisition* opens with reference to objections to the argument and to the "diversity of opinion" (paragraph 100), including the ultimate source of this diversity. He has mentioned opinion before, typically in connection with great or dangerous errors; opinion as distinguished from knowledge or science (paragraphs 44ff., 86ff., 100ff.). The supposition in question is introduced here because, although it may be supposed that a free press as the organ of public opinion may remedy the defects of absolute government by undermining all artifices of authority and establishing reasonableness, or that it may, as an authority in its own right, interpose itself as a formal or informal constitutional check against the abuse of power and defeat absolutism, it in fact may merely infeeble or corrupt the operation of government and render constitutional government less practicable than it otherwise is or might be by replacing timely action with public controversy or masterly inactivity with foolish haste (paragraph 100).[28] It surely renders the elevation of those possessed of wisdom and weight of character unlikely. This is because "what is called public opinion," the opinion of which the press is the organ, is typically rather only the opinion or voice of the dominant numerical majority or minority of the whole community. It is not the opinion of the disinterested whole, the "public," the "voice of the people" itself, the *res publica*, but only of an interested part (paragraphs 44, 61).[29] It actually speaks for a part in the struggle with other parts. It is oppositional. This fact is not altered according to whether it possesses the government itself or not. The "public" is that which is shared or held in common by the community, that which makes the community a community, as distinct from the "private" or what is not shared or held in common. The press is actually the organ of the parties growing out of partial interests composing the community and is less a forum for the expression or formation of genuinely public opinion than for molding and manipulating popular or mass opinion for selfish or interested purposes.[30] It hides rather than reveals the public. (This insight has been systematically developed as though the operation were a positive good in the work of Lasswell and his successors, who abandon or evade the essential problem it raises, if not its consequences: *Disquisition*, paragraph 13). Its rise is, thus, not the rise of reason but of opinion and prejudice, if not of fanaticism. Hence it does not simply represent the rule of reasonableness. In fact, it may effectively check such rule, for as an organ of party it would be but the conduit through which the factious feelings of the day would enter and contaminate deliberation, the only possible check on vulgar symbols and stereotypes, at its source. The press, no less than, say, tax policy, is also the object of domination, with all its attendant struggles. For this reason, whatever its utility for promoting conformity and standardization—or division and anarchy—may be, the power of the press is no less problematic than suffrage itself in regard to the construction and practicability of constitutional government.[31] Calhoun has shown how the principle of suffrage may be completed and fulfilled in its aim. The question thus arises now as to how this "new" power may be checked or held responsible to the community and hence to reason.

Constitutional government, according to Calhoun, is government most according to the ends of human nature. Paragraph 113 and the beginning and end of the paragraph 114 on the nature of man succinctly redact the theme of the *Disquisition's* introductory part (paragraphs 1-18). This phenomenon, human nature, had become controversial and was even denied long before *A Disquisition on Government* was conceived. It has remained no less controversial since that time in many political and educational circles, and particularly in thought that is meant to pertain to the object and policies of human government. Often the phenomenon is obscured or lost sight of altogether in speculation about the "open society" (following Mill), Habermas' "ideal speech situation" (or "emancipatory communicative action"), or Gouldner's technocratical "culture of critical discourse," to say nothing of historicism or speculation about "elitism" and varieties of *apparatchiki* (following Pareto and Mosca). For Calhoun, the phenomenon exists as he has set it forth from the beginning. The distinction between reason and opinion, or the character of opinion *qua* opinion, is not altered by the emergence of an unchecked press as a political power. This distinction exists as a limit or boundary of humanity that is signaled by the existence of government itself, to say nothing of government in the plural (the true end of "pluralism," i.e., the rediscovery of post-Lockean human nature as inequality). No religion, education, stage of society, condition of society, progress of civilization, production of wealth, level of affluence, form of constitution, party platform or other formulation or communication of political ideas have changed or can change it. Were it otherwise, to say nothing of other things, there could be no conception of "progress," in the first place, or, if there were, there could then be no conception of progress as in any way problematic.

This does not mean that the press or mass media are without significant potential for good. The middle of paragraph 114 is devoted to the educational and practical achievements that might be expected from the increasing power and influence of the press.[32] Calhoun provides, in the subjunctive case, an optimal outline of all of these desirable potentialities. The influence of the press might do much to stimulate the progress of knowledge and information, and hence might aid the cause of education and bring about salutary changes in society. Improvement in the cause of education might do much to promote and teach the understanding of government, for example, along with everything else that it promotes. Salutary changes in social conditions might do much to achieve the ordained ends of government, including securing universal preservation and expanding the sphere of liberty and contracting the sphere of power. For social changes to be salutary, there must be correspondent genuine progress in knowledge and virtue; otherwise, it is at best merely mitosis, and most probably retrograde or even cataclysmic. Arguably, to the extent that the press might actually contribute to such progress, it might actually be a medium of genuine enlightenment, that is, open and disinterested reason among impartial patriotic reasoners. It might to that extent be advantageous. It is with this in mind that Calhoun has composed *A Disquisition on Government*: "I have not dilated, but left truth, plainly announced, to battle its own way" in the flux of skepticism and conflicting popular opinions, including prominent hypothetical histories and states. In a "period of transition," one can only make one's way amid unsettled and untrue opinions by following all political opinions genuinely to elementary principles and by tracing circumstances that seem likely to effect changes in political condition to their sources, and follow them out to their consequences.

Calhoun's *A Disquisition on Government* itself is presented as a check, indeed, as *the* check, in theory or in principle, to the unlimited diffusion of intelligence, information, and opinion throughout all ranks of human society around the globe.

"But all this kind" of achievement, according to him, including however high attainments of education and whatever changes in social conditions, and the rest, would, nevertheless, not in the least supersede the need for constitutional government (paragraph 78 end, paragraph 27). Actual, effectual constitutional government, to whatever extent it is successful (paragraph 41), only fulfills and does not supersede the need for itself, as is indicated by the ultimate decline of even of the most solidly founded constitutional regimes. The new power of the organs of mass opinion, which is the political expression ultimately of the advance of applied science technology, for which it here stands (and, practically, if not theoretically, just as little constitutionally checked or guided), will lead to great social and political changes, but it will do nothing to affect human nature or the fact of human politics and government.

Paragraphs 118-126:
The Forms of Government and Constitution

It is with the great social and political changes that are portended in mind that Calhoun now turns to the subject of the forms of constitutional regimes and regime formation. This section of the *Disquisition* continues the general subject of political construction as part of the science of government (paragraph 99), of which the intervening question of practicability in emergency situations is an essential criterion, and roughly corresponds to the passages in Plato's *Statesman* (269ff.) on the forms of regimes and their degeneration and regeneration; in Aristotle's *Politics*, V, on the causes of political decay and revolution and the means of preserving the forms of regimes; and in Polybius' *Histories*, VI, on the natural and necessary cycle of regimes. It follows or picks up again the "second question" discussed in paragraphs 15-18, in which the leading concern is "aggrandizement," and of which the prior question of the principles of constitutional government is necessarily the preliminary part (paragraphs 19-98), and turns to the question of founding or the opportunities for founding. The last word in the section is "constructed" (paragraph 131 end).

The subject of practicability is here continued with a view to social and political change (paragraph 112: "great changes," paragraph 131: "great changes"), and finally concluded (paragraphs 140ff) with a view to stability. We may note in passing that, for reasons that have been set forth and explained throughout the *Disquisition*, it should be clear that the original distinction between absolutism and constitutionalism remains in the section on the forms of government the fundamental distinction for politics and the study of human events. It summarizes and transcends other dichotomic concepts, such as "tradition and modernity" as it is found in the works of Maine, Tonnies, Durkheim, and their successors, which, whatever their variations, actually are *au fond* primarily economic or "civil" (e.g., "modernization," "development") and find their ultimate origin and theoretical impetus in the doctrine of the "state of nature." This is obviously not to deny that these schools ostensibly aim not at Hobbian or Lockean philosophy but at the circumstantial habits and long-held opinions that give communities empirical coherence, that is, at the impressions received by the human *tabula rasa* as set forth by Locke.

Paragraph 118-120

Numerical majoritarianism has an advantage over a constitutional majority in that it is relatively facile, an advantage in construction that all absolute regimes have over constitutional regimes (paragraph 118).[33] Calhoun calls this advantage into question ("if, indeed, it can be called an advantage"), because, although it is lower, believing that what all or almost all men share in common is more important than virtue or intelligence, it is also a less "solid" construction (paragraph 107). While it requires little or no intelligence, virtue, or refinement, it is for this very reason constantly agitated and volatile and depends much more on force and police presence (paragraph 58). Nevertheless, all constitutional regimes can be objected to on the ground that they require more of the citizenry than absolute regimes. However, such an objection merely amounts to an assertion or admission that the subjects of absolute regimes are unworthy of liberty (paragraphs 84-86). It is characteristic that in constitutional regimes this requirement is welcomed and warmly embraced, while in absolute regimes it is merely imitated or in one or another way set aside as a kind of burden or distraction or other evil.

The natural tendency in all government is toward decline from the more complex to the more simple, and, finally, to decline into absolute monarchy, the simplest or most primitive in construction and also the most common of all regimes (paragraphs 119, 68-69). As the natural tendency in all government is toward decline, there is, also, a natural human tendency toward the peaks from which the tendency to decline is visible as such. The latter arises from the social or sympathetic feelings, including the love of truth and justice. But it is not stronger than the tendency toward decline, which arises from the strength of the individual or selfish feelings, including in the decisive case personal ambition. Descent is easy, ascent is hard. Constitutional governments are, therefore, the most complex and difficult of effective formation and maintenance. The highest order of wisdom and virtue has, therefore, had less import in constructing the more complex forms than "favorable combinations of circumstances." Were wisdom and virtue more common, the phenomenon would be otherwise. As it is, complex forms of government come about primarily by chance. Fortunate circumstances have betimes placed necessity on the side of the social feelings and the common good (cf. paragraph 107). The struggle of interests to which history testifies and that is characteristic of political life may sometimes fortunately issue, and potentially always could issue, in a compromise by which both parties obtain a separate, effectual voice in the government, or in a fortunate circumstance that forces such a compromise. This has been the historical root of constitutional regimes.[34] Thus, it appears that the primary practical orientation of political science in constitutional regimes will typically be first toward maintenance or conservation rather than founding toward preservation of the political *status quo* rather than toward great social changes, although, at the same time, it will avoid mere orthodoxy. It will take its lead from Cicero and from Burke.

In a long paragraph, Calhoun discusses the limitations of all wisdom or science in connection with this consideration in terms of three general ways in which deliberately forming constitutional governments has exceeded human sagacity (paragraphs 119, 14). In order of rank, the first concerns the wise as wise, about which Calhoun typically says the least; the second concerns statesmen or the wise as statesmen, about which he says about twice as much; and the third concerns the subject of communities themselves, with which he completes the paragraph. With respect to the first, "it would seem almost impossible" for one to possess both parts of the philosophy or science of government. Full knowledge of the elementary principles of constitutional government is the theoretical and more remote part of the science; sagacity or judgment, reducing the principles to application in given cases, is the practical and more immediate part (cf. paragraph 41). Both are sufficiently difficult, but Calhoun stresses that the practical part has always required the aid of fortunate necessity or chance, and the tendency to political decline being constant and pervasive, it will probably always be required. With respect to the second, it is a different and fuller if less abstract or theoretical order of study and application than the first, although it is of course ultimately dependent upon the first. Hence it is perhaps not surprising that, given some knowledge of political principles and their practical applications, "it would seem almost impossible," also, for any man or even for any group of men to know adequately the whole people and interests of any particular community, above all in the advanced or most civilized stage of human society, sufficiently to be able to organize a constitutional government comprehensively suited to their condition. In such a case, the emphasis must be almost altogether upon the turns of fortune. Thirdly, in respect to communities, "even were [all] this possible," Calhoun says, "it would be difficult" to find a community already sufficiently wise and virtuous to consent to a complex government without the aid of fortunate necessity. Such communities are rare enough, if not rarer than the statesmen just mentioned.

Calhoun evidently disdains the ancient (and not only ancient) sages who traveled and drafted laws and "constitutions" for foreign countries and peoples as "ignorant of their trade." This is the way of the conqueror, whatever his stated aims, not the way of the statesman. There is nothing rote or standardized, about constitutional government; the necessary laws and powers cannot execute themselves (paragraph 13). Elementary principles do not provide a blueprint for action, and they are liable to grave difficulties when applying them to practical uses (paragraph 41). In any case, constitutional government cannot be imposed or "lavished" on a community or people (paragraph 86). It must be attained from within and then preserved. It must "spring from the bosom," from the common heart of the whole community in order to succeed, or as it were come from below, as well as from above. It is vivacious, not lethargic or dull of sense. This necessity cannot be overemphasized. It is in political terms the relation of differences and protection of liberty described earlier. For this, it must be intimately and spontaneously attached "in the comprehensive sense" (paragraph 19) in the intelligence, character, and "multifarious" conditions of the whole people considered individually, the concrete, as distinct from abstract, individuals. This spontaneity, willingness, or openness is the character of constitutional liberty and hence of constitutional government. The point might be annotated in terms of the principle assigning the spheres of power and liberty by saying that the sphere of power is limited by just that amount of virtue as is spontaneous among the people. "The laws ought, in all cases, to fit the permanent and settled character of the community."[35] It must begin within or be where the people or community itself already is, so to speak, and proceed then in accordance with the elementary principles of government in order to elevate the community (10, 78). Otherwise, what is supposed a constitutional form of government will immediately be appropriately simplified in accordance with the actual character and pursuits of the people, as in the hypothetical case of the regime proposed by Hippodamus. All these things are so many marks of the natural and definitive limitations of ordinary human reason (cf. paragraph 16: "limited reason and faculties of man," "great diversity," "various other causes"). The elementary problem of the perfection of government altogether to one side, the natural tendency of governments to decline into ever simpler forms itself presents a challenge that is equal to or greater than ordinary human reason. These observations are true always and everywhere, but they take on particular emphasis in the light of the new political element—universal diffusion of information—that has become characteristic of the modern or contemporary age, the "period of transition."

"It would seem," then, Calhoun concludes, that governments originally were simple absolute forms that were well-suited to the original conditions of their communities (paragraph 120). In communities that achieve some progress in their condition and pursuits, political struggles lead either (typically) toward the simplest form of all, military despotism, or (rarely), aided by prompting necessity, toward the foundation of constitutional government, "to be afterwards matured and perfected" (cf. paragraphs 25, 66), by inclusion of the respective parties in control of the government. This maturation, when not derailed altogether, is gradual. If it is too much to say that Calhoun is the first philosopher of political participation, compromise and participation are surely the core themes of his doctrine of constitutionalism. ("Participation" is mentioned five times in this section on construction. Concurrent participation, for Calhoun, is of course not the same thing as the fragment of Rousseauism now sometimes celebrated as "participatory democracy," but it alone may absorb all that is supposed desirable in participatory democracy without instability. Cf. paragraphs 70, 42). He emphasizes that the efficient cause of these governments has been chance, not political theory, still less zealous philanthropy. It is only in the maturation of the regime that the community as a whole begins to earn or possess the regime, and only in possessing and being possessed by the regime that the community matures (paragraph 78). Strictly speaking, this is why it is difficult or impossible for one people simply to imitate the constitutional example of another, although the constitutional example may be inspiring to others or favorably influence them, for the different communities must naturally differ in the comprehensive sense. The best that can be done is to study the principles exhibited in such examples and attempt to apply them in their own cases.

Paragraph 121

However distinguished are all the forms of constitutional government from all forms of absolute government (paragraphs 20, 57), each actual constitution is also clearly distinct from every other and has a distinct historic and hence social origin. The different forms of government reflect the different forms of society. What they all have originally in common is both a resistance to oppression and abuse and a resistance to that resistance, that is, "a struggle for the whole" (paragraph 121), or, ultimately, about justice and the common good. This is also why it is crucial for communities to "terminate all civil conflicts" by compromise that prevents the complete domination of either party. Because politics is the means to the natural human ends, compromise is no less than violence or the appeal to arms the decisive political act. The foundation of constitutional government is thus always possible, however unlikely it may always be, or even had a constitutional government never come to be, if only the respective parties are able to gain a voice in the control of the government. This is not *mere* chance, for the results of such participation are always the same, in accordance with its quality and extent, nor is it *mere* fate, for it requires some deliberation and choice, the original reasonable nature of man, aided by prompting necessity. The following paragraphs address the problems of constitutional forms on the basis that is set forth in this paragraph: all constitutional governments have an historical or material and spiritual or moral origin. This is the true key to understanding "fortune and misfortune in history."[36]

The principles of constitutional government are the same in all cases, but, as there are a variety of communities in differing conditions, there occur different elementary constitutional forms. The elementary forms of constitutional government are the popular, the aristocratic, and the monarchic forms (paragraph 121). Of all these forms, the popular constitution is the most complex. Hence it is the most difficult form of all to construct successfully, and, when constructed, to maintain. The United States, which has already been cited, with England, as a striking example of the combination of civilization and liberty (paragraph 95), is here alluded to as also the unique significant example of a purely popular constitution. Its constitution at that time is, therefore, the most complex and hence, in some ways, the most interesting government known. The complexity of popular constitutional forms arises because, in contradistinction to the popular form, the other constitutional forms are characterized by communities arranged into different social orders, estates, or classes (paragraph 69). These social arrangements are artificial or conventional and derive from the diversity of men within the variety of historical circumstances in which they are found. With the removal of such divisions, and where there is more or less equality of condition, the community and hence the government becomes more or less anonymous, and there is increasingly little to grasp onto apart from the abstraction of the "average man" ("common man," "working man," "mass man," etc.). The power of the press, mass opinion, will be difficult to check effectively. Without divisions and with broad equality of condition, the course of affairs will thus follow the outline begun in the twenty-fifth paragraph and following (cf. paragraphs 64ff.), resulting in the increasing coalition of the government, economic corporations, and wealthy interest groups.[37]

Such an absence of arrangement is also perhaps defective in that, lacking distinct or formal orders or classes, the rear rank will increasingly straggle and be left increasingly behind (paragraph 70 end, paragraph 84). If the most talented individuals of all orders or classes are for the most part retained in their class, their own efforts over time will elevate their classes as a whole, and therewith the community, and provide them with leadership, whereas, on the other hand, if the most talented are allowed simply to elevate themselves, the rear rank is deprived of its natural leaders and left behind. Some organism in the community itself may eventually prove necessary to overcome this difficulty (paragraph 39). For example, as the majority of the wealth in such regimes is increasingly effectively controlled by fewer than five or ten percent of the total population, these might be made personally responsible and accountable for the lives and expenses of the much greater percentage of all those who control nothing at all under some procedure of indenture or similar arrangement.

In the aristocratic form the political interests are simplified into two: the nobles and the commons or people, understood as distinct interests. As the simplest constitutional form, it may appear the strongest and most durable. Rome, the greatest ancient and most distinguished of all constitutional examples, is the example of an aristocratic constitution that Calhoun will treat at (relative) length in the *Disquisition*, and it receives from him the highest praise of all. This praise must be distinguished from that connected with the constitutional governments in the eighteenth paragraph. In that case, Calhoun's praise was not so much for the regimes themselves, which were certainly praiseworthy as constitutional regimes, as it was for the founders and statesmen of those regimes. In the case of the Republic Rome, the regime itself is equally praised, even from the point of view of the individual citizen (163). In the monarchic form, the political interests are three: the monarch, the nobles, and the people (or "commons"), the latter understood as an interest distinct from the others. Britain (with the United States the greatest of modern examples), is the example of a monarchic constitutional form that Calhoun treats at some length in the *Disquisition*. Complex as the constitutional forms are, they are quite competent to provide for the security of the community. The greatest example of a popular constitutional form, the United States, which is also the only one of "any considerable significance," is not treated in the *Disquisition* at all. This is in part because it is the most complex of all popular constitutions, as well as the most recent (paragraph 165), and because available information about its origin is uniquely complete.[38] It is the subject of the subsequent *Discourse on the Constitution and Government of the United States*, which work is introduced by *A Disquisition on Government*. The latter two facts are connected with the "new and important political element" that Calhoun mentioned in an earlier paragraph (112): popular government hence assumes an extremely and even uniquely complex "new form" (paragraph 130, end).

Paragraphs 122-126

With respect to popular constitutions, which have not the advantages of the simpler forms in regard to construction, Calhoun here leaves it at the observation (paragraphs 122-123) that compromise is more difficult in absolute popular governments than it is in the other forms (paragraphs 49, 51) because of the greater number of interests and the fact that, while more numerous, these are less distinctly marked and more anonymous than in other forms (paragraph 69).[39] This does not obstruct the natural tendency of government to decline (paragraph 119), but it obstructs or confuses any tendency to rise. The political interests arise not with the different social orders, which are artificial, but from the natural pursuits of the community: the aggregated diversity of pursuits, conditions, situations, and characters among the people. As has been explained, these will form coalitions with respect to the action of the government in the struggle to obtain control of it and, with it, the whole (paragraph 26). For these reasons, the form of concurrent majority that is required to establish a constitution and overcome the tendency of popular government to decline is more complex than those required in aristocratic or monarchic constitutions, where the interests are more clearly marked. This is true of popular government in all stages of society, but it is especially the case in the most advanced stages. Popular government in the most advanced and complex stage of society will require the most advanced and complex form of constitution. Otherwise, it can attain only a simple form of absolute government.

Aristocracy has also the advantage because in the struggle for political ascendancy the original object of the people or commons as against the nobles or aristocrats is not to overthrow the whole, for they much respect "the descendants of a long line of distinguished ancestors," but to participate in the government and correct its abuses with respect to themselves (paragraph 124). This respect, which was a guiding principle in Confucian China, is as crucial as it is tenacious in moderating the ambition of the commons. Reasonable nobles who are influential may for a time take advantage of the habitual respect of the people for the nobility and lead a judicious compromise that includes the elevation of the people to participation in the government with the nobles. It is in this manner that constitutional government may come about in aristocracies. However, the peoples' respect for the nobles may erode, or the nobles may prove too strong. Success depends, therefore, on the presence of a reasonable and patriotic noble who is influential and who has the timely opportunity to interpose. Such men are rare (*Politics*, 1308a *ad fin*). (The only occurrence of the term "individuals" in this section is found in this paragraph. In all the relevant places in the *Disquisition* one is tempted to infer that Calhoun's preferred constitutional form is the aristocratic form.) In other words, it depends crucially on chance.

The process of constitutional construction in a monarchy is different (paragraph 125). It may follow a course that is closer to necessity than to aristocracies, and that is less dependent on virtuous and well-placed individuals. In military despotisms, however, the people either have the government they deserve or, if they have the fiber to resist, in the effort to throw it off or improve on it they necessarily are either defeated or are successful only in changing dynasties. The experiences of Russia, China, and various African states provide the most obvious examples in the twentieth century. Yet, as Montesquieu says, if the monarch is surrounded by a hereditary nobility who wish to dissipate his authority and honor, the people may be advantaged by developing struggles between him and them for the ascendancy, and, if no action in this conflict is decisive for a sufficiently long time, they will "almost necessarily" be gradually elevated to participation in the government with both as a consequence of the influence of necessity on each of the others to cultivate them in such circumstances. We may speculate that this is necessarily the most common origin of constitutional governments, as it requires little original intelligence or virtue on the part of any of the parties. This inference is almost immediately confirmed (paragraph 127). In any event, we note that the author does not even pause to discuss in passing whether constitutional government might be brought about by some Praetorian action or *coup d'etat* in this case.

In contradistinction to aristocracies or monarchies, in democracies party conflicts "can hardly ever terminate in compromise," for the object in such conflicts is not participation in the government but control of the whole, which is reminiscent of political conflicts in absolute or military monarchies, as has been shown (paragraphs 126, 37, 64-69). In the process, every apparent success by either party only widens the actual gulf between them and carries the government further from constitutional compromise, a process that influential leaders will increasingly stimulate and exacerbate on their own behalf (paragraph 70). For these reasons, as well as others to which he alludes, constitutional governments are more easily formed in aristocratic and monarchic than in popular governments. Hence popular constitutions are the most difficult of construction (paragraph 121). The rest of the section (paragraphs 127-131) is devoted to the discussion of monarchies, which are the easiest of construction and the most prevalent and powerful of constitutional and of absolute forms.

Paragraphs 127-131:
Monarchy and Constitution

This part begins and ends with reference to what has been the case up to now and what will be the case from now on, or at least for an unforeseeably long time.[40] The tendency in question is the theme of the concluding paragraph, discussed in terms of what is "new" in the advanced stage of society (paragraph 130) and the "great changes" that this effects (paragraphs 131, cf. 112: "great changes — social and political"). However, as neither the new things nor the great social and political changes they have effected reach to essential human nature, and hence to the elementary questions of political science, this theme is here not new but is essentially the same as the theme of the forty-third paragraph, which was there set forth without any reference to a particular stage of society. The fundamental tendency that is not effected by new political elements and great social and political changes is the tendency of government to decline in the scale of liberty (paragraphs 118, 82-85). Not progress in civilization and intelligence, to say nothing of wealth, but only constitutional government can arrest this tendency (cf. paragraph 18 end).

Monarchy is or has up to now been the typical form of government because it is the simplest and, generally, the most powerful and durable, given the general ignorance of the mankind, on the one hand, and, as has been indicated, its easy, almost natural assimilation to military power for its preservation, on the other (paragraph 127). All regimes tend ultimately in the direction of the most absolute and the simplest form, or military despotism. Hence all regimes except absolute monarchy tend to changes in the form of government, while absolute monarchies tend only to changes in dynasty (paragraph 69, cf. 37). The exceptions have been described (paragraphs 121-125). There are, however, "other causes of a higher character" than these which also contribute to the prevalence and permanence of monarchies (paragraph 128). These causes are important, as they may to some extent apply as well to absolute democracies (in regard, e.g., to the tax-paying and tax-consuming classes) which, in power and other respects, not merely the relative intelligence of the communities, are so similar, if not identical, to absolute monarchies.

All regimes, as we have seen, even the most absolute and the most constitutional, are more or less mixed. Strictly, there is no "simple" regime in this sense.[41] In practice, they all depart more or less from their preservative principles (paragraphs 55-58, 62). Among the higher causes which contribute to the stability of monarchies, above all "the leading one is" that they are the most susceptible of improvement (paragraph 128). Just as they most easily assimilate to military power and the simplest absolutism, they are also most easily

(Calhoun says "almost naturally") modified in the direction of constitutional government "without assuming the constitutional form in its strict sense." That is, they may, to a limited extent, by habit and custom, almost naturally limit themselves in oppression an abuse of power (cf. paragraph 55). It would seem that, as it is set forth in the *Disquisition*, the form "monarchy" (which implies one power), as distinguished, on the one hand, from "absolute" monarchy, and, on the other, from strictly constitutional monarchy, is susceptible of some of the same ambiguities as the form "polity" (which means "regime" or "political order"), as distinguished from "democracy" or the rule of the multitude in Aristotle's presentation of the forms of regimes in the *Politics*. Both are habitually and for aims of their own concerned with the rule of the whole itself for the good of the whole. Where Aristotle stresses interests in this connection, Calhoun here stresses habit and custom, though neither writer is silent about the other element. However this may be, Calhoun cites hereditary monarchy as the first and oldest important modification of the monarchic form in its strict sense (absolutism), which he proceeds to explain. In the process of time, its natural tendency, if not interrupted, is toward paternalism and away from oppression and abuse of power. Hereditary possession tends strongly to identify the interests of monarch and subjects, and, in the process of time, in the absence of oppression and abuse, mutual security and custom "naturally" replaces fear and police in familial feelings of paternal benevolence and loyal devotion.[42] Such kindly or social feelings, which begin to approach toward the more exalted feelings of constitutional governments, are powerful and substantial, and often characteristic of hereditary monarchies, accounting for much of their strength and moral power. Nevertheless, such a form of government is not political but absolute, such as, in certain optimal cases, the government of hereditary masters and slaves.

The second such improvement to which monarchies are readily susceptible is related to the first, the extension of the hereditary principle to other families (paragraph 129). In the process of time, as has been explained (paragraph 125), this circumstance strongly tends to the elevation of the people to a participation in the powers of the government and a transformation of the regime into a constitutional government, which amounts to the extension of the hereditary principle to the people, or as far as it can be extended, that is, toward citizenship (paragraphs 21ff., 70). (In principle, one begins with suffrage or a democratic principle; in practice, one begins with monarchy.) Even when this does not actually happen, the people nevertheless gain increasing "respect," without which citizenship is impossible and which, on their part, they already have for the nobles. In this state of increased mutual respect, which is an improvement upon the benevolent familial or paternalist state of hereditary monarchy, in the process of time, law or precedent and "fixed rules of action" that the sovereign is compelled to respect will usually come to strengthen customary feelings. In these ways, then, monarchy can over time come to imitate the advantages of constitutional government without changing its unconstitutional form. Calhoun points to the "enlightened monarchies of Europe" as pertinent examples, with the attendant "advances in power, intelligence, and civilization." His point, however, is that it is not enlightenment as such, and above all not what is called the European "Enlightenment" or the alleged progress in the science of government that has been mistakenly supposed derivable from it, but circumstances and the susceptibility of monarchical form have produced these improvements in monarchies.

To these higher causes of susceptibility to regime improvement Calhoun adds also the greater capacity that monarchies of whatever modification, absolutism, or constitutional arrangement have exhibited over others to hold under subjection extended populations, and hence to gain in power over others to the extent that size and number are elements of power (paragraph 130). Almost all large or significant empires have been monarchical in form, and the few great exceptions, including even the greatest and most striking exceptions, such as the Roman Republic, which apparently irresistibly transformed itself into a military despotism, have in the process of time been absorbed by the monarchical form. Extended republics present all the essential problems of imperial regimes, of which they are potential instances. To the extent that all regimes, including constitutional regimes, tend toward empire, they tend toward absolutism and monarchy, and monarchy, although it may to some extent limit itself with respect to oppression and abuse of power, if it cannot limit itself in the tendency toward empire, will be checked by some external power or by its own internal decay. It appears, then, that all non-monarchical forms of government are exceptions to the general rule of monarchism, or that monarchism of some kind is the most necessary or practical form of government.

It remains now to be seen, Calhoun concludes, whether this state of things will continue as it has heretofore or whether it might in the future be altered under the great and growing influence of both the new political element he has described, and which has equally emerged both in the old and the new world, and the new and imposing form of popular government that has emerged only in the United States in the new world, that is, as opposed to the form that emerged in the old world in France following the French Revolution, which (as Burke had predicted) led to the Terror and military despotism, conquest, and reconstruction.

These new things have both "already effected" great changes adverse to the monarchic form, "and will probably effect still greater" (paragraph 131). Still, "For reasons which have been explained," says Calhoun, these changes have "as yet" (1850) tended rather toward the absolute rather than the constitutional form of popular government. (He takes it for granted that, whatever the other particulars to which it may be traced, the greatest change yet generally effected both by the new political element and by the example of the war of the English colonies in America for independence and their new government, has been the French Revolution.) If this tendency toward the absolute rather than the constitutional form of popular government should continue, the prevalence of monarchy will continue, not to say military despotism. Worldwide, then, the fundamental political alternative from the time of the completion of the *Disquisition* onward will foreseeably be largely determined not by the old but the new world. It will be between the convergent forms of absolute democracy, on the one hand, and more or less absolute monarchy, on the other. We here leave it with the observation that, if this should prove the case, we would have what in Calhoun's terms was then already the general political condition of Latin or South America.

He immediately continues that if, on the contrary, the great changes following upon these things should incline rather toward the constitutional form of popular government, then in the process of time the monarchical form of government will cease to be the prevalent form. Calhoun takes the long view. Whether the great and future changes actually take this direction will, he says, "for a long time" —which may mean only the emergent epoch or simply for so long as man remains as he is and has been (cf. paragraph 17, first sentence) —depend both upon the success of the complex constitutional form in the United States and on a "correct understanding" of the principles upon which constitutional governments are constructed. We may note that it does not depend primarily upon the influence of the press or the influence of what is called public opinion, which, in this connection, Calhoun here drops altogether and replaces with "correct understanding" (cf. paragraph 49).

Paragraphs 132-139:
Progress and the Forms of
Government in the Current Age

The following section returns from this vantage to the subject of the paragraphs immediately preceding the section on the different forms of government, a free press as the organ of mass opinion and hence of social and political change (paragraphs 112-117). To comprehend correctly the import of this new political element, it is necessary to consider its causes. All of these, which finally culminate in the influence of public opinion and hence the press, are "adverse to the monarchical form" as it has been familiar heretofore.[43] The great import of what, in connection with the press, is called public opinion—mass opinion, publicity, organized popularity—depends upon the existence of a mass urban public and the means to use it. This phenomenon, as distinct from the "commons" however otherwise understood, is in a sense "new," although it is not unique.[44] It has arisen now as a consequence of the development of natural science and, more especially, if secondarily, of the application and diffusion of that development through technology and its relation to warfare and to the commercial market. As we have noted, Calhoun typically distinguishes the present broadly from the past primarily in terms of the development of natural science and its influence, on the one hand, and the emergence of the modern credit system — what has come to be called "finance capitalism" — and its influence, on the other. Here, he refers only to the developments in natural science as the essential or fundamental cause of the existence of this mass public. For it is these discoveries and inventions and their practical application that underlies industrialism, urbanization, in short, "modernization," including "public opinion." It is not "civil society" that is "new" or distinctively "modern," *pace* Hegel, but, rather, the acceptance of the idea of "civilization" as itself, per Bacon, the final "ideal" or aim of "history" or "progress." This aim is implicit in the original presentations of the concepts of the "state of nature" and the "social contract."

Paragraphs 133-135

Calhoun mentions two kinds of discoveries and inventions based on their primary field of application. (The crucial term "application" occurs seven times in paragraphs 133-134.) The first group or kind primarily concerns application in global exploration, war, and knowledge or information. The second group or kind mentioned concerns primarily production, long-distance transportation, and long-distance communication. The result is commerce that is global and increasingly interdependent as distinct from merely local or regional.[45] Calhoun summarizes that the "joint effect" of all of these discoveries and inventions and their applications has been "a great increase and diffusion of knowledge," which has inspired "an impulse to progress and civilization heretofore unexampled in the history of the world — accompanied by a mental energy and activity unprecedented" (paragraph 135). It could seem that Calhoun agrees with Condorcet that "the history of civilization is the history of enlightenment." In fact, Calhoun understands the term civilization, as it was originally introduced into English about 1600, as "bringing out of barbarism." Now, that phenomenon is global. It is part of the supremacy of the advanced stage of society Calhoun mentioned in the ninety-fifth paragraph. When this end is achieved, however, the original problem of government will not have been altered in the slightest but will remain just as it was and has ever been. The progress of civilization does not overcome this original problem, which was the original and essential or deepest aim of the original state-of-nature theorists. At any rate, one must not lose sight of the fact that the characteristics described in these paragraphs (134-135) are what is certainly most striking and most admirable in the advanced stage of society, in contradistinction to all other characteristics and to all other stages of society. Calhoun here (and typically) summarizes these characteristics as the "light and blessings of civilization."[46]

The light of civilization is its knowledge. Hence Calhoun immediately describes the results of developments in the art of printing. These have been the preservation and wide diffusion of old and new knowledge, both the "fruits of observation and reflection" and knowledge of discoveries and inventions. This has happened before to only a very limited extent, thanks to commerce and to books or writing. One may note that the wide diffusion of knowledge here emphasized is, more than any advance in knowledge, specified by Calhoun as the essential difference between the advanced stage of society or the present age and the earliest ages (paragraph 18). This diffusion, combined with developments in the weapons of war, have in principle guaranteed, by insuring the ascendancy of civilization over barbarism (paragraph 95) and by spreading knowledge to all peoples globally, that whatever accumulated knowledge there is or may hereafter be gained will never again be lost, as it often was before, when diffusion was limited even within the community, and the Alexandrian and Ninevan libraries destroyed, for example, or Rome itself fell to barbarians or Constantinople to the Turks.[47] Any threat in this respect is now entirely internal, not external. The whole earth or mankind would have to be destroyed for it to be lost. As for the blessings of civilization, these are, first, its informed leisure, its improvements over harsh scarcity, and its material products. Hence the many-fold increase in the "productive powers of labor and capital" has resulted first and most importantly of all, according to Calhoun, in greatly increasing "the number who may devote themselves to study and improvement." Secondly, the consequent increase in commerce carried on by those who do not so devote themselves also greatly increases the wealth of the civilized countries and, more particularly, the condition of the less advanced portions of the globe, where the progress of civilization is thus initiated. The light and blessings of civilization are genuine goods, but they are not sufficient to replace or to establish constitutional government.

It is in connection with Calhoun's emphasis here on "an all-pervading commerce" and productivity, including his reference to commercial exchanges and the advantages of the spread of civilization for the less advanced portions of the globe, that we may briefly pause to sketch his views of free trade and protection. He does not present these views in the *A Disquisition on Government*, nor, so far as I am able to see, are they specifically entailed in what he does present. He subsumes them entirely under the political argument of the *Disquisition*.[48] Calhoun follows Montesquieu and Smith in regard to the procedures and benefits of international trade. He especially follows Smith in his opposition to what Physiocrats had called the "mercantile system" of monopolies, duties, and protection serving the rising manufacturing and merchant interests.[49] The touchstones of Calhoun's political economics are found in his considered remarks on the stability of currency and independence from debt.[50] Together, these represent the height of "enlightened self-interest" and the lowest part of political science, or what Smith had called "a branch of the science of the legislator or statesman."[51] He agreed with Smith that, although the great power of civilized peoples allowed them to do as they liked in regard to the less advanced peoples, ultimately, through the development of commerce, "the inhabitants of all the different quarters of the world may arrive at that equality of courage and force which, by inspiring mutual fear, can alone overawe the injustice of independent nations into some sort of respect for the rights of one another."[52] When power checks power, then conquest may be supplanted with commerce. However, according to Calhoun, for this end to be achieved the first or primary aim is not the development of manufacturing or mercantile interests but, as is implicit in many of the Physiocratic writings, the protection of established agricultural interests. This protection is best afforded by strict adherence to free trade. Without this "natural" protection, the agricultural interest, which is both stable and stabilizing, will be increasingly overwhelmed by the manufacturing interest, the "mercantile system," not as a result of the market, which, depending on conditions, will reward both interests in varying degrees and provide the stimulus for progress, but of the operation of the government. Otherwise, that is, if either agriculture or mechanics are developed for international trade under the impetus of the government interest or imperialism, the result will only be fraud and, ultimately, despotism. The view of Calhoun and Smith with respect to the character of the British East India Company and its effects, for example (or the core of Lenin's characterization of imperialism), is the same.[53] The progress of civilization among all peoples may most steadily and easily proceed under the protection of the agricultural interests in each country, for it is only in this way that its social and political destruction can be avoided and its social and political progress balanced.

The forceful defense of agricultural interests associated with Calhoun has rightly been seen in connection with issues of American sectionalism.[54] He also saw it in this light, although he did not limit its application to any particular American section, and he looked with great favor on the manufacturing interest as such. His views are compatible with those familiar from the Physiocracy, as well as, to be sure, English Tory social thought or the Cavalier South, but they are not the same. Calhoun defends the agricultural interest not primarily on feudal grounds but primarily on the grounds that it is only on such a basis that a country can ultimately rest.[55] This is because in an advanced stage of society the agricultural interest of the country alone is self-sufficient and hence independent, while the others are dependent upon currency fluctuations, the banking system, economic cycles, international markets, and so forth, to say nothing of the struggle of capital and labor.[56] Should the agricultural interest become similarly dependent, the community will be uprooted. It is the agricultural interest and only the agricultural interest that ultimately anchors the community. In less advanced communities, it is enough that agricultural trade be left free, and that, where circumstances impose such a necessity, the more advanced engage in the civilization of the less advanced with a view to the interests of the latter. Otherwise, as has been indicated, the latter will be destroyed and the former corrupted.[57]

Paragraphs 136-137

The discoveries and inventions described by Calhoun are ongoing and exercise now a more or less ubiquitous influence. No people is exempt from its consequences. Still, they have not yet attained anything like what will be their maximum force. He points out that not one of these revolutionary discoveries and inventions has probably yet produced its full effect, while several are very recent, and others — "probably of equal or greater force" — still await their discovery and application. In a reciprocal process, one discovery or invention leads to others; one application leads to others. It is difficult for anyone to estimate the force that these inventions and applications will give to public opinion for ubiquitous social and political change in the course of their inexhaustible operation, or upon their full effect (paragraphs 136-137). These unexampled changes will increasingly characterize the emerging unprecedented global epoch of advanced civilization, and only the process of time will present their ultimate bearing. However, the outlines of this bearing had been suggested in the previous section on the forms of government, as well as elsewhere. That bearing necessarily will be either in the direction of absolute government or constitutional government, and the attendant struggles, including the characteristic media of the new political element, will be accompanied by unprecedented advances in weaponry. Wars will not retard the progress in the application of new discoveries and inventions to matters of warfare, they may only accelerate that progress, and with it the power of government, in future as they have in the past, or, rather, beyond what was the case in the past (cf. paragraph 28).

With respect to these ongoing and projected changes we may note two possibilities in connection with the new political estate under discussion, the power of the press as the organ of social and political change. The first is that all journalists may be genuine philosophers or scientists, or participate in specialized communication with regard to public opinion and the whole. In this way all the advantages of the press that were outlined earlier might be secured (paragraph 114). The second, less absurd possibility is that the freedom of the press will be controlled in accordance with the principle laid down in paragraphs 80-83, that is, in accordance with the principles of constitutional government and the organism of concurrent majority, both morally and legally. Only the concurrent majority can remedy party struggles (paragraph 114), and, in so doing it may to that extent act as a control on the press. In this case, some of the advantages outlined earlier might also be approached. Yet, in any case, legal control will be difficult if not impossible, however perfect the constitution or the organism of concurrency. Even the most absolute regimes cannot entirely control this power (paragraphs 136, 132). This would seem to mean that there is now a political element or power that cannot be controlled, or that is itself in a sense more absolute than the formerly absolute regimes, and against which the concurrent majority not only offers no remedy but is typically, rather, itself the target of that power. This is a grave problem, for it is this power which characterizes the period of transition to which Calhoun now turns to draw explicit attention.

Culture, however it is understood or whatever its style, is always political in its nature. Now it is clear to all but the meanest capacities that civilization, science itself, the least of all "culturally relative" things, is inescapably political. "Civilization" is the popularization and hence politicization of science. Calhoun's term for this phenomenon throughout the *Disquisition* is "diffusion" (paragraphs 18, 34), the provision of the attitudes and products of science to non-scientists. For this provision to be unprovisionally beneficial as, for example, Descartes and Bacon wished, however, it must be accompanied by constitutional government, or more fully, by the virtue set forth in the sections of the *Disquisition* on community (paragraphs 72-78) and harmony (paragraphs 98, 104-109), and, ultimately, by the science of government itself, including its diffusion, not merely internally or domestically but globally, to all communities, beginning with the most advanced communities. Otherwise, the progress of civilization will tend to be only the progress of destruction and absolutism on a scale heretofore unimagined, a scale almost equal to Creation itself. The project of exporting numerical majoritarianism and making the world safe for numerical majoritarianism, according to Calhoun, will only mean the unprecedented and fundamental insecurity of the world.

It would be impious, according to Calhoun, to suppose that all the changes that are presently underway will ultimately do other than improve the human condition, for this would be to suppose that the Creator had so constituted man that the employment of his highest and most distinctive faculties, his intellectual faculties, by which the materials agents of nature are mastered, would be the cause of permanent evil (paragraph 137).[58] This is conceivable. Yet, "if such a supposition be inadmissable," as it must be, given the whole impulse and structure of his argument from the beginning, Calhoun concludes, then, that "they must, in their orderly and full development, end in his permanent good." His next sentence begins with the word "but." If this is to be, piety notwithstanding, and whatever the status of man's creation, the ultimate political effect of the changes underway must be to give ascendancy to constitutional government as to that form of government which most fulfills the ordained end of perfection of the human moral as well as intellectual faculties, even if this should ultimately be an act of the human creative will. If it were the case that man is not created for good, then he must, by the hypothesis, create himself in accordance with reason.[59] It is thus that constitutional government may be shown on Hobbes' own grounds to be the only justifiable and enlightened government, *pace* Hobbes. For it is hardly possible that other than permanent evil should arise from unconstitutional government in the present condition of society, to say nothing of the conquest and mastery of the material agents of nature. This is a *summum malum* worthy of Hobbes' reconsideration, an "end of history" requiring Hegel's rephenomenologization.

Since, according to Calhoun, it is easier to maintain free institutions among communities lacking civilization than among communities characterized by civilization, the triumph of civilization over barbarism is become, at the best, politically ambiguous, if only because the triumph of civilization does nothing to ensure the triumph of constitutional government. This fact alone here calls into question—as distinct from in any way halting or slowing—the globalization of civilized society, whether driven primarily by political or commercial ambitions, or both. It is not driven by scientific considerations in the strict or more usual sense. It is no accident that the only explicit illustration we are given of the celebrated contemporary confrontation between the more and the less advanced communities, among the latter of which man's moral as distinct from intellectual qualities may be "much more easily sustained...than among a civilized people," is that of the tragic confrontation between the enlightened European imperial monarchies and the constitution of the aboriginal Iroquois confederacy, or that we should find a kind of praise for hereditary monarchies, the "original" absolute form of government, in certain conditions, set forth in the most trenchant work on constitutional government yet written.

The problem that Calhoun's consideration of the extreme progress of civilization brings sharply but fairly to light in the advanced stage of contemporary society is an essential one that exists independently of advanced society and has always existed whether or not there is progress in civilization beyond the level of barbarism. The replacement of primitive superstition by mass opinion—which, to the extent that it is impious is merely that much more superstitious than primitive superstition—does not and can not alter the existence and character of this problem, which is coeval with man, but only deepens and complicates it on a single or one-dimensional (if global) plane (paragraphs 116-117, 138). The "well-being of our race," that is, the human race, depends so completely on good government that it is hardly possible that any changes from whatever causes that lead away from good government could prove to be a permanent good, that is, progress (cf. paragraph 69). Rather, it would be the absolute rule for their own ends of a few hundreds or thousands over many millions or billions.[60]

Paragraph 138

Even if the changes that are now underway, whether social or political or both, should somehow ultimately tend toward permanent good in some unforeseen and hence unknown and unknowable future epoch, now, "many and great" evils will immediately follow in their train not because of their proclaimed or nominal ends, whatever these may be, nor even only because of the violence and calamities that everywhere characterize their progress, but merely because they are rapid, and leave anticipation behind (paragraph 138). They are blind. They are not controlled. For this reason alone it is impossible to argue from progress in the control and manipulation of the material agents of nature to progress in the mastery of nature as such. There is no such mastery apart from the individual's mastery of himself and constitutional government. Among the dangers invited by the rapidity of communication that has just been emphasized (paragraph 134) is that the different pace of ordinary human thought and deed or habit may be forgotten in the fervor and excitement of acceleration. Human society is in this respect intractable. The development of morals and manners requires time and habituation (paragraphs 6, 124, 142-155). Great changes of almost any description might be made very gradually, "imitating the beautiful process which we sometimes see of a wounded or diseased part in a living organic body gradually superseded by the healing process of nature," but rapid and imposed changes bring calamities and do not reach the end hoped for and piously promised. Thus, when Calhoun writes elsewhere that society seems to be "rushing toward a new and untried condition" it is not difficult to see what he envisions. As new discoveries and applications continue to be altered and overcome what had seemed to be natural limits and barriers, there will be an increasing tendency to uproot the conventions and distinctions in society which reflect natural distinctions, and which, as such, are not susceptible of abolition, and to replace them with artificial projects of social engineering and control.[61] This is a necessary consequence of understanding man and society as essentially matter in motion, whether rationalized in accordance with Hobbesianism or Epicureanism. Hence Calhoun here refers to a law that apparently operates with as great a force in the political as in the material world. The law to which he refers is, in political terms, the law of recapitulation or cyclical metamorphoses of forms of government in accordance with the tendency of regimes to decay and decline, as explained in previous sections (paragraphs 118-131, 62-69). It is not "eternal" but it *is* a historical "law," in so far as all human history is political history.[62]

According to this political or historical law, "great changes cannot be made, except very gradually, without convulsions and revolutions."[63] (It goes without saying that Calhoun uses the term "revolution" in its radical or strict sense, to turn over or to turn back, and not in a contemporary French or salvific sense.[64]) This is because the first effect will be, through the power of the press, to unsettle long-established opinions and the principles in which recent or long-established governments originated and upon which habituation is based.[65] As Burke has shown in an earlier context, this will lead progressively in the case at hand not to political virtue or new self-mastery but merely to predictable destruction and familiar despotism. The freedom of thought that is necessary to the progress of science or of taste becomes, as Tocqueville and Mill each foresaw, only doctrine or license in the popular press, and, to the extent that it *or* established principle does not conform to popular opinion, blindly execrated. In this way, in contradistinction to threats from without, liberty may be lost within while popular knowledge, say, of mass weaponry or the procedures of mass banking, and hence of mass production and related arts, is retained. The interval between the decay of the old and the establishment of the new is, therefore, "a period of transition which must always be one of uncertainty, confusion, error, and wild and fierce fanaticism." That is, it is a period essentially reminiscent of anarchy and, hence, that, to the extent that it is not actually already simply absolutist, tends increasingly and all but inexorably toward absolutism.

Paragraph 139

The governments of the more advanced and civilized portions of the world, according to Calhoun, are now in the midst of this period, and are thus almost as inferior to themselves morally as they are materially superior to communities of the more barbarous or "poor" and less advanced or "developed" portions (paragraph 139). It is only the vague sense or realization among many of the essential emptiness of civilization or a globally standardized "civil society" as in itself the highest and final human end, that is, the realization that civilization in fact does not and can not in the least replace politics or the ends of human nature, that has led to the so-called "crisis" or transition of the West, with which all are now familiar. Yet this vague realization is perhaps due less to civilization or technology as such (*pace* Heidegger, among others), much less to science as such, than to the sense of its accompanying tendency toward absolutism for the reasons Calhoun has indicated.[66] This is typically presented by academic and popular writers in terms of a general "anomie," loss of identity, nostalgia, impotence, sense of helplessness, or what have you. It is in fact the uneasy but increasingly ubiquitous sense or realization that liberty has been lost.[67]

So long as this state of things continues, the more advanced portions of the globe will necessarily disseminate as much darkness as light, however much wealth and mastery of the material world might be increased and concentrated (and including eventual technical mastery of the problems of environmental degradation that are often pursuant to economic development). Nothing is "transvalued"; all is merely devalued. The challenges to statesmanship will be most difficult, and, many times, perhaps, impossible to meet. This does not alter the fact that they must be met. The brightest shaft of light that shines into this period is found in the fact that whatever knowledge is now accumulated will not be lost, and is available to those who may devote themselves to study and improvement (paragraph 134). What is most needful in these governments is for statesmen to perceive and carefully distinguish between the voice of the community as a whole, or what is truly the "public" or "common" opinion, and the pressure or agitation of merely a dominant majority (or minority), and formulate policies in accordance with the protection of the whole. As has been explained, this is sufficiently difficult in itself, and it is further complicated in this period by the irresponsible power of the press. To effect it would be to take steps toward constitutional government, whatever the orientation of dominant opinion (paragraphs 47, 52, end). Otherwise, the period of transition or crisis will merely continue as a confused, progressive transition to a permanent absolutism whence there is no recourse.

For this to be avoided, according to Calhoun, one must become aware of and begin to see the foundations of modern life in light of the principles of government. Again, where, in less striking but related circumstances, Plato had Socrates say in the *Republic* that political problems would end only when absolute kings philosophized or philosophers became absolute kings, Calhoun here as much as says that they would improve only when the whole people, the governors and the governed themselves, should become political philosophers, which, as he has indicated, is hardly possible (paragraphs 139, 119-120, 43). Under such conditions, it would perhaps be possible to speak unequivocally of human progress, of an increase in self-mastery that is commensurate with the increase in intelligence, or of "the past" becoming in some sense "past." It is for those extraordinary constitutions in the future, then, whose aspiration is first for such understanding, that the *Disquisition on Government* is ultimately written. Calhoun's countryman Faulkner, who towered over contemporaries but little less than Calhoun had done, observed that one can present the truth plainly or put it in a chalice. Either achievement is extraordinary, he thought, under the best of circumstances. *A Disquisition on Government* represents the opportunity to discover that one may, also, do both.

The period of crisis or transition here outlined by Calhoun "will endure" on earth until rulers and ruled understand better the ends for which government is ordained: security of the whole and perfection of the human moral and intellectual faculties, particularly the perfection of the moral faculties, and the elementary principles and benefits of the forms of government most in accord with nature and most adaptable to all the circumstances in which communities may find themselves (paragraphs 139, 44). This is the object of the science of government (*Disquisition*, paragraphs 1, 15).

With this conclusion, which remains open, Calhoun turns briefly to exemplify these elementary principles as they are found in the most remarkable constitutional governments that have as yet come about by chance.

AFTERWORD

Calhoun and the New Age

LIKE THAT OF HOBBES, WHOM HE MEANT TO CORRECT ONCE AND FOR ALL, THE thought of Calhoun arose in the shadow, or in the foreshadow, of civil war, when the political consciousness of the people came into crisis. Calhoun's thought, like all political philosophy, raises acutely—the standard examples in our time are those of Martin Heidegger and Ezra Pound—the question of the relation of philosophy or poetry to what we now call the historical moment or the "historical consciousness." In Calhoun's terms, the regime, the political community, is itself the most comprehensive expression of a people's "historical consciousness," which, like all human consciousness, includes some original notion or awareness of the good and the true, and which, as such, transcends time and place.

The general question is familiar, though it emerges in cases always individually distinct. In philosophy, it may be traced at least to the career and trial of Zeno of Elea, or, more properly, to the career of Solon of Athens,[1] and, in poetry, it may be traced at least to Aristophanes' comedy *Frogs*, in which the god Dionysus finally comes to judge between rival tragedians according the wisdom of their recommendations for the *polis*, if not to Hesiod's criticism of Homer for seeming indiscriminately to praise war. In any case, investigation of the question requires in each instance, first, an effort of mind equal to the rediscovery of the passed world or context in which it arose, or, in Schleiermacher's celebrated gloss, that we first and above all understand the principals as they understood themselves.[2] The same strictures apply in the case of Calhoun.

According to his German biographer of the 1880s, Herman von Holst, professor at the University of Freiburg and visitor and student of the United States, "every day it becomes more difficult really to understand" the career of Calhoun, even though, "As the years roll on, the fame of Daniel Webster and Henry Clay is gradually growing dimmer, while the name of Calhoun has yet hardly lost anything of the lurid intensity with which it glowed in the political firmament of the United States toward the end of the first half of this century. Nor will it ever lose much of this."[3] Yet the world in which Calhoun actually lived and breathed is irretrievably passed away:

Even the present generation [1882], which has grown to manhood since the civil war, hardly realizes that it is not a soul-stirring romance but sober history.[4] The next generation will find it easier to form an adequate conception of the life of the ancient Indians and Egyptians than of that of their own grandfathers; for there is no instance in all the history of the world where two civilizations of two different ages, with their antagonistic principles and modes of thinking and feeling, have been so intricately interwoven as in the United States during the slavery conflict. It is only the part played by Calhoun in this conflict which puts him into the very first rank of the men who have acted on the political stage of the United States, though he has done enough else to secure for his name a permanent place in the annals of the country.[5]

As we have sufficiently noted, Calhoun, for his own part, was perfectly aware that his lifetime fell in an age of transition, soberly predicted the secession of the Southern states within a decade of his death, and the war, and foresaw, beyond that, the "new phase" of the age: finance-driven commerce, egalitarian, characterized by accelerating diffusion of information and technological development, and tending "when perfected," to a global communication state "endowed with sensitiveness," in which "whatever touches on one point, will be instantly felt on every other." We have also noted that he attempts across all divides to address directly posterity—to speak to the coming generations described by Professor von Holst, those in the midst of what he styles an age of transition, in his posthumous writings, A Disquisition on Government and the unfinished A Discourse on the Constitution and Government of the United States.

In the elementary or fundamental part of A Disquisition on Government, the opening paragraphs in which he addresses the first question of the science of government, Calhoun attempts this address via an appeal to "nature." The discussion of the first question, the Disquisition from the beginning, where he says, "In order to have a clear and just understanding of the nature and object of government" (paragraph 1) up to where he says, "With these remarks I proceed to the important and difficult [i.e., second, or higher] question" (paragraph 15), amounts to a treatise on human nature.[6] His introductory discussion of the higher question in the remainder of the introductory part of the Disquisition (through paragraph 18) and beyond, depends on this prior discussion.[7] Calhoun does not in the opening part of the Disquisition fully present or question the condition or cause that "nature," including "human nature," is—A Disquisition on Government, like, say, Aristotle's Ethics or Politics, is not a work like Aristotle's Categories or Physics—yet his meaning would nowhere be altered if his usage of the term "nature" were replaced in every instance with the term "being."

Calhoun's contemporaries, for their part, proved unresponsive to *A Disquisition on Government*, particularly those in the South, where one might have expected that it would be most warmly received, for these wished in the rising heat of the political crisis above all that the awaited explication of "the Calhoun constitution" would contain, whatever else it might include, a forthright and irrefragable statement of the claims of the South as the planter class understood them, which, however, the work does not so much as notice.[8] As part of his long summation of Calhoun's career, Charles Wiltse, his finest biographer, includes this thought: "It is not likely...that the result [of the political crisis] would have been materially changed had he never lived. He did not create but only formulated and expressed the attitude of the planter class to which he belonged, seeking always to direct the Southern discontent into nonviolent channels."[9] While containing important truth, this is surely an overstatement. After all, to cite another, not unrelated example, who can say whether political support for the second war with Britain would have been as effectively built and sustained as it was, or perhaps the war itself victoriously concluded, or even engaged in, had Calhoun never lived?[10] (Besides, have we not heard that even the shape of Cleopatra's nose materially might be said to have altered the course of historic events?) Yet, even allowing the suggestion to be taken as true, either in some sense or altogether, may we not then ask, following Wiltse's analogy, whether the result might have been *spiritually* changed had Calhoun never lived? Might not he have made a moral difference?

We seek, we demand a moral judgment. In the case of Calhoun, this means above all that we understand his argument that the institution of slavery as it existed in the section where providence had cast his lot is a "positive good." Although he makes this argument openly and unambiguously in some of his senatorial speeches, *A Disquisition on Government*, specifically, is of little use in arriving at it. This is both because, according to him, in laying the foundation of the science of government and understanding the elementary principles of constitutional government it is not necessary to consider the constitution including the American Constitution, "in its most comprehensive sense" (paragraph 19), entailing all the social, commercial and agricultural, educational, and religious arrangements of the population, and, similarly, because the achievement of constitutional government is typically "the product of [historical or social] circumstances," or fortune (paragraphs 119-120). Calhoun's argument that African slavery in the American South was a positive good, i.e., that it was good for the slaves and for the community as a whole, allowing the closest possible proximity and familiarity between the races, depends ultimately on the view that the African presence in the community was itself a positive good, and was always a distinctly minority position, even characteristic primarily if not only of Calhoun himself, although like all his positions, certainly, it was in part precedented. The majority position, South as well as North, was, rather, that the institution was a "necessary evil," evil for the community as a whole, whether or not it might be in some sense good for the slaves, and reduces to the view that the presence of Africans in the community is a positive evil. This presence is the evil that, for reasons of security, tranquility, decorum, and organized management, together with long-established habit, render slavery much the lesser or necessary evil. The defense or excuse of slavery as a necessary evil is an argument from circumstance that is often accompanied with a condemnation of slavery in principle or in the abstract and that ultimately (if often vaguely) finds its aim in the complete separation of the races through the removal of Africans.

On the basis primarily of the beginning of the Declaration of Independence in 1776, it is sometimes insisted that some or many of the Framers envisioned (among other, more pressing things) an eventual disestablishment of institutionalized slavery, which had existed in the colonies for a century and a half by the time of the convening of the State delegates in Philadelphia in 1787, in framing the proposed new orders of confederal government. This opinion is acceptable provided one does not evade the collateral and concomitant envisioning of African colonization or other such ultimate redispersal of the root problem on the part of most of these same Framers. Jefferson, who, as the chief drafter of the Declaration of Independence, whose *Notes on the State of Virginia* in the 1780s deplores the existence of African slavery as fundamentally corrupting to all concerned with it, and who elsewhere variously expresses a sense of guilt and concern, must be accounted the most apt of all examples, developed a draft plan, which (instead of being presented to the Virginia legislature for actual consideration) is also presented in the *Notes*, for the manumission of *all* the slaves in Virginia on a date to be specified; for their vocational education or job-training by tax-supported organizations until they reach maturity; and, finally, "for their removal to another locality on reaching maturity." The slaves would not merely be abandoned, and, in this way, Virginia would be divested of the institution and its traces within a relatively short span of time. Jefferson's draft plan does not specify whence the former slaves will be removed—merely to somewhere else.[11]

A generation later, in 1824, the year Calhoun was first elected to the vice presidency, the editor of Boston, Massachusetts' influential periodical, the *North American Review*, denounced "the living pestilence of a free black population" (largely the result of manumission in that section after independence).[12] This same view extends similarly (if not always uniformly) to following generations. In 1852, for example (Calhoun had died in the spring of 1850), Abraham Lincoln's honest eulogy of Henry Clay, Lincoln's political model and co-founder of the American Colonization Society (*sc.* the American Society for Colonizing the Free People of Color of the United States), concludes with the peroration that Clay's glorious dream of "restoring a captive people to their long lost fatherland" (the motto of the Society: [removal] "to the land of their fathers"), might be speedily realized. This removal, according to Lincoln, by superannuating African slavery in the United States and redispersing the former captives in Africa or abroad (perhaps in a territory or reservation), would represent the "capstone" of Clay's illustrious career, his greatest achievement on behalf of liberty.[13]

If it is the case that, in Lincoln's terms, the slave population is not socially and politically equal to the citizenry, and may never become so,[14] then it would seem that either the inherited institution should be sustained, for otherwise the house would merely become irrevocably divided against itself as two nations or races, or, if the political weight of the South can no longer be brooked in this or other respects, then its alteration or abolition should be the subject of careful planning and preparation, along the lines pointed to by Jefferson, including relevant vocational and other training of both races, North and South. As Calhoun pointed out, if its abolition is brought about by force of arms, the result will be catastrophic for all concerned, for the slaves and for the community as a whole, and no genuinely liberal aim actually arrived at.[15] What will become of the former slaves, whose material well-being on average had equaled or exceeded that of Northern workers (Calhoun's famous "Marxism," which we discussed in connection with Hegel),[16] or of those whose slaves had been confiscated "by an act of war," a value computed, in 1913 English pounds, "at four hundred millions sterling"?[17] In this context, the purport of Calhoun's "positive good" argument may be summarized in the proposition that, if the special, or, in his familiar phrase, "peculiar institution" did not already exist stably by long inheritance, it would have to be invented from scratch in some continuing form, if only, then, as a "necessary evil," in order that the house so divided against itself might stand.[18] For it is not to be supposed that life itself or the political community, however profoundly altered and simplified, will cease with the end of the war, or that there will be an "end of history."

In 1913, Charles Francis Adams observed to an English audience that Americans "at the close of our Civil War found ourselves with a race issue on our hands and a section of our common country seething with discontent—in a word, perplexed in the extreme by a condition of great unrest." He explained the outcome:

> Strange indeed as it sounds, the remedy for the ills consequent to the war was found in a recourse to the system which had caused it.... the principle of State Sovereignty applied in its extreme form in practice led to the trouble; but, fifteen years later, that same principle of State Sovereignty in it proper form, now known as Local Self-Government, or, in other words, Home Rule, brought to a close the unrest and disturbance which naturally ensued from the strife. Operating as a charm, it worked a miracle.[19]

While, in pointing to "the principle of State Sovereignty in its proper form" by way of explaining this miracle, Adams tacitly and perhaps unwittingly in fact points back to the program of Stephen A. Douglas, he points at the same time and primarily to a quasi expulsion, the special (or "peculiar") development of parallel communities ("separate but equal"), in which the contact between the two races, living in some proximity, is governed by elaborate mores and sanctions.[20] Although it brings peace and superficial concord, this new condition is exactly similar to that addressed by Calhoun almost a century earlier in state papers we have already cited in connection with deficient Indian policy (American authority should govern them directly in their own interest), particularly as bearing on "independent" ("sovereign") tribal reservations: "To tribes thus surrounded, nothing can be conceived more opposed to their happiness and civilization than this state of nominal independence. It has not one of the advantages of real independence, while it has nearly all the disadvantages of a state of complete subjugation. The consequence is inevitable."[21] We may note in passing that Calhoun thus exposes, *avant le lettre*, in the course of his remarks on the reservation system and its underlying policy the fallacy of the later South African attempt to retain original multicultural integrities by means of apartheid, for the original cultures (which are not originally "book" cultures) are not maintained but lost in such as system. Calhoun points out: "They lose the lofty spirit and heroic courage of the savage state, without acquiring the virtues which belong to the civilized."

It is conceivable that, in spite of achievements by exceptional individuals, this condition may continue indefinitely, if it is not interrupted by a change in policy. In regard to this form of the peculiar institution—segregation, black codes, Jim Crow laws—Charles Francis Adams held that

> Every political issue, every step in the process of political evolution, be the same upward or downward, is a question of *pro* and *con*, a balancing of advantages. Sometimes, and not infrequently, as we all know, it of necessity becomes a balancing of public and general good against private hardship and individual wrong. As an abstract proposition, however, subject of course to proper limitations, the general public good is the end to be kept in view.[22]

In general, Adams's whole presentation in this connection should be read in the light of *Disquisition* paragraphs 81ff. Yet, in view of his review of "pros and cons," it is impossible to avoid the specific inference that Adams regards at least the aspect of American "State sovereignty in its proper form" pertaining to the circumstances he is presenting as a necessary evil. His conclusion in this respect is not complacent but tempered:

...the Africans, once slaves, we were honor bound to protect.... As a nation we were under the deepest obligations to the Afro-American.... The problem of the advance and present condition of the African race in what was once their land of bondage is with us in America much debated and involved in doubt. Into it, though most interesting, I do not propose here to enter. It is unquestionably one of the numerous great issues, as yet only partially solved and not become historical, resulting from the outcome of our War of Secession. One one point, however, no question remains: it has passed out of the forum of political discussion.[23]

It is conceivable, in spite of surpassing achievements of exceptional individuals in education and natural science (it suffices to recall to the name of Carver), that such a condition might continue—and it did continue—for generations, until it reenters the forum of political discussion. However, the arrangement proved sufficiently stable to produce black troops who served with distinction in American armed forces in the two world wars and Korea, and, as American forces (including blacks) were committed in South Vietnam, the demand was raised by blacks for full citizenship, much as the Athenian slaves who had served with distinction in the naval victories of the Persian Wars had then demanded Athenian citizenship with full political rights. This demand was acceded to in the Southern states with less unrest and violence than might reasonably have been expected, given their history, and, setting aside conventional rhetoric on all sides of the controversy, incomparably less than attended contemporaneous "race riots" in Northern states then and thereafter.[24]

On the heels of this demand and the related acts of government pursuant to it, there quickly arose the concomitant demand for a special institution, "affirmative (i.e., "positive") action," to ensure that the purport of these acts be materially fulfilled, that some progress in—not to say equality of—condition be guaranteed or enforced by the government.[25] In spite of the achievements of many individuals in the uppermost ranks of domestic economics and politics, blacks taken as a group in America at the turn of the twenty-first century lag behind other groups in economic categories, and almost half (45 percent) of all black American families are headed by women alone, with one third (33 percent) of the total black population in America being under eighteen years of age.[26] With the simplification of the regime, it may appear that the "liberal" and "conservative" positions have altered in respect to this issue, among others. The "liberal" argument defending the institution of affirmative action is typically weak (and even fundamentally blurred and subverted in the cooption or attempt to exploit the institution by various subpolitical or "civil" groups—women, homosexuals, resident aliens, temporary immigrants with green cards, rising numbers of new immigrants, etc.), but it is animated by a genuine insight into the—in spite of the achievements of very many individuals—accelerating "marginalization" of a daily expanding domestic population,[27] who are fully counted for purposes of taxation and representation, but who otherwise remain fractional ("second class") citizens. This process will continue as the consequences of spiraling immigration, raising other issues of its own, compound. When apologists assert that this controversial special institution should be enforced for at least as long as the institution of slavery itself existed, i.e., for centuries, on behalf of American blacks who, like all citizens, are now free to go but are determined on staying—and why not?—one is then but a step from the original conventional view of the institution of slavery. The "conservative" opposition to the peculiar institution, on the other hand, on the ground that the evident achievement of very many American blacks sufficiently demonstrates that their "integration," desired by all significant parties (or at least opposed by none), is entirely possible without any special policy, which unnecessarily and unwisely risks instituting equality of condition as a guarantee of the fundamental law,[28] while in a sense true, is, with respect to the actual and continuing condition of a significant and increasing portion of this American citizenry, open to the charge of a certain "abstractionism," or, in short, to much the same criticism Marx made of *Hegel's Philosophy of Right*, which we have sufficiently noticed.

Moreover, once it is seriously proclaimed by its defenders that the institution of affirmative action (presumably restricted to blacks, or to certain blacks) stretch out for centuries, it requires but little mental effort to conceive of the institution of slavery itself, seen as a positive good, as but a circumstantial form of affirmative action.[29] It is at least possible, certainly, that in the process of centuries the institution would have in some way followed the course of the plebs in the example of Rome or that of the commons in the example of Britain, as these are presented in the *Disquisition*. This possibility, however remote (*sc.* centuries), cannot be simply ruled out, for, the presumption of Professor Spain in his *Political Theory of John C. Calhoun* notwithstanding, Calhoun never rested his position on slavery on the "natural" or "innate" or "abstract" inferiority of black Africans (nor on any biblical argument), like most apologists of slavery, North and South, and his position, in this case as in many others, should not be simply assimilated to theirs.[30] His argument is political, concerning the juxtaposition of distinct, numerous, and more and less advanced (citizen and noncitizen) domestic populations. Professor Spain is correct, certainly, in stressing Calhoun's Aristotelianism in all his political thinking, but he overlooks the fact that Calhoun's Aristotelianism, which, as we have noted, is profound, is characterized strikingly—arrestingly—by the absence anywhere in his writings or speeches of the argument about the "slave by nature," with which Aristotle all but opens the *Politics*. (Aristotle's position is sometimes dismissed as referring merely to persons with obvious mental or physical defects, who must be closely cared for, etc., but Aristotle of course does not mean this, for he elsewhere says that infants with obvious mental or physical defects ought to be exposed at birth, since they cannot live a fully human life. And yet, might one not propose, rather, that, as the slaves by nature cannot live a fully human life either, and still are allowed to live, might it not be as well that those with more obvious defects be also allowed to live, unless, in virtue of their mental defect, they pose a threat to others, even though they must be closely cared for, for Aristotle also says that all living things seem to love life?) Besides, Calhoun manumitted at least one of his own slaves, which he obviously would not have done had he supposed that the slave population was "innately" inferior or "naturally" slavish. It may be that this individual was exceptional, as in some sense he doubtless was, but this only proves that for Calhoun the black race is capable of producing exceptional individuals, or in other words that it is not "innately inferior" to other races possessing that capacity, and on that ground alone its presence might be received as a positive good.

It is true that the difference of complexion between the white and black races provides an added obstacle in this case (the freedman returned after a time in New York requesting to remain always at Fort Hill), and Calhoun often points to this difference, along with everyone else, for it is obvious to all and, for that reason, all the more more formidable, even though it might be no more than what he in another context calls "a common error" to presume (like Jefferson) that it is in any sense fundamental, or any more fundamental than in the case of the red Indians.[31] In this connection, particularly, he mentions "complexion" in the catalog of causes that, "with various other causes," have led to the separation humanity into a multitude of independent communities acting independently of each other (*Disquisition*, paragraph 16), but it is of no greater rank or import than any of the other causes, some of which are clearly not fundamental, and the communities themselves to which these causes have helped give rise, are of course not there ranked in any way. We know that he in fact considered other causes of division to be much more fundamental than differences in complexion, for in the course of a speech we have cited repeatedly he says, stressing especially two of the causes he mentions in the catalog in *Disquisition*, paragraph 16: "Those who know the human heart best know how powerfully distance tends to break the sympathies of our nature. Nothing—not even *dissimilarity of language* tends more to estrange man from man" (emphasis added). Apart from physical inaccessibility, dissimilarity of language is the greatest of the dividing features among mankind. Differences of complexion presents, then, only a formidable obstacle at best, certainly not a natural impossibility, in the advancement of black Americans in any condition in the process of time. It is unnecessary to note that the whole subject today of special policies concerning the advancement of American blacks provides the occasion for much passion and controversy, for this is but a way of saying, in Charles Francis Adams's phrase, that it has reentered "the forum of political discussion." In any case, the investigation and judgment of Calhoun's own position, which itself was always a minority position and always controversial, is amply afforded and even invited by his speeches and papers, where it is openly and unambiguously presented repeatedly, and for which *A Disquisition on Government* is neither sufficient nor necessary.

The demand for moral judgment on such issues is itself as clear a proof as anyone could wish that the new world foreseen beyond his own and addressed by Calhoun in *A Disquisition on Government*, however changed and "developed" it may be or seem, and however remote from it or undeveloped Calhoun's world may seem in its light, remains in every essential respect a "political" or human world. The demand for morality and moral judgment is "natural." The demand for moral judgment, not to say outright moralism, in fact underlies all the hand-wringing about the relation of philosophy and history (i.e., moral responsibility). (Indeed, it is little wonder that some hold that it is only by active and hence conscious evasion or suppression of moral questions as such that one can pretend to "historicism.") For Heidegger, who, like Rousseau, begins by displacing or expanding the focus of Hobbes' "state of nature" into the original sweet "sense" of human experience (for Heidegger, the original "experience" of "thrownness" and the arising or potency of self-discovery and "struggle" for authenticity, "Kampf"), and whose thought is proclaimed as the culmination of historicism, politics seems, in the first place, a matter of race. For Calhoun, of course, this is perfectly true, so long as by "race" we understand, as presented in the *Disquisition*, the human race, the humans as distinct from the animals. The highest aim of humanity as such is in principle open to all "races." As we have noted, the *Disquisition* includes examples of constitutional government among many races: Egyptians, Indians, Chinese, Jews, Europeans, and Iroquois. (The Iroquois, a "red" race of men in the savage or hunting and gathering state, is not in principle distinct from original "Africans." Among the latter, over the ages there may well have been constitutional governments of which we are unaware.) Yet, Heidegger means, rather, the Germans, the German nation, and also the ancient Greeks, at least as these have been understood by modern Germans since Hegel and Winckelmann, if not merely by Heidegger himself from the *Introduction to Metaphysics* onward, (i.e., the "pre-Socratic" Greeks). However modulated, politics—the political dimension or sphere of human nature—always unavoidably exhibits something of an "aristocratic" tincture or bias. It is natural. This bias is easily discovered in *A Disquisition on Government*, where, in part, it displays a "paternalistic" character, or orientation toward protection of the weak against the strong, of which, in Heidegger, of course, there is no trace. For Heidegger, this is a delusion belonging to "those who speak of 'values' and 'totalities,'" including, above all, "political wholes," for, while he often speaks of "world" where we might have expected reference to the community or regime, the question of the [political] whole that seems decisive for him is never that of the government or the constitution (either in the strict or the comprehensive sense) but, first, the race-language group. Hence, the "aristocratic" bias is present in Heidegger's thought first in the assumed place or rank of the Germans (and pre-Socratic Greeks) in relation to the rest of the race (not to say to the "barbarians"). This is what leads to his national socialism: destiny demands the rule of the strong for the sake of the strong, which is at the same time the authentic leadership of the world.

The [political] vocation, according to Heidegger in 1935 and still in 1953, of the "extra-ordinary" or "most metaphysical of nations," greater Germany, which is the core or peak of "the West" as such, is now demanded, by the fact that Europe itself is "caught in a pincers" between Russian communism on the one hand and American liberal capitalism on the other. This situation is the same as the decline of the West, it defines the decline of the West into the metaphysical indistinguishability of the rest of humanity ("multiculturalism"). Heidegger calls this the "night" or "darkening" of the World, a dark age darker than the Dark Ages, which Heidegger also styles the "age of information," by which phrase he means precisely what Calhoun means whenever he speaks of the "wide diffusion of intelligence" (e.g., *Disquisition*, paragraph 18, and related passages). "From a metaphysical point of view, Russia and America are the same; the same dreary technological frenzy, the same unrestricted organization of the average man" (*Introduction to Metaphysics*, 37; 45: "Europe lies in a pincers between Russia and America, which are metaphysically the same, namely in regard to their world character and relation to the spirit," etc.). Yet, might one observe that Russian communism, that is, "Marxism," is itself German, or, now, the primary legacy of Germany?[32] Heidegger is resolute in opposing any such counterfeit legacy. According to him, the vocation of the most metaphysical of all the nations, i.e., of the most extraordinary people, is, therefore, to take "a *creative view of its tradition*" and "move" or lead "the history of the West beyond the center of their future 'happening' and into the primordial powers of being" (*Introduction*, 38-39). This somewhat ambiguous statement refers both to the leadership of the West (and hence the human world) out of the ordinary by the New Germany, that is (one necessarily infers), by German National Socialism, and to Heidegger's own creative and epochal program of return to Western origins among the ancient Greeks.[33] However, when Heidegger elsewhere (on Holderlin's *Der Ister*) says: "One does not at all serve the knowledge and appraisal of the uniqueness of National Socialism if one interprets Greek humanity [i.e., mere "greekness"] such that one could suppose that the Greeks have already all been 'National Socialists,'" he means that most or even almost all of them (merely in virtue of their greekness or their part among an extraordinary or superior metaphysical people) have not been so, but that some among the Greek philosophic poets have been National Socialists. The converse, it must be noted, thus also holds. Many or no doubt most of those Germans who called themselves National Socialists or were camp-followers of various kinds, perhaps some or even many among those most associated in the minds of Germans and non-Germans with "National Socialism," are not National Socialists, but only those Germans who represent the highest, because the most creative, grandeur yet attained by Western civilization, the "inner truth of National Socialism."[34] Hence, however dependent it may be upon "spirit" and the German language itself, the issue is by no means merely a question of race in the conventional sense and can in no sense be reduced to biology. Be this as it may, the extraordinary people are now in the *Introduction to Metaphysics* of 1935, in a historic position to make the "great decision" for Europe (the allusion is to Spengler's *Hour of Decision*, which followed his *Decline of the West*), that is, for "the West," and hence for humanity itself or the human world.

The realization of human destiny, for Heidegger, is or lies beyond every ordinary form of utilitarianism in the "primordial realm of the powers of being" (*Introduction*, 38). This is to say, it is or points to a discovery of politics as a dimension, or of human nature as political, only above and beyond mere utilitarianism or technology and the organization of average men—but *also*, following Calhoun, one must immediately add: beyond ordinary, everyday tyranny or the rule of the strong—to the distinctively human clearing between the existing things as they are and being as such. Heidegger, in spite of his vaunted return to the Greeks among whom political philosophy and many of our own political terms themselves originated, does not make this turn. He says only: "From a metaphysical point of view, Russia and America are the same; the same dreary technological frenzy" (Carl Schmitt said the same, referring to economism), while "the inner truth and grandeur of National Socialism," on the contrary, extra-ordinarily achieves or anyway attempts "a satisfactory relationship to the essence of technology," or "enframement,"[35] that is, understands human being or man as man is in truth. The outer appearance or practice of National Socialism, not National Socialism as it is in itself according to Heidegger, but as it is seen by all non-National Socialists (including party hangers-on), may or (to the extent that it seemed to conceive of itself as almost a biologism) may not have seemed to live up to this inner truth or attempt at truth, but it is the shadow or trace of Heideggerism in the place of politics, i.e., imperial tyranny based on the destiny of true German spirit at this historical moment (*fuhrerprinzip*). The only question, then, that the average, ordinary non-National Socialist might seem to have would be who is the true representative and hence redeemer of this true German spirit, Heidegger or Hitler—or, even, rather, Bonhoeffer or Count von Stauffenberg?[36]

For Heidegger, such an ordinary question does not reach the deeper issue but only points to it, for the issue as he raises and answers it in *An Introduction to*

Metaphysics is extra-ordinary. Yet, much as one might sympathize with his complaint in a crucial paragraph of the *Introduction* that "time as history" — that is, time as authentic human being — "has has vanished from the lives of all peoples" (including, above all, greater Germany), when "mass meetings attended by millions are looked on as a triumph" (viz., the great rally at the 1934 Nuremberg Party Congress — Heidegger's allusion is to Leni Riefenstahl's celebrated film, *Triumph of the Will*),[37] one must nevertheless concern oneself in the first instance with the rediscovery or disclosure of the "outer truth" of human being, ordinary politics as such, and, ultimately, for those who can resolutely live up to it, the science of government itself. Here (*Introduction to Metaphysics*, 37-38), however, just before Heidegger offers his adaptation of Max Weber's *vocation*,[38] and in the course of what amounts to a thorough (if quiet, or typically Heideggerean) denunciation in 1935 of Hitlerite leadership (the allusions to Riefenstahl and Schmeling) amid a brilliant if almost silent (tacit) collocation of all modern German thought as the collapse of the philosophy of freedom — "vanished history," alluding to Kant ("universal history") and Hegel ("end of history") and their successors (Nietzsche: "use and abuse of history") — Heidegger himself merely exclaims, alluding to the opening sentence of Marx's *Communist Manifesto* (Marx spoke of the true beginning of human history, which was still in the revolutionary future), that " — then, *yes then*, through all this turmoil, a question still haunts us like a specter: *What for?*" (Emphasis added.)

An answer to this question would have to begin with an investigation of the nature of human society and its relation to the political community and the individual, in short, an effort of the kind Calhoun has made in *A Disquisition on Government*. Heidegger, however, does not follow the path of this haunting question but, rather, "destructs" the question in the course of his "creative" review of the Western tradition. In other words, the supposedly or allegedly extra-ordinary and epochal turn in "enframement" represented by Heideggerism turns out to be merely an extraordinary path of embracing the ordinary and immemorial inclination toward absolutism to which "every page of [ordinary] history testifies." By the close of the "Fundamental Question of Metaphysics" (*Introduction to Metaphysics*, 49-51, including the explicit citation there of the *Rektoratsrede*, Heidegger's address upon assuming the rectorship of the University of Freiburg a generation after the death of Hermann von Holst), one may be willing to entertain the vision or thought-path of a "true" or National Socialist movement of one authentic human being (viz. Heidegger), even (what is here the same thing) of a "nation [master of language and fate] in the center of the Western world" that is both "historical" and "destined" of one authentic human being, when the author speaks there of the spirit and the "powers of the essent as such and as a whole," etc., and of "our entire constitution." One may be willing, in other words, to appreciate that the "inner truth and grandeur of National Socialism" and even the attainment out of ordinary time of the primordial and hence authentic history itself is proposed to be nothing more and nothing else than the thought of Heidegger as we have it before us in *Being and Time*, the *Rektoratsrede*, *Introduction to Metaphysics*, and wherever else (e.g., in the reinterpretation of Aristotle's *Physics* in the attempt to restore the hardened West on its fluid, pre-Socratic foundation), and his consequent action, and to learn that, in this manner and only in this manner, time and humanity as such are redeemed before being or fully (humanly) reciprocate being. However, though it supposes far otherwise, this simultaneous denunciation and thought-path, while not without a certain gloomy grandeur, does not yet arrive at Aristotle's *Ethics* and *Politics*. It is not yet adequate even for us to distinguish the rival *Fuhrers*, for Hitler, the other, "outer" and "inauthentic" *Kaiser novus*, also subordinated the "state" to the "folk": he also said "First came the *Volk* [i.e., the German, if not Aryan, nation or race]. Only then came the *Reich*," and, "In 1918 the bourgeois [ordinary] politician only saw the state in front of him; I saw the *Volk*, the substance: *For me the state was then nothing but a purely external, a restrictive framework* [*Zwangsform*]," i.e., something genuinely if only vaguely or partially and imperfectly (because merely "external") *constitutional* in what Calhoun calls the strict sense (emphasis added).[39] In the name of what god, or in the name of what authority, one might ask, might one find anything to choose between these German National Socialist party members and leaders, or enter into partnership with them, who see the regime (state) in this way? Aristophanes' Dionysus, judging according to the wisdom of their advice to the *polis*, or to follow these leaders, to the *Volk*, new and unaccustomed as he is to the consideration of such weighty matters, would obviously choose somebody else altogether—and who is a "pre-Socratic" Greek philosopher poet if not Aristophanes?

For Heidegger, after the second world war (1953), one who notices still finds his authenticity, that is, his humanity, his whole *lifetime*, threatened "in a pincers" between a metaphysically indistinguishable Marxist communism on the one hand and Lockean capitalism on the other, that is, between modern Western conventionalities of politics that are at once merely ordinary and also entirely false, amounting to the same thing, and to which the only possible alternative remains authentic National Socialism, i.e., Heideggerism. The present and its conventionalities must be abandoned in order to recover the primordial experience that originally gave rise to the enveloping hardened counterfeit systems and cancel them, or, as the epigoni say, "place them under erasure." This recovery and its conscious and active reaffirmation is, for Heidegger, the core of "authentic resolution," the truly *moral*, that is, the only true dimension or site of ethics and politics, the truly human dimension, authentic "history," which must be discovered and recovered and then reaffirmed in the union of thought and action itself and which one is always seeking along the way in Heidegger.[40] For

Heidegger, the primordial experience toward which one tends is the "truly" or authentically political, which is to be arrived at via "true" or authentic National Socialism. This is not "politics" but a species of warrior heroicism in its place—an "authentic" Siegfried as Uber-Legislator amidst the *Volk*, etc.—of dubious authenticity, however "spirited" or libidinous. Dwelling toward the folk heroic in "rushing toward death"—in place of the either truly private or inauthentic (unspirited) "vocation" (Max Weber) of a mere boxer-goliath (Max Schmeling)—Heidegger quests anew for an equivalence of the spontaneous decision-experience of the Rebel Yell.[41]

For Calhoun, the case is the reverse: the political is the primordial for human beings: humanity is originally and already ordinarily political, and that is itself the first object to be understood. On his own showing, Heideggerism, authentic or inauthentic, may well achieve non-paternal despotic government and its concomitant destruction in the reaffirmation of one's primordial experience (although such is perhaps achieved easily enough already without all this), but, authentic or inauthentic, it has no means of achieving constitutional government, or even any awareness of it: it is simply a forgotten question and, hence, a forgotten quest. Heideggerism is, thus, not yet fully human, however extraordinary; bold, but not yet "authentic," merely pretend. Desiring to transcend Lockean civil society in all its versions, it merely abandons the field of politics to the enveloping conventionalities and forces in the guise of "destructing" them, while actually arming and unleashing extraordinary but surely authentic "savages" to "run into death" with technologically sophisticated weaponry. Little wonder it is gloomy. As Professor von Holst might say, National Socialism may, by Kolakowski, for example, whom we have cited in this connection, be remembered as "sober history," it will not be remembered by anyone as "romance." Since it on principle or, rather, by decision closes and seals itself to all transcendence and embraces radical temporality for the sake of discovering authentic spirit and stoking it up in resolution, it amounts practically to the resolution to shoot one's way out, but, as there is only immanence at hand, there is no out, "no exit." Sartre, Heidegger's popularizing pupil, explained the condition silently expressed in the absence or active suppression of the political in original Heideggerism by saying, "Hell is other people." Yet Heidegger himself might have said, rather, that Hades was merely the wasteland of commercial or civil society, to which those who have eyes are in no way restricted, but, for him, this answer lacked grandeur.[42] This is why Heideggerism is characterized by lack statesmanship, while longing to be the leader.

We conclude that Heidegger and Hitler are doubtless illustrative of some of the poles of the Wagnerian spirit, but that Bonhoeffer and the brave Count von Stauffenburg, rather, are truly exceptional cases, and better instances, at that "moment," ("rising to the task at hand") of the authentic German spirit, and, therewith, also of the simply human spirit.[43]

However, when the political *is* discovered or recovered or otherwise "arrived at," whether in postrevolutionary or transitional or modern or post-modern or other ages, all the principles and issues presented in *A Disquisition on Government* immediately come into play. And, whenever one should notice (or, in Heidegger's terms, hears or obeys the "call" of past authentic history), they are all found, as when one begins at night to notice the stars and planets, to be long since already and always in play, as though, skin intact, one has stepped from out of the gloom into the sunlight. As T. S. Eliot said, echoing a line of Sophocles, "In my beginning is my end," meaning by this the recognition that in one's beginning, the "ordinary," is a part of the whole truth, and not something merely to be resolutely "canceled" or "destructed" and replaced with one's own "authentic" self-made assertion (i.e., decayed, or international-individualist Heideggerism) or with one's struggle for sacrificial immersion into a warrior Volk-spirituality (original "nationalist" Heideggerism).[44] For Calhoun, this is the ordinary or typical state of human nature, or the primordial human condition which he begins to unveil in the opening sentence of *A Disquisition on Government.*

Yet, if politics is shared by all humanity, and all humanity is the same in this essential respect, as we have said, that is, in its human nature, or if politics is the necessary condition for humanity, politics does not unite all humanity. Rather, its very actuality and performance implies divisions. This observation is but a way of returning to Calhoun's point that the political is always the historical, including the personal and even merely private, and this truth holds for the reader of *A Disquisition on Government* today no less than for its original author. We have already had occasion to quote from one of his speeches this statement in which he describes the philosophic inquirer of the future: "To avoid all personal feeling, I shall endeavor to recede, in imagination, a century from the present time, and from that distant position regard the events to which I allude, in that spirit of philosophical inquiry by which an earnest seeker after truth, at so remote a day, may be supposed to be actuated." While he so addresses and hence invites his immediate audience of leading politicians to adopt a philosophical spirit there and then, he also indicates the manner in which the posterity addressed in *A Disquisition on Government* may begin to take it up. In either instance, for they are in this the same, his fundamental supposition, and the supposition on which his address in *A Disquisition on Government* itself ultimately depends, is nothing else than that this "spirit of philosophical inquiry" is at least genuinely possible for human beings, even if it is only the exceptional case, even if it is always the most exceptional case, that one may love the truth itself plainly and truly as one's own, or as what it means in truth *to be,* beyond all personal feeling and all historical and political separations or divisions, and so exert oneself in seeking it.

Calhoun's foundation of the science of government was inspired not only in the foreshadow of the war for Southern independence, which posterity may yet remember as a historico-romance, to adapt the terms of the Professor of Freiburg, or in Daniel Lucas's "The Land Where We Were Dreaming."[45] Primarily, as we have mentioned, it arose in the awareness that, beyond the social conditions provided by the wide diffusion of information necessary for accelerating scientific and technological progress, there is no connection between scientific and technological progress—which, along with entertainment, longevity and weight loss, now absorbs civil society—and social progress, including progress of individuals as individuals. Mass technological society remains in every way as divided as any other, even moreso.

To begin to progress beyond or transcend without forgetting these divisions historical, political, and socio-individual, we may make use of the catalog of some of the causes of human separation and difference in *Disquisition*, paragraph 16. The causes of difference there listed by Calhoun include "the limited reason and faculties of man, the great diversity of language, customs, pursuits, situation, and complexion, and the difficulty of intercourse, among other causes." Some of these familiar causes of separation are, also, however, if secondarily, often occasions or overlap or sharing. A certain language, for example, or complexion, to cite those we have already mentioned, are by no means always restricted only to a certain community. They may be distinctions shared, or more or less shared, among various communities. Let us consider in particular Calhoun's central term: "pursuits." Certain pursuits may characterize political communities, but, particularly among communities of some advancement, they may also provide certain affinities between otherwise different and distinct communities. Artisans are the classic example, for artisanship is an individual skill, and hence points primarily to skilled individuals, and not primarily to communities.

Two pursuits of this kind in particular are especially important in the very beginning of *A Disquisition on Government*. These are, first, because most obvious, the pursuit of the science of astronomy. For the order of the sun, moon, and stars is of course exhibited in all times and places, and remains unaffected by the character of any regime, however apparently absolutist or relativistic its climate of opinion. It is the same for Aztecs and Mayans alike, and for ourselves. The other is the pursuit initiated there by Calhoun, the science of government understood as the perfection of the human mind. However different and distinct political communities may be, and however difficult the application of even the most elementary principles may seem in particular circumstances, the principles of government themselves do not change from society to society or from time to time or place to place, irrespective of whether they are recognized as such or not.[46] It is this challenging but rewarding pursuit that one must take up earnestly for oneself, in full awareness of the limited reason and faculties of man, as a seeker after truth,[47] whatever one's race or regime or time or place, in beginning the study of *A Disquisition on Government*.

Notes:

Foreword

---

[1] More than a century after his death, Calhoun in 1957 was named one of the five great United States Senators through all United States Congresses by an advisory panel of 150 scholars and the vote of the Senate during the 85th Congress. Senator John F. Kennedy (D-Mass.), chair of the Senate selection committee averred that Calhoun was "the most notable political thinker ever to sit in the Senate, whose doctrine of the concurrent majorities has permanently influenced our political theory and practice," and Professor Allan Nevins, speaking on behalf of the scholarly advisory committee, said that "Calhoun made the most original and profound contributions to constitutional theory. His doctrine that a concurrent majority is much to be preferred in government to an absolute majority has force." (See *Congressional Record*, 85th Congress, 1st sess., May 1, 1957, 103, pt. 5: 1026ff, and context, quoted in *John C. Calhoun*, Margaret Coit ed. (Prentice-Hall, "Great Lives Observed Series": Englewood Cliffs, N.J., 1970) 165ff. In 1930, British historian Christopher Hollis ranked Calhoun among the four greatest U.S. statesmen (*The America Heresy*, New York; see Coit, 119ff, 169). In 1847, British writer Sarah M. Maury (*The Statesmen of America*) held Calhoun to be the greatest statesman in the Euro-American world: "If this distinguished statesman could be prevailed upon to visit England, either in a public or a private capacity, he would command more admiration, and attract more interest than any other man of Europe or of America" (see Coit, 72ff). Thirty years after Calhoun's death, contemporary Congressman John W. Wentworth wrote (*Congressional Reminiscences*, Chicago, 1882): "After having heard all the Senators speak, if a stranger should select the one, irrespective of doctrine, who came nearest a saint, he would select Mr. Calhoun" (See Coit, 78ff.). Abolitionist Oliver Dyer (*Great Senators of the United States Forty Years Ago*, 1889) recalled that "Calhoun's kindness of heart was inexhaustible. He impressed me as being deeply but unobtrusively religious, and was so morally clean and spiritually pure that it was a pleasure to have one's soul get close to his soul—a feeling that I never had for any other man. He seemed to exhale an atmosphere of purity, as fresh...and bracing as a breeze from the prairie, the ocean, or the mountain. He was inexpressibly urbane, refined, gentle, winning; and yet he was strong and thoroughly manly with an elegant and engaging invincibleness pervading his softness and gentleness" (Coit, 82).

Contemporary Frederick Douglass (*Frederick Douglass Papers*, vol. 2, November 24, 1854) wrote: "The late John C. Calhoun—one of the mightiest men that ever stood up in the American Senate—probably studied the [anti-slavery] movement as deeply, though not as honestly, as Gerrit Smith or William Lloyd Garrison [and]...showed himself a master of the mental, moral, and religious constitution of human society.... To [Daniel Webster and Calhoun]—the two greatest men to whom the nation has yet given birth—may be traced the two great facts of the present—the South triumphant, and the North humbled. Their names may stand thus: Calhoun and domination—Webster and degradation" (see Coit, 94ff; John Greenleaf Whittier makes essentially the same points in respect to Calhoun and

Henry Clay: see Merrill D. Peterson, *The Great Triumvirate: Webster, Clay, and Calhoun* [Oxford, 1987], 288-89). The greatest American under the original Constitution as it came from the Framers is also the most immoral, since slavery is immoral. A decade later, John Smith Dye (*History of the Plots and Crimes of the Great Conspiracy to Overthrow Liberty in America*, New York, 1866), published that Calhoun had established the Slave Power in the United States and was personally responsible (directly or indirectly) for an assassination attempt on President Jackson, and was probably immediately responsible for the suspicious deaths of Presidents Harrison and (in principle) Taylor, after these had defied Calhoun's imperium, as well as, probably, other political murders and similar crimes. (See David Brion Davis, *The Slave Power Consipiracy and the Paranoid Style*, Louisiana State University Press, 1969, 8 ff.) William Henry Channing (*The Civil War in America*, Liverpool, 1861): there has been for years "*a conspiracy of the Slave Oligarchy to ruin, because they can no longer rule, the Republic of the United States*. By Conspiracy is meant a plot of treason.... and the Grand-Master of the conspirators was the late John C. Calhoun." Calhoun was "a man of soaring ambition, that knew no bounds; and his dauntless self-confidence brooked no superior. He was professionally a politician, and from early life he planned to manage the Democratic party, so as to serve the exclusive ends of the Slave-power.... [and] to elect Presidents and Vice-presidents, Speakers of the House of Representatives, Secretaries of State, Treasury, and War, Chiefs of Army and Navy, Judges of the Supreme Court and foreign Ambassadors.... In Nullification, Mr. Calhoun craftily planted the germ of Secession." Calhoun at once both ruled the whole country for a generation and wholly subverted it. (See Coit, 102f; Davis, 69ff.)

It is fair to observe that Channing's *The Civil War* (which has been called a propaganda pamphlet) does not notice Jefferson and Madison's 1798 Virginia and Kentucky Resolutions (which, following Channing, in some circles has been similarly called "pure political party propaganda": e.g., the popular textbook, *America Past and Present*, Robert A. Divine, et al., eds. [New York: Harper Collins, 1986, 1990), 121-22), and the emphasis in these resolutions on the states' rights of inter-position and nullification. In this connection, see, also, John Taylor of Caroline, *Construction Construed, and Constitutions Vindicated* (Richmond, 1820), 9-28, 77-89, 133-34. Cf. Dumas Malone, *The Sage of Monticello*, vol. 4 of *Jefferson and His Time* (New York, 1977, 1981), 356-59 (and nn. 37, 39, 45), and context: "After reading this difficult author's latest work, *Construction Construed*, he [Jefferson] pronounced it the best treatise in republicanism that had appeared since the adoption if the constitution," i.e., since *The Federalist*. Incidentally, in tracing the theoretical source of President Buchanan's 1860 doctrine that the United States government, once expelled from a State, lacks constitutional authority to subdue that State by force to Madison's doctrine of state interposition in the 1798 Virginia Resolutions, when Professor Edward Corwin ("National Power and State Interposition, 1787-1861") speaks of "the brilliant but irresponsible direction of an opportunist doctrinaire," as against "the true and authoritative sources of constitutional construction" (i.e., "the people of the United States of this day and hour"), Corwin's editor Professor Richard Loss is mistaken in saying that "Corwin may have identified Thomas Jefferson as the guilty party because of his influence over James Madison." Rather, over and above Madison and Jefferson, Corwin means Calhoun: according to this celebrated scholar, "Not till Calhoun" and Nullification did the term "sovereign" in regard to individual states and the Constitution become an issue. *Corwin on the Constitution*, vol. 3: *On Liberty against Government*, Richard Loss, ed. and intro. (Ithaca, New York: Cornell University Press, 1988), 20, 186, 199, cf. 199: "this ridiculous parcel of puns, pseudo-philosophy, and falsified history," "Calhoun's theory," "all theories of secession," and context. However, see William Rawle's esteemed textbook, *A View of the Constitution of the United States of America* (Philadelphia, 1825). 295ff: States of the Union possess the right to secede peaceably from the Union.

2 *Union and Liberty: The Political Philosophy of John C. Calhoun*, Ross M. Lence, ed. (Indianapolis: Liberty, 1992), xii; *The Essential Calhoun*, Clyde Wilson, ed. and intro. (New Brunswick: Transaction Publishers, 1992), introduction, first paragraph. The parenthetical quotations may be found in Wilson, *The Papers of John C. Calhoun*, W. Edwin Hemphill, Robert Merriwether, and Clyde Wilson, eds. 14 vols. (Columbia, SC: 1959-), 10:xiii; and, e.g., Peterson, *The Great Triumvirate: Webster, Clay, and Calhoun* (New York: Oxford University Press, 1987), 95, 344. For the quotation from Thomas Ritchie, editor of the Richmond *Enquirer*, that follow, see, e.g., Peterson, *The Great Triumvirate: Webster, Clay, and Calhoun*, 3, 26-27: "The Twelfth Congress of the United States, convening on November 4, 1811, was a watershed in the history of the republic. It marked the entry into national politics of a new generation of leaders who had had no part in the founding of the republic and whose highest aspiration was to preserve it.... All considered, despite his limited experience, Calhoun entered the national arena with powers of mind and character, of reason and sensibility, unsurpassed in his generation," with Irving H. Bartlett, *John C. Calhoun: A Biography* (New York: Norton, 1994), 380 and context: "Calhoun's contributions to the Union in the early years of the Republic were not surpassed by any other leader of his generation.... [and he] probed more deeply into the nature and weaknesses of popular government than any of his contemporaries." For the following quotation from Webster's eulogy of Calhoun, see Coit, *John C. Calhoun*, 92-94.

3 Coit, p. 86. The repellent tribal chief "Nulli" in Melville's *Mardi: and A Voyage* Thither is supposed a depiction of Calhoun as almost supernatural: "...wonderous eyes—bright, nimble as the twin corposant balls, playing about the ends of ship's royal-yards in gales...." The impression made by his eyes is commonplace in the descriptions of Calhoun by his contemporaries: e.g., Nathaniel Willis: "his eyes, bright as coals, move with jumps, as if he thought in electric leaps from one idea to another"; Varina Davis: "the most glorious pair of yellow brown shining eyes, that seemed to have a light inherent in themselves...He lowered them less than anyone I have ever seen...they had an almost mesmeric power.... He always appeared to me rather as a mental and moral abstraction..."; Peterson: "He was truly Emerson's 'transparent eyeball,' knowing nothing but seeing all, 'head bathed by the blithe air and uplifted into infinite space' by the exhiilaration of his own truth" (Coit, pp. 88, 76-78; Peterson, pp. 406-408). Sarah Maury, already cited, may stand for all: "I have seen but one alone with eyes so beautiful. Sometimes their intense look is reading each thought of your bosom; sometimes they are beaming with the inspirations of his own. I believe they give out light in the dark" (emphasis original; Coit, p. 74.)

A striking description is given by Oliver Dyer, already cited: "The rabid abolitionists... of whom I was one...felt towards Calhoun...[as] the 'Great Secessionist,' the 'Great Nullifier,' the 'Great Disunionist' and the 'Great' bad man generally....His appearance [in the late 1840s] satisfied me completely....Had I come across his likeness in a copy of Milton's *Paradise Lost*, I [would] have at once accepted it... as a masterpiece of some great artist who had a peculiar genius for Satanic portraiture..." (Coit, p. 81).

⁴ The text of *A Disquisition on Government* was originally included with *A Discourse on the Constitution and Government of the United States* in the first volume of *The Works of John C. Calhoun*, Richard K. Cralle, ed., 6 vols. (Charleston, S.C.: 1851-1856). Peterson, pp. 477, 497: "Few copies of the volume were sold, despite frequent notices in newspapers and periodicals." Peterson (e.g.) cites reviews in the *Southern Literary Messenger* (1854), which praised the work, and the *North American Review* (1853), which did not, but in some ways the most important American notice was published in New York in 1860 in the concluding parts of the ten-part sociological "Review, Historical and Critical, of Social Philosophy," in Freeman Hunt's *Merchant's Magazine and Commercial Review*, nos. 5 and 6 (discussed in chapter three), in which Calhoun is seen as the completion and fulfillment of the "modern" or Machiavellian–Lockean school of social philosophy, as against the "ancient" or Platonic-Aristotelian school of social philosophy. With Calhoun's final fulfillment and completion of the last of these great Western philosophic schools in *A Disquisition on Government*, the world is declared henceforth to be in a post-philosophic age.

⁵ This prediction is recounted in most lives of Calhoun or histories of the era. The statement here is from John Niven, *John C. Calhoun and the Price of Union: A Biography* (Baton Rouge: Louisiana State University Press, 1988), p. 1. Cf. p. 332: "Throughout the *Disquisition on Government* there is an inherent, though never expressed argument, for the perpetuation of slavery, concealed behind the facade of minority rights and geographic distinctions." As much might be asserted as well of the inherency "though never expressed" arguments for *all* his characteristic positions — on the War of 1812, the tariff, the Force Bill, the bank, the occupation of the Yucatan, the Mexican War, and the rest. However, in fact, Calhoun never speaks at all of "minority rights and geographic [sectional] distinctions" in the *Disquisition*, or of any other peculiarly American circumstances or conditions, still less erects a "facade" of them. Those topics are explicitly and concretely addressed by Calhoun elsewhere. See e.g., "Report on the Circulation of Abolitionist Petitions" (February 4, 1836), *Works*, V, pp. 202-205: "diversity of the races..."; "On the Reception of Abolition Petitions" (delivered in the Senate, February 6, 1837), II, pp. 625ff.; and "On His Resolution in Respect to the Brig Enterprise" (March 13, 1840), III, p. 479, and context; "On the Amendment to Extend the Missouri Compromise Line" (delivered in the Senate, August 12, 1849), IV, pp. 513-535; "On the Slavery Question" (delivered in the Senate, March 4, 1850), IV, pp. 542ff. The truth in Nevin's statement lies merely in the fact that *A Disquisition on Government*, which is meant to establish the science of government, is also a statement (*apologia*) of Calhoun's elementary principles, and hence is in some sense, apart from its own preliminery general scope and rational purpose, necessarily related even to his own particular life and historic career and its circumstances. This relation of course does not vitiate the *Disquisition* but even renders it the more interesting.

In fairness to Professor Nevin, he acknowledges in the preface to his biography that he does not make the attempt to consider Calhoun's positions on slavery in the South or on the nature of the American union objectively (p. xv). As for the man himself, "like most men of his time and station," according to Professor Nevin, Calhoun (at least until he was already over 40) "accepted the rhetoric of the American Union without much thought . . . " (p. 4), and he was "a thoughtless advocate of war in 1811" (p. 5), while, in age, he "rejected the evidence of his own senses and became more enmeshed in abstract rationalizations" (p. 336), and, so enmeshed, "he failed to reckon with the transient, flexible nature of human institutions, which, even as he wrote, were changing with time and circumstance." In short, "Calhoun did not realize how much the current political and social scene guided his thoughts," etc. (p. 330). Nevertheless, in spite of all thoughtlessness, changing times and circumstances, and the spirit of the age itself, Professor Nevin does assert that he "found Calhoun to be more consistent in his political career than his contemporaries or his previous biographers have given him credit." Yet, he explicitly treats *A Disquisition on Government*, Calhoun's masterpiece, as "almost" an instance of political "pamphletering." E.g., according to him (author of a biography of Martin Van Buren), American readers, at least, ought to think especially of President Van Buren whenever Calhoun touches upon the subject of spoils (pp. xv, 330). Be it so. More importantly, however, Professor Nevin also asserts that Calhoun's *Disquisition* and *Discourse* "bespeak an originality in American thought that remains unequaled"; that "It still remains difficult, if not impossible, to settle the problem of sovereignty, which Calhoun himself raises"; and (perhaps most remarkably) that "His analysis of the imperfections and dangers of majority rule *has never been refuted in practice* or in theoretical explanation" (emphasis added), and, finally and most importantly, he admits in the end what is actually the best beginning, that, so far as Calhoun himself was concerned, at least, that author "thought that he was writing a scientific explanation of government complete with irrefutable laws of human behavior, in the style of the great political theorists of the past...[and] of a general nature and presumably universal application" (pp. 328-334). It is this thought that leads to our interest in *A Disquisition on Government*.

Chapter 1

[1] Calhoun to his daughter, Anna Maria Clemson, June 15, 1849. Quoted in *Calhoun: Basic Documents*, John M. Anderson, ed. and introduction (State College, Pa.: Bald Eagle Press, 1952), 29.

Calhoun was sixty-seven at the time of this writing and suffering from advanced tuberculosis. The text of *A Disquisition on Government* here cited is that originally included with *A Discourse on the Constitution and Government of the United States* in the first volume of *The Works of John C. Calhoun*, Richard K. Cralle, ed., 6 vols. (Charleston, S.C.: 1851-1856), (hereafter *Works*). See nn. 85-86 below.

The *Disquisition* is 165 paragraphs long. All references to the *Disquisition* will be to the paragraph.

[2] E.g., Alan Pendleton Grimes, *American Political Thought*, rev. ed. (New York: Holt, Rinehart, and Winston, 1960), xi: "Calhoun arose as probably the most original American political theorist"; Ralph Henry Gabriel, *The Course of American Democratic Thought* (New York: Ronald Press, 1956), "A Footnote on John C. Calhoun," 107ff; William S. Carpenter, *The Development of American Political Thought* (Princeton: Princeton University Press, 1930), 143ff. Cf., e.g., Charles Merriam, *A History of American Political Theories* (1903; New York: Russell & Russell, 1968), 267: "John Calhoun is the great political philosopher of the South"; Louis Hartz, *The Liberal Tradition in America* (New York: Harcourt Brace, 1955), 173: "It is Calhoun we are constantly rediscovering..." and context. Cf. Vernon Parrington, *Main Currents of American Thought* (New York: 1930), 2:77; Peter Drucker, "Calhoun's Pluralism," in *Men, Ideas and Politics* (New York: Harper & Row, 1971), 105ff. Best are Michele Surdi, "Introduzione," in *John Caldwell Calhoun, Disquisizione sul governo e Discorso sul governo e la constituzione degli Stati Uniti* (Rome: Instituto della Enciclopedia Italiana fondata da Giovanni Treccani, 1986) and Marshall L. DeRosa, "John C. Calhoun, The Confederate Phoenix" in *The Confederate Constitution of 1861: An Inquiry into American Constitutionalism* (Columbia, Mo.: University of Missouri Press, 1991), 18-37.

The best points of entry for studying Calhoun's life and thought today are Clyde Wilson's introductions to individual volumes of *The Papers of John C. Calhoun*, W. Edwin Hemphill, Robert Merriwether, and Clyde Wilson, eds. (Columbia, S.C.: 1959-). Charles Wiltse's three volumes on the life of Calhoun (Indianapolis, Ind.: Bobbs-Merrill, 1944-1949) are, with Douglas Southall Freeman's on Lee and Washington, the finest in American political biography. Also excellent is Margaret L. Coit, *John C. Calhoun: An American Portrait* (Boston: Houghton Mifflin, 1950) and ed., *John C. Calhoun* (Englewood Cliffs, N.J.: Prentice-Hall, 1970), "Great Lives Observed." The most convenient and insightful recent life is Irving H. Bartlett, *John C. Calhoun: A Biography* (New York: Norton, 1994): "What most of his friends, to say nothing of his enemies, did not understand was that although Calhoun would never leave the political arena, his ultimate ambition was not to become President but to be known as the statesman who finally placed political science on the same solid foundation as physical science" (351).

Recent collections of Calhoun's writings and speeches are Wilson, ed., *The Essential Calhoun* (New Brunswick: Transaction Publishers, 1992) and Ross M. Lence, ed. *Union and Liberty: The Political Philosophy of John C. Calhoun* (Indianapolis: Liberty, 1992).

³ See n. 82 below.

⁴ Aristotle, *Politics*, 1253a.

⁵ Plato, *Republic*, 464d8-9 and context, 416d5-6; *Laws*, 739c7-d1.

⁶ Nietzsche, *Thus Spake Zarathustra*, prologue, 3.

⁷ *Disquisition*, paras. 5-7; para. 9: "twofold constitution"; cf., "On the Oregon Bill" (delivered in the Senate, June 27, 1848), *Works*, 4:509-510:

The social state [of man is necessary for] the existence of his race and the development of the high faculties, mental and moral, with which he is endowed by his creator.... [Since the social state does not and can not exist without government,] it is the political [state], which includes the social, that is his natural state. It is the one for which his creator formed him—into which he is irresistably [*sic*] impelled—and in which only his race can exist and all its faculties be fully developed. Such being the case, it follows that any, the worst form of government, is better than anarchy...."

⁸ Calhoun to Andrew Pickens, May 23, 1803, in Merriwether, Wilson, eds., *The Papers of John C. Calhoun* (Columbia: University of South Carolina Press, 1959), 1:9-10, and context: "For what is a greater incitement to men than honor?"

⁹ Calhoun, "On the Proposed Occupation of Yucatan" (delivered in the Senate, May 15, 1848), *Works*, 4:454. Cf. Aristotle, *Politics*, 1319b33-36, and context; Hume, *Essays III*, "That Politics May Be Reduced to a Science," first paragraph: "I...should be sorry to think that human affairs admit of no greater stability than what they receive from the casual humours and characters of particular men."

¹⁰ This subject occupied Calhoun all his adult life. The text of his address as Yale University's leading graduate in the class of 1804 on the subject of "The Qualifications Necessary to Make a Statesman" has not survived. He knew Latin and Greek and it seems likely that his remarks reflected his study of this subject at that time in the writings of Aristotle and Cicero, as well as his celebrated discussions with New England Federalist Timothy Dwight, Yale's president. Although not a professional academician, Calhoun's study of these and other writers was concentrated and lifelong, and in no sense narrow. To take an out-of-the-way example, he composed an informal grammar of Hebrew in order to teach himself that language and study the history of the Hebrew government in the Old Testament original (cf. *Disquisition*, 18). (It is not known if Calhoun ever completed this project.)

¹¹ E.g., Gunnar Heckscher, "Calhoun's Idea of 'Concurrent Majority' and the Constitutional Theory of Hegel," *American Political Science Review* 33/4 (August 1939): 585-90. Heckscher's scholarship is perspicacious, but he fails to reach the fundamental issues. Perhaps the relation of Calhoun and Hegel is best seen in assessments like these: In Hegel's writings "there emerges the model of a modern state [that tries] to strike a balance between *homo economicus* and *zoon politikon*," and "The political theory of Calhoun was a fusion, original in some respects, of elements drawn from Greek philosophy, modern European and English philosophy, and earlier American experience." See, Shlomo Avineri, *Hegel's Theory of the Modern State* (Cambridge: Cambridge University Press, 1972), 240, and

August O. Spain, *The Political Theory of John Calhoun* (New York: Bookman Associates, 1951), 263-66, 278. In any case, to say nothing of other things, for Calhoun, Napoleon was merely a despot, and the Prussian "constitutional monarchy" was not exemplary of the best regime. (See Merle E. Curti, "John C. Calhoun and the Unification of Germany," *American Historical Review* 40 [April 1935]: 476; also, Edward G. Elliot, "*Die Staatslehre* John C. Calhouns," [1903], 70, *Staats-und volkerrechtliche Abhandlungen*, 4, no. 2, Dunker und Humblot, Leipzig; D. Zwicker, *Der Amerikanische Staatsmann John C. Calhoun, ein Kämpfer gegen die "Ideen von 1789"* [Berlin: Ebering, 1935], 179ff and context.) According to Leo Strauss, Hegel's fundamental political doctrine was based on Hobbes' doctrine of the "state of nature": *The Political Philosophy of Hobbes, Its Basis and Its Genesis* (Chicago: University of Chicago Phoenix Books, 1963), 57-58, and "Restatement on Xenophon's Hiero" in *On Tyranny* (New York: The Free Press, 1963), 189ff.

Richard Hofstadter, "John C. Calhoun: The Marx of the Master Class," in *The American Political Tradition* (New York: 1948), and Richard Current, "Philosopher of Reaction," in John L. Thomas, ed., *John C. Calhoun, A Profile* (New York: Hill and Wang, 1968), 151ff. Calhoun himself often emphatically said that he was the adherent of no class or party. In any case, for two centuries the plantation regime of the American South had no alienated Marxian proletariat or, in Calhoun's lifetime, any prospect of one. According to Marx, of course, Hegel himself was already the "Marx" of the master class, which it was the whole point for Marxism to demystify and change.

Ralph Lerner, "John C. Calhoun," in *American Political Thought: The Philosophic Dimension of American Statesmanship*, Morton J. Frisch and Richard G. Stevens, eds. (New York: Charles Scribner's Sons, 1971), 99ff.: "Calhoun was one of the first to construct a science of politics...that we can fairly identify as belonging to today's behavioral political science." Yet, Calhoun speaks throughout the *Disquisition* of the "common good," which is antithetical to behaviorism. Not Calhoun but Hobbes, rather, is typically presented as the father of behaviorial political science: e.g., Floyd W. Matson, *The Broken Image* (Garden City, N.Y.: Doubleday, 1966), chaps. 1-2. However, similarly, A. J. Beitzinger, *A History of American Political Thought* (New York: Dodd, Mead & Company, 1972), 386: Calhoun's "emphasis of groups and interests has become, as the work of Arthur Bentley and, more recently, David Truman, shows, a basic aspect of American political science." Cf., also, Drucker, "Calhoun's Pluralism," cited in n. 2 above. However, Calhoun emphasizes the ambition of individuals as much as or even more than the tendencies of political estates or interests. What seems most helpful in any of these suggestions will be taken up in due course in later chapters.

[12] Calhoun is studied in particular connection with Madison and majoritarianism in Lacy K. Ford, Jr., "Inventing the Concurrent Majority: Madison, Calhoun, and the Problem of Majoritarianism in American Political Thought," *Journal of Southern History* 60 (1994): 19-58; and "Recovering the Republic: Calhoun, South Carolina, and the Concurrent Majority," South Carolina Historical Magazine 89 (1988): 146-59; and in H. Lee Cheek, Jr. "Republicanism Revisited: Jefferson, Madison and Calhoun," a paper delivered at the 1997 Annual Meeting of the American Political Science Association, Washington, D. C., August 28-September 1, 1997.

[13] John Stuart Mill, "Bentham," in *Mill's Essays on Literature and Society*, J. B. Schneewind, ed. (New York: Collier Books, 1965), 255. Calhoun carried his learning easily: "Mr. Calhoun had no youth, to our knowledge. He sprang into the arena like Minerva from the head of Jove..." (a contemporary quoted in Merill D. Peterson, *The Great Triumvirate: Webster, Clay, and Calhoun* [New York: Oxford University Press, 1987], 27). "He borrowed nothing...from authors of the past" (a contemporary quoted in Margaret L. Coit, *John C. Calhoun: An American Portrait* [Boston: Houghton Mifflin, 1950), 77]. The opposite impression was equally widespread and forceful. For example, one contemporary said that he knew it for a fact that one of Calhoun's most celebrated speeches was closely modeled on Demosthenes' "On the Crown," yet none of Calhoun's major writings ever explicitly refer to that work (Coit, *John C. Calhoun*, 86).

[14] Hegel, *Natural Law*, T. M. Knox, trans. (Philadelphia: University of Pennsylvania Press, 1975), 92. Apart from the constitution or political life itself, the idea of the "people" is but an "indeterminate abstraction" Hegel, *Philosophy of Right*, T. M. Knox, trans. (New York: Oxford University Press, 1952), para. 279. Cf. Burke, "Appeal from the New to the Old Whigs" in *Works* (London: Rivington, 1815-1827), 6:216. Calhoun to William Smith, July, 1843: "...the people, as has been stated, are regarded as constituting a body politic, or State; and not merely as so many individuals. It is only when so regarded that *they possess any political rights*" (emphasis added)(cited in Clyde Wilson, ed., *The Essential Calhoun* [New Brunswick: Transaction Publishers, 1992], 49).

[15] *Disquisition*, para. 89, cf. para. 18. Although he is unnamed, a particular individual drawn by Calhoun from Livy's *Ab Urbe Condita* plays a significant role in the course of Calhoun's illustration of constitutional principles in a simple republican regime, cf. paras. 145 and 163, discussed in chap. 3, below. Mindful of the context of Calhoun's marked silence in regard to all writers and schools, the reader is in a position to discover the tacit prominence in his thought of, to take only the most obvious example, those who assert the hypothesis of the "state of nature" (para. 89), even in the crucial arguments near the beginning of the *Disquisition* that bear directly on the hypothesis, although Calhoun does not explicitly say so.

[16] Calhoun rarely discusses methodism or logic, but he typically praises judgment: e.g., "what may be wise and expedient under certain circumstances might be eminently unwise and impolitic under different circumstances" ("On the Resolutions Giving Notice to Great Britain of the Abrogation of the Convention of Joint Occupancy," delivered in the Senate, March 16, 1846, *Works*, 4:268; cf. *Disquisition*, 41). "On the Repeal of the Embargo and Non-Importation Act" (delivered in the House, April 6, 1814), *Works*, 2:109 and context:

> I know regard ought always to be had to this trait [sc. consistency], so valuable in governments and individuals; but it is not the duty of men to regulate their conduct without any regard to events. True wisdom consists in properly adapting our conduct to circumstances. Two things may change our conduct on any particular point: a change of our own opinion, or of exterior circumstances, which entirely change the reason of our former conduct. Men cannot always go straight forward, but must regard the obstacles which impede their course.

[17] Calhoun, "On Mr. Crittenden's Amendment to the Land Bill" (delivered in the Senate, January 30, 1841), *Works*, 3:591: "Burke." Spain, *The Political Theory of John C. Calhoun*, 35: "Aristotle and Burke were without doubt his favorite authors." William M. Meigs, *The Life of John C. Calhoun* 2 vols. (New York: 1917), 2:100: "He was an exceedingly well-informed man, but a great reader of books we know he was not. He rather saturated himself with a few books than hurried through hundreds. He had been a close student of Aristotle's *Politics* and often spoke of Machiavelli's *History of Florence*. There was no writer of whom he was fonder than Burke." Cf. Charles M. Wiltse, *John C. Calhoun: Nationalist* (New York: 1944), 381-83, and *John C. Calhoun: Sectionalist* (New York: 1951), 420: "Plato and Aristotle, Machiavelli, Hobbes and Locke...Burke...John Taylor of Caroline...Adam Smith..."; Arthur Styron, *The Cast-Iron Man: John C. Calhoun and American Democracy* (New York: Longmans, Green and Co., 1935). "...Greek and Roman political writers, and the Eighteenth Century philosophers such as Locke, Burke, and Montesquieu...." It is to works such as these that *A Disquisition on Government* must be compared if its core animus is to be actively grasped. John Nevin, *John C. Calhoun and the Price of Union* (Baton Rouge: Louisiana State University Press, 1988), 331: the notions that characterize Calhoun's *Disquisition* derive "in part" from his "close reading of Aristotle's *Politics* and *Nichomachean Ethics* and his embibing of the political skepticism of Machiavelli, Hobbes, and Hume."

[18] Hume, *A Treatise of Human Nature: Being An Attempt to Introduce the Experimental Method of Reasoning into Moral Subjects*, L. A. Selby-Bigge, ed. (Oxford: The Clarendon Press, 1888), introduction. The discussion of "solidity" occurs in pt. 4, sec. 4, "Of the Modern Philosophy," in bk. 1. Cf., Locke, *Essay on Human Understanding* (London: Ward, Lock, n.d.), 76: "solid"; consider in this connection also Tocqueville, *Recollections*, George Lawrence, trans., J. Mayer and A. P. Kerr, eds. (Garden City: Doubleday, 1970), 65-66: "solid ground" ["terra firma"] in connection with the period of transition through which the European world was passing. Cf. Descartes, *Meditations*, 1:144; Bacon, *The Great Instauration*, *Proemium*: "foundation."

[19] Aristotle, *Politics*, 1282b13ff: "Since in all the sciences and arts the end is some good, it is the greatest and primary good in that which is the most authoritative of all; this is the political capacity. The political good is justice, and this is the common advantage." Cf. *Politics*, first sentence. Also, *Nichomachean Ethics*, 1094a22-28 and context, 1094b1-28, and related passages.

[20] Hume, *Treatise*, 401-402; 486, 493: arising from the gravitational principle in "that natural appetite betwixt the sexes," man's "very first state and situation may justly be esteemed social." Hume's point of departure is the origin and association of a herd. *Enquiry into the Principles of Morals*, L. A. Selby-Bigge, ed. (Oxford: Clarendon Press, 1902), 219: "It is needless to push our researches so far as to ask why we have...a fellow feeling with others. It is sufficient that this is experienced to be a principle in human nature." Cf., Cicero, *De officiis* 2.73: "Men naturally tend to congregate together...." Rousseau, *A Discourse on the Origin of Inequality*, in *The Social Contract and Discourses*, G. D. H. Cole, trans. (London: Dent, 1913), 171: "The only gods he [sc. man as man] recognizes in the universe are food, a female, and sleep; the only evils he fears are pain and hunger."

[21] Hume adopts a similar argument in regard to Locke, *Treatise*, 549. Cf. "Of the First Principles of Government" (in *Essays Moral, Political and Literary*) near the beginning: "It is

sufficiently understood that the opinion of right to property is of moment in all matters of government. A noted author has made *property the foundation of all government*, and most of our political writers seem inclined to follow him in that particular. This is carrying matters too far, but still it must be owned that the opinion of right to property has a great influence in this subject." (Emphasis added.) This says no more than that "opinion," not property, is the foundation of government. Cf. *The Philosophical Works of David Hume*, T. H. Green and T. H. Grose, eds. 4 vols. (London: Longmans, Green, 1882), 3:109-110. Calhoun, "On the Loan Bill" (delivered in the House, February 25, 1814), *Works*, 2:91: "Opinion is power." Unless I am mistaken, the term "property" does not occur in *A Disquisition on Government*.

[22] *Disquisition*, para. 6: the "peculiar relations" ("as that of a mother and her infant") derive from Hume's "first and original" social relations; para. 89: "parental authority." "On his Resolutions in Reference to the War with Mexico" (delivered in the Senate, January 4, 1848), *Works*, 4:411: political diversity and inequality of what Calhoun calls "the human family." *Disquisition*, para. 16: political diversity of "the human race"; para. 85: "the race." Cf. Aristotle, *Politics*, I. xii. 1259b10, and context: paternal or kingly rule is non-political rule. This could sometimes seem to be the whole issue between Locke and Filmer.

[23] *Disquisition*, paras. 2-3, n. 7, above.

[24] Hobbes, *De Cive*, in *English Works*, William Molesworth, ed. 11 vols. (London: John Bohn, 1839), 1, chap. 7.

[25] Hobbes, *De Corpore*, in *English Works*, 1, chap. 8.

[26] Leo Strauss, *The Political Philosophy of Hobbes: Its Basis and Its Genesis*, 2, 152-53. Cf. Hume, "Of Justice," in *An Enquiry Concerning the Principles of Morals*, ad fin: "It is entirely agreeable to the rules of philosophy and even of common reason, where any principle has been found to have great force and energy in one instance, to ascribe to it a like energy in all similar instances. This indeed is Newton's chief rule of philosophizing." Bacon, *Novum Organon*, in *The Works of Sir Francis Bacon*, J. Spedding, R. L. Ellis and D. D. Heath, eds. (Boston: Little Brown, 1861 and following), 1:79-80, 120: the Baconian method is applicable to all knowledge. Calhoun, "On the Independent Treasury Bill" (delivered in the Senate, February 15, 1838), *Works*, 3:214: "If the argument is good in one case, it is good in all similar cases." Probably the classical statement of the principle is found in Galileo's discussion of "motion" in *Dialogues and Mathematical Demonstrations Concerning Two New Sciences*, Crew and De Salvio, trans. (New York, 1914), 95ff. Cf. R. H. Hurlbutt, *Hume, Newton and the Design Argument* (London: 1965); and R. Kuhns, "Hume's Republic and the Universe of Newton," in *Eighteenth Century Studies Presented to A. M. Wilson*, Peter Gay, ed. (Hanover, N.H.: 1952). Cf. A. B. Arons, "Newton and the American Political Tradition," *American Journal of Physics* 43/3 (1975); R. E. Butts and J. E. Davis, *The Methodological Heritage of Newton* (Toronto: 1970); Woodrow Wilson, *Constitutional Government* (New York: Columbia University Press, 1961), 54-57, and *The State: Elements of Historical and Practical Politics* (Boston: D.C. Heath, 1895), 597 and context: Newtownian and Darwinian constitutionalism. In Wilson, what is called Darwinian or "evolutionary" constitutionalism, in contradistinction to Newtonian constitutionalism to which it is superior, gradually reduces to the career of a single increasingly predominant power and its claims, which Calhoun has identified as absolute rather than constitutional rule (*Disquisition* 56). Cf. Arthur Bullit, *Woodrow Wilson and the League of Nations* with Calhoun's position in R. W.

Faulkner, "Taking John C. Calhoun to the United Nations," *Polity* 15 (Summer 1983): 473-91; Mitchell Franklin, "The Roman Origin and the American Justification of the Tribunitial or Veto Power in the Charter of the United Nations," *Tulane Law Review* 22 (October 1947): 24-61; and Walter Berns, "Where the Majority Rules: A U.N. Diary," in *In Defense of Liberal Democracy* (Chicago: Gateway Editions, 1984), 81ff.

[27] John Stuart Mill, *A System of Logic* (London: Longmans, Green, 1941), xv.

[28] Jeremy Bentham, *A Fragment on Government*, F. C. Montague, ed. (London: Oxford University Press, 1899), 154.

[29] Quoted in David Baumgardt, *Bentham and the Ethics of Today* (Princeton: Princeton University Press, 1952), 62.

[30] *Disquisition*, paras. 22-25, 118. Cf. Cicero, *De Republica* iii.45.; ii.57; i.55. Legare connects Cicero with Burke at length in "Cicero *de Republica*" [1829], *Writings of Hugh Swinton Legare*, Mary Legare, ed. 2 vols. (Charleston, S.C.: 1845), 2:216-53, esp., 244ff. In his *The Southern Tradition at Bay* (New Rochelle: Arlington House, 1968), Richard Weaver mispeaks in suggesting that Alexander Stephens, who is sometimes asserted to be Calhoun's foremost successor, modeled his *A Constitutional View...Presented in a Series of Colloquies at Liberty Hall* on Cicero's *Tusculan Disputations*. Rather, *The Constitutional View*, 2 vols. (Philadelphia: National Publishing Company, 1868-1870) is conceived on the model of Cicero's *Republic*, which it imitates and is implicitly in part meant to rival: 1:13-14, 33, 204-205. (This must provide the subject of another study.) Calhoun (who is not present) takes the place of Cicero's Scipio and appears in the dialog through his speeches. On the point made above, compare John Stuart Mill, *Essay on Liberty*, in *Utilitarianism, Liberty, and Representative Government* (New York: E. Dutton, 1951), 87: "the nation...tyrannising over itself."

[31] *Disquisition*, paras. 132ff, 117.

[32] John Stuart Mill, *Autobiography* (New York: Columbia University Press, 1924), 116. Cf. Elie Halevy, *The Growth of Philosophical Radicalism* (New York: A. M. Kelly, 1949), 6: "Utilitarianism...can be defined as nothing but an attempt to apply the principles of Newton to the affairs of politics and morals." Cf. Legare, "Jeremy Bentham and Utilitarianism" (1831), in *Writings of Hugh Swinton Legare*, 2:449-81: "His nomenclature or terminology is a study of itself—as complicated, if not quite so systematic, as that of the chemists. This wrapping up of plain matters in the mysteries of artificial language...is Jeremy's great title to the admiration of the world."

[33] James Mill, *A Fragment on Mackintosh* (London: Longmans, Green, et al., 1870), 29, 37, and context. Cf. Hobbes, *Leviathan*, ad fin.

[34] John Stuart Mill, *Autobiography*, 45-46, 93. *The Early Draft of John Stuart Mill's 'Autobiography'*, Jack Stillinger, ed. (Urbana: University of Illinois Press, 1961), 74ff.

[35] James Mill, "Periodical Literature," *Westminster Review* 1 (January 1824): 207-208. John Stuart Mill, *Autobiography*, 64-65. Cf. e.g., Calhoun, "On the United States Bank Bill" (delivered in the House of Representatives, February 16, 1816), *Works*, 2:162: "public opinion," "control over the press"; "On the Repeal of the Non-importation Act" (delivered in the House of Representatives, June 24, 1812), ibid., 24: "interests" and "opinion."

[36] *Disquisition*, para. 132. Cf. Legare (1827): "The press, once so humble, so insignificant, known only to the closets of the studious, of the privileged intercourse of the learned,

addressing itself to the few in ancient and exclusive language, has in modern days, in consequence of the wide diffusion of education, been directed to the great mass of society with decided effect, and now exercises an almost despotic control over the opinions of mankind." Quoted in Linda Rhea, *Hugh Swinton Legare* (Chapel Hill: University of North Carolina Press, 1934), 237.

[37] *Disquisition,* para. 117. John Stuart Mill, *Autobiography,* 72; 141: "My father's intellect was emphatically polemical." *Autobiography,* chap. 4, "Youthful Propagandism, *The Westminster Review,*" passim: "...the review made a considerable noise in the world, and gave a recognized status in the arena of opinion and discussion to the Benthamic type of radicalism quite out of proportion to the very small number of its adherents...." Cf. *Considerations on Representative Government,* 246: "One person with a belief is a social power equal to ninety-nine who have only interests." Of course, there are none who only have "interests." Cf. Joseph Hamburger, *James Mill and the Art of Revolution* (New Haven, Conn.: Yale University Press, 1963), *passim.*

[38] John Stuart Mill, *Autobiography,* 111ff.; *A System of Logic,* 546, 587, 242-47. (Cf. Kant, "Enquiry Concerning the Clarity of the Principles of Natural Theology and Ethics" [1763] in *Kant: Selected Pre-Critical Writings and Correspondence,* G. B. Kerferd and D. E. Walford, trans. [Mancester: University Press, 1968], 17 and context: philosophy should be formed according to the model of Newtonian physics and not according to the model of Euclidean geometry.) Benthamism is a belief masked as science which unmasks or strips off the varnish of private or "sinister interests" only to reveal that "sinister interests," however elaborately aggregated, are all that is (this is "demystification"). Cf. Hume, *Enquiry Concerning the Principles of Morals,* 296-97: Hume reproves the desire of "an epicurean or a Hobbist...to explain every affection to be self-love, twisted and molded, by a particular turn of imagination into a variety of appearances." Cf. Hobbes, *English Works,* 4, chap. 13.

[39] John Stuart Mill, *Autobiography,* 111-13; and "Bentham," 244-45, 256, 269: "If Bentham had merely continued the work of Hume, he would scarcely have been heard of in philosophy." He took the "warfare against absurdity" that had been initiated by Hume against what Hume had called "epicureans and Hobbists," among others ("abstruse philosophers"), "into things practical." There Bentham had swept away, in particular, the "Augean stable" of "Ciceronian trash" which bolstered traditional morality. *Bentham, Deontology, or the Science of Morality,* arranged and edited by John Bowring 2 vols. (London: Longmans, Green, et al., 1834), 1:42, 227, 300-301. Cf. Mary Mack, *Jeremy Bentham, An Odyssey of Ideas* (New York: Columbia University Press, 1963), 110. Compare Hume: "Cicero's *De Officiis* I had in my eye in all my reasonings." *Letters of David Hume,* J. Y. T. Greig, ed. 2 vols. (Oxford: Clarendon Press, 1932), 1:34.; *Philosophical Works,* 29-30.

[40] See n. 37, above. John Stuart Mill, "Remarks on Bentham's Moral Philosophy," in *Mill's Utilitarianism: Text and Criticism,* James Smith and Earnest Sosa, eds. (Belmont, Calif.: Wadsworth Publishing Company, 1969), 27: "By the promulgation of [his political and philosophical axioms], and by a general tone of thought and expression perfectly in harmony with them, I conceive Mr. Bentham's writings to have done and to be doing very serious evil.... The effect is still worse on the minds of those who are not shocked and repelled by this tone of thinking, for on them it must be perverting their whole moral

nature." In the context of this perversion, compare Tocqueville's remarks on "self-interest" in *Democracy in America*.

⁴¹ John Stuart Mill, *A System of Logic*, 582-83.

⁴² Mill's abandoned "system of political philosophy," the system of the Philosophic Radicals, appears to be restored as, rather, and merely, a "practical political creed," the creed of a political radical, answering (he asserts) to "the requirements of my own time and country," i.e., to the time of greatest and still increasing advancement in the most advanced country. John Stuart Mill, *Autobiography*, 120. Cf., especially, in this context, "M. de Tocqueville on Democracy in America," in Alexis de Tocqueville, *Democracy in America in Two Volumes with a Critical Appraisal of Each Volume by John Stuart Mill* (New York: Schocken Books, 1961), passim.

⁴³ Willmoore Kendall, "Conservatism and the 'Open Society,'" in *The Conservative Affirmation* (Chicago: Regnery Co., 1963), 100-101; Tocqueville, *Democracy in America*, Phillips Bradley, ed. (New York, 1945), I.434: "Until our time..."; also, 438; II.351, 102-103.

⁴⁴ Kendall, "Conservatism and the 'Open Society.'" Cf. Mill, *Considerations on Representative Government*, 265ff., and related passages. Calhoun, *Disquisition*, paras. 95, 119, 66. Calhoun always means by the term "community," which he implicitly distinguishes from mere "society," what Aristotle means by the term *polis* or "regime." It is unimportant whether this understanding is entailed in the term's origin or implied in much general usage, and so on: it is Calhoun's own understanding. More specifically, for Calhoun, "community" equals "technically" (a) "society," understood as mere human sociability (sc. human nature) in some given context (natural + historical circumstances), plus (b) "government" in whatever form. This understanding is developed in the opening paragraphs of the *Disquisition*. Similarly, by the term "civilized" Calhoun means "having or characterized by a high development of the arts and sciences," as distinct from "savage," which is human life in the absence of these, i.e., hunting-gathering, herding, elementary ("primitive") agriculture. Savage life may be noble (or not—it depends on the government), and in so far as it is so, fully human and deserving of the high reward of liberty, but it is not "intelligent," and, in so far as it is not so, it does not express the fullest in humanity. Intelligence completes liberty, which graces it.

⁴⁵ John Stuart Mill, *Autobiography*, 94.

⁴⁶ Alfred North Whitehead, *Science and the Modern World* (New York: Macmillan, 1925). I am citing the 1967 Free Press edition, 4, 16: "Some variant of Hume's philosophy has generally prevailed among men of science. But scientific faith has risen to the occasion, and has tacitly removed the philosophic mountain." Heisenberg is the most celebrated current representative, although one may note that the progress of science has not slowed. Cf., especially, Stanley Jaki, *The Road of Science and the Ways to God* (Chicago: University of Chicago Press, 1978), 102-103, 369-70; and the same writer's "Introduction" to Kant, *Universal Natural History and the Theory of the Heavens*, S. L. Jaki, trans. (Edinburgh: Scottish Academic Press, 1981).

⁴⁷ Kendall, "Conservatism and the 'Open Society,'" 114-15; Kendall's position is stated in Mill's *Logic*, 10th ed., 2:520ff.

⁴⁸ Cf. Tacitus, *Annales* 16.22: "To overthrow authority, they uphold liberty: when authority is overturned, they will attack liberty." With Mill, see (e.g.) Kant, "What is

Enlightenment?": political freedom means "to make public use of one's reason at every point"; the "scholar" is a citizen of the world; and Fichte, *The Vocation of the Scholar:* because he "sees not merely the point which humanity now occupies, but also that to which it must advance...the scholar [as distinct from the statesman, or as the true statesman] is the guide to the human race." (*The Vocation of the Scholar* is most accessible in English in volume 1 of *The Popular Works of Johann Gottlieb Fichte,* William Smith, trans. [Bristol: Thoemeus Press, 1999)

[49] *Disquisition,* paras. 108-109.

[50] Cf. John Stuart Mill, *Considerations on Representative Government,* chap. 1, *Essay on Liberty,* "Introductory." Rousseau, [Considerations on the] *Government of Poland,* Willmoore Kendall, trans. (Bobbs-Merrill Company, 1972), 2: "As one reads the history of Poland, it is hard to understand how a state so oddly constituted can have survived for so long.... There, to my mind, you have one of the strangest spectacles that ever forced itself upon the attention of a thinking man."

[51] John Stuart Mill, *Early Draft,* 48, 62, and related passages; *Essay on Liberty,* 113-14, 137, etc.; *Mill's Ethical Writings,* J. B. Schneewind, ed. (New York: Collier Books, 1965), 276. Drawing on Herodotus, Calhoun refers to Marathon, Platea, Salamis, Miltiades, and Themistocles in, e.g., "On the Force Bill," (delivered in the Senate February 15-16, 1833), *Works,* 2:238-39, 244ff.

[52] Lewis Henry Morgan, *League of the Iroquois* (1851; reprint, Secaucus, N.J.: Citadel Press, 1962), 55. According to Morgan, men's "progress has been found to be in exact proportion to the wisdom of the institutions under which their minds were developed." Cf. *Disquisition,* para. 18. Morgan's classic presentation of the Iroquois League is largely in Calhounian terms.

> The legislators of the Iroquois united the several tribes into independent nations, and between these nations established a perfect and harmonious union.... The central government was organized and administered upon the same principles which regulated that of each nation in its separate capacity; the nations sustaining nearly the same relation to the League, that American States bear to the Union.... For all purposes of a local and domestic, and many of a political character, the nations were entirely independent of each other.... Each nation had an equal voice, and a negative on the others [in council].... In this council resided the animating principle by which their political machinery was moved. It was, in effect, the government.... The sovereignty of the nations, by this mode of giving assent, was not only preserved, but made subservient to the effort itself to secure unanimity.... Oratory, from the constitutional organization of the council, was necessarily brought to high repute...[cultivation and exercise of which]...opened the pathway to personal distinction...[and the]...highest degree of personal consideration.... All the sachems of the League, in whom originally was vested the entire civil power, were required to be of 'one mind,' to give efficacy to their legislation. Unanimity was a fundamental law. The idea of majorities and minorities were entirely unknown [to them].... It was a system sufficiently ample to enfold the whole Indian race. [*League,* 58, 62, 69, 93-94, 105, 111-12]

Also, Lewis Henry Morgan, *Ancient Society: Researches in the Lines of Human Progress from Savagery through Barbarism to Civilization* (1877; reprint, Tucson: University of Arizona Press, 1985), pt. 2, "Origin of the Idea of Government," chaps. 2-5, on the Iroquois.

[53] "On His Resolutions in Reference to the War with Mexico" (delivered in the Senate January 4, 1848), *Works*, 4:411. Cf. Morgan, *League*, 82-83, 91-94; Rousseau, *The Government of Poland*, 67ff, 82ff.

[54] Cf. *Federalist* 9, first paragraph: "perpetual vibration between the extremes of tyranny and anarchy," "waves of sedition and party rage," "vices of government." Third paragraph: "the science of politics, however, like most other sciences has received great improvement. The efficacy of various principles is now well understood, which were either not known at all, or imperfectly known to the ancients." Also James Monroe, *The People the Sovereigns, Being a Comparison of the Government of the United States with Those of the Republics which Have Existed before, with the Causes of Their Decadence and Fall* (1825-1829, published 1867), Samuel L. Gouverneur, ed. (Cumberland, Va.: James River Press, 1987), chap. 2, "Athens, Lacedemon, and Carthage."

[55] Morgan, *League*, chap. 6, 127ff. passim. The Greeks are "brilliant," and particularly admirable in virtue of their imaginative myths. Nevertheless,

All things considered, the Iroquois [regime] excites a belief in its superiority over those of antiquity.... It would be difficult to describe any political society in which there was less of oppression and discontent, more of individual independence and boundless freedom.... In its construction the latter was more perfect, systematic and liberal than those of antiquity.... Those of Greece were exceedingly unstable, and therefore incline us to regard them as transition states of their institutions; while that of [the Iroquois] was guarded in so many ways for the resistance of political changes, that it would have required a very energetic popular movement for its overthrow.

Page 107: comparison of the "ambitious Roman" and the "proud Indian" as equivalent. Cf. *Disquisition*, para. 163.

[56] Cf. Morgan, *League*, 4, 29, 139, 143-45:

Our country they once called their country.... It is well understood that the decline of the Iroquois commenced with their first intercourse with Europeans. The possession of firearms, and their use in Indian warfare, [...] and their incessant conflicts with [Europeans and their allies], were calculated to waste them away with great rapidity.... [After] the treaty of peace between Great Britain and the United States in 1783...the political transactions of the League were substantially closed. This was, in effect, the termination of their political existence.... Race has yielded to race, the inevitable result of the civilized with the hunter life.... They fell under the giant embrace of civilization.

Cf. Mill, *Considerations on Representative Government*, 238: "Nothing but foreign force would induce a tribe of North American Indians to submit to the restraints of a regular and civilized government." See Hume, *Enquiry into the Principles of Morals*, 191, and *Disquisition*, para. 95. Cf. James Fenimore Cooper, *The Last of the Mohicans: A Narrative of 1757* (New York: W. A. Townsend, 1859), viii, and context: "the advances, or it might be termed the inroads of civilization"; 1.11: "there was no recess of the woods so dark, nor any secret place...that it might claim exemption from the inroads of those who had pledged [themselves to]...vengeance, or...cold and selfish policy...." This is Cooper's equivalent of Conrad's faraway Kurtz's "Exterminate the brutes!" or Twain's closer to home "Battle of the Sand-Belt," *A Yankee in King Arthur's Court*, chap. XLIII.

Engels, whose *Origin of the Family, Private Property, and the State* was inspired by Morgan's *Ancient Society* and Marx's interpretive digest of it, writes, following Morgan in accordance with Marx-Engels: "The [primitive] constitution in its best days, as we saw it in America, presupposed an extremely undeveloped state of production and therefore an extremely sparse population over a wide area.... The power of this primitive community had to be broken, and it was broken...[by] the new, civilized class society...." (*Origin of the Family*, chap. 3, "The Iroquois Gens," concluding paragraph). Yet many peoples have enjoyed an extremely undeveloped state of production and sparse population over wide areas. Not these items but rather constitutional government itself, according to Calhoun, provided the Iroquois with their "best days."

[57] "On the Passage of the Tariff Bill," delivered in the Senate, August 5, 1842, *Works*, 4:196. Morgan, *League*, 3-4: "They now stand forth on the canvass of Indian history, prominent alike for the wisdom of their civil institutions, their sagacity in the administration of the League, and their courage in its defense"; *Ancient Society*, 148-50.

[58] *Disquisition*, para. 86; *Works*, 4:511: "the highest reward that can be bestowed on our race." Cf. Rousseau, *Government of Poland*, 29-31: "Proud, sacred liberty!" Tocqueville, *Democracy in America* (Bradley ed.), 2:305, 340-41; Tocqueville to Henry Reeve, March 1837, in *Memoir, Letters, and Remains of Alexis de Tocqueville* (London: 1861), 39-40.

[59] See n. 34 above. Mill, *Essay on Liberty*, 100-101:

[S]ome of these modern reformers who have placed themselves in strongest opposition to the religions of the past, have been noway behind either churches or sects in their assertion of the right of spiritual domination: M. Comte, in particular, whose social system, as unfolded in his *Systeme de Politique Positive*, aims at establishing (though by moral more than by legal appliances) a despotism of society over the individual, surpassing anything contemplated in the political ideal of the most rigid disciplinarian among the ancient philosophers.... [A] strong barrier...[should] be raised against the mischief.

Otherwise, "we must expect, in the present circumstances of the world, to see it increase." Tocqueville, *Recollections*, 71: "...the really new element in the old picture." See n. 65 below.

[60] Kendall, 'Conservation and the 'Open Society,'" 107, 111. Cf. Kendall, "Freedom of Speech in America" in Kendall, *The Conservative Affirmation*, 77-82., and Calhoun, *Works*, 2:465ff; 509ff.

[61] John Stuart Mill, *Essay on Liberty*, chap. 3, para. 1.

[62] John Stuart Mill, *Considerations on Representative Government*, 268, and context; 292ff.

[63] Mill, *Considerations*, 439, Mill's "fundamental maxim of government" is drawn from Calhoun's *Disquisition*. Cf. Mill, *Dissertations and Discussions*, 2d ed., 3 vols. (London: Longmans, Green, et al, 1867), 3:65 and context. Also, Calhoun, e.g., "On the Bill to Repeal the Force Act" (delivered in the Senate, April 9, 1834), *Works*, 2:386-87: "governments in which a single power predominates...are necessarily despotic—whether that power be wielded by the will of one man, or that of an absolute and unchecked majority." Calhoun

to General Hamilton (August 28, 1832), ibid., 6:188ff, etc.; and *Disquisition*, paras. 39-43. Mill refers to the *Disquisition* only once in his *Considerations on Representative Government* (502, cf. 498), describing it as "a posthumous work of great ability" by "a man who has displayed powers as a speculative political thinker superior to any who has appeared in American politics since the authors of the *Federalist*." His own discussion of the forms of government of Egypt, China, the Jews, and the Hindoos (268-71) is occasioned by the reference to them in *Disquisition*'s great paragraph 18, but it is not a Calhounian discussion.

[64] Essentially the same introduction to Calhoun's place, with due qualification and reorientation, as that just briefly described could have been reached had we taken our point of departure not from Hobbes and Hume up to J. S. Mill but from Locke's *Two Treatises* and Rousseau's merging of nature and history in the *First and Second Discourses* and the *Social Contract* up to James Monroe's fragmentary comparison of republican governments, *The People the Sovereigns, Being a Comparison of the Government of the United States with Those of the Republics which Have Existed before, with the Causes of Their Decadence and Fall* (n. 54, above), particularly his first chapter, "A Comparative Elementary View of Government and of Society." Through his careful survey and interpretive redactions of "the writers on the subject of government, ancient and modern," in the second chapter, Monroe praises most highly Aristotle among the ancients and Montesquieu among the moderns, that is, as the foremost political thinkers of what he identifies as the first two human "epochs." These writers are the "most comprehensive, systematic, and truly descriptive," of the "state of society" and of the "circle of the science" of government in the epochs they represent. Monroe's own work itself is modeled on Aristotle's collection of constitutions and guided by Montesquieu's attention to societies and governments "differently circumstanced." According to Monroe, however differently they may be circumstanced, all free governments would be improved by a judicious application of Montesquieu's principle of the separation of powers. Nevertheless, whatever might appear to be true of the letter of the *Comparison* (the "method" or preference for Montesquieu), its spirit is not that of its apparent models but the spirit, even, at times, against the letter, of Locke and, above all, Rousseau. It is through Rousseau, specifically, through his study of Rousseau's version of the "state of nature" and the emergence of man and civilization via the "social contract," that Monroe at length discovers the third and greatest human epoch in the completion of the "social contract," i.e., the emergence of the perfect government, blending "liberty and humanity," out of the "state of nature" of the new American society. Although itself unfinished and incomplete, Monroe's comparison of republican governments is meant to represent the "circle of the science of government" as drawn by Rousseau and Locke and achieved by the constitution of the United States. If the state of that science sometimes seems contradictory as presented and developed by Monroe, the contradictions are already the contradictions of greater writers the fame of whose doctrines is rivaled only by the fame of their contradictoriness.

We may note in this connection particularly that although some scholars have held that the *Comparison* was left unfinished because the former president was persuaded not to continue the effort by associates who felt that such arguments as those of Adams' political writings and the *Federalist*, etc., had, with the successful establishment of the US Constitution, long since become *passe*, Monroe actually abandoned the work only in the course of the development of the Nullification crisis in the wake of Calhoun's *South Carolina Exposition and Protest* and the *Fort Hill Address*, and related matters, which largely overtook his thesis.

[65] Cf., e.g., Jeremy Bentham, *Deontology*, 1:48-49: A benefit of utilitarianism will be that "the work of the legislator will be lighted, and the moralist [i.e., the journalist] will assume many of the legislator's functions. The great court of public opinion will take charge of the decision of many questions which are now in the keeping of penal judicature." The full character of the new moralist's administration is set forth by Bentham in the *Panopticon*, his plan for the perfect prison. *Works*, 4:39-72. 63-64: Systematic utilitarian moralism, over and above any traditional orthodoxy, would bring prison management to the "pitch of perfection." Bentham's title foreshadows the famous slogan from Orwell's *1984*.

[66] *Disquisition*, paras. 2, "scale of being," "brute creation"; 10: "first in the order of things," [first in] "dignity of...object"; 12, "Infinite Being," "Creator of all"; 14, "great ends...ordained," "divine ordination," "Infinite ordained"; 15, "end...ordained"; 79, "ends...ordained," 86, "Providence," "dispensation"; 89, "Creator"; 90, "ends...ordained"; 95, "brute creation," 137, "impious," "Being," "Creator of all," "ends...ordained"; 139 "ends...ordained". Compare Hobbes, *Leviathan*.... "general Providence." Aristotle, *Metaphysics*, i.982b; xii.1074b, and related passages. One acquaintance, a pronounced Comptean Positivist, speaks of Calhoun's "theologies of government, almost the only subject on which his thoughts are employed...," (Harriet Martineau, quoted in Coit, *John C. Calhoun*, 71).

Calhoun's understanding and usage of the crucial term "Infinite" seems identical to that set forth in Descartes, *Meditations on First Philosophy*, III, secs. 23-24.

In light of Calhoun's theme in many contexts of "one harmonious system," we may suppose that for Calhoun the inanimate world must be understood as only "materially" inanimate, or "brute": the materially inanimate world is animated formally by the laws of Providence. Cf. Aristotle, *Physics*, 250b14 and context; cf. also, Joseph Priestley, "Disquisitions Relating to Matter and Spirit" (1777), *Priestley Writing's on Philosophy, Science, and Politics*, John A. Passmore, ed. (New York: 1965); also Steven Shapin, "Of Gods and Kings: Natural Philosophy and Politics in the Leibniz-Clarke Disputes," *Isis* 72 (February 1981): 187-215.

[67] Mary Chesnut, *Mary Chesnut's Civil War*, C. Vann Woodward, ed. (New Haven, Conn.: Yale University Press, 1981), 21-22. Cf., e.g., Coit, *John C. Calhoun*, 396-97.

[68] "On the Force Bill," *Works*, 2:232-33; cf. also, Calhoun, *Congressional Globe*, 25th Congress, 2nd Session, 176-81, quoted in *Calhoun: Basic Documents*, 14:

...the powers of analysis and generalization [are] those higher faculties of the mind...which decompose and resolve into their elements the complex masses of ideas that exist in the *world of mind*...and without which those deep and hidden causes which are in constant action, and producing such mighty changes in the condition of society, would operate unseen and undetected [emphasis added].

[69] *Mathematical Principles of Natural Philosophy*, Andrew Motte, trans., with introduction by F. Cajoni (Berkeley: 1966), 1:xviii, 2:398, 547: "This is incomparably the best way of philosophizing." *Opticks*, 4th ed. (1730; Dover Publications, 1952), *Query* 23/31, 404-405; also, Descartes, *Meditation, Second Responses*, ad fin. Hobbes, *English Works*, 1:10, 66-69. Cf.

Aristotle, *Nichomachean Ethics*, 1112a-1113a14, 1095aff; *Posterior Analytics* i. 2. 72a, ii. 19. 100b.

E.g., Laplace: "It is by comparing phenomena together, and by endeavering [*sic*] to trace their connection to each other, that he [the scientist] has succeeded in discovering these laws, the existence of which may be perceived even in the most complicated of their effects." *Exposition du Systeme du Monde* (Paris: 1798); English translation by J. Pond as *The System of the World* (London: 1809) 1:206. Also, Laplace, *A Philosophical Essay on Probabilities* (London: 1902), 176.

[70] See nn. 25-26 above. Alistair Crombie, *Robert Grosseteste and the Origins of Experimental Science* (Oxford: University Press, 1953), 59: Calcidius' commentary on the *Timeaus*: "Resolution or analysis is the method used in arriving at the material principles of things; compositivo or synthesis is the means whereby one learns the formal relationships of these principles, enabling us to grasp God's harmonius order and his providential role." Cf. Ernst Cassirer, "Galileo's Platonism," in M. Ashley Montegue, ed., *Studies and Essays in the History of Science and Learning* (New York: 1946), 229ff.

[71] Cf. "On the Independent Treasury Bill" (delivered in the Senate, February 15, 1838), *Works*, 3:217: "More than half of the errors of life may be traced to fallacies originating in an improper use of words." Locke, *Essay on Human Understanding*, IV.8.3.

[72] Cf. Hume, *Treatise*, I.iii.16; II.i.12; II.ii.12; *Enquiry Concerning Human Understanding*, vol. 1, sec. 9: "reason does not fundamentally distinguish men and beasts"; also, "An Inquiry Concerning the Principles of Morals": "sufficient sagacity..." and context. Rousseau, *A Discourse on the Origin of Inequality*, in *The Social Contract and Discourses*, 170: "Every animal has ideas, since it has sense; it even combines those ideas in a certain degree; and it is only in degree that man differs, in this respect, from the brutes." Cf. also Locke, *Essay on Human Understanding*, II.xxvii.8; III.ii.2-11, 20, and related passages.

[73] *Disquisition*, para. 7: "...a phenomenon not of our nature only, but of all animated existence throughout its entire range, so far as our knowledge extends...the great law of self preservation which pervades all that feels, from man down to the lowest insect or reptile...this all-pervading and essential law of animated existence." (With *Disquisition*, para. 2, see "On the State Rights' Resolutions" [delivered in the Senate, January 12, 1838], *Works*, 3:165: "It is only the ignorant and the brute creation over whom they ["abstractions," "abstract truths"] have no control.")

This distinction, the "highest" intellectual power from all that is touched by any "feeling" however pervasive, is characteristic of Calhoun's thought, although he does not always express himself in the same terms. In the speech quoted in the text the distinction is drawn between this highest or "metaphysical" intellectual power and "mere" sagacity. In the speech "On the Resolutions Giving Notice to Great Britain..." (delivered in the Senate, March 16, 1846), *Works*, 4:286., he points to the highest intellectual power in speaking of the "profoundest sagacity and wisdom." In this instance, the "profoundest sagacity" is "a sagacity which looks into the great causes in the physical, moral, and political world, which, by their incessant operation, are ever changing the conditions of nations for good or evil." The associated "wisdom" "knows how to use and direct them." Together, these represent the "highest elements of statesmanship." (One notes that these high elements here specifically refer to times "when [the great causes] are acting favorably," and hence indicate a policy of "wise and masterly inactivity." The opposite case is not addressed. (Cf. "On Crittenden's Amendment to the Land Distribution Bill," delivered in the Senate, January 30, 1841, *Works*, 3:599-600: the feature most strongly distinguishing the "firm and enlightened statesman.")

See especially Burke, "Conciliation With the Colonies," *Works*, 8 vols. [Bohn's *British Classics: 1854-1889*], 1:642 and context: "wise and salutary neglect." Cf. *Disquisition*, 139, "sagacity...and...good sense and firmness"; 14, "human wisdom"; 119 "human sagacity"; 20, "wisdom and skill." E.g., "On the Oregon Bill," *Works*, 4:507: "a philosophical turn of mind...disposed to look to more remote and recondite causes...." Aristotle, *Politics*, 1308a25ff (Barker, trans.): "those who take thought for the regime should...make the far away near...to recognize an ill as it arises in the beginning belongs not to an ordinary person but rather to a man expert in politics," and context. Cicero, *Republic* VI.i.1: "What you look for, then, is an account of this ruling statesman's prudence in its entirety, a quality which derives its name from foreseeing." As is sometimes noted, the Latin *prudence* is derived from "foresight."

[74] *Disquisition*, paras. 14, 1; cf. 43, 139.

[75] Cf. Rousseau, *Discours sur les sciences et sur les arts*, Francois Bouchardy, ed. (Paris: Gallimard, 1964), 29: Bacon is "*le plus grand, peut-etre, des philosophes.*" Hume, *Enquiries*, 14, of Newton: "a philosopher determined the laws and forces, by which the revolutions of the planets are governed and directed."

[76] Cf. "On Mr. Clay's Resolutions" (delivered in the Senate, March 16-17, 1842), *Works*, 4:440: "...a sort of metaphysical idea!" and context. Cf. also, Jonathan Edwards, *Works*, E. Williams and E. Parsons, eds. (Leeds: 1806-11), 1:410: "...we have no strict demonstration of any thing, excepting mathematical truths, but by metaphysics."

[77] Cf. *Leibniz Selections*, P. Weiner, ed. (New York: Charles Scribner's Sons, 1951), 69, 320. Newton, *Opticks*, Query 20/28. *Principia*, Cajoni, ed., xvii-xviii. *Disquisition*, paras. 10, 14; n. 63, above. Calhoun to Anna Marie Clemson, November 21, 1846, cited in Coit, *John C. Calhoun*, 521: "What I dread is that progress in political science falls far short of progress in what relates to matter, and which may lead to convulsions and revolutions, that may retard, or even arrest the former." There is progress in human arts and sciences but none in human nature, which is the decisive thing. It is for this reason that political science is ever the supreme science in all eras or all stages of human progress.

[78] Cf. Plato, *Laws*, 643e-644b. Calhoun to his son Patrick upon his graduation from West Point: "You must not think you have finished your education, but on the contrary, that you have not more than begun. We ought to consider life itself but as a school, and that our education terminates only in death," *Calhoun Papers*, 16:559. Cf. note 10, *supra*.

[79] *Disquisition*, paras. 137-139. Cf. 61, "impiety," "the Voice of God," "impious"; 78, "scale of patriotism and virtue"; 86, "scale of liberty" (twice), "some fixed law"; 105, "a sacrifice...a free-will offering on the altar of the country"; 106, "greatest possible achievement of the science of government"; 138, "a law in the political as well as in the material world." Cf., "On the Veto Power" (delivered in the Senate, February 28, 1842), *Works*, 4:93-94: "*vox populi vox Dei,*" "Deity of our political system"; "On the Compensation Bill" (delivered in the House of Representatives, January 17, 1817), ibid., 2:179: "*vox*

populi...vox Dei," "first orb in the political creation." Cf. Rousseau, *Social Contract,* IV, chap. 8.

[80] *Disquisition,* paras. 2-3, 106, 78. The moral faculties are distinctively human: humans are open and receptive to morality or moral virtue, unlike other creatures ("none of the moral virtues arise in us by nature" simply [Aristotle, *Nicomachean Ethics,* 1103a29], yet all, more or less, love justice [*Disquisition,* 104]).

[81] *Disquisition,* paras. 14; 81-86, 138-139, cf. n. 73, above. Of course, a science of politics alone cannot achieve this.

[82] In connection with Calhoun's apportioning, the statement attributed to Churchill: "One has a public life, a private life, and a secret life." Sarah M. Maury, *The Statesman of America* (Philadelphia: 1847), 169, quoted in Margaret Coit, ed., *Great Lives Observed: John C. Calhoun* (Englewood Cliffs: Prentice Hall, 1970), 75; C. Gordon Post, ed., "Introduction," "*A Disquisition on Government" and Selections from the "Discourse"* (Indianapolis: The Liberal Arts Press, 1953), vii. The *Discourse* is not a finished work. Calhoun was composing and revising it up to the evening of his death, and its publication required the editor's hand. See Cralle, *Works,* 1:viii, e.g.; 323. Stephens correctly distinguishes the intent, character, and audience of Calhoun's two works: "His treatise on the Constitution of the United States is the greatest that ever was penned on the subject, [but] his *Disquisition on Government* generally is one of the few books of this age that will outlive the language in which it was written." *A Constitutional View,* 1:341, and context.

[83] "On the Bill to Set Aside the Bank Bill Dividends" (February 4, 1817), *Works,* 2:190-91, and context. Calhoun introduces this remark by saying, among other things, "We are great, and rapidly—I was about to say fearfully—growing. This is our pride and our danger; our weakness and our strength. Little does he deserve to be intrusted [sic] with the liberties of this people, who does not raise his mind to these truths." Cf. "On the Compensation Bill" (delivered in the House of Representatives, January 17, 1817). (Also, *Works,* 2:182: "No one is fit for legislation who does not constantly bear in mind that our republic is distinguished from all others that have ever existed by the extent of its territory. While we derive from this distinction many advantages, we are liable to great and menacing dangers"; *Disquisition,* para. 25.) See n. 73 above.

[84] Cf. generally in this connection Grotius, "Prolegomena: 30, 41; 1, 8, 9, 11," *De Jure Belli et Pacis,* I. 60, 66-67, 5th ed., William Whewell, trans. 3 vols. (Cambridge: Cambridge University Press, 1853); Pufendorf, *Of the Law of Nature and Nations,* trans. Basil Kennett (London: Walthoe, 1729), 1-3 (bk. 1, chap. 1); Burlamaqui, *The Principles of Natural and Politic Law,* Thomas Nugent, trans. 2 vols. (Cambridge: Hilliard, 1807), 1:134-40 (pt. 2, chap. 6); 2:16-24 (pt. 1, chap. 3); 2:38-49 (pt. 1, chap. 7); Locke, *Second Treatise,* 12.87-89, 135.

[85] Cf. Locke on the "plain style." Calhoun was virtually illiterate until the age of thirteen, when he taught himself to read by studying Rollin's *Englished Ancient History* and Locke's *Essay on Human Understanding.* (E.g., Peterson, *The Great Triumvirate,* 20; Niven, *Calhoun,* 14: "The thirteen year old lad then set himself to studying John Locke's dense *Essay Concerning Human Understanding,* which he worked over so diligently that he suffered from eye strain, lack of exercise, and bad eating habits.") Cf. Jonathan Edwards, *The Nature of True Virtue* (Ann Arbor: University of Michigan Press, 1960). Edwards began his lifelong study of Locke's *Essay* at fifteen. Ola Elizabeth Winslow, *Jonathan Edwards* (New York:

Macmillan, 1940), 61. These are America's profoundest students of Locke, but this must provide the subject of another study. See Edwards, *Freedom of the Will*, ed., Paul Ramsey (New Haven: Yale University Press, 1957), 1, 47-65. Cf. Meigs, *The Life of John C. Calhoun*, 2:93-94: "Calhoun and Jonathan Edwards were endowed with the greatest minds the country has produced...."; also, Rufus Griswold, *Prose Writers of America*, 173: "Edwards," "Locke," "Calhoun."

Bartlett, *John C. Calhoun*, 353: "He is able to achieve a kind of stripped-down elegance and power in the *Disquisition* that is unexcelled in American political writing."

[86] Cralle, ed., *Works*, 1:viii. See nn. 1 and 71 above. In studying the *Disquisition* we may be well guided by a contemporary writer on political and religious oratory saying of Calhoun's speeches that "his language is exceedingly choice" and his "bright imagination" subject "only to reason" (quoted in Coit, *John C. Calhoun*, 87), and attempt to understand each word in its place. "It is an easy task, by misstating or garbling, to distort the most elevated and correct sentiment." ("Reply," delivered in the Senate, March 22, 1838, *Works*, 3:299.) At the same time, while guided by this precept, we must also bear in mind Calhoun's often repeated statements that he cared not for words but for things, not for form but for substance, e.g., "I like to attend to things, not to the names by which they are called." ("Reply," delivered in the Senate, March 5, 1850, *Works*, 4:578.)

Having put forward this much, we may note that Calhoun himself provided no introduction or preface to the *Disquisition*. The following quotation, taken out of its original context ("On the Loan Bill, already cited, *Works*, 2:71-72), could hardly be improved on:

I must beg an attentive and deliberate hearing; for a correct mode of thinking on this subject I sincerely believe to be necessary to the lasting prosperity of our country. I say an attentive and deliberative hearing, for it is not sufficient that the mind be fixed on the discussion, but should also be free from those passions and prejudices unfavorable to the reception of truth. The fact that discussion here [in the House] assumes the form of debate produces a state of things unfavorable to dispassionate attention. In debate here, as between two individuals, the opposite sides are much more disposed to find objections to an argument, be it ever so clear, than they are to receive it with a proper degree of assent. In their zeal the interest of the country is too often forgotten, and mere recriminations made to take the place of earnest endeavors to discover and enforce the claims of truth. I hope what I have to say will not be viewed as a mere exercise of skill in discussion, in which those who hear me have little or no interest, but as containing principles believed to be essential to the public interest. I trust I hold in proper contempt the spirit of idle debate. Its heat and zeal are momentary. Not so with our principles and measures. On them must depend our future prosperity and happiness.

Cf. *Disquisition*, para. 100. Cf. Hume, *Treatise of Human Nature*, Introduction, first two paragraphs.

[87] "On the Force Bill" (delivered in the Senate, February 15-16, 1833), *Works*, 2:211.

[88] See n. 15 and the text at nn. 55-58 above; also "On the Force Bill" (February 15-16, 1833), *Works*, 2:246: "I know how difficult it is to communicate distinct ideas on [complex political] subjects through the medium of general propositions without particular illustrations...." The *Disquisition* itself introduces the *Discourse*, which sets forth the most

complex of constitutional examples. Apart from the reference to the "limits of our country" already mentioned (para. 110), see paras. 95: United States and Great Britain founded on constitutional principles "as will be shown hereafter"; 121: United States the "only popular constitutional government; 131: "our government"; 140: "our own more complex system"; 141: "our own far more refined, artificial, and complex form"; 165: "character, origin, structure of the government of the United States."

[89] "On the Non-importation Act" (delivered in the Senate, June 24, 1812), *Works*, 2:28-29 ("People are not in the habit of looking back beyond immediate causes"): "The difference is great between the passive and the active mind." Cf. Kant, *Critique of Judgment*, sec. 40: "passive reason." See nn. 68, 72-74 above.

[90] Calhoun, *Works*, 4:258: "[political or moral] laws [are] as uniform and certain in the moral world as [the law] of gravitation is in the physical." "On the Repeal of the Force Bill" (delivered in the Senate, April 9, 1834), *Works*, 2:387: "There is no event—no, not in the political or moral world, more than the physical—without an adequate cause." Cf., passim, Comte, *Cours de Philosophie Positive*, First Lecture.

[91] See citations at n. 83 above. Cf. Mills' review of Tocqueville, 1:xxxix, vii: newspapers and mass opinion; 2:xvi: "The newspapers and the railroads are solving the problem of bringing the Democracy of England to vote, like that of Athens, simultaneously in one agora; and the same agencies...are making us more than ever a homogenous people." Rousseau, *Discourse on the Moral Effects of the Arts and Sciences*, in *The Social Contract and Other Discourses*, 140: breeding place of a "herd of textbook authors" and the spread of error. See nn. 35-36 above.

[92] "On the Resolutions Giving Notice to Great Britain," *Works*, 4:283-84, cf. *Disquisition*, paras. 132-39. Cf. Whitehead, *Science and the Modern World*, 96:

> It was not until the nineteenth century that the [scientific movement] came to that full development and peculiar balance characteristic of the sixty years following the battle of Waterloo. What is peculiar and new to the century, differentiating it from its predecessors, is its technology. It was not merely the introduction of some great isolated inventions. It is impossible not to feel that something more was involved.... The greatest invention of the nineteenth century was the invention of the method of invention.... that is the real novelty, which has broken up the foundations of the old civilization.... Both the material and the spiritual bases of social life were in process of transformation...."

Cf. Bacon, *New Atlantis*, passim, *Novum Organum*, 1.79-80, 120, 129.

[93] "The new electronic interdependence recreates the world in the image of a global village," McLuhan, *The Medium is the Message: An Inventory of Effects* (New York: Bantam, 1967), 67; cf. *The Mechanical Bride: Folklore of Industrial Man* (New York: Vanguard, 1951), "the image of the world as a single city" (10).

[94] The Agrarian position is stated most authoritatively in John Crowe Ransom, Donald Davidson, Allen Tate, Andrew Lytle, Frank Owsley, et al., *I'll Take My Stand: The South and the Agrarian Tradition, By Twelve Southerners* (New York: Harper Brothers, 1930), see especially, Lyle H. Lanier, "A Critique of the Philosophy of Progress." Cf. *Also Who Owns America?* Herbert Agar and Allen Tate, eds. (Boston: 1936), with Walter Prescott Webb, *Divided We Stand*. The principal Agrarian view of Calhoun is given in Andrew Lytle, "John

C. Calhoun," in *The Hero with the Private Parts*, with an introduction by Allen Tate (Baton Rouge: Louisiana State University Press, 1966), 205-26. Consider also Gamaliel Bradford, "John Caldwell Calhoun" in *Southwest Review*, 13/2 (Winter, 1928): 195-216, and Anne W. Amacher, "Myths and Consequences: Calhoun and Some Nashville Agrarians," *South Atlantic Quarterly* 59 (Spring 1968): 251-64.

[95] *Disquisition*, paras. 28, 95. Cf. Andrew Bard Schmookler, *The Parable of the Tribes: The Problem of Power in Social Evolution* (Boston: Houghton Mifflin), 21-22ff and passim:

no one is free to choose peace, but anyone can impose upon all the necessity for power.... Power can be stopped only by power, and if the threatening society has discovered ways to magnify its power through innovations in organization or technology (or whatever), the defensive society will have to transform itself into something more like its foe in order to resist the external force.... *A selection for power among civilized societies is inevitable. This is the new evolutionary principle that came into the world with civilization.* (Emphasis added.)

Calhoun, "On the Loan Bill" (delivered in the House, February 25, 1814), *Works*, 2:102: "The ambition of a single nation can destroy the peace of the world." Aristotle makes the point also at *Politics*, 1331a (and context) and 1267a16-20. Cf. also the factual case at Plato, *Laws*, 706b, 707b-d.

[96] Calhoun believed that the defeat of Napoleon at Waterloo was a victory for liberty (just as he believed that the American defeat of the British in the War of 1812 was a victory for liberty), a victory all but comparable even to the defeats of the Turks before Vienna. Yet, by reason of the very advances that he enumerates in almost the same breath, he did not believe that it was in any sense a decisive victory against Bonapartism or "The Revolution." Napoleon suffered a great failure in Russia, but it was not a decisive failure. Cf. "On the Report of the Secretary of the Treasury" (delivered in the Senate, June 21, 1841), *Works*, 3:646: "Bonaparte...in the name of ideology" (referring to Napoleon's explanation of the revolutionary army's collapse in Russia). With the speech excerpted in the text, see particularly "On the Motion to Repeal the Direct Tax" (delivered in the House of Representatives, January 31, 1816), *Works*, 2:140-43: "the most formidable power in the world."

[97] Burke, *Works*, 3:340: "We all must obey the great law of change. It is the most powerful law of nature, and the means perhaps of its conservation. All we can do, and that human wisdom can do, is to provide that the change shall proceed by insensible degrees.... This gradual course will prevent" both aggressive subversion and political delusion. Bacon, *Essays* (24): "...if time of course alter things to the worse, and wisdom and counsel shall not alter them to the better," then "it were good that men in their innovations would follow the example of time itself; which indeed innovateth greatly, but quietly, and by degrees scarce to be perceived." (But nature works universally, while men work in this or that regime, which then fling itself on unsuspecting others.) Cf. Thomas Aquinas, *Summa Theologica*, Ia, IIae, 94.5. Calhoun, *Disquisition*, para. 138; cf. his characterization of the process of constitutional government in "On the Bill to Recharter the United States Bank" (delivered in the Senate, March 21, 1843), *Works*, 2:363-64 and context: to avoid shocks equal to savage conquest in alleviating egregious wrongs, "a new and safe system must gradually grow up under and replace the old; imitating, in this

respect, the beautiful process which we sometimes see of a wounded or diseased part in a living organic body gradually superseded by the healing process of nature." But for this, of course, time, stability, and rest are necessary.

Something of Calhoun's vision or orientation in *A Disquisition on Government* may already be glimpsed in Professor Spain's assessment:

Calhoun did attempt to set forth a social philosophy that was internally consistent and universally valid.... Although in his time he did not directly concern himself with world federation to keep the peace, his doctrine would clearly insist that ambitious present day projects in orchestration of world community be wary of building structures without assuming final responsibility for federal devolution to preserve enduring national interests and ways of life. (*The Political Theory of John C. Calhoun*, 266ff)

[98] Cf. Tocqueville, *Recollections*, 65-66, "intermittent anarchy," 71-76: "restlessness in the minds of the people..." "the modern world." The term "period of transition" is the same in both Calhoun and Hegel, "Preface," *Phenomenology of the Mind (1807)*, J. B. Baillie, trans. (New York: 1967), 75:

Our epoch is a birth time and a period of transition. The spirit of man has broken with the old order of things hitherto prevailing, and with it the old ways of thinking, and is in the mind to let them all sink into the depths of the past and to set about its own transformation. It is indeed never at rest, but carried along on the stream of progress ever onward....

Mill's *Autobiography* is meant to be a self-conscious mirror of the human mind reflecting such a period: "In an age of transition of opinions there may be somewhat both of interest and of benefit in noting the successive phases of any mind which was always pressing forward..." (1). The peculiarly American and perhaps finest example of all such efforts is *The Education of Henry Adams*.

[99] Cf. Whitehead, *Science and the Modern World* (1925), who turns finally toward the problem set forth by Calhoun in his concluding chapter entitled "Requisites for Social Progress":

At the present time...society is decaying.... The pace of progress requires a greater force of [wise] direction if disasters are to be avoided.... In the immediate future there will be less security than in the immediate past, less stability. It must be admitted that there is a degree of instability which is inconsistent with civilization.... The world is now faced with a self-evolving system which it cannot stop. There are dangers and advantages in this situation. It is obvious that the gain in material power affords opportunity for social betterment. But the material power in itself is ethically neutral. It can well work in the wrong direction. The problem is not how to produce great men, but how to produce great societies. The great society will put up the men for the occasions...."

Both Whitehead and Hegel seem more optimistic than Calhoun (cf. *Science and the Modern World*, closing two paragraphs; *Philosophy of Right*, "Preface," para. 7ff). However, twenty-five years later, Whitehead wrote: "Today...I see no hope for the future of civilization apart from world unity based on sympathetic compromise within a framework of morality which the United Nations Organization now represents." "An Appeal to Sanity," in *Essays in Science and Philosophy* (New York: Philosophical Library, 1948), 44. This represents Whitehead's final position. See Faulkner, "Taking John C. Calhoun to the United Nations," in *Polity*, 15/3 (Summer, 1983): 473ff., also Walter Berns, "Where the Majority Rules: A U.N. Diary," and related pieces at note 26. *supra*.

[100] See n. 1, above. The term "philosophy" does not occur in the *Disquisition*. Calhoun to General Hamilton (August 28, 1832), *Works*, 6:189: "philosophy of government."

Chapter 2

1 Laplace, *Exposition du Systeme du Monde* (Paris: 1798) English translation by J. Pond, *The System of the World* (London: 1809), 1:206. Cf. Diogenes Laertius, *Lives of the Famous Philosophers*, 7.139 and 149 and context and, also, Adam Smith, "The Principles which Lead and Direct Philosophical Enquiries, Illustrated by the History of Astronomy," in *Essays on Philosophical Subjects*, Dugald Stewart, ed. (London: Cadell, J. & W. Davies, and W. Creech, 1795), 90-96.

2 Cf. Hume, *Treatise of Human Nature*, introduction, para. 6.

3 *Leviathan* (Macpherson, ed.), 238. This is the vision of the absolute state, the Hobbesian state of unlimited state sovereignty. Locke's reaction to Hobbes is to compose these individuals as the "community" or "civil society," as distinct from the "state," and as retaining "a Supream Power" against the state: *An Essay Concerning the True Original, Extent, and End of Civil Government*, in *Two Treatises of Government*, Peter Laslett, ed. (New York, 1963), 413 and related passages. Locke's *Essay* is sometimes said to present the "constitutional" vision of the state as against the absolute vision of Hobbes. The Lockean view of restraining or restricting the state tends to the view of government or the state as a necessary evil, and at last finds its end in the reaction to Burke's *Reflections on the Revolution in France* of Thomas Paine, for whom men in the state of nature are attracted to commerce "as naturally as gravitation acts to a center," and government and politics wither away in to the "cordial unison" of civil "commercial" society (*Rights of Man*, Henry Collins, ed. [Harmondworth, 1977], 185-86; cf. e.g., Ayn Rand, *The Ethics of Capitalism, The Virtue of Selfishness*). This school of thought, including our observations on the subject in our first chapter, is the immediate background or context of the opening paragraph.

4 For Kant himself, "Two things fill the mind with ever new and increasing admiration and awe: the starry heaven above me and the moral law within me" (*Critique of Practical Reason*, "Conclusion"). However, he does not indicate the connection in government between the "starry heaven above" and the "moral law within." (Cf. Edgar Poe, *Eureka: A Prose Poem, An Essay on the Material and Spiritual Universe* [1848] in Edgar Allen Poe, *Poetry and Tales* (New York: The Library of America, 1984), 1, 261ff.) Cf. Cicero, *Laws*, I.vii.22-24ff; cf. also, Calhoun, e.g., "On the Bill to Repeal the Force Act" (delivered in the Senate, April 9, 1834), *Works*, 2:382-83.

5 *Federalist* 51, "But what is government itself but the greatest of all reflections on human nature? If men were angels, no government would be necessary." Kant, *Perpetual Peace, A Philosophic Sketch*, 112-13 (and the whole context): "Many say that a republic would have to be a nation of angels, because men with their self-seeking inclinations are not capable of a constitution of so sublime a nature....The problem of organizing a state, as hard as it may sound, can be solved even for a race of devils, if only they possess understanding." Cf. John Adams: "The best republics will be virtuous, and have been so; but we may hazard a conjecture that the virtues have been the effect of the well ordered constitution rather than the cause. And, perhaps, it would be impossible to prove that a republic cannot exist even among highwaymen by setting one rogue to watch another; and the knaves themselves may in time be made honest men by the struggle" (*Defence of*

Constitutions of Government of the United States of America in *The Political Writings of John Adams*, George A. Peek, Jr., ed. (Indianapolis: Bobbs-Merrill, 1954), 162.

6 *Publius Valerius Publicola* ("public man" or "people's friend"): Madison and Hamilton assumed the name of *Publius Valerius* because he was the first leading man to speak up for the people and to help their cause with the patricians after the overthrow of the kings. Madison takes the name from Plutarch's comparison of *Publius Valerius* with Solon of Athens. See Cicero, *Republic*, 2:53-55. Calhoun refers to the *Federalist* repeatedly in his speeches, e.g., "On the Loan Bill" (1814), *Works*, 2:100 (*Federalist* 10); "Reply to Simmons" (delivered in the Senate, February 20, 1847), *Works*, 4:350; and it is a useful companion to parts of the *Disquisition* and to the *Discourse* as a whole. Cf. *Discourse*, 150-61.

7 Cf. Aristotle, *Politics*, bk. 1, passim, 1282b, 15ff; cf. *Nichomachaen Ethics*, 1160a11-15.

8 Aristotle, *Metaphysics*, 1074a30 and context, 1026a18; *Physics*, 196a33ff, and context. *Nichomachaen Ethics*, 1140b34ff: "It may be argued that man is superior to the animals, but this makes no difference: since there exist other things far more divine in their nature than man, for instance, to mention the most visible, the things of which the celestial order ["cosmos"] is composed."

9 This was the view Calhoun held of constitutional government throughout his mature life. Cf. e.g., "On the Compensation Bill" (delivered in the House of Representatives, January 17, 1817), *Works*, 2:179: "This body [the House of Representatives] is the first orb in the political creation..."; "On the Merchants' Bonds," (delivered in the House of Representatives, December 4, 1812), *Works*, 2:37: "The operation of this government is an interesting problem. I wish to see the whole in full possession of its primitive power, but all of the parts confined to their respective spheres." He held a like view of empires: e.g., "On the Loan Bill" (delivered in the House of Representatives, February 25, 1814), *Works*, 2:76: "the vortex of her [imperial] system"; 87: "That counteracting influence, that repulsive power [viz., a defensive power] by which she [the imperial power] was bound to her proper orbit...," etc. Cf. Aristotle, *Politics*, 1326a 33: "...a task requiring divine power, which is what holds together the whole itself." Cf. also, *Disquisition*, para. 61. See chap. 1, n. 10 above.

10 Consider Locke, *Essay on Human Understanding*, vol. 4, chap. 12, 4-8 and related passages.

11 J. S. Mill, *A System of Logic* (London: Longmans, Green and Company, 1941), 546. Cf. Aristotle, *Nichomachaen Ethics*, X. ix. 1179a30-1180b22; Consider Tacitus, *Annals*, IV. 33.1.

The opening phrase of the *Disquisition* is "in order..." (1); the phrase closing its introductory part is "progress and improvement" (18) The phrase, "order," here taken as referring to natural or necessary or logical order, or what is necessary in order to understand, the order of things, as indicated in the remarks on causes mentioned in the previous chapter, and that of "progress," referring to the historical progress of human artifice in what is permitted to man's volition, may be broadly taken to summarize and illustrate the twofold constitution and the whole character of Calhoun's political thought.

Compare J. S. Mill, *Considerations on Representative Government*, chap. 2:249ff. Cf. Preston King, *The Ideology of Order: A Comparative Analysis of Jean Bodin and Thomas Hobbes* (London: George Allen & Unwin, 1974), para. 1. See Aristotle, *Nichomachaean Ethics*, 1103b26-1104a12, 1105b12-18; Cicero, *Republic*, I. 2.

¹² Cf. Jonathan Edwards, *The Freedom of the Will*, II, sec. 3.

¹³ See text at nn. 66-68 below.

¹⁴ *Philosophy of Right*, preface, para. 13. See chap. 1, n. 11 above. Steven B. Smith, *Hegel's Critique of Liberalism: Rights in Context* (Chicago: University of Chicago Press, 1989), 136, 104: "the Philosophy of Right [is] perhaps the most formidable and austerely written text in the history of political philosophy." This is perhaps an exaggerated (not to say comic) notion of "austerity."

¹⁵ *Jenaer Realphilosophie*, J. Hoffmeister, ed. (Hamburg: F. Meiner, 1969), 246-48. *The German Constitution* in Hegel's *Political Writings*, T. M. Knox, trans., "Introductory Essay" by Z. A. Pelzynski (Oxford: Clarendon Press, 1964), 218-23. See Aveneri, *Hegel's Theory of the Modern State*, 230; Smith, *Hegel's Critique of Liberalism*, 94-95.

¹⁶ *Philosophy of Right*, para. 189A: "Smith, Say, and Ricardo." For Hegel, political economy is to practice ("understanding") as astronomy is to theory ("reason"): Addition to para. 189: this practical science "has a parallel in the solar system which displays to the eye only irregular movements, though its laws may none the less be ascertained."

¹⁷ Cf. Aveneri, *Hegel's Theory of the Modern State*, 111, n. 76: "The resemblance of this paradigm [i.e., Hegel's presentation of the overthrow of superfluous tyranny by a people] to Marx's *Aufhebung* of the state through the dictatorship of the proletariat is truly remarkable. The dialectics of *Aufhebung* calls forth this necessary abolition of both types of dictatorships once their aim has been achieved." By means of the dialectical materialist *Aufhebung*, specialization of labor will be abolished, while the industrial system of production with its technological differentiation will be retained. This is one of Marx's materialist advances beyond the metaphysics of Hegelianism.

¹⁸ Cf. Adam Smith, *Wealth of Nations*, V.i.iii, articles 2 and 3.

¹⁹ *Jenaer Realphilosophie*, 249-51; George Armstrong Kelly, *Hegel's Retreat from Eleusis* (Princeton: Princeton University Press, 1978), 190, nn. 12, 217-20; Aveniri, *Hegel's Theory of the Modern State*, 111-12. On this and the following point consult Michael B. Foster, *The Political Philosophies of Plato and Hegel* (Oxford, 1967).

²⁰ Cf. Adriaan Peperzak, *Philosophy and Politics: A Commentary on the Preface to Hegel's Philosophy of Right* (Dordrecht: Martinus Nijhoff Publishers, 1987), commentary on paras. 9-12. Kelly, "Politics and Philosophy in Hegel," *Hegel's Retreat from Eleusis*, 8ff. Aveniri, *Hegel's Theory of the Modern State*, 87: "...while Hegel's main concern was always the attempt to achieve a comprehensive system of general philosophic speculation, his preoccupation with problems of a social and political nature consistently remained as the focus of his theoretical interest." Smith, *Hegel's Critique of Liberalism*, 190-91: "The concept of *Aufhebung* is the centerpiece of the Hegelian dialectic, if any concept is....the concept of *Aufhebung* is profoundly consistent with Hegel's larger political project of restoring harmony and unity to a broken world."

²¹ Cf., Garry Wills, "The Convenient State" in Frank S. Meyer, ed., *What is Conservatism?* (New York: Holt, Rinehart and Winston, 1964).

²² *Critique of Hegel's 'Philosophy of Right'*, Anette Jolin and Joseph O'Malley, trans., with an introduction and notes by Joseph O'Malley (Cambridge: Cambridge University Press, 1978), 14. Page xiv: "the *Critique of Hegel's 'Philosophy of Right'* developed into the whole program of research and writing which occupied Marx for the remainder of his life."

23 See chap. 1, n. 11 above. *Manifesto of the Communist Party*, first sentence.

24 For Marx, the state according to Hegel is the true modern state. Cf. Calhoun, "On the Bankrupt Bill" (delivered in the Senate, June 2, 1840), *Works*, 3:519:

> Sir, I am not to be caught by words; I have too much experience for that. It is vain that I am told that this is a contest between corporations and individuals—the artificial legal person called a body politic and the individual man, as formed by his Creator. All this is lost on me. I look not to where the blow is professedly aimed, but beyond, where it must fall. The corporate, ideal thing at which it is said to be directed is intangible, and without the capacity of hearing, seeing, or feeling; but there are beneath thousands on thousands, not shadows, but real, sensitive human beings, on whom the blow will fall with a vengence [*sic*]. Before we act, let us look at things as they really are, and not as we may imagine them, in the fervor of debate.

Also Burke, "A Letter to a Member of the National Assembly," in *Works* (Bohn's), 2:537: "benevolence to the whole species" removes care for "the single human being." Cf. *Reflections* in Bohn, *Works*, 2:337, 341, 350: "in the groves of the [Parisian philosophers'] academy, at the end of every vista, you see nothing but the gallows."

Hegel's "speculative" philosophy surely does not intend to be merely "abstract"; he in no sense approves of mere "abstractionism": see section 82, *Encyclopedia of Philosophical Sciences*.

25 Cf. Marx, *Capital*, foreword, in *Marx-Engels Reader*, Robert C. Tucker, ed., 2nd German ed (New York: W. W. Norton, 1978), 301-302: "mystification which dialectic suffers in Hegel's hands," the method "must [be] turned right side up again," etc. O'Malley, "Introduction," xxvii-xxxii; Kelley, *Hegel's Retreat from Eleusis*, 164ff.

26 See text at notes 39ff, chap. 1, above.

27 *Critique*, comment on para. 279 (32):

> It is obvious that the political constitution as such is perfected for the first time when the private spheres have attained independent existence. Where commerce and property and land are not free, not yet autonomous, there is also not yet the political constitution....The abstraction of the state as such belongs only to modern times because the abstraction of private life belongs only to modern times. The abstraction of the political state is a modern product.

Almost all of Marx's time spent under Proudhon, whom he regarded as a first-rate intellect, was taken up in attempting to instruct him in Hegelianism. (Marx complained that Proudhon could not understand Hegelianism because he could not speak German.)

28 Richard Hofstadter, "John C. Calhoun: The Marx of the Master Class," 69:

> Although his concepts of nullification and the concurrent voice have little more than antiquarian interest for the twentieth century mind, he also set forth a system of social analysis that is worthy of considerable respect...Before Karl Marx published the *Communist Manifesto*, Calhoun laid down an analysis of American politics and the sectional conflict which foreshadowed some of the seminal ideas of Marx's system. A brilliant if narrow dialectician, probably the last American statesman to do any primary political thinking, he placed the central ideas of

"scientific" socialism in an inverted framework of moral values and produced an arresting defense of reaction....

Professor Hofstadter does not see that, were this interpretation accurate, Calhoun would merely have stood Hegel's system back up as it was before Marx "inverted" it, and that Calhoun's thought would then have to be reconceived and interpreted in that light. He takes the idea of Calhoun's pre-Marxism from Professor Richard Current's earlier "John C. Calhoun: Philosopher of Reaction," of which his own critique is an extension; cf. also, William W. Freehling, "Spoilsmen and Interests in the Career of John C. Calhoun," *Journal of American History*, 52/2 (June 1965).

More importantly, it should be observed in passing that Calhoun's concepts of nullification or veto power and concurrency are not yet entirely of antiquarian interest for the twenty-first century mind. To take only the most celebrated example, the American Secretary of State, Cordell Hull, wrote soon after the founding of the United Nations, hopeful harbinger of world federation, that "our Government would not remain there a day without retaining the veto power." The reasoning behind this statement is perfectly Calhounian. *The Memoirs of Cordell Hull*, 2 vols. (New York: Macmillan, 1948), 2:1164, quoted in Faulkner, "Taking John C. Calhoun to the United Nations," 479, cf. Walter Berns, "Where the Majority Rules: A U.N. Diary" (see chap. 1, n. 26, end, above); cf. also, Owen J. Roberts, John F. Smith, and Clarence Streit ("Publius II"), *The New Federalist* (New York: Harper, 1950), and Gunville Clark and Louis B. John, *World Peace through World Law* (Cambridge: Harvard University Press, 1966).

29 Madison, *Federalist* 10, also: "Theoretic politicians...have erroneously supposed that by reducing mankind to a perfect equality in their political rights, they would at the same time be perfectly equalized and assimilated in their possessions, their opinions, and their passions." Cf. Douglas Adair, "'That Politics May Be Reduced to a Science': David Hume, James Madison, and the Tenth Federalist," in *Fame and the Founding Fathers: Essays by Douglas Adair*, Trevor Colbourn, ed. (New York: W. W. Norton, 1974), 93ff.

30 Martin Diamond, "Democracy and *The Federalist*: A Reconsideration of the Framers' Intent," *American Political Science Review* 53 (March 1959): 52-68. The argument on *Federalist* 10 is outlined rather than explored. Professor Diamond has primarily in mind refuting the Beard thesis, itself a mild elaboration of Marx's and related doctrines, according to which *Federalist* 10 is "a masterly statement of the theory of economic determinism" (Charles Beard, *An Economic Interpretation of the United States*, [New York: Macmillan, 1954], 15.). Professor Diamond's thesis hardly improves Beard's thesis: "interests" as Professor Diamond understands them is not what "Madison's whole system" amounts to. If it were, then one could only explain the engagement of men like Washington, Jefferson, Hamilton, Madison, and others (Calhoun) on the basis of Beard's thesis. This is obviously inadequate. Professor Diamond's Madison merely goes the way of Professor Hofstadter's Calhoun. It is more interesting to note that at the end of his life, in one of the last (if not the last) articles he wrote, after a long professional career of interpreting the American Founding, *The Federalist*, and "federalism," Professor Diamond discovered that: "it is instructive, and perhaps disconcerting, to learn that our modern distinction between confederalism and federalism derives [*sic*] from John Calhoun....[Calhoun's thought] appears to have been an important source of our contemporary understanding of federalism," but this would not

seem to jibe with his own views of *The Federalist* and the Federalists' view of Federalism. He begins to see a light at the end of the tunnel of "interests," but he goes no further. "The Federalist on Federalism: Neither A National Nor A Federal Constitution" in *As Far As Republican Principles Will Admit: Essays by Martin Diamond*, William A. Schambra, ed. (Washington, D.C.: American Enterprise Institute Press, 1992), 169ff. (Diamond seems to have been unaware of the *Discourse*.) The issue begins to be drawn in Drew R. McCoy, *The Last of the Fathers: James Madison and the Republican Legacy* (Cambridge: Cambridge University Press, 1989), the chapter on Nullification and the citations there. Cf. also, Garry Wills, *Explaining America: "The Federalist"* (Garden City, N.Y.: Doubleday, 1981), xiv: "Madison was for [Beard] what Calhoun would later be called, the Marx of the ruling class." This *is* the "Beard thesis."

31 Perhaps the observation by Manfred Fuhrmann that "[t]hrough his [political] thought...Cicero shows himself to be a Hegelian before the term existed" is truer than he imagined: *Cicero and the Roman Republic* (Oxford: Blackwell, 1992), 115. Much twentieth-century European politics is portended in this only apparently antiquarian question: consult especially Walter Bagehot, "Caesarism as It Existed in 1865," *Literary Studies (Miscellaneous Essays)*, 3 vols., R. H. Hutton, ed. (1865, London, 1902-1905), 3:72f: In the name of the "unorganized people," Julius Caesar "said to the numerical majority of Roman citizens: 'I am your advocate and your leader: make me supreme, and I will govern for your good, and in your name.'"

The contemporary issues are popularly drawn in Thomas De Quincey, "The Caesars," *The Works of Thomas De Quincey* 14 vols. (1832, London, 1878), 7:7f: saviour, master, "godlike man"; and Anthony Trollope, *Life of Cicero* 2 vols. (London, 1880); cf., also, H. J. Haskell, *This Was Cicero* (New York: Knopf, 1942), last chapter: "Alexander H. Stephens," "Guizot." Consult in this connection, Cicero, *Second Philippic*, 116; *De Officiis*, 1. 26, 64. Cf. *Disquisition*, para. 149 (10th sentence); also para. 124 (3rd sentence).

32 Marx, *German Ideology*: "The state is overcome in Communist society, where nobody has an exclusive range of activity, but everybody can train himself in every branch; where society regulates general production and thereby makes it possible for me to do one thing today and another thing tomorrow, to hunt in the morning, to fish in the afternoon, to be a husbandman in the evening, and to indulge in critical work after supper, as it pleases me, without any necessity for me ever to become a hunter, fisherman, husbandman, or critic." That is, everyone will be a Victorian English squire or gentleman.

33 A glimpse of this may be why Cassirer said "Hegel dreamed of becoming a second Machiavelli," *The Myth of the State* (New Haven: Yale University Press, 1946), 122 (referring to the German Constitution). More especially, cf. Hegel, *Philosophy of History*, 35, 447-51; *Philosophy of Right*, preface, para. 7ff.

34 Cf. Kelly, *Hegel's Retreat from Eleusis*, 140: Hegel "was prepared for the hereditary monarch to be a nitwit..."; 190: "Hegel's sovereign cannot simply be discarded as an 'unintelligible exception' to his theory....he makes bold to conclude that his theory of sovereignty is 'the higher principle of the modern age'...which Plato was unacquainted with." Hegel's view is that this coincidence represents the historical resolution, understood by him, of the dichotomy between philosophy and political life or the private and the public thematically emphasized by Plato. Yet, it actually does not achieve this. Cf. Harry

Brod, *Hegel's Philosophy of Politics: Idealism, Identity, and Modernity* (Boulder: Westview Press, 1992), 157: "Ultimately, the institution of the monarchy within Hegel's system may be understood as an attempt to fuse the idea of Plato's philosopher-ruler with the idea of the pedagogic state of German idealism....This attempt fails, however, at least as far as the consciousness of the citizens is concerned [i.e., decisively], because...the symbolism of the monarchy remains too esoteric, too much in need of technical philosophic decoding, to have the required impact on the citizens, [etc.]." The issue is of continuing import for students of German political thought because it leads to the equally vexed question of Professor Heidegger's view of the spiritual role of the *Fuhrer* of the German *volk* and of his personal role as *Fuhrer* of the German university world.

35 Mill, cf. text at chap. 1, nn. 37 above.

36 O'Malley, "Editor's Introduction," x-xi: "Of the whole corpus of Marx's writings, the *Critique*, largely because we have it just as it flowed from his pen, especially exemplifies what Wilhelm Liebknect meant when he observed that 'if Buffon's phrase holds good of anyone, it holds good of Marx: the style is the man—Marx's style is Marx himself.'" Also, Marx to Engels, November 27, 1867: "I must be diplomatic with the Fenians. I cannot entirely keep quiet, but I do not wish that these guys include in a critique of my book that I am a demagogue," in *Marx und Engels, Briefwechsel*, 3:538. This style leads as well to national socialism as international socialism. Jaspers, "Philosophical Memoir," in *Philosophy and the World*, E. B. Ashton, trans. (Chicago: Henry Regnery, 1963), 278: "it is no accident that both National Socialism and Bolshevism would regard philosophy as their deadly spiritual foe." See the text in chap. 1, n. 41 above.

Calhoun takes the term "French philosophy" (a familiar enough term of the day) from Burke. See Burke, *Works* (Bohn's), 2:284-87, 299-302, 338-39, 361-62, 382-84, 403-405, 414, 423; 2:87-91, 350-54, 376-79, 442-43, 456-57, and related passages. According to Burke, the French Revolution is significant because it is the first in which "the spirit of ambition is connected with the spirit of speculation." Burke presents this revolution in so many words as the secularized Reformation conceived fifty years later by Marx in the Introduction to the *Critique of Hegel's 'Philosophy of Right'*, 131-38.

The term "false philosophy" as used by Calhoun means purposes and schemes which are not philosophic presented as philosophy or immediately following from philosophy by persons who are not philosophic posing as philosophers. The philosophers, for him, are men such as the authors of Aristotle's *Politics* or Cicero's *Offices*.

37 O'Malley, "Editor's Introduction," *Critique of Hegel's Philosophy of Right*, xxiii. Smith, *Hegel's Critique of Liberalism*, last sentence: "to the extent that modern critical theory remains wedded to a belief in the self-realization of reason, its problems remain the problems of Hegel." It should be observed that this is already Hegel's own position in the *Philosophy of Right* itself, cf. preface, paras. 7ff ("sophists").

38 Chap. 1, n. 40 above. The term "totalitarianism" was apparently coined by Mussolini, who took it from the Hegelianizing thought of Gentile and Croce. It is essentially Hegelian in its origin, for it is he who is always speaking of "totalities" and their understanding and mastery, etc. (Kant had sometimes used the term.) Cf. Georg Lukacs, *History and Class Consciousness*, Rodney Livingstone, trans. (Cambridge, Mass., 1971), 27:

"The primacy of the totality...the catagory of the totality...is the essence of the method which Marx took from Hegel and transformed into the basis of a wholly new science...."

39 Cf. Aristotle, *Nichomachaen Ethics*, 1160a10ff; *Politics*, 1259a5ff: monopoly and competition, supply and demand, etc. See Leo Strauss, "On Aristotle's *Politics*," in *The City and Man* (Chicago: University of Chicago Press, 1964), 30-34.

40 Hobbes, *De Cive*, Preface: "I took my beginning from the very matter of civil government, and thence proceeded to its generation and form, and the first beginning of justice....that we [might] rightly understand what the quality of human nature is, in what matters it is, in what not, fit to make up a civil government, and how men must be agreed amongst themselves that intend to grow up into a well-grounded state."

41 Calhoun, "On the Bill to Recharter the United States Bank" (delivered in the Senate, March 21, 1834), *Works*, 2:356 and context ("disease"). Marx's *Critique* does not criticize Hegel's discussion of war. Its place is taken in Marx's thought by *"ad hominem critique"* itself, "hand-to-hand combat," which is a "kind of combat" against the noble, the equal, and the interesting (introduction, 133, 137).

42 Cf. Hegel, *Philosophy of Right*, preface, para. 15.

43 Cf. also, Hume, *Enquiry Concerning Human Understanding*, L. A. Selby-Bigge, ed. (Oxford: Clarendon Press, 1902), 83-84: "Would you know the sentiments, inclinations, and course of life of the Greeks and Romans? Study well the temper and actions of the French and English.... Mankind are so much the same, in all times and places, that history informs us of nothing new or strange in this particular. Its chief use is only to discover the constant and universal principles of human nature." Hume's view that "the philosophy of the ancients" is "entirely hypothetical," that is, it rests "more upon invention than experience," is taken over by Hegel and re-presented on the (invented) grounds of historicism, which he understands as the logically necessary if non-Humean consequence of the ground established by Hume's empiricism. (The quotation of Hume is from *The Letters of David Hume*, J. Y. T. Grieg, ed. 2 vols. [Oxford: Oxford University Press, 1932], 1:16.).

44 Cf. Avineri, *Hegel's Theory of the Modern State*, 10: "In the polis and in the Church, Hegel was looking for a paradigm for a kind of universality which was lacking in the political system of the modern state. Being aware of the achievement of modernity—he quotes Hume as the historian who looked for the integration of the individual in a political universality—Hegel is conscious of its burden as well." Cf. the preface to the *Philosophy of Right* and the introduction to the *Treatise of Human Nature*.

45 Cf. Smith, *Hegel's Critique of Liberalism*, 115ff: "Every bit as much as Hobbes or any other contractarian, Hegel explains the origins of rights by reference to a putatively natural condition which is one of maximum conflict and deprivation"; x: "The central feature of Hegel's theory of the state is its respect for rights, crucially including the [natural] right to recognition." Cf., also, J. W. N. Watkins, *Hobbes' System of Ideas* (New York: Barnes and Noble, 1965), the concept of the person.

46 *Disquisition*, para. 9; Jenaer, *Realphilosophie*, 270, and context. See Avineri, *Hegel's Theory of the Modern State*, 113. Note Whitehead, "Immortality," in *Essays in Science and Philosophy* (New York: Philosophical Library, 1948), 61ff: "...The Two Worlds."

---

[47] Quoted in Hofstadter, "John C. Calhoun: The Marx of the Master Class," in *The American Political Tradition*, 78; see Wilson, *The Essential Calhoun*, 429. The reference to happiness as the end of this effort is drawn from Calhoun's speech on the Force Bill, n. 54 below. See chap. 1, n. 78 above.

[48] Cf. Hume, *Treatise*, III.iii, 414-15ff: "We speak not strictly and philosophically when we talk of the combat of reason and passion."

[49] *Disquisition*, paras. 52, 75-78, with *Philosophy of Right*, remark on paras. 301, 302 and remark on paras. 302, 303, and related passages. Marx's commentary on these sections in his *Critique* fails to reach the issue. He most closely approaches Calhoun when he quotes Hegel's remark that

> The organic unity of the powers of the state itself implies that it is one single mind which both firmly establishes the universal and also brings it into its determinate actuality and carries it out, [and then says:] but it is precisely this organic unity which Hegel has failed to construct. The various powers each have a different principle, although at the same time they are all equally real. To take refuge from their real conflict in an imaginary organic unity, instead of developing the various powers as moments of an organic unity, is therefore an empty, mystical evasion. (59)

Hegel's concern is with depicting the completeness of the constitutional state historically understood as containing what he identifies to his satisfaction as "all the essential moments of the state," etc. Calhoun's concern is with this completeness politically understood as the problem of justice or the common good of the whole, i.e., with the nature of constitution itself. Calhoun discusses constitutional monarchy at *Disquisition*, paras. 125, 152-60.

[50] Cf. "On the Loan Bill" (February 25, 1814), Works, 2:98; Aristotle, *Politics*, 1261a15-30, *Nichomachaen Ethics*, 1132b33ff.

[51] See the text at chap. 1, nn. 24-25 above.

[52] Seneca, *Epistulae*, 121.17: "The animate being is first attached to itself, for there must be something to which other things are related." Cicero, *De Finibus*, iii.16-17: (Cato:) "As soon as it is born, for we should start here, any animate being feels an attachment and attraction to itself.... Hence we should conclude that it is self-love which is the starting point *(principium)*."

[53] Calhoun takes this term, the "sympathetic" or social feelings, from Hume, *A Treatise of Human Nature*, ii.1.11ff; 316-24, 363-65; 487, which it is probable he associates with the view set forth in Aristotle, *Rhetoric*, 1941b, 1385b13-16. It could appear that Calhoun straightforwardly adopts the theory of passions (including "habits") set forth by Hume in the *Treatise*, although this is questionable. In any case, the systematic investigation of Calhoun's own view properly begins with the *Treatise* and the *Enquiries*, if not the *Rhetoric* itself, and not, for example, with Smith's *Theory of Moral Sentiments*, which is ultimately based on Hume's associationism. In Calhoun, reason takes the place of the imagination as presented in Smith's "History of Astronomy" *(Essays on Philosophical Subjects)*. Smith's understanding of the imagination and its essential role in science and in what is now called the structure of scientific revolutions is drawn from Hume's theory of our belief in the persistence of the external world. Cf. also, Adam Ferguson, *An Essay on the History of Civil*

Society (Edinburgh: Edinburgh University Press, 1966), 16ff. See Hume, *Treatise*, iii.7, "Of the Origin of Government," first two paragraphs.

54 See chap. 1, n. 5, above; n. 51, above.

55 Plato, *Laws*, 731d-e (Stranger from Athens:) "...The truth is that the cause of all sins [wrongdoings] in every case lies in one's *excessive* love of self....So, all men should flee *excessive* self-love. . ." (emphasis added.) Aristotle, *Politics*, 1263b1ff: "Selfishness is justly blamed; but this is not merely having affection for oneself, but rather having more affection than one should—just as in the case of the greedy person, for practically everyone has affection for things of this sort." *Nichomachaen Ethics*, 1148a25ff: "Men are not blamed merely for regarding or desiring or liking naturally desirable or neutral things, for instance, money, gain, victory, honor, but for doing so in a certain way, namely, to excess"; with what follows in the *Disquisition*, cf. 1168a28ff. Seneca, *Ep.*, 87.15, 22, 28ff. Cf., also, Rousseau, *Discourse on the Origin of Inequality* (Second Discourse), note o. Consider the distinction between individualism and egoism drawn in Tocqueville, *Democracy in America*, II.2.2.

56 Consider Hume, *A Treatise of Human Nature*, 487, 500-501, and context: "tho' it be rare to meet with one, who loves any single person better than himself; yet 'tis as rare to meet with one, in whom all the kind affections, taken together, do not over-balance all the selfish."

57 "On the New Army Bill" (delivered in the House of Representatives, January 14, 1813), *Works*, 2:54: "The love of present ease and enjoyment, the love of gain, and party zeal.... These constitute the *weakness* of our *nature*. We *naturally* lean that way without the arts of persuasion," or stronger checks (emphasis added). Cf. Plato, *Phaedrus*, 237d6ff; *Laws*, 626d1-627d6. See also, "On the Second Resolution reported by the Foreign Relations Committee" (delivered in the House of Representatives, December 12, 1811), *Works*, 2:3: "the human tongue," etc. Aristotle, *Nichomachaen Ethics*, 1181a12-19.

58 Aristotle, *Nichomachaen Ethics*, 1097b9-12ff, 1162a16-22ff, 1168a25-27ff; *Politics*, 1253a19ff. Cf. Locke, *First Treatise*, sec. 56.

59 Cicero, *Laws*, i.29: "No individual thing is so like another individual thing, so comparable, as all of us are to each other. Indeed, if bad habits and false beliefs did not distort weaker minds and bend them in different directions, no one would be so like himself as he would be like all the others." See *Disquisition*, paras. 3 and 104, also the text at nn. 46-47 above.

60 Cf. Aristotle, *Nichomachaen Ethics*, 1179b22; Calhoun, "Reply to Clay" (delivered in the Senate, March 10, 1838), *Works*, 3:274: "The faculties of our mind are the immediate gift of our Creator, for which we are no further responsible than for their proper cultivation, according to our opportunities, and their proper application to control and regulate our actions."

61 "On the Force Bill" (delivered in the Senate, February 15-16, 1833), *Works*, 2:199: "moral and intellectual acquirements"; 215: "the most commanding talents and acquirements." Chap. 1, n. 58 above. Cf. "On the Repeal of the Direct Tax" (delivered in the House of Representatives, January 31, 1816), *Works*, 2:152-53:

It is immutable—it is in the nature of things. The love of present ease and pleasure, indifference about the future—that fatal weakness of human nature – has never failed, in individuals or nations, to sink to disgrace and ruin. On the contrary, virtue and wisdom, which regard the future, which spurn the temptations of the moment, however rugged their path, end in happiness. Such are the sentiments of all wise writers, from the didactics of the philosopher to the fictions of the poet. They agree and inculcate that pleasure is a flowery path, leading off among groves and gardens, but ending in a dreary wilderness; that it is the siren's voice, that he who listens is ruined; that it is the cup of Circe, of which whosoever drinks is converted into a swine. This is the language of fiction. Reason teaches the same lesson. No effort is needed...to impel us the opposite way.

(Cf. Plato, *Republic*, 378d and context; Homer, *Odyssey*, IX, X, XII) Contemporary moral or invisible defects are most visible and tangible in their future consequences.

[62] E.g., Calhoun, "On the Compensation Bill" (delivered in the House of Representatives, January 17, 1817), *Works*, 2:180-83: "Cato, Phocion, and Aristides," "human nature as it is," "duties of legislation." "On the Bill to Separate the Government from the Banks" (delivered in the Senate, October 3, 1837), *Works*, 3:116-17: "bearing on the moral and intellectual development of the community," "development of the higher mental qualities, intellectual and moral," "science, literature, philosophy, statesmanship," "mount up the rugged steep of science," "advance of civilization," and context. Burke, *Works*, John C. Nimmo, ed., 12 vols. (London: 1887), 4:468.

[63] Hobbes, *Leviathan*, chap. 44. Hobbes' argument here points to or confirms Machiavelli's doctrine of *"fortuna"* in the *Prince* and the *Discourses on Livy*. See Leo Strauss, *Thoughts on Machiavelli* (Glencoe, Ill.: The Free Press, 1958), 174ff: "Machiavelli's Teaching." Hegel, *Philosophy of Right*, para. 49R.

[64] Cf., e.g., Hume, *An Enquiry Concerning the Principles of Morals*, L. A. Selby-Bigge, ed., revised by P. H. Niddich (Oxford: Clarendon Press, 1975), 296-97: "An Epicurean or a Hobbist readily allows that there is such a thing as friendship in the world, without hypocrisy or disguise; tho' he may attempt, by a philosophical chemistry, to resolve the elements of this passion, if I may so speak, into the elements of another, and explain every affection to be self-love, twisted and moulded [*sic*], by a particular turn of the imagination, into a variety of appearances."

[65] Cf. Coit, *John C. Calhoun: American Portrait*, 395: "I have never been more convinced of Mr. Calhoun's genius...than while he talked to us of a flower"; 384-86, 322, 179, 282. Bartlett, *John C. Calhoun*, 374: "Joseph Henry, director of the Smithsonian and finest scientific mind in the country [wrote of Calhoun that] no man in Washington was more interesting in conversation...no one so quick to catch an idea and give it back to you enlarged and improved."

[66] Aristotle, *Politics*, 1263a8 and context; Cicero, *Offices*, I.157 and context.

[67] N. 48 above.

[68] Cf. Jean Bodin, *Method for the Easy Comprehension of History* (New York: 1945), vide *"humanitas"*, 117, 227; Gobineau, *Essai sur l'Inegalite des Races Humaines*, 4 vols. (Paris: Firmin-Didot, 1853-5), 1:11-12: *"societe"*; Oswald Spengler, *The Decline of the West*, passim: "the problem of 'civilization'," "'culture' as organism"; J. Huizinga, *In the Shadow of Tomorrow* (New York: W. W. Norton, 1936), 18-19, 39-51, 187-89, 217-20. Also, Christopher Dawson, *The Dynamics of World History*, John J. Mulloy, ed. (New York: Sheed and Ward, 1956), 43-

52; Eric Voegelin, *The New Science of Politics* (Chicago: University of Chicago Press, 1952), 107-32.

⁶⁹ Cf. Freud, *The Future of an Illusion*, sec. 1, paras. 3-4:

Human civilization, by which I mean all those respects in which human life has raised itself above its animal status and differs from the life of beasts—and I scorn to distinguish between culture and civilization—presents, as we know, two aspects to the observer. It includes on the one hand all the knowledge and capacity that men have acquired in order to control the forces of nature and extract its wealth for the satisfaction of human needs, and, on the other hand, all the regulations necessary in order to adjust the relations of men to one another and the especially the distribution of available wealth.

Its defect, however, owing to human nature, particularly the nature of the human "masses," is that "while mankind has made continual advances in its control over nature and may expect to make still greater ones, it is not possible to establish with certainty that a similar advance has been made in the management of human affairs." The masses and also non-masses are actually enemies of civilization. Following Rousseau, Freud traces this essential defect to childhood and the lack of effective "cultural regulations." He supposes that further advances in our control over nature ("civilization") and the elaboration of the new science of psychiatry might provide the desirable regulations. The distinction he scorns to make thus remains in full force, even if, as it were, only subconsciously. In this way, i.e., by placing the "state of nature" in the human subconscious, Freud proposes that domestic relations or the family come to take the place of politics and the city, economics ("civil society") the place of polity or community, and psychiatry and the psychotherapist the place of political science and statesmanship. This is the final end of the lowering or abolition of the political as such, and, accordingly, Calhoun's science of government must be seen as relatively worthless and dated. In the *Future of An Illusion*, Freud's contribution to this desired control in psychiatry is the place of political science. This is necessary since the "state of nature" exists primarily in the human unconscious. Freud states the problem (in what histories sometimes call the "classic statement of the problem") in the same manner Calhoun stated it already almost one-hundred years earlier: "While mankind has made continual advances in its control over nature and may expect to make still greater ones, it is not possible to establish with certainty that a similar advance has been made in the management of human affairs."

⁷⁰ For example, Calhoun always mentions fiction under the aspect of government or morals, as he does arts and sciences. The aim of the poets and political philosophers or scientists is the same in this regard, and points us to "community" rather than to "civilization." Fiction is superior even to positive law in this respect. While studying law in his mid-twenties, Calhoun wrote to a friend: "Many things I study for the love of study, but not so with law. I can never consider it but as a task which my situation forces on me. I therefore often lay it aside for the more delicious themes of the muses, or the interesting pages of history." Quoted in Gerald Capers, *John C. Calhoun: Opportunist, A Reappraisal* (Gainesville: University of Florida Press, 1960), 15. Aristotle *Politics*, on collecting laws. See n. 72 below; chap. 3 below.

[71] Plato, *Laws*, 672b10-c, etc. Aristotle, *Politics*, i.1.1252b 20-26; iii.5.1278a 1ff, and context. Cf. Locke: "No man at birth can have a right to anything." Quoted in Ruth Grant, *John Locke's Liberalism* (Chicago: University of Chicago Press, 1987), 134, n. 48; *First Discourse*, sec. 2; *Some Thoughts Concerning Education*, sec. 103, 105: "I told you before that children love *Liberty*,...I tell you now, they love something more, and that is *Dominion*: And the first original of most vicious Habits...." Bentham: "Every child during his period of weakness, every man for the first 16 or 18 years of his life is a slave....Your republic if it has parents and children in it, will after all be but a cluster of little monarchies." Quoted in Gertrude Himmelfarb, "Bentham's Utopia" in *Marriage and Morals among the Victorians* (New York: Alfred A. Knopf, 1986), 136. Consider Aristotle, *Nichomachaean Ethics*, 1095b1-13; 1178a33-1180a11, and the *Politics* on paternal rule; Rousseau, *Emile*, introduction, on maternal rule. Also, *Disquisition*, para. 16.

[72] Cf. La Rochefoucauld, preface to *Maximes* (in *Oeuvres*, Paris: Hachette, 1923, 1:30): "By the word 'interest' I understand not always an interest in wealth but most often an interest in honor or glory." Also, Hobbes, *De Cive*, 1:ii; 5:5; *Leviathan*, chap. 27, etc.: Men are not naturally social but nevertheless tend naturally toward "vanity," and hence toward the *bellum omnium contra omnes*. *Federalist* 10: "As long as the connection subsists between [man's] reason and his self-love, his opinions and his passions will have a reciprocal influence on each other; and the former will be objects to which the latter attach themselves." Cf. Hegel, *Philosophy of Right*, remark to para. 289: "...civil society is the battlefield where everyone's private interest meets everyone else's, so here we have the struggle...." Kant, "*Idea for a Universal History with Cosmopolitan Intent*," Fourth Principle.

[73] In light of the above, compare Hume, *Treatise*, III.2.7; Hobbes, *De Cive*, ii.3.25 and 27; *Leviathan*, 14. 7-8.

[74] Aristotle, *Politics*, first sentence. Cf. Solzhenitsyn, *The Gulag Archipelago: An Experiment in Literary Investigation*, Thomas P. Whitney, trans., 3 vols. (New York: Harper and Row, 1976), vol. 1, chap. 1: "there are as many centers of the Universe as there are living beings in it." See n. 50 above; *Disquisition*, first paragraph.

[75] Hobbes, *De Cive*, i. 2-3, 12. With due qualification, something of the spirit of Calhoun's conception is captured in James Monroe, *The People the Sovereigns*, 26: "Man is by nature a sociable being, and pursuing the impulse derived from nature, clings to his fellow-man. As soon as such numbers are collected, no matter from whence they come, or how thrown together, as to merit the name, a society is formed, and over it such government as they are capable of forming," as though the latter activity, forming a government, is itself the purpose from the beginning. Cf. also, Cicero, *Republic*, I, 39-42; also, Aristotle, *Nichomachaean Ethics*, 1102a5-1103b25, 1140a24-1140b30, 1142a32-1142b34, 1144b-1145a7; 1170b10; Montesquieu, *The Spirit of the Laws* I, chap. ix: "Constitution of our being."

[76] Cf. Plato, *Laws*, 875a; Aristotle, *Politics*, i. 2. 1253a1-19; Cicero, *Laws*, I. 27-30; II. 12-13.

[77] Noted in Coit, *John C. Calhoun*, 383; contrast Monroe, *The People the Sovereigns.*, 51: "Plato composed a work on the subject of politics. He drew two projects, but they are so theoretical and objectionable in every view; so little applicable to us, and even to the age in which they were written, that they need not be noticed." Cf. Meigs, *The Life of John C. Calhoun*, 2:100: "Plato and Aristotle, he thought, had sounded the depths of human knowledge and taught the world all the wisdom it ever learned."

[78] Cf. Burke, "On the State of the Representation of the Commons in Parliament" (May 7, 1782), *Works* (Beaconsfield), 7:97: "Whenever I speak against theory, I mean always a weak, erroneous, fallacious, unfounded or imperfect theory: and one of the ways of discovering that it is a false theory is by comparing it with practice. This is the true touchstone of all theories which regard man and the affairs of men, — does it suit his nature in general? — Does it suit his nature as modified by his habits?"

[79] Calhoun to Anna Marie Clemson in Spain, *The Political Theory of John C. Calhoun*, 87: the French standard of liberty is "ideal."

> It belongs to that kind of liberty which man has been supposed to possess in what has been falsely called a state of nature — a state supposed to have preceded the social and political, and in which, of course, he must have lived apart, as an isolated individual, without society, without government. In such a state, if it were possible for him to exist in it, he would have, indeed, two of the elements of the French political creed, liberty and equality, but no fraternity. That can only exist in the social and political, and the attempt to unite the other two, as they would exist in a supposed state of nature, in man, as he must exist in the former, must and ever will fail. The union is impossible, and *the attempt to unite them is absurd*.... (emphasis added.)

Fraternity, as distinct from liberty and equality, involves "recognition" — this, incidentally, is almost the whole purport of Hegel's philosophy of politics as presented in the *Philosophy of Right*. Hence the project to see the Hegelian "end of history" merely in the liberal principles of the French Revolution, "liberty and equality" (Fukuyama) and the modern "universal and homogeneous state" united therein (Kojeve), without "fraternity," is absurd. It amounts to saying that the "end of history," without community or fraternity, must be for Hegel the beginning of politics, which, for Hegel, is nonsense (although for, say, Hume, it makes perfect sense).

See Francis Fukuyama, "The End of History?" (*The National Interest* 16 [Summer 1989]: 3-18), 6: "the ideas of liberty and equality"; and *The End of History and the Last Man* (New York: Macmillan, 1992), 64: "When Hegel declared that history had ended after the Battle of Jena in 1806...he was saying that the principles of liberty and equality" were established; cf. 67: "the principles of liberty and equality that emerged from the French Revolution, embodied in what Kojeve called the "universal and homogenous state..."; 199ff, "The Universal and Homogeneous State," and context. Rather, the universal and homogeneous state, as we have seen from the *Disquisition*, is merely the nondescript (civil) social state (nature) that is defined by diverse governments (history, i.e., nature and community or fraternity). Fukuyama follows Alexander Kojeve, *Introduction to the Reading of Hegel*, James Nichols, trans., Allan Bloom, ed. (New York: Basic Books, 1969). However, cf. 95-97: where Hegel is everywhere always firm that the modern constitutional state is necessarily composed of different or diverse elements or parts, etc., Kojeve says that the Hegelian state is "homogeneous" (i.e., is in principle essentially the same as Locke's "civil society"), and one is merely back at the beginning of consideration either of a science of politics or of a discipline of statesmanship, if not merely left with absolutism and empty desire for honor. See also Fukuyama, *The End of History and the Last Man*, 144 and n. 3.

[80] With paragraph 11 and the first part of paragraph 10, cf. Mandeville, *The Fable of the Bees*, F. B. Kaye, ed., 2 vols. (Oxford: Clarendon Press, 1957), 1:51, 116, etc., and Hume, *Treatise*, 500 and context. Rousseau, *Social Contract, Second Discourse*, First Part ("Fable of the Bees"), *Emile*. With what follows, consider Aquinas, *De Veritate*, q. 10, a. 12, ad. 7: "*et sic nullus potest cogitare se non esse cum assensu: in hoc enim quod cogitate aliquid, percipit se esse.*" See also Thomas Eschmann, "Studies on the Notion of Society in St. Thomas Aquinas," *Mediaeval Studies*, 1944, 8:1-42.

[81] See the text at n. 62 above. Rousseau, *Second Discourse*.

[82] "Letter to the Honorable William Smith" (July 3, 1843), *Works*, 6:222.

[83] Cf. Burke, *Reflections* (London: World Classics, 1950), 107: "Without...civil society man could not by any possibility arrive at the perfection of which his nature is capable, nor even make a remote and faint approach to it....He who gave our nature to be perfected by our virtue, willed also the necessary means of its perfection--He willed therefore the state--He willed its connexion with the source and original archetype of all perfection."

Also e.g., Bohoeffer, *Ethics*, III.1., final paragraph: "The term government does not imply any particular form of society or any particular form of state. Government is divinely ordained authority to exercise worldly dominion by divine right."

[84] Cf. Laplace, *A Philosophical Essay on Probabilities*, F. W. Truscott and F. L. Emory, trans. (1814, New York: Dover, 1951), 4: generalized, the human mind points to a superior intelligence "which would comprehend all the forces by which nature is animated and the respective situation of beings who compose it—and intelligence sufficiently vast to submit these data to analysis—it would embrace in the same formula the movement of the greatest bodies and the lightest atoms; for it, nothing would be uncertain and the future, as the past, would be present to its eyes."

Calhoun's conception goes further than that of Laplace not only because he speaks of the Creator but primarily because he sees that the omniscient superintendent has left perfection and hence freedom to depend in some part on human judgement coupled with volition and effort (*Disquisition*, para. 14).

Consider T. D. Weldon, *Introduction to Kant's Critique of Pure Reason*, (Oxford: Clarendon, 1958), 210: "The type of physical theory that Kant himself had underwritten in the Second Analogy forced philosophers to ask themselves how freedom could be squared not with divine but with potential human omniscience. The claim of Laplace to predict, in principle without limitation, all future states of the universe made "choice" and "activity," except in drastically redefined senses, words for which enlightened language could have no use." For Calhoun, in all future states of the universe as determined by Laplace government will remain the paramount human challenge and that which most vivifies and dignifies human choice and activity.

[85] Consider Cicero, *Republic*, III, 37 (Laelius:) "Do we not observe that dominion has been assigned by nature to the best in the interest of the weak? Why else does god rule man, the mind rule the body, reason rule desire and anger and the other vicious parts of the mind?..." *Laws*, I. 22-30., III. 2-3.15. Cf. also, Montesquieu, *The Spirit of the Laws*, I. 1, passim; I. 3 (para. 11). Cicero, *Republic*, I. 56, III. 33; *Laws*, I. 18, II. 11-12, 15-16; Aristotle, *Metaphysics*, xii. 9. 1074bff. With *Disquisition*, paras. 3, 7, 12, 14, 89, see Aristotle, *Historia Animalia*, 588b-599a; *Politics*, 1253a, 1332b; Plato, *Timaeus*, 90a-c.

[86] Aristotle, *Nichomachaean Ethics*, 1168 16-22; cf. *Politics*, iii. 6. 1278b25-30: "For there is perhaps something fine in living just by itself, provided there is no great excess of hardships. It is clear that most men will endure harsh treatment in their longing for life, the assumption being that there is a kind of enjoyment inherent in it and a natural sweetness." Cicero, *De Officiis*, i.11.

[87] Chap. 1, nn. 95-96 above. Cf. also, Marx to Engels (June 18, 1862): Darwinism "is Hobbes' *bellum omnium contra omnes*, and it is reminiscent of Hegel in the *Phenomenology*, where bourgeois society represents a spiritual animal kingdom, while for Darwin the animal kingdom represents bourgeois society." See the citations of Wilson at chap. 1, n. 26 above.

[88] Rousseau, *Letters Written from the Mountain* in *Oeuvres completes*, Bernard Gagnebin and Marcel Raymond, eds. (Paris: Gallimand: Bibliotheque de la Pleiade, 1959-), 3:808-809.

[89] Cf. Cicero, *Republic*, I. 12; also, I. 20 (Laelius to Manilius), and the discussion of astronomy in bk. I (xv-xxxiv), e.g., II. 45, beginning, III. 34, Scipio's *Dream*.

[90] The term "society" occurs three times and the term "state," used, uncharacteristically for Calhoun in the *Disquisition*, in the sense of the political whole, occurs for the first and only time in this section. The context in which it occurs makes it clear that in this instance the term "state" is used as synonymous with "community," including government, as it looks outward, as opposed to inward. Para. 17: "full command of the power and resources of the state"; "full command of the resources of the community." As we have noted, Calhoun does not distinguish between the "state" and "society" in the usual manner, but between the community and culture, on the one hand, and the social and political nature of man, on the other. See "On the Force Bill" (delivered in the Senate, February 15-16, 1833), *Works*, 2:229: "political existence of the state," "the sovereign community," "defence of the state." For the phrase "quantum of power," see e.g., "On the Oregon Bill" (delivered in the Senate, June 27, 1848), *Works*, 4:510. Calhoun takes the term from Burke's *Reflections*. Cf. Hegel, "Quantum," in *Science of Logic*, W. H. Johnston and L. G. Struthers, trans. (London: George Allen & Unwin, 1929), 217-332. In connection with what immediately follows in the text, see Machiavelli, *Prince*, chap. 15.

[91] "On the Force Bill" (delivered in the Senate, February 15-16, 1833), *Works*, 2:248-51.

[92] Plato, *Laws*, 832c; 714a-715d. Aristotle, *Politics*, 1278b6-14; 1279a25ff; 1289a11-20; 1283a26-29. Cicero, *Republic*, III, 43 end-45.

[93] Cf. J. S. Mill, *Principles of Political Economy* (London: Longmans, Green, People's Edition, 1966), v. i. 2. 482: "[T]he admitted functions of government embrace a much wider field than can easily be included within the ring or fence of any restrictive definition...it is hardly possible to find any ground of justification common to them all, except the comprehensive one of general expediency, nor to limit the interference of government by any universal rule, save the simple and vague one that it should never be admitted but when the case of expediency is strong."

[94] Cicero, *Republic*, i. 1. Cf. Locke, *Second Treatise on Government* in Peter Laslett, ed., *Two Treatises on Government* (Cambridge: Cambridge University Press, 1963), para. 134: "the first and fundamental natural law,...the preservation of society...." Burke, "On a Bill for the Relief of the Protestant Dissenters," *Works* (Beaconsfield), 7:44: "For as self preservation in individuals is the first law of Nature, the same will prevail in societies, who will, right or wrong, make that an object paramount to all other rights whatsoever." Calhoun, "On the

Care of McLeod" (delivered in the Senate, June 11, 1841), *Works*, 3:620: "The Laws of nations are but the Laws of morals, as applicable to individuals, so far modified, and no further, as reason may make necessary in their application to nations." Cf. "On the Loan Bill" (delivered in the House of Representatives, February 25, 1814), *Works*, 2:84: "Nations are, for the most part, not restrained by moral principles, but by fear. It is an old maxim that they have heads, but no hearts. They see their own interests, but they do not sympathize in the wrongs of others." A strong nation "can only be restrained by power."

95 Cf. Calhoun, "South Carolina Exposition" (December 1828), *Works*, 6:33, and context. Cf. Smith, *Theory of Moral Sentiments*, VI. II. ii. Locke, *Second Treatise on Government*, para. 6: in the "Community of Nature" "every one as he is bound to preserve himself, and not quit his Station wilfully; so by the like reason when his own Preservation comes not in competition, ought he, as much as he can, to preserve the rest of Mankind." Cf. Locke, *Second Treatise*, para. 229: "The end of Government is the good of Mankind, and which is best for Mankind...." Cf. Toynbee, *A Study of History*, 12 vols. (London: Oxford University Press, 1934 et seq.), 1:9ff: "unlike their articulations called states"; the "intelligible field of historical study," etc.; especially, 12:526-27, 536-37, 279.

96 "On the Bill to Set Aside the Bank Dividends," delivered in the House of Representatives, February 4, 1817, *Works*, 2:190; cf. p. 189: belief of "the most profound political philosophers." See, e.g., Aristotle, *Politics*, 1326a35-b7, and context; Montesquieu, *The Spirit of the Laws*, viii. 16.

97 Cf. Plutarch, "On the Fortune or Virtue of Alexander," *Moralia*, 329c:
> Zeno wrote an admirable *Republic*, based on the principle that men should not separate themselves off into cities and peoples each with its own particular laws, for all men are fellow-citizens, since they share a single life and a single cosmos. What Zeno had written as it were in a dream, Alexander brought into reality. He brought together, as it were in a mixing bowl, all the people of the earth; he commanded that they consider the cosmos their country, the army their acropolis, moral men their kin and bad men as aliens.

Kant, *Perpetual Peace: A Philosophic Sketch*: "law of world citizenship," etc. Cf. Calhoun, "On the Force Bill" (delivered in the Senate, February 15-16, 1833), *Works*, 2:242: "a...citizen of the world...would be a perfect nondescript..."

98 Kant, *Perpetual Peace: A Philosophic Sketch*, 113-14 (and context): "The idea of international right presupposes the separate existence of many independent adjoining states. And such a state of affairs is essentially a state of war, unless there is a federal union to prevent hostilities breaking out. But in the light of the idea of reason, this state is still to be preferred to an amalgamation of the separate nations under a single power which has overruled the rest and created a universal monarchy.... Thus nature wisely separates the nations...." According to Kant, nature "uses two means to separate the nations and prevent them from intermingling—linguistic and religious differences," which, however, failed to restrain Alexander. See Toynbee at n. 97 above; John Dewey, *Characters and Events: Essays in Social and Political Philosophy*, Joseph Rattner, ed. 2 vols. (New York: Henry Holt, 1929), 1:798-814. See the citations at chap. 1, n. 26 above.

99 Calhoun, "On the Loan Bill" (delivered in the House of Representatives, February 25, 1814), *Works*, 2:85-87, 89, 102; "On His Resolutions" (delivered in the Senate, February

26, 1833), *Works*, 2:303: "the peace of despotism…the peace of death, where all the vital functions of liberty have ceased." Cf. Kant's mention of the Dutch innkeeper's signboard depicting a graveyard: *Perpetual Peace*, first sentence; and 114: "that universal despotism which saps all men's energies and ends in the graveyard of freedom."

100 "On the Proposed Occupation of the Yucatan" (delivered in the Senate, May 15, 1848), *Works*, 4:472; "On the Oregon Bill," *Works*, 4:509, 511-12. *Disquisition*, para. 117. See "On His Resolutions with Reference to the War With Mexico" (delivered in the Senate, January 4, 1848), *Works*, 4:416: "it is a sad delusion"; *Disquisition*, para. 46: "delusive hope." Cf. Tocqueville, *The Old Regime and the French Revolution* (New York: Anchor Books, 1955), 146: "They gave the substance of reality to what our philosophies were only dreaming about" and context.

The most important speech of Calhoun in connection with this paragraph of the *Disquisition* in this regard is probably "On His Resolutions in Respect to the Brig Enterprise" (delivered in the Senate, March 13, 1840), *Works*, 3:462-87 passim.

101 Calhoun's list here is summary; see, e.g., "Reply to Mr. Webster on the Independent Treasury Bill" (delivered in the Senate, March 22, 1838), *Works*, 3:287: "distinguished by…soil, climate, situation, institutions, and productions." Cf. Hume, "On National Character," and Montesquieu on climate and national character; J. S. Mill, *Considerations on Representative Government*, chap. 16: "race and descent"; "language and religion"; "geographical limits"; "identity of political antecedents." Strauss, "On Aristotle's Politics," *The City and Man*, 15: "…climate, character of a territory, race, fauna, flora…"

102 Cf. *Federalist* 6: it has become "a sort of axiom in politics that vicinity, or nearness of situation, constitutes nations' natural enemies." Kant, *Perpetual Peace: A Philosophical Sketch*, 102, 105: "Peoples who have grouped themselves into nation states may be judged in the same way as individual men living in the state of nature, independent of external laws; for they are a standing offense to one another by the very fact that they are neighbors.…Just like individual men they must renounce their savage and lawless freedom, adapt themselves to public coercive laws, and thus form an international state *(civitas gentium)*, which would naturally grow…[into] a world republic."

As the world republic is now impossible, "this can at best find a negative substitute in the shape of an enduring and gradually expanding federation likely to prevent war."

103 Oswald Spengler, *The Hour of Decision*, C. F. Atkinson, trans. (New York: Alfred A. Knopf, 1934), 11, 34-35: "Human history in the period of the high cultures is the history of political forces. The form of this history is war. But peace is also part of it, for it is the continuation of war with different means—the attempt of the vanquished to shake off the consequences of the war in the shape of treaties, the attempt of the victor to maintain them.… Internal politics exist only to secure the strength and unity of external politics.…" Cf. Carl Schmitt, *The Concept of the Political*, George Schwab, trans. (New Brunswick: Rutgers University Press, 1976), 30-37 (the translator cites Clausewitz). Hobbes, *Leviathan*, chap. 13.

Cf. Heraclitus (frag. 52): "War is the beginning/rule of all things…"

104 "The law of nations is composed, principally, of usages originating in mutual advantages." "On the Loan Bill" (delivered in the House of Representatives, February 25, 1814), *Works*, 2:76-77; cf. 86 (of international law courts): "…one of the principal

ornaments of the civilization of modern times," "international law," "free trade." See Richard Cox, *Locke on War and Peace* (Oxford: Clarendon Press, 1960). Hegel, *Philosophy of Right*, para. 324ff. Cf. Montesquieu, *The Spirit of the Laws*, I. 3: "law of nations"; Aristotle, *Politics*, iii. 9. 1280a30-1281a10; vii. 7. 1327b20-33.

105 Calhoun briefly discusses the Twelve Tribes of Israel with regard to the consequences of tax policy, e.g., in his speech "On the Force Bill" (delivered in the Senate, February 15-16, 1833), *Works*, 2:244-45. His study of the Hebrews focused primarily on Samuel and the Davidic dynasty, the priesthoods of Shiloh and Hebron, and ultimately, on the secession of the Northern tribes from the pharaonical Solomonic kingdom in the time of Rehoboam and Jeroboam. So far as I am aware, the best or most complete kind of Calhounian study of these subjects now available are Bernard Halpern, *The Constitution of the Monarchy of Israel* (Harvard Semitic Monographs: Decatur, Ga.: Scholars Press, 1981), and "Sectionalism and the Schism," *Journal of Biblical Literature* 93 (1974): 519-32. Secondarily, his study concerned the secession of the the followers of Moses from Egypt and the influence of the latter on the former, as similar to the influence of the Greeks on the Romans or of Great Britain on the United States. He perhaps considered the kingdom and priesthood of Israel a case of former parts of constitutional regimes adopting a similar form of government (*Disquisition*, para. 66, end). Contrast Coit, *John C. Calhoun*, 396-97.

106 Consider in this connection Confucius, *Analects*, First Analect.

107 Cf. Hume, "Of the Rise and Progress of the Arts and Sciences," in *Works*, 3:176-77, etc. Consult Hegel, *Lectures on the Philosophy of History*, ad init: China, Egypt, India; Voegelin, *Israel and Revelation*, vol. I of *Order and History* (Baton Rouge: Louisiana State University Press, 1956): "China," "Egypt," India," "cosmological empires"; cf. Marx, *Capital* vol 3, the way of the orient.

108 Perhaps Whitehead does not quite know what he means when he says, first, "China and India long ago attained to types of life with more aesthetic and philosophic appreciations, in some respects, than our Western type. But they reached a level and stayed there…[yet p]olitical stability is not the point," and, then, "care should be taken to avoid the indiscriminate extension of European legal ideas into a social life to which they are alien….A sensitive response to the real facts of the life around is required. The simplicities of abstract thought must be shunned. These warnings are commonplace. Unfortunately they are required." "An Appeal to Sanity," *Essays on Science and Philosophy*, 51, 58. For Calhoun, political stability is the most important of the real facts of the life around and must be the first point emphasized in any appeal to "sanity." Cf. Plato, *Laws*, 634d7-e4, 757d-e, 875a-d5; Aristotle, *Politics*, 1269a15ff, and related passages (Bk. 5).

109 Smith, *Wealth of Nations*, vol. 1, chap. 3, penultimate paragraph: "It is remarkable that neither the ancient Egyptians, nor the Indians, nor the Chinese, encouraged foreign commerce, but all seem to have derived their great opulence from…inland navigation." All the examples here cited by Calhoun shared this "Hebraism." Cf. Plato, *Laws*, X: "strangers."

110 Tocqueville, *The Old Regime and the French Revolution*, 163-64. See Joseph Needham, "Review of Karl A. Wittfogel, *Oriental Despotism*," *Science and Society* (1958): 61ff: "the emperors were served in all ages by a great company of profoundly humane and disinterested scholars." Cf. Joseph R. Levinson, *Modern China and Its Confucian Past: The*

Problem of Intellectual Continuity (Garden City, N.Y.: Anchor Books, 1964), 59ff, and *Confucian China and Its Modern Fate* 3 vols (London: 1958-1965).

Calhoun, in the speech "On his Resolution in respect to the Brig Enterprise" (delivered in the Senate, March 13, 1840) *Works*, 3:483, said of China "Let me add to her other claims to respect and veneration, that, of all despotic governments, it seems to me (judging from the scanty evidence we have of a people so secluded), it is the wisest and most parental."

111 "It is certainly difficult for a European to realize how long-established in China were practices [of administrative organization and communications] that in the West we associate mainly with the modern age." Otto Van Der Sprenkel, "Max Weber on China," in *Studies in the Philosophy of History*, G. H. Nadel, ed. (New York: Harper Torchbooks, 1965), 207. Certainly, Calhoun held that suffering despotism was a worse evil. He distinguished between just and unjust wars, although not primarily on the lines laid down by Suarez. See "On the Bill to Encourage Enlistments" (delivered in the House of Representatives, January 17, 1814), *Works*, 2:57-58: "I will lay it down as a universal criterion that a war is offensive or defensive not by the mode of carrying it on, which is an immaterial circumstance, but by the motive and cause which lead to it. If it has its origin in ambition, avarice, or any of the like passions, then it is offensive; but if, on the contrary, designed to repel insult, injury, or oppression, it is of an opposite character, and is defensive....the difference between an offensive and a defensive war is of the moral kind." Cf. Plato, *Laws*, 628d-e; also, John Kautsky, *The Politics of Aristocratic Empires* (Chapel Hill: University of North Carolina Press, 1982), 144 ff. The conditions of war often vitiate the aims for which it is fought. Calhoun, "On the Resolutions Giving Notice to Great Britain" (delivered in the Senate, March 16, 1846), *Works*, 4:287: "great and free."

Chapter 3

---

[1] Daniel Webster, "Eulogy of Calhoun," from *Obituary Addresses* (Washington, D.C.: John T. Towers, 1850), quoted in Margaret Coit, *John C. Calhoun*, "Great Lives Observed Series" (Englewood Cliffs, N.J.: Prentice-Hall, 1970), 92-94. One must turn to Ben Jonson's praise of Shakespeare in the First Folio of 1623 for a comparably generous tribute in English from a contemporary and rival like Webster's summary on Calhoun. The complete passage runs as follows:

> Mr. Calhoun was calculated to be a leader in whatsoever association of political friends he was thrown. He was a man of undoubted genius, and of commanding talent. All the country and all the world admit that.... His demeanor as a Senator is well known to us all — is appreciated, is venerated by us all. No man was more respectful to others; no man carried himself with greater decorum, no man with superior dignity. I think there is not one of us but felt when he last addressed us from his seat in the Senate, his form still erect, with a voice by no means indicating such a degree of physical weakness as did, in fact, possess him, with clear tones, and impressive, and I may say, an imposing manner, who did not feel that he might imagine that he saw before us a Senator of Rome when Rome survived.... He is now an historical character. Those of us who have known him here will find that he has left upon our minds and our hearts a strong and lasting impression of his person, his character, and his public performances, which, while we live, will never be obliterated. We shall hereafter, I am sure, indulge in it as a grateful recollection that we have lived in his age, that we have been his contemporaries, that we have seen him, and heard him, and known him. We shall delight to speak of him to those who are rising up to fill our places. And, when the time has come for us to go, one after another, in succession, to our graves, we shall carry with us a deep sense of his genius and character, his honor and integrity, his amiable deportment in private life, and the purity of his exalted patriotism.

Regarding Webster's reference to Rome, consult the chapter on "Roman Virtue" in Howard Mumford Jones, *O Strange New World* (Cambridge, Mass., 1970); M. E. Bradford, "A Teaching for Republicans: Roman History and the Nation's First Identity" in *A Better Guide Than Reason: Studies in the American Revolution* (LaSalle, Ill., 1979), 3-27, and *"Romanitas* in Southern Literature" in *Generations of the Faithful Heart: On the Literature of the Old South* (LaSalle, Ill., 1983), 17-28; and, for the Founding period in particular, M. N. S. Sellers, *American Republicanism: Roman Ideology in the United States Constitution* (New York, 1995).

[2] "Address on the Relations of the States and Federal Government" (July 26, 1831), in *The Works of John C. Calhoun*, Richard K. Cralle, ed., 6 vols. (Charleston, S.C.: 1851-1856), 6:62-63: "It has been said by one of the most sagacious men of antiquity that the object of a constitution is to restrain the government, as that of the laws is to restrain individuals. The remark is correct; nor is it less true where the government is vested in a majority than when it is vested in a single or a few individuals — in a republic, rather than a monarchy or aristocracy."

Cf. also, James Monroe, *The People the Sovereigns, Being a Comparison of the Government of the United States with Those of the Republics which Have Existed before, with the Causes of Their Decadence and Fall*, 7-8, 10-13, 17-18: "That the government [the law-making, judicial, and executive powers, as constituted] be separated from the sovereignty [the constitution or constitution-making power itself]" is the "first," "fundamental and invariable" principle of government"; and Rousseau, *The Social Contract and Discourses*, translated by G. D. H. Cole (London: Dent, 1913), III, xv, passim.

³ See "On the Oregon Bill" (July 27, 1848), *Works*, 4:507-512: "...Locke and Sydney...." Cf. especially Monroe, *The People the Sovereigns*, 61: "His refutation of the work of Filmer..."; "...to refute the doctrine of Filmer..."; and Calhoun, "Letter to the Honorable William Smith on the Rhode Island Controversy" (July 3, 1843),*Works*, 6:229-32: "Sir Robert Filmer...and...Locke and Sydney"; also, "Address to the People of South Carolina" (1831), *Works*, 138-39: "right to govern."

⁴ See chap. 5, n. 1 below. Cf. Carl Schmitt, who is unaware of Calhoun, *The Crisis of Parliamentary Democracy*, Ellen Kennedy, trans. (Cambridge: MIT Press, 1985), 2:

> Whoever wants to find out what [the characteristic ideas of parliamentarianism] are will be forced to return to Burke, Bentham, Guizot, and John Stuart Mill. He will then be forced to admit that after them, since about 1848, there have certainly been many new practical considerations but no new principled arguments.... Therefore one has to concern oneself with those "mouldy" greats...because what is specific to parliamentarianism can only be gleaned from their thought, and only there does parliament retain the particular character of a specially founded institution that can demonstrate its intellectual superiority to direct democracy as well as Bolshevism and Fascism.

⁵ The following descriptions and citations are drawn from "Review, Historical and Critical, of Social Philosophy," Freeman Hunt's *Merchant's Magazine and Commercial Review*, no. 5, 545, 554-55 and context; and no. 6, 659ff., and context. The author of this review of all political philosophy up to the mid-nineteenth century and the emergence of sociology is not named in these numbers. According to the author, the "first" or "modern" class of social philosophy, which emphasizes security and individual rights, includes, among others, Machiavelli, Milton, Locke (especially), according to whom the majority have rights over against the prince, Montesquieu ("the most masterly"), Rousseau ("an elongation of Locke," but more "abstract or ideal"), Thomas Paine, Alexander Hamilton and the *Federalist*, Jefferson, Tocqueville, and finally Calhoun, who completes or perfects the class and stands for it. Montesquieu and Tocqueville are seen to be somewhat problematic as "exponents" of this class; all are discussed at relative length. According to the moderns, the end of government is to make men free. The "second" or "ancient" class, which emphasizes virtue, includes, presumably among many who are not named, only Plato and Aristotle. "In short, the grand end of government, according to Aristotle, is *to make men virtuous*," "Review, Historical and Critical, of Social Philosophy," *Merchant's Magazine and Commercial Review*, no. 6, 663 (emphasis original).

The aim of the ten-part survey as a whole, which is an interpretation of all thought to the present, is stated in the eighth part: "the very aim of the present undertaking...is to condense what has already been stated at large, to compress sermons into texts, volumes into paragraphs, and to *express*, as it were, in a literal sense, the very *marrow*, or *most interior existence*, of all that is valuable, either in the speculation or the practice of former times, and of the various races of men, in relation to the philosophy and science of human society" (no. 3, 277, emphasis original).

6 The modern school begins properly with Machiavelli's *Il Principe* and his "valuable historical contributions," but the author asserts that the *Discourses on Livy* is his greatest work. "Yet even in this work it appears manifest that Machiavelli took a very unfavorable view of human nature, and held mankind in a rather low estimation." There is also in Machiavelli "too prominently an appeal to the fears" of man. The writer takes the *Prince* as standing for Hobbes' *Leviathan* and slights Hobbes in favor of Locke. Locke's "essay on Civil Government...[may be taken as] the great representative work, if not the parent work, of a more exhaustive class of political disquisitions and speculations than has appeared in this or any age." Withal, apart from those already mentioned, the author deals with Newton, Descartes, Leibnitz, Condillac, Humbolt, Schelling, Guizot, and others, but above all, with Bacon: "No two minds, perhaps, scarcely excepting that of Confucius, have ever exerted a greater or more lasting influence on the direction and character of human thought than Aristotle and Bacon" (no. 3, 291).

7 "Review, Historical and Critical, of Social Philosophy," *Merchant's Magazine and Commercial Review*, no. 5, 555, emphasis original. The *Disquisition* "may be briefly characterized as a powerful reaction, springing up in the heart of the [Lockean] spirit of the age, against *the idea that the majority have the unlimited right to rule the minority*." The sociologist is thus inspired by the *Disquisition* in the same manner as Mill in the *Considerations on Representative Government*. The writer understands and admits that this is not Calhoun's own characterization of the work: "It is true that his aim is somewhat differently and more comprehensively stated by him. Thus, he informs us in one place that the grand aim of society should be 'a government so constituted as to suppress the expansion of all partial and selfish interests, and to give a faithful utterance to the sense of the whole community in reference to its common welfare' — an end almost as impracticable as that aimed at by Rousseau, yet surely desirable."

The historian does not consider it, yet it is this "more comprehensive" view of Calhoun that we are trying to understand. (In regard to the "Review's" characterization of the Lockean "spirit of the age," see Willmoore Kendall, *John Locke and the Doctrine of Majority Rule* [Urbana: University of Illinois Press, 1965], 68ff., 132ff.).

8 "Review, Historical and Critical, of Social Philosophy," *Merchant's Magazine and Commercial Review* no. 6, 659, 661, all emphases omitted. The author continues with a half-page of Platonic desiderata, concluding as follows: "[L]lastly, though not leastly, if not primarily and of paramount importance, the strictest attention should be paid to the laws of genealogy and population; to the former, by means of judicious crosses, with a view to the production of the noblest offspring; to the latter, by means of encouraging or restraining marriages, with a view to maintaining a just equilibrium of numbers in the community, so that the population may be neither too small nor too large" (662).

Cf. Ernest G. McClain, *The Pythagorean Plato: Prelude to the Song Itself* (York Beach: Nicholas-Hap, Inc., 1978), 17ff.

9 E.g., Hegel, *Philosophy of Right*, para. 261A.

¹⁰ See Calhoun, "On the Veto Power" (delivered in the Senate, February 28, 1842), *Works*, 4:83, on the formation of constitutional government:

> There is but one way in which it can possibly be accomplished; and that is by a judicious and wise division and organization of the Government and community, with reference to its great and conflicting interests,—and by taking the sense of each part separately, and the concurrence of all as the voice of the whole.... But on what principle is such a division and organization to be made to effect this great object, without which it is impossible to preserve free and popular institutions? To this no general answer can be given. It is the work of the wise and experienced [*Disquisition* 18: "wise and good," "wisdom and skill," "consummate wisdom and skill"],—having full and perfect knowledge of the country and the people, in every particular—for whom the Government is intended. It must be made to fit; and when it does, it will fit no other, and will be incapable of being imitated or borrowed.

¹¹ Hippodamus is referred to by Karl Popper as the first "social engineer" (*The Open Society and Its Enemies* 2 vols. [London: Routledge & Kegan Paul, 1962], 1:210-211: "As the first social engineer one might describe Hippodamus of Miletus," citing *The Poverty of Historicism*, pt. 3. Popper traces the term "social engineering" to Roscoe Pound, although he notes that some say it was originated by the Fabians a little before Pound. See *The Open Society*, chap. 9: "utopian social engineering.") Hippodamus is repeatedly praised by Professor Pound in several law review articles, including *Harvard Law Review* 57/1, 57/10 (1943); "Individual Interests of Substance—Promised Advantages," *Harvard Law Review* 59/1, 59/11 (1945); and "The Role of Will in Law," *Harvard Law Review* 68/1 (1954). According to Popper, the term "social engineering" was introduced into English, or at any rate American, by Professor Pound in his *An Introduction to the Philosophy of Law* (New Haven: Yale University Press, 1922), 99. Cf. Edwin L. Earp, The Social Engineer (New York: Eaton and Maine, 1911). The term "social control" was introduced in Edward A. Ross, *Social Control: A Survey of the Foundations of Social Order* (New York, 1901), as an item of sociology. The emergence of these and similar terms are characteristic of the eclipse of Calhounism following the 1860s.

All of substance that is known of Hippodamus today is drawn from the second book of Aristotle's *Politics* and the presentation of him in Aristophanes' *Knights*. See John C. Hogan, *Hippodamus on the Best Form of Government and Law* (Santa Monica, Calif.: The Rand Foundation, n.d.), who outlines the attention of Pound. Most discussions of Hippodamus have focused on such questions as whether he may or may not have been a Pythagorean or a Sophist, and whether or not Aristotle is fair to Hippodamus in his presentation of Hippodamus' perfect community or regime. See Franz Susemihl and R. D. Hicks, *The Politics of Aristotle*, and, also, Kathleen Freeman, *The Pre-Socratic Philosophers* (Oxford: Oxford University Press), 211ff. So far as I know, none of the discussants have defended Hippodamus' proposal as actually representing the best regime for man or the regime most according to nature. The supposed textual problemata in the *Politics* mentioned by some are, I believe, merely apparent and arise from failure to follow Aristotle's somewhat uncharacteristic presentation.

¹² Aristotle obviously does not mean either that Hippodamus was the first city planner or the first man to speculate on these things. Such speculation is evident in the whole edifice of the ancient Egyptian temple cities and tomb monuments, e.g., where, as Hippodamus' association of architecture or engineering and astronomy perhaps suggests, he may have gotten some of his ideas (cf. Herodotus, *Histories, I:*"Thales," "Solon," "Pythagoras.").

¹³ E.g., among others, Demosthenes, "Against Timocrates," 192: "There are two sorts of problems, men of Athens, with which the laws of all peoples are concerned. First, what are the principles which we associate with one another, have dealings with one another, define the obligations of private life, and, in general, order our relations? Secondly, what are the duties that every man among us owes to the polity, if he chooses to take part in public life and professes any concern for the city?"

¹⁴ Murray N. Rothbard, "The Anatomy of the State" in *Egalitarianism as a Revolt Against Nature, and Other Essays* (Washington, D.C.: Libertarian Review Press, 1974), 43-48. Professor Rothbard is described in the foreword as a "free market anarchist social philosopher," that is, a Lockean who wishes to out-Locke Locke. At the opposite extreme of this kind of thing one would find, say, Bakuninism.

¹⁵ Professor Rothbard's discussion turns on Charles L. Black, *The People and the Court* (New York: Macmillan, 1970), 35ff., on Calhoun and the role of the Supreme Court in the passage of the New Deal; J. Allen Smith, *The Growth and Decadence of Constitutional Government* (New York: Henry Holt and Co., 1930), 87-88, and Calhoun. The discussion of the *Disquisition* represents the peak of the essay.

¹⁶ A "consistent theory of concurrence would imply veto power by every individual, i.e., some form of 'unanimity principle.' When Calhoun wrote that it should be 'impossible to put or to keep it [the government] in action without the concurrent consent of all,' he was, perhaps unwittingly, implying just such a conclusion. But such speculation begins to take us away from our subject, for down this path lie political systems that could hardly be called 'states' at all" (citing Herbert Spencer, *The Right to Ignore the State*), "Anatomy of the State," 48. We may merely note that Calhoun was sufficiently aware of the reach of his argument that he devoted two paragraphs of the *Disquisition* to the example of the constitution of Poland, which Professor Rothbard does not notice. According to the "Review, Historical and Critical, of Social Philosophy" (*Merchant's Magazine and Commercial Review* no. 5, 554): "In short, Mr. Calhoun would have a government organized somewhat after the plan of the Polish Diet, where every nobleman had a veto on all the rest, or of a jury where each juryman has the same power, and unanimity is necessary to a decision. He admits, however, that this would be carrying the principle rather too far...." (Calhoun does not make this "admission," rather Professor Rothbard has used the *Disquisition* for predetermined purposes.

¹⁷ Professor Rothbard writes, "just as the right of nullification for a state logically implies its right of secession, so a right of individual nullification would imply the right of any individual to "secede" from the state under which he lives. (Calhoun nowhere denies the right of citizens to immigrate.) The end of all this kind of Lockean argument is shown in Professor Joseph Leondar Schneider's "Transcendental Nullification: The Unity of

Thoreau's 'Civil Disobedience' and Calhoun's 'Exposition and Protest'," (Duke University, 1964, Unpublished papers).

[18] Nn. 12-13 above. As has been indicated, the author of the "Review, Historical and Critical, of Social Philosophy" denominates Calhoun as "a powerful reaction springing up in the very heart of the great democratic spirit of the age," and hence as the polar reaction or diametrical opposite to Locke, although he does not use these terms (*Merchant's Magazine and Commercial Review* no. 5, 554, 545). (According to the author, Locke is the great "conservative" side of this school, while Rousseau is the great "radical.") However, he had already written that "[t]he principles of Locke's 'Essay on Government' are diametrically opposed, in most respects, to those of Machiavelli's *Prince*, or are developed from a diametrically opposed standpoint" (542). The author most associates Calhoun's own aim with the aim of Rousseau, although, when he does so, he does not call it "radical." This confusion is not cleared up in the article, with the result that the treatment of Calhoun most closely resembles that of "the justly celebrated" Montesquieu. After a (relatively) lengthy critique, the author, who apparently cannot figure out to whom Montesquieu is most diametrically opposed, decides that Montesquieu had only a vague idea "of the legitimate ends of government." It should be observed that when he asks the question about partitioning the community, it is possible that he means no more than the question: "should there be something more than a house of representatives, a senate, a president, and a judiciary department?" (554-55).

[19] Smith begins the fourth book of the Inquiry into the *Wealth of Nations* by defining political economy as "a branch of the science of a statesman or legislator," which is how Calhoun understood it. In the fifth book, Smith confirms that "civil government, so far as it is instituted for the security of property, is in reality instituted for the defence [sic] of the rich against the poor, or those who have some property against those who have none at all," which is what Marx wished to overcome. The accumulation of property does not exhaust the ends of man, according to Smith, but its protection is the primary aim of the state. For Professor Rothbard, just as for Marx, "the State is born of conquest and exploitation," i.e., in the attempt of parasites and robbers to seize the property of others. It is in this way that private property occasions the emergence of the State.

"The State provides a legal, orderly, systematic channel for the predation of private property" (ibid., 37). Both agree that "ideology" is what sustains this predation, and both desire the withering away of the government. The difference is that for Marx (as for Calhoun) the "individual" without society is a fiction, and for Rothbard, the "public sector" is a fiction ("illusion").

[20] Cf. Garry Wills, "The Convenient State" in *What is Conservatism*, Frank S. Meyer, ed. (New York: Holt, Rinehardt and Winston, 1964), chap. 9, 152ff.: "Calhoun's maxim" and newly-emerging nations in the Third World. Cf. Irving Kristol, "'Moral Dilemmas' in Foreign Policy," *Wall Street Journal*, February 28, 1980: "It is the fundamental fallacy of American policy to believe, in the face of the evidence, that all peoples, everywhere, are immediately 'entitled' to a liberal constitutional government—and a thoroughly democratic one at that." Professor Kristol traces this fundamental fallacy to the thought and policies of Woodrow Wilson, former president of the American Political Science and Historical

Associations. Before Wilson, according to Kristol, thinking was moored "in the real world." *Disquisition*, para. 86.

21 See chap. 1, n. 82 above. The *Discourse* has its own introduction (111-112) and its own conclusion (400-406), neither of which make any reference to the *Disquisition*. What would represent the concluding section of exemplary constitutions presented in the *Disquisition* is presented in the *Discourse* not immediately but only in a relatively late section and without reference to the *Disquisition*. Cf. *Disquisition*, paras. 142: "It is well known, to the least conversant with their history, that the Roman people..."; para. 151: "The origin and character of the British government are so well known that a very brief sketch..."; *Discourse*, 188-89: "It is known to all, in any degree familiar with our history, that the region embraced by the original States of the Union.... It is also known...." These comments follow paragraphs beginning, "I have now established...," and "I have already shown...," which begin the section (187-188).

22 Cf., e.g., the relevant passages in August O. Spain, *The Political Theory of John Calhoun* (New York: Bookman Associates, 1951).

23 Montesquieu, *Spirit of the Laws*, XI, chap. 13.

24 Montesquieu's *Considerations on the Grandeur of the Romans and Their Decadence*, which contains a comparison and critique of Great Britain, presents Rome more in the light of the Senate and the end of the Republic in light of the superannuation of the Senate (e.g., *Romans*, IX, para. 4). See also *Romans*, I, paras. 15-16; IV: "Carthage," "commercial powers"; VIII end; X, last para., and related passages.

25 Consult Livy, *Annals* IV.iii. 4-5 and context; R. Syme, *Tacitus* 2 vols. (Oxford: Oxford University Press, 1958), 1:317-19.

26See A. dell'Oro, *La formazione dello stato patrizio-plebe* (Milan-Varese, 1950). Cf. Cicero, *Republic*, ii.37.

27 See Livy, *Annals*, iii.48ff; Macaulay, "Virginia"; cf. Machiavelli, *Discourses on Livy*, III,5; 26, and related passages.

28 Cf., Machiavelli, *Discourses*, I, chap. iii, end; *Disquisition*, paras. 142, 125, 129. Shakespeare, *Rape of Lucrece*.

29 Livy, *Annals*, II.23ff., and context. Some scholars have doubted the factual authenticity of the story itself, believing that the author invented or embellished it "in place of a political essay." Others question Livy's dates for the original *tribini plebis*. Livy places the plebeian secession in the fifteenth year of the republic, less than half a generation after the expulsion of the Tarquins. Calhoun follows closely, if inimitably, the argument of Machiavelli in the Polybian introduction of the *Discourses on Livy*, I, chaps. ii-iii, iv-vi: "tribunes of the people"; and related passages. Calhoun omits, as does Livy, the forgiveness of plebeian debts included in the compromise.

30 Cf. Livy on the patrician Caius Marcius Coriolanus in this context, Plutarch, "Life of Coriolanus," and Shakespeare, *Coriolanus*. The general Coriolanus is reminiscent of Lucrece, and the opposite of Livy's old centurion.

31 Where Calhoun refers to "a superficial observer" (para. 147), Machiavelli refers to "whoever will carefully examine the result...," *Discourses*, I.iv. Calhoun has referred to superficial observers once before (para. 101), in connection with Polybius and the united strength and energy of the whole in the hour of danger. See the text at chap. 5, n. 6 below.

[32] Polybius, I.5-6ff.

[33] Montesquieu, *Romans*, IX, para. 11.

[34] Polybius (VI.50.3) implies in this connection that at least to some extent expansionist imperialism is a matter of choice rather than necessity. According to Machiavelli (*Discourses*, I.ii.6), imperialism is necessary.

[35] Cf. the two causes discussed in Montesquieu, *Romans*, chap. IX.

[36] Montesquieu, *Spirit of the Laws*, XI.17; cf. 19, first para.: "Such was the distribution of the three powers in Rome. But they were far from being thus distributed in the provinces. Liberty prevailed in the center and tyranny at the extreme parts."

[37] E.g., Remarks "On the Proposition to Establish Territorial Governments in New Mexico and California" (in the Senate, February 24, 1849), *Works*, 4:535-41; remarks "On the Ten Regiment Bill" (in the Senate, March 17, 1848), *Works*, 4:439-50. The theme is consistent throughout Calhoun's speeches.

[38] In tracing the decline of the republic to the decline of the tribunate after the Gracchi, Rousseau mistakes the effect for the cause (*Social Contract*, III, v, paras. 5-8). As a result, his recommendations will not reach the issue. Calhoun implicitly follows or agrees with Cicero, *Republic*, III.35,41: the violations of the treaties with foreign peoples; IV.7; *Laws*, III.9,17; *Offices*, II.27. As has been observed by Marshall Hammond, it is noteworthy that, "Tiberius and Gaius Gracchus [were] the two sons of an upright senator who had distinguished himself by what was rare at the time, honorable dealings with the Spanish barbarians against whom the Romans had been conducting intermittent warfare for nearly a century and whom they treated with the same disregard for honor that the white men displayed toward the Indians in the New World" (*City State and World State in Greek and Roman Political Theory until Augustus* [Cambridge: Howard University Press, 1957], 83).

This point is not incidental but central. See James Mill, *An Essay on Government* (1819, London, 1955), 60-61: "...the ruling *one or* the ruling few would, if checks did not operate in the way of prevention, reduce the great mass of the people subject to their power at least to the condition of Negroes in the West Indies."

[39] Calhoun to Vandeventer, March 24, 1833, quoted in *The Essential Calhoun*, 47: "It is not in the power of any single or few individuals to preserve liberty. It can only be affected by the people themselves, by their intelligence, virtue, courage, and patriotism."

[40] Cf. Polybius, xi. 2. 1-11; xxx. 7. 2ff.

[41] Machiavelli, *Discourses*, I, 33, 52. The uncertainty of Octavian was easy to foresee, and was foreseen. "The army" to which Machiavelli refers was Octavian's army, in the absence of a Senatorial army from Brutus or Cassius. What was more difficult to foresee was the deaths of the Consuls Hirtius and Pansa in the complete defeat of Antony's legions at Modena, while Antony himself survived. Cicero remarked that, if it was necessary to kill Caesar, then the liberators should have killed Antony at the same time as Caesar to finish what was begun. (Cf. also, *Offices*, I.76.) Later Imperial writers, Plutarch, Appian, and Dion Cassius, also write against Cicero (long after his death under a ban of silence as an enemy of the state). Montesquieu speaks of the tragedy of the abandoned republic toward the end of the chapter. See Montesquieu, *Considerations on the Causes of the Greatness of the Romans and Their Decline*, David Lowenthal, trans. (Ithaca, N.Y.: Cornell University Press, 1968), 116, translator's note. Rousseau speaks of the need for foresight and

of the love of glory as opposed to the love of country in the critique given in the chapter of the *Social Contract* on "Dictatorship," which follows that on "Tribuneship."

⁴² Admittedly, Machiavelli's view is not so clear as it might appear, especially in connection with Cicero. Setting aside Ciceronian inspiration of the so-called "Renaissance Man," that is, the true or complete human being, one may wonder, for example, what extent Locke's view of Cicero as one of the few "truly great men" sheds light on his distance from Hobbes, who was primarily critical of Cicero, except (like Rousseau), on rhetorical topics. In Marx's opinion, which is perhaps less than authoritative on the subject, "Cicero knew as little about philosophy as the president of the United States of America" ("Notebooks on Epicurean Philosophy"); cf. Bentham at chap. 1, n. 39 above; chap. 2, n. 71 above.

⁴³ Cf. Livy, *Annals*, I. viii, 4: the city walls were originally made wider than necessary "in the hope of a greater multitude to come"; cf. Montesquieu, *Romans*, III, end; VIII first sentence. Plutarch, "Life of Marcus Cato," 1ff., Pliny, *Natural History*, XXIV, i. 1; *Dio Cassius*, LX. xvii. 5; Seneca, *Apokolokyntosis*, III; Tacitus, *Annals*, I. XI. xxiii; n. 35, supra. See also, Mark Hulliung, *Montesquieu and the Old Regime* (Berkeley: University of California Press, 1976), 160-61.

⁴⁴ Cf. Cicero, *Laws*, III. iii. 9; Livy, II. xviii. 30, III. xx. 8; and related passages; Polybius, III. 86-87; Machiavelli, *Discourses*, I, xxxiii, xlix. Cf. *Disquisition*, para. 85. Plutarch, *Roman Questions* lxxxi: "The tribunes do not cease from their functions when a dictator is chosen, but although he transfers every other office to himself, the tribunes alone remain, not as being officials but as holding some other position."

⁴⁵ Cf. Montesquieu, *Spirit of the Laws*, IX.19: Rome and Sparta; cf. VIII.16: "it is natural to a republic to have only a small territory"; with IX.11: "If a republic is small, it is destroyed by a foreign power, if it be large, it is destroyed by an internal imperfection. Consequently, a monarchy is better." *Disquisition*, para. 130.

⁴⁶ C f. Montesquieu, *Romans*, VIII, toward the end: "censorship"; Rousseau, *Social Contract*, IV.vii: "The Censorship."

⁴⁷ His model is Odysseus (XII. 27). Cf. e.g., *Histories*, III. 4. 7-8; IX. 20. 5-6: "motion," useful to future readers, I. 2. 6, III. 6. 1, and context: "causes," "most true explanation"; Thucydides I. i: "motion"; future readers, I. 23. "causes," "most true explanation." F. W. Walbank's interpretation and reconstruction are questionable, e.g. *A Historical Commentary on Polybius* (Oxford: Calrendon Press, 1957), 1:727. The interpretation of Polybius is admittedly difficult because so much of the original is lost. The best introduction is Kenneth Sacks, *Polybius on the Writing of History* (Berkeley: University of California Press, 1981); cf. Leonard Dean, "Sir Francis Bacon's Theory of Civil History-Writing," *ELH*, VIII (1941), 161-83: "Polybius."

⁴⁸ Polybius, I. 1. 5-6, 2. 7., 4. 1; III. i. 4, 9; 2. 6, 3. 9, 4. 2, 118. 9; VI. 2. 3 and related passages; VIII. 2. 3; XXXIX. 8. 7; on Sparta, VI. 10, 50. 3-4, 6: balance of power, equilibrium, "*kata ton tes antipathias logon*"; the future, VI. 3. 1-4 with 9-14; 57. Montesquieu, *Romans*, V: "the war they waged with Antiochus..."; VI "universal conquest..."; IX: second para.

We may note that these remarks by Polybius, as well as many other ancient writings we have cited, are sufficient to show that the checks-and-balances view of political organism, the view with which Calhoun is (rightly) most associated, and that is now associated above all with Newtonian natural science, does not depend in any fundamental way on Newtonianism, and still less on those political schools attempting to build directly upon Newtonianism, or Hobbesianism.

⁴⁹ Cf. Voegelin, *Order and History*, vol. 4, *The Ecumenic Age* (Baton Rouge: Louisiana State University Press, 1974), 122 (the title of the volume is drawn from Polybius): Polybius "lays down the principle that the object of the study has to emerge as self-apparent from the ideas themselves. (That is the very principle which in its general form—that the order of history emerges from the history of order—is employed throughout [the five volumes] of the present study.)" The differences in agreement Voegelin notes in regard to Polybius ultimately turn on the questionable understanding of the Polybian *somatoiedes* as referring essentially to "chance" and "history" instead of to the matter constitution and empire in the *Histories*. History is perhaps more than the history of experience, and even than the awareness of experience. Cf. also, Toynbee, *A Study of History*, 10:233: Polybius' vision "has been my own principle inducement and stimulus in the work which I have undertaken." Constitution is not central for Toynbee. According to Toynbee's Polybius: "the coincidence by which all the transactions of the world have been oriented in a single direction and guided towards a single goal is the extraordinary characteristic of the present age" (Toynbee, trans.). The specific coincidence in question is that of the strength of the Republican constitution in the face of "the laws of fortune on a grand scale." This is here Calhoun's primary concern. Cf., H. Strasberger, "Posidonius on the Problems of the Roman Empire," *Journal of Roman Studies* 55 (1965): 40ff.

⁵⁰ Louis Hartz, *Liberalism in America*, 162: "When Locke accepted majority rule, he was more pessemistic than Calhoun, the great pessimist, would permit himself to be." Calhoun is only a pragmatic pessimistic or skeptic.

⁵¹ Montesquieu, *Romans*, IX: "Sulla"; XI: "Sulla"; XIII: comparison of Sulla and Augustus; Cicero, *Offices*, II. 8: comparison of Sulla and Caesar (quoted by Montesquieu in IX, para. 7.).

⁵² Plutarch, *Stoic Contradictions*. Cf. Montesquieu follows Cicero in *Romans*, X, first sentence, and following. Rousseau, *Social Contract*: "I hope our enemies are of this opinion."

⁵³ Livy, XLII. 47. 9; Polybius, I. 3. 6; XXX-XXXIII; XXXVI. 2, 9; n. 55 above. Consideration of "pretexts" in connection with law, custom, and opinion is the key to understanding Polybius' presentation of "causes" and "true explanations." Calhoun discusses domestic ambition and avarice in connection with large civil and military establishments in paragraph 28. He discusses pretexts in terms of "liberal" (majoritarian) and "strict" (minoritarian) construction of written constitutions in paragraphs 49-51. Consider in this connection Livy, IV. 58. 9-10; XXXI. 7. 3. Cf., also, Voegelin, *Order and History*.; J. Briscoe, "Q. Marcius Philippus and *nova sapientia*," *Journal of Roman Studies*, 54 (1954): 66-77; F. W. Walbank, "Polybius and Rome's Eastern Policy," *Journal of Roman Studies* 53 (1963): 1-12. Cf. chap. 2, n. 114 above, with Cicero, *De Officiis*, I. xi. 35-36. In connection with Polybius' conception of "pretexts," consider Hegel, *Philosophy of History*, introduction: "At no time as much as in our own have such general principles and notions been advanced with so much pretentiousness. At other times history seems to present itself as a struggle of passions. In our time, however, though passions are not wanting, history exhibits partly and predominantly a struggle of justifiable ideas and partly a struggle of passions and

subjective interests under the mask of much higher pretentions. These pretentions, regarded as legitimate in the name of the supposed destiny of reason, are thereby validated as absolute ends...." With but little amendment, this is perhaps as good an orientation as anyone needs for beginning to study Polybius' *Histories*. Consider, also, Posidonius, *History after Polybius* in Theiles, ed., *Poseidonius: Die Fragmente*, vol. 1: *Texte*, vol. 2: *Erlanterungen* (Berlin: Walter de Gruyter, 1982); cf. David E. Hahn, "Posidonius's Theory of Historical Causation," *ANRW* 2.36.3 (1989): 1325-63, esp. 1334ff.

54 "It was to Polybius...to whom the Romans owed the conception of the Empire as an ecumenical organism," according to the commonplace claim, and the Augustan age and beyond abounded with every kind of claim of world dominion. Lidia Storoni Mazzolani, *The Idea of the City in Roman Thought: From Walled City to Spiritual Commonwealth*, S. O'Donnell trans. (Bloomington: Indiana University Press, 1970), 56ff. (One must wonder, however, whether the pragmatic imperial movement that is designated in this subtitle is not actually just the reverse. Cf. Montesquieu, *Romans*, 9) Writers disagree, have always disagreed, on the extent to which all these claims, or certain kinds of them, were meant only to be taken metaphorically, as "in a manner of speaking," or more literally and concretely, and similar citations are often presented from among many lessor or insignificant peoples or countries as proofs that such speaking is not unique to Rome or that Rome itself, at least in this respect, is not unique. This is Polybius' beginning place. Rome is unique because it made them concrete, and understood that it had done so.

55 Livy, XXXVI. xvii. 14-16: Manius Acilius Glabrio is made to say: "You will open a way for the Roman power into Asia and Syria, and the most opulent realms to the extremity of the east. What, then, must be the consequence, but that, from Gades to the Red Sea, we shall have no limit but the Ocean, which encircles in its embrace the whole orb of the earth; and that all mankind shall regard the Roman name with a degree of veneration next to that which they pay to the divinities? Nerve yourselves to be worthy of such high rewards!" (Mazzolani, trans.). One may then investigate whether Polybius thought there is such a limit. Cf. Strabo, *Geog.* 2.3.2 (Posidonius, *On the Ocean*), 2.3.7; 4.1.14; *Dis Chrysostom, Ovations* 12.2730; also, Voegelin, *History and Order*, 202-211. See also, Lidia Storoni Mazzolani, *The Empire without End*, Mario Pei and Joan McConnell Mammarella, trans. (New York: Harcourt Brace Jovanovich, 1976).

56 Cf. Montesquieu, *Romans*, VI, last six paras.

57 The term "organic mechanism" is drawn from *Disquisition*, para. 19; cf., e.g., Whitehead, *Science and the Modern World*, 80, 107 and context: "...an individual entity, whose own life-history is a part within the life-history of some larger, deeper, more complete pattern, is liable to have aspects of that larger pattern dominating its own being, and to experience modifications of that larger pattern reflected in itself as modifications of its own being. This is the theory of organic mechanism." For Calhoun, it is the purposeful internal instrumentality that is moved by that which is outside itself, the various parts or interests of the community as a whole, like the bodies of material nature, to counterbalance and adjust the preponderances of the animate whole in accordance with the good of the whole.

58 "On the Treasury Report" (delivered in the Senate, June 21, 1841), *Works*, 3:647; "On the Commercial Convention with Great Britain" (delivered in the House of

Representatives, January 9, 1816), *Work*, 2:32 and context; "On the Loan Bill," *Work*, 2:98. See chap. 4, n. 83 below.

⁵⁹ Cf. Hume, *The History of England from the Invasion of Julius Caesar to the Abdication of James the Second, 1688* (1778 edition), vol. I, chap. 1. first para.: the early history of Britain properly begins with "the state of the inhabitants as it appeared to the Romans on their invasion of this country," and context.

Calhoun is the precursor of the Wilsonian scholars Charles Homer Haskins and Joseph Strayer who later thought they found in the Norman conquest and government of England the seed of the modern bureaucratic state. See Charles Homer Haskins, *The Normans in European History* (New York: Frederick Ungar, 1959), *Norman Institutions* (Cambridge: Harvard University Press, 1918); Strayer, *On the Medieval Origins of the Modern State* (Princeton: Princeton University Press, 1970). In the *Disquisition*, the commons include the Anglo-Saxons.

⁶⁰ Cf. Hume, *History*, VI, chap. lxxi: "Newton was the greatest and rarest genius that ever arose for the ornament and instruction of mankind." Whitehead, *Process and Reality* (New York: Macmillan, 1929), II.iii, 144: "it cannot be too clearly understood that, within the limits of its abstraction, what the Scholium says is true, and that it is expressed with the lucidity of genius. Thus, any cosmological document that cannot be read as an interpretation of the *Scolium* is useless."

⁶¹ Edwards, *The Nature of True Virtue*, 3: "There is a beauty of order in society...which is of the secondary kind [of beauty]"; 7: "Among the Romans, love to their country was the highest virtue; though this affection of theirs so much extolled, was employed as it were for the destruction of the rest of mankind." Cf. Rousseau, *Social Contract*, III.11.1: "If Sparta and Rome perished, what state can hope to last forever?"

⁶² Cf. Hume, *History of England*, vol. I, chap. iii: "Edward the Confessor": "The English flattered themselves that, by the succession of Edward [a Dane], they were delivered forever from the dominion of foreigners," to the end of the chapter; also chap. 4: "...the king [William of Normandy] intended to rely entirely on the support and affections of foreigners"; "William the Conqueror, the most potent, the most haughty, and the most vigorous prince in Europe, was not, among all his splendid successes, secure from the attacks of [Pope Gregory VI]"; passim. Hume concludes (chap. 4, penultimate paragraph) that, as distinguished from "the Roman state, which spread its dominion over Europe," "except for the former conquest of England by the Saxons themselves...it would be difficult to find in all history a revolution more destructive, or attended with a more complete subjection of the ancient inhabitants" than that of the Norman conquest of England. This—the midst of subjection and destruction—is Calhoun's characteristic beginning place. Order begins in evident chaos.

⁶³ Hume, *History of England*, vol. I, appendix II, first sentence: "The feudal law is the chief foundation both of the political government and of the jurisprudence established by the Normans in England," and passim. The lords "were the generals of a conquering army, which was obliged to continue in a military posture, and to maintain great subordination under their leader, in order to secure themselves from the revolt of the numerous natives, whom they had bereaved of all their properties and priviliges [sic]." Vide also chap. iv, passim; appendix I; nn. F and K.

[64] Hume, *History,* vol. I, Appendix II. See Victor Wexler, *David Hume and the "History of England"* (Philadelphia: American Philosophical Society, 1979), preface, second para.: "The History of England evolved into an extension of Hume's study of the 'science of man'."

[65] Ibid.

[66] Hume, *History,* I, chap. xi.

[67] Hume, *History,* II, chap. xi, and context: From this beginning, the House of Commons "soon proved...one of the most useful, and, in process of time, one of the most powerful members of the national constitution." This is Calhoun's point. Cf. also, George L. Haskins, *The Growth of English Representative Government* (University of Pennsylvania Press, 1948), chap. 3.

[68] Hume, *History,* II, chap. xiii: "Digression on the Constitution of Parliament" and the waning of feudalism; and n. F. "In rising by these slow degrees, the commons "in their progress made arts and commerce, the necessary attendants of liberty and equality, flourish in the kingdom." However, under constant pressure of the issues of taxation, "it was found that no laws could be fixed for one order of men without affecting the whole, and that the force and efficacy of laws depended entirely on the terms employed in wording them." Cf. *Disquisition,* paras. 25ff., 80ff.

[69] Hume, *History,* II, chap. xvii: "The first dawn of the arts and good government in that age, had excited all the minds of the populace...to wish for a better condition," and related passages. The immediate cause of the rebellion was a vaguely-worded tax.

[70] Hume, *History,* II, chap. xxi: "complaints against the numerous abuses in government," and context. Cf. in this connection 6, chap. 71: "Extremes of all kinds are to be avoided, and though no one will ever please either faction by moderate opinions, it is there we are most likely to meet with truth and certainty," and context.

[71] Hume, *History,* III, chap. xxix: Upon the imposition of a new tax, "[a]n insurrection was begun in some places, but as the people were not headed by any considerable person, it was easy to induce the ringleaders to lay down their arms and surrender themselves as prisoners.... The king, finding it dangerous to punish criminals engaged in so popular a cause was determined, notwithstanding his violent, imperious temper, to grant them a pardon..."

[72] Hume, *History,* V, chap. liv: e.g., "noble ancients," context, and related passages; passim. Wexler, *David Hume and the "History of England,"* 20: Hume "was the first (if not the last) historian to make the rise of the Commons the central issue in a fully developed constitutional history of England.... Despite the inevitable revisions of more recent scholarship, Hume's interpretation, at least in kernal form, remains a classic." It is the kernel of that kernel which is distilled and completed in Calhoun's sketch of the British constitution in *A Disquisition on Government.*

[73] Hume, *History,* V, chaps. lv-lxii, and nn. I and K.

[74] Hume, *History,* V, chap. lxii.

[75] Hume, *History,* VI, chap. lxv "defects of the constitution," and related passages.

[76] Hume, *History,* VI, chap. lxxi: "The convention annexed to this settlement of the crown a declaration of rights, where all the points which had of late years been disputed between the king and the people, were finally determined; and the powers of royal

prerogative were more narrowly circumscribed and more exactly defined, than at any former period of the English government."

⁷⁷ Cf. Montesquieu, *Spirit of Laws*, bk. XI and following, bk. XIX and following, with Locke, *Second Treatise on Government*, chaps. xi-xiv.

⁷⁸ Cf. Hegel, *Philosophy of Right*, sec. 273:

> Here again, as in so many other places, we must recognize the depth of Montesquieu's insight in his now famous treatment of the basic principles of the forms of government. To recognize the accuracy of his account, however, we must not misunderstand it. As is well known, he holds that "virtue'" is the principle of democracy since it is in fact the case that that type of constitution rests on sentiment.... But Montesquieu goes on to say that in the seventeenth century, "England provided a fine spectacle of the way in which efforts to found a democracy were rendered ineffective by a lack of virtue in the leaders," and again he adds '"when virtue vanishes from the republic, ambition enters hearts which are capable of it and greed masters everyone...." These quotations call for the comment that in more mature social conditions and when the power of particularity has developed and become free, a form of rational law other than the form of sentiment is required, because virtue in the heads of state is not enough if the state as a whole is to gain the power to resist disruption and to bestow on the powers of particularity, now become mature, both their positive and their negative rights...[and] the fact that Montesquieu discusses "honor" as the principle of monarchy at once makes it clear that by "monarchy" he understands not...the type organized into an objective constitution, but only feudal monarchy.

(Cf., also, *Spirit of the Laws*, III.7; V.19: "true honor"; *Disquisition*, para. 76: "high and glittering prize.")

⁷⁹ Cf. Burke, "Thoughts on the Cause of the Present Discontents": "This was the most noble and refined part of our constitution. The people, by their representatives and grandees, were entrusted with a deliberative power in making laws; the king with the control of his negative. The king was entrusted with the deliberative choice and election to office; the people had the negative in a parliamentary refusal of support.... If the use of this power of control on the system and persons of administration is gone, everything is lost, Parliament and all" [and context].

⁸⁰ *Disquisition*, paras. 44, 45, 46, 48, 86, 87, 89, 108; 112.

⁸¹ From the Trinitarian "sovereign law of unity and variety," Donoso Cortes arrives at a Calhounian view of political sovereignty according to which, in its "internal organism," the British constitution was not a division of powers and that the House of Lords was "the only true Power in the State." According to him, the British constitution therefore has more in common with medieval parliaments than with modern European parliamentarianism. *Vide* "Donoso Cortes and the Meaning of Political Power" in Frederick D. Wilhelmsen, *Christianity and Political Philosophy* (Athens: University of Georgia Press, 1978), 139ff. Cf. Haskins, *The Growth of English Representative Government*, 2: "Although representative assemblies were common features of the countries of Western Europe in the

Middle Ages, the English alone was not eclipsed — temporarily or otherwise — by the rise of the national monarchies in the fifteenth and sixteenth centuries."

82 Hume, *History*, VI, chap. lxxi. Cf. Whitehead, "The Study of the Past," in *Essays in Science and Philosophy*, 116: "So far as sheer individual freedom is concerned, there was more diffused freedom in the City of London in 1633, when Charles the First was King, than there is today in any industrial city of the world."

83 See nn. 56-57 above. The theme of technical superiority and ready adaptability on the part of Rome as crucial to her rise is emphasized by Montesquieu from the beginning, e.g., *Romans*, I, para. 5. Only Carthage under the ingenious Hannibal imitated the Romans in this respect, with the result, Montesquieu says (IV), that in "the Second Punic War...we have before us the finest spectacle of antiquity." It is this spectacle that Calhoun has in mind in his remarks on the proposed notice to Great Britain, quoted above (chap. 1, nn. 92ff.). In connection with what was said above, cf. Burke, "Remarks on the Policy of the Allies," *Works* (Bohn's), III.448: "...this astonishing, this hitherto unheard of power...," and context.

84 E.g., Cicero, *Republic*, II, 40. Cf. Orwell, *1984*, "proles."

85 N. 45 above.

86 Cf. Calhoun, "On the Repeal of the Direct Tax" (delivered in the House of Representatives, January 21, 1816), *Works*, 2:146, and context ("that heroism which nations in modern times may admire..."): "All the free nations of antiquity..."; "On the Force Bill" (delivered in the Senate, February 15-16, 1833) ibid., 259: "...all free states ancient and modern..."; "Reply to Mr. Webster on the Rights of the States" (delivered in the Senate, February 26, 1833) ibid., 306: "every free state from the remotest antiquity"; also Disquisition, para. 110. (Cf. Herman von Holst, *John C. Calhoun* [1899, New York: Chelsea House, 1980], Clyde Wilson, introduction, 45-49.) As we have noted, the example of the Iroquois Confederacy (para. 110) leads in the *Disquisition* not only to the introduction of modernity (paras. 112ff.), of which it is so far (or for Calhoun) the noblest victim, but also and above all to the introduction of the Republic of Rome (para. 111).

Consider "On Its Resolutions in Respect to the Brig Enterprise" (delivered in the Senate, March 13, 1841), *Works*, 3:482-83: "There never before existed on this globe a nation that presented such a spectacle as Great Britain does at this moment.... A spirit of conquest and domination not surpassed by Rome in the haughtiest days of the Republic.... She works against herself.... She is preparing the way for universal discord, within and without...." This whole speech should be studied in connection with the comparison of Rome and Great Britain and Calhoun's understanding of the present age of transition.

87 N. 23 above.

88 E.g., Coit, *John C. Calhoun*, "Young Hercules," 7:87ff; Peterson, *The Great Triumvirate*, "Young Hercules," 1:18ff. Calhoun's view parallels that of Smith. See *Wealth of Nations* V.iii.92; also, *The Economic History of Britain since 1700*, Roderick Floud and Donald McCloskey, eds., (Cambridge: Cambridge University Press, 1987), "Overseas Trade and Empire," 1:90ff., especially 94-102.

Chapter 4

1 *Politics*, 1279a and context.

2 Cf. Burke, *Works* (Bohn's), V. 124; Alexander Stephens, *The Constitutional View*, 2 vols. (Philadelphia: National Publishing Company, 1868-1870), 1:7-8, 118:

> The organic laws, which enter into the structure of any Association, Society, Community, Commonwealth, State, or Nation, by whatever name it may be designated, form what may be styled the Constitution of that particular Organism. These are the elementary principles, from which spring the vital functions of the Political Being, thus brought into existence, and upon which depend, mainly, the future development of the Organism, and the character, as well as the standard of its civilization. But, while these Structural laws act upon Society in its *embryo* state, as well as shaping its subsequent development, Society is also acting back upon them. As individual life, in all its forms and stages, is said to be the result of a war between opposing agencies, so it is with the political life or existence of every body politic.

Calhoun goes further than Stephens in introducing the strict distinction between constitution and absolutism in considering the political organism. Cf. Burke, *Works*, V. 153. See Leslie Stephen, *History of English Thought in the Eighteenth Century* 2 vols. (London, 1876), 2:230-48.

3 Burke, *Works*, II. 307:

> Our political system is placed in a just symmetry with the order of the world, and with the mode of existence decreed to a permanent body composed by transitory parts; wherein, by the dispensation of a stupendous wisdom, moulding together the great mysteries of the human race, the whole, at one time, is never old, or middle-aged, or young, but, in a condition of unchangeable constancy, moves on through the varied tenor of perpetual decay, fall, renovation, and progression.

Cf. the celebrated passage in Woodrow Wilson, *The New Freedom* (1913, Garden City: 1931), 40-46. As Whitehead has indicated, the contrast of "organism" with "mechanism" may easily appear more profound than it is. Cf. Montesquieu, "Causes That Can Effect Minds and Characters": "the body a machine..."; Burke, *Works*, V. 124: "These analogies between bodies natural and political, though they may sometimes illustrate, furnish no argument in themselves."

4 Cf. Aristotle, *Politics*, 1254a28-34: "harmony."

5 Cf. Plato, *Statesman*, 291e-292a; also, 258e-259d, 295.

6 Calhoun, "On the Right of Petition" (delivered in the Senate, February 13, 1840), *The Works of John C. Calhoun*, Richard K. Cralle, ed., 6 vols. (Charleston, S.C.: 1851-1856), 3:445: "The moral is like the physical world. Nature has encrusted the exterior of all organic life for its safety. Let that be broken through and all is weakness within. So in the moral and political world."

7 Calhoun, "On the Force Bill" (delivered in the Senate, February 15-16, 1833), *Works*, 2:229, and context: "Death is not the greatest calamity." Cf. Cicero, *De Officiis*, 1.23: "Death is to be chosen before slavery and base deeds."

The failure mentioned in the text is the basis of the right of rebellion or secession. Otherwise, it would be always right for right to acquiesce before might: it would then be meaningless to speak of "right" or of ought instead of only might or force. The ruled will naturally resist the oppression of the rulers whenever possible. The right of rebellion or secession may be resorted to "rightfully," Calhoun elsewhere says, "only where government has failed in the great objects for which it was ordained, the security and happiness of the people, and then only where no other remedy can be applied" — when the aim is not the capture of the government or the whole but independence. (Quoted in *The Essential Calhoun*, 49-50).

⁸ Cf., e.g., Aristotle, *Politics*, 1296b38-40, 1297a6-7: "a lasting polity," "more lasting [polity]"; Burke, *Works* (Bohn's), V. 124; Calhoun, "On the Veto Power" (delivered in the Senate, February 28, 1842), *Works*, 4:93-94.

It should be noted that Calhoun begins his discussion of the question posed in paragraph 20 where Locke had begun the *Second Treatise* as a whole (first chapter): the right of suffrage is the right of making laws. From this beginning, Locke arrives at the end wherein "all private judgement of every particular Member being excluded, the Community comes to be Umpire, by settled standing Rules" (*Two Treatises of Government*, Laslett, ed., 342). This end is, of course, reminiscent of Rousseau's "general will." According to Calhoun, neither the contract doctrines nor, certainly, the special educational projects of either thinker, whether taken separately or together, will rationally or actually arrive at the desired end. The relation of Calhoun to Locke may be seen by merely noting that, for Locke, the government and the community are the same: "...*political society* [sic], where everyone of the Members hath quitted this natural Power, resigned it up into the hands of the Community in all cases..." (*Two Treatises of Government*, Laslett, ed., 342). As Calhoun elsewhere observes, this is the principle of "Asiatic polity and civilization" that was beaten back at "Marathon, Platea, and Salamis" ("On The Force Bill" [delivered in the Senate, February 15-16], 1833, *Works*, 2:238). According to Calhoun, there is a kind of hidden absolutism or despotism in Lockean civil society arising from the fiction of the "state of nature" doctrine.

⁹ Aristotle, *Politics*, 1287b 5-10: "The regime is an arrangement of the city with respect to its offices, particularly the one which has authority over all matters. For what has authority in the city is everywhere the governing body, and the governing body is the regime. I mean, for example, that in democratic regimes the many have authority, while by contrast the few in oligarchies. The regime, too, we say is different in these cases, [and the political virtue that is found in each]."

¹⁰ Calhoun, "On the Bill to Regulate Commerce Between Britain and the United States" (delivered in the House of Representatives, January 9, 1816), *Works*, 2:130; cf. "On the Veto Power" (delivered in the Senate, February 28, 1842), *Works*, 4:81-82: "If one *must be* sacrificed to the other, it is better that the few be sacrificed to the many than the many to the few"; cf. *Disquisition*, para. 85.

¹¹ See, e.g., "On the New Army Bill" (delivered in the House of Representatives, January 14, 1813), *Works*, 2:46: "indispensable agents"; "On the Loan Bill" (delivered in the House of Representatives, February 25, 1814), *Works*, 2:99. 71-74, and context: "...the most material [substantive] elements of power"; "spontaneous and concurring zeal of its

citizens"; "On the Motion to Repeal the Direct Tax" (delivered in the House of Representatives, January 31, 1816), *Works*, 2:150-51, and context: "...for all the powers of government, the power of the moral kind is most to be cherished. We had better give up all our physical power than part with this. But what is this power? The zeal of the country, and the confidence it reposes in the administration of the government." Cf. *Disquisition*, paras. 96-98.

¹² E.g., Calhoun, "On the Compensation Bill" (delivered in the House of Representatives, January 17, 1817), *Works*, 2:177-80: "Instructions"; Burke, "Speech to the Electors of Bristol": "Your representative...." Calhoun's position is identical to that of Burke as described by Professor Hannah Pitkin: The representative or agent "is to pursue the interest of his constituency rather than do its bidding." Professor Pitkin adds that "the characteristic feature of Burke's approach is that such a contrast is possible and even highly meaningful." *The Concept of Representation* (Berkeley: University of California Press, 1972), 187, and context. Of course, without such a distinction, it would be impossible for the conception of self-*government* even to occur or to find any contrast between, say, self-interest and doing or not doing whatever one might will, and thus there would be "no reason" for Calhoun to point out the necessity of enlightenment on the part of the people. In other words, it represents the distinction and contrast between reason and desire.

¹³ Calhoun does not specify any particular extent of this right. Later, under certain further conditions, he says that it might be made more "universal," i.e., it might extend to "every male citizen of mature age," as a head or potential head of a household (para. 70). He never considers whether it might extend to women or to children or to adult males who are not citizens, such as resident aliens or bondsmen. Hence, even though Calhoun does not find the essential or natural root of human society in the kinship of the family, he does imply that the family "unit," the household, however understood, is the elemental social phenomenon and the most basic exponent of society and the community (cf. para. 89). The family is "first for us."

¹⁴ Aristotle, *Politics*, 1261b 31ff, etc.: "the city is in its nature a sort of multitude...the city is made up not only of a number of human beings, but also of human beings differing in kind: a city does not arise from persons who are similar..."

¹⁵ James Madison to Thomas Jefferson, *Papers of James Madison*, Robert A. Rutland, et al., eds. 10 vols. (Charlottesville: University of Virginia Press, 1979), 10:212.

¹⁶ *Disquisition*, para. 8. Cf. *Federalist* 10, sixth para.: "...reason and self-love," "diversity in the faculties of men...," "protection of these faculties...." Cf. Bacon, *Works*, 3:418: "[some have taught well] How (I say) *to set affection against affection and to master one by another....* for as in the government of states it is sometimes necessary to bridle one faction with another, so it is in the government within." Hobbes, *Leviathan*, xiii: "passions and desires of men" motivating aggression; "passions that incline men to peace." Hume, *Treatise*, II. iii. ii: "Nothing can retard the impulse of passion but a contrary passion." John Dewey: "power must contravene power," "Newtonianism is valid in politics."

Calhoun refers to the discussion of faction, including "majority faction," in the tenth *Federalist* in "On the Loan Bill" (delivered in the House of Representatives, February 25, 1814), Works, 2:100-101. He particularly agrees with the view that in a free country a majority faction ceasing "to consult the general interest" is more dangerous than a minority faction, but he particularly denies, on both the ground of experience and reason, that "all the follies and miseries of free states originated in the follies of majorities." In the *Disquisition*, the principal allusion to the tenth *Federalist* occurs in paragraph 25: "the more diversified the conditions and pursuits of its population; and the richer, more luxurious, and dissimilar the people...." Cf. e.g., "On the New Tariff Bill" (delivered in the House of Representatives, January 17, 1817), *Works*, 2:184: "...extent of...territory," and context; chap. 1, n. 83 above.

The perspective of the *Disquisition* (and *Discourse*) is different than that of the *Federalist* (it goes without saying that Calhoun was a Jeffersonian rather than a Hamiltonian, and regarded the Virginia Resolutions of 1799 as Madison's greatest work), yet it may be noted that he was of the opinion that "we were indebted to Mr. Madison, at least as much as to any other man, for the form of government under which we live. Indeed, he might be said to have done as much for our institutions as any man now living, or that had gone before him" (February 18, 1837, quoted in *The Essential Calhoun*, 365.)

[17] Aristotle, *Politics*, 1289b 27-1290a 14ff: "The reason for their being a number of regimes is that there are a number of parts in any city.... There are necessarily, therefore, as many regimes as their are arrangements based on the sorts of preeminence and the differences of the parts." See n. 9 above. Cf., *Politics*, 1294a19-1296b2ff, 1301a36-b4ff; *Eudemian Ethics*, 1235a5-29; Cicero, *De Officiis*, 1. 25; *Republic*, I. 32. 49, 55; II. 23. 42-43, 39. 65-66, 43. 69, and context; Polybius, VI. x. 44.

[18] Calhoun, "On the Force Bill" (delivered in the Senate, February 15-16, 1833), *Works*, 2:229. Cf. "On the Relations of the States and the General Government" (July 26, 1831), *Works*, 6:83: "the great end of government and without which it is a curse and not a blessing—justice..."; "On the Tariff Bill" (delivered in the Senate, August 27, 1842), *Works*, 4:207: "Justice and equality—justice rigidly enforced, and equality between citizen and citizen...and one portion of the country and another, are essential elements of [constitutional] governments"; "On Presenting His Resolutions" (delivered in the Senate, February 19, 1847), *Works*, 4:344: "The whole system [must be] based on justice and equality—perfect equality between the members of [a] republic." Cf. Aquinas, *Summa Theologiae*, I Part II (Qu. 90-97) "Treatise on Law."

[19] Calhoun, "Reply to Mr. Simmons" (delivered in the Senate, February 20, 1847), *Works*, 4:351. Cf. "On the Amendment to Mr. Webster's Bill on Pubic Deposits" (delivered in the Senate, June 28, 1838), *Works*, 3:357: "He knows nothing of the human heart, or the working of a political system over so wide a country, who does not see that there must be a constant tendency on the part of the stronger portion to monopolize all the advantages for itself and to transfer all its burdens to the weaker. Nor is he less ignorant who does not see that such a tendency must in the end prove fatal to the government if not steadily and successfully resisted." Cf. *Federalist* 15: "the love of power," and context.

[20] Aristotle, *Politics*, 1269a 9ff: "Just as in the case of the other arts, so with regard to political arrangements it is not possible for everything to be written down precisely, for it is necessary to write them in generalities, while actions concern particulars."

[21] Calhoun, "On the Merchant's Bonds" (delivered in the House of Representatives, December 4, 1812), *Works*, 2:35. Cf. "On the Independent Treasury Bill" (delivered in the Senate, February 15, 1838), *Works*, 3:217-31, beginning with the statement, "More than half

of the errors of life may be traced to fallacies originating in an improper use of words...,"
and climaxing in the phrase, "...would form a despotic *money-cracy* (if I may be permitted
to unite an English and a Greek word), altogether irresistable." See chap. 5, n. 58 below.

22 See chap. 2, n. 74 above. In the text, the quotation of the Homeric line is drawn
from Aristotle's discussion of the egalitarian regime proposed by Phaleas of Chalcedon,
Politics, 1266a 35ff: "Political division occurs not only because of inequality of possessions,
but also because of inequality of honors, though in an opposite way in each case; for the
many become seditious because possessions are unequal, but the refined [or: "more
elevated"] do so if honors are equal—hence the verse 'in single honor, whether wicked or
worthy.'" Aristotle immediately refers to philosophy in this context. In connection with the
Homeric verse, cf. Isocrates, *Areopagiticus*, 21-22, and *Disquisition*, paras. 77-78.

23 Cf. William W. Freehling, "Spoilsmen and Interests in the Thought and Career of
John C. Calhoun," in *The Journal of American History* 52/2 (June 1965): 25-42, outlines some
of the problems that render the formation of constitutional government difficult. Professor
Freehling asserts that the subject of "emergent spoilsmen is the neglected theme in the
thought and career of the Carolinian." He believes that contradictions "between the
theory of interests and the theory of spoilsmen"—i.e., in Calhoun's *metaphy*sics of politics
and morals—"destroyed his political philosophy," but, somewhat inconsistently, at the
same time, that "the problem with the *Disquisition* lies not in its diagnosis but rather in its
exaggerations of weakness in a republic." (According to Freehling, Calhoun particularly
exaggerated the neglected theme of spoilsmen, who are not such a problem as Calhoun
supposed in a republic, Professor Freehling believes: republics are strong. Of course, in the
interest of historical accuracy, one must not overlook the fact that the phenomenon to
which Calhoun drew such attention led in due time, among other things, to the second
American presidential assassination. To be sure, the establishment of a "civil service"
subsequent to this assassination to blunt the violent edges of the party struggles is partly
Calhounian in conception. See "On the Bill to Prevent Interference in Elections"
(delivered in the Senate, February 22, 1839), *Works*, 3:382ff. However, such an institution
nevertheless simultaneously perforce immeasurably extends the government interest or
party.) Cf. Aristotle, *Politics*, 1279a 13-21, Plato, *Republic*, 345a-347a, and context; e.g.,
Cicero, *Pro Sestio*, 21, 96-99ff., 105. In any case, it is primarily to the most capable of such
ambitious men that the philosophy of government itself as presented in the *Disquisition* is
addressed. Cf., e.g., "On the Bill to Repeal the Four Year's Law and Regulate the Power of
Removal" (delivered in the Senate, February, 1835), *Works*, 2:426ff.; "On the Bill to Reduce
Certain Tariff Duties" (delivered in the Senate, February 25, 1837), excerpted in *The
Essential Calhoun*, 335.

Essentially similar concerns as discussed by Calhoun are raised with greater pungency
if no more insight in Henry Adams, "The Session" (1868-1869, Fortieth Congress), "The
Session, 1869-1870," and "Civil Service Reform," in *The Great Secession Winter of 1860-61 and
other Essays*, George Hochfield, ed. (New York, 1958), esp. 65-75. Similarly, Adams's 1874
review of Hermann von Holst, *The Administration of Andrew Jackson* (collected in *Sketches
for the North American Review*, Edward Chalfant, ed. (Hamden, Conn., 1986). "What had
commenced in Jackson's time was now reaching its full fruition in the age of Grant,"
Brooks D. Simpson, *The Political Education of Henry Adams* (Columbia, S.C., 1996), 87; cf. xiv,

103, 113, 119: "In many ways, Henry Adams was one of the last defenders of the republican idea in its original form," "republic of the Founding Fathers...," "...theory of the Ameria Constitution...." See also Mark Wahlgren Summers, *The Era of Good Stealings* (New York, 1993).

Cf. also, William Graham Sumner's centennial essay, "Politics in America, 1776-1876," in *The Forgotten Man and Other Essays*, A. G. Keller, ed. (New Haven: Yale University Press, 1919), 329: "It seems sometimes that the prophecy of Calhoun had turned into history...."

24 See particularly Leonard D. White, "John C. Calhoun," in *The Jeffersonians: A Study in Administrative History 1801-1829* (New York: The Free Press, 1965), 246ff.; cf. *The Federalists: A Study in Administrative History: 1789-1801* (New York: The Free Press, 1948), "War: 'A Difficult and Unpopular Department'." On the subject of military organization and preparation, John Adams wrote to Benjamin Rush, July 10, 1812: "Mr. Calhoun speaks as I think," in *The Spur of Fame: Dialogues of John Adams and Benjamin Rush, 1805-1813*, John A. Schutz and Douglass Adair, eds. (San Marino, California: Huntington Library, 1966), 231-32. E.g., "Report on the Reduction of the Army" (December, 1818) and "Report on Roads and Canals" (January, 1819), *Works*, 5:25ff., 40ff.

25 Para. 76: "public and private morals." See "On the Passage of the Tariff Bill" (delivered in the Senate, August 15, 1842), *Works*, 4:197-200, on the relation of inequitable tax policy and degeneration in "politics and morals" or "private as well as public morals." Cf., also, "On the Bill to Establish a National Bank" (delivered in the House of Representatives, February 26, 1816), *Works*, 2:162, and context: "the health of the body politic, which depend[s] on public morals...." See n. 22 above.

26 Calhoun's most expressive practical formulation of this phenomenon is found in his speech "On the Bill Making Alterations in the Pay Department of the Army" (delivered in the Senate, May 14, 1846), *Works*, 4:294-96, 301-303; see the "Report on the Extent of Executive Privilege" (February 9, 1835), *Works*, 5:138ff.; *Calhoun Papers*, 12:452ff., and context; 495.

27 Jerold L. Waltman, *The Political Origins of the U.S. Income Tax* (Jackson: University of Mississippi Press, 1985), 3. Calhoun, "On Crittenden's Amendment to the Land Distribution Bill" (delivered in the Senate, January 30, 1841), *Works*, 3:591: "The wisest of modern statesmen, and who had the keenest and deepest insight into futurity (Edmund Burke), truly said that the revenue is the state; to which I add that to distribute the revenue, in a confederated community, among its members, is to dissolve the community." Cf. Aristotle, *Politics*, 1281a17-18; 1308b26-31: "Taking all the citizens into consideration, if the majority distributes among itself the things of a minority, it is evident that it will destroy the city.... A remedy for this is always to place actions and offices in the hands of the opposing parts—I speak of the respectable as opposed to the multitude, and the poor as opposed to the well-off...." This separation and balance of powers among the parts of the community is the heart of the Aristotelian mixed regime or "polity."

According to Calhoun, the fiscal operation of the government is, "in the present condition of the world," the same as the growth and centralization of the government interest and power. See "On the Independent Treasury Bill" (delivered in the Senate, February 15, 1838), *Works*, 3:234 (emphasis added): "Burke has wisely said that the revenue is the state *in modern times*. Violence and coercion are no longer the instruments of government in civilized communities. Their reign has passed. Everything is now done by money. It is not only the sinew of war, but of politics, over which, in the form of patronage, it exercises almost unlimited control." Again referring to Burke, the same position is developed in Calhoun's speech "On the Distribution Bill" (delivered in the Senate, August 24, 1841), *Works*, 4:9. The whole speech on the Distribution Bill should be read in connection with this section of the *Disquisition*. (The metaphor of money as the blood of the modern state is taken from Hobbes, *Leviathan*, chap. XXIV.) The subject treated in paragraphs 29-37 rightly follows that mentioned in the immediately preceding paragraphs 27-28, for, as Burke also observed "with sagacity": "an instance is not to be found of a high-minded nation sinking under financial difficulties." "On the Repeal of the Direct Tax" (delivered in the House of Representatives, January 31, 1816), *Works*, 2:139-40; see 150, 152.

   28 Calhoun's treatment of this phenomenon as essentially political in its character and object has since been developed, for example, in the work of the Virginia School of Public Choice. See James M. Buchanan, *The Limits of Liberty: Between Anarchy and Leviathan* (Chicago: University of Chicago Press, 1975). Cf., also, with *Disquisition*, paras. 29-35, and 119, Hayek, *Law, Legislation, and Liberty*, vol. II, *The Mirage of Social Justice* (Chicago: University of Chicago Press, 1976), and Robert Nozick, *Anarchy, State, and Utopia* (New York: Basic Books, 1974).

   29 Among other places, this characteristic argument is set forth at length by Calhoun in his famous Senatorial speeches "On the Independent Treasury Bill" (February 15, 1838), *Works*, 3:233-35, 237; "Reply to Mr. Clay on the Independent Treasury Bill" (March 10, 1838), *Works*, 3:275; and, especially, "Reply to Mr. Webster on the Independent Treasury Bill" (March 22, 1838), *Works*, 3:310-11, 325-26; "On the Engrossment of the Bill to Graduate the Price of the Public Lands" (January 5, 1839), *Works*, 3:380ff: "the revenue power converted into a penal and stipendiary power..."; and, especially, "On the Report of the Secretary of the Treasury" (June 21, 1841), *Works*, 3:636ff: "Who is meant by the country?...tax consumers...tax payers...fiscal action of the government." It is already sketched in, e.g., "On the Bill to Establish a National Bank" (delivered in the House of Representatives, February 16, 1816), *Works*, 2:162: "inequality of taxation...notwithstanding the taxes were laid with strict regard to...their equality...."

   Consult, also, in this regard, Charles Adams, *Those Dirty Rotten Taxes: The Tax Revolts That Built America* (New York, 1998), on the ante-bellum U.S. tariffs; then, Ludwell H. Johnson, *Division and Reunion: America, 1848-1877* (New York, 1978), 110: Between 1861 and 1865, the tariff rose 18.84 percent to 47.56 percent, and stayed above 40 percent in all but two years of the period concluded with the election of Woodrow Wilson, working to "facilitate a massive transfer of wealth, satisfying the dreariest predictions of John C. Calhoun."

   30 Richard C. Current, "John C. Calhoun, Philosopher of Reaction" in *Antioch Review* 3/2 (Summer 1943): 223-34: "Historians have completely overlooked the key to Calhoun's political philosophy. That key is the concept of the class struggle...."

   31 Cf. e.g., Demosthenes, "Against Aristocrates"; James Monroe, *The People, the Sovereigns*, 7-13, 18-20ff; Mill, *Essay on Liberty*, 87-89. In connection with the points made in paragraph 37 (cf. 64-65), consider Chinua Achebe, *A Man of the People*, chap. 12, particularly the speech of the new party spokesman and the reply of the local elder, and

context. Calhoun, e.g., "Remarks On the Letter of General Jackson" (made in the Senate, June 9, 1837), 8: the reprimand of the view that "to the victor belong the spoils."

    32 Calhoun, "In Reply to Mr. Simmons" (delivered in the Senate, February 20, 1847), *Works*, 4:358. See e.g., *The Essential Calhoun*, 50: "You will see that if I am opposed to a government based on the principle that a mere numerical majority has a right to govern, I am equally opposed to the government of a minority. They are both the government of a part over a part. I am in favor of the government of the whole...a government based on the concurrent majority—the joint assent of all the parts, through their respective majority of the whole." This and only this is constitutional government worthy of the name, or the political rule that is naturally right. Aristotle, *Politics*, 1279a 13-21.

    33 See also Calhoun, "Public Letter to General Hamilton" (August 28, 1832), *Works*, 6:189-91. J. Arthur Thomson's late-nineteenth century history of biology, *The Science of Life* (London and New York: 1899, 103), cites a comment of the biologist Schwann in 1839: "The [biological] organism subsists only by means of the reciprocal action of the single elementary parts." Cf. n. 3 above.

    The purpose of the *Disquisition* is understanding, not action, although, to be sure, it points to a certain kind of action. As is clear in its following paragraph (41), this "pointing" is the obliging character of reason or right itself. Cf. Locke, *Essays on the Law of Nature*, W. von Leyden, ed. (Oxford: Clarendon Press, 1958), 135: "...a rational apprehension of what is right puts us under an obligation..." Calhoun, "On the President's Protest" (May 6, 1834), *Works*, 2:415: duties are the obligations of rights.

    34 Consider Kant, *Prolegomena to any Future Metaphysics*, Lewis White Beck, trans. (New York: Bobbs-Merrill, 1970), 364:

> The practical value, which merely speculative science might have, lies without the bounds of this science, and can therefore be considered a scholium [sc. Newton physics] merely, and like all scholia does not form part of the science itself. This application, however, surely lies within the bounds of philosophy, especially of philosophy drawn from the pure sources of reason, where its speculative use in metaphysics must necessarily be at one with its practical use in morals.

Calhoun's vision of the application of the elementary principles in question in paragraph 41, statemanship (cf. 139), is not developed in the *Disquisition*. See "On the Veto Power" (delivered in the Senate, February 28, 1842), *Works*, 4:82-83:

> What then is to be done, if neither the majority nor the minority, the greater nor less part, can be safely trusted with exclusive control? What but to vest the powers of the Government in the whole—the entire people; to make it, in truth and reality, the government of the people, instead of a dominant over a subject part, be it the greater or less—of the whole people—self-government; and, if this should prove impossible in practice, then to make the nearest approach to it, by requiring the concurrence in the action of the government of the greatest possible number.... But how is this to be effected? Not, certainly, by considering the whole community as one, and taking its sense as a whole by a single process, which, instead of giving the voice of all, can but give that of a part. There is but one way in which it can possibly be accomplished; and that is by a judicious and wise

division and organization of the Government and community, with reference to its great and conflicting interests,—and by taking the sense of each part separately, and the concurrence of all as the voice of the whole.

His closing sentence on this point bears upon the issue raised in paragraph 41: "Each may be imperfect of itself; but if the construction be good, *and all the keys skillfully touched*, there will be given out, in one blended and harmonious whole, the true and perfect voice of the people." (Emphasis added.) The role of one who can apply elementary principles to this purpose, the statesman, is ineliminable, even in the perfection of constitutional government. The science of government does not produce Calhounian statesmen or Rousseauan legislators, but these presuppose the science.

See the text at chap. 3 note 10 above.

35 Cf. James Burnham, *Congress and the American Tradition* (Chicago: Henry Regnery and Company, 1965), 313-15: "methods for calculating the majority." A surprising introduction to the Calhounian approach to more recent politics in the United States is found in Willmoore Kendall's important essay, "The Two Majorities." (Kendall was unaware of the *Disquisition* when he composed "The Two Majorities.") Consult Calhoun, "On the Veto Power" (delivered in the Senate, February 28, 1842), *Works*, 4:90 and context. Cf. Arend Lijphart, "Majority Rule versus Democracy in Deeply Divided Societies," *Politikon* (December 1977): 118: "consociational democracy," "Calhoun."

36 Consider the passage in the "Letter to the Honorable William Smith," July 3, 1843, *Works*, 6:238-39: "Its very complication—[constitutional democracy]—is calculated to give a force to discussion and agitation never before known—and to cause a diffusion of political intelligence heretofore unknown in the history of the world, [if not upset by mere physical force,] as an element of change—and keeping wide open the door for the full and free action of all the moral elements in its favor."

37 Arthur F. Bentley, *The Process of Government* (1908; San Antonio: Principia Press at Trinity University, 1949), 175-80, 203-222, 258-71, 351-52; David Truman, *The Governmental Process* (New York: Alfred Knopf, 1951), 38ff., 14-24. In Benthamism, the political whole is shown clearly only as one among the abstruse notions that are set at distance in the beginning of Hume's science of man. Cf. John Dewey, *The Public and Its Problems*, in *The Middle Works of John Dewey*, J. A. Boydston, ed. (Carbondale: Southern Illinois University Press, 1968), 308, 314ff.: "If a public exists...Hume."

According to Dewey, what he called the "Great Society," the mass of modern democratic mankind, must transform itself into the "Great Community," a genuinely democratic government and state. This crucial transformation is less a matter of political organization than an "intellectual problem, in a degree to which the political affairs of prior ages offer no parallel." Following Walter Lippmann, whose *Public Opinion* he held was "the most effective indictment of democracy as currently conceived ever penned," his effort was to identify "a kind of knowledge and insight which does not yet exist," but upon which the future of democratic government principally depends. He thus arrives at the position of Mill upon his rejection of Benthamism, which is, also, the primary impulse of Benthamism. See chap. 5, nn. on paras. 112ff. below; chap. 1, text at n. 39ff.,and n. 65 above; as well as Lasswell's efforts on scientific techniques for manipulating public opinion.

38 E.g., Aristotle, *Politics*, 1252a 1-6, 1283a 23-b4, 1290a 7-11, 1294b 13-18, 1297a 4-13.

³⁹ E.g., Tocqueville, *Democracy in America* (New York: Alfred A. Knopf, 1945), 2:318-19; cf. the text at chap. 1, n. 42 above. One cannot export (or import) "self-determination." (This is almost the whole subject of Machiavelli's *Prince*.)

⁴⁰ On the same grounds, the same dogma may be offered on behalf of absolute monarchy. Hobbes, *Leviathan*, chaps. XIV and XVIII: "because the major part hath by consenting voices declared a Soveraigne: he that dissented must now consent with the rest; that is, be contented to avow all the actions he shall do, or else be justly destroyed by all the rest."

⁴¹ Calhoun to Duff Green (September 20, 1834): "...the phantom of strict construction—a good thing in the abstract, but in practice not worth a farthing without the right of interposition to enforce it.... Everybody is for strict construction...but, in fact, it will ever be found to be the construction of the permanent minority against the permanent majority, and, of course, itself valueless." Quoted in *The Essential Calhoun*, 67; cf. p. 46: "It is the part of political wisdom not to trust when it can make secure, and in a case of...vital importance, it will not confide in the strongest probabilities. Faith is an article of religion, but not of politics."

⁴² Cf., e.g., *Federalist* 15: "...an instructive lesson to mankind, how little dependence is to be placed on treaties which have no other sanction than the obligations of good faith, and which oppose general considerations of peace and justice to the impulse of any immediate interest or passion." Patrick Henry: "Tell me not of checks on paper; but tell me of checks founded on self-love. The English Government is founded on self-love. This powerful irresistable [*sic*] stimulus of self-love has saved that Government. It has interposed the hereditary nobility between the King and Commons..." (spoken at the Virginia Ratifying Convention, June 9, 1788. *The Complete Anti-Federalist*, Herbert Storing, ed. 5 vols. [Chicago: University of Chicago Press, 1981], 5:233ff.). Also, e.g., Churchill, *Blood, Sweat, and Tears* (New York: Putnam, 1941), 45ff.: "...it is vain to imagine that the mere perception or declaration of right principles, whether in one country or in many countries, will be of any value unless they are supported by those qualities of civic virtue and manly courage—aye, and by those instruments and agencies of force and science which in the last resort must be the defense of right and reason..."

Calhoun, "On Congratulating the French Nation on the Success of Their Revolutionary Struggle" (delivered in the Senate, March 30, 1848), *Works*, 4:451: "The real work [was not the revolution but] is [yet] before them. They have decreed a republic, but it remains for them to establish a republic."

⁴³ Cf. e.g., Mill, *Essay on Liberty*; also, *Principles of Political Economy*, IV. vii. secs. 1-2.

⁴⁴ See Calhoun's remarks on the Monroe Doctrine in his speech "On the Proposed Occupation of the Yucatan" (delivered in the Senate, May 15, 1848), *Works*, 4:454-66ff, especially 466:

...no general [declaration] can be laid down to guide us on [every] question. Every case must speak for itself—every case must be decided on its own merits. Whether you will resist or not, and the measure of your resistance—whether it shall be by negotiation, remonstrance, or some immediate measure, or by a resort to arms, all this must be determined and decided on the merits of the question itself. This is the only wise course. We are not to have quoted on us, on every occasion, general declarations to which any and every meaning may be attached. See nn. 20-21 above.

45 E.g., "Brunetiere says that the more he read *The Spirit of the Laws* the less he could discern its true purpose" (quoted in George Sorel, *The Illusions of Progress*, John and Charlotte Stanley, trans. [Berkeley: University of California Press, 1969], chap. 2, n. 39).

In connection with the argument set forth in paragraph 52, see Calhoun to Robert S. Garnett (July 3, 1824) [source for letter]: "If there is one portion of the [United States] Constitution which I most admire, it is the distribution of power between the State and General government. It is the only portion that is novel and peculiar. The rest has been more or less copied; this is our invention and is altogether our own." These thoughts lead Calhoun immediately to Montesquieu:

I consider it to be the greatest improvement in the science of government after the division of power into Legislative, Executive, and Judicial. Without it, free states in the present [i.e., civilized or modern] condition of the world could not exist, or must have existed without safety or respectability. If limited to a small territory, they must be crushed by the great monarchical powers, or exist only at their discretion; but if extended over a great surface, the concentration of power and patronage necessary for government would speedily end in tyranny.

Quoted in *The Essential Calhoun*, 298-99. See, e.g., Montesquieu at chap. 3, n. 45 above. According to Calhoun, it is federalism or state rights that provides the only possible means of overcoming the disadvantages of an extended republic. Cf. *Spirit of the Laws*, bk. XI, chap. iv: "To prevent the abuse of power it is necessary to have power check power.

46 "On the Treasury Report" (delivered in the Senate, June 21, 1841), *Works*, 3:647.

47 "On the Veto Power" (delivered in the Senate, February 28, 1842), *Works*, 4:83: "one blended and harmonious whole, the true and perfect voice of the people"; 93ff., and context: "...of which the government itself is but a creature"; also, "On the Compensation Bill" (delivered in the House of Representatives, January 17, 1818), *Works*, 2:179-80: "...the all powerful voice which spake our government into existence, and made us politically what we are."

See Calhoun at chap. 2, nn. 3 and 8 above. Reference is usually made to the chapter 35 of Francis Leiber, *On Civil Liberty and Self-Government* (Philadelphia: 1880). Leiber had taught for a time in South Carolina, and was familiar with Calhoun's thought. Nevertheless, it is useful to note that Calhoun's usage has nothing to do with Leiber's discussion, but, rather, is to be immediately compared with Locke's identification of reason as "the Voice of God in man," above all with respect to the "strong desire of Self-preservation," which Calhoun calls the "great law of self preservation which pervades all that feels," and Hegel's identification of the state as "the march of God through the world" (Philosophy of Right, paras. addition to 258; 260, 270; cf. *Philosophy of History*, J. Sibree, trans. (New York: Dover, 1956), 457: the [rational] constitution is "the true *Theodicea*, the justification of God in history."). We began to discuss the implications of Calhoun's usage in the course of our remarks on *Disquisition*, para. 7. See Locke, *Two Treatises* (Laslett, ed.), 311; also, e.g., Diogenes Laertius, *Lives of the Famous Philosophers*, VII. 83.

⁴⁸ Cf. Aristotle, *Politics*, 1247a 6-8, especially, 1292a 4-24; Demosthenes, "On the Liberty of the Rhodians." It is possible that Calhoun also has in mind the career of Publius Claudius Pulcher ("Clodius"), including the affair concerning Caesar's wife. Cf. Calhoun, *Works*, 6:Appendix, 349ff.; also, Calhoun to Alexander Hamilton, Jr. (March 1830), quoted in Wilson, *The Essential Calhoun*, 348.

⁴⁹ Cf. Aristotle, *Politics*, 1265b 27-38, 1288b 22-1289a 25, 1291a 8-19, 1295b 39-1296a 3, 1326b 27-1327a 32; Plato, *Republic*, 421d; *Laws*, 704d-705b, 707d 1-6, 737a 5-b 4, 744d 1-8.

⁵⁰ See chap. 1 at nn. 85-86 above.

⁵¹ See Mill at chap. 1, n. 97 and the text at chap. 1 n. 51 above. Cf. Aristotle, *Politics*, 1263b 25ff., and context: "In the *Republic*, after all, Socrates has discussed very few matters: how things should stand concerning the partnership in women and children, possessions, and the [social] arrangement of the regime.... Otherwise, he has filled up the argument with extraneous discourses, particularly concerning the sort of education the guardians should have.

⁵² See the volumes of Wiltse's life and Coit's *John C. Calhoun: An American Portrait*. Varina Davis observed that "it was one of the sources of his power over the youth of his country that he assumed nothing except a universal, honest, co-intelligence between him and the world, and his conversation with a girl was on the same subjects as with a statesman" (quoted in Coit, *John C. Calhoun: Great Lives Observed*, 77). Calhoun to Anna Maria: "I am not one of those who think your sex ought to have nothing to do with politics. They have as much interest in the good conditions of the country as the other sex, and tho [*sic*] it would be unbecoming them to take an active part in political struggles, their opinion, when enlightened, cannot fail to have a great and salutary effect" (quoted in Bartlett, *John C. Calhoun*. 261) Cf. e.g., Niven, *John C. Calhoun and the Price of Union*, 223-24).

⁵³ The English geologist George Washington Featherstonhough, who held Calhoun to be "the most perfect gentleman I ever met," believed that Calhoun's only shortcoming was his failure to recognize his obvious superiority to others. Paul Hamilton Hayne: "I was impressed at the simplicity of Mr. Calhoun's manners. There is no assumption of that *chilling dignity* which the Great so frequently exercise towards inferior, but with an *intuitive perception* of courtesy grounded in real benevolence of heart, Mr. Calhoun adapts his conversation to the peculiar pursuits of the individual with whom he speaks & always leaves in the mind of his hearer a favorable opinion of his character — as a gentleman of tact & discernment" (quoted in Bartlett, *John C. Calhoun*, 277, emphasis original). Visiting the New York studio of Matthew Brady with Anna at her request in 1848, Calhoun who was ill, "showed a knowledge of the scientific process of photography" in his explanations to her which surprised Brady himself. See Coit's life, 479.

⁵⁴ Calhoun, "On the Bill Reported by the Select Committee of Executive Patronage" (delivered in the Senate, February 13, 1835), *Works*, 2:456: "Nature, said Mr. Calhoun, has bestowed her gifts very unequally and partially upon men. To some she has given one quality, to others another." "On the Independent Treasury Bill, in reply to Mr. Clay," *Works*, 3:, cf. 274 and 250: "The faculties of our mind are the immediate gift of our Creator, for which we are no further responsible than for their proper cultivation, according to our opportunities, and their proper application to control and regulate our actions." Human life is both for the sake of and the means to knowledge and goodness.

Cf. e.g., Calhoun to Andrew Jackson, June 4, 1826: "If I had no higher object than personal advancement, my course would be easy. I would have nothing to do but to float with the current of events." Calhoun to Micah Sterling, July 26, 1838:

> Had I gone with the crowd and the current of the times and aimed at advancing my popularity and influence, instead of struggling to preserve our free institutions and the liberty of the country, I could have passed for a first rate patriot.... What is really remarkable is this. Almost all allow me to possess abilities and sagacity, and yet altho' I have done the most unpopular acts, of which I could not but see the consequences even in performing them, I have been charged with motives of popularity and ambition.

Quoted in *The Essential Calhoun*, 423, 426. See the opening of "In Reply to Mr. Benton of Missouri" (delivered in the Senate, February 24, 1847), *Works*, 4:362ff.

55 Cf. Calhoun at n. 16 above: not all the disadvantages of such governments originate in the follies of numerical majorities. Aristotle, *Politics*, bk. V, *passim*, especially 1305 b22ff. The general point made in the text is the tacit problem addressed already in paragraph 27. In a sense, it is *the* problem.

56 Calhoun, "On His Resolution in Respect to the Brig Enterprise" (delivered in the Senate, March 13, 1840), *Works*, 3:483-84, and context: "wisest and most parental..."

57 Calhoun, "On the Bill to Recharter the United States Bank" (delivered in the Senate, March 21, 1834), *Works*, 2:355. *Works*, 2:79: "Such generous sympathy for those who stand connected with us only by the ties of citizenship...constitutes our real union. The rest is form." See n. 11 above.

There is nowhere in the *Disquisition* any concern for a special political education of children such as those propounded in Locke's *Thoughts on Education* or Rousseau's subsequent *Emile*. Calhoun's view that all of life is for education is opposed in spirit to the highly-structured inculcations or socialization projects represented by these efforts. These projects are not secondary or ephemeral, they are the characteristic expression of political thought based on the hypothesis of the "state of nature." Their Cartesian origin is evident in their respective emphasis on methodology and epistemology, not to say therapy, as well as authority, in perfecting the human faculties and attaining their natural ends. They are attempts, on this basis, to educate the children, beginning with the children's educators, to certain kinds of laws (Aristotle, *Politics*, 1310 a13-38), but they fail in educating virtue, which, according to Calhoun, is the aim of politics, as the ubiquity of government among all peoples at all times, shows whatever their education or level of intellectual and moral culture or, in other words, their place in the scale of patriotism and virtue. Calhoun addresses this issue directly in this section of the *Disquisition*.

58 Only the terms "society" (two times), "individuals" or "each [individual]" (four times), and "government" in reference strictly to its "primary end," which Calhoun again specifies as "protection" (three times), occur in paragraph 18. His discussion immediately returns from "society" and "individuals" to the "community" and the "people." Neither "society" nor "individuals" occurs again until paragraph 85. Para. 81: "community," "the great ends [of] government,"; para. 82: "community" (two times); para. 83: "community" (three times); "self-government" (two-times), as opposed to "absolute and despotic government"; para. 84: "community"; "people" or "they" (five times); "the race," under-

stood as so many human individuals or as human society (two times); the lower and the higher ends of government. In the whole discussion of the relation of the highest natural end of government, intellectual perfection, which is only rarely attained, and its primary end, which is protection in all circumstances, Calhoun increasingly treats the terms "liberty" and virtue (or "moral causes") or "self-government" as equivalent.

⁵⁹ See Locke, *An Essay Concerning Human Understanding* (Niddich, ed.), 43-46: "busy mind." Locke's root is Hobbes' *Leviathan*, chap. 13, on insecurity of property: "...in such a condition there is no place for industry; because the fruit thereof [cf. Calhoun: "fruits of their exertions"] is uncertain: and consequently no cultivation of the earth, no navigation, nor use of the commodities that may be imported by sea; no commodious building; no instruments of moving, and removing such things as require much force...." In connection with what follows, see Hume, "Of Commerce": "Our passions are the only causes of our labor."

⁶⁰ Cf. Smith, *The Wealth of Nations*, Edwin Cannon, ed. (New York: Random House, Modern Library, 1937), 324-27:

> An augmentation of fortune is the means by which the greater part of men propose and wish to better their condition [for] it is the means the most vulgar and obvious. [Nevertheless,]...the uniform, constant and uninterrupted effort of every man to better his condition, the principal from which public and national, as well as private opulence [the wealth of nations], is originally derived, is frequently powerful enough to maintain the natural progress of things toward improvement, in spite of both the extravagance of government, and the greatest errors of administration. Like the unknown principle of animal life, it frequently restores health and vigor to the constitution, in spite, not only of the disease, but of the absurd prescriptions of the doctor.

Its most invigorating spur is to be "protected by law and allowed by liberty."

⁶¹ Calhoun, "On the Bill to Recharter the United States Bank" (delivered in the Senate, March 21, 1834), *Works*, 2:344ff., and "On the Bill to Separate the Government from the Banks" (delivered in the Senate, October 3, 1837), *Works*, 3:102ff., 116ff.: the emergence of what Calhoun calls the "first era" of the system (Bank of Amsterdam, 1609-Bank of England, 1694) was "destined to effect a revolution in the condition of modern society." Withal, "never was an engine invented better calculated to place the destiny of the many in the hands of the few, or less favorable to that equality and independence which lie at the bottom of all free institutions.... its most fatal effects originate in its bearing on the moral and intellectual development of the community." See "On the Bill to Regulate the Deposits of the Public Money" (delivered in the Senate, May 28, 1836), *Works*, 3:534-69; "On the Loan Bill" (delivered in the Senate, July 19, 1841), *Works*, 4:1-13.

It is of course generally recognized that the concerns evinced in the passages cited are thematic in Calhoun's speeches, but the subject has not been systematically studied. See nn. 25 and 27 above; also, in connection with the speeches, G. M. Dickson, *The Financial Revolution in England: A Study in the Development of Public Credit 1688-1756* (London: 1967).

⁶² E.g., para. 80: "...his condition [of individuals and human desire]"; para. 84: "...their condition [of a people or political wholes]"; para. 88: "...equality of *condition* [with respect

to the condition of each]," "...their condition [with respect to the desire of each]"; para. 91: "the condition of the community."

Calhoun's attack on avarice is thematic throughout his public career and speeches (it is the root of his attack on spoilsmen or patronage, for example, no less than on the alliance of the government and the banking system or the system of disposing of public lands); e.g.: "...making money. The practical language of the Government to the people was—it is better to be rich than to be virtuous. Can we, then, wonder at the alarming growth of avarice? It is to be traced back, in part, to this original sin of our Government" ("On the Loan Bill" [delivered in the Senate, February 15, 1815], Works, 2:81, and context).

63 We note in passing that, while Calhoun here stipulates that "progress and improvement" among the population ("individuals") will be retarded by this turning back or decline, he omits any reference to "civilization," which he had mentioned earlier in the paragraph in connection with these. The development of the high arts and sciences, that is, technology or applied science, will continue, including its application to warfare, owing to the necessity both to provide for defense against external dangers and to maintain control against internal opposition (cf. para. 133).

64 Burke annotates the principle assigning liberty and power their proper spheres in his "Letter to a Member of the National Assembly" (in The Writings and Speeches of Edmund Burke, vol. VIII, L. G. Mitchell [Oxford: 1989], 332): "Men are qualified for civil society in exact proportion to their disposition to put moral chains upon their own appetites.... Society cannot exist unless a controlling power upon will and appetite be placed somewhere, and the less of it there is within, the more there must be without. It is ordained in the eternal constitution of things that men of intemperate minds cannot be free, Their passions forge their fetters." Government is this "controlling power" (Disquisition, para. 8).

65 Cf. e.g., Orlando Patterson, Freedom in the Making of Western Culture (New York: Basic Books, 1991), x:

There is nothing at all self-evident in the idea or, more properly, the high esteem in which we in the West hold freedom. For most of human history, and for nearly all of the non-Western world prior to Western contact, freedom was, and for many still remains, anything but an obvious or desirable goal.... Indeed, non-Western peoples have thought so little about freedom that most human languages did not even possess a word for the concept before contact with the West...

(Some chose a word whose primary meaning had been "licentiousness" to translate the Western idea, as all peoples, Western or non-Western, have a word for licentiousness. This reaction, which is historically not a reaction to Plato or Cicero—"Greece" or "Rome"—but to Hobbes and Locke—England—certainly deserves more attention than Professor Patterson devotes to it, for it evinces a sure awareness that Hobbism somehow reduces virtue to vice.) This is an important insight, which, however, ought to be extended to the Western concept of "equality," as well. Freedom or liberty is necessarily conceived in contradistinction to unfreedom or power or necessity, not in contradistinction to slavery, as is shown by the fact, observed by Professor Patterson, that the institution of slavery is universal, while the Western idea of freedom is not, as well as by the fact that freedom itself has often been understood in the West as "slavery to the law." Equality, in contradistinction to inequality, may or may not originally have been conceived, among other things, in contradistinction to slavery.

Professor Patterson's dogmatic sociology of Western culture is in fact animated by primarily a certain kind of Western egalitarianism (viz., "the latent ideology of the anti-slavery movement"), according to which inequality, not lack of liberty, is identified as "social death." The ideology of egalitarianism as the only way out of what is ideologically classified as "social death" need never arrive at the idea of liberty, and may even lose the substance of the term "licentiousness" as universally understood. Hence it is not surprising that, on the basis of Professor Patterson's sociology, one is incapable of distinguishing between the regime of German National Socialism and that of, say, the Tupinamba (ibid., 9ff.: "historical dead end," 404ff.: "the bleak sociohistorical truth..."). Nor is it surprising that the project should attempt to culminate in an attack on Plato and Cicero, as Hobbism itself had originally begun in such an attack (Aristotle).

Admittedly, equality and liberty are united to some extent, viz., politically, for liberty and hence inequality presuppose equality, but they are different ideas. To understand the emergence of the idea of liberty, it is necessary to understand the principles of constitutional government, whether Western or any other.

⁶⁶ Calhoun, "On the Oregon Bill" (delivered in the Senate, June 27, 1848), Works, 4:507-512: "Locke and Sydney..., vastly more [difficult]"; Hume, Treatise of Human Nature, "mere philosophical fictions," "fallacious and sophistical," and context.

⁶⁷ E.g., Aristotle, Politics, 1308b 11-15, and related passages. With respect to this important paragraph of the Disquisition, it may be noted that Calhoun spoke in just the same way in 1816. See "On the Repeal of the Direct Tax" (delivered in the House of Representatives, January 31, 1816), Works, 2:146: "I know that I utter truths unpleasant to those who wish to enjoy liberty without making the efforts necessary to secure it. Her favor is never won by the cowardly, the vicious, the indolent. It has been said by some physicians that life is a forced state. The same may be said of freedom. It requires efforts; it presupposes mental and moral qualities of a high order to be generally diffused in the society where it exists." And "On His Resolutions in Reference to the War with Mexico" (delivered in the Senate, January 4, 1848), Works, 4:416: "We make a great mistake in supposing all people are capable of self-government. Acting under that impression, many are anxious to force free governments on all the people of this continent, and over the world, if they had the power."

⁶⁸ Consult in this connection, Kant, Metaphysics of Morals, pt. 2, "Doctrine of Virtue," paras. 38-39: "...the idea of man who, as such, as a moral being, can never lose every inclination toward what is good," and context. This is the basis of the Scholastic moral doctrine of the natural law: Thomas Aquinas, Summa Theologiae, IaIIae, q. 94, a. 6. Consider Disquisition, paras. 2-3, 16 end, with 104.

In regard to the principle laid down in this paragraph, consider the distinct but related observation in Thomas Szasz, The Second Sin (New York: Anchor, 1973), 42: "Punishment is no longer fashionable. Why? Because—with its corollary, reward—it makes some people guilty and others innocent, some good and others evil; in short, it creates moral distinctions among men, and to the 'democratic' mentality this is odious. Our age seems to prefer a meaningless collective guilt to meaningful individual responsibility."

69 Certainly, one may think of Manifest Destiny and the doctrine popular sovereignty. Cf. Lewis Cass (Democrat U.S. presidential candidate from Michigan in 1844 and 1846) in support of the War with Mexico: "We want almost unlimited power of expansion. That is our safety valve" (e.g., Peterson, *The Great Triumvirate*, 424). See note 67, above.

Calhoun, "On His Resolution in Respect to the Brig Enterprise" (March 13, 1840), *Works*, 3:480-82: "a higher and more intellectual class...the Abbe Lamennais," some of whose writings are quoted; "social and political slavery..."; "the serfs of this era...." Lamennais' ideal social condition was then that of the early Christian church or the monastic community (like Tolstoy's influence on Israeli *kibbutzim*). (Some of Marx's phraseology and sermonic tone in the *Manifesto of the Communist Party*, which further degrades Christian socialism in the direction of R. H. Tawney's Christian Marxism and of "liberation theology," is reminiscent of Lamennais.) See generally L. B. Namier, *1848: The Revolution of the Intellectuals* (London, 1944): the revolts were inspired by the political ideologies of journalists, professors, philosophers, lawyers, and students; and P. Robertson, *Revolutions of 1848* (Princeton, 1952). Consult in this connection Timothy Messer-Kruse, *The Yankee International: Marxism and the American Reform Tradition* (Chapel Hill, 1998), 24ff.

Calhoun, "On His Resolutions in Reference to the War with Mexico" (delivered in the Senate, January 4, 1848), *Works*, 4:416, and context: "It is a sad delusion"; 405, "antiquated notions—obsolete ideas"; nn. 38-39 above; *Disquisition*, paras. 46, 119. In connection with the points made in the text, see Orestes Brownson to Calhoun, Oct. 13, 1841, in *Papers of John C. Calhoun*, 15:791.

See Kolakowski, *Main Currents of Marxism*, 3 vols. (Oxford, 1978, rep. New York, 1982), 3:323-24 and context: "the greatest fantasy...."

70 Cf. Aristotle, *Politics*, 1266 a31-1267 b20; n. 22 above.

71 Equality before the law means that none are not subject to law, not necessarily that there is equality of laws. However, compare, e.g., Kant "Theory and Practice," in *Kant's Political Writings*, Hans Reiss, ed. (Cambridge University Press, 1970), 76: equality before the law means that no citizen can enjoy hereditary privileges [private, not common, laws] against other citizens.

72 Cf. Smith, *The Theory of Moral Sentiments*, I. iii. chap. 2, "Of the Origin of Ambition, and of the Distinction of Ranks": "...the most agreeable hope and...the most ardent desire of human nature," etc. The phrase quoted in the text above is taken from the *Wealth of Nations*, bk. V. Cf. the English agrarian Charles Hall, *The Effects of Civilization on the People in the European States* (1805, London, 1850), 106:

> Civilization we have defined to consist in the improvements of the sciences, and in the refinements of manufactures, by which the luxuries of life are furnished. These [improvements, refinements, and, especially, luxuries] could have had no existence unless the bulk of mankind had been reduced to be manufacturers; that is to say, till they were reduced to that degree of poverty as to be compelled to work at those trades for their subsistence."

73 Calhoun, "On the Compensation Bill" (delivered in the House of Representatives, January 17, 1817), *Works*, 2:184: "...the most deserving citizens. Talent in this country is

principally from the middle and lower classes..."; "...men who, by nature and study, are endowed with requisite talents for public service..."Also Bartlett, *John C. Calhoun*, 107: Calhoun, touching upon a characteristic principle of Ciceronianism (e.g., *De Oratore*, III.61): "I deem it...the duty of any man of education and leisure to bring himself forward in the publick business." Cf. Marmor, *John C. Calhoun: Politician, Social Critic, Political Philosopher*, 110: "Calhoun was neither egalitarian nor aristocratic, but meritocratic."

The multiplication of wants created by the march of progress represents a constant temptation to luxury and corruption. This is not a new temptation, although, as has been noted, it is strongest in civilized regimes. In fact, it constitutes the characteristic weakness of civilized regimes. Like other temptations, it must be controlled by discipline or self-government, and constitutional government is the most effective means of nourishing both attachment to a common center and self-government (paras. 77-78, 96-97).

74 What may seem the sum total of Calhoun's position on slavery in America in this connection, or of what is called his "reactionary" anticipation of Marx, is, ultimately, a response to Locke's assertion in the *Essay on Civil Government* that in America "a King of a large and fruitful Territory there feeds, lodges, and is clad worse than a day laborer in England": Calhoun's reply is that, without kings, a slave in America is better fed, lodged, clad, and cared for than a day laborer is in England. Cf. Smith, writing a little more than a century after the *Essay on Civil Government* in *The Wealth of Nations*:

> Observe the accommodation of the most common artificer or day laborer in a civilized and thriving country.... Compared, indeed, with the more extravagant luxury of the great, his accommodation must no doubt appear extremely simple and easy; and yet it may be true, perhaps, that the accommodation of an European prince does not always so much exceed that of an industrious and frugal peasant, as the accommodation of the latter exceeds that of many an African king, the absolute master of ten thousand naked savages.

For Smith, the difference between these "accommodations" is ultimately to be found in the progressive condition of commercial society. Nevertheless, or rather because of this, his economic science tends to become, and is originally conceived as, a kind of political science, "a branch of the science of the statesman or legislator" (*Wealth of Nations*, IV, introduction). In Smith, however, this "branch" all but absorbs statesmanship and legislation. For Calhoun, politics necessarily comes first; political economy (economics as other than "home economics") is secondary, because it depends on politics to understand itself. It is possible for men in the savage state to be more noble, more manly, than men in the civilized state, to say nothing of peasants or of men under absolute rule. The case of the Iroquois is an obvious example, otherwise it would not be an example "deserving notice" (*Disquisition*, para. 110). That they depend primarily on their constitution, not on their "accommodations" or conditions, is what the statesman must first understand (*Disquisition*, para. 83).

75 Calhoun to John O'Sullivan (October 14, 1838): "I am of the progress party; but events must move slowly and in their proper order, in order to move successfully. I am of the impression [that] the progress party are too much disposed to simplify in politics.... successful application in any given case requires a highly refined organic arrangement, just

as we see the application, in practice, of all the great laws of nature." Quoted in *The Essential Calhoun*, 48-49.

According to Smith, the aim of the true statesman is the "progressive" state (including progressively rising wages), which, as Calhoun read him, can only be achieved by insuring that the "market" (supply and demand) checks or provides a negative on organized economic interests. It is only thus that a "free market" is free. This means, in the first place, that economic interests (and above all, the banks) must be separated from the government, whose protection they will earnestly seek. *Wealth of Nations*, I. vi. 43; II. iii. 6; IV. ii. 43, and related sections. The best introduction of which I am aware is Knud Haakonssen, *The Science of the Legislator: The Natural Jurisprudence of David Hume and Adam Smith* (Cambridge: 1981): the subject discussed in paragraph 80ff. of the *Disquisition* is treated on 100-101, 131ff.), and George Stigler, "Smith's Travels on the Ship of State," in *Essays on Adam Smith*, A. S. Skinner and Thomas Wilson, eds. (Oxford: 1975), 237-46. See also n. 96, below.

Calhoun elsewhere repeatedly speaks of the rise of banking and credit as the most salient feature of modernity, and carefully and even masterfully traces its history and application to politics, but he nowhere touches upon this important subject in the *Disquisition*. Banking historian Bray Hammond has written that Calhoun was "distinguished among American statesmen in his realization that banking is a monetary function, that regulation of the currency is the duty of the federal government and that the duty is to be exercised through a state bank; not for more than a century would such an understanding of the subject be expressed again in Congress" (quoted in Bartlett, *John C. Calhoun*, 207.)

76 Cf. Bertrand de Jouvenal, *The Ethics of Redistribution* (Indianapolis: Liberty Press, 1990), 12:

> The promise that the State [which exists only to protect Lockean property] will wither away, because [of] the disappearance of antagonisms is the fundamental aim of socialism; but it has somewhat suffered from being bandied about in political controversy. Some shrewd critics of socialism have very properly taken the withering away of the State as a criterion of socialist success, thereby causing annoyance to their opponents. In the dust of combat the fact that the State is supposed to wither away as an instrument of repression and police power has been somewhat lost sight of, and in fairness it does not seem that enlarged functions of the State, by themselves, prove a failure of socialism but only the preservation and *a fortiori* the enlargement of police powers. It is, however, only too evident that police powers are at their greatest where the destruction of private property has been most achieved—a plain fact which refutes socialist belief.

Cf., similarly, John Dunn, *Western Political Theory in the Face of the Future*, 2nd ed. (Cambridge: Cambridge University Press, 1993), 111-12:

> The experience of post-revolutionary socialist countries under Marxist auspices...make it apparent that the relationship between Marxism as a monopolistic system of belief and a ruling Marxist party which is in a position to exert the rights which it claims to derive from the exercise of a monopoly of moral insight and practical sagacity is, in the absence of *effective political restraints*, quite

appallingly dangerous. Both Marx and Lenin appear to have assumed that socialized production and a very high degree of responsibility of governmental power to society and economy were quite readily compatible. But their reasons for believing this were not well articulated [*viz.*, that after the revolution human nature would change]; and the organized political legacy which they have, however unwittingly [*sic*], left behind them has made their hopes seem more than a little callow. This is not a matter about which it is either forgivable or sensible to be discreet. If Marxist political theory is to learn how to realize its own emancipatory project, it needs to develop a quite new level and style of reflection [*sic*] on the question of how in practice and in principle the battle of democracy could be won.... But the extent to which governments can in fact be rendered responsible to those over whom they rule (an extent which, unless it can be increased rather than diminished, will preclude forever the construction [*sic*] of a society in any way resembling the aspirations of Marx) is still a very obscure question and one which urgently demands reflection. [Emphasis added.]

Indeed, according to Calhoun, it is what the science of government comes down to, as well as its occasion (*Disquisition*, para. 15: "the important and difficult question...").

The quotation in the following paragraph is taken from Calhoun, "On the Oregon Bill" (delivered in the Senate, June 27, 1848), *Works*, 4:512.

77 Calhoun, "Remarks on the State Rights Resolutions in Regard to Abolition" (delivered in the Senate, January 12, 1838), *Works*, 3:164-65: "The fact is that it is abstract truths only which deeply impress the understanding and the heart, and effect great and durable revolutions; and the higher the intelligence of a people, the greater their influence. It is only the ignorant and brute creation over whom they have no control."

78 Kant, "Conjectural Beginning of Human History." Cf. *Critique of Judgement*, sec. 41.

79 Kant, "Conjectural Beginning of Human History": "the safe and harmless state of childhood"; "Idea for a Universal History," Ninth Thesis, and Mill's reference in the *Essay Liberty* to all those peoples still in the "nonage" of the race; Locke, *Thoughts Concerning Education:*"nonage" (i.e., childhood).

Cf. Charles Beard, xxvi, xl:

Viewed in the large, history reveals a great gulf between the primitive savagery with which mankind began and the best [i.e., most "progressive"] social orders. This may be said without overlooking the tragedy and cruelty that mark the way from the beginnings; and technology by continually demonstrating potentialities, will surely strengthen the idea of progress until a new synthesis is provided which may enormously accelerate the blundering pace inherited from the past. But after all this has been said, does the idea of progress take on the validity of a law of nature, the law of gravitation, for instance?...The answer must be negative.... [Yet] conceding for the sake of the argument that the past has been chaos, without order or design, we are still haunted by the shadowing thought that by immense efforts of will and intelligence, employing natural science as the supreme instrumentality of power, mankind may rise above the necessity into the kingdom [*sic*] of freedom, subduing material things to humane and rational purposes.

The quotation concerning children immediately following in the text is taken from Calhoun, "On the Loan Bill" (delivered in the House of Representatives, February 25, 1814), *Works*, 2:91; cf. "On the Repeal of the Direct Tax" (delivered in the House of Representatives, January 31, 1816), *Works*, 2:137: "The first symptom of decay has ever appeared in the backward and negligent discharge of [the duty of prompt defence of the country]. Those who are acquainted with the historians and orators of antiquity know the truth of this assertion. The least decay of patriotism, the least verging toward towards pleasure and luxury, will there immediately discover itself."

[80] One may be tempted to say that Calhoun's view of history is epitomized in the historical works of Gibbon and Hume (the latter of which he clearly held in almost the same regard as did Hegel), but, so far as I am aware, he nowhere unequivocally indicates as much. Apart from his thematic references to posterity and the judgment of later ages, his own view is found in such statements as: "To avoid all personal feelings, I shall endeavor to recede, in imagination, a century from the present time, and from that distant position regard the [immediate] events to which I allude, in that spirit of philosophical inquiry by which an earnest seeker after truth, at so remote a day, may be supposed to be actuated." "On the Bill to Repeal the Force Act" (delivered in the Senate, April 9, 1834), *Works*, 2:392. See chap. 1, n. 75, and context. Calhoun's own actions are meant by him to be seen in this light: this is a key to Calhoun's politics. More importantly, it is also the key to *A Disquisition on Government*.

[81] Cf. Locke, *First Treatise*, first chapter; more especially, Filmer, *Patriarcha*, in *Patriarcha and Other Political Works*, Peter Laslett, intro. and ed. (Oxford: Basil Blackwell, 1949), 331-35. Calhoun sides with Filmer, not Locke, although on what might be called Lockean grounds. Cf. "Letter to the Honorable William Smith," *Works*, 6:229-30: "Filmer," "Locke and Sydney"; "On the Loan Bill" (delivered in the House of Representatives, February 25, 1814), *Works*, 2:96: the "country...stands in the place of the common parent of all." See n. 13 above; also, particularly, Burke, "Speech on the Opening Articles of Impeachment": "This great law..."

[82] Locke, *Second Treatise*, 323: "another way of entrance into the World," and context; Calhoun, "On the Oregon Bill" (delivered in the Senate, June 27, 1848), *Works*, 4:507-509ff.

[83] See n. 56 above.

[84] Louis Hartz, *The Liberal Tradition in America* (New York: Harcourt Brace, 1955), 60. Professor Hartz is followed in this general view by Hannah Arendt (*On Revolution*) and various others.

[85] The account of this conversation is drawn from its record in Adams' diaries, and presented in the better lives of Calhoun. Calhoun's position on the relation of civilized to less advanced peoples is analogous to that of Burke with regard to British rule in India. See Calhoun at n. 96 below; Burke, "Speech on Fox's East India Bill," "Speech on Opening the Articles of Impeachment," "Speech at the Close of the Impeachment"; cf. Cicero, "Against Verres"; text at n. 48ff above. Burke's oft-cited comment that he would rather be remembered for his protection of the peoples of India than for anything else, as well as the controversy about him in this regard (e.g., James Mill, *The History of British India*, vol. 5) should be seen in this context; Conor Cruise O'Brien, *The Great Melody: A Thematic Life of Edmund Burke* (Chicago: University of Chicago Press, 1992), xxxiv-xxxviii; chaps. 4 and 6.

[86] Cf. "On Abolition Petitions" (delivered in the Senate, March 9, 1836), *Works*, 2:484: "The power of resistance, by an universal law of nature, is on the exterior..."; "On the Loan Bill (delivered in the House of Representatives, February 25, 1814), *Works*. 2:99: "Like the system of our State and General Governments—within they are many—to the world but one." See n. 6 above. Cf. Thomas Jefferson to James Madison (December 16, 1786, Ford, IV, 333): "To make us one nation as to foreign concerns, and keep us distinct in domestic ones, gives the proper outline of the proper division of power between the general and particular governments."

[87] See n. 9 above. This phenomenon is the root of Aristotle's contention that a good man can be a good citizen only in a good regime, and Machiavelli's contention that what is called vice in a bad regime may be necessary and desirable, that is, virtue. (With Calhoun's reference to liberty as "little more than a name," see Solzhenitsyn, *Letter to the Soviet Leaders*: life by lies; the acknowledged or "open" lie, and similar remarks by Vaclav Havel in connection with the corruption of public life and hence private morality.)

[88] Cf. Monroe, *The People, the Sovereigns*, 7-11, 13, 17-18.

[89] Cf. Machiavelli, *The Prince*, chap. 2, and related passages.

[90] E.g., "Address on the Relations of the States and Federal Government" (1831), *Works*, 6:92. "On Mr. Clay's Resolution in Relation to the Revenues and Expenditures of the Government" (delivered in the Senate, March 16, 1842), *Works*, 4:103.

[91] The term is taken from Heidegger's essays, "The Question About Technology" and "The Turning" in *The Question Concerning Technology and Other Essays*, William Lovitt, trans. and intro. (New York: Harper and Row, 1977). We use it here in its primary sense as "valuing." While, for Heidegger, enframing conceals existing things as they are in themselves, it confronts one at the same time with the question of being as such and hence with the possibility of the revealing or unconcealment of being, or of one's recognizing the simultaneous concealment and unconcealment of being as such. This recognition of concealment itself for what it is, what Heidegger calls one's "turning" from the concealment of being in enframed things to openness for being as such, and the assumption of one's own individual finitude, is the return to the true human home. Only thus is one (man himself) not forgotten but discovered (disclosed) for what one is. The turning or disclosure or authentic being can only be achieved individually through questioning being, and it is the definitive human task. However, this interesting way of thinking from enframing to one's discovery or knowing of being as such, or the "is" of beings, and the assumption of finitude, worldliness, and caring, forgets the original problem of things as problems. Receiving the disclosure of being, one still does not see existing things as they are. One is even led away from this question or into forgetfullness about it, particularly in the most important instance, the problem of tyranny as such or of the existence of tyrants. Heideggerism does not recognize this most characteristic of human problems as a distinctively human problem, which is to say, Heideggerism does not recognize human being as essentially political: man, although social or possessing technology (language), and hence possessing the possibility of human being, is in the decisive sense not yet a political animal. Human freedom is trans- or other-than-political in the traditional sense.

Yet there is in Heidegger an erstaz political thinking, or a thinking in place of the political in the traditional sense, of what is between the existing things as they are and the disclosure of being as such. This is the place of "standing up," which means the same thing as "living up" in English, to the greatness of a "spiritual world," or in accord with the values of an original worldview (*An Introduction to Metaphysics*, Ralph Manheim, trans. [New Haven, 1959], 45-46). This is the role or "vocation," as Heidegger adapts and develops Weber's thought of "Politics as a Vocation," of a "nation" or "people," such as ancient Greeks and modern Germans (*Introduction*, 38). This vocation is to attain or destin the extra-ordinary in the world (whereas "to philosophize...is an extra-ordinary inquiry into the extra-ordinary," 13-14), what Calhoun has called the exceptional case, "something extraordinary" (*Disquisition*, para. 6; cf. e.g., paras. 79: "striking," 99: "striking," 104: "wonder"). In discussing this vocation, Heidegger puts all the weight on what Calhoun describes as the "spring from the bosom of the community" (*Disquisition*, para. 119), i.e., just as government itself springs from human society, and none on government itself, still less on extraordinary (i.e., constitutional) government as such. In other words, he thinks only of the fact that a people gives a government (or gets the government it deserves, as the saying is), and not at all of the fact that the government also makes or forms the people (*Disquisition*, para. 78), or is indeed the most important thing. (Otherwise, one is left merely with the idea of race.) In other words, because he presupposes that an extraordinary people, say, in Heidegger's terms (*Introduction*, 38), the "most metaphysical of nations," will give or "wrest" an extraordinary government ("Spirit is destiny"), he forgets the question of government, as though it were given or taken-for-granted or some kind of standing reserve. According to Calhoun, however, this question, which itself is the truly extraordinary and characteristically human question, cannot be forgotten but must remain uppermost even for a people capable of "high intellectual and moral culture," and even especially and above all for such a people (*Disquisition*, para. 7ff), beginning with the question of perfection of the moral faculties generally, since the familiar virtues are, like government, found in some sense in all communities, or, if this is (on the argument) declared impossible, then with the question of how the intelligent may come to lead the community and protect the weaker against the stronger parts for the good of the whole (*Disquisition*, paras. 21, last sentence, 71ff).

How can now absent history be seized and begun and truly human being disclosed? This haunting question, this "enframing" (in the sense we have used it in the text) question in the very midst of the fundamental question of being, is here the *political* question *par excellence*, in the end, the question of the nature and object of government. Is there not walled off in these paragraphs of *An Introduction to Metaphysics* the question that if human being is only in its being disclosed or understood, what is it for? Here is portent of the clearing for politics, the becoming of good and right.

Heidegger's original ontology bespeaks a commonplace politics, one in which the clearing of politics is filled with the "I" (Latin *Ego*) of the speaking *princeps*. In short, this "relation to being" (51) is here nothing extra-ordinary, and much less something distinctively "Greek." (Consult in this connection especially Simone Weil, "The Great Beast" ["*Quelques reflexions sur les origines de l'Hitlerism*"], passim, in *Selected Essays* [London: Routledge & Kegan Paul], 1957.) On the contrary, the destination of the "creative view" — that is to say, for Heidegger (following Neitzsche) the destruction — of the Western tradition in the will to power of a tribe (or tribes) or its leader is not merely "pre-Socratic" but even pre-Homeric, not to say pre-literate. It is the effort mounted by strong German thinkers whose thought is not yet so strong as their German. The characteristic symptom of such an ambition, the willful attempt to destruct the Western tradition as such as a way with and in words *and* deeds, may be said to show itself most expressively in Heidegger's attack on the statesman Cicero in the same lecture: *An Introduction to Metaphysics* (13 and context, 51). Cf. esp., chap. 2, n. 31 and context, above; Cicero, *Academica Posteriori* I, 4ff.

For the themes Heidegger develops in the portion of the *Introduction to Metaphysics* mentioned here, dereliction (*Geworfenheit*, see *Being and Time*, paras. 38, 40), national spirit, and technicity, compare generally Simone Weil, *The Need for Roots* (*L'Enracinement*). Weil's interest in manual labor is comparable to what has been called Heidegger's Swabian agrarianism and to the critique of "progress" in Southern Agrarianism.

⁹² The most immediately relevant comparison is that of the "four stages" of historic development outlined by Smith in his lectures on jurisprudence and in *The Wealth of Nations* (cf. especially the remarks on the application of gunpowder to warfare):

In ancient times the opulent and civilized found it difficult to defend themselves against the poor and barbarous nations. In modern times the poor and barbarous find it difficult to defend themselves against the opulent and civilized. The invention of fire-arms, an invention which at first sight appears to be so pernicious, is certainly favorable both to the permanency and to the *extension* of civilization. [emphasis added, *Wealth of Nations*, bk. V.i.a.44]

Cf. Haakonssen, *The Science of the Legislator: The Natural Jurisprudence of David Hume and Adam Smith*, 155ff; and Istvan Hont, "The Language and Sociability of Commerce: Samuel Pufendorf and the Theoretical Foundations of the 'Four-Stages Theory'," in L. Pagden, ed., *The Languages of Political Theory* (Cambridge: 1987), 253ff. See also Monroe, *The People, the Sovereigns*, 20-21, 24-33, 39-40, 47-48, 50ff.; there was doubtless considerable discussion between Calhoun and Monroe on this subject, particularly as it immediately bore on Indian policy.

Cf., also, e.g., J. S. Mill, *Auguste Comte and Positivism* (London: 1865), and *Cours, the Positive Philosophy of Auguste Comte*, Harriet Martineau, ed. and trans. (London: 1853).

⁹³ Cf. e.g., Aristotle, *Politics*, 1268b 38-41, and context.

⁹⁴ As Rousseau says in the *Emile*, it is only *history* that rises at dusk, or "when a people is already in decline." On the other hand, in Kant's conjectural sketches toward a universal history, he points to the same time to which Hegel points as a "period of transition" after the "end" of history. Taken in themselves or within the limits of their own ground, the peak statements of this school: Rousseau's "legislator," Kant's world "republic of republics," and the constitutional monarchy of the *Philosophy of Right*, can and do only retard the politics of this stage of society. Perhaps (as one might expect of private persons who did not engage in politics), they provide little guidance for the statesman.

⁹⁵ E.g., Calhoun, "On the Motion to Repeal the Direct Tax" (delivered in the House of Representatives, January 31, 1816), *Works*, 2:136-53; "On the Abolition Petitions" (delivered in the Senate, March 9, 1836), *Works*, 2:475: "...nearly all that has been gained for liberty in modern times..."; "On the Resolutions Giving Notice to Great Britain" (delivered in the

Senate, March 16, 1846), *Works*, 4:278: "...a struggle for mastery between the greatest power in the world on the one side, against the most growing on the other," and context; in connection with this paragraph in particular, "On the Distribution Bill" (delivered in the Senate, August 24, 1841), *Works*, 4:13-43.

[96] Cf. Twain, *A Yankee in King Arthur's Court*, chap. XLIII, "The Battle of the Sand-Belt." (The Connecticut arms-manufacturer replaces Modred, or "Medraut," in the novel.)

The view is essentially the same in Melville's novels of the South Seas: e.g., *Typee*: "Civilization, for every advantage she imparts, holds a hundred evils in reserve..." Cf, Ahab in *Moby-Dick*: "All my means are sane, my motive and my object mad."

[97] Two instances in which Calhoun presented this comparison in other terms are noteworthy in this context. In his speech "On the Proposed Increase in the Army," ([delivered in the Senate, February 16], 1837, *Works*, 3:28ff) he compares the condition of the Indians, whom he more typically referred to as "aborigines," in relation to a civilized army to unwary and benign animals in relation to human hunters. The speech (unfortunately, only reported) should be studied in its entirety, including its context, from the beginning.

The emphasis on agents and fortunes in these speeches just cited points to Calhoun's concern with trade as distinct from conquest. In his "Report on the System of Indian Trade" (December, 1818, *Works*, 5:8ff.), he explains that "the Indians themselves are not the proper judges of their own interests," that is, they are implicitly in the condition of children in relation to predatory adults, in respect to trade with civilized peoples, and, if not protected accordingly, they only "become the instruments of the most cunning and vicious of the traders." "It is their very ignorance and weakness" in the face of fraud and violence, "which render it necessary for the Government to interfere." Awareness of this fact presents a necessary and crucial exception to the doctrine of free trade as it is usually understood (21-24: "a greater effort of reason"). As "the Indians are not so situated to leave it to time and experience to effect their civilization," but will otherwise rapidly be utterly destroyed, protection is necessary in order to ensure genuinely free trade, and its blessings, including increased civilization, among them, and thus benefit all those who would trade with them. Otherwise, a few vicious individuals will merely steal fortunes and retard progress. After discussing the character and aims of this protection, Calhoun says: "A deep conviction of the importance of the subject, and a strong desire to arrest the current of events, which, if permitted to flow in the present channel, must end in the annihilation of those who were once the population of the country, must be my apology for this digression."

The importance of the subject concerns the proper relation of civilized and non-civilized peoples existing in immediate proximity. This relation or the problem it poses characterizes the present condition of the world. The protection in question is connected with economics, to be sure, but it is a political protection and its ends are essentially political. It is a question of what Calhoun understood, perhaps better than any other figure after Burke and Smith, what was once understood as "political economy," which is the only genuine economics. The condition of the American aborigines in this respect is exemplary of the condition of savage in relation to civilized peoples:

The nations of Indians who inhabit this portion of our continent, were, on its first discovery, in a state of the most perfect commercial independence. Their knowledge of the useful arts was, indeed, very limited, but it was commensurate with their wants and desires. With their rude implements of husbandry, their hook and bow, in the construction of which they were well instructed, they drew a scanty but (for them) a sufficient supply from the soil, the water, and the forest. A great change has since taken place, such as appears to be inevitable by a fixed law of nature, in the intercourse between a civilized and savage people. Helplessness has succeeded independence. While their wants have been greatly multiplied and enlarged by their intercourse with their more civilized neighbors, their knowledge even of their former rude arts has been lost, without acquiring those which are necessary in their new condition. The manufacture of the axe and hoe, by which they now clear and cultivate the soil, and the gun and ammunition, by which they take their game, are far above their skill; and with the exhaustion of their present stock, without a new supply, they would be reduced to extreme want. On trade, then, with those from whom they can draw these and other supplies, they are wholly dependent...their capacity of paying for the goods purchased must...in a great measure, depend upon the proceeds of the soil.

In short, in the light of political economy, the relation of the savage peoples to the civilized begins to stand in the present condition of the world as that of the agricultural to the manufacturing interest in a civilized community or country. This fundamental relationship must be borne in mind in beginning to study all of Calhoun's speeches and reports touching upon this celebrated but as yet little understood feature of his thought, for it is not unconnected to his view that agriculture is superior to manufacturing, to say nothing of banking, as a human way of life.

[98] Cf. Monroe, *The People, the Sovereigns*, 25-27: "brute creation...extinct"; passim, "the obligations of humanity..." Walter A. Fairservis, Jr., *The Threshold of Civilization* (New York: Scribner and Sons, 1975), 5: "The societies of primitive man are virtually extinguished when they come in contact with civilizations."

[99] "If there be a political proposition universally true—one which springs directly from the nature of man, and is independent of circumstances—it is that irresponsible power is inconsistent with liberty, and must corrupt those who exercise it." "Exposition and Protest," *Works*, 6:29ff. Aristotle, *Politics*, 1318b38-1319a1: "For to be under constraint and unable to do everything one might resolve to do is advantageous. The license to do whatever one wishes cannot defend against what is base in every human being." Montesquieu, *Spirit of the Laws*, XI. iv. first para.: "*une experience eternelle...*"

[100] E.g., Michael Howard, *War in European History* (New York: Oxford University Press, 1976).

[101] Calhoun, "On the Resolutions Giving Notice to Great Britain" (delivered in the Senate, March 16, 1846), *Works*, 4:279: "I allude not to the ravages or devastations—to the oceans of blood that must flow, and the manifold losses and miseries which would accompany the war. They are common to all wars; but however vividly painted, they have but little effect in deterring a brave people from resorting to it." Cf. "On the Tariff Bill" (delivered in the House of Representatives, April 6, 1816), *Works*, 2:165:

We cannot, he presumed, be indifferent to dangers from abroad, unless, indeed, the House is prepared to indulge in the phantom of eternal peace, which seems to possess the dream of some of its members. Could such a state exist, no foresight or fortitude would be necessary to conduct the affairs of the republic; but as it is the mere illusion of the imagination, as every people that ever has or ever will exist is subjected to the vicissitudes of peace and war, it must ever be considered as the plain dictate of wisdom in peace to prepare for war.

102 Cf. Thackeray, "*De Juventute*" (1860), in *The Works of William Makepeace Thackeray* 26 vols. (New York: Harper Brothers, 1898-1921), 21:232. What Thackeray calls the "old world" of his childhood was the world of "stage coaches, more or less swift, riding-horses, pack-horses, highway-men, knights in armour, Norman invaders, Roman legions, Druids, Ancient Britons, painted blue, and so forth.... Your railroad starts the new era, and we of a certain age belong to the new time and the old one. We are of the time of chivalry as well as the Black Prince of Sir Walter Manny. We are the age of steam." Such observations are common. This is is part of what Calhoun calls the continuing "age of transition."

103 Cf. Montesquieu, *Pensees*: "Voltaire will never write a good history. He is like the monks who write not for the subject they are concerned with but for the greater glory of their order: Voltaire is writing for his monastery" (*Oeuvres*, II, 419).

104 For example, Calhoun speaks of religion as "the sacred cause," "the most sacred of all things, the medium of divine communion, our consolation as mortals," and believes that joining the interests of religion and politics results now in injury to "the interest of both." ("On the New Army Bill" [delivered in the House of Representatives, January 14, 1818], *Works*, 2:54.) Fanaticism is, on the other hand, a kind of caricature of religion's relation to reason, is related to religion or to politics in the same way: "Fanaticism, from its nature, breaks out into violent movements, and soon exhausts itself by its extravagence and folly, unless it comes to be combined with some more steady and permanent cause of action. The reason is to be found in the fact that fanatics, as a class, have far more zeal than intellect – and are fanatics only because they have. There can be no fanaticism but where there is more passion than reason" ("On the Amendment to the Oregon Bill" [delivered in the Senate, August 12, 1849], *Works*, 2:519).

105 Calhoun, "On the Loan Bill" (delivered in the House of Representatives, February 25, 1814), *Works*, 2:99: "Government, it is true, can command the arm and hand, the bone and muscle, of the nation; but these are powerless – nerveless, without the concurring good wishes of the community. He who, in estimating the strength of a people, looks only to numbers and physical force, leaves out the most material elements of power – union and zeal. Without these, the former is inert matter. Without these, a free people is degraded to the miserable rabble of a despotism; but with these, they are irresistable [sic]." Throughout his speeches, Calhoun typically refers to all the elements here mentioned in reference to moral power as the "virtue of the people." See nn. 11, 56 above.

106 See n. 79 above. Cicero, *Republic*, I.34.51. Cf. Thomas Jefferson to John Adams, October 28, 1813: "That form of government is the best which provides the most effectually for a pure selection of natural *Aristoi* into offices of the government."

Chapter 5

---

[1] John D'Alberg, Lord Acton, "Political Causes of the American Revolution," in *Essays on Church and State*, Douglas Woodruff, ed. (New York: Viking Press, 1953), 315, 316. The quotation is a composite of two Acton sentences. "Writing...at the age of twenty-seven, Acton said that Calhoun's arguments in this passage were the perfection of political truth," wrote G. E. Fasnacht, and he "expressed substantially the same view" through the end of his life; Fasnacht, *Acton's Political Philosophy: An Analysis* (New York: Viking Press, 1953), 95.

Acton actually had said, in reference to certain of Calhoun's speeches and reports, that "Calhoun [delivered] arguments which are the very perfection of political truth, and which combine the realities of modern democracies and medieval freedom." The reference by Fasnacht to what he identifies as "this passage," however, actually denotes no passage by Acton himself but, rather, Acton's three-page synopsis of the whole *Disquisition* (about half of which is reproduced in Fasnacht's *Acton's Political Philosophy*), which constitutes the center and theoretical peak of his great essay. The synopsis is given in excerpts from the *Disquisition*. Acton introduces his synopsis by saying that "in his disquisition on government, Calhoun has expounded his theory of a constitution in a manner so profound and so extremely applicable to the politics of the present day, that we regret we can only give a very feeble notion of the argument in a few extracts for which we can make room."

The relation of Calhoun's political philosophy to Acton's thought (or Mill's) is another study. However, we may note that the synopsis excerpts from paragraphs 13 and 14 (describing the "constitution"), and from paragraph 126 (describing the "struggle for the whole"). All of Acton's other excerpts are taken from the section 19-98: specifically, from paragraphs 21, 22, 26, 36, 37, 39, 40, 54, 57, 70, 72, 74, 88, 89. Of these, Acton devotes the most space to the extracts from 13-14, 22, 36-40, 54, 70, 88, and 126.

[2] Even his better biographers (Wiltse, Coit, Meigs, Bartlett, etc.) perhaps have not sufficiently wondered about or been guided in their reflection upon Calhoun's career by the almost Dionysian epithets of personal praise and derision that surrounded him throughout his public life from his first significant speech in the House of Representatives ("the voice of the age"). There is nothing comparable in American political history.

[3] E.g., Kant, preface to "On the Common Saying: This May be True in Theory, but it does not Apply in Practice," in, *Kant's Political Writings*, H. S. Reiss, ed., H. B. Nisbet (Cambridge: Cambridge University Press, 1977), 61.

[4] "On the Loan Bill" (delivered in the House of Representatives, February 25, 1814), *Works*, 2:91. See, e.g., Plutarch, *Aud.*, 39d; *Profect. Virt.*, 80b-c.

[5] Cf., e.g., Aristotle, *Politics*, 1263a4, and context: "In general, to live together and be partners in any human matter is difficult." Cicero, *De Officiis*, I.i.46, iii.8; III.ii,13-16.

[6] Taking up the qualities introduced in paras. 96-98 in this section Calhoun especially emphasizes the "*disposition to harmonize*" (102, emphasis in the original); this is its theme. Cf. Polybius, *Histories*, VI.4.2, 6.11-12, 8.1, 9.1, 10.14, 18.1, 46.7.

[7] Consider Calhoun's various references in his speeches, e.g., to Burlemanqui, the *Federalist*, "the elementary texts on the subject," and others.

[8] Francis Lieber, in *On Civil Liberty and Self-Government* (Philadelphia: 1880). It is curious that in many academic surveys of the history of American thought one finds reference to Lieber (or others) where one should have expected Calhoun.

[9] Consider, in this connection, the article "Juries" in the *International Encyclopedia of the Social Sciences*, David L. Sills, ed. (New York: 1968). Cf. Frederick Pollock and F. W. Maitland, *The History of English Law before the Time of Edward I*, 2d ed., 2 vols. (Cambridge: Cambridge University Press, 1898) particularly the years 1215 and following; and John Phillip Reid, *Constitutional History of the American Revolution* (Madison: University of Wisconsin Press, 1986), chap. 6, 47ff; also, Leonard W. Levy, *The Palladium of Justice: Origins of Trial by Jury* (Chicago: Ivan Dee, 1999).

[10] Cf. Reid Hastie, Steven Penrod, and Nancy Pennington, *Inside the Jury* (Cambridge: Harvard University Press, 1983), 228-29, 115-16: In the "best and most complete study of juries and their deliberations done to date," the authors conclude that,

> although it is up to policy makers and perhaps the voting public to assign appropriate weight to these empirical results...the unanimous rule appears preferable to majority rules because of the importance of deliberative thoroughness, expression of individual viewpoints, and protection against sampling variability effects of initial verdict preference [i.e., learning, moderation or compromise]. Furthermore, because respect for the institution of the jury is a critical condition for public acceptance of jury decisions, the lower postdeliberation evaluation of the quality of their decision by jurors in nonunanimous juries and the larger number of holdouts who reject the jury's verdict under these rules greatly diminish the usefulness of the majority rule jury as a mechanism for resolving legal disputes.

"Nonunanimous juries discuss both evidence and law during deliberation far less thoroughly than do unanimous rule juries...[and also lack] the moderating influence of the longer, more thorough deliberations under the unanimous rule..." See also 2-6.

[11] "On the Loan Bill" (delivered in the House of Representatives, February 25, 1814), Works, 2:71; see also 94, bottom. (Calhoun then almost immediately refers to the example of Rome.) See chap. 1, n. 86 above. This view is represented in much the same language throughout Calhoun's speeches. E.g., "On the Independent Treasury Bill, in reply to Mr. Clay" (delivered in the Senate, March 10, 1838), *Works*, 2:248-49ff.; "On the Independent Treasury Bill, in reply to Mr. Webster" (March 22, 1838), *Works*, 2:305-306; and, e.g., "Reply to Mr. Webster on the Report of the Select Committee" (March 3, 1840), *Works*, 2:462, last two sentences.

[12] Carl Schmitt, *The Crisis of Parliamentary Democracy*, Ellen Kennedy, trans. (1923, 1916; Boston: MIT Press, 1985), 4-6 ("Preface to the Second Edition"). "The situation of parliamentarianism is critical today because the development of modern mass democracy has made argumentative public discussion an empty formality." Schmitt's position toward parliamentarianism is essentially that adopted by Mosca. Cf. *Disquisition*, paras. 112ff., 116-117. In this connection, see also, Jeffrey Abramson, "The Jury and Democratic Theory," *The Journal of Political Philosophy* 1/1 (March 1993): 45ff., especially last three paragraphs; and contrast Lysander Spooner, *An Essay on the Trial by Jury* (Boston, 1852), chapters 1 and 10.

[13] E.g., Machiavelli, *Discourses on Livy*, III.12: "As has been written by some moral philosophers, man's hand and tongue, two most noble instruments for ennobling him, would not have done their work perfectly nor would they have carried the works of men to the heights to which they are seen to have been carried, if they had not been driven on by necessity."

[14] Calhoun, "On the Bill to Encourage Enlistments" (delivered in the House of Representatives, January 17, 1814), *Works*, 2:62-63. The whole speech should be studied in this light, as well as in the context of his great speeches in the Senate on the Force Bill and the Oregon Bill. Cf. in the same connection, "On the Bill to Recharter the United States Bank" (delivered in the Senate, March 21, 1834), *Works*, 2:349-50, and context: "not...a systematic opposition...cheerfully..."

[15] The characterization of Calhoun as Calvinist is usually found in connection with descriptive references to his "stern" reasoning and austerity of style and public habits, etc. It is inaccurate. It merely mistakes what is now taken for the "look" of Calvinism for what was once known as the characteristic style and manner of "republicanism" or republican virtue, even of *gravitas* and *dignitas*. This mistake is an easy one for writers primarily influenced by liberalism, for if liberalism is not democratic (e.g., Mill, Schmitt) neither is it republican (it celebrates neither citizenship nor austerity), to say nothing of Calvinist. It is the characteristic thought of Locke's "civil society" as based on Hobbes' removal of the grounds for submitting private wishes to public good. What it cannot identify openly as virtue, since such an identification would necessarily imply the capacity to identify vice, and since liberalism stands or falls by the refusal to identify vice as such, it will wish to identify as "Calvinism," if not as "Puritanism."

[16] Scotus: "*Potentia Naturalis*," "*Potentia Liberia* "; liberty is human perfection: "*Propter Perfectionem Totius*"; cf. also, *De Primo Principio*: "infinite." Cf. e.g., Thomas Aquinas, *Summa Theologica*, Ia, 95, i, 4, "*In Puris Naturalibus*," and related passages; John Scotus Erigena, *De Divisione Naturae*, "created" and "uncreated." Kant, e.g., *Critique of Practical Reason*, Lewis White Beck, trans. (Indianapolis: Bobbs-Merrill, 1956), 3: "keystone of the whole architecture...," 32: "Infinite Being...," 109-110: "embodied...," "...pure world of the understanding" (with Calhoun: "world of mind"), 130: "reason..."; *Critique of Pure Reason*, Norman Kemp Smith, trans. (London: Macmillan, 1929), 424: "foundation stone...."

The question of the comparative coherence of Calhoun's system or science in relation to such thinkers is a study that can be distinguished if not ultimately detached from the study of his political science—or, if one likes, it can be separated from the rest of his thought to such an extent as the rest of Aristotle's philosophy can be separated from the *Politics* and *Ethics* and *Rhetoric* or Hobbes' from the *Leviathan*, etc., whereas Marxism, for example, cannot be grasped at all apart from Marxist theoretical history and hence from its dependence on Hegel and Hegelianism, and similarly for the Heidegger case.

[17] Cicero, *De Officiis*, I.i.17; cf. in this connection, on Polybius (VI.56), Vico, *New Science*, no. 179; consider also, Descartes, *The Passions of the Soul*, article 50: "There is no will so weak that it cannot, if properly directed, acquire absolute power over its passions." Cf. Kant, *Metaphysics of the Principles of Virtue*, James Ellington, trans. (Indianapolis: Bobbs-Merrill, 1964), 39n: "...voice of duty," and related passages, with, e.g., Calhoun, "On the

President's Protest" (delivered in the Senate, May 6, 1834), already cited, *Works*, 2:415: duty is obligation imposed by right.

[18] Burke, "Appeal from the New to the Old Whigs," (Beaconsfield) IV. 176ff.: "A true natural aristocracy is not a separate interest in the state or separable from it. It is an essential integral part of any large body rightly constituted." Cf. Theodore R. Marmor, *The Career of John C. Calhoun: Politician, Social Critic, Political Philosopher* (New York: Garland Publishing, 1988), 248: "The figures of the scientist and doctor were Calhoun's metaphoric representation of this cluster of roles. The political scientist, like the physicist, was to frame the laws of motion that apply to the polity. The doctor of the body politic was to be both diagnostician and curer. It was in the application of cures that the natural aristocrat best fulfilled his promise in republican politics."

[19] Cf. Kierkegaard:

The exception explains the general and itself. And if one wants to study the general correctly, one only needs to look around for a true exception. It reveals everything more clearly than does the general. Endless talk about the general becomes boring: there are exceptions. If they cannot be explained, then the general also cannot be explained. The difficulty is usually not noticed because the general is not thought about with passion but with a comfortable superficiality. The exception, on the other hand, thinks the general with an intense passion.

This passage from Kierkegaard's *Repetition* is quoted in Carl Schmitt, *Political Theology: Four Chapters on the Concept of Sovereignty*, George Schwab, trans. (1922, Cambridge: MIT Press, 1985), 15; *vide*, chap. 1, "Definition of Sovereignty," 13-15. The *Disquisition* should be understood in this light from paragraph 6 forward: constitutional government is the most striking of all exceptions.

[20] Burke, ibid., IV, 62ff., "this short digression..."; *Disquisition*, para. 14.

[21] *Disquisition*, para. 100: "Experience provides many examples...the most familiar..."; 108: "History furnishes many examples...[the most] extreme..."; 110: "Another example, not so striking...but deserving of attention"; 111: "the most distinguished of all examples." Cf. *Discourse*, 393: "the two most distinguished constitutional governments of antiquity, both in respect of permanence and power.... I refer to those of Sparta and of Rome."

As we have noted, Calhoun does not refer to the constitution of Sparta in the *Disquisition*, although he does so in the *Discourse*. In chapter 6 of the *Considerations on the Government of Poland*, Rousseau emphasizes the dangers Poland would risk in immediately freeing the serfs (cf. chap. XIII); cf. Montesquieu, *Spirit of the Laws*, II, 3; XI, 5. Cf. Elizabeth Rawson, *The Spartan Tradition in European Thought* (Oxford: 1969). Machiavelli, *The Art of War*, bk. I: Sparta enjoyed liberty for eight hundred years; Rome for only four hundred; cf. Montesquieu, *Spirit of the Laws*, VIII, 16: "The long duration of the republic of Sparta was owing to her having continued in the same extent of territory after all her wars." Sparta was not imperial.

[22] Burke, "Appeal from the New to the Old Whigs." This observation is almost immediately preceded by the observation that "in our judicial trials we require unanimity either to condemn or absolve."

[23] Burke, *Reflections*: The Christian religion is "one great source of civilization [here used in Calhoun's sense of "culture"] amongst us, and amongst many other nations..."

Churchill took his understanding of the term "civilization" from Burke (*Blood, Sweat, and Tears*), 45ff.:

> There are few words which are used more loosely than the word "Civilization" [Calhoun's "culture"]. What does it mean? It means a society based upon the opinions of civilians. It means that violence, the rule of warriors and despotic chiefs, the conditions of camps and warfare, of riot and tyranny, gives place to parliaments where laws are made, and independent courts of justice in which over long periods those laws are maintained. That is Civilization—and in its soil grow continually, freedom, comfort, and culture [Calhoun's "civilization"].... The central principle of Civilization is the subordination of the ruling authority to the settled customs of the people and to their will as expressed through the Constitution....

Except for his reference to "comfort," Churchill's Burkean understanding of the terms "civilization" and "culture" is the inverse of Calhoun's understanding, while the understanding of constitutionalism is the same. It is culture, particularly political culture, that gives rise to civilization. Civilization, the development of the high arts and sciences — technology — is ambivalent and can more or less easily be transplanted, not to say gratuitously lavished among all alike; culture, the constitution, cannot be so transplanted, but must be earned.

[24] Georges Sorel, *The Illusions of Progress*, John and Charlotte Stanley, trans. (Berkeley and Los Angeles: University of California Press, 1969), chap. 4, sec. iii, 106-111: "...Father Charlevoix's book on New France...influence on Turgot and Rousseau was probably especially great." The quotation given in the text is taken from among Sorel's excerpts. See chap. 1, nn. 52-58 above; also, Francis Jennings, *The Ambiguous Iroquois Empire* (Norton, 1984), chaps. 5, 10, 19.

[25] The hypothesis or supposition here discussed by Calhoun is usually associated with the celebrated career and writings of Guizot (*History of the Origins of Representative Government in Europe*), perhaps hardly less so with Benjamin Franklin. See also Jefferson to Carrington (January 16, 1787, The Writing of Thomas Jefferson, Paul Leicester Ford, ed., 10 vols. [New York: 1892-1899], 4:359-60). It represents the culmination of the original aim of the Enlightenment as it is found in Hobbes and Bacon. Cf. *The Papers of John C. Calhoun*, Clyde Wilson, et al., eds., 10:130-31, 16-17; and the discussion of Mill's concern about propagandism in chap. 1, above, and, especially, Tocqueville, *Democracy in America*, II.1.2, 2.2: "intellectual authority."

[26] In light of Calhoun's comments see Walter Lippmann, *Liberty and the News* (New York: Harcourt, Brace, 1920), 5-13: "In an exact sense the crisis of western democracy is a crisis in journalism..." and context. Lippmann sketched an ambitious journalism that was "cosmopolitan" and "universalistic," and conceived of the journalist as "scientist." In connection with what follows, see Schmitt, *The Crisis of Parliamentary Democracy*, 2-8, 35-39, and elsewhere. Schmitt's general view is somewhat thinned out and filigreed in Jurgen Habermas, *The Structural Transformation of the Public Sphere*, Ellen Kennedy, trans.

(Cambridge: MIT Press, 1985). Consult, more especially, Mark Wahlgren Summers, *The Press Gang: Newspapers and Politics, 1865-1878* (Chapel Hill, 1994).

[27] Cf. Marx, himself an impassioned propagandist, to Kuglemann, July 27, 1871: "Hitherto one believed that the creation of civil myths and fables under the Roman empire was possible only because the printing press was not yet invented. But it is just the opposite: the daily press and telegraph, which spreads the inventions of the press in a few seconds over the whole globe, fabricate more myths in a single day than could be produced formerly in a century." One may take this as an occasion and illustration of the theories of Sorel and Mosca about what they called "political mythology." See Marx at chap. 2, n. 34 above.

Cf. John Dewey (following Lippmann), *The Public and Its Problems* (Chicago: Swallow, 1927), 348: "A genuine social science would manifest in its reality in the daily press, while learned books and articles supply and polish the tools of inquiry," for only thus, according to Dewey, can public opinion ever be cleansed of propaganda. See chap. 2, n. 34 above; *Disquisition*, para. 138; and nn. 28-31 below. See Mary O. Furner, *Advocacy & Objectivity: A Crisis in the Professionalization of American Social Science, 1865-1905* (Lexington, Ky., 1975), and Thomas Haskell, *The Emergence of Professional Social Science: The American Social Science Association and the Nineteenth-Century Crisis in Authority* (Urbana, 1977). The profession gradually emerged as essentially progressive democrat in Woodrow Wilson: "A new age is before us in which, it would seem, we must lead the world" (Inaugural Address at Princeton University, October 26, 1902), and became assimilated to marketing and merchandising.

What Dewey calls the "scientific attitude" (which he sometimes confused with a Germanic kind of practice and effect), or what it would be if adequately filled out, qualified, and developed, points to Calhounian political science. Cf., e.g. Dewey, *Freedom and Culture* (New York: Putnam, 1939), 148ff.

Similarly, Lani Guinier, *The Tyranny of the Majority, Fundamental Fairness in Representative Democracy* (New York: Simon and Schuster, 1994), argues in a superficially Calhounian way about "society," but lacks a genuine conception of the political regime (i.e., community or whole), actually emphasizing instead many "communities" (i.e., "societies" or even, parties). The forward to the book by Stephen L. Carter discusses the role of press and political "symbol."

Cf. Twain, *A Connecticut Yankee in King Arthur's Court*, chap. 9: "...for it was my purpose, by and by, when I should have gotten the people along far enough, to start a newspaper.... You can't resurrect a dead country without it; there isn't any way..."

[28] See, e.g., Walter Lippmann, *Essays in the Public Philosophy* (Boston: Atlantic-Little Brown, 1955), 13-25f., and context, 63; and John Dewey, "Review of Walter Lippmann, *Public Philosophy*," *New Republic*, May 3, 1922, 286ff. Lippmann's idea of countervailing powers (business-labor, etc.) looks toward concurrency.

[29] Cf. Schmitt, *Crisis of Parliamentary Democracy*, 17, 25-29, and context:

[D]ictatorial and Caesaristic methods not only can produce the acclamation of the people but can also be a direct expression of democratic substance and power.... Everything depends on how the will of the people is formed [*sic*]. The ancient dialectic in the theory of the will of the people has still not been resolved: the minority might express the true will of the people; the people [numerical majority] can be deceived, and one has long been familiar with the techniques of propaganda and the manipulation of public opinion. This dialectic is as old as democracy itself and does not in any way begin with Rousseau and the Jacobins.

Nevertheless, the press weights this familiar dialectic in unfamiliar ways. Calhoun observed that in all popular governments, "the laws cannot be much above the tone of public opinion." Cf. Ortega, *Revolt of the Masses*, chap. 1, especially first paragraph; chap. 14.

[30] Cf. Walter Lippmann, *The Phantom Public: A Sequel to "Public Opinion"* (New York: Macmillan, 1925), 48 and context:

> Since the general opinions of large numbers of persons are almost certain to be a vague and confusing medley, action cannot be taken until these opinions have been factored down, canalized, and made uniform. The making of one general will out of a multitude of general wishes is not an Hegelian mystery...but an art well known to leaders, politicians, and steering committees. It consists essentially in the use of symbols which assemble emotions after they have been detached from their ideas. Because feelings are much less specific than ideas, and yet more poignant, the leader is able to make a homogenous will out of a heterogenous mass of desires. The process, therefore, by which general opinions are brought to cooperation consists of an intensification of feeling and a degradation of significance.

It all but goes without saying that government by these "symbols" and what Lippmann called "stereotypes" is the opposite of what Calhoun intends by reasoning government or government by reason. Cf. Schmitt, *Crisis of Parliamentary Democracy*, 6-7, 88: "...the great distinction between absolutism and constitutional regimes...," and context. Hegel, *Philosophy of Right*, secs. 302 and context, 317-18: mass opinion may easily be "a powerful *bloc* in opposition to the organized state," i.e., the whole or rational community, and the true legislator should ignore much of public opinion, in any case, because it contains so much that is false.

The first systematic work on public opinion, A. L. Lowell, *Public Opinion and Popular Government* (New York, 1913), follows Calhoun's distinction between the true "public" and a numerical majority, or what is now called a "public opinion poll," which is a phase of merchandising.

For Calhoun, unequivocal public opinion is "one blended and harmonious whole, the true and perfect voice of the people." "On the Veto Power" (delivered in the Senate, February 28, 1842), *Works*, 4:83, and related passages. Compare Kant, *The Metaphysical Elements of Justice*, J. Ladd, trans. (New York: Bobbs-Merrill, 1965), (speaking of the legislature as the essence of the State): "the united will of the people."

[31] Calhoun to Samuel Gouverneur (November 9, 1823):

> Can a combination of powerful individuals, by securing many of the long established and influential presses, bring into disrepute an administration, which has acted wisely and virtuously, but which has only relied on the people for support? This is the point *now* on trial, and it is one of the deepest moment. On

its determination depends the fact, whether our government can be administered in reference to principles and policy, or whether it will be necessary for it to throw itself into the hands of those who, by any means, may obtain a control over leading presses, and what is called party machinery.

(Quoted in Wilson, *The Essential Calhoun*, 46, emphasis added. The letter was written a year before the founding of the *Westminster Review*.) See Calhoun at chap. 1, n. 35 above.

Cf. Alan Ware, "Political Parties," in *New Forms of Democracy*, D. Held and C. Pollitt, eds. (Beverly Hills: Sage, 1986), 110-34, on media, parties, and "special interests"; also, Edward S. Herman and Noam Chomsky, *Manufacturing Consent: The Political Economy of the Mass Media* (New York: Random House, 1988). See n. 12 above.

Walter Lippmann, *Public Opinion* (1922, New York: Macmillan, 1947), 266ff. on Machiavelli: "The world, as he found it, was composed of people whose vision could rarely be corrected, and Machiavelli knew that such people, since they see all public relations in a private way, are involved in perpetual strife. What they see is their own personal, class, dynastic, or municipal version of affairs that in reality extend far beyond the boundries [*sic*] of their vision. They see their aspect. They see it as right. But they cross other people who are similarly self-centered."

Consult *Federalist* 10: "opinions"; Hegel, *Philosophy of Right*, sec. 246; *Disquisition*, paras. 5-13.

[32] Hegel, *Philosophy of Right*, sec. 315-318: "[While the press provides people] with a potent means of development and a theater of higher distinction, it is at the same time another antidote to the self-conceit of individuals singly and *en masse*, and another means—indeed one of the chief means—of their education," yet, "to be independent of common opinion is the first formal condition of achieving anything great or rational whether in life or in science."

Cf. *Philosophy of Right*, secs. 116-117, 288-290, 301-302, 308-309, 311. What is decisive that true public opinion recognize all the parts of the totality.

[33] Burke, *Reflections*:

The nature of man is intricate; the objects of society are of the greatest possible complexity; and therefore no simple disposition or direction of power can be suitable either to man's nature, or to the quality of his affairs. When I hear the simplicity of construction aimed at and boasted of in any new political constitutions, I am at no loss to decide that the artificers are grossly ignorant of their trade, or totally negligent of their duty. The simple governments are fundamentally defective, to say no worse of them. If you were to contemplate society in but one point of view, all these simple modes of polity are infinitely captivating. In effect, each would answer its single end much more perfectly than the complex is able to attain all its complex purposes. But it is better that the whole should be imperfectly and anomalously answered, than that, while some parts are provided for with great exactness, others might be totally neglected, or perhaps materially injured, by the over-care of a favorite member.

[34] See the text at chap. 2, n. 23 above.

[35] "On the Compensation Law" (delivered in the House of Representatives, January 17, 1817); cf. Aristotle, *Nichomachean Ethics*, 1181a 12-19. Cf. Plutarch, "On the *Republic* of

Zeno"; also, "On the Fortune of Alexander" I. vi and viii: "Alexander desired to render all upon the earth subject to one law of reason and one form of government, and to reveal all men as one people." According to Calhoun, this is the natural tendency of the unchecked press. Aristotle is sometimes blamed for the desire of Alexander just mentioned; the merest familiarity with the *Politics* or the *Nichomachean* or *Eudemian Ethics* makes it obvious that Aristotle does not deserve this blame: rather, it is inspired by the example of Persia (Iran), whose kings preceded Alexander in the attempt to unify the nations under Persian law. Cf. in this connection, among others, Plato, *Republic*, 426ff; Rousseau, *Social Contract*, II. vii, and his writings on Corsica and Poland; and the relevant passages of Burke's *Reflections*.

We may note in passing that Calhoun here (and elsewhere) gives a beforehand answer to the suggestion, familiar a century later in the 1950s and 1960s among academicians that the British parliamentary "model" be adopted in the United States (cf. *Disquisition*, paras. 124-125, 151-160). These recommendations did not go so far as to suggest the division of the population into distinct social classes, however.

Among other things, Calhoun responded to the request of the Prussian Minister to the United States to review and comment on the proposed German Imperial constitution (May 28, 1848): "Every constitution, to succeed, must be adapted to the community for which it is made, in all respects; and hence no one in forming a constitution for itself can derive much aid from that of others" (quoted in *The Essential, Calhoun*, 45); also, "On the Veto Power" (delivered in the Senate, February 28, 1842), *Works*, 4:82-83: With respect to circumstances, "no general answer can be given. It is the work of the wise and experienced—having full and perfect knowledge of the country and the people in every particular—for whom the Government is intended. It must be made to fit; and when in does, it will fit no other, and will be incapable of being imitated or borrowed."

Cf. Montesquieu, *The Spirit of the Laws*, bk. XXIX, chap. xiv: "we must not separate the laws from the circumstances in which they were made."

[36] Cf. Burckhardt, "Fortune and Misfortune in History." Also, Plato, *Laws*, 751b-c: "...although the giving of laws is a grand thing, even where a city is well-equipped, if the magistrates established to administer the well-formulated laws are unfit, then not only would the laws no longer be well-founded, and the situation ridiculous, but those same laws would be likely to bring the greatest harm and ruin to those cities."

[37] See Calhoun at chap. 2, n. 24 above; n. 39 below, and related passages. Political conceptions arising within such problematic circumstances, such as "pluralism," John Dewey's "democratic pragmatism," Robert Dahl's "polyarchy," and so on, are all attempts to work toward Calhoun's doctrine of the constitutional majority. See, e.g., Robert A. Dahl, *A Preface to Democratic Theory* (Chicago: University of Chicago Press, 1956), 150-51: "...incredibly complex society," and *The Dilemmas of Pluralist Democracy* (New Haven: Yale University Press, 1982); cf. Iris Marion Young, *Justice and the Politics of Difference* (Princeton: Princeton University Press, 1990), chap. 6, "The Politics of Difference," and, e.g., Josette Feral, "The Powers of Difference" in *The Future of Difference*, Hester Eisenstein and Alice Jardine, eds. (Boston: G. K. Hall, 1980), 88-94. Peter Drucker, "Calhoun's Pluralism: The Key to American Politics." Pluralism has no meaning except in the context of the whole. Of course, to the extent that what is called "pluralism" actually means no more than capitulation to consolidated power or neutralization of opposition to that power, it is the

same as what Calhoun typically refers to as sinking into "acknowledged inferiority," whether it is publicly acknowledged by its claimants or not. (As for cultural pluralism, what is it today but the claim of those in savage or tribal costumes demanding all the rights and privileges of Lockean Englishmen, as once was demanded "citizenship" in imperial Rome?)

Indeed, it is in just such a condition of society that Calhoun believes the numerical majority to be most important:

> Let me not be misunderstood. I object not to that structure of Government which makes the numerical majority the prominent [sic] element: it should perhaps be so in all popular constitutional governments...which exclude classes. It is necessarily the exponent of the strongest interest, or combination of interests in the community; and it would seem necessary to give it the preponderance in order to infuse into the Government the necessary energy to accomplish the ends for which it was instituted. The great question is—how is due preponderance to be given to it without subjecting the whole, in time, to its unlimited sway? ["On the Veto Power" (delivered in the Senate, February 28, 1842), Works, 4:92-94]

In such a circumstance, the numerical majority is the lowest level to which the whole can be degraded, and, except in quantity, is no different than its being degraded to the rule of a fewer few or of one with some help. This is a part with which the whole must be constructed. For all these reasons, Calhoun is interested in the political whole, and only secondarily and derivatively in "pluralism."

In such a condition, like others, according to Calhoun, the most important initial steps are reduction of debt and reduction of taxes. "The relation of creditor and debtor," in the present condition of the world, is "the all-pervading one" ("On the Bankrupt Bill" [delivered in the Senate, June 2, 1840], Works, 3:506); cf., e.g., "On the Treaty of Washington" (delivered in the Senate, August 28, 1842), Works, 4:326-37.

[38] Calhoun, Discourse, in Works, 1:188:

> ...we have the advantage (possessed by few people, who, in past times, have formed and flourished under remarkable political institutions), of historical accounts, so full and accurate, of the origin, rise, and formation of our institutions, throughout their stages, as to leave nothing relating to either the causes and circumstances which led to the formation, in all its parts, of our present peculiar, complicated, and remarkable system of government to vague and uncertain conjecture.

Cf. Locke, Second Treatise, 352: "...Government is everywhere antecedent to records..." It is important to see that Calhoun here means both that the history of the United States thus obviously does not arise out of the "state of nature," and, what is of much—not to say infinitely—greater significance by the time one has arrived at the conclusion of the Disquisition and the beginning of the Discourse, that this history up to his own time should be self-consciously studied now, in his own time, in the light of and as on a strict par with that of the Roman Republic itself, and, also, the constitutional monarchy of Great Britain (Disquisition, para. 165). This exemplary history, like that of Livy, Cicero, and Hume, is the subject of the unfinished Discourse on the Constitution and Government of the United States. Taking this view seriously is the first step in beginning to be able to see what Calhoun believed he was doing, or beginning to study Calhounian or modern statesmanship in its own right or in the light of what is naturally and politically best, i.e., Burkean statesmanship theoretically grounded. Cf. also, Bacon, *Advancement of Learning* in *The Works of Francis Bacon*, Spedding, Ellis, and Heath, eds., 14 vols. (London: Longman and Co., 1857-1874), 3:333-37 (perfection of history and the history of Great Britain); Calhoun on the British example, chap. 3, above.

[39] Cf. Willmoore Kendall, "The Intensity Problem and Democratic Theory" (with George Carey), in *Willmoore Kendall Contra Mundum*, Nellie Kendall, ed. (New Rochelle, Arlington House, 1971), 469ff.

[40] *Disquisition*, paras. 127: "heretofore"; 130: "heretofore," "I say heretofore — for it remains to be seen whether they will continue..."; 131: "changes have tended...in the same direction," "whether they will take this direction...will depend...." These questions will take several generations, perhaps, centuries, to settle with clarity.

[41] *Disquisition*, para. 62, and context, paras. 90ff; Hume, "Of the Origin of Government": "In all governments, there is a perpetual intestine struggle, open or in secret, between *authority* and *liberty*; and neither of them can ever absolutely prevail in the contest. A great sacrifice of liberty must be made in every government, yet even the authority, which confines liberty, can never, and perhaps ought never, in any [government] to become quite entire and uncontrolable [sic]."

[42] In Tocqueville's *Democracy in America* a somewhat similar discussion in which some of the same points are made is carried on in connection with the general theme of "servants."

[43] Cf. Burke, "Second Letter on a Regicide Peace": "The press, in reality, has made every government, in its spirit, almost democratic." See chap. 1, nn. 36, 91 above.

[44] Rome grew to possess such an urban population (Cicero's *proles*), during which time, while Caesar was Consul and at his direction, an equivalent of the contemporary newspaper developed out of the *Acta Diurna*, the daily proceedings of the Senate, which was posted in the Forum and copied and circulated at large together with other news. It was Caesar's intention to gain support for his agenda by appealing in this manner beyond Senatorial (mainly Cicero's) opposition.

[45] E.g., "On the Tariff Bill" (delivered in the Senate, August 5, 1842), *Works*, 4:171ff.:
We have...reached a remarkable point in the progress of civilization, and the mechanical and chemical arts, and which will require a great change in the policy of nations. Within the last three or four generations, they have received an impulse far beyond all former example, and have now obtained a perfection before unknown. The result has been a wonderful increased facility of producing all articles of supply depending on those arts.... In consequence of this increased facility, it now requires but a small part, comparatively, of the labor and capital of a country to clothe its people and supply itself with most of the products of the useful arts; and hence all civilized people, with little exception, are producing their own supply, and even overstocking their own market. It results that no people, restricted to the home market, can, in the present advanced state of the useful arts, rise to greatness and wealth by manufactures. For that purpose, they

must compete successfully for the foreign market, in the younger, less advanced, and less civilized countries.

Cf. "On the Motion of Mr. Benton to Strike Out the 19th and 20th Sections of the Independent Treasury Bill" (delivered in the Senate, January 16, 1840), *Works*, 3:431ff.: the outline of what will come to be known as "supply-side economics": "command of the foreign market," "currency," "labor," "wages."

[46] Calhoun, "On the Tariff Bill," August 5, 1842 [source of speech]: "According to my conception, the great advance made in the arts by mechanical and chemical inventions and discoveries, in the last three or four generations, has done more for civilization and the elevation of the human race than all other causes combined in the same period."

Cf. *Disquisition*, paras. 132-138 with John Adams, "Preface," *A Defence of the Constitutions of Government of the United States of America*, in *The Works of John Adams*, ed. Charles Francis Adams, 10 vols. (Boston:, 1850-1856), 5:283.

[47] This passage and the close of paragraph 18 could appear to redact a celebrated comment of Gibbon (whose work Calhoun admired and recommended for study, following upon "all the ancient classicks") in *The Decline and Fall of the Roman Empire*, chap. XXXVIII: "gradual advances in the science of war...," and related passages. However, one need only observe that Calhoun's emphasis here on diffusion of knowledge and information is absent in Gibbon's remarks, and, more importantly, any reference to "wisdom," by which the ancient statesmanship is explicitly characterized by Calhoun in paragraph 18, is absent throughout his consideration of the causes of the influence of the press and public opinion. Cf. Condorcet, *Outlines of an Historical View of the Progress of the Human Mind*, eighth-tenth periods: "mass of the people," "public opinion," "progress of light and that of freedom...."

With regard to Calhoun's repeated recommendation of the ancient classics (and Gibbon), compare Hobbes' repeated recommendation in the *Leviathan* and *Behemoth* (which recommendation, it goes without saying, he did not follow himself) against Aristotle and "the reading of the books of policy and histories of the ancient Greeks and Romans," as too liable to foment discontent with the "social contract" and hence disloyalty under the monarch.

With respect to the point made in the text, one might wonder about natural planetary catastrophes that may have occurred in the past and destroyed the gains of humanity, and that may happen again. It seems that Calhoun does not believe that there have ever been any such catastrophes. The relevant "catastrophes" that unquestionably have destroyed the gains of humanity in the past have all been political catastrophes ultimately traceable to human agency. Such catastrophes may certainly continue in future—recognition of the possibility, not to say likelihood, of such phenomena is part of the occasion of the *Disquisition* and the *Discourse*.

[48] This fact alone is more than sufficient to distinguish the ground of Calhoun's political economy from that of Smith's political economy, although they are otherwise similar. Cf. Smith, "Introduction," *Wealth of Nations*:

Little else is required to carry a state to the highest degree of opulence from the lowest barbarism, but peace, easy taxes, and a tolerable administration of justice; all the rest being brought about by the natural course of things. All governments which thwart this natural course, which force things into another channel or which endeavor to arrest the progress of society at a particular point, are unnatural, and to support themselves are obliged to be oppressive and tyrannical.

According to Calhoun, government itself is the essential and most natural part of this natural course, the aim of which is only incidentally wealth or opulence as it strengthens the community against external enemies and promotes civilization.

[49] Smith, *The Wealth of Nations*, bk. IV. See also, *Free Trade and Other Fundamental Doctrines of the Manchester School*, Francis W. Hirst, ed. (New York: August M. Kelley, 1903).

[50] E.g., "On the Passage of the Tariff Bill" (delivered in the Senate, August 5, 1842), *Works*, 4:178-201; "On the Assumption of State Debts" (delivered in the Senate, February 5, 1840), *Works*, 3:407ff.

[51] E.g., "Mr. Calhoun spoke in reply...at some length, expressing his surprise that, at the present enlightened age of political science, any proposition for retaliating duties should be countenanced..." (quoted in *The Essential Calhoun*, 216). See chap. 4, nn. 71, 72 above.

[52] Smith, *The Wealth of Nations*, IV. vii. c. 80, and context. As Calhoun observes, the case is otherwise "in the midst of civilized society," where the force of uncivilized nations has in fact been broken and there is no likelihood, in the circumstances, of their ever rekindling it. In such cases, the civilized people should be immediately guided not merely by what is but what *ought* to be. Speaking in the "Report On Indian Trade" (1818), quoted earlier, of the neighboring aboriginal nations in the United States, Calhoun writes (*Works*, 5:18-19):

> The time seems to have arrived when our policy toward them *should* undergo an important change. They neither are, in fact, nor *ought* to be, considered as independent nations. Our views of their interests, and not their own, *ought* to govern them. By a proper combination of force and persuasion, of punishments and rewards, they *ought* to be brought within the pales of civilization. Left to themselves, they will never reach that desirable condition. Before the slow operation of reason and experience can convince them of its superior advantage [i.e., as opposed merely to obtaining some of its products], they must be overwhelmed by the mighty torrents of population. Such small bodies, with savage customs and character, cannot, and *ought* not to be permitted to exist in an independent condition in the midst of civilized society. Our laws and manners *ought* to supersede their present savage manners and customs. Beginning with those most advanced in civilization and surrounded by our people, they *ought* to be made to contract their settlements within reasonable bounds, with a distinct understanding that the United States intend to make no further acquisition of land from them, and that the settlements reserved are intended for their permanent home. The land *ought* to be divided among families; and the idea of individual property in the soil carefully inculcated. Their annuities would constitute an ample school fund; and education, comprehending as well the common arts of life as reading, writing, and arithmetic, *ought not* be left discretionary with parents. Those who might not choose to submit, *ought* to be permitted and aided in forming new settlements at a distance from ours. When sufficiently advanced in civilization, they would be

permitted to participate in such civil and political rights as the respective States within whose limits they are situated might safely extend to them. It is only by causing our interest to prevail, that they can be saved from extinction. Under the present policy, they are continually decreasing and degenerating. [Emphasis added.]

Calhoun tactfully associates this recommendation with an argument about the "strong interests" in connection with the new policy, which was only partly adopted. Cf. the speeches delivered in the Senate, 1839-1841, *Works*, vol. 3, especially, "On the Prospective Pre-emption Bill," 3:541ff.: "Without pretending to the spirit of prophecy, I feel I hazard nothing in predicting that what is deemed so easy to be done when out of power, will be pronounced impracticable when in...."; "In Reply to the Speeches of Mr. Webster and Mr. Clay on Mr. Crittenden's Amendment to Distribute the Revenue from the Public Lands Among the States," 3:602ff.: "If I do not greatly mistake the tendency of the system as it stands, it is to extinguish the Indian titles far more rapidly than the demands of our increasing population require.... the occupation of the aborigines, whom we are so rapidly expelling..."; also, "Report on the Public Lands" (May 13, 1840), *Works*, 5:208ff.

The first thing that might be said about Calhoun's policy with respect to the aborigines is that, while reason is understood to be the ultimate standard of sovereignty, it becomes decisive only in such circumstances he has described and only in such circumstances. It does not provide grounds for the conquest and subjection of uncivilized peoples. In the abstract, there is no such thing as a "burden" of one people to civilize others. Nevertheless, the great power of civilized peoples in immediate relation to uncivilized peoples makes it likely that this great power, as the uncivilized peoples cannot check it, will be abused to the utmost. It can only be checked by the civilized peoples themselves in accordance with such a policy as Calhoun suggests. Otherwise, apart from the fact that it will immediately destroy the uncivilized people as a people, it will gradually corrupt and degrade the civilized people from within. (Contrast Lewis Hanke, *Aristotle and the American Indians: A Study of Race Prejudice in the Modern World* [London: Hollis and Carter, 1959], 12ff.; 28-61.) Cf. chap. 1, n. 56 above.

Secondly, it is clear from what has been said that Calhoun has nothing to do with what later became celebrated for a time as the idea of the "melting pot," or any notion of "pluralism" that might have to do with it. The "melting pot" is the characteristic of empire, of Urdu, which is precisely what Calhoun wishes to avoid as degrading to the community. In view of the fact that linguistic, ethnic, and related features of differing peoples are immiscible, it is necessary in the circumstances at hand that those features be removed: civilizing the aborigines means making them "like us." Making them "like us" does not mean making them men. They already are men. That is why, in the circumstances described, they *should* be civilized, and why the civilized people *should* take that responsibility to make them like "we" are, so that we are attached to them and them to us as citizens, i.e., as all having a common center of primary attachment. If the civilized people do not take up this responsibility, however fraught with difficulty, they will then be responsible for the extinction of a portion of humanity and for using a portion of humanity for their own ends, that is, for tyranny. This is inhumane, and no good can come of it. It can only corrupt the civilized people. (Calhoun once famously rebuked Sam Houston for medizing and showing up for official meetings of state with Indian chieftains dressed in the tribal garb of aborigines. The incident usually receives more notice in the lives of Houston than of Calhoun.) We may note in passing that this was identical to Calhoun's position on the international African slave trade (whether practiced by Europeans, Africans themselves, or Arabs). (E.g., "On the Bill to Regulate Commerce Between the United States and Great Britain" [delivered in the House of Representatives, January 9, 1816], *Works*, 2:133: "I feel ashamed of such a tolerance..."; "On the Treaty of Washington" [delivered in the Senate, August 28, 1842], *Works*, 4:226-35.) The good that is sometimes said to come from such evils comes in fact only from the efforts of those to act as they should, in view of the circumstances and the consequences of their actions, to "mitigate the evils."

Thirdly, we may also note that where Marx (as distinct from some later "Marxists") holds that it is historically impossible to move directly from the agricultural to the Communist state, Calhoun holds that the transition from the savage to the civilized condition requires habits arduously inculcated by reason and experience over time, as such is how the civilized state originally emerged and can only emerge from the savage state. The desire to alter Marx's historicist doctrine on this point (Leninism, Maoism) is the desire to abolish theoretical history, not to fulfill it. This abolition amounts to an attempt to rediscover human nature under the overlay of theoretical history while retaining its historicist end.

Much thought was, doubtless, expended in the preparation of these attempts. Yet with what result? About the time Freud published *The Future of an Illusion*, of which we have already made mention, with its modest reluctance to speak of the future of the bold new Bolshevik experiment, Ortega wrote:

It is not a question of being, or not being, a Communist or a Bolshevist. I am not discussing the creed. What is inconceivable and anachronistic is that a Communist of 1917 should launch out into a revolution which is identical in form with all those which have gone before, and in which there is not the slightest amendment of the defects and errors of its predecessors. Hence what has happened in Russia possesses no historic interest, it is, strictly speaking, anything but a new start in human life. On the contrary, it is a monotonous repetition of the eternal revolution, it is the perfect commonplace of revolutions..." [Ortega, *Revolt of the Masses* (1930), chap. 10]

According to Calhoun, the only thing that breaks this monotony, the only thing that is genuinely "historic" in the sense intended, the only thing that is genuinely "new" or exceptional, is constitutional government. Now, since he wished to reserve judgment on Lenin and Stalin, what might any "normal" (minimally psychotic, etc.) and "well-adjusted" person think, that he or she might learn more, or at least genuinely learn something, from Freud's theoretical opinions about the American Lenin, Wilson, and his many neuroses, or from a Calhounian analysis of Wilson's (or of Lenin's) actual domestic and international policy? Cf. Albert Einstein and Sigmund Freud, *Why War?*, Stuart Gilbert, trans. (Geneva: League of Nations, 1933).

[53] Smith, *The Wealth of Nations*, IV, vii. c. 91ff.; Calhoun, "On His Resolutions in Respect to the Brig Enterprise" (delivered in the Senate, March 13, 1840), *Works*, 3:478-79.

[54] E.g., "Fort Hill Address" (July 26, 1831); "On the Force Bill" (delivered in the Senate, February 15-16, 1833), *Works*, 2:197ff. Cf. also, e.g., *Who Owns America? A New Declaration of Independence*, Herbert Agar and Allen Tate, eds. (Boston: Houghton Mifflin, 1936), Walter Prescott Webb, *Divided We Stand*. Calhoun's thought is associated with agrarian traditionalism in the writings of Vernon Parrington and, in Britain, of Christopher Hollis.

Although, strictly speaking the following observation belongs properly in a discussion of the *Discourse*, with respect to Calhoun's American "sectionalism" and "nationalism," it might be asserted that this subject as he understood it is typically misconceived in hindsight. Stripped of its rhetoric and tact, Calhoun's position is that the South is equal or superior to the North. It produces and has produced superior men, both in deliberation and in the field, men, like Washington and Jefferson, who are equal or superior to the greatest contemporary English or European men, and acclaimed as such. Since the South is the superior portion, it is obvious that the fundamental or crucial struggle in American constitutionalism is necessarily not primarily a struggle between the North and the South, but lies *within* the "South" itself. The North, so to speak, is neither here nor there, except as a constant brute force or kind of quantity. To grasp Calhoun's "sectionalism" in this context, the context of Madison and Marshall, one is gradually led to see that the great drama of American constitutionalism, and hence of modern constitutionalism or free government, finds its true and fully self-conscious peak not primarily in the battle fields of the war for Southern independence from the Northern States, or any other *war*, but ultimately in the city of Washington itself in the political struggle of Calhoun and General Jackson—or, if you like, that of "Jeffersonianism" or the "old Virginia" school, and "Jacksonianism," the populist "new" South, as represented variously by Clay, Foote, Houston, and others, and their several policies and programs. This is the original and fundamental tension in the American spirit, however obscured it may become. In one or another expression, it is the fundamental tension of every government.

These comments should not be taken as implying any slight (which is entirely absent from Calhoun's thought) to any of the great men of the North, some of whom, after all, were more "Jeffersonian" than many in the South. Calhoun praised or at any rate spoke well of Franklin, the celebrated friend of Voltaire. But he observed that the greatest men of the North, or, if you like, outside the South, Hamilton, above all, and the elder Adams, were both of the opinion that the best government in truth was the British monarchy: "the wisest and best ever formed by man" (see "On the Bill to Prevent Interference in Elections" [delivered in the Senate, February 22, 1839], *Works*, 3:390ff.: "The great difference between them [Jefferson and Hamilton] is that Jefferson had more genius, Hamilton more abilities; the former leaned more to the side of liberty, and his great rival more to that of power.") (The same view of Britain was held by Emerson.) They are, thus, distinct from Madison and Jefferson. The contrast of the Jeffersonian and Hamiltonian schools is original and systematic in Calhoun's writings. Cf. also, e.g., "On the Force Bill," mentioned above, 387ff., especially 391: "I, said Mr. Calhoun, avail myself of the occasion to avow my high respect for both of the great parties which divided the country in its early history..."; "On the Joint Resolution in Reference to the Madison Papers" (delivered in the Senate, February 20th, 1837), *Works*, 3:37ff.; "In Reply to Mr. Simmons on His Resolutions" (delivered in the Senate, February 20, 1847), *Works*, 4:353ff.

[55] E.g., Calhoun, "On the Tariff Bill" (delivered in the House of Representatives, April 6, 1816), *Works*, 2:166:

> ...the general nature of wealth. Neither agriculture, manufactures, nor commerce, taken separately, is the cause of wealth; it flows from the three combined, and cannot exist without each. The wealth of any single nation or an individual, it is true, may not immediately depend on the three, but such wealth always presupposes their existence. He viewed the words in their most enlarged sense. Without commerce, industry would have no stimulus; without manufactures, it would be without the means of production; and without agriculture, neither of the others can subsist.

Calhoun does not defend agricultural—or "sectional"— interests primarily on the familiar basis of Southern feudalism, for, setting aside the question of "cultural affinities," the economic notion is too imprecise. Cf. the American authority on the subject, Joseph Reese Strayer, *Feudalism* (Princeton: Princeton University Press, 1965): "A [non-political "economic"] definition which can include societies as disparate as those of the Ancient Middle East, the late Roman Empire, medieval Europe, the southern part of the United States in the nineteenth century, and the Soviet Union in the 1930s is not much use in historical analysis." It could easily apply to contemporary corporate "neo-feudal" economies, as well. See Calhoun, n. 53 above; n. 56 below.

Cf. Jefferson to Mason (February 4, 1791, Ford, V, 275): "The only corrective to what is corrupt in our present form of government will be the augmentation of the numbers of the lower house so as to get a more agricultural representation, which may put that interest above that of the stock-jobbers." See *Notes on the State of Virginia*: "...the manners and spirit of a people which preserve a republic in vigor," etc.

[56] E.g., "On Mr. Clay's Resolutions in Relation to the Revenues and Expenditures of the Government" (delivered in the Senate, March 16, 1842), *Works*, 4:134-35: "A plantation is a little community of itself—which, when hard pressed, can furnish within itself almost all of its supplies...," and context; "Reply to Webster on the Independent Treasury Bill" (delivered in the Senate, March 22, 1838), *Works*, 3:317-18ff: "plantations," as opposed to "a fictitious mass of credit piled on credit...bank stocks...," and context. Compare the study of Aristotle's understanding of the role of the extended household in the *polis* in, e.g., R. G. Mulgan, *Aristotle's Political Theory* (Oxford, 1977), 38.

[57] See chap. 4, n. 95 above.

[58] Cf. Lewis White Beck, *Commentary on Kant's Critique of Practical Reason* (Chicago: University of Chicago Press, 1960), 277: "...the ultimate teleology of the world is moral, not natural. The final purpose of creation is moral; it is the *summum bonum*." Also, e.g., Thomas Aquinas, *Summa Contra Gentiles*, "The Activity of the Wise."

[59] The thought here expressed by Calhoun may be supposed essentially Stoic; cf. Marcus Aurelius, *Meditations*, IX. 28: "If everything happens by chance, do not be ruled by chance yourself": it is in fact the thesis of the *Disquisition* from the beginning: however the world is made that we never made, one is nevertheless always free to govern oneself. See the text at chap. 3, nn. 60 and 97 above. Cf. e.g., "On the Oregon Bill" (delivered in the Senate, June 27, 1848), *Works*, 4:494 and context: "But admit, for the sake of argument, that I am mistaken, and that the objections I have urged...are groundless..."; 500 and

context: "But, if mistaken—if my arguments, instead of being sound and true, as I hold them beyond controversy to be, should turn out to be a mass of sophisms..."

[60] See n. 53 above.

[61] Cf. Locke, "Of the Conduct of the Understanding," the whole section on "Haste"; e.g., Marlowe, "*Doctor Faustus*" in *Christopher Marlowe: The Complete Plays*, J. B. Steane, ed. (Harmondsworth: Penguin, 1969), 330 (Chorus).

[62] Aristotle, *Politics*, 1264a 1-5, and related passages.

[63] See chap. 1, nn. 96-97; chap. 4, n. 72 above; Ortega, *Man in Crisis*.

[64] In his reply to the request of the Prussian Minister in 1848, Calhoun wrote:

I look to Germany with deep interest. If France has taken the lead in pulling down the old government, it is reserved for Germany, if I do not mistake, to take the lead in the more glorious task of constructing the new on true principles. The character of the people is well suited to establish and maintain constitutional governments, and has ample and excellent materials wherewith to construct them—far better than France or any other country on the continent of Europe. On her success will depend not only the successful consummation of what the recent revolutions aimed at in Germany, but in the rest of Europe. If she fails, all others probably will. [*The Essential Calhoun*, 45.]

Events on the continent in the century following Calhoun's death retarded the possibility noted. See the text at chap. 2, nn. 30-31 and following.

[65] Calhoun, "On the Admission of Michigan" (delivered in the Senate, January 5, 1837), *Works* 2:611-12:

I know that it is difficult to define complex terms; that is, to enumerate all the ideas that belong to them, and exclude all that do not; but there is always, in the most complex, some prominent idea which marks the meaning of the term, and in relation to which there is usually no disagreement.... If you wish to mark the first indications of a revolution, the commencement of the profound changes in the character of a people which are working beneath, before a ripple appears on the surface, look to the change of language; you will first notice it in the altered meaning of important words, and which, as it indicates a change in the feelings and principles of the people, become in turn a powerful instrument in accelerating the change, till an entire revolution is effected...

See chap. 1, nn. 97-98 above, and the relevant citations of Burke in chapter 2.

Tocqueville, *The Old Regime and the Revolution* (1856), on the revolutionary intelligensia: "...taste for reshaping institutions on novel, ingenious, original lines," "desire to reconstruct the entire constitution...," etc. Alvin Gouldner, *The Future of Intellectuals and the Rise of the New Class* (New York, 1979), the "culture of critical discourse" carried on by the "emancipatory" elite continues Kant's notion of "scholars" ("What is Enlightenment?")

Calhoun (*Works*, 2:613) acknowledges, "It has, perhaps, been too much my habit to look more to the future and less to the present, than is wise; but such is the constitution of my mind, that, when I see before me the indications of causes calculated to effect important changes in our political condition, I am led irresistibly to trace them to their sources, and follow them out to their consequences."

[66] Cf. John Dunn, *Western Political Theory in the Face of the Future*, 132-37, and context: "If the globe can be humanly inhabitable for the next century or two (let alone for longer), it will have to be so in the last instance by political skill or political luck.... The key question already is whether human beings still have a world that they can reasonably hope to keep. This is a starkly conservative question.... It puts an unnerving weight on the capacity for self-education of modern populations...."

[67] Cf. Rousseau, *Social Contract*, III. 15. 9, 10 (in the context of remarks about the constitution of Sparta): "...you are more concerned about your profit than your freedom; and you fear slavery far less than poverty...you, modern peoples, you have no slaves, but you are slaves. You pay for their freedom with your own. You boast of this preference in vain; I find more cowardice than humanity in it, [because it is motivated by desire for profit]...."

Tocqueville, *Democracy in America* (Bradley, ed.), II.317-18; Calhoun, "On the Loan Bill" (delivered in the House, February 25, 1814), *Works*, 2:81: "To do our duty is more important than to be rich."

Afterword

1 For Zeno, consult Diogenes Laertius, *Lives of the Famous Philosophers*, IX. 25-29, cf., also, *Parminides* and *Apology of Socrates*, the "first" and the penultimate "Socratic" dialogs of Plato. The career of Solon is discussed in Diogenes Laertius *Lives*, the first book of Herodotus' *Histories*, and elsewhere.

2 Freidrich Schleiermacher, *Hermeneutics: The Handwritten Manuscripts*, H. Kimmerle, ed., J. Duke and J. Forstman, trans., (Missoula, Montana: Scholars Press, 1977), 112.

3 *John C. Calhoun* (1882), 3, cf. chap. 1, n. 2, above. Holst traces Calhoun's "lurid" luminosity to the unshakeable hold slavery exerted over his mind, so that he came to personify the issue, whence it is taken over by Christopher Hollis and later writers. Analogous statements in regard to many issues can be found among Calhoun's contemporaries: the War of 1812, the bank, the tariff, etc. As William Matthews wrote in 1879: "It may be said of Calhoun that the ideal of his life was to gather statistics of the United States and work them up into theories of State Rights and Nullification." (Quoted in Coit, *Calhoun: Great Lives Observed*, 87.) Probably the most judicious observation was rendered by the abolitionist Oliver Dyer, whom we have already had occasion to cite, in 1889: "There were at least two Calhouns, perhaps there were several[;]…the man himself seemed to be a different personage at different times, according to the question or subject before him. His faculties were simply a confederacy, and every one of them was a sovereign faculty, which could think and act for itself" (quoted in Coit, ibid., 82-83).

Professor von Holst sees and treats of Calhoun as a "doctrinaire" or incompetent, who, as such, is unable to examine his true political premises (or, in short, more or less as Hans-Georg Gadamer interprets Heidegger in "The Political Incompetence of Philosophy," in T. Rockmore and J. Margolis, eds., *The Heidegger Case: On Philosophy and Politics* [Philadelphia: Temple University Press, 1992], 364ff.). That is, remarkably enough, von Holst sees and treats of Calhoun just as he does of Alexis de Tocqueville, the only true predecessor whom, with grave qualifications, he acknowledges: "The great French scholar was a 'doctrinarian,'" who is characterized by "the weakness of his political reasoning," and the "unhistorical and unpolitical turn of his mind," Holst, *The Constitutional and Political History of the United States* (Chicago: Callaghan and Company, 1877), vii-viii, and (especially) 67, note.

4 In his preface to the 1877 volume of his *The Constitutional and Political History of the United States*, vii, Professor von Holst characterizes this generation thus: "The United States are about to commence the second century of their life as an independent commonwealth as a republic. It is a curious fact that, at the same time, they evidently are entering upon a new phase of their political development. The era of buoyant youth is coming to a close: ripe and sober manhood is to take its place." One may consult Henry Adams's novel, *Democracy* (1880), for a sober contemporary American presentation of this "new phase," or, e.g., a generation later, Vachel Lindsay's 1928 poem "romantically" threatening the sober tribe of "Babbitt," "The Virginians Are Coming Again."

5 Von Holst, *John C. Calhoun*, 3. Comparing Calhoun to Alexander Hamilton, "America's greatest political genius" (2), Professor von Holst concludes that Calhoun "has no claims on the gratitude of his country, although his name will forever remain one of the

foremost in its records. But, in common with Alexander Hamilton, he is still waiting for the only monument worthy of his memory, a biography which does him full justice."

⁶ Cf. Paras. 1: "law of our nature"; 4: "phenomena of our nature"; 5: "phenomena appertaining to our nature"; 6: "law of our nature"; 7: "our nature"; 8: "constitution of our nature"; 9: "twofold constitution of his [man's] nature"; 10: "his [man's] nature"; 13: "same constitution of our nature"; 14: "principle of our nature."

⁷ Cf. Paras. 16: "same constitution of our nature"; 21: "same constitution of our nature"; 26: "same constitution of our nature."

In para. 30, Calhoun speaks of the "nature of the process" (of taxation). Consider particularly in this connection para. 159: "habitually and naturally, the most powerful interest...*the tax-consuming interest*...the interest that lives by the government." Cf. paras. 64-65: "process of the struggle," "process of time," "earlier stages of the process," "very first stages of the process" (twice); also, 117: "party warfare"; 119: "struggles of conflicting interests"; 126: "struggle for the whole."

Calhoun refers in various places to "the constitution of man" and, once (67) to the "nature of popular government." In para. 89, of course, he refers to the hypothesis of the "state of nature," and the "natural state of man." "His [man's] natural state is the social and political."

⁸ Peterson, *The Great Triumvirate: Webster, Clay, and Calhoun*, 477: "Few copies were sold, despite frequent notices in newspapers and periodicals. It provided the first authoritative exposition of 'the Calhoun constitution'...But the threads were spun so fine, terminating in such airy conclusions, that for all the praise heaped upon it in the South the volume commanded little interest, while in the North it scarcely commanded respect." This reception only reflects the fact that *A Disquisition on Government* contains no blueprint for any party programs, but, in place of this, emphasizes statesmanship. Unsurprisingly, Alexander Stephens, in his great post-war exposition of the issues and legality of secession, *A Constitutional View of the Late War Between the States*, makes no appeal to *A Disquisition on Government*, but, rather, to various of Calhoun's public papers and senatorial speeches, one of which he manages to find occasion to recite in its entirety in the course of his Ciceronian "dialog." Of this work, Professor von Holst writes in opening his chapter "The Worship of the Constitution, And Its Real Character": "Only a thorough study of American history can solve the enigma how a man [*sc.* Stephens]of so much acuteness as a thinker, and of so much intelligence, one who has spent his whole life in the study of political questions, could honestly say that his views and his actions were in complete harmony." *The Constitutional and Political History of the United States*, 64-65. In raising this question, Professor von Holst points to the most engaging topics afforded by American studies.

⁹ Wiltse, *John C. Calhoun: Sectionalist*, 480ff. Similarly, in his 1931 *American Mercury* essay assessing of the praise and, more particularly, the blame due leading American statesmen, North and South, up to secession and war, "Stephen A. Douglas," Edgar Lee Masters, if I am not mistaken, mentions Calhoun by name only once:

> Douglas, ever since the deaths of Webster and Clay in 1852 and of Calhoun in 1850, had been the master mind of the Senate, as well as the undisputed leader of the Democratic party. As chairman of the Committee on Territories he had charge of the most important legislation of the time. He had out-argued Seward and

Chase and Sumner, and routed them over and over again, until they were wary of engaging in debate with him. He knew more than they did. He was readier with his knowledge.
The American Mercury Reader, Lawrence E. Spivak and Charles Angoff, eds. (Philadelphia: Blakiston Company, 1944), 216ff. Masters' essay antedates George Fort Milton's *Eve of Conflict: Stephen A. Douglas and the Needless War* (New York: Houghton Mifflin, 1934).

¹⁰ Cf. Von Holst, *The Constitutional and Political History of the United States*, 195ff,254ff, 260-71. The more pronounced Federalists "endeavored to incline the northern states [in case of the election of Jefferson] to a division of the Union." The Connecticut *Courant* wrote: "The northern states can subsist as a nation, as a republic, without any connection with the southern...I shall in future papers consider some of the grave events which will lead to a separation of the United States." An "intimate coalition of the northern states" would get rid "of the 'tyranny of the south' and establish a just 'balance of power.'" More extreme Federalists "did not consider this possible," there must be "division of the union." Von Holst quotes one of these: "There can be no safety to the northern states [owing to Southern anti-commercialism], without a separation from the confederacy" [sic]. The more moderate sentiment continued among Federalists, including a report of the joint committee of the two houses quoting the Virginia and Kentucky resolutions (Von Holst: the principle of state interposition was "'the spirit of our Union'": "The whole report was in fact a second edition of the Virginia and Kentucky resolutions") until, in "culmination of an inner struggle from 1801-1815" at what was supposed the height of the War of 1812, the Federalist congresses of Massachusetts, Connecticut, and Rhode Island sent delegates into convention at Hartford, along with delegates sent from conventions called for the purpose in Vermont and New Hampshire, to consider their grievances and, if deemed necessary, "to adopt measures to have a convention of all the states called for the purpose of revising the constitution." As it happened the convention adopted a report repeating "almost verbatim the declaration of faith laid down in the Kentucky resolutions of 1798."

> They had learned from Madison that a state had not only the right but the duty to "interpose their authority" as a shield between its citizens and the federal powers; and Jefferson had taught them that the fundamental principle of the autocrat c right of of deciding in strifes between parties without a common umpire applied to the relation of the states to the Union.
>
> The report was adopted by the legislatures of Massachusetts and Connecticut. Both these states thus formally declared their acceptance of the constitutional theories maintained in it as their own.

The strife which reached its culmination in the Hartford Convention was dissolved in the timely successful conclusion of the war. The Federalists were exploded by the perception of their palpable tardiness in supporting the country in war. Fifteen years after the Hartford Convention, during the presidency of Jackson, a similar strife (arising from the oppression of Southern agriculture), and the spirit of the Virginia and Kentucky resolutions themselves, culminated among the Jeffersonians in Calhoun's doctrine of Nullification. Cf. Malone, *Jefferson And His Time*, 6:355, of Jefferson's draft of the Kentucky Resolutions of 1798: "Jefferson claimed for the states the right to judge not only the infractions of the compact but also [the mode and measure of redress]. He asserted that the proper remedy for infractions of the compact was nullification..." Charles Francis Adams provides a summary statement (*Trans-Atlantic Historical Solidarity*, 45ff):

> Two whole generations passed away between the adoption of the Federal Constitution in 1789 and the War of Secession in 1861. When that war broke out, the last of the Framers of the Constitution had been a score of years in his grave [viz. since the 1840s]. Evidence, however, is conclusive that, until the decennium between 1830 and 1840, the belief was nearly universal that in the case of a final, unavoidable issue, sovereignty resided in the State and to the State its citizens' allegiance was due.

[11] Cf. Jefferson, *Notes on the State of Virginia* in *The Complete Jefferson*, Saul K. Padover, ed. (New York: Duell Sloan & Pearce, 1943), 665 and context: "Among the Romans emancipation required but one effort. The slave, when made free, might mix with, without staining the blood of his master. But with us a second is necessary, unknown to history. When freed, he is to be removed beyond the reach of mixture."

[12] Quoted in Dumas Malone, *Jefferson And His Time*, 6 vols. (Boston: Little Brown and Company, 1977), 6:319; vide 316ff.

[13] Quoted in Peterson, *The Great Triumvirate: Webster, Clay, and Calhoun*, 488-9. Clay often said "I wish every slave in the United States was in the country of his ancestors," cf. e.g., the quotation of Clay in *The Collected Works of Abraham Lincoln*, Roy Basler, ed. (Rutgers University, 1943), 2:132:

> There is a moral fitness in the idea of returning to Africa her children, whose ancestors have been torn from her by the ruthless hand of fraud and violence. Transplanted in a foreign land, they will carry back to their native soil the rich fruits of religion, civilization, law and liberty. May it not be one of the great designs of the Ruler of the universe (whose ways are often inscrutable by short-sighted mortals,) thus to transform an original crime into a signal blessing to that most unfortunate portion of the globe.

Apart from its omission of any reference to the longstanding and widespread practice of slavery in Africa, both among Africans themselves and trading to the whole Islamic world, before the advent of the international slave trade to the New World, this declamation is merely the original justification of the New World slave trade in reverse. In the ratification debates concerning the U.S. Constitution in South Carolina, Rawlins Lowndes argued that the international slave trade, at least as it concerned the South, "could be justified the principles of religion, humanity, and justice; for certainly to translate a set of human beings from a bad country to a better was fulfilling every part of these principles" (quoted in M. E. Bradford, "Preserving the Birthright: The Intention of South Carolina in Adopting the United States Constitution" in *Original Intentions: On the Making and Ratification of the United States Constitution* [Athens: University of Georgia Press, 1993], 63.). For Calhoun, such defenses of the international slave trade merely mask what amounts to an offensive war on innocent peoples (vide chap. 2, n. 111), and is no better a justification than that which might in the same or similar terms accompany a policy to "force free governments" on various peoples over the world. In a speech we have already cited, Calhoun held in the House of Representatives that the international slave trade was shameful and inhumane, and did not countenance the uprooting of the African population in America for colonization in "Africa" as it would be, if possible, even more shameful and inhumane. The project was opposed on similar grounds by organizations of free blacks in Massachusetts and New York.

14 E.g., in his Peoria speech of 1854 (*Collected Works*, vol. 2), making a point which he repeated elsewhere, Lincoln asks: "What next? Free them, and make the politically and socially our equals? My own feeling will not admit of this; and if mine would, we well know that those of the great mass of white people will not. Whether this feeling accords with justice and sound government, is not the sole question, if indeed it is any part of it. A universal feeling, whether well or ill- founded, can not be safely disregarded."

15 In a speech already cited, Calhoun observes the growing prejudice according to which institutions pertaining even to such as the Russian serfs and the "vast plantation" of English Hindoostan may be regarded as not illiberal, but, of all, only the institution of slavery in the South is illiberal and despotic. An apt illustration of his meaning is found in, e.g., James A. Michener, *My Lost Mexico: The Making of a Novel* (New York: Tor, 1993), 4-5, where Michener writes of an episode in the life of Harriet Beecher Stowe. (Charles Francis Adams treats at length of the popular impact of *Uncle Tom's Cabin, or Life Among the Lowly* in *Trans-Atlantic Historical Solidarity*, 70, 79-84: "a more immediate, considerable and dramatic world-influence than any book ever printed," etc.; 124: quoting the French writer Eugene Pelletan, "the presidency of Abraham Lincoln sprang from the presidency of Uncle Tom," etc.) James Michener writes:

> Her book [1852] was wildly successful both in America and Europe, was translated into twenty-three other languages, and made her an international heroine of liberal-thinking people. It was incomprehensible that only a few years later, in 1856, when she traveled to England and Scotland to wild acclaim, her critical faculties seem to have become addled. Accepting social courtesies from the Duke of Sutherland and reveling in them, she blinded herself to his hideous behavior. As owner of vast estates in the northeast corner of Scotland, he was an arrogant leader among the group of wealthy land owners who evicted crofters whose families hand rented the lands for generations. Bundling them up, often with police or military assistance, he drove them off his lands, refusing to worry about how or where they were to find another place to live.

He made himself anathema to decent Scots, who felt that, whereas an owner did have certain rights to his lands, including hunting and the raising of cattle and sheep, he also inherited certain moral obligations to exercise those rights without harming poorer citizens who had served his forebears for generations. An understandable outcry rose against the Duke's unfeeling inhumanity, and he suffered a besmudged image and reputation which was more or less whitewashed by a stout defense of his policies written by his personal friend, the American abolitionist Harriet Beecher Stowe. Emotionally incapable of seeing that the clearances committed by a Scottish noblemen were just as intolerable as the slavery administered by a Georgia planter, she excused Sutherland's excesses as the mere and inescapable consequence of good land management.

It is here but a step to excusing the lay-off of 5000 or 2000 retainers on the ground that a Fortune 500 stock corporation "merge" with another one, or be "streamlined." For Calhoun, the error lies in not seeing that the Georgia planter unites moral obligations moral and economic interests that the landowner (though styled with a feudal title entailing particular obligations) and his apologist evade on grounds of economism.

16 Consult, e.g., Robert Fogel and Stanley Engerman, *Time on the Cross: The Economics of American Negro Slavery*, 2 vols. (Boston: Little Brown, 1974)., 1:4-6, especially enumerated items 8-10; 117ff, and related passages.

17 Charles Francis Adams, *Trans-Atlantic Historical Solidarity* (Oxford: Clarenden Press, 1913), 113-14, 180: "It may not unfairly be doubted whether a people prostrate after civil conflict has often received severer measure than was dealt out to the so-called reconstructed Confederate States during the years immediately succeeding the close of strife.... over and above [the confiscation of slaves amounting 400 millions sterling], a simultaneous reconstruction subjected the disenfranchised master [and disenfranchised yeoman] to the rule of the enfranchised bondsman"...[and] thus placed by alien force under the civil rule of a different and distinctly inferior race..." guided by "mistaken recourse" to a "policy of force and repression." On the Southern yeomen, consult generally Frank L. Owsley, *Plain Folk of the Old South* (Baton Rouge: Louisiana State University Press, 1949).

18 Cf. Calhoun, in a speech we have already had occasion to cite: "But without [social and political] equality, to change the present condition of the race, were it possible, would be but to change the form of slavery."

19 Adams, *Trans-Atlantic Historic Solidarity*, 175. Adams immediately adds for his Oxford audience: "In this result, historically complete in our case [sic], is there a lesson beneficially to be studied by Great Britain in disposing of the issues long and still confronting it in Ireland? I do not know; nor would it be for me to express an opinion did I hold one." Consider, however, the concluding paragraph of his lectures (180).

20 Adams, *Trans-Atlantic Solidarity*, 177: "Deprived of the franchise in open disregard of the fundamental law enacted for his [the emancipated African's " — our Ulster—"] protection in it [the Reconstruction Amendments], throughout large sections of the common country [North and South] he was not, nor is he now, practically the equal of the white in presence of the law. I state the case in its full extent and in the baldest way. But, on the other hand, general peace, goodwill, and loyalty were restored; throughout the land unrest ceased. How under such circumstances do we look for the balance in the weighing of the *pros* and *cons*?" 176: "Slavery had ceased to exist." On the Reconstruction Amendments in this connection, *vide* M. E. Bradford, "Changed Only a Little: The Reconstruction Amendments and the Nomocratic Constitution of 1787" in *Original Intentions: On the Making and Ratification of the United States Constitution*, 107ff. These amendments, of course, do not touch on the Indian populations.

21 At the turn of the twenty-first century, more than 150 years after Calhoun first spoke on the floor of the United States Senate on the globalization of communications via electricity, California state ballot propositions for approval of gambling casinos and public liquor licenses on Native American lands were marketed to the electorate by supporters as a belated means for bringing electricity, televisions, standardized housing, and consistently potable water to many Indian reservations.

Von Holst, *John C. Calhoun*, 46-47, in discussing Calhoun's distinctly minority views on Indian policy writes:

Whether his theorizing propensities had anything to do with his taking such a favorable view of the capability and desire of the Indians to raise themselves out of the darkness and sloth of their savage state need not here be inquired into [sic]. In judging this question Calhoun was, at all events, a sufficiently matter-of-fact man to see that, in spite of this supposed natural capability for becoming civilized, their actual civilization was impossible so long as the leading principle of the Indian policy hitherto pursued was not abandoned.

On the other hand, von Holst sees the "peculiar institution" primarily and even almost only as a "barrier to progress," which only-too-obvious fact, he repeatedly complains, Calhoun is either too theoretical in his bent or to matter-of-fact to grasp.

[22] Adams, *Trans-Atlantic Historical Solidarity*, 176-77.

[23] Adams, *Trans-Atlantic Historical Solidarity*, 179-80.

[24] E.g., Peter Jennings and Todd Brewster, *The* [20th] *Century* (New York: Doubleday, 1998), 401, 538-39:

> Yet in one of the sixties' many ironies, it was the success of the civil rights movement in the South that seemed to inspire violence in the North...[In Watts,] thirty-four people died, almost all of them black. More than nine hundred people were injured and more than four thousand were arrested. Watts quickly inspired rioters into the streets of other cities, too, including Chicago, Hartford, San Diego, Philadelphia, and Springfield, Massachusetts [and Newark and Detroit], leading to the pattern of urban rioting that would dominate the middle sixties in America. Altogether, between 1965 and 1968, there would be over one hundred riots in American cities, in which more than eight thousand people were either killed or injured.... Twenty-seven years after the "first" L.A. riots in Watts...[after the first "Rodney King verdict"] Los Angeles erupted into what would be the worst scene of civil unrest in America in this century, bigger than Watts, bigger than Detroit. In three days of unrest, fifty-four people were killed and more than 900 million worth of property damaged.

[25] Cf. Mickey Kraus, *The End of Equality* (New York: Basic Books, 1992), chaps. 7-8; page 17: "What really bothers liberals about American society?" He offers a half-dozen rhetorical queries, of which the most important are "Is it that a whole class of Americans—mainly poor, black Americans—have become more or less totally isolated from the rest of society, and are acquiring the status of a despised foreign presence? Is it that the wealthiest 20 or 30 percent of Americans are 'seceding' as Robert Reich puts it, into separate, often self-sufficient suburbs where they rarely even meet members of non-wealthy classes, except in the latter's role as receptionists or repairmen?" Cf., similarly, the culmination of Theodore Lowi's *The End of Liberalism: Ideology, Policy, and the Crisis of Public Authority* (New York: Norton, 1969), 195ff, 277ff. According to Professor Lowi, white (and to some extent uppwardly-mobile black) suburbanization amounts to the attempt to retain all the substance of the old "separate but equal" codes without the name, and must be opposed on the same grounds, along with black separatism.

[26] These statistics may be found at the U.S. Census Bureau's website, http://www.census.gov. Cf. John W. Blassingame, *The Slave Community: Plantation Life in the Antebellum South*, revised edition (New York, 1979), 173-77.

27 E.g., Andrew Hacker, *Two Nations: Black and White, Separate, Hostile, Unequal* (New York: Ballentine Books, 1992); cf. Stephan Thernstrom and Abigail Thernstrom, *America in Black and White: One Nation, Indivisible* (New York: Simon and Schuster, 1997). Morton Auerbach, *The Conservative Illusion* (New York: Columbia University Press, 1959), 5: "The only possible direction in which liberalism can continue to develop is towards increasing equality."

28 E.g., Jim Sleeper, *Liberal Racism* (New York: Viking 1997); Dinesh D'Souza, *The End of Racism: Principles of a Multiracial Society* (New York: Free Press, 1995); Clarence Thomas, "Affirmative Action Goals and Timetables: Too Tough? Not Tough Enough!" *Yale Law & Policy Review*, vol. 5, no. 2 (Spring/Summer 1987): 402ff.; cf. Nathan Glazer, *We Are All Multiculturalists Now* (Cambridge: Harvard University Press, 1996), and, more generally and especially in this context, Thomas Sowell, *The Quest for Cosmic Justice* (New York, Free Press, 1999).

29 Calhoun, "Report on the Circulation of Abolition Petitions," *Works*, 5:204: "It may, indeed, be safely asserted, that there is no example in history in which a savage people, such as their ancestors were brought into the country, have ever advanced in the same period so rapidly in numbers and improvement."

30 It is true that in a speech we have already cited that Calhoun, according to whom no political institution lasts forever, once replied to a repeated assertion of the innate fragility and insecurity of the institution of slavery in the South by saying that it might last "forever among us" if left undisturbed by outside intervention. It would not foreseeably die out or be overthrown by itself. Writing more than a generation after it had been overthrown, Charles Francis Adams asserted in his lectures on *Trans-Atlantic Historical Solidarity* (178-79):

> The plain historic truth is that African slavery, as it existed in the United States anterior to 1862, an evil institution at best, yet constituted a mild form of servitude, as servitude then existed and immemorially had almost everywhere existed. And this was incontrovertibly proven by the course of events subsequent to the issue of the [Emancipation] Proclamation. Before 1862, it was confidently believed that any open social agitation within, or violent disturbance from without, would inevitably to a Southern servile insurrection. As I have already elsewhere shown [viz., in his first and third lectures], the Proclamation when first issued was denounced almost universally and in no measured terms. It was stigmatized as a measure unwarranted in warfare. From its practical operation unimaginable horrors [sc. Southern servile rebellion and race war] would surely ensue.
>
> What actually occurred is now historic. The confident anticipations of our English brethren were, not for the first time, negatived; nor is there any page in our American record more creditable to those concerned than the attitude held by the African during the fierce internecine struggle which prevailed between April, 1861, and April, 1865. In it there is scarcely a trace, if indeed there is any trace at all, of such a condition of affairs as had developed in the Antilles in 1790 and in Hindustan in 1850. The attitude of the African towards his Confederate owner was submissive and kindly. Although the armed as masterful domestic protector

was at the front and engaged in deadly, all-absorbing conflict, yet the women and children of the Southern plantation, with unbarred doors, slept free from apprehension, much more from molestation.

At the turn of the twenty-first century, some generations after Charles Francis Adams, this portrayal, even by an Adams, may be asserted by some to be misleading or merely apologist. Yet, e.g., Peter J. Parish, who is surely in no way comparable to Adams, in his *[American] Slavery: History and Historians* (New York: Harper & Row, 1989), 152-52, observes:

> For all the transient slave population on the move within the South, and for all the urban and industrial slaves and the military laborers, it was still true that, in large areas of the Confederacy and for much of the war, the bulk of the slave population remained down on the farm or plantation. But even here the war exerted a far-reaching, if less-dramatic influence.... Discipline on the plantations was inevitably relaxed, and slaves generally worked less hard than before...

In short, viewed from any historical angle, the institution proved as internally stable as Calhoun always said it was, even when enveloped in war.

31 Merrill D. Peterson, *The Great Triumvirate: Webster, Clay, and Calhoun*, 91, on Calhoun as head of the War Department: "The ultimate goal of government Indian policy was, of course, the incorporation of the natives into white society.... Calhoun believed this was the only alternative to extinction."

32 Cf. Herbert Marcuse, *Soviet Marxism: A Critical Analysis* (New York: Columbia University Press, 1958). Marcuse, the so-called "Heideggerean Marxist," does not refer to Heidegger.

33 Wagner wrote in 1883: "The German races are granted by going back to their roots a competence which has been lost by the entire Semitized [Christian] so-called Latin world." Hans Mayer, *Portrait of Wagner*, [New York: Herder and Herder, 1972], Robert Nowell, trans., 168. The *Ring* is Aeschylus redivivus, etc. Cf. chap. 4, n. 91, above.

34 Heidegger's (later or original) clarification of this phrase "inner truth and grandeur" with the parenthetical addition, "namely, the encounter between global technology and modern humanity," has no other meaning than the identification of his own thought as authentic National Socialism. His relation to Hitler is as that of Nietzsche to Wagner, with the professor-leaders attempting to claim that the poet-politicians are pandering, insufficiently Volkish and revolutionary and, hence, (extraordinarily) inauthentic. (Adolf Hitler's own notion of his struggle, in Heidegger's phrase, to "achieve a satisfactory relationship to the essence of technology" was merely that of establishing an effective personalized ["charismatic"] arrangement [i.e., "*Mitteilung*," as Heidegger often understands it: "command"] between himself and Krupp, Messerschmitt, Porsche, von Braun, et al., or, in other words, the immediate task of German rearmament.) Heidegger's later addition (if it is later), like many similar clarifications and re-presentations of (and omissions from) his earlier thought and action, is now increasingly well known and controversial, and considered in many places. It is not without interest that celebrated figures associated in one way or another with Heidegger's doctrine of radical "historicism" —Heidegger himself, Sartre, de Man, etc.—should typically lie about their own personal pasts, in this way surreptitiously reintroducing the whole realm of myth, romance, "metaphysics," and the rest, along with every day, ordinary politics, into their

official "lives" (*Daseine*). This feature, actually, is an essential characteristic of their thought and of their lives. For the case of Sartre, consult, e.g., Paul Johnson's breezy *The Intellectuals* (London: Weidenfeld and Nicolson, 1988) chap. 9; for that of de Man, consult, e.g., David Lehman, *Signs of the Times: Deconstruction and the Fall of Paul de Man, With a New Afterword* (New York: Poseidon Press, 1992).

35 Heidegger, "Only a God Can Save Us," W. J. Richardson, trans., in Thomas Sheehan, ed., *Heidegger: The Man and the Thinker* [Chicago: Precedent, 1981], 55ff.

36 However, cf. Leszek Kolakowski, "A Comment on Heidegger's Comment on Nietzsche's Alleged Comment on Hegel's Comment on the Power of Negativity," in *The Heidegger Case: On Philosophy and Politics*, Tom Rockmore and Joseph Margolis, eds. [Philadelphia, 1992], 260: "...Germany's expansion and the extermination of foreign tribes would not be qualitatively different from a shark's swallowing smaller fish. In both cases, we are faced with the law of life, to condemn which would be as silly as to condemn being itself." Yet it is of course precisely such animalization of the human world and spirit, rather, that it is the whole quest of Heideggerism to avoid, and by which it must stand or fall.

37 Heidegger, *Introduction to Metaphysics*, 37-38; cf. L. Riefenstahl, *Hinter den Kulissen des Reichparteitag-Films* (Munich, 1935). Note also the derogatory reference in this context to the former German world heavyweight boxing champion, Max Schmeling, whom Hitler celebrated.

38 Among others with which this passage is studded, the allusion to Weber's "vocation" should not be underemphasized. In "Politics as a Vocation" (*From Max Weber: Essays in Sociology*, H. H. Gerth and C. Wright Mills, eds. and trans. [New York: Oxford University Press, 1958], 77-128), Weber stresses the need for human dominion or force for political order ever to emerge from the chaos of nature, and for justification (he classifies various kinds) then to be developed as a kind of afterthought, whether mythical or rationalized or personalized, to sustain it. This amounts to Weber's supplying an answer for what Rousseau in discussing the origin of human society had left blank ("How this came about, I do not know."). It is perfectly identical with Calhoun's dictum, for example, that mere appeals to "reason, truth, justice," are folly without physical force to command attention (*Disquisition*, para. 51), but only with the decisive caveat that these notions are already originally present there within in the disorder, i.e., with force at hand for their ordering. Otherwise, as has been set forth in the study of the introductory portion of the *Disquisition*, the violence and domination is merely brute, and as indistinguishable as the chaos itself.

39 Adolf Hitler is quoted in, e.g., John Lukacs, *The End of the Twentieth Century and the End of the Modern Age* (New York: Ticknor & Fields, 1993), 213-14; cf., generally, Hitler, *Mein Kampf*, Ralph Manheim, trans., 23rd edition (Boston: Houghton Mifflin, 1971), the chapter "Federalism as a Mask," 554ff.

40 Consider, e.g., Mark Blitz, *Heidegger's "Being and Time" and the Possibility of Political Philosophy* (Ithaca: Cornell University Press, 1981), and Frederick A. Olafson, *Heidegger and the Ground of Ethics: A Study of "Mitsein"* (Cambridge: Cambridge University Press, 1998).

41 Consult Johannes Fritsche, *Historical Destiny and National Socialism in Heidegger's "Being and Time"* (Berkeley: University of California Press, 1999), 3ff, and related passages,

and chap. 3, sec. E: *"Verlaufen zum Tod,"* etc.; *"Entschlossen in den Tod vorlaufen,"* "to resolutely run ahead in to death," the "heroes of Langemarck," the "heroes of Verdun," etc.

42 Cf. Aristophanes, *Frogs*, ll. 173ff.; *Ploutos*.

43 A century earlier, Calhoun's remarkable praise of "the Teutonic race" (in which he included Britain and the United States, as well as the German-speaking peoples) in the course of his speech "On the Force Bill" (delivered in the Senate. February 15-16, 1833, *Works*, 238-39), drew attention to the federal organization of the various ancient German governments, going so far on the occasion as actually to quote an authority by name. The core of the passage is as follows: "Every ancient Teutonic monarchy must be considered as a federation; it is not a unit, of which the smaller bodies politic therein contained are the fractions, but they are the integers, and the state is the multiple which results from them." We have had occasion to mention Calhoun's opinion that the future of Germany for attaining a constitutional government seemed promising, given good luck and guidance. What impressed Calhoun most about this impressive race is the same thing that impresses him about the Iroquois people or, if you like, "Volk." Indeed, the touchstone for and the sufficient impetus to all German (and other) seeking for meaning and guidance out of das Volk (or *das gemeine Volk*) is not found in Lutheranism or Pietism but, rather, in the original reception in Germany (and elsewhere) of Rousseau's hypothesis of the "noble savage" (which, following Sorel, we have observed itself is constructed out of reports of the Iroquois) as set over against "civilized" man, and the ultimate aim and value of all such romantic archeology, questing, recovering, and hypothosizing is set forth once and for all in Calhoun's example of the constitutional politics of the Iroquois confederation (*Disquisition*, paras. 108-111).

44 Here, we may point also to the essential connection, which is not yet fully appreciated, between the struggling, sacrificial phenomenological "paths" of the Freiburg school of Husserl-Heidegger in this period and the Vienna-Zurich school of Freud-Jung, including the quest to recover for the contemporary West or the commercial "world" what is living in "pre-Socratic" (i.e., pre-Platonic) Greece and, beyond, in the (Aryan-Volk) East (ancient Iran and India). (The relation may be blurred by the characteristic insistence on "higher consciousness" and its attendent guildism and its esotericism in Jungism, which is absent in Heidegger.) One might begin by considering the (re)turn to radical temporality or experiences in themselves in relation to the popular evolutionary (historicist) dictum of recapitulation, for the question of ontology recapitulates (German-Greek) philology toward unveiling authentic Volk spirit in the "transition" to a "new reality" (Heidegger), and the quest of ontogeny ("individuation") recapitulates phylogeny (Volk unconscious) toward (re)birth of authentic psyche (ubermensch) in the "initiation" of a "new reality," "new order," or "new age" (Jung), and, also, by comparing the relevant passages of Heidegger, Nietzsche (David Farrell Krell, ed. and trans., 4 vols. [San Francisco: Harper, 1991-]), Jung's Nietzsche's "Zarathustra": Notes of the Seminar Given in 1934-1939 (James Jarrett, ed., 2 vols. [Princeton: Princeton University Press. 1988]), and the section of "On the Psychology and Pathology of So-Called Occult Phenomena" (*The Collected Works of C. G. Jung*, Herbert Read, Michael Fordham, Gerhard Adler, eds., 20 vols. [Princeton: Princeton University Press]), in which Jung discusses the derivation of crucial portions of *Thus Spake Zarathustra*.

The clearest proto-instance of the relation in question of which I am aware is the brief 1912 essay by Jung's associate, Sabina Spielrein, *Die Destruktion als Ursache des Werdens*, translated by Kenneth McCormick in the *Journal of Analytical Psychology* (39 [1994], 187ff.) as "Destruction as the Cause of Coming-Into-Being."

45 Daniel Bedinger Lucas, "The Land Where We Were Dreaming" (1865) in, e.g., Louis Manly, ed., *Southern Literature: From 1579-1895* (Richmond: B. F. Johnson Publishing Co., 1895), 388-89.

46 Consider *Disquisition*, para. 25: "pursuits, productions, or the degrees of civilization," and context, i.e., identical operation of essential aspects of government in all communities, however diverse.

47 Calhoun, quoted in Bartlett, *John C. Calhoun*, 51: "I always feel myself in the best health when studying closely."

Selected Index